The New Civil Court in Action

David Barnard, BA

of Gray's Inn and of the South-Eastern Circuit, Barrister,
Sometime Reader in Civil and Criminal Procedure at the
Inns of Court School of Law

Mark Houghton, BA

of the Middle Temple and Lincoln's Inn, Barrister,
Senior Lecturer in Law at Kingston University,
Sometime Lecturer in Law at the Inns of Court School of Law

Butterworths
London, Dublin, Edinburgh
1993

United Kingdom	Butterworth & Co (Publishers) Ltd, 88 Kingsway, LONDON WC2B 6AB and 4 Hill Street, EDINBURGH EH2 3JZ
Australia	Butterworths, SYDNEY, MELBOURNE, BRISBANE, ADELAIDE, PERTH, CANBERRA and HOBART
Belgium	Butterworth & Co (Publishers) Ltd, BRUSSELS
Canada	Butterworths Canada Ltd, TORONTO and VANCOUVER
Ireland	Butterworth (Ireland) Ltd, DUBLIN
Malaysia	Malayan Law Journal Sdn Bhd, KUALA LUMPUR
New Zealand	Butterworths of New Zealand Ltd, WELLINGTON and AUCKLAND
Puerto Rico	Equity de Puerto Rico, Inc, HATO REY
Singapore	Butterworths Asia, SINGAPORE
USA	Butterworth Legal Publishers, AUSTIN, Texas; BOSTON, Massachusetts; CLEARWATER, Florida (D & S Publishers); ORFORD, New Hampshire (Equity Publishing); ST PAUL, Minnesota; and SEATTLE, Washington

A CIP Catalogue record for this book is available from the British Library.

ISBN 0 406 00268 1

Typeset by Phoenix Photosetting, Chatham, Kent
Printed and bound in Great Britain by Latimer Trend & Co Ltd, Plymouth

Preface

The New Civil Court in Action is intended to make civil litigation understand-
able and interesting. It is designed to be used both by law students taking
university and professional examinations and by busy practitioners who
need a clear summary of the rules of court and case law. We firmly believe
that the best way of explaining civil procedure is to show how the principles
are applied in real instances; to that end, we have illustrated each procedural topic with worked-out examples (including the relevant pleadings
and forms). A feature of this edition is the emphasis on the skills the practising lawyer needs to acquire in order to conduct litigation efficiently; in
particular, we have added practice notes under various headings setting out
the sort of advice which the beginner might receive from a more experienced practitioner before venturing into court.

When *The Civil Court in Action* was first published in 1977 the system of
civil procedure was overly complicated, time consuming and expensive.
One of the major achievements in law reform in recent years has been the
development of rules designed to improve the process of litigation – most
notably the advance disclosure of witness statements, the revival of the use
of interrogatories, the submission of written openings and skeleton arguments and the integration of the jurisdiction and procedures of the High
Court and county courts. It is not an exaggeration to say that the effect of
these changes (which are continuing) is the creation of a new Civil Court in
almost every respect radically different from the Civil Court fifteen years
ago – hence our title *The New Civil Court in Action*.

We wish to thank the editorial staff at Butterworths for their assistance
and patience in the preparation of this edition. We are grateful to the editors
of the *County Court Practice* for their kind permission to reproduce the diagram on pre-trial review, originally produced by Mr R Gregory QC for the
Rule Committee. We are again indebted to Mr Edward Davidson who for
the third time running has looked over and made numerous helpful suggestions on Chapter 16 and our thanks are due to Susan Budaly for her
useful researches. We are also very conscious of the help and assistance we
have received from our colleagues at the Bar and at Kingston University.
As much as to anyone we owe a debt of gratitude to our students who have
never been slow in pointing out our mistakes or in warning us when we
have become incomprehensible.

The teaching of procedural law and the skills required in the preparation
and presentation of cases in court is now recognised as an essential

component of a lawyer's training. This was not always so. Not so many years ago, civil procedure was considered a topic worthy of only a part paper in professional examinations. The idea of skills training was unknown. It was our privilege to work at the Inns of Court School of Law under Charles Morrison QC, the Dean from 1968 to 1984. He encouraged and developed the imaginative teaching of civil litigation as a core subject at the School of Law and understood the importance (but also the limitations) of training in practical litigation skills. It is in a similar spirit that this book is written.

David Barnard
Mark Houghton
Bedford Row
August 1993

Acknowledgments

The publishers and authors wish to thank the following for permission to reproduce material from the sources indicated:

High Court and Insolvency-Bankruptcy forms are reproduced by kind permission of the Solicitors' Law Stationery Society Ltd.

Forms N201, N1, N9A, N9B, N16A, N117, N205A, N337 and N56 are Crown copyright.

The Mareva and Anton Piller precedents were originally produced for the *Civil Litigation Review 1991* and are reproduced by kind permission of Temple Lectures Limited.

Contents

Table of Statutes

References in this Table to Statutes are to Halsbury's Statutes of England (Fourth Edition) showing the volume and page at which the annotated text of the Act will be found. Page references printed in **bold** type indicate where the section of the Act is set out in part or in full.

Table of Statutory Instruments

Page references printed in **bold** type indicate where the Rule/Regulation is set out in part or in full.

List of Cases

Oliver Twist v West Middlesex Salvage Co Ltd

Twist v West Middlesex Salvage Co Ltd

On 1 March 1991 Oliver Twist (who was just 17) began working at a factory in Southall belonging to the West Middlesex Salvage Company. Oliver had only just left school and this was his very first job. His employers were a company who had a contract with the local council for disposing of bulky salvage. One of the machines Oliver was going to learn to work consisted of a large press. Cardboard boxes, crates, paper, etc. were forced into a special compartment by a hydraulic ram while at the same time a press came down and pressed the salvage into a compact bale. This machine was always operated by a man called Sikes. Oliver used to watch Mr Sikes working the press and pretty quickly understood how it worked. There was one snag; sometimes odd boxes would spill out of the press compartment. When that happened Sikes would grab the box and pull it away while the ram was working and before the press descended. Of course this should have been done with the machine switched off but since there was always a lot to be done and since Sikes was anxious to earn the biggest possible bonus every week, he used to pull the boxes out quickly before the ram had stopped moving and the press had fully descended. It all looked very easy.

After Oliver had been working at the factory for a month, Sikes let Oliver have a go on the press and Oliver showed he knew just how to work it. There was a great deal to be done and it was a help to Mr Sikes to have a boy available who could take over when he was busy.

One Wednesday when Oliver had been at the factory for about six weeks Sikes left him in charge of the machine whilst he went over to the manager's office. Oliver went on working the press quite happily for about a quarter of an hour until to his annoyance he saw one of the cases was coming out of the compartment. Oliver did not bother to stop the machine – Mr Sikes never did that. He just went over to the press compartment and started to tug the box. It would not come out and Oliver grasped the top of the box and tried to get it free. Oliver realised the press was coming down but had not appreciated the force of the ram because quite suddenly he realised he could not get his hand free. 'Help!' he shouted, 'Bill come quickly'. Luckily for him Mr Sikes was just coming out of the manager's office – he ran to the machine and threw the master switch and everything stopped, but by this time Oliver was unconscious because his hand been crushed by the ram. Sikes put the machine in reverse while one of the men telephoned for an ambulance.

Oliver spent a month in hospital. There was very little the doctors could do for his hand. His thumb and a finger were amputated, but they managed to save the remaining three fingers. After he had been in hospital for about a week the shop steward came round to see Oliver. When Oliver started work he had joined the union and had regularly paid his dues. He only had a very hazy idea about the union's activities and one of the things he had not realised was that trade unions will assist members who are injured at work to recover compensation. Some unions fund the litigation but Oliver's union did not do this; that, in fact, did not matter because, as we shall see Oliver would be able to obtain Legal Aid.

The shop steward explained to Oliver that:

(*a*) Everybody who is injured at work is entitled to benefit under the state-run National Insurance Scheme. The state, the employer and the employee contribute to provide a fund to assist persons injured at work irrespective of questions of fault. Oliver was told to apply at once to the local DSS office for benefit.

(*b*) *In addition* to obtaining compensation through the state scheme, Oliver could sue his employers for damages for the injuries he received. Whether Oliver would succeed in such an action would depend on whether his employer was in some way at fault. The shop steward thought the machine should have been guarded so that Oliver could not have put his hand in the way of the moving parts. He strongly advised Oliver to consult the union's solicitors who were very experienced in handling this type of litigation.

A couple of days after Oliver left hospital he went to see the trade union's solicitors and met Mr Wilkins, the solicitor who would be dealing with his claim. The first thing Mr Wilkins did was to complete a standard form questionnaire which he used in all such cases. The questionnaire covered, amongst other things:–

(*a*) how the accident occurred;
(*b*) the names and addresses of any witnesses;
(*c*) a plan of the machine;
(*d*) details of Oliver's loss of pay.

He also told Oliver that he would like to arrange for a medical inspection by a specialist in hand injuries. The second thing Mr Wilkins did was to complete a Legal Aid Application Form. He explained to Oliver that to qualify for Legal Aid he had to satisfy two conditions:–

(i) he had to show that he had reasonable grounds for taking a court action and that it was reasonable to grant Legal Aid in the circumstances (this is called the *merits test*);

(ii) he had also to show that his savings and his income were within the current limits (the *means test*). In Oliver's case since his only income was sickness benefit and he had no savings there would be no question that he would qualify financially.

Six weeks later Mr Wilkins received a certificate from the Legal Aid Area Office granting Oliver legal aid for the purposes of bringing actions against his employers. After he obtained the Legal Aid certificate, Mr Wilkins wrote to Oliver's employers telling them that he was acting for Oliver and that on the information he had it was clear that his client's injuries had been caused by their negligence and breach of statutory duty under the Factories

Act. In due course Mr Wilkins received a reply from the insurers who acted for the company denying all liability and saying the accident was entirely Oliver's fault for putting his hand into a moving machine. Mr Wilkins was not in any sense distressed by this letter; indeed, he would have been very surprised if it had said anything else. He noted that the letter ended: 'Without prejudice, we would be grateful for the opportunity of arranging our own medical examination of your client'.

Mr Wilkins wrote back agreeing to such an examination on condition that the insurers were responsible for his client's expenses in attending the consultant. He also asked in this letter for the name and address of the company's solicitors so that he could effect service of a writ upon them. This last remark was not pure belligerence. Although Mr Wilkins fully expected the action eventually to be settled out of court, he knew that the insurers were more likely to treat Oliver's claim expeditiously if litigation was commenced against the employers. It followed that it was in Oliver's interest for proceedings to be issued at the earliest possible moment. As Oliver was under 18, it was technically necessary for the action to be brought in his father's name and so Mr Wilkins wrote and obtained authority from Mr Twist to bring the case. Mr Wilkins had already decided that Oliver's case should be brought in the High Court rather than at the local county court. Personal injury actions *must* be brought in the county court where the value of the claim (ie the amount which it is expected will be awarded) is £50,000 or less. Mr Wilkins believed the damages awarded to Oliver would exceed £50,000 and so he decided to commence High Court proceedings.

The day after Mr Wilkins received written authority from Oliver's father he sent his clerk down to the Law Courts to *issue* a writ. A writ is a formal document issued under the authority of the Lord Chancellor telling a defendant that a claim has been brought against him and that he must deliver 'an acknowledgement of service', ie place himself on the court record, or judgment will be given against him. Every writ must have written on the back a statement, usually only in general terms, of the nature of the case against the defendant. In the present case it can be seen from the writ contained in counsel's brief (p 15, post) that this 'general indorsement' states the nature of the cause of action (ie negligence and breach of statutory duty), the date upon which the cause of action arose and the type of relief claimed (ie damages). The writ is prepared in the solicitor's office and the clerk takes three copies to the Central Office of the Law Courts. These copies are sealed with the court seal and one of them is stamped to show that a fee has been paid. The copy with the stamp is then retained by the court and the other copies are given back to the solicitors; they will retain one (the 'original') and in due course serve the other copy on the defendants.

The next step was for Mr Wilkins to arrange for the writ to be *served*. In theory this could have been done by posting a copy of the writ to the company's registered office but, since Mr Wilkins had received a reply from the company's insurers stating the name of the solicitors instructed to accept service, he effected service on those solicitors. This was quite simply done by sending the original writ and the sealed copy to the defendants' solicitors who retained the copy and sent the original back indorsed with a note to the effect that they accepted service on behalf of their clients. If you look at the writ (p 15, post) you can see the indorsement in the margin. At the same time the defendants' solicitors completed an 'acknowledgement of service' form (see p 17) which they sent to the Central Office. The purpose of the acknowledgement of service is that the defendants have thereby placed themselves on the court record and indicated their intention of defending the action. The court keeps a record of all acknowledgements of service and sends a copy of the completed form to the plaintiff's solicitors.

Several months now went by while both solicitors collated the evidence and obtained their medical reports. Both sides hoped that the case could be settled out of court. There were really three issues that concerned Mr Wilkins:

(1) Was there any negligence on the part of the defendants at all? He felt confident there was. Nobody, let alone an inexperienced employee, should be allowed to operate a machine with moving parts that are not fenced in.

(2) Was there contributory negligence on the part of Oliver? Where an employee is also to blame for his accident the court has the power to reduce his damages 'to such extent as the court thinks just and equitable having regard to the claimant's share in the responsibility for the damage' (Law Reform (Contributory Negligence) Act 1945). If Oliver had been an experienced workman, then Mr Wilkins had little doubt that the judge would have held him substantially to blame for the accident. The position, however, seemed different in the case of a young boy just starting his first job.

(3) Finally Mr Wilkins was concerned to have an estimate of the damages Oliver would be likely to receive.

Mr Wilkins decided to send the papers to counsel to advise on the above matters and to settle a statement of claim. First he took a very full statement from Oliver. (This would be the first draft of the witness statement which would in due course be sent to the other side as advance notice of Oliver's evidence. The text was typed on a word processor and kept on disk. From time to time as the case proceeded and more information came to light it would be necessary to amend and amplify the statement.) Counsel asked to see Oliver in conference. At the conference he made Oliver go through the history of the accident in detail. He told Mr Wilkins that he had no real doubt that Oliver would succeed in establishing liability and also that, in view of Oliver's inexperience, the court would be unlikely to make any substantial deduction for contributory negligence. Counsel suggested that Mr Wilkins should obtain a report from a consulting engineer with knowledge of safety precautions in industry. Counsel also agreed to advise in writing on quantum.

In due course counsel advised that Oliver was likely to be awarded a sum in the region of £62,000. The way in which this was calculated was as follows:–

1. *Damages for pain and suffering* caused by the injury (including the permanent handicap – Oliver was right handed – and the cosmetic defect in having a maimed hand): *£24,000.* The starting point in making such an assessment is the *Guidelines for the Assessment of General Damages in Personal Injury Cases* issued by the Judicial Studies Board. (These Guidelines are published by Blackstone Press; they are also reproduced in *Kemp and Kemp on Damages*, Sweet and Maxwell). The *Guidelines* state:–

   '*Serious Hand Injuries*: For example, loss reducing hand to 50% capacity with, eg several fingers amputated and rejoined to hand leaving it clawed, clumsy and unsightly or amputation of some fingers together with part of the palm resulting in gross diminution of grip and dexterity and gross cosmetic disfigurement: up to *£20,000.*

Maximum for *Total Loss of Index Finger: £7500.*

Loss of Thumb: £15,000–£20,000.'

Counsel considered that the court would be likely to award a sum in the region of £24,000 for the loss of fingers and thumb in the dominant hand. In coming to this conclusion he took into account that Oliver had always enjoyed mechanical work but would not be able to pursue a career involving deft movements of the hand and fingers.

2. *Loss of Earnings.* In October 1991 Oliver started work as a messenger boy for a newspaper publishing company in Wapping. His take home pay of £80 per week had to be contrasted with his net salary at the defendants' factory where he had been earning £90 per week. His loss of earnings (after tax and national insurance) therefore was:

April – 7 October: £90 net per week for 27 weeks	£2430
October to date of Advice (4 January 1992) 13 weeks at £10 per week	£130

(Note that while Oliver was out of work he had been receiving sickness benefit of £1500; if Oliver succeeds in his claim this will be deducted by the defendants from the sum they pay over to Oliver and sent instead to the Department of Social Security at the Compensation Recovery Unit.)

3. *Past Expenses.* Oliver had to pay bus fares while he was going to physiotherapy (£25) and his shirt was ruined in the accident (£15).

4. *Future Loss of Earnings.* It seems likely that Oliver would always be earning less than if he had continued in the sort of work he was doing at the defendants' factory. Mr Wilkins has obtained details from the defendants of the sort of salary he would have been receiving from them: it appeared his wages would have risen from £90 net per week at seventeen to £150 per week at twenty-one. In the newspaper job he would only be earning about £120 per week at that age. It appeared therefore that there was a continuing loss from 21 at the rate of £30 per week. Of course these figures can only give a rough estimate and counsel advised that clearer evidence needed to be obtained but nonetheless it looked as if there would be a continuing loss of about £30 per week or £1560 per year. Oliver would probably work until he was 65 so that at first sight it would seem as if his loss from 21 was £1560 × 44; this is *not*, however, how such loss is calculated. The reason is that the plaintiff is obtaining the damages for future loss as a capital sum instead of as income spread over many years. The way the loss is calculated is to apply a multiplier (typically 17–18 years for a young man) to the net loss. Counsel advised that the court would be likely to award Oliver: £1560 × 18 = £28,000 to cover the continuing loss of earnings during his working life.

5. *Handicap on the Labour Market.* If Oliver lost his job at any time he would have to compete for a new job with people who did not have his handicap. The courts recognise that persons with a disability are likely to be out of work between jobs longer than other people and will make an award to cover this contingency. The amount which would

be awarded depended on (a) the likelihood that during Oliver's career he would find himself out of work and looking for a job; (b) how many times this was likely to occur; (c) how much longer it would take Oliver than an able-bodied person to find employment. Obviously this head of damage involves a substantial degree of speculation but it is nonetheless an important head of damage. (Personal injury lawyers refer to this as the *Smith v Manchester Corporation* award after one of the first cases (unfortunately only reported in 17 Knights Industrial Reports 1). The leading case which should be consulted is *Moeliker v A Reyrolle & Co Ltd* [1977] 1 All ER 9.) Counsel advised by reference to the current level of awards in cases similar to Oliver's claim that the court might well award up to £5000.

6. *Future Expenses.* Prior to the accident Oliver (who was very interested in cars) had done his own servicing; he was also adept at home decoration. In future he would incur extra expense each year in garage bills and on occasions he would have to pay for decorating at home which, but for the injury to his hand, he would have been able to carry out himself. Counsel advised that he was likely to be awarded £2000 to cover the extent his living expenses would be increased because of his disability (this is sometimes called a 'Do It Yourself' claim).

7. *Interest.* Finally counsel pointed out that Oliver would be entitled to interest under the Law Reform (Miscellaneous Provisions) Act 1934. He would be entitled to:

   (1) Interest at 2% per annum from the date of service of the writ on the damages for pain and suffering.
   (2) Interest at 7% (half the average rate paid on money held by the court for litigants) from the date of the accident.

(Details of how this is calculated are set out at p 309, post.)

One can summarise counsel's advise as follows:–

1. Pain and suffering and disability	£24000
2. Interest thereon at 2% from service of writ	[ ]
3. Loss of Earnings (which was continuing)	£ 2560
4. Past Expenses	£ 40
5. Interest on 3 and 4 at 7% from accident	[ ]
6. Future loss of earnings	£28000
7. Handicap on labour market	£ 5000
8. Future Expenses	£ 2000

It can be seen that (ignoring the interest calculation) counsel believed the likely award would be in the region of £61,000. As stated above counsel did not believe any substantial deduction would be made for contributory negligence: he considered that Mr Wilkins in negotiating a settlement should be prepared to discount by about 15% to cover the uncertainty inherent in any calculation of quantum and the possibility of a finding of a small degree of contributory negligence.

It will be remembered that Mr Wilkins had also instructed counsel to settle a statement of claim. Before any civil action case comes to court, both sides are required to prepare a written statement of the allegations they intend to make. In the present case the statement setting out Oliver's claim would show:

(1) that on the relevant date the accident took place while Oliver was working for the defendants;
(2) that it was caused by the negligence of the defendants;
(3) that as a result Oliver sustained injuries and suffered loss and expense (ie special damage).

The rules of court require the plaintiff's solicitor to annex to the statement of claim an up-to-date medical report and a schedule setting out the details of the loss and expenses claimed. The schedules must also show the calculation of future loss of earnings. Note the claim for interest which appears on the writ and the statement of claim.

The statement of claim is set out at pp 19–21 in counsel's brief. When counsel's draft came back, Mr Wilkins checked one or two details and then had the pleading typed on special A4 paper (know as 'judicature') and sent it by post to the defendants' solicitors.

It was then the defendants' turn to file a pleading in reply to the statement of claim. Although they knew that it was likely that the court would hold them to a substantial extent to blame for the accident, their pleaded case would be that Oliver was wholly responsible for his own misfortune. Therefore they denied liability and counter-pleaded Oliver's negligence. So far as the injuries were concerned, they knew as a matter of common sense that what was set out in the pleading and the accompanying medical report was likely to be correct but they were not prepared to concede that at this stage; for that reason counsel had used the form of words: 'the Defendants *do not admit* . . .'. The remaining matters which had to be dealt with were the allegations of past and future loss. The rules of court require the defendants' counsel to plead particulars of any fact upon which he will rely at the trial as to the amount of damages. The defendants' insurers were not prepared to accept the thinking behind the calculation of future loss but at this stage had no positive evidence to put forward: therefore the formula 'do not admit' was used again. The defence is set out at p 22 in counsel's brief.

While counsel were drafting the pleadings, negotiations continued between the solicitors. However, it gradually became clear that there was a serious difference of opinion between the two sides as to the extent to which Oliver was the author of his own misfortune. The defendants were prepared to accept that they were two-thirds to blame. They calculated that on the basis of full liability Oliver would be awarded damages in the region of £45,000 and so were prepared to offer £30,000 as an opening gambit. Mr Wilkins was not prepared to reduce the claim by more than 15 per cent to cover Oliver's carelessness so that, on the basis of the advice he had received from counsel on quantum, he was not willing to accept at this stage less than £54,000. It gradually became more and more likely that the action would be fought and so Mr Wilkins started making serious preparations for trial.

Now the Supreme Court Rules provide a timetable which is to be followed by practitioners once the pleading stage has been completed. In a straightforward personal injury claim such as the one we are considering the pleadings are deemed to be 'closed' 14 days after the defence is served. Order 25, rule 8 provides that the parties' solicitors:

(*a*) must compile and exchange lists of documents within 14 days of *close of pleadings*

(*b*) must within 14 weeks serve on the other side statements setting out the evidence the parties and their witnesses will give at the trial

(*c*) must exchange medical and other expert reports also within 14 weeks of the close of pleadings

(*d*) must within 6 months set the action down for trial.

(In practice these time periods (except those in relation to exchange of witness statements – see RSC Ord 38, r 2A(2)) are often extended by agreement between the parties.) We must now consider each of these steps in the context of Oliver's case.

The first step was for *both* sides to exchange lists of all the documents held by them at any time which related to the case. This is the way by which each side in an action can find out in advance what documentary evidence has been in the possession of their opponents. Each side will be entitled to inspect all relevant documents which are not privileged. This process is know as *Discovery and Inspection*. It will be appreciated that this is an important step in the preparation of the case for trial. You will see in the defendants' notice (at pp 23–25) in counsel's brief) that the list of documents is divided into three sections:

(1) documents held by them which they are prepared to reveal;

(2) documents held by the defendants which they refuse to disclose on the ground of privilege (for example, anything prepared with a view to the proceedings such as reports, counsel's advice etc);

(3) documents which were formerly in their possession but are no longer with them.

The form concludes with a statement of the date and time when the other party can *inspect* these documents. In practice, the solicitors usually photocopy for each other the documents which are required. In Oliver's case, Mr Wilkins would have been especially interested in seeing the report of the incident in the company's Accident Book. He might well also have wanted to see any operating instructions provided by the manufacturers of the machine. It will be seen from the defendants' list that no such documents were revealed. In those circumstances Mr Wilkins wrote to the defendants' solicitors asking whether such instructions did exist and also whether the defendants were prepared to disclose them. In the event they replied sending copies. If they had not been prepared to do this Mr Wilkins would have applied to the court for an order for *specific discovery*. Such an application is made by issuing a summons notifying the other side of the date and time when the district judge (called a 'Master' at the Royal Courts of Justice) would decide this procedural (or *interlocutory*) dispute. Any evidence would be set out in the form of a sworn *affidavit*. At the same time as discovery was taking place Mr Wilkins and his opposite number at the defendants' solicitors would have been obtaining statements from their witnesses and further medical reports. As stated above these should be exchanged within 14 weeks of the 'close of pleadings'. Mr Wilkins also obtained a report from a consulting engineer experienced in safety procedure who strongly criticised the system of work and the layout of the work area.

After discovery and exchange of witness statements and reports had taken place Mr Wilkins sent all his papers back to counsel to 'advise on evidence'. This enabled counsel to undertake a review of the material so far collected. In particular he made a résumé of:

(a) the issues;
(b) the evidence at present available on each issue; and
(c) any extra evidence required.

Thus, for example, on the question of Oliver's own negligence the only evidence Mr Wilkins had was Oliver's own statement. Counsel noted that Sikes' witness statement which had been served by the other side made no reference at all to earlier occasions when he had pulled material out of the press. Counsel therefore asked that an effort should be made to interview other employees to see if they would confirm what Oliver had said had happened in the past. Counsel also asked for a letter to be obtained from the Inspector of Factories who would have investigated the case. He also asked the solicitors to endeavour to agree with the other side the items of special damage. This meant in effect agreeing Oliver's average pre-accident earnings, the amount he would have been likely to receive if he had continued with the defendants and the amount he had in fact received from his new employers. If the defendants were not prepared to agree these figures it would be necessary to serve the relevant correspondence on them with notice under the Civil Evidence Act 1968 and it would then be put in at the trial without the witnesses attending court unless the other side insisted they needed to cross-examine them.

Another matter which counsel considered was whether there should be a *split trial*; in other words whether the court should be asked to determine *liability* (and the issue of contributory negligence) first and only then, if Oliver succeeded in establishing liability, go on at a later date to decide *quantum*. This is often a good idea where, for example, the prognosis in respect of the plaintiff's injury is uncertain. In Oliver's case, however, the extent of his permanent disability was established and counsel therefore thought there was no advantage in seeking an order for a split trial.

The last matter counsel dealt with in his advice was the question whether Oliver should apply for an *interim payment*. Typically it takes at least two years for a case to come to trial and so where it is clear from the outset that the plaintiff will recover substantial damages and he is suing a defendant covered by insurance, the court can make an *interim* award. Counsel (perhaps rather conservatively) advised that liability was too much in dispute and so an application should not be made.

After Mr Wilkins had received counsel's advice he sent his court clerk to *set the action down for trial*. This was done quite simply by lodging at court a request that the action should be entered in the list of cases for trial in the Queen's Bench Division and filing copies of the pleadings, the legal aid certificates, a statement that the value of the claim was not less than £50,000 and a time estimate by counsel of the likely length of the trial.

Now at this stage it was fairly obvious to the defendants that the action was not going to be easily settled. It was also obvious, and they had been so advised by counsel, that Oliver would recover *some* damages from them. In other words he would be able to establish some negligence by them even though his damages might be reduced because of his own carelessness. If the defendants did nothing at this stage then, even though Oliver only recovered a fairly small award at the trial, they would still have to pay his costs (which after a two day trial might well amount to several thousand pounds). In a sense this would not be fair because, as we have seen, the defendants had already made a substantial offer to Oliver. The fair course would be to place this offer formally on record and say that if Oliver did not get more than the offer he should pay the legal fees incurred by defendants thereafter. This is the system known as *payment into court*. The defendants are entitled to estimate what they consider a claim is worth and deposit this sum with the court together with a notice to the plaintiff's solicitors of this formal offer. Mr Wilkins was not therefore very surprised when he received a letter from the defendants' solicitors notifying him that they had paid £45,000 into court. This figure is a great deal more than the £30,000 already offered in negotiation. For Oliver the action now became a gamble. He could take the money paid into court *and* recover all his costs to date or he could continue the case.

It is very important to understand how the system of payment-in works and the consequences which can follow if the wrong decision is made about accepting the offer (this matter is dealt with in detail in Chapter 11 at p 263 post). In simple terms the position was as follows:–

1. The Legal Aid Board were entitled to deduct from any damages and costs Oliver recovered a sufficient sum to pay his own solicitors' charges (known as legal 'costs').
2. The costs to date incurred by Mr Wilkins were £3000.
3. If Oliver accepted the sum of £45,000 he would also automatically receive a further sum from the defendants to cover almost all his costs. In effect he would receive something very nearly £45,000 (less repayment of DSS benefit which would be sent directly to the Department by the defendants' insurers).
4. If he did not accept the offer and proceeded to trial and recovered more than £45,000 he would still receive an additional sum from the defendants which would pay almost all his costs.
5. Suppose, however, he was only awarded £45,000 (ie he failed 'to beat the payment-in'). The position then would be as follows:–
   (a) He would still recover almost all his costs up to the date of payment-in – ie £3000.
   (b) But the defendants would be entitled to deduct from the £45,000 their costs incurred after the payment-in. In practice the most expensive items in litigation are the costs incurred in preparing for trial and at the hearing itself. The costs might well be £7500. So Oliver's solicitors would receive (£45,000 + £3000) – £7500 = £40,500 from the defendants.
   (c) His solicitors would then have to deduct their costs incurred under the Legal Aid Certificate. It might well be their costs *after* payment-in would amount to £7500 as well. The total deduction to cover their costs would be £3000 + £7500 = £10,500.
   (d) The net sum therefore which would be left for Oliver would be £30,000.

In other words Oliver stood to lose £15,000, which was a lot of money to him, if he made the wrong decision.

In fact Oliver decided that he wanted to proceed with the case. He said he would accept £55,000 but not a penny less. Mr Wilkins then began the final preparations for trial. In particular he prepared the 'court bundle'. This consisted of the documents the judge would need to have in front of him at the trial. The bundle prepared by Mr Wilkins (with the agreement of his opposite number) comprised:

(i) the witness statements
(ii) the medical reports
(iii) the report from the consulting engineer
(iv) the documents which supported Oliver's claim for past and future loss of wages.

At the same time Mr Wilkins prepared an up-to-date schedule showing precisely how the loss of wages claim was calculated. The defendants served a counter-schedule setting out their calculations.

All this time Mr Wilkins was expecting the defendants would increase their offer. It is quite a common tactic for insurance companies to wait until the last moment and then make an increased offer a few weeks before the trial. A month before the trial this happened: the insurers paid into court another £5000. Mr Wilkins and counsel both felt that Oliver should take the money offered. The effect would be that his costs would be paid by the other side. Oliver however remained adamant; he was not taking less than £55,000.

Mr Wilkins was very worried that unless the defendants increased their offer at the court door (which seemed unlikely) the matter was obviously going to be fought out. The next step therefore was for Mr Wilkins to prepare his brief to counsel.

We now set out part of the brief Mr Wilkins delivered to counsel shortly before the case was due to be heard. Study the documents, especially the pleadings, carefully, before reading the transcript which follows. For reasons of space we have omitted some of the documents which would have been included in counsel's brief, in particular the bundle of correspondence. A full list of the documents which would normally be contained in the brief is set out in counsel's instructions.

In the High Court of Justice   1992-T-No. 3102

Queen's Bench Division

    Between:

Oliver Twist

(a Minor, by his father and

next friend, Arthur Albert Twist)   Plaintiff

and

West Middlesex Salvage Company   Defendants

Limited

Brief to Counsel for the Plaintiff

Counsel has herewith:

(1)   Bundle of Pleadings including Writ, Acknowledgment of Service, Statement of
      Claim, Defence, Lists of Documents, Legal Aid Certificates
(2)   Schedule of Special Damage and Defendants' Counter-Schedule
(3)   Court Bundle Comprising:-
          (a) Witness Statement of Plaintiff
          (b) Defendants' witness statements
          (c) Medical Reports
          (d) Report from Consulting Engineer
          (e) Statements of H.M. Inspector of Factories
          (f) Plan of Machine
          (g) Documents in support of Schedule of Special
              Damage and Civil Evidence Act Notices
(4)   Notices of Payment into Court and CRU Certificate
(5)   Correspondence between instructing solicitors and defendant insurers and their
      solicitors
(6)   Previous papers before counsel and his Advice thereon

    Counsel is instructed on behalf of Oliver Twist (who is now 19 years of age) and who is
claiming damages for serious injuries to his right hand sustained in an accident at the
defendants' premises in Southall in April 1991. Counsel will see from the witness statement
of Mr. Sikes that he makes no mention of there being earlier occasions on which he had
removed material manually from the press compartment while the machine was working.
It had been intended that the Inspector of Factories and Consulting Engineer should be
called as witnesses but the defendants have agreed that the statements from them can be
read at the trial. We anticipate that the defendants will not dispute our contention that
the machine was dangerous in that it was inadequately fenced. It appears therefore that
the real issue will be whether our client's damages should be reduced because of
contributory negligence on his part. Counsel will note that the defendants have paid into
court the sum of £50,000. Counsel is accordingly instructed to attend on behalf of the
plaintiff and endeavour to secure an award of damages and costs.

COURT FEES ONLY

IN THE HIGH COURT OF JUSTICE

Queen's Bench Division

[**District Registry]**

19 92— T.—No. 3102

Between

OLIVER TWIST
(a Minor, by his father and next friend,
ARTHUR ALBERT TWIST)

Plaintiff

AND

WEST MIDDLESEX SALVAGE COMPANY LIMITED

Defendant

(1) Insert name.

To the Defendant (¹)   WEST MIDDLESEX SALVAGE COMPANY LIMITED

(2) Insert address.

~~of (²)~~   whose registered office is at 201 Uxbridge Road, Southall
in the area of Greater London

This Writ of Summons has been issued against you by the above-named
Plaintiff   in respect of the claim set out on the back.

Within 14 days after the service of this Writ on you, counting the day of service, you
must either satisfy the claim or return to the Court Office mentioned below the
accompanying **Acknowledgment of Service** stating therein whether you intend to
contest these proceedings.

If you fail to satisfy the claim or to return the Acknowledgment within the time stated,
or if you return the Acknowledgment without stating therein an intention to contest the
proceedings, the Plaintiff   may proceed with the action and judgment may be entered
against you forthwith without further notice.

~~(3) Complete
and delete as
necessary.~~

Issued   from   the   ~~(³)~~ [Central   Office]   ~~[Admiralty   and   Commercial   Registry]~~
[~~District Registry]~~ of the High Court
this   26th   day of   July   19 92.

NOTE: —This Writ may not be served later than 4 calendar months *(or, if leave is
required to effect service out of the jurisdiction, 6 months)* beginning with
that date unless renewed by order of the Court.

IMPORTANT

Directions for Acknowledgment of Service are given with the accompanying form.

The Plaintiff's claim is for

damages (and interest pursuant to section 35A of the Supreme Court Act 1981) for personal injuries loss and expense arising out of an accident at the Defendant's premises at Southall in the area of Greater London on 1st April 1991 caused by the Defendant's negligence and breach of statutory duty under the Factories Act 1961.

This Writ includes a claim for personal injuries but may be commenced in the High Court because the value of the action for the purposes of Article 5 of the High Court and County Courts Jurisdiction Order 1991 exceeds £50,000.

(1) If this Writ was issued out of a District Registry, this indorsement as to place where the action arose should be completed.

(2) Delete as necessary.

(3) Insert name of place.

(4) For phraseology of this indorsement where the Plaintiff sues in person, see *Supreme Court Practice*, vol. 2, para 1.

(¹) [(²) [The cause] [One of the causes] of action in respect of which the Plaintiff claim relief in this action arose wholly or in part at (³) in the district of the District Registry named overleaf.]

(⁴)**This Writ** was issued by

of

[Agent for

of

Solicitor   for the said Plaintiff

Evans and Bartlam
5 South Square
Gray's Inn
London WC1

whose address   (²) [is] [are]

25 Acacia Gardens,
Ealing, London W5.

Solicitor's Reference

Tel. No:

]

Acknowledgment
of Service of Writ
of Summons
(Queen's Bench)

IN THE HIGH COURT OF JUSTICE

Queen's Bench Division

19 92.— T .—No. 3102

*The adjacent
heading should
be completed by
the Plaintiff*

Between

OLIVER TWIST
(a Minor, by his father and next friend,
ARTHUR ALBERT TWIST)

Plaintiff

AND

WEST MIDDLESEX SALVAGE COMPANY LIMITED   Defendant

If you intend to instruct a Solicitor to act for you, give him this form IMMEDIATELY. Please complete in black ink.

IMPORTANT. Read the accompanying directions and notes for guidance carefully before completing this form. If any information required is omitted or given wrongly, THIS FORM MAY HAVE TO BE RETURNED. Delay may result in judgment being entered against a Defendant whereby he or his solicitor may have to pay the costs of applying to set it aside.

See Notes 1, 3, 4 and 5

1   State the full name of the Defendant by whom or on whose behalf the service of the Writ is being acknowledged.   West Middlesex Salvage Company Limited

2   State whether the Defendant intends to contest the proceedings (*tick appropriate box*)   ☑ yes   ☐ no

See Direction 3

3   If the claim against the Defendant is for a debt or liquidated demand, AND he does not intend to contest the proceedings, state if the Defendant intends to apply for a stay of execution against any judgment entered by the Plaintiff (*tick box*)   ☐ yes

See Direction 4

4   If the Writ of Summons was issued out of a District Registry and

   (*a*)   the Defendant's residence, place of business or registered office (if a limited company) is NOT within the district of that District Registry AND

   (*b*)   there is no indorsement on the Writ that the Plaintiff's cause of action arose wholly or in part within that district,

state if the Defendant applies for the transfer of the action (*tick box*) ☐ yes

If YES, state—
(*tick appropriate box*)

   ☐ to the Royal Courts of Justice, London:
   OR
   ☐ to the*   District Registry

*State which Registry

Service of the Writ is acknowledged accordingly

(*Signed*)

1st August 1992

†*Where words appear between square brackets, delete if inapplicable. Insert "Defendant in Person" if appropriate*

†[Solicitor] [Agent for   ]

Address for service (**See notes overleaf**)

Freeman's Court, Cornhill, London EC3

Please complete overleaf

Indorsement by Plaintiff's solicitor (or by Plaintiff if suing in person) of his name address and reference, if any, in the box below.

Evans and Bartlam
5 South Square
Gray's Inn
London   WC1

Notes as to Address for Service

Solicitor. Where the Defendant is represented by a Solicitor, state the Solicitor's place of business in England or Wales. If the Solicitor is the Agent of another Solicitor, state the name and the place of business of the Solicitor for whom he is acting.

Defendant in person. Where the Defendant is acting in person, he must give his residence OR, if he does not reside in England or Wales, he must give an address in England or Wales where communications for him should be sent. In the case of a limited company, "residence" means its registered or principal office.

OYEZ The Solicitors' Law Stationery Society Ltd, Oyez House, 7 Spa Road, London SE16 3QQ

10 92 F23306

5044213
• • • • •

High Court E22 (PR)

In the High Court of Justice   1992-T-No. 3102

Queen's Bench Division

(Writ issued the 26th day of July, 1992)

Between:

OLIVER TWIST

(a Minor, by his father and

next friend, ARTHUR ALBERT TWIST)   Plaintiff

and

WEST MIDDLESEX SALVAGE COMPANY

LIMITED   Defendants

Statement of Claim

---

1. The Plaintiff was at all material times employed by the Defendants as a trainee machine operator at their premises at Southall in the area of Greater London being premises to which the provisions of the Factories Act 1961 applied.

2. On 1st April 1991 the Plaintiff whilst so employed by the Defendants was injured at work when his right hand was trapped in a hydraulic ram and press.

3. The Plaintiff's injuries were caused by the Defendants' negligence and/or breach of statutory duty under the Factories Act.

Particulars of Negligence and Breach of Statutory Duty

The Defendants their servants or agents:-

(a)   Permitted the Plaintiff to operate the ram and press when the moving parts thereof were unfenced.

(b)   Failed to give the Plaintiff any or adequate instruction or supervision in the operation of the said machine.

(c)   Failed to warn the Plaintiff of the danger of placing his hand into the press compartment when the machine was operating.

(d)   Failed to provide any emergency switch or other mechanism by which the Plaintiff could switch off the machine upon his hand being caught in the said compartment.

(e)   Failed in the matters set out in paragraphs (a) - (d) herein to provide the Plaintiff with a safe system of work or safe plant.

(f)   Failed to fence the said machinery contrary to section 14 of the Factories Act.

4.   By reason of the matters aforesaid the Plaintiff has sustained personal injury loss and expense.

Particulars of Injuries

The Plaintiff, who was aged 17 at the date of the accident, sustained a traumatic amputation of the thumb and index finger of the right hand and fractures of the ring and little fingers. The Plaintiff was detained in hospital for 5 weeks and thereafter received physiotherapy and underwent a course of rehabilitation. He was off work for 6 months.

The Plaintiff is right handed.

He has effectively lost complete use of the right hand. The stumps are unsightly and constitute a substantial cosmetic defect. [There is annexed hereto the report of Mr. L. Spratt dated 1st June 1992]

Particulars of Special Damage

[Particulars of the Plaintiff's Loss and Expense to date and an estimate of future loss of earnings and likely expense are set out in the Schedule annexed hereto. The Plaintiff will contend at the trial that by reason of his injury he will suffer serious disadvantage whenever during his working life he should be seeking employment]

5.   Further the Plaintiff claims interest pursuant to Section 35A of the Supreme Court Act 1981 on the damages to be awarded at such rate and for such period as the Court shall think fit.

And the Plaintiff claims DAMAGES and INTEREST pursuant to section 35A of the Supreme Court Act 1981

JONATHAN SLOPE

Served this 1st day of September 1992 by Evans and Bartlam of 5 South Square, Grays Inn, London WC1. Solicitors for the Plaintiff.

Schedule of Special Damages and Future Loss

(as at anticipated date of trial: 1st May 1993)

Part One   Loss to date of trial

Loss of Earnings

(1)	From 1.4.91 to 7.10.91;		
	27 weeks at £90 per week		£2430
(2)	From 7.10.91 to 4.1.92;		
	13 weeks at £10 per week		£130
(3)	From 5.1.92 to 4.1.93		
	52 weeks at £15 per week		£780
(4)	From 5.1.93 to 1.5.93		
	22 weeks at £17.50		£385
		Total	£3725

[Note: Social Security Benefits were received during the above period and are subject to recoupment]

Expenses

(1)	Shirt ruined in accident		£15.00
(2)	Fares to hospital		£25.00
		Total	£40.00

Part Two

Future Loss

Annual Amount	Multiplier	Total
£910	1	£910
£1248	1	£1248
£1560	16	£24960
		£27116

Extra Expenditure

Vehicle Servicing		
£300 per annum	x 18	£5400
Decoration etc		
£50 per annum	x 18	£900
		£6300

[In addition the plaintiff claims further damages for handicap on the labour market]

<u>In the High Court of Justice</u>   <u>1992-T-No. 3102</u>

<u>Queen's Bench Division</u>

   Between:

OLIVER TWIST

(a Minor, by his father and
next friend, Arthur Albert Twist)   <u>Plaintiff</u>

and

WEST MIDDLESEX SALVAGE COMPANY <u>Defendants</u>
LIMITED

Defence

1. Paragraphs 1 and 2 of the Statement of Claims are admitted.

2. Paragraph 3 of the Statement of Claim is denied.

3. It is not admitted that the Plaintiff sustained any injury loss or expense as alleged in paragraph 4 of the Statement of Claim or at all. The Defendants will plead further to the Schedule of Special Damage after discovery and further particulars have been delivered.

4. Causation is not admitted.

5. If the Plaintiff sustained any such injury loss or expense the same was wholly caused by or alternatively contributed to by his own negligence.

<u>Particulars of Contributory</u>
<u>Negligence</u>

The Plaintiff:
(a) placed his hand in the said machine when it was unsafe so to do,
(b) failed to stop the said machine before inserting his hand therein,
(c) failed to summon the assistance of a more experienced employee
  before attempting to remove the obstruction,
(d) failed to notice and/or heed the lateral motion of the ram
  mechanism and withdraw his hand from the said machine.

6. Save as is hereinbefore expressly admitted the Defendants deny each and every of the allegations contained in the Statement of Claim as if the same were here each set out and separately traversed.

SEBASTIAN SNUBBINS

Served this 1st day of October 1992
by Dodson and Fogg of Freeman's Court,
Cornhill, London EC3. Solicitors for
the Defendants.

List of
Documents
(O.24 r.5)

IN THE HIGH COURT OF JUSTICE　　19₉₂.— T.—No. 3102

Queen's Bench　**Division**

Between

OLIVER TWIST
(a Minor, by his father and next friend,
ARTHUR ALBERT TWIST)　　　　　Plaintiff

AND

WEST MIDDLESEX SALVAGE COMPANY LIMITED　　Defendant

LIST OF DOCUMENTS

　　The following is a list of the documents relating to the matters in question in this action which are or have been in the possession, custody or power of the above-named(¹)

(1) Plaintiffs (*or* Defendant(s)) A.B.

　　DEFENDANTS

and which is served in compliance with Order 24, rule 2 [*or* the order herein dated the day of　　　　, 19　].

(2) Plaintiff(s) *or* Defendant(s).

　　1. The (²)　DEFENDANTS　　have in their possession, custody or power the documents relating to the matters in question in this action enumerated in Schedule 1 hereto.

　　2. The (²)　DEFENDANTS　　object　to produce the documents enumerated

(3) State ground of objection.

in Part 2 of the said Schedule 1 on the ground that (³)

　　the said documents are by their very nature privileged

　　3. The (²)　DEFENDANTS　　have had, but have not now, in　their possession, custody or power the documents relating to the matters in question in this action enumerated in Schedule 2 hereto.

　　4. Of the documents in the said Schedule 2, those numbered　1 and 2

(4) Plaintiff's *or* Defendant's.
(5) State when.

in that Schedule were last in the (⁴)　DEFENDANTS'　possession, custody or power on (⁵)　1st May 1992　　and the remainder on (⁵)

(6) Here state what has become of the said documents and in whose possession they now are.

　　(⁶)　　when they were sent to H.M. Inspector of Factories, Ealing District Office, Uxbridge Road, Ealing W5.

　　5. Neither the (²) Defendants nor　their　Solicitor　nor any other person on their behalf,　have　now, or ever had, in their　possession, custody or power any document of any description whatever relating to any matter in question in this action, other than the documents enumerated in Schedules 1 and 2 hereto.

SCHEDULE 1.—Part 1.

(Here enumerate in a convenient order the documents (or bundles of documents, if of the same nature, such as invoices) in the possession, custody or power of the party in question which he does not object to produce, with a short description of each document or bundle sufficient to identify it.)

Description of Document	Date
1. Open correspondence between the Defendants and their insurers on the one part and Plaintiff's solicitors on the other:	1.6.92 to date

SCHEDULE 1.—Part 2.

(Here enumerate as aforesaid the documents in the possession, custody or power of the party in question which he objects to produce.)

Description of Document	Date
Correspondence and communications between the Defendants' Solicitors and the Defendants' Insurance Co. with the Defendants and their agents, Instructions to and Opinion of Counsel; drafts of pleadings and other documents settled by Counsel; statements and proofs of witnesses and other correspondence and documents prepared and obtained for the purpose of this action.	

SCHEDULE 2.

(Here enumerate as aforesaid the documents which have been, but at the date of service of the list are not, in the possession, custody or power of the party in question.)

1.	Letter to H.M. Inspector of Factories	29.4.82

Dated the   17th   day of December   , 1992 .

NOTICE TO INSPECT

Take notice that the documents in the above list, other than those listed in Part 2 of Schedule 1 [and Schedule 2], may be inspected at [the office of the Solicitor of the above-named (7)

(7) Plaintiff(s) *or* Defendant(s) (*insert address) or as may be.*

Defendants

]

on the   21st   day of   December   , 1992 , between the hours of 10.30 am.   and 4.30pm .

(8) Defendant(s) (*or* Plaintiff(s) C.D.

To the (8)   Served the   17th   day of   Dec.   , 1992 .
   Plaintiff   by   Dodson and Fogg
               of   Freemans Court, London EC3
and his Solicitor   Solicitors for the   Defendants

WITNESS STATEMENT

Oliver Twist
25 Acacia Gardens, Ealing W5

1. I left school at Christmas 1990 and started work at West Middlesex Salvage Co's factory at Southall in March 1991. I was employed as a trainee fitter. My foreman was Mr Sikes.

2. One of our jobs was to operate a ram press for compressing salvage into bales. I had watched Mr Sikes do this many times and I understood how it worked and, in due course, I was allowed to operate the machine myself.

3. On 1st April 1991 I was operating the machine when some boxes began to spill out of the ram compartment. I tried to pull them out and that was how my hand was caught in the machine. I had seen Mr Sikes do this on many occasions and nobody had told me not to do it.

4. I was kept at Ealing General Hospital for one month and lost my right thumb and index finger. I was off work for 6 months attending physiotherapy and rehabilitation courses.

5. I now have a job in Wapping working as a messenger for a newspaper company. I have seen the Schedule of Special Damage and can confirm that the information contained therein is correct.

6. My great interest has always been mechanical things. Before my accident I enjoyed working on the family car and did the servicing for my father. I can still drive a car but cannot do any sort of mechanical work. I also cannot do any home decorating or similar work.

7. I should add that I am very disappointed that I am not able to pursue a career as a fitter because I feel I had a real aptitude for mechanical work.

Signed   Oliver Twist
2nd April 1993

WITNESS STATEMENT

William M Sikes
126 Scrubbs Lane
Acton W3

1. I have been employed by the Defendant Company since 1985. My current position is senior fitter and that is the position I held at the date of the Plaintiff's accident.

2. On the day of the accident I had left the Plaintiff operating the press-ram. He was fully familiar with the operation of the machine and I had no hesitation in leaving him to operate it.

3. I was at the door of the manager's office when I heard Oliver shout out, I ran over to the master switch and immediately stopped the machine.

Signed William M Sikes

FACTUAL STATEMENT OF MR C.J. BARKER

H.M. INSPECTOR OF FACTORIES, HOUNSLOW

On 1 May 1991, I visited the salvage pressing plant of W. Middlesex Salvage Company at Southall. It had been reported to H.M. District Inspector of Factories that Mr. Oliver Twist had been injured in an accident on 23 April whilst operating a ram/press at the above works.

I was shown a ram/press which consisted of (i) a compartment in which material for compression had been placed (ii) a ram/press mechanism operated on a hydraulic principle with the hydraulic pump driven by an electric motor. A control panel consisting of an on/off switch was situated beside the motor unit some 6' from the nearest point of the press compartment. Marked on the motor control panel were the following words "Murdstone Manufacturing Company, Blackfriars, England. BHP 75; Speed 1440; Volts 400/440; Phase 3; Cycles 50; Amps 98; Motor no. 17849'.

The press compartment comprised a box of fabricated steel some 3' in height. On the control side of the machine a wire screen 18" in height enclosed the area above the compartment. This screen appeared to be a temporary structure since there were location points for the insertion of a solid guard which would have extended to a height of 7' from the ground and corresponded to the guard on the opposite side of the compartment.

I have no first hand knowledge as to how the accident occurred.

C.J. Barker

15.8.93

071-242 1873   MR. LANCELOT SPRATT
                                                            267 Wimpole Street
                                                            London W1

                                  REPORT ON

Name   Oliver Twist

Address   25 Acacia Gardens, Ealing, W5

Occupation   Messenger   Age 18   Date 1st June 1992

<u>Previous Trouble</u>:   Nil

<u>Present Injury</u>:   Mr. Twist states that he was injured on 1st April 1991 when his
right hand was caught in a hydraulic ram he was in the process of operating. From
the records made available I note that he was taken to Southall General Hospital
where the stumps of his right thumb and index finger were cleansed and sutured
under general anaesthetic. X-rays were taken of the right hand and revealed
displaced fractures of the terminal phalanges of the 3rd and 4th digits: these were
reduced under anaesthetic and splints applied. He was discharged home on 26th May
and thereafter underwent an intensive course of physiotherapy for 2 months
commencing 1st July 1981. He returned to work in November 1991 as a
messenger.

<u>On Examination</u>
The right thumb and index finger have been amputated at the metacarpo-phalangeal
joint. The stumps are well-healed and pain-free. The fractures of the right ring and
little fingers have united well and there is full range of movement in these fingers
although Mr. Twist complains that they become swollen and ache on occasions. The
appearance of the hand is obviously unsightly and Mr. Twist tells me that he find this
embarrassing and is very conscious of having a misshapen hand.

<u>Conclusion</u>
This young man sustained injuries involving the thumb and index finger of his right
hand (his dominant hand). In as much as it is generally accepted that one-half of the
manual capacity of the hand is attributable to the thumb, the injuries sustained by
Mr. Twist mean that for most practical purposes he should be treated as a one-handed
man.

                                               Lancelot Spratt, F.R.C.S.
                                               Hon. Consultant,
                                               St. Swithuns' Hospital, N1

Notice of Payment
into Court
(O.22,rr.1,2)

IN THE HIGH COURT OF JUSTICE

19 92 .— T.—**No.** 3102

Division

Between   OLIVER TWIST
(a Minor, by his father and next friend,
Arthur Albert Twist)   **Plaintiff**

AND

WEST MIDDLESEX SALVAGE COMPANY LIMITED   **Defendant**

Take Notice that—

(1) If by a particular
Defendant insert
name.

The Defendant (¹) s

ha ᵥₑ paid £ 50,000   into Court.
The said £ 50,000   is in satisfaction of [the cause of action] [all the causes
of action] in respect of which the Plaintiff claims [and after taking into account and
satisfying the above-named Defendant's cause of action for

in respect of which   he   counterclaim]

or

The said £   is in satisfaction of the following causes of action
in respect of which the Plaintiff   claim , namely,

[and after taking into account and satisfying the above-named Defendant's cause of
action for

in respect of which   he   counterclaim]

or

Of the said £   , £   is in satisfaction of the
Plaintiff's cause[s] of action for

[and after taking into account and satisfying the above-named Defendant's cause of
action for

in respect of which   he   counterclaim]

and £   is in satisfaction of the Plaintiff's cause[s] of action for

[and after taking into account and satisfying the above-named Defendant's cause of
action for

in respect of which   he   counterclaim].

[The Defendant has withheld from this payment into court the sum of
£ 3,307.50   in accordance with paragraph 12(2)(a)(i) of Schedule 4 to the Social
Security Act 1989]

Dated the 21st   day of   April   19 93 .

To   MESSRS EVANS AND BARTLAM
5 SOUTH SQUARE, GRAY'S INN, WC1

[   ]   of

The Plaintiff's Solicitor   [Agent for

or Agent
[and to [   ]   of

Solicitor for the Defendant (²) [   ]   Solicitor for the Defendant
[   ]]

(2) If there are
co-Defendants a
copy of the notice
must   also   be
served upon their
Solicitors.

OLIVER TWIST V WEST MIDDLESEX SALVAGE CO LIMITED

BEFORE MR JUSTICE STARELEIGH

[5 MAY 1993]

Transcript

(The Law Courts, Strand, London. It is just before half past ten o'clock and the parties are waiting in Court for the judge to arrive. Behind counsel sit their respective solicitors and behind them Oliver and other witnesses. Since these are civil proceedings the witnesses are permitted to remain in court and hear the evidence unless an application is made to the judge to exclude them. As the clock strikes the half hour the usher calls for silence and the judge enters, bows to counsel and sits down. The associate, who is wigged and gowned and sits immediately below the judge, then rises and calls the action on.)

Associate: Twist against West Middlesex Salvage Company.

Judge: Yes, Mr Slope.

Counsel for the plaintiff: May it please you, my lord, I appear in this matter for the plaintiff and my learned friend Mr Snubbins appears for the defendant. Milord, this is a claim for damages for personal injuries sustained in an accident at the defendants' factory at Southall in April 1991. The defendants, milord, are concerned in the collection and processing of paper and cardboard as salvage and to that end have a machine which compresses the salvage into bales which can be marketed. Milord there is an agreed plan which perhaps I could put in at this stage.

Judge: Yes, let that be marked exhibit P1.

Counsel: Your lordship will see from the plan that the machine consists of a ram which moves horizontally and compresses material contained in the compartment marked A – does your lordship see that? – while at the same time, milord, a press descends from above. Your lordship will also note that the wire screen which encloses the sides of the compression compartment only extends some 18 inches above the edge of the compartment.

Judge: Are there any photographs of this machine?

Counsel: Milord, no; I regret not.

Judge: Well, why on earth not? I would have thought it was quite obvious if I am expected to try this action I would need a set of photographs of the machine in question.

Counsel: Milord it was thought that the plan would be adequate.

Judge: I find that quite amazing. Well, we are certainly not going to waste any time by adjourning this matter. If the parties don't choose to prepare the case properly they must take the consequences.

(Counsel confer.)

Counsel: Milord, those instructing me will endeavour to obtain a set of photographs this afternoon but I understand from my learned friend that the machine has been considerably modified since the accident.

Judge: I have no doubt it has. What I am complaining about is the failure of your solicitors to take the elementary step of photographing the machine before it was modified. We had better get on as best we can.

Counsel: Well, Milord, the plaintiff began work with the defendants at the beginning of March 1991, he had just left school. . .

Judge: Mr Slope I have read the pleadings and, of course, the documents in the court bundle. There is no need for you to open the case in any detail.

Counsel: I'm very much obliged: then your lordship will have seen that the basis of the plaintiff's case is set out in the allegations in paragraph 3 of the statement of claim – in effect that this young man should have been given proper instructions as to the operation of the machine and that the machine itself was dangerous in that the emergency switch was not readily accessible.

Judge: And of course the defendants say that the plaintiff was the author of his own misfortune in putting his hand into the compartment.

Counsel: Milord, yes, but we say that the important factor in this case is that this was not an experienced operator but in effect a lad who had just left school and had no experience whatsoever in handling dangerous machinery.

Judge: How old is your client now?

Counsel: Milord I'll take instructions *(he confers with Oliver)*. Milord, I am instructed he is now 19 years of age.

Judge: Has notice been filed that he is adopting this action? The papers before me show him to be suing as an infant by his next friend.

Counsel: *(counsel again confers with his solicitors)* Milord, it appears that those instructing me have overlooked this point.

Judge: The practice is quite clear. It's here in the White Book, paragraph 80/2/12. Your solicitors had better undertake to file a notice forthwith.

Counsel: Milord, yes, I'm very much obliged.

Judge: This isn't just pedantry you know – it could have an effect on any order as to who pays the costs.

Counsel: Milord, yes.

Judge: Very well. Now what about the medical reports. Why isn't there an agreed report?

Counsel: Milord, the reports in the Court Bundle are agreed.

Judge: If there is agreement on the medical evidence, wouldn't it have been more sensible to put one report before me? I suppose I am now going to have to wade through pages of repetition.

Counsel: Milord, there is no discrepancy between the doctors' findings or conclusions.

Judge: Well then I wholly fail to see why I have to read through *two* reports. What is the position with regard to the special damage?

Counsel: Milord, your Lordship will have seen the schedule and counter-schedule.

Judge: I have but why is it necessary to have two schedules. The practice now is for one schedule to be prepared for the purpose of the trial showing the respective contentions of each party. That is what should have been done here. (*To the Defendants' counsel:*) Mr Snubbins, is there any dispute about the loss to date?

Counsel for the defendants: Milord, no, but there is dispute about the estimates of future loss of earnings.

Judge: Very well, that is a point in issue. Mr Slope I have seen the plaintiff's witness statement. Is there any reason why that should not stand as his evidence-in-chief?

Counsel: Milord, both myself and my learned friend agree that questions of credibility may arise in this case and that the better course would be for the witnesses on each side to be taken through their evidence-in-chief.

Judge: Very well then, Mr Slope, you had better call the plaintiff.

(Oliver now goes into the witness box and is sworn and gives his account of the matter which is taken down by the judge in his note. We rejoin the hearing at the crucial point, where Oliver deals with the suggestion of contributory negligence.)

Counsel for the plaintiff: Had you ever seen Mr Sikes put his hand in the compartment?

Oliver: Yes.

Counsel: How often?

Oliver: Not often.

Counsel: How many times do you think?

Oliver: Two or three times I should think.

(This of course contradicts Oliver's witness statement where he says that Sikes had put his hand in the compartment 'on many occasions'; counsel, however, is not permitted to refer his own witness to an earlier statement inconsistent with the evidence now given nor, as we shall see, to cross-examine his own witness.)

Counsel: Only two or three times!

Oliver: Yes.

Counsel: That is all you remember?

Counsel for the defendants: Milord, my learned friend has already received his answer to that question.

Judge: Yes, I think you had better move on to something else, Mr Slope. You wouldn't want to embarrass Mr Twist by cross-examining him, would you?

Counsel for the plaintiff: If your lordship pleases. *(To Oliver)* Do you remember the last time you had seen him trying to pull salvage out of the compartment.

Oliver: Yes. He had to do it on the morning of the accident . . .

Counsel: Had he ever told you not to put your hand into the machine?

Oliver: No.

Counsel: And of course there were no notices in the factory warning you?

Counsel for the defendants: Milord, that is a grossly leading question.

Judge: Well, it is leading, but are you suggesting that there were notices?

Counsel for the defendants: No, we don't suggest that.

Judge: Then I cannot see there is anything improper in the question. There is no reason why counsel shouldn't ask leading questions on matters not in dispute . . .

(Oliver then goes on to deal with his efforts to get a job and the extent of his present disability. After his examination-in-chief by his own counsel is concluded, counsel for the defendants is entitled to cross-examine.)

Counsel for the defendants: Did you do metal work at school?

Oliver: Yes.

Counsel: I think you were quite proficient at it.

Oliver: Yes.

Counsel: Did that involve operating lathes?

Oliver: Yes.

Counsel: Other machinery?
Oliver: Yes.
Counsel: And you were always aware of the need to take care with moving machinery?
Oliver: Of course.
Counsel: This machine you operated at the factory, it's quite simple, isn't it?
Oliver: Yes, it's easy.
Counsel: It's simply two presses: one coming from above and one from the side.
Oliver: Yes.
Counsel: And it is obviously dangerous to put your hand into the pressing compartment.
Oliver: Yes, it is.
Counsel: You don't need to be a mechanic to see that, do you?
Oliver: I suppose not.
Counsel: If you'd thought for a moment, you'd have realised the stupidity of what you were doing?
Oliver: I suppose so, but Mr Sikes did it.
Counsel: You didn't need Mr Sikes to tell you it was dangerous?
Oliver: No . . .

(After Oliver's cross-examination is concluded, his own counsel is entitled to re-examine on any points that had arisen during the cross-examination.)

Counsel for the plaintiff: Who showed you how to operate the machine?
Oliver: Mr Sikes.
Counsel: Did he ever tell you about the safety precautions?
Oliver: No.
Counsel: Did he ever tell you not to pull boxes out of the way like he did?
Oliver: No.
Counsel: Milord, that's all the questions I have.
Judge: Very well, thank you Mr Twist.

(The witness withdraws.)

Counsel: Milord I wonder if your Lordship would be kind enough to look at the statement from HM Inspector of Factories – at page 22 in your Lordship's Bundle – and milord it's an agreed document. Your lordship will also see the report from Mr Edwards the consulting engineer and your Lordship will see the comments on the failure to provide fencing and the location of the emergency switches. My Lord notice of our intention to put in this report has been served under the Civil Evidence Act 1972.
Judge: The 1972 Act covers expert opinion evidence of course. Just give me a moment *(he reads the statement and the report)*. It seems fairly clear from this that there was a breach of duty in not fencing the machine. What do you say about this Mr Snubbins?
Counsel for the defendants: Milord I have obviously considered this very carefully with those instructing me – we do not propose to dispute the contention that the machine was not adequately guarded.
Judge: Then the real issue will be as to contributory negligence.
Counsel: Milord, yes.
Judge: Very well.

Counsel for the plaintiff: Milord I would now put before your lordship two letters, and milord notice has been given under the Civil Evidence Act 1968. Your lordship sees the first letter is from the Transport and General Workers Union and sets out details of the present average earnings of machine operators according to their age and position. The second letter milord is from the same union and gives details, milord, of earnings which the plaintiff could expect in the sort of unskilled work it appears he will now be following.

Judge: Yes, it seems that at the moment he has a continuing loss of earnings of about £30 per week.

Counsel: Milord, yes. Milord, that then is the case for the plaintiff.

(Counsel for the defendant then calls his evidence. The factory manager deposes that there had never been any previous incident at the machine and he had never noticed anybody putting their hand into the press compartment. Sikes then gives evidence . . .)

Counsel for the defendants: Have you ever put your hand in the press compartment while the machine was operating?

Sikes: I have pulled boxes and bits of cardboard clear when they have spilt over the top of the compartment.

Counsel: Did that involve putting your hand into the compartment?

Sikes: Once or twice I've had to pull something clear which has been stuck.

Counsel: Have you ever done that in front of the plaintiff?

Sikes: I can remember doing so that morning, but I warned young Oliver not to try it himself.

(This answer catches counsel for the defendants by surprise since there was no suggestion in Sikes' witness statement that he had given any warning to Oliver. It also surprises counsel for the plaintiffs.)

Judge: Are you saying you had told this boy not to do it?

Sikes: I said to him 'we shouldn't really do this'.

Counsel for the plaintiff: Milord, I must protest. This is a very serious allegation and it's nowhere suggested in the defence that the plaintiff had been warned.

Judge: Let me just see the defence . . . yes, that's quite correct. Mr Snubbins, why isn't this matter pleaded?

Counsel for the defendants: Milord, it takes me as much by surprise as it does my learned friend.

Judge: Well, assuming Mr Sikes hasn't made this up, it suggests that those instructing you have been very seriously at fault. It was quite clear at an early stage what the issues were in the case and it should have been obvious what questions ought to have been asked of the witnesses. It should have appeared in the pleadings and if, because of some mistake, it didn't appear at that stage, it should certainly have been set out in the witness statement. Where does this leave us now?

Counsel for the defendants: Milord, I think I must formally ask for leave to amend the defence to raise the allegation that the plaintiff disregarded a warning from his foreman.

Judge: What do you say, Mr Slope?

Counsel for the plaintiff: Milord, I take the strongest possible objection to the course proposed by my learned friend. In my submission, it's far too late in the day now for the defendants to amend to plead, in effect, a totally different case, a case which of course hasn't been put to my client in cross-examination.

Judge: Well, I have a great deal of sympathy with what you say Mr Slope; as I've already indicated, it is disgraceful that the plaintiff should be confronted with such an allegation at the trial in this way. It makes a mockery of the whole idea of exchange of witness statements. However, it seems to me I cannot now prevent the defendants raising this point, but I shall certainly grant you an adjournment and the costs thrown away if you desire it. Perhaps it would be convenient if I rose for a few moments so that you can take instructions.

(The learned judge rises. Counsel for the plaintiff has now to decide whether to continue with the case that day or have the matter adjourned to see if he can produce any evidence concerning the alleged conversation. Having discussed the matter with Oliver who cannot remember anything at all except that there had been an incident earlier that morning when Sikes pulled out some boxes which were coming out of the press, counsel decides not to ask for an adjournment. Sikes' evidence is then continued and finally Oliver is recalled to say he has no recollection of any warning given by Sikes. Counsel for the defendants then addresses the judge on the question of contributory negligence and also upon Oliver's potential loss of future earnings. After he has finished his address, counsel for the plaintiff rises to address the judge . . .)

Judge: I needn't trouble you on the question of liability and contributory negligence, Mr Slope.

Counsel: I'm very much obliged, milord.

Judge: Are there any particular matters you wish to refer to on the issue of quantum?

(This exchange which might have appeared confusing to a spectator tells counsel that the judge has decided to find for Oliver on the issue of liability without any deduction for contributory negligence. Where a judge decides that the plaintiff should succeed there is no point in his counsel addressing the judge further; where, however, counsel for the plaintiff is called on, it does not necessarily mean that he has lost the case for it may be that the judge is still uncertain.)

Judge: In this case, the plaintiff, Oliver Twist, who was an infant when these proceedings were commenced but has since attained his majority and adopted this action, sues his former employer for damages for personal injuries sustained whilst he was operating a mechanical press at their premises in Southall. *(The learned judge goes on to recite the facts of the case.)* The plaintiff contends (and it is not now disputed) that the defendants were in breach of duty at common law and by statute in permitting him to work at machinery which was not securely fenced. I find the absence of fencing clear evidence of such breach of duty. If it was necessary to consider further I would also hold that the relative inaccessibility of the emergency switch rendered it dangerous to permit the machine to be operated by one man. The real issue in this case, however, has been as to the extent to which, if at all, the plaintiff's damages fall to be reduced by reason of his own negligence. The defendants' case as pleaded and put to him in cross-examination was that he should himself have realised the danger inherent in what he was doing and was therefore the author of his own misfortune. I reject that contention. The plaintiff had started work only one month before the accident; he had seen his foreman removing boxes in exactly the manner which led to the accident; he had received no formal instruction concerning the safe operation of the machine. I am not prepared in the circumstances to make any finding of contributory negligence. At a late stage in the proceedings counsel for the defendants applied for leave to amend the defence so as to include an allegation that the plaintiff had disregarded a warning given to him that morning by the foreman. This amendment was necessary because the foreman, one Sikes, had raised the matter in his evidence-in-chief although, apparently, he had never disclosed it to the defendants' solicitors. I permitted the amendment to be made. The plaintiff was in due course recalled and gave evidence that he had no recollection of such a warning. I was impressed by the plaintiff as a witness – I found him truthful and accurate and where his evidence conflicts with that of Mr Sikes, I prefer his account. Therefore I reject Mr Sikes' evidence on this point. He may now believe that he gave such a warning but, if it had been given in the explicit terms suggested, he would have been bound to have mentioned the matter to his employers after the incident. *(The learned judge then dealt with the medical evidence and the question of loss of future earnings.)* I have decided that the appropriate sum for general damages for pain and suffering is £26,000. In so deciding I have taken into account the fact that this young man has lost the opportunity of pursuing a career involving mechanical work and that he obviously had an aptitude for such work. I shall add the sum of £900 being interest at 2% from the date of service of the writ. Loss and expense to date is agreed at £3765 to which will be added £550 to cover interest from the date of the accident. I assess future loss of earnings at £27,000. (The defendants contended that the multiplicand of £1560 suggested by the plaintiffs was too high; the plaintiffs put in evidence from the research department of the Transport and General Workers Union which was not contradicted by any data provided by the defendants. In those circumstances I accept the plaintiff's contention.) I accept also that there will be extra future recurrent expenditure which I assess at £6000. There is a real and substantial handicap on the labour market for which I award £5000.

Counsel for the plaintiff: Milord, I ask for judgment for £69,215 and costs to be taxed on the standard basis. I also ask for a legal aid taxation of the plaintiff's costs.

Judge: So be it. Is there any payment into court?

(The Associate hands the judge a copy of the notice of payment in.)

Judge: I will order that the sum of £50,000 paid into court by the defendants be paid out to the plaintiff's solicitors in part satisfaction.

Counsel for the plaintiff: I am very much obliged.

Part Two

The rules of civil procedure

Chapter 1

Preliminary matters

HIGH COURT OR COUNTY COURT?

Civil proceedings in England and Wales are brought either in the High Court or in a county court. High Court cases are begun by the issue of proceedings in the Central Office at the Royal Courts of Justice in London or at one of the district registries in the provinces. The trial of a civil action takes place before a *High Court Judge* sitting in London or at the local 'trial centre'. Procedural disputes before the case gets to trial are decided by a *Master* in London or by a *District Judge* if the action is proceeding in a district registry.

County courts exist in almost every major town and since July 1991[1] their jurisdiction has been enlarged to make them the appropriate tribunal for relatively large, as well as small and medium-sized claims. County court actions are tried before a *Circuit Judge*; procedural disputes (and claims for up to £5000) are heard by a *District Judge*. It should be noted that a District Judge may deal with procedural disputes both at the local High Court district registry and at the county court.

The allocation of business between the High Court and the county courts is now governed by the rules set out in the High Court and County Courts Jurisdiction Order 1991; these rules make provisions relating to the *jurisdiction* of each court, the *commencement* of proceedings and the *trial* of actions. A plaintiff with a choice of court in which to bring proceedings will usually wish to do so in the local county court, where the expense of obtaining and enforcing judgment is likely to be lower.

(a) Jurisdiction

The detailed rules defining the types of case in which the county courts have jurisdiction are set out in the Appendix on page 400. We have also set out overleaf a table showing a summary of the jurisdiction of the county courts over the most common forms of civil action.

In many cases both the High Court and the county courts have concurrent jurisdiction over proceedings;[2] for example, in actions for debt or damages in contract or tort the county courts have jurisdiction along with

---

1 The High Court and County Courts Jurisdiction Order 1991, SI 1991 No 724 (L 5)
2 In general, a county court will either have full jurisdiction whatever the amount involved or the value of any fund or asset connected with the proceedings or jurisdiction subject to monetary limits or other conditions.

Type of Action	Jurisdiction	Statutory Provision
Debt, rent, contract, tort (other than personal injury), recovery of chattels	High Court and county courts have jurisdiction irrespective of value. Claims may be commenced in the High Court or a county court. The decision as to the court of trial depends on the criteria set out in art 7(5) of the Jurisdiction Order namely – financial substance of the action, importance of issues to parties and public, complexity of facts, legal issues, remedies or procedures involved, whether transfer will result in a more speedy trial. Claims having a value of £50,000 or more will usually be tried in the High Court; claims having a value of less than £25,000 will almost invariably be heard in a county court. There is an overlap in the case of claims having a value of £25,000 or more but less than £50,000. Such claims may be heard in the court in which they are commenced or transferred in the light of the criteria in art 7(5).	County Courts Act 1984, s 15; High Court and County Courts Jurisdiction Order 1991 SI 1991 No 724 (L5)
Personal injury cases	High Court and county courts have jurisdiction irrespective of value. Claims must be commenced in a county court unless value (excluding interest and deductions for contributory negligence) is £50,000 or more. In the High Court the writ must be indorsed before issue with a statement of value signed by the plaintiff's solicitor.	High Court and County Courts Jurisdiction Order 1991 arts 5 and 9; QBD Practice Direction [1991] 3 All ER 452
Possession of land where title in dispute or against trespassers	Claims may be commenced in the High Court or a county court, which have jurisdiction whatever the value of the action, but the decision as to where disputed actions will be *tried* depends on the criteria in art 7(5) of the 1991 Jurisdiction Order.	County Courts Act 1984, s.21; 1991 Jurisdiction Order arts 2, 7 and 9
Claims for possession by mortgagees (e g banks and building societies)	High Court has jurisdiction in all cases. County courts have jurisdiction where amount owing does not exceed £30,000.	1991 Jurisdiction Order art 2(4)
Claims for possession against residential tenants	The High Court and county courts have jurisdiction. Almost invariably proceedings are brought in a county court in Rent Act cases because costs are usually not recoverable in the High Court.	Rent Act 1977, s 141; Housing Act 1980, s 86
Applications for new tenancy of business premises	Both the High Court and county courts have jurisdiction. Applications will be tried by the High Court or a county court according to the criteria in art 7(5).	Landlord and Tenant Act 1954, s 63(2); 1991 Jurisdiction Order art 2(1)(d) and Schedule 1
Disputes between co-owners as to sale of land	High Court and county courts have jurisdiction. Proceedings will be allocated for trial according to the art 7(5) criteria.	Law of Property Act 1925, s 30; 1991 Jurisdiction Order art 2(1)(a)
Equity proceedings	High Court has jurisdiction in all cases. County courts have concurrent jurisdiction where the value of the fund or property does not exceed £30,000.	County Courts Act 1984, s 23; County Courts Jurisdiction Order 1981, art 2

the High Court, whatever the amount claimed by the plaintiff.[3] Although this appears to give a plaintiff a choice of forum, the plaintiff's choice is limited in two ways. The rules prescribe firstly that certain proceedings *must* be commenced in a county court,[4] and secondly, that certain claims, although they may be started in the High Court, must be *tried* at a county court, and must be transferred to that court for trial. The rules restricting commencement and trial, which mainly depend on the nature of the claim and its monetary value, are explained below.

(b) Commencement of proceedings

Where both the High Court and the county courts have jurisdiction an action may be started in either court. Proceedings where the value of the claim is less than £25,000 will usually be commenced in the county court because they will be tried in that court. However, it is important to note that debt or contract proceedings will still often be commenced in the High Court in claims for comparatively small sums. This will occur where the plaintiff's solicitor hopes to obtain default or summary judgment and then use the efficient High Court procedures for enforcing the judgment.[5]

> *Example 1.* Albert intends to bring proceedings against Benjamin for £12,000 being the price of goods sold and delivered. He cannot see that Benjamin has any answer to the claim. It is likely that his solicitor will bring proceedings in the High Court in the hope of obtaining within a few weeks a default judgment (see page 93) or summary judgment (see page 149). The judgment will then be enforced in the High Court. If Benjamin intends to defend the claim and raises a triable issue, the case will be transferred under s 40(2) of the County Courts Act 1984 for trial at a county court.
>
> *Example 2.* Charles intends to sue Donald for damages amounting to £12,000 in respect of a lorry purchased from Donald. There has been extensive correspondence in which Donald has repeatedly claimed that the lorry broke down because of lack of maintenance by Charles. Donald has instructed solicitors to act for him. Such a case will be commenced in a county court as there would be no point in starting proceedings in the High Court; the case would inevitably be transferred to a county court for trial.

There is one important exception[6] to the general rule that proceedings where both courts have jurisdiction can be started in either court: article 5 of the 1991 Jurisdiction Order provides that proceedings which include a claim for damages in respect of personal injuries *must* be commenced in a county court, unless the value of the action is £50,000 or more:[7]

> '5.–(1) Proceedings in which county courts have jurisdiction and which include a claim for damages in respect of personal injuries shall be commenced in a county court, unless the value of the action is £50,000 or more.
>
> (2) In this article "personal injuries" means personal injuries to the plaintiff or

---

3 The High Court and County Courts Jurisdiction Order 1991, art 2(1)(1).
4 Ibid, art 4.
5 Particularly when it is intended to enforce a judgment wholly or partially by execution against goods (writ of *fi fa*), which may be enforced only in the High Court where the sum involved is £5000 or more: High Court and County Courts Jurisdiction Order 1991, art 8.
6 Another, less important, exception is applications and appeals under ss 19 and 20 of the Local Government Finance Act 1982 (dealing with the legality of items of local government expenditure) which must be commenced in the High Court: art 6.
7 Ibid, art 5(1).

any other person, and includes disease, impairment of physical or mental condition, and death.'

The 'value of the action' for this purpose is determined at the time the
action is commenced;[8] the plaintiff excludes the amount he is likely to be
awarded in interest[9] and ignores the possibility that the eventual award
may be reduced because of a finding of contributory negligence.[10] In order
to give effect to this rule, where a writ which includes a claim for personal
injuries is issued in the Queen's Bench Division of the High Court it must
first be indorsed with a statement of value, signed by the plaintiff or his
solicitor as follows:

> 'This writ includes a claim for personal injury but may be commenced in the
> High Court because the value of the action for the purposes of art 5 of the High
> Court and County Courts Jurisdiction Order 1991 exceeds £50,000.'[11]

If an action where the value of the claim is clearly less than £50,000 is
brought in the High Court, the other side can apply for an order under
section 40(1) of the County Courts Act 1984 which provides:

> '(1) Where the High Court is satisfied that any proceedings before it are required
> by any provision of a kind mentioned in subsection (8) to be in a county court it
> shall
>   (*a*) order the transfer of the proceedings to a county court; or
>   (*b*) if the court is satisfied that the person bringing the proceedings knew, or
>   ought to have known, of that requirement, order that they be struck out.'

> (8) The provisions referred to in subsection (1) are any made–
>   (*a*) under section 1 of the Courts and Legal Services Act 1990; or
>   (*b*) by or under any other enactment.'

> *Example.* Mona has commenced High Court proceedings against Edgar in respect
> of personal injuries caused by Edgar's negligent driving. Mona suffered a
> fractured rib and was forced to stay away from work for one month. Her solicitor
> indorsed the writ with a statement that the value of the action exceeded £50,000.
> Edgar has served a defence denying negligence. Edgar can apply to the court for
> an order under section 40(1) that the action should be struck out. The High Court
> will either transfer the action or strike it out on the grounds that Mona's solicitors
> must have been well aware that the claim could not have been worth more than
> £50,000 (or indeed anywhere near that sum).

(c) Trial of proceedings
Sections 40–42 of the County Courts Act 1984 provide for the transfer of
proceedings between the High Court and a county court. Article 7 of the
Jurisdiction Order deals with the question whether a case should be transferred. In theory, proceedings in which the High Court and the county
courts have jurisdiction may be tried in either court. However, article 7
establishes certain *presumptions* as to place of trial based on the value of the
claim and also certain *criteria* which are to be applied in deciding whether to
transfer a case for trial:

8 The High Court and County Courts Jurisdiction Order 1991, art 10(a).
9 Ibid, art 9(2)(b).
10 Ibid, art 9(4)(b), unless the plaintiff admits contributory negligence, when a reduction in
   value should be made.
11 QBD *Practice Direction*, 21 June 1991 [1991] 3 All ER 352.

'(2) The following provisions of this article apply to proceedings in which both the High Court and the county courts have jurisdiction, . . . save that paragraphs (3) and (4) do not apply to proceedings which have no quantifiable value.

(3) An action of which the value is less than £25,000 shall be tried in a county court unless–
  (*a*) a county court, having regard to the criteria set out in sub-paragraphs (a) to (d) of paragraph (5), considers that it ought to transfer the action to the High Court for trial and the High Court considers that it ought to try the action; or
  (*b*) it is commenced in the High Court and the High Court, having regard to the said criteria considers that it ought to try the action.

(4) An action of which the value is £50,000 or more shall be tried in the High Court unless–
  (*a*) it is commenced in a county court and the county court does not, having regard to the criteria set out in sub-paragraphs (a) to (d) of paragraph (5), consider that the action ought to be transferred to the High Court for trial; or
  (*b*) the High Court, having regard to the said criteria, considers that it ought to transfer the case to a county court for trial.

(5) The High Court and the county courts, when considering whether to exercise their powers under section 40(2), 41(1) or 42(2) of the County Courts Act 1984 (Transfer) shall have regard to the following criteria–
  (*a*) the financial substance of the action, including the value of any counterclaim,
  (*b*) whether the action is otherwise important and, in particular, whether it raises questions of importance to persons who are not parties or questions of general public interest,
  (*c*) the complexity of the facts, legal issues, remedies or procedures involved, and
  (*d*) whether transfer is likely to result in a more speedy trial of the action,

but no transfer shall be made on the grounds of sub-paragraph (d) alone.'

In effect, it can be seen that the Article defines three categories of actions:

  (i) actions with a value of less that £25,000;
  (ii) actions with a value of £50,000 or more;
  (iii) actions with a value of £25,000 or more but less than £50,000.

In practice transfer *from* a county court to the High Court is almost unknown; transfer *from* the High Court *to* a county court is very common, particularly in cases falling within the last category (ie where the claim is less than £50,000 but not less than £25,000). Either party may apply for transfer but even if no application is made the master or district judge will review the case after setting down and may order transfer to a county court.

ASSESSING THE VALUE OF AN ACTION

For the purposes of many of the above provisions it is clearly very important to identify the value of an action. Where the plaintiff claims a sum of money, the value of the action is the amount which the plaintiff reasonably expects to recover, whether or not the sum is specified in the claim.[12] If the plaintiff's claim is not for a sum of money, but for other specified relief, the value of the action is the sum of money which the plaintiff could reasonably state to be

---

12 Ibid, art 9(1)(a). Where there is more than one plaintiff, the value is the aggregate of their expectations: art 9(3).

the financial worth of the claim to him.[13] If the plaintiff could not reasonably state any financial worth of the relief claimed, the action is treated as having no quantifiable value.[14] In every case, no account is to be taken of unspecified further or other relief;[15] interest, other than contractual interest; costs; possible findings of contributory negligence, except to the extent that it is admitted; or the possibility of further future damages where an award of provisional damages is sought.[16] Further, the amount which the plaintiff reasonably expects to recover must be reduced by the amount of any *debt* which the plaintiff admits is owed to the defendant provided it arises from the circumstances which give rise to the action.[17]

> *Example 1.* Roger and Mary commence proceedings in the High Court against the Aler Brewery for breach of contract after they are dismissed without notice from their jobs as co-managers of one of the brewery's public houses. Under their contracts, they are entitled to six months' notice of termination and their salaries are £20,000 each. The Aler Brewery claims that the plaintiffs' bad management justified their dismissals. If they win the action, they could reasonably expect to recover £1,500 in statutory interest and £5,000 costs in addition to damages of £10,000 each. The value of the action will be £20,000 for the purposes of trial allocation because the values of each plaintiff's claim for damages must be aggregated, but the statutory interest and legal costs are ignored. The action will therefore be transferred to a county court for trial unless there are good reasons, based on the criteria in article 7, justifying a High Court trial.
>
> *Example 2.* Brian commenced High Court proceedings against Thack claiming the return of £40,000 which Brian lent Thack and which has not been repaid. Thack claimed that the agreed period of the loan was three years which had not yet expired. Because the value of the action is between £25,000 and £50,000 there is no 'presumption' as to place of trial. Neither party applied for transfer to the local county court but the Master on his own motion decided to transfer the action and the court served notice of the decision on the parties. They had the right to serve *notice of objection* to this decision in which case the issue of transfer would be decided after the Master had heard argument from both parties. The argument would turn on the application of the statutory criteria to the facts of the case.
>
> *Example 3.* Wendy wishes to bring proceedings for negligence against her former employer, Simon's Fashions Ltd, in respect of inaccurate references provided by the company to Wendy's prospective employers. Wendy was refused employment on the basis of the references and is advised by her solicitors that the damages recoverable are in the region of £55,000. Wendy admits that she has not yet paid Simon's Fashions the sum of £10,000 being the price of the company car which she recently bought from the company. Although Wendy admits the debt, it does not arise from the circumstances which gave rise to the action so it does not affect the value of the action. There is accordingly a presumption that the action will be tried in the High Court.

The presumptions relating to place of trial based on the value of the action apply to all proceedings in which both the county courts and the High Court have jurisdiction except:

(i)   Equity proceedings under ss 23 and 24 of the County Courts Act 1984 – art 7(2). In practice most equity proceedings will continue to be dealt with in the Chancery Division of the High Court.

13 The High Court and County Courts Jurisdiction Order 1991, art 9(1)(b)(i).
14 Ibid, art 9(1)(b)(ii).
15 Ibid, art 9(2)(a).
16 Ibid, art 9(2), (4).
17 Ibid, art 9(4)(a).

(ii) Probate proceedings under s 32 of the County Courts Act 1984 – art 7(2). Probate proceedings are almost always brought in the High Court and this practice is likely to continue.

(iii) Proceedings which have no quantifiable value. Proceedings have no quantifiable value if they include a claim for relief other than a sum of money, and the plaintiff cannot reasonably state the financial worth of the claim (e g a claim for an injunction for nuisance caused by noise).[18] In such proceedings there is no 'presumption' as to place of trial so that such cases may be tried in either court; but in considering whether to exercise their powers of transfer the courts will have regard to the criteria contained in art 7(5) (see below).

Example. Maureen commences proceedings in the High Court to obtain a declaration that her neighbour Albert is building an extension to his pigeon shed on Maureen's land and an injunction restraining Albert from continuing with the work and compelling him to demolish the structure already built. Maureen is not claiming a sum of money and if there is no amount which she can reasonably state to be the financial worth of the claim to her, the action has no quantifiable value for the purposes of determining where the case should be tried. Nevertheless the criteria (discussed below) will probably require the case to be transferred to the local county court for trial.

The criteria

In every case, when considering where the trial should take place, the High Court and county courts must have regard to four criteria in art 7(5):

(a) the financial substance of the action, including the value of any counterclaim;[19]

(b) whether the action is otherwise important and, in particular, whether it raises questions of importance to persons who are not parties or questions of general importance;[20]

(c) the complexity of the facts, legal issues, remedies or procedures involved;[21]

(d) whether transfer is likely to result in a more speedy trial of the action.[22]

The following types of action have been identified as potentially suitable for High Court trial under the above criteria, whatever the value of the claim:[23] (1) professional negligence; (2) fatal accidents; (3) fraud or undue influence; (4) defamation; (5) malicious prosecution or false imprisonment; (6) claims against the police.

INJUNCTIONS

Section 38 of the County Courts Act 1984[24] empowers a county court to 'make any order which could be made by the High Court if the proceedings were in the High Court'. This removes the former restriction under which a

18 The High Court and County Courts Jurisdiction Order 1991, art 9(1).
19 Ibid, art 7(5)(a).
20 Ibid, art 7(5)(b).
21 Ibid, art 7(5)(c).
22 Ibid, art 7(5)(d).
23 *QBD Practice Direction*, 26 June 1991 [1991] 3 All ER 349, para 9.
24 As amended by s 3 of the Courts and Legal Services Act 1990.

county court could normally grant an injunction only in connection with a monetary claim.

However, the County Courts Remedies Regulations 1991 prohibit a county court from granting Mareva injunctions or Anton Piller orders,[25] other than in very limited circumstances.[26]

QUEEN'S BENCH OR CHANCERY DIVISION?

When High Court proceedings are to be brought, the plaintiff must decide in which *division* of the High Court to start the action. Commencement in the wrong division will not be fatal, as each division has wide powers of transfer if the court considers that it is inappropriate for the type of action which has been brought. To some extent, the plaintiff has a choice of division, which should be exercised according to the nature of the case and issues raised by it. Broadly, the judges of the Chancery Division will possess specialist knowledge and expertise in particular areas of practice, such as sale of land, trusts, company law, patents and taxation, making cases raising such issues appropriate for commencement in the Chancery Division. Certain actions *must* be commenced in particular divisions. Schedule 1 to the Supreme Court Act 1981 allocates civil actions between the Queen's Bench and Chancery Divisions as follows.[27]

'DISTRIBUTION OF BUSINESS IN THE HIGH COURT

Chancery Division
1. To the Chancery Divisions are assigned all causes and matters relating to –

    (a) the sale, exchange or partition of land, or the raising of charges on land;
    (b) the redemption or foreclosure of mortgages;
    (c) the execution of trusts;
    (d) the administration of the estates of deceased persons;
    (e) bankruptcy;
    (f) the dissolution of partnership or the taking of partnership or other accounts;
    (g) the rectification, setting aside or cancellation of deeds or other instruments in writing;
    (h) probate business, other than non-contentious or common form business;
    (i) patents, trade marks, registered designs or copyright;
    (j) the appointment of a guardian of a minor's estate;

and all causes an matters involving the exercise of the High Court's jurisdiction under the enactments relating to companies.

---

25 See pp 244–262, post.
26 If a Mareva injunction or Anton Piller order is sought, in practice the proceedings will be begun in the High Court (although article 3 of the 1991 Jurisdiction Order enables the High Court to grant such relief in proceedings begun in a county court).
27 Schedule 1, paragraph 3 also allocates the business of the Family Division.

Queen's Bench Division
2. To the Queen's Bench Division are assigned–

    (a) applications for writs of habeas corpus, except applications made by a parent or guardian of a minor for such a writ concerning the custody of the minor;

    (b) applications for judicial review;

    (c) all causes and matters involving the exercise of the High Court's Admiralty jurisdiction or its jurisdiction as a prize court; and

    (d) all causes and matters entered in the commercial list.'

It is important to remember that Schedule 1 sets out only those actions which are exclusively assigned to a particular division. Many categories of actions, such as claims for breach of contract, may be brought in either division depending on the 'flavour' of the action.

> *Example.* The plaintiff company, which manufactures fire alarms, sued the defendants, former employees of the company, for, *inter alia*, breach of contract arising from the defendants' alleged misuse of confidential information which they acquired whilst they were employees. The provisions of Schedule 1 do not assign the case to the Chancery Division and the plaintiff commenced the action in the Queen's Bench Division. But early in the proceedings the action was transferred to the Chancery Division which is the more appropriate division of the High Court to determine an action including claims for misuse of confidential information and passing off.[28]

HIGH COURT ACTIONS – CENTRAL OFFICE OR DISTRICT REGISTRY?

Although the High Court is based in London, it is possible for a plaintiff outside London to commence High Court proceedings through one of the 133 district registries of the High Court. The district registries usually cover a number of county court districts and High Court proceedings commenced in a registry will continue to be dealt with there (for example, summary judgment applications or other interlocutory questions), unless the court otherwise orders.[29] Interlocutory matters arising in proceedings commenced in a district registry are heard, not by masters, but by district judges.

WHICH COUNTY COURT?

If the case is to be in a county court the plaintiff may have a choice of court in which to bring the action. Suppose a plaintiff living in Brentford has been supplied with goods by a defendant trading in Cleethorpes. In such a case, it will obviously suit the plaintiff better to use the Brentford County Court, but this may be very inconvenient for the defendant. Whether the plaintiff can use his local county court depends on the nature of the claim. The basic rules[30] as to where an action may be commenced are as follows:

    (i) In the case of a *default action* (i e where the plaintiff is claiming a sum

---

28 See *Lock International plc v Beswick* [1989] 3 All ER 373.
29 RSC Ord 32, r 24(1).
30 CCR Ord 4, r 2. Note throughout the text CCR refers to the County Court Rules 1981; RSC refers to the Rules of the Supreme Court 1965.

of money or damages *only*), the case can be brought in any county court. But the case may be transferred to the *defendant's* home court:

(a) where the claim is for a *liquidated sum* (i e a debt or a sum which is alleged to have been agreed, such as the price of goods), the case is *automatically* transferred to the defendant's home court if the defendant files a substantive defence.[31] If the plaintiff objects, he may then apply to the defendant's home court for further transfer elsewhere;[32]

(b) where the claim is for an unliquidated sum (such as damages for personal injury), there is no automatic transfer, but the parties (usually the defendant) may apply to have the case transferred to another county court.

(ii) In cases other than default actions (i e where the plaintiff claims a remedy other than money, such as possession of land or recovery of goods), the plaintiff must bring the action either:

(a) in the court for the district in which the *defendant* or one of the defendants *resides* or *carries on business; or*

(b) in the court for the district in which the *cause of action wholly or in part*[33] *arose.*

Example 1. Eric, who lives in Brentford, orders some furniture from a firm called Furniture Express in Manchester. He fails to pay for the goods. Proceedings by Furniture Express could be brought in any court but will automatically be transferred to Brentford County Court once Eric files a defence disputing the claim because this is a liquidated claim.

Example 2. Clive, who also lives in Brentford, is driving in Norwich when his car is damaged in a road accident with a lorry owned by Ben's Haulage of Portsmouth. Clive's claim is for damages and is therefore a default action; he may bring the claim in Brentford County Court. If Ben's Haulage files a defence, the case will not be transferred automatically as Clive is not claiming a liquidated (i e contractually defined) sum but Ben's Haulage may apply to have the case transferred to Portsmouth County Court or to Norwich County Court.[34]

THE PARTIES

(a) Joinder of parties
The basic rule is that two or more persons must sue or be sued in one action where they are jointly entitled to the relief claimed or jointly liable under any contract on which the plaintiff sues. In addition two or more persons may sue or be sued in one action where:

---

31 CCR Ord 9, r 2(8)(a).
32 CCR Ord 16, r 4(2).
33 In contract cases, the cause of action will arise *in part* at the place where the contract is made and in part where it is broken. A contract by exchange of letters is *made* where the letter of acceptance is posted: see *Byrne & Co v Leon Von Tienhoven & Co* (1880) 5 CPD 344. Where a contract is entered into by telephone it is deemed to have been made by the acceptor so that it is his location which determines where the cause of action arises; similarly where the agreement is made by telex: see *Brinkibon Ltd v Stahag Stahl und Stahlwarenhandel GmbH* [1983] 2 AC 34, [1982] 1 All ER 293, HL.
34 Applications for transfer to another county court are made in writing and the parties' attendance is not necessary: CCR Ord 16, r 1.

(i) if separate actions were brought a *common question of law or fact* would arise in all the actions, *and*

(ii) the claims arise out of the *same transactions or series of transactions.*[35]

Example 1. Albert and Mary rent a flat from Bernard. There is a written lease. They fall into arrears of rent and fail to keep the interior of the premises in proper repair. One action for forfeiture will be brought against them both as they are jointly liable under the terms of the lease.

Example 2. Eric is driving a lorry owned by his employer David when he knocks down a pedestrian, Peter. Peter can sue David alone and will normally do so since the employer will be vicariously liable for his employees' negligence. He can also sue Eric alone or he may sue both David and Eric in one action. This would be appropriate where a question arose whether Eric was acting within the course of his employment at the relevant time.

Where two or more persons *sue* as co-plaintiffs they must employ the same solicitor and counsel, the theory being that as there should be no conflict of interest between them, the employment of separate counsel and solicitors would duplicate work and increase costs.

Example. The Daily Telegraph published an article to the effect that the police were investigating the affairs of a certain company. The chairman of the company and the company itself brought actions alleging libel. The company went into liquidation but the liquidator carried on the action. Differences arose between the liquidator and the company chairman who then obtained separate representation. The Court of Appeal held this was improper. Per Russell LJ: 'Prima facie, co-plaintiffs, whether in one original action or in an action consisting of consolidated actions must be jointly represented by solicitor and counsel. In a proper case, an order may be made authorising severance in part of representation but this must be, I think, rare and should only be done to avoid injustice' (*Lewis v Daily Telegraph Ltd (No 2)*).[36]

An example of a case where separate representation was permitted on the ground of substantial conflict of interest between co-plaintiffs is *The Bosworth*:[37]

Example. At Christmas 1957 *The Bosworth* was carrying a cargo of coal from Scotland to Norway when she developed a list in a heavy gale. A trawler called the *Wolverhampton Wanderers* stood by in answer to a distress call and eventually took off the crew. Another trawler, *The Faraday*, put four men on to *The Bosworth* and towed her into Aberdeen. Both trawlers sued the owners of the collier for salvage but since there was a substantial dispute between them as to the proper apportionment of the sum recovered, they were allowed separate representation.

(b) Consolidation

What happens if parties who could sue as co-plaintiffs instead bring separate actions? Generally speaking, the defendant will wish to have the matters which each action has in common with the others tried at one time to save costs. There are a number of possibilities open to the court in such cases:

(i)   to order that one action be tried first and that the remaining actions be stayed until the result of the test case is known. Usually the

---

35 The above is a paraphrase of RSC Ord 15, r 4(1) and CCR Ord 5, rr 1 and 2 which are for practical purposes identical. For the purposes of this rule 'transaction' includes a set of circumstances and is not restricted to contractual relationships: *Re Beck* (1918) 87 LJ Ch 335, CA.

36 [1964] 2 QB 601 at 623.

37 [1960] 1 All ER 146, [1961] 1 WLR 312.

defendant, in whose interest such an order is made, undertakes to be bound by the decision in the subsequent actions. This is the usual order in cases where the issue of liability is the same, e g railway or aircraft accidents;

(ii) to order that the actions come on one after the other so that the judge hears the evidence in all the cases before giving judgment;

(iii) to order that the actions be consolidated, i e treated as one action;[38]

(iv) to order that the actions be consolidated so far as the common issues are concerned but thereafter tried separately.

An example which illustrates this problem is *Healey v A Waddington & Sons*.[39]

Example. Six miners were killed and two seriously injured in a colliery accident. The injured men and the dependants of the deceased brought separate actions in negligence against the mine owners. The judge ordered that one action should be tried first as a test case on the issue of liability. However, the defendants felt that somewhat different questions on liability arose in respect of the different claims and so would not have been satisfied with the result of a test case. Nevertheless it was obvious that six separate cases would cause great expense: the Court of Appeal therefore ordered that there should be consolidation of the actions on the question of liability, i e so that the slightly different issues in respect of each action could be heard together and determined at one time, but that there should then be separate trials with separate representation on the issues of quantum.

(c) Representative actions

There will be some cases where so many people have an interest in proceedings that it would be impracticable for them all to be joined as co-plaintiffs or co-defendants. To cover this eventuality RSC Order 15, rule 12[40] provides that:

'Where numerous persons have the same interest in proceedings[41] . . . the proceedings may be begun and, unless the Court otherwise orders, continued by or against any one or more of them as representing all or as representing all except one or more of them.'

The essence of such a 'class action'[42] is that all the persons represented have a common interest which is threatened and that the relief claimed benefits them all.

Example 1. A cleaner employed by the City Livery Club fell at work and sued the secretary and chairman of the club 'on their own behalf and on behalf of all other members of the club'. The court ordered that the persons sued should represent all the members of the club as at the date of the accident (*Campbell v Thompson*[43]).
Example 2. The Duke of Bedford was granted a charter by statute to run a market at Covent Garden. The market gardeners of Middlesex obtained preferential rights for themselves under the statute as 'growers' to sell their produce at lower tolls than the middlemen or merchants. The Duke was alleged to have levied excessive tolls. In a representative action by four growers for a declaration and an

38 RSC Ord 4, r 9; CCR Ord 13, r 9.
39 [1954] 1 All ER 861n, [1954] 1 WLR 688, CA.
40 And CCR Ord 5, r 5.
41 Special rules apply to proceedings concerning the administration of a deceased's estate, property subject to a trust, or the construction of an instrument, including a statute, where all the members of the class cannot be ascertained: RSC Ord 15, r 13.
42 For a recent example of such a class action see the 'Opren' litigation: *Nash v Eli Lilly & Co* [1993] 1 WLR 782, CA. See also 'Guide for use in Group Actions' available from Lord Chancellor's Department.
43 [1953] 1 QB 445, [1953] 1 All ER 831.

account, the Duke took the point that the four could not represent anyone but themselves since the growers had no *proprietary* rights in common. This argument was rejected by the House of Lords. Per Lord McNaughton: 'Given a common interest and a common grievance, a representative suit is in order if the relief sought is in its nature beneficial to all whom the plaintiffs propose to represent' (*Duke of Bedford v Ellis*[44]).

It should be noted that the conditions stated by Lord McNaughton must all apply before a representative action can be brought.

Example 1. A ship carrying various cargoes from New York to Japan was sunk by a Russian cruiser during the Russo-Japanese war because some of the cargo was contraband. An action was brought against the shipowners for breach of contract in permitting contraband on board. The case was brought by a number of cargo-owners 'on behalf of themselves and other owners of cargo lately laden on board the steamship *Knight Commander*'. The shipowners objected on the basis that the cargo-owners did not have common rights; thus though some were ignorant of the contraband, others knew it was on board and had separate contacts with the shipowners. The objection was sustained. The cargo-owners could have joined together as co-plaintiffs but a representative action was not in order because the rights of the parties were not identical. *Semble* where the claims by the cargo-owners and any defence of the shipowners are identical a representative action would be appropriate (*Markt & Co Ltd v Knight SS Co Ltd*[45])

Example 2. Cardiff Corporation decided to increase the total rent income from council houses by an increase payable by tenants of over a certain income. An action was brought by four tenants acting 'on behalf of themselves and all other tenants of houses provided by the defendants under [the Housing Act 1936]' claiming a declaration that the scheme was ultra vires. It was held that since the scheme did not affect *all* the council tenants adversely, the representative action as brought was misconceived.[46]

It should be carefully noted that the essence of a representative action is that the eventual judgment *binds the persons represented although not appearing personally.* Therefore a plaintiff suing representative defendants must obtain an order of the court that the persons he has nominated are to act as representatives of the class.[47] If the plaintiff is purporting to represent a class of persons but some of them object, they are entitled to take part in the proceedings by being added as defendants to the action.

(d) Claims against the plaintiff
A defendant who wishes to bring a claim against the plaintiff may, instead of bringing separate proceedings, bring a counterclaim against the plaintiff in the same action. The counterclaim will be pleaded as part of the defence: no other document need be served (see p 133, post). It should be remembered that under RSC Ord 15, r 2 (CCR Ord 9, r 2 in the county court) a

---

44 [1901] AC 1.
45 [1910] 2 KB 1021, CA.
46 *Smith v Cardiff Corpn* [1954] 1 QB 210, [1953] 2 All ER 1373, CA. Note that today a person seeking to establish that the decision of a public authority infringes rights which he is entitled to have protected under public law must as a general rule proceed by way of an application for judicial review under RSC Ord 53 rather than by bringing proceedings claiming a declaration. See *O'Reilly v Mackman* [1983] 2 AC 237, [1982] 3 All ER 1124, HL and *Cocks v Thanet District Council* [1983] 2 AC 286, [1982] 3 All ER 1135, HL. But see also *Roy v Kensington and Chelsea and Westminster Family Practitioner Committee* [1992] IRLR 233, HL (public law issue incidental to private law rights). It seems therefore that representative actions are no longer appropriate as means of obtaining declarations in cases involving public rights.
47 RSC Ord 15, r 12(2), CCR Ord 5, r 5.

defendant is permitted to raise *any* counterclaim against the plaintiff, whether or not it arises out of, or is otherwise connected with the plaintiff's claim.[48] But if, for any reason, the court considers that a counterclaim ought to be disposed of by a separate action, or tried separately, it may make an order accordingly.[49]

> *Example.* Teddy sues his landlady, Hilda, for damages arising from breach of covenant to repair. With her defence, Hilda serves a counterclaim which alleges that Teddy has libelled Hilda. Although Hilda was free to serve a counterclaim for libel, there is unlikely to be any saving of time or costs by hearing the two claims together. Further, the joinder is inconvenient because Hilda's claim may have to be tried by a jury. The court will therefore order Hilda's counterclaim either to be tried separately, or struck out completely, leaving Hilda to bring separate proceedings against Teddy.

(e) Counterclaims against additional parties

Sometimes, a defendant may also wish to bring proceedings against a person who is not a party to the action. A defendant who is counterclaiming against the plaintiff may also include other persons as *defendants to the counterclaim* in the following cases:

(i)   if the defendant alleges that an additional party is liable to him *along with the plaintiff in respect of the subject-matter of the counterclaim*;

(ii) if the defendant claims against the additional party *any relief relating to or connected with the original subject-matter of the action.*[50]

> *Example.* Following a road accident involving a number of vehicles, Edward sues Elizabeth for damages for repairs to his Mercedes car. Elizabeth, who denies negligence, suffered serious injuries in the accident and she alleges it was caused by Edward and another driver, George. Furthermore, Elizabeth wishes to claim damages in respect of further damage caused to her BMW car by Freda, who carelessly drove into the back of the car immediately after the main accident. Since Elizabeth is counterclaiming against Edward, she can also include a counterclaim against:
>
> (i)   George, because he is alleged to be *liable along with* the plaintiff; and
> (ii) Freda, because the claim *relates to or is connected with* the original claim for damages brought by the plaintiff.[51]

(f) Order for separate trials

The rules governing the joinder of parties under RSC Order 15 and CCR Order 5 (including those relating to the bringing of counterclaims) set out the circumstances in which parties may be joined *without the leave of the court*. But even where the requirements of the above rules are not satisfied, the court may nevertheless grant leave for parties to be joined when there are advantages to be gained from doing so.[52] Conversely, there may be circumstances where the joinder of parties falls within the rules, but with the consequences that the trial may become over complicated or unwieldy, because, for example, different witnesses will need to be called in respect of

48 *Gray v Webb* (1882) 21 Ch D 802.
49 RSC Ord 15, r 5(2); CCR Ord 21, r 4(3).
50 RSC Ord 15, r 3(1).
51 Note that this is not an appropriate case for commencing third party proceedings against Freda under RSC Ord 16 as Elizabeth is not claiming relief in respect of the same loss as that claimed by Edward. See RSC Ord 16, r 1(1)(b).
52 See RSC Ord 15, r 4(1).

each party. The court is therefore given power to order the severance of such a joinder by RSC Order 15, r 5:

'(1) If claims in respect of two or more causes of action are included by a plaintiff in the same action or by a defendant in a counterclaim, or if two or more plaintiffs or defendants are parties to the same action, and it appears to the Court that the joinder of causes of action or of parties, as the case may be, may embarrass or delay the trial or is otherwise inconvenient, the Court may order separate trials or make such other order as may be expedient.

(2) If it appears on the application of any party against whom a counterclaim is made that the subject-matter of the counterclaim ought for any reason to be disposed of by a separate action, the Court may order the counterclaim to be struck out or may order it to be tried separately or make such other order as may be expedient.'

(g) Intervening

A person who is not a party to an action may be added as a party either by the court of its own motion or on the application of an existing party or the 'intervener'. RSC Order 15, r 6(2) provides that a party may be added under the rule if either:

'(a) the presence of the intervener is necessary to ensure all matters in dispute are fully determined; or

(b) it would be just and convenient to determine a question or issue relating to the relief already claimed between the intervener and an existing party at the same time as determining the existing action.'

The court will exercise its power under these rules in cases where the intervener may be affected by the outcome of the action, such as where the Motor Insurers' Bureau will become liable for damages awarded against an untraced or uninsured driver.[53] Likewise, the Attorney General may wish to intervene to represent the public interest where matters of public policy arise in an action. Applications are made by summons in the High Court and by notice of application in a county court. In each case, where the application is made by the intervener, it must be supported by an affidavit showing the intervener's interest in the proceedings.

(h) Corporate bodies etc

Much of the business and public life of the country is carried on by individuals grouped together in associations. Some of these groupings are recognised by the law as having corporate status, thus a district council or a limited company can sue and be sued as if it was an individual. Other groupings do not have corporate status but it is considered convenient that actions should be brought by or against the groups as a whole, eg partnerships and trade unions. It is of vital importance to ascertain at the commencement of proceedings the exact legal identity of the parties. The table on pp 58–60 sets out the principal entities which the beginner is likely to encounter. The student should note in particular the methods whereby partners and sole traders can be sued.

---

53 The intervening party's interest must, however, relate to the subject matter of the action; a mere commercial interest in the outcome, such as that of a creditor, is not sufficient: *Sanders Lead Co Inc v Entores Metal Brokers Ltd* [1984] 1 All ER 857, CA.

MINORS[54]

Persons who have not attained their majority (ie who are under 18) can neither bring proceedings nor defend save through the agency of an adult acting on their behalf. In the case of a minor plaintiff, the adult is called his 'next friend'; in the case of a minor defendant, he is called the 'guardian ad litem'. We set out below the procedure adopted in the High Court and county court respectively.

High Court
The procedure is regulated by RSC Ord 80. The next friend of a minor plaintiff *must* employ a solicitor to act for him. In the Queen's Bench Division the title of an action by such a plaintiff shows that he is suing by his next friend; in the Chancery Division the title merely records that he is a minor and the details as to his next friend are set out in the body of the writ or originating summons. The next friend is liable to the defendant for costs if they are awarded against the plaintiff but has a right of indemnity against the minor. Where a minor is sued, service should not be effected on him but on his father or guardian or the person with whom he resides or in whose care he is.[55] If that person so chooses he may agree to be the guardian ad litem. In that case he must appoint a solicitor to represent the minor and file at court a written consent to act and a certificate by the solicitor to the effect that the guardian has no interest in the action.[56] He will then file an acknowledgment of service in the usual way. Where no acknowledgment is filed, the plaintiff cannot enter judgment in default but must apply to the court for the appointment of a guardian ad litem; if no one is prepared to act, then the court will appoint the Official Solicitor to act as guardian ad litem. The guardian ad litem is liable to an order for costs subject to a remedy over against the minor.

County court
In the county court a minor may bring proceedings in his own right to recover wages up to £5000.[57] A minor may be sued to judgment in respect of a liquidated sum[58] without the intervention of a guardian ad litem.[59] In all other cases a next friend or guardian ad litem must act for him. Where a minor sues by his next friend, the next friend must sign an undertaking at the court office to be liable for any costs awarded to the defendant, before process will issue;[60] he is, of course, entitled to be indemnified by the minor. Where proceedings are brought against a minor, service is to be effected upon his father, guardian etc.[61] If that person or other responsible adult is prepared to act as guardian he delivers to the court office the form of defence or admission together with a certificate to that effect stating that he has no adverse interest in the proceedings to the minor's; once this is done, he automatically becomes the guardian ad litem.[62] If no defence is delivered

---

54 Similar provisions apply to mental patients. See RSC Ord 80; CCR Ord 10.
55 RSC Ord 80, r 16(2)(a).
56 Ibid, r 3.
57 County Courts Act 1984, s 47.
58 Eg a debt.
59 CCR Ord 10, r 8.
60 Ord 10, r 2.
61 Ord 10, r 4.
62 Ord 10, r 5.

and the plaintiff knows that the defendant is a minor, he must apply for the court to appoint a person to act as guardian.[63] If it only appears at the hearing that the defendant is under age then the court will at that stage appoint a guardian to act for him.[64] If judgment is entered against a defendant who does not appear and it subsequently transpires that he was a minor, the judgment may be set aside. In county court proceedings, the guardian is not personally liable for any costs unless the same were occasioned by his personal negligence or misconduct.[65]

In both the High Court and county court where the minor attains majority during the course of the action, a notice that he adopts the proceedings should be filed at court and served on the other parties.[66] It should be noted that special rules apply as to the settlement of claims on behalf of minors and as to investment of sums awarded to them.[67]

---

63 Ord 10, r 6.
64 Ord 10, r 7.
65 Ord 10, r 9.
66 See *Oliver Twist v West Middlesex Salvage Co Ltd*, p 32, ante.
67 See pp 271–272, post.

Entity	Sues or is sued as	Example	Rules	Service (if not on solicitor)	Commentary
Limited company	Company name	Mammoth Law Book Public Limited Company (*public company*) *or* Brighter Law Books Limited (*private company*)	Companies Act 1985, s 725	Registered office	Leave at, or send writ to, registered office. Overseas company trading in England is required by s 691(1)(*b*)(ii) to provide Registrar with name and address of person resident and authorised to accept service. If overseas company fails to do so, service may be effected by leaving the writ (or posting it) to the company's established place of business in England – s 695(2). If company in liquidation by order of the court, leave is necessary to issue the writ and it is served on liquidator
Partners	Firm name	Smith and Jones (a firm)	RSC Ord 81 CCR Ord 5, r 19	Either one partner or person in charge at principal place of business. In High Court proceedings, the acknowledgement of service is not in the name of the firm but in the names of all the partners. Where partners sue or are sued they must on demand serve a notice of the names of all persons who were partners at the date the cause of action occurred	It is also possible to sue partners as individuals, eg 'John Smith and Peter Jones (trading as Smith and Jones)', but this mode of action has the disadvantage that execution cannot levy against the firm's property except after a special application. This method is employed, however, where the firm does not carry on business within the jurisdiction. It should also be noted that many partnerships carry on business in the style 'Smith, Jones and Co' although they are not a limited company. Again persons may trade in a name distinct from the firm name. However the true identity of such a body should be discoverable because s 4 Business Names Act 1985 requires the name of each partner to be stated in legible characters on all business letters, written orders for goods or services, invoices and receipts and demands for payment of debts
Individual carrying on business in name other than his own	Can be *sued* in his own or business name	Joseph Soap (trading as Mick's Café)	RSC Ord 81, r 9 CCR Ord 5, r 10	Service as partnership	The true identity of the owner can usually be ascertained in the same way as in the case of a partnership – ie by consulting business correspondence, orders, etc. If it cannot be found it is permissible to describe the defendant by his trade name thus 'Mick's Café (a trade name)'

Entity	Sues or is sued as	Example	Rules	Service (if not on solicitor)	Commentary
Members clubs	(a) Contract: persons authorising contract (b) tort: representative action	(a) Albert Smith and John Higgins (b) Albert Smith and John Higgins on behalf of themselves and all members of the Gray's Inn Rugby Club	RSC Ord 15, r 12 CCR Ord 5, r 5	Service on individuals named	(a) In contract cases, the committee members authorising the contract sue or are sued as individuals (b) In tort cases, the appropriate procedure is by way of representative action – see *Campbell v Thompson* (1953) 1 QB 445, supra (c) Property disputes are usually brought by or defended by trustees
Government departments	Name of department	Home Office, Department of Employment	Crown Proceedings Act 1947, s 17	Solicitor of Department or Treasury Solicitor	A list is periodically published setting out (a) departments which have their own solicitor, eg Commissioners of Inland Revenue, Department of Employment, and (b) those for whom the Treasury Solicitor acts, eg Home Office, Department of Environment, HM Stationery Office. The list should be checked in the current SC or CC Practice. If no department appears to be the appropriate defendant, proceedings are brought against the Attorney-General and served on the Treasury Solicitor
Local authorities	Name of county, district or parish council	Hampshire County Council, Rushmoor District Council, Hook Parish Council	Local Government Act 1972, ss 2(3) and 14(1)	Solicitor to authority, chairman, clerk of the council	Or chairman, town clerk or similar officer – see Ord 65, r 3
State schools	Name of education authority	Hampshire County Council		Solicitor to authority, chairman, clerk to the council	Education Act 1944 provides for county councils to be responsible for education. In the case of private schools, it is necessary to investigate their constitution in order to determine the proper plaintiffs or defendants
Hospitals	Regional Authority, District H Authority, Special Health Authority, Family Health Services Authority (FHSA), National Health Service Trust	North East Thames Regional H Authority, East London and the City District H Authority, Hammersmith and Queen Charlotte's Special H Authority, City and E London FHSA, West London Healthcare NHS Trust	National Health Service Act 1977, ss 8–10 and National Health Service and Community Care Act 1990	Solicitor appointed Chairman or Secretary of board, Chairman of board of directors of NHS Trust.	Family Health Services Authorities are responsible for primary health care, Regional and District Authorities for secondary care. NHS trusts have corporate status under s 5(5) of the 1990 Act and have legal capacity where appropriate. Either District Health Authorities or a Special H Authority are the responsible bodies in proceedings involving teaching hospitals

Entity	Sues or is sued as	Example	Rules	Service (if not on solicitor)	Commentary
Trade union	Name of union	Transport and General Workers Union	Trade Union and Labour Relations (Consolidation) Act 1992, s 10(1)(b)	At Head or Main Office	Unions even though not registered are entitled to sue and be sued in their own names
Police	In London Metropolitan Police Receiver; elsewhere Chief Constable	Sir A B (Chief Constable of the Rutland Police Authority)	Police Act 1964	Solicitor to Authority	
Trusts	Trustees	A B and C D (as trustees of the Estate of E F deceased)	RSC Ord 15, r 14	Trustees personally	Trustees, executors and administrators may sue and be sued on behalf of the fund or estate without joining the persons beneficially entitled. The pleading is headed 'In the Matter of the Trusts of the Will (Deed) of EF [deceased]' Where an action is brought against trustees, executors or administrators for the administration of a fund or estate it will normally be proper to add the beneficiaries interested as defendants
Minors	In own name but as plaintiffs by 'next friend' and as defendants by 'guardian ad litem'	A B, a minor (by his father and next friend C B) or A B, a minor (by his guardian ad litem C B)	RSC Ord 80 CCR Ord 10, r 1 et seq	On father, guardian, person with whom he resides or in whose care he is	In Chancery Division the next friend's name is *not* referred to in the title

LEGAL AID

The state provides assistance out of public funds for persons who wish to bring or defend civil proceedings under a statutory scheme administered by the Legal Aid Board.[68] For the purposes of day to day administration, the country is divided into *legal aid areas*, each with an area director and area committee, which determine individual applications. The scheme distinguishes between (*a*) preliminary advice and assistance and (*b*) legal representation in court proceedings.

Advice and assistance

A client is entitled to obtain assistance from a solicitor belonging to the scheme provided his means fall within certain limits. The solicitor fills in a questionnaire (the 'green form') designed to show:

(a) his client's disposable income, i e his net income after deductions are made for tax, national insurance contributions etc and due allowance given for his dependants;

(b) his client's disposable capital, i e the value of capital such as savings, car etc. but generally ignoring the value of the house he lives in.

Provided his disposable income and capital do not exceed the statutory limit the client will be entitled to assistance either free of charge or subject to a contribution.[69]

The work which can be done at this stage includes drafting letters, negotiating with the other side and obtaining an opinion from counsel,[70] provided the cost does not exceed the prescribed limit.[71] Advice or assistance which is likely to exceed the limit will require the prior approval of the area director.

Legal aid for civil proceedings

If the client wishes to bring or defend proceedings then his solicitor prepares an application to the area director for a *legal aid certificate*. A certificate will normally only be granted to litigants who are *individuals*; so that companies and other unincorporated bodies (such as trustees or a trade union) are not eligible.[72] The decision whether a certificate should be granted depends on

(a) the merits of the case: the applicant must show 'reasonable grounds for taking, defending or being a party to the proceedings';[73]

(b) the suitability of the case for civil legal aid;[74]

(c) the applicant's means, as determined by the Department of Social

---

68 Established by the Legal Aid Act 1988, s 3.
69 The limits are changed from time to time. As at 12 April 1993, if the client's disposable capital is not more than £3000 and his income not more than £147 per week he will be entitled to advice under the scheme. If his disposable income is £61 or less he will not have to make any contributions: Legal Advice and Assistance Regulations 1989, SI 1989 No 340 (as amended).
70 In fact there is nothing that a solicitor would normally do for a paying client that cannot be done under the 'green form' except taking a step in the proceedings.
71 Legal Aid Act 1988, s 10; Legal Advice and Assistance Regulations 1989, reg 4.
72 Ibid, s 2(10).
73 Ibid, s 15(2).
74 Ibid, s 15(3).

Security in accordance with the limits currently prescribed.[75] Frequently, the certificate will be subject to the condition that the assisted person pays a contribution by monthly instalments based on his disposable income. He may also be required to make a capital contribution from his savings before a certificate is issued.

The certificate issued, unless specially limited, will cover the ordinary steps in the litigation but a further application should be made for express authority to take any unusual steps, eg obtaining experts' reports. Where a certificate is issued, notice of issue (but *not* the certificate itself) *must* be served on all other parties to the proceedings and a copy filed with the court. This is very important because a party who is sued by or sues a legally aided litigant will only be able to obtain a limited order for costs against him.[76] This may have an important bearing on his future conduct of the litigation. It should also be noted that the Legal Aid Board has a *first charge*[77] on any damages or property recovered or preserved for an assisted litigant in order to cover the costs incurred by the Board to the extent that they are not paid by the other party.

Example. Colin, a former director of High Tech Computers Ltd, is sued by the company for specific performance of a contract under which the plaintiffs allege that Colin agreed to transfer shares in the company worth £15,000 upon ceasing to be a director. Colin maintains that there was no such agreement and the shares were given to him as an inducement to leave his former employment. Colin is granted legal aid with a nil contribution. At the county court trial the judge finds in favour of Colin and the plaintiffs' claim is dismissed. The Legal Aid Board has incurred legal costs of £4000 on Colin's behalf but through cash flow difficulties High Tech Computers are able to meet only £2500 of the award of costs against them. Since Colin's shares were preserved by him in the proceedings, the Board has a first charge against the shares for £1500 being the shortfall between the Board's actual costs and those recoverable from the plaintiffs.

IS THE ACTION STATUTE BARRED?

(a) The general rules
The law requires that proceedings should be brought within a limited time from the date on which the matters of complaint occurred (*a*) because of the destruction of evidence as time elapses and (*b*) because of the unfairness to a defendant if matters could be litigated many years after they had occurred. Proceedings are 'brought' for the purposes of limitation when a writ is *issued*. The principal periods of limitation are set out in tabular form below.

---

75 See the Civil Legal Aid (Assessment of Resources) Regulations (1989 SI 1989 No 338) as amended by the Civil Legal Aid (Assessment of Resources) (Amendment) Regulations 1993 (SI 1993 No 788). The limits since 12 April 1993 are: disposable capital not more than £6750; disposable income £6800; where disposable capital is below £3000 and income is below £2294 the applicant will not have to make any contribution.
76 See Legal Aid Act 1988, s 18 and p 316, post.
77 Legal Aid Act 1988, s 16(6).

Type of case	*Period in years*	*Statute*	*Notes*
Contract	6	Limitation Act 1980, s 5	Time runs from the breach complained of
Contract under seal	12	s 8	Called an action 'upon a specialty'
Sum recoverable under statute	6	ibid, s 9	eg unlawful premium paid on grant of Rent Act tenancy
Action for an account	6	s 23	
Tort	6	s 2	If the tort is actionable *per se*, time runs from date of commission of tort (eg trespass, libel); if actionable only on proof of damage, from date damage occurred (eg nuisance, *Rylands v Fletcher* situation)
Personal injury cases	3 (in exceptional cases can be overridden)	s 11	Applies to 'actions for damages for negligence, nuisance or breach of duty (whether the duty exists by virtue of a contract or of provision made by or under a statute or independently of any contract or any such provision)'. When the damages claimed by the plaintiff consist of or include damages in respect of personal injuries, time runs from date of cause of action or knowledge, see p 67, post
Fatal accident cases	3 (in exceptional cases can be overridden)	s 12	Special rule applies where plaintiff unaware of cause of action
Other cases by or against deceased persons		Proceedings Against Estates Act 1970	The appropriate period now depends only on the type of case involved – there are now no special rules
Defamation actions	3 (or 1 year from date of knowledge)	s 4A s 32A	
Claims under the Latent Damage Act 1986	3	ss 14A 14B	3 years from date of knowledge subject to 15 year longstop from act of negligence
Claims under the Consumer Protection Act 1987	3	s 11A	Subject to 10 year longstop from date product supplied

Type of case	Period in years	Statute	Notes
Claims for equitable relief	no period	s 36	There is no prescribed limitation period where the plaintiff is claiming an equitable, ie *discretionary* remedy. Such remedies have their own 'built in' limitation period since any unfair or prejudicial delay in bringing proceedings is likely to lead to the refusal of equitable relief.
Recovery of land	12	s 15	Action arises as at date of dispossession; where plaintiffs' interest not then vested, it runs from date he became entitled to possession
Informal personal loans	6	s 6	Loans between members of family and friends: time usually does not begin to run until demand is made for payment
Rent	6	s 19	
Mortgagee's claim for foreclosure and sale	12	s 20	As from date when right to sue occurred
Mortgage interest	6	s 20(5)	
Recovery of trust property from trustee	no period	s 21(1)	
Fraudulent breach of trust	no period	s 21(1)	
Other breaches of trust	6	s 21(3)	Eg claims against trustee for unauthorised investment
Claim for Contribution	2	s 10	Where a defendant is held liable or settles an action, a claim by him under the Civil Liability (Contributions) Act 1978 for contribution must be made within 2 years of the judgment or date of settlement

(b) When does time begin to run?

As the above table shows, limitation periods begin to run at different points in time and on the happening of different events depending on the cause of action on which the plaintiff bases his claim. The nature of the action is the decisive factor in determining when the relevant period of limitation begins to run. Generally, in claims for breach of contract the limitation period begins to run from the date of the breach, because at this point the plaintiff can establish all the elements of the claim, i e the *agreement*, the relevant *term* and the date on which the *breach* occurred. Greater difficulties can arise in actions in *tort*, where (apart from those torts which are actionable per se, such as libel) the cause of action does not arise until the plaintiff suffers some damage.

> *Example 1.* In 1984 P is dismissed from his position as managing director of D Co. Between 1985 and 1989 he pursues his statutory claim for unfair dismissal before an industrial tribunal and thereafter on appeal to the Employment Appeal Tribunal and the Court of Appeal. In 1991 P issues and serves proceedings in the High Court against D Co alleging wrongful dismissal in breach of the terms of his contract. D Co have a complete defence to the action in that the limitation period of six years from the date of the alleged *breach* of contract has expired.
>
> *Example 2.* In 1984 D Co, who are sub-contractors on a building site owned by P, negligently damaged part of the structure which had already been built. P issues proceedings against the main contractor T Co in 1987 but these are stayed when T Co go into liquidation in 1991. P then commenced proceedings in the High Court directly against the sub-contractors D Co for negligence. D Co have a complete defence to the claim because the cause of action arose in 1984 when the negligence caused *damage* to P's property.

It should be noted that the expiry of the limitation period prevents an action being pursued only if the defendant expressly raises the point either by pleading the matter in his defence or applying to strike out the proceedings.

(c) *Extension of period*
The limitation periods would work injustice if the law did not permit exceptions in some cases. There are six exceptional cases where the general rules are modified:

(i)   where the plaintiff is under a disability;
(ii) where the right of action arises out of fraud or mistake or has been concealed;
(iii) personal injury cases;
(iv) cases involving latent damage;
(v)   claims under the Consumer Protection Act 1987;
(vi) some claims in defamation.

We shall consider each of these cases in turn.

(i) *Plaintiff under a disability*
The general rule is that where a plaintiff was an infant or mental patient when the cause of action accrued and subsequently attains majority (or recovers), he may bring the action within six years of his majority (or recovery). In personal injury cases, the relevant period is three years from the date on which the disability ended.[78]

(ii) *Fraud, concealment and mistake*
Section 32 of the Limitation Act 1980 provides that where an action is based on the defendant's fraud (e g an action in deceit or to recover damages for fraudulent misrepresentation) or for relief against the consequences of mistake, time does not begin to run until the plaintiff has discovered the

---

78 Limitation Act 1980, s 28.

fraud or mistake or could with reasonable diligence have discovered it.[79] It should be noted that this section does not apply wherever the plaintiff has made a mistake about his legal position; it only applies where the claim is for equitable relief from the consequences of a mistake.

> *Example 1.* A solicitor entered into a contract of employment whereby she would receive a share of profits from the practice. She was underpaid by mistake for twelve years. The defendants pleaded the statute of limitation in respect of the first six years. She claimed that her action was 'for relief against the consequences of a mistake'. Held: her action was to recover monies unpaid under a contract and not for relief against mistake. Per Pearson J: 'It seems to me that [the statutory] wording is carefully chosen to indicate a class of actions where a mistake has been made which has had certain consequences and the plaintiff seeks to be relieved from those consequences. Familiar examples are, first, money paid in consequence of a mistake: in such a case the mistake is made, in consequence of the mistake the money is paid, and the action is to recover that money back. Secondly, there may be a contract entered into in consequence of a mistake and the action is to obtain the rescission or, in some cases, the rectification of the contract. Thirdly, there may be an account settled in consequence of mistakes; if the mistakes are sufficiently serious there can be a re-opening of the account . . . Probably [this provision] applies only where the mistake is an essential ingredient of the cause of action, so that the statement of claim sets out, or should set out, the mistake and its consequences and prays for relief from those consequences.'[80]
>
> *Example 2.* In 1970 the plaintiff bought from the defendants, a reputable gallery, a drawing which was believed by both parties to be an original by a famous nineteenth century artist. In 1981, after a number of subsequent insurance valuations which raised no questions as to its authenticity, the drawing was discovered to be a worthless reproduction. The plaintiff brought an action for the recovery of the purchase price and rescission of the contract on the ground of a mistake of fact. The parties reached an agreement whereby the defendants conceded liability in a stated sum. In the event the judge found that the plaintiff could not with reasonable diligence have discovered the mistake before the expiry of six years from the date of purchase. The defendants expressly agreed *not* to take the point that the action was not 'for relief against the consequences of mistake'. Nevertheless Webster J (*obiter*) commented: 'It may well be the case that, where attribution forms a term of the contract, either as a condition or as a warranty, and where that attribution is mistaken, then in those circumstances s 32(1)(c) does not apply either because it is not a mistake within the meaning of that subsection or because, where goods are sold with a condition or warranty as to attribution which is broken because the seller is under a mistake, the price paid is not to be regarded as money paid in consequence of a mistake.'[81]

Section 32 also provides that where any fact relevant to the plaintiff's right of action has been *deliberately concealed* by the defendant or his agent, time shall not begin to run against the plaintiff until he has discovered the concealment or could have done so with reasonable diligence. What does the expression 'deliberately concealed' mean? There are logically two possibilities: *either* it could mean 'concealed by a deliberate act of deception' *or* it could mean 'concealment in circumstances amounting to a reckless

---

79 These provisions are not to operate so as to defeat the right of third parties who have acquired property in ignorance of the fraud or mistake in question.

80 *Phillips-Higgins v Harper* [1954] 1 QB 411 at 418. Note that the mistake need not be that of the plaintiffs, e g the cases on equitable tracing: *Re Diplock, Diplock v Wintle* [1948] Ch 465, [1948] 2 All ER 318, CA; affd sub nom *Ministry of Health v Simpson* [1951] AC 251, [1950] 2 All ER 1137, HL.

81 *Peco Arts Inc v Hazlitt Gallery Ltd* [1983] 3 All ER 193, at 203e.

disregard of the defendant's duty to tell the plaintiff the true situation'. It is this second, more extensive definition which was adopted by the courts in interpreting the predecessor of this section which spoke of the right of action being 'concealed by . . . fraud'.

> *Example 1.* In 1935 P deposited certain packages containing jewellery with D. In 1940 D's agent who was closing the business because of the war opened the packages, decided the jewellery was of no value and gave it to the Salvation Army. In late 1946 (after six years had elapsed) P discovered her jewellery had been disposed of and sued D who pleaded the limitation period. Denning J at first instance held that D had not acted with any dishonest motive and consequently could not be said to have 'concealed the right of action by fraud'. The Court of Appeal reversed this decision and held that the very act of conversion without attempting to give notice to P amounted to 'fraudulent concealment'. Per Lord Greene MR: 'the conduct of the defendants by the very manner in which they converted the plaintiff's chattels in breach of the confidence reposed in them and in circumstances calculated to keep her in ignorance of the wrong they had committed amounted to a fraudulent concealment of the cause of action'.[82]
>
> *Example 2.* F purchased certain shares in the names of his children. Subsequently he sold the shares but placed the proceeds of sale into deposit accounts in the names of his children. Thereafter he drew on those accounts and never replaced the monies therein. These matters came to light many years later on his death. The children sued the executors as creditors of the estate. The executors raised the defence that the claim was statute-barred. The Court of Appeal rejected this argument. Per Denning LJ: 'When he drew the money from the bank, either he intended to use the children's money as his own, or he did not. If he did intend to use it as his own and told them nothing about it, then the very nature of his dealing amounted to a fraudulent concealment from them of their right of action; and the period of limitation did not start to run until the children discovered it: see section [32(1) of the Limitation Act 1980] . . . If the father did not intend to use the money as his own, but on behalf of the children as he ought to have done, then he was a trustee of it and he has since converted it to his own use and the children are not bound by any period of limitation . . . see also section [21(1) of the Limitation Act 1980].'[83]

(iii) *Personal injury cases*

In cases involving personal injury or fatal accidents special rules exist which permit a plaintiff in some circumstances to bring such proceedings outside the ordinary limitation periods. These rules enable the court (a) to extend the time for bringing proceedings where the plaintiff was unaware he could bring a claim; and (b) to exercise its discretion to disapply the ordinary limitation period where it is just to do so.

(a) Plaintiff not aware he can sue. It has already been stated that in tort cases where damage is an essential ingredient of the cause of action time begins to run from the date when the damage occurred. What is the position, however, if

---

82 *Beaman v ARTS Ltd* [1949] 1 KB 550, at 566. See also *UBAF Ltd v European American Banking Corpn* [1984] QB 713, [1984] 2 All ER 226, CA (defendants' continuing concealment from plaintiffs of insufficiency of security for loan).

83 *Re Shephard, Shephard v Cartwright* [1953] Ch 728, at 756, CA. See also *Kitchen v RAF Association* [1958] 2 All ER 241, CA; *King v Victor Parsons & Co* [1973] 1 All ER 206, [1973] 1 WLR 29, CA and *Tito v Waddell (No 2)* [1977] Ch 106, [1977] 3 All ER 129, per Megarry VC at 244: 'as the authorities stand, it can be said that in the ordinary use of language not only does "fraud" not mean "fraud" but also "concealed" does not mean "concealed", since any unconscionable failure to reveal is enough'.

that damage remains dormant for many years and is only discovered after the period of limitation has elapsed?

> *Example 1.* A miner contracts pneumoconiosis whilst working in a colliery but the symptoms do not appear for many years.[84]
> *Example 2.* An operation is performed to prevent conception. Four years later the woman conceives a child.
> *Example 3.* A is injured at work but does not realise he could sue his employers. Four years after the accident he reads of a similar case in a newspaper and at once consults solicitors.[85]

Section 11 of the Limitation Act 1980 seeks to solve this problem in claims arising out of personal injuries and death[86] by providing that in such cases the three-year period of limitation begins to run either from the date the cause of action accrued *or* from the date upon which the plaintiff became aware or should reasonably have become aware of his right to sue the defendant:

> '(3) An action to which this section applies shall not be brought after the expiration of the period applicable in accordance with subsections (4) and (5) below.
> (4) Except where subsection (5) below applies, the period is three years from –
>   (*a*) the date on which the cause of action accrued, or
>   (*b*) the date of knowledge (if later) of the person injured.
> (5) If the person injured dies before the expiration of the period mentioned in subsection (4) above, the period applicable as respects the cause of action surviving for the benefit of his estate by virtue of section 1 of the Law Reform (Miscellaneous Provisions) Act 1934 shall be three years from –
>   (*a*) the date of death, or
>   (*b*) the date of the personal representative's knowledge, whichever is the later.'

Section 12 makes similar provision in cases brought on behalf of the dependants of a deceased person under the Fatal Accidents Act 1976.

Section 14 provides a definition of the expression 'date of knowledge'–

> '(1) In sections 11 and 12 of this Act, references to a person's date of knowledge are references to the date on which he first had knowledge of the following facts–
>   (*a*) that the injury in question was significant, and
>   (*b*) that the injury was attributable in whole or in part to the act or omission which is alleged to constitute negligence, nuisance or breach of duty, and
>   (*c*) the identity of the defendant, and
>   (*d*) if it is alleged that the act or omission was that of a person other than the defendant, the identity of that person and the additional facts supporting the bringing of an action against the defendant,
>   and knowledge that any acts or omissions did or did not, as a matter of law, involve negligence, nuisance or breach of duty is irrelevant.
> (2) For the purposes of this section an injury is significant if the person whose date of knowledge is in question would reasonably have considered it to be

---

84 *Cartledge v E Jopling & Sons Ltd* [1963] AC 758, [1963] 1 All ER 341, HL.
85 *Harper v National Coal Board* [1974] QB 614, [1974] 2 All ER 441, CA.
86 Section 11(1) applies to 'any action for damages for negligence, nuisance or breach of duty . . . where the damages claimed . . . consist of or include damages in respect of personal injuries . . .' The statutory language does not cover personal injury claims arising from *intentional* torts, such as battery: see *Stubbings v Webb* [1993] 1 All ER 322, HL (claim for personal injuries arising from sexual abuse).

sufficiently serious to justify his instituting proceedings for damages against a defendant who did not dispute liability and was able to satisfy a judgment.
(3) For the purposes of this section a person's knowledge includes knowledge which he might reasonably have been expected to acquire–
    (*a*) from facts observable or ascertainable by him, or
    (*b*) from facts ascertainable by him with the help of medical or other appropriate expert advice which it is reasonable for him to seek,
but a person shall not be fixed under this subsection with knowledge of a fact ascertainable only with the help of expert advice so long as he has taken all reasonable steps to obtain (and, where appropriate, to act on) that advice.'

In the examples above the Act would work as follows:

(1) The miner would be able to bring an action within three years of the date he realised that he was suffering from pneumoconiosis *and* that this was attributable to some action or omission by his employer (see ss 11 and 14(1)(*b*)).
(2) The woman who conceived after a sterilisation operation could bring an action within three years of the date upon which she received (or should reasonably have received) expert advice indicating that she had a cause of action against the hospital (ss 11, 14(1) and (3)).
(3) So far as the example of the employee who did not realise he had a legal right to sue his employer is concerned, s 14(1) provides that in fixing the relevant date when the plaintiff first had knowledge of the matters complained of, the fact that he was not aware at that time that he had a legal right to sue is irrelevant. The limitation period would have started to run at the date of the accident and would have expired. However, this might be a case where the court would exercise its power to override the limitation period under s 33 (see below).

In cases brought on the basis of expert advice, deciding when the plaintiff had knowledge of the relevant facts can be difficult. The plaintiff will be regarded as lacking the knowledge that his injury or condition is attributable to the acts of the defendant if the causal link could only be appreciated with the benefit of expert guidance (unless the plaintiff has unreasonably failed to take steps to obtain or act on such advice).

Example 1. In August 1987 S issued proceedings claiming damages for mental illness allegedly caused by abuse by her adoptive father and brother during a period beginning in 1959. S attained her majority in January 1975 but did not commence proceedings because she did not appreciate that her psychological problems might be attributable to the abuse she had suffered. In September 1984 she had a consultation with a psychiatrist specialising in child abuse. The Court of Appeal held that the date of S's knowledge was September 1984 so the claim was brought just within the three-year limitation period. S did not appreciate until she received expert advice in September 1984 that there was a causal link between her mental condition (which she knew to be 'significant') and the defendants' acts. Knowledge could not be imputed to S under s 14(3) even though the expert advice, which she failed to seek until September 1984, would have revealed it. Per Bingham LJ: 'The plaintiff did not, it is true, seek expert medical advice on the possible existence of this causal link, but unless she suspected such a link she could not reasonably be expected to do so.'[87]

87 *Stubbings v Webb* [1992] 1 QB 197, [1991] 3 All ER 949, CA (D's appeal to the House of Lords succeeded on different grounds—see p 68, n 86).

Example 2. The plaintiff, H, was the mother and administratrix of the estate of a 16 year old girl who was stabbed to death in April 1978. The second defendant was acquitted of her murder in November 1978 but he made statements implicating the first defendant, who was his stepfather. The evidence cast doubts on which of them had caused the death, but clearly showed that no other person could conceivably have been involved. A subsequent campaign to persuade the authorities to prosecute the first defendant failed. It was not until April 1987, when new solicitors advised the plaintiff that a civil action on behalf of her daughter's estate was feasible, and after legal aid was obtained, that a writ was issued. The Court of Appeal held that the proceedings had been commenced outside the primary limitation period. Legal advice did not fall within the category of 'appropriate expert advice' under s 14(3) so the three-year limitation period began to run at the latest at the conclusion of the second defendant's trial, when H obtained the necessary knowledge that her daughter's death was caused by one or other, or both of the defendants.[88]

(b) Discretionary power to override limitation period. In some limited circumstances the court is given power to allow an action to proceed although under the rules discussed above the limitation period has expired. Section 33 of the Limitation Act 1980 provides that in personal injury and fatal injury cases the court can override the statutory time limits if it would be just to do so:

'(1) If it appears to the court that it would be equitable to allow an action to proceed having regard to the degree to which
   (a) the provisions of sections 11 or 12 of this Act prejudice the plaintiff or any person whom he represents, and
   (b) any decision of the court under this subsection would prejudice the defendant or any person whom he represents
   the court may direct that those provisions shall not apply to the action, or shall not apply to any specified cause of action to which the action relates.'

The relevant factors to be taken into account are set out in subsection (3):

'(3) In acting under this section the court shall have regard to all the circumstances of the case and in particular to
   (a) the length of, and the reasons for, the delay on the part of the plaintiff;
   (b) the extent to which, having regard to the delay, the evidence adduced or likely to be adduced by the plaintiff or the defendant is or is likely to be less cogent than if the action had been brought within the time allowed by section 11, section 11A or (as the case may be) by section 12;
   (c) the conduct of the defendant after the cause of action arose, including the extent (if any) to which he responded to requests reasonably made by the plaintiff for information or inspection for the purpose of ascertaining facts which were or might be relevant to the plaintiff's cause of action against the defendant;
   (d) the duration of any disability of the plaintiff arising after the date of the accrual of the cause of action;
   (e) the extent to which the plaintiff acted promptly and reasonably once he knew whether or not the act or omission of the defendant, to which the injury was attributable, might be capable at that time of giving rise to an action for damages;
   (f) the steps, if any, taken by the plaintiff to obtain medical, legal or other expert advice and the nature of any such advice he may have received.
(4) In a case where the person injured died when, because of section 11 or subsection (4) of section 11A, he could no longer maintain an action and

88 *Halford v Brookes* [1991] 3 All ER 559, CA.

recover damages in respect of the injury, the court shall have regard in particular to the length of, and the reasons for, the delay on the part of the deceased.

(5) In a case under subsection (4) above, or any other case where the time limit, or one of the time limits, depends on the date of knowledge of a person other than the plaintiff, subsection (3) above shall have effect with appropriate modifications, and shall have effect in particular as if references to the plaintiff include references to any persons whose date of knowledge is or was relevant in determining a time limit.'

It is worth remembering that the court is not confined to the factors specified in s 33(3). In *Donovan v Gwentoys Ltd*[89] the House of Lords confirmed that in exercising its unfettered discretion the court was not restricted to considering only those matters set out in s 33(3) but could also take account of matters such as the overall delay in notifying the defendant of the claim. The plaintiff was injured at work in December 1979 when she was 16. The limitation period expired in April 1984, three years after she attained her majority. Shortly before that date she consulted solicitors who failed to issue proceedings until October 1984, five and a half months after the expiry of the limitation period. Looking at the wording of s 33(3)(b), the judge at first instance held that he was confined to considering the minimal prejudice caused to the defendants by the five and a half months' delay between the expiry of the limitation period and the issue of the writ; on that basis he exercised his discretion in favour of the plaintiff and allowed the claim to proceed. The House of Lords held that this approach was wrong and allowed the defendants' appeal. The judge had an unfettered discretion under s 33(1) having regard to the degree to which the plaintiff and defendant would be prejudiced. Adopting the words of Stuart-Smith LJ in the Court of Appeal, Lord Griffiths said:

'The time of the notification of the claim is not one of the particular matters to which the court is required to have regard under s 33(3), although it may come in under para (e). But to my mind it is an extremely important consideration . . . I cannot accept [counsel for the plaintiff's] contention that it is irrelevant, presumably because it is not specifically referred to in s 33(3).'

Therefore, having regard to the delay of five years after the accident in notifying the defendants of the claim against them the balance of prejudice was heavily in favour of the defendants. Per Lord Griffiths:[90] 'It would not be equitable to require the defendants to meet a claim which they would have the utmost difficulty in defending when the plaintiff will suffer only the slightest prejudice if she is required to pursue her remedy against her solicitors.'

In a number of cases the question has arisen whether the plaintiff can use the provisions of s 33 to start a second action when an action commenced within the limitation period cannot proceed – for example, because the writ has expired or the original action is liable to be struck out for want of prosecution.

Example 1. In 1969 the plaintiff contracted an industrial disease. In 1971 a writ was issued and served but no further steps were taken by the plaintiff's solicitors. In 1972 the limitation period expired. In 1976 new solicitors, realising the first action would be struck out for want of prosecution, issued a new writ and applied

89 [1990] 1 All ER 1018, HL.
90 Ibid, at 1025a.

under section 33 for the action to proceed notwithstanding the limitation period had expired. The House of Lords held section 33 only applied where '*the provisions of section 11 . . . prejudice the plaintiff*'; the plaintiff was not prejudiced by that section because an action had been brought within the limitation period: accordingly there was no power to allow a second action to proceed under section 33 (*Walkley v Precision Forgings Ltd*[91]).

Example 2. In 1971 the plaintiff was injured in an accident. In June 1974 a writ was issued but not served. The limitation period expired in August 1974. In 1976 the writ was renewed but the defendants upon being served applied successfully to set the writ aside on the grounds that it should not have been renewed once the limitation period had expired. In May 1978 the plaintiff's solicitors issued a second writ and applied under section 33 for the action to proceed. The Court of Appeal held that section 33 had no application where proceedings had originally been issued within the limitation period but had proved abortive (*Chappell v Cooper*[92]).

Example 3. On 7 October 1977 the plaintiff sustained serious injuries which rendered him paraplegic. On 23 August 1979 a writ was issued but not served because negotiations were continuing with the defendant's insurers for settlement. On 4 August 1980 the insurers paid £5000 by way of interim payment. On 23 August the writ expired without being renewed. On 7 October 1980 the limitation period expired. The plaintiff's solicitors then issued a new writ and applied for leave to proceed under section 33. The application was refused on the grounds section 33 did not apply at all where an action had been begun within the limitation period (*Deerness v John R Keeble & Son (Brantham) Ltd*[93]).

These decisions have produced the paradoxical result that where a solicitor has been negligent to the extent of failing altogether to issue a writ during the limitation period, he can issue subsequently and apply under section 33 whereas the solicitor who issues but then, perhaps because negotiations are continuing, fails to serve while the writ is current cannot take any step to preserve the claim after the limitation period expires.[94]

(iv) *Latent damage*

The rule that a cause of action in negligence arises as soon as damage is caused could work serious injustice where many years pass before the fact that damage has been caused is appreciated.

Example. In January 1979 Jerry Construction Ltd negligently install a damp proof course in the basement of A's house which they are in the process of renovating. The building is sold to P in 1980. As a result of the inadequate damp proofing, damage is caused to the basement walls by January 1981 but this is not appreciated until June 1987 when a serious infestation of dry rot occurs which requires substantial works to be carried out.

Under the old law time would begin to run in January 1981 and the limitation period would have expired in January 1987 (see *Pirelli General Cable Works Ltd v Oscar Faber & Partners*[95]). The Latent Damage Act 1986 was passed to deal with this problem. It inserted sections 14A and 14B into

---

91 [1979] 2 All ER 548, [1979] 1 WLR 606, HL.
92 [1980] 2 All ER 463, [1980] 1 WLR 958, CA.
93 [1983] 2 Lloyds Rep 260, HL.
94 See *Thompson v Brown Construction (Ebbw Vale) Ltd* [1981] 2 All ER 296, [1981] 1 WLR 744, HL where *no* writ had been issued during the limitation period, the House of Lords held that section 33 was applicable and the fact that the plaintiff would have had a claim in negligence against his solicitor was not necessarily a reason why the court should not give permission for an action brought outside the limitation period to proceed.
95 [1983] 2 AC 1, [1983] 1 All ER 65, at 72, HL.

the Limitation Act 1980 providing that in negligence claims[96] the limitation period should be:

(a) either 6 years from the date when the cause of action accrued (ie when damage occurs); *or*

(b) 3 years from the date when the plaintiff had (or might reasonably be expected to have had) knowledge of the material facts (if that period expires later)[97]; *but*

(c) no action can be brought more than 15 years from the date of the negligent act or omission in question.[98]

In the problem above, the house owner would be able to bring proceedings against the builders in the three year period commencing June 1987. If the damage however had not become apparent before January 1994 no proceedings could be brought because of the 'long stop' provided by section 14B.

Suppose the expert witnesses agree that P should have realised by August 1984 that damage had occurred; the three year time period would begin to run from that date in 1984. P would still have time to issue a writ on discovering the damage in June 1987 provided he does so before the limitation period expires in August 1987.

The provisions of sections 14A and 14B are likely to be important:

(i) in building cases where a claim is brought arising from damage to property resulting from negligent construction by a contractor or builder;[99]

(ii) in cases where a claim is brought arising out of negligent advice (for example, by a solicitor or broker).[100]

(v) *Defective products*

Section 11A(4) of the Limitation Act provides that claims in respect of injury or damage caused by defective products must be brought within 3 years of the date on which the cause of action accrued or 3 years of the date of knowledge (whichever is later). Section 11A(3) provides for a 'long stop': no action shall be brought after 10 years have elapsed from the relevant time. This provision was introduced to implement the EC Council Directive 85/374 concerning product liability.

(vi) *Libel or slander*

No action for libel or slander may be brought after the expiration of 3 years

---

96 The provisions do not apply to actions framed in contract, ie claims for so called 'contractual negligence': see *Société Commerciale de Réassurance v ERAS (International) Ltd* [1992] 2 All ER 82n, CA and *Iron Trade Mutual Insurance Co Ltd v J K Buckenham Ltd* [1990] 1 All ER 808.

97 Limitation Act 1980, s 14A(4).

98 Ibid, s 14B(1).

99 But note that such claims have been severely restricted by the decisions of the House of Lords that generally no action can be brought in negligence where the plaintiff is effectively seeking to recover for pure economic loss: see *D & F Estates Ltd v Church Comrs for England* [1989] AC 177, [1988] 2 All ER 992, HL; *Murphy v Brentwood District Council* [1991] 1 AC 398, [1990] 2 All ER 908, HL; *Department of the Environment v Thomas Bates & Son Ltd* [1991] 1 AC 499, [1990] 2 All ER 943, HL.

100 For example, in *Bell v Peter Browne & Co (a firm)* [1990] 2 QB 495, [1990] 3 All ER 124 CA, failure of a solicitor to register a charge protecting his client's interests not discovered until eight years after the omission (and so statute-barred); today, the plaintiff could rely on section 14A.

from the date on which the cause of action accrued (Limitation Act 1980, s 4A). This is subject to the extension of the period in cases of disability or concealment of the cause of action. Further, the High Court has power under s 32A to grant leave for an action to be brought within 1 year from the earliest date when the plaintiff knew all the facts relevant to his cause of action.

Chapter 2

Starting High Court proceedings

PROCESS IN THE HIGH COURT

Note: the reader is referred to the short description of the issue and service of a writ in Part 1 at p 5.

(a) The writ of summons

High Court proceedings are normally commenced by writ.[1] A writ is a document addressed to the defendant giving him notice that a High Court action has been commenced against him and requiring him to place himself on the court record by delivering an acknowledgment of service to the court office. The writ is prepared by the plaintiff's solicitor who must take particular care to comply with the following:

(i)   The parties are correctly described in the title of the action (see table pp 58–60).

(ii)   That on the back of the writ he has set out 'a concise statement of the nature of the claim made or the relief or remedy required in the action'.[2] This is known as the *'general indorsement'*. In an action for breach of contract the indorsement should state the date of the contract, whether oral or written, the breach complained of and the remedy claimed, thus:

> 'The Plaintiff's claim is for damages (and interest thereon pursuant to section 35A of the Supreme Court Act 1981) for breach by the Defendant of a written contract dated the 1st day of March 1990 whereby the Defendant agreed to appear at the Plaintiff's theatre at Drury Lane for six months commencing the 7th day of May 1990 and for an injunction restraining the Defendant from appearing at any other theatre during the said period in breach of the aforesaid contract.'

In an action for tort, the indorsement should state the date, place and nature of the alleged tort, thus:

> 'The Plaintiff's claim is for damages for personal injuries, loss and expense arising out of a road traffic collision on the 16th August 1990 at Chancery Lane, London WC1 caused by the negligent driving of an

---

1 In Chapter 16 we shall consider the principal alternative form of process, namely the *originating summons* which is used extensively in the Chancery Division usually in matters where the issues of fact are not substantially in dispute.

2 RSC Ord 6, r 2.

omnibus by the Defendants' servant. The Plaintiff further claims interest upon such damages pursuant to section 35A of the Supreme Court Act 1981 to be assessed. (This writ includes a claim for personal injury but may be commenced in the High Court because the value of the action for the purposes of Article 5 of the High Court and County Courts Jurisdiction Order 1991 exceeds £50,000.)'

In an action for recovery of possession of land the indorsement must state whether the premises comprise a dwelling house[3] and, if so, their rateable value:

'The Plaintiff's claim is for possession of shop premises known as 23 Victoria Road in the London Borough of Hammersmith and for mesne profits from [date of expiry of notice to quit] until judgment.'

The purpose of the general indorsement is to provide a short summary of the nature of the claim and the relief sought. It should not be confused with the *statement of claim* which is the formal and detailed expression of the plaintiff's case served either after the defendant has acknowledged service or along with the writ in place of a general indorsement (see below).

(iii)   If the plaintiff's claim is only for a fixed sum (eg a debt, the price of goods or a sum claimed for services by way of quantum meruit), then there is set out on the back of the writ a statement telling the defendant that provided he pays the amount claimed and costs within the 14-day period limited for delivering an acknowledgment of service, further proceedings will be stayed.[4] The form of words used is set out in the example on p 80. This sort of claim, i e where the amount due is fixed or can be calculated by reference to the contract itself without needing to be assessed by the court, is known as a liquidated claim.

(iv)   If the writ is issued out of a district registry and the cause of action in respect of which relief is claimed wholly or in part arose in that district, an indorsement to that effect must be inserted.[5]

(v)   If the claim is for personal injuries then the writ must be indorsed with a statement that the value of the claim exceeds £50,000[6] (see illustration above).

(vi)   Where the claim is to recover possession or delivery of goods a statement must be provided of the value which the plaintiff puts on the goods.

(vii)   Where the claim relates to a consumer credit agreement the plaintiff's solicitor must certify that section 141 of the Consumer Credit Act 1974 does not apply, ie that the action is not to enforce a 'regulated agreement' or any security relating to it or to enforce a 'linked transaction' (because the county court has exclusive jurisdiction over such matters).

(viii)   If the claim is for a debt or liquidated demand expressed in a

---

3   If the claim relates to a dwelling house the indorsement should state whether the Rent Acts apply. Generally, actions to recover possession of a dwelling house let on a protected or statutory tenancy will be brought in a county court because no costs are awarded if such a claim is brought in the High Court: Rent Act 1977, s 141.

4   RSC Ord 6, r 2(1)(b).

5   RSC Ord 6, r 4; Ord 12, r 1(3); Ord 4, r 5(3).

6   QBD *Practice Direction*, 21 June 1991 [1991] 3 All ER 352.

foreign currency a certificate must be inserted stating the sterling equivalent at the rate current in London for the purchase of such currency at the close of business on the preceding day.

Once the writ has been drafted, the plaintiff's solicitors take copies to the Central Office or Chancery Chambers in London or the local district registry in the provinces for the writ to be formally *issued*.[7] One copy of the writ (the 'original') is sealed with the court stamp and returned to the solicitors. Another copy is sealed and stamped (to show the fee has been paid) and signed by the solicitors issuing; this copy (the 'duplicate') is retained by the court. Other copies of the writ are sealed and given to the plaintiff's solicitor for service on each of the defendants. Before sealing, a reference number is assigned to the action. The writ is issued the moment it is sealed. An entry recording (a) the reference number of the action, (b) the date and time of issue, (c) the name of the plaintiff's solicitor and (d) the names of the parties is made in a ledger called the 'Cause Book'. The Cause Book also records details of the subsequent steps in the action.

(b) Specially indorsed writs

The plaintiff may if he wishes serve his *statement of claim* at the same time that he serves the writ. He may, for example, have wished to do this if he thought the defendant had no defence to the action and so intended to apply in due course for *summary judgment*,[8] ie an order giving him judgment on the basis the defendant could not show even a *prima facie* defence. In such a case, instead of serving the statement of claim as a separate document, the plaintiff may, instead, set out the statement of claim on the back of the writ in place of the general indorsement. Although this can be a fully drafted statement of claim running to several pages, this practice is usually only followed in simple actions in debt or for the balance of an account. In such cases it is accepted that an abbreviated statement of claim may be used (see copy writ on p 79).

(c) Service of writ

Once the writ has been issued it is the plaintiff's task to effect service; service is not effected by the court.[9] In practice this is normally done by sending a copy of the writ and the sealed original to the defendant's solicitors who return the original with a dated indorsement stating that they accept service on behalf of the client.[10] If the defendant has no solicitor authorised to accept service on his behalf, the plaintiff will either serve the writ by post or try to effect personal service. *Postal service*[11] is effected by sending a sealed copy of the writ by ordinary first-class post to the defendant at his usual or last known address. For this purpose, the transmission of a writ to the

---

7 The plaintiff's solicitors may apply by post for the issue of a writ. This involves sending copies and the fee to the court office where the copies will be sealed. This method is not much employed because if there is any error on the draft writ it must be returned to the plaintiff's solicitors for correction. Where there is personal attendance the writ can be amended and issued at once. See *Practice Direction* [1980] 3 All ER 832, [1980] 1 WLR 1441.

8 See p 149.

9 This is in contrast with county court actions, where service of proceedings is usually effected by the court.

10 RSC Ord 10, r 1(4). See the case of Oliver Twist, p 5.

11 RSC Ord 10.

Writ indorsed with
Statement of Claim
[Liquidated
Demand]
(O.6, r. 1)

IN THE HIGH COURT OF JUSTICE

Queen's Bench Division

[GUILDFORD   **District Registry]**

19 93 .— H .—No. 267

Between

ALBERT HIGGINS   Plaintiff

AND

THE GOLDEN GRIFFIN RESTAURANT
(a firm)   Defendant

(1) Insert name.   **To the Defendant(¹)** THE GOLDEN GRIFFIN RESTAURANT

(2) Insert address.   of (²)   201 Wellington Road, Aldershot in the County of Hampshire

This Writ of Summons has been issued against you by the above-named Plaintiff in respect of the claim set out overleaf.

Within 14 days after the service of this Writ on you, counting the day of service, you must either satisfy the claim or return to the Court Office mentioned below the accompanying **Acknowledgment of Service** stating therein whether you intend to contest these proceedings.

If you fail to satisfy the claim or to return the Acknowledgment within the time stated, or if you return the Acknowledgment without stating therein an intention to contest the proceedings, the Plaintiff may proceed with the action and judgment may be entered against you forthwith without further notice.

(3) Complete
and delete as
necessary.

Issued   from   the   (³)   [Central   Office]   [Admiralty   and   Commercial   Registry]
[GUILDFORD   District Registry] of the High Court
this   3rd   day of   June   19₉₃

NOTE:—This Writ may not be served later than 4 calendar months *(or, if leave is required to effect service out of the jurisdiction, 6 months)* beginning with that date unless renewed by order of the Court.

IMPORTANT
Directions for Acknowledgment of Service are given with the accompanying form.

Statement of Claim

The Plaintiff   claim is for the sum of £25,000 being the price of goods sold and delivered to the Defendant on 23rd February 1993 and for the further sum of £1,027.00 being interest thereon at 15% per annum from 23rd February 1992 to the date hereof and further interest at the aforesaid rate (ie £10.27 per day) to judgment or sooner payment.

(Signed)   *Bullen and Leake*

If, within the time for returning the Acknowledgment of Service, the Defendant pay s
the amount claimed and £ 80.25   for costs and, if the Plaintiff obtain s an
order for substituted service, the additional sum of £ 43   , further proceedings
will be stayed. The money must be paid to the Plaintiff ,   h   Solicitor   or Agent

(1) If this Writ
was issued out of
a District Registry,
this indorsement
as to place where
the cause of action
arose should be
completed.

(2) Delete as
necessary.

(3) Insert name of
place.

(4) For phrase-
ology of this
indorsement where
the Plaintiff sues in
person, see
*Supreme Court
Practice,* Vol 2,
para 1.

(¹) [(²) [The cause] [One of the causes] of action in respect of which the Plaintiff
claims relief in this action arose wholly or in part at (³)
in the district of the District Registry named overleaf.]

(⁴) **This Writ** was issued by   BULLEN and LEAKE

of   213 Union Street, Aldershot, Hants

[Agent for

of   ]

Solicitor for the said Plaintiff whose address   (²) [is] [are]

42 Crimea Road, Aldershot, Hants

Solicitor's Reference: FB/LIT/HIGGINS/0041   **TEL No:** 0252 756481

defendant by fax does not constitute good service.[12] Unless the contrary is shown, the writ is deemed to have been served on the seventh day after posting. As an alternative to sending the writ by post it may be inserted through the defendant's letter box at his last known address;[13] again it will be deemed to have been served on the seventh day after insertion:

Order 10, r 1:
'(2) A writ for service on a defendant within the jurisdiction may, instead of being served personally on him, be served –
   (a) by sending a copy of the writ by ordinary first-class post to the defendant at his usual or last known address, or
   (b) if there is a letter box for that address, by inserting through the letter box a copy of the writ enclosed in a sealed envelope addressed to the defendant . . .
(3) Where a writ is served in accordance with paragraph (2) –
   (a) the date of service shall, unless the contrary is shown, be deemed to be the seventh day (ignoring Order 3, rule 2(5)) after the date on which the copy was sent to or, as the case may be, inserted through the letter box for the address in question;
   (b) any affidavit proving due service of the writ must contain a statement to the effect that –
     (i) in the opinion of the deponent (or, if the deponent is the plaintiff's solicitor or an employee of that solicitor, in the opinion of the plaintiff) the copy of the writ, if sent to, or, as the case may be inserted through the letter box for, the address in question, will have come to the knowledge of the defendant within 7 days thereafter . . .'

In order for service to be properly effected under Ord 10, r 1(2) the defendant must be physically present within the jurisdiction at the time 'service' is effected.[14] 'Service' of the writ may occur *after* the writ is posted or inserted through the defendant's letter box. Where the defendant is abroad service is not effected on him until he returns and learns of the documents which have been sent to him.

Example. The plaintiff inserted the writ through the letter box of the defendant's Buckinghamshire flat two hours before the defendant arrived in England. The defendant was met at the airport by the caretaker of the flat who informed him that an envelope had been delivered by special messenger. On receiving this news the defendant did not visit the flat, but went to a hotel and left the country the following day. On the question of whether the writ had been properly served, the House of Lords held that the defendant had to be within the jurisdiction at the date the writ was served to satisfy the requirements of r 1(2). The House held, however, that the words 'unless the contrary is shown' in Ord 10, r 1(3)(a) allowed the plaintiff to displace the deemed date of service (i e 7 days after insertion through the letter box) by showing that the defendant acquired knowledge of the writ at some other date. Therefore, although the defendant had been outside the jurisdiction when the writ was inserted through his flat's letter box and by the seventh day thereafter, he *had* been within the jurisdiction at the time he became

---

12 But the transmission by fax of many documents in the course of litigation, such as chambers summonses, lists of documents etc, will constitute good service under RSC Ord 65, r 5 provided they are not documents required to be served personally or which initiate proceedings, see *Hastie & Jenkerson (a firm) v McMahon* [1991] 1 All ER 255, CA. See RSC Ord 65, r 5(2B) for the conditions under which ordinary service may be made by fax.
13 RSC Ord 10, r 1(2)(b).
14 *Barclays Bank of Swaziland Ltd v Hahn* [1989] 2 All ER 398, HL.

aware of the writ and at that point service was properly effected under r 1(2)(b) (*Barclays Bank of Swaziland Ltd v Hahn*[15]).

The result would be the same where the defendant while out of the jurisdiction but within the 7 day period learns of the writ; the date of service would be the date when he returned to the jurisdiction.

> *Example*. The plaintiff's agent inserted a sealed envelope containing a copy of the writ through the defendant's letter box on 5 September 1988. At that time, the defendant was in India, but she returned to England on 29 May 1989. The question arose whether the writ had been properly served during its period of validity (then 12 months). No affidavit was filed to the effect that the writ would have come to the knowledge of the defendant within 7 days as required by Ord 10, r 1(3)(b)(i). The court therefore could not be satisfied of the *likelihood* that the writ had come to the defendant's attention within 7 days as required so the writ had not, therefore, been properly served. The court went on to say that provided, however, the plaintiff could properly depose to the likelihood of the writ being brought to the attention of the defendant within the period of 7 days after insertion through the letter box (or posting) it would not matter if the defendant was then outside the jurisdiction. The writ would be deemed to be served under Ord 10, r 1(3)(b)(i) at the moment the defendant returned to the jurisdiction (*India Videogram Association Ltd v Patel*[16]).

What emerges from the above cases is that the rules for proper service under RSC Ord 10, r 1 are wide enough to include the situation where the defendant is outside the jurisdiction at the time the writ is posted or inserted through his letter box, even if he does not return to the jurisdiction until after the expiry of the 7 day period specified in Ord 10, r 1(3)(a), provided some person had brought the writ to his attention during the seven day period. In all such cases the plaintiff *must* depose to the likelihood of the writ coming to the defendant's knowledge within 7 days of posting or insertion. If there were no such requirement:

> '. . . that would mean that a plaintiff, who was aware that the defendant had locked up his house and gone abroad leaving it unoccupied for a period of months, could nevertheless rely on r 1(2)(b) by serving through the letter box and waiting for service to take effect months later when the defendant came back. I do not think that such delayed action service was contemplated by the rule.'[17]

Personal service is used where for one reason or another postal service is not appropriate (e g in urgent cases where the plaintiff intends to apply on notice for an interlocutory injunction and does not wish to wait for seven days before service is deemed to be effective). Personal service is effected as follows:

> (i) *On individuals*. The server satisfies himself that the person to be served is the defendant and gives him a sealed copy of the writ.[18] If the defendant refuses to accept the copy writ, it is sufficient to tell him the nature of the document and leave it as nearly in his possession or control as possible.[19]

---

15 [1989] 2 All ER 398, HL.
16 [1991] 1 All ER 214, Hoffmann J.
17 Ibid, at p 217J, per Hoffmann J.
18 RSC Ord 65, r 2.
19 It is not sufficient, however, to give the writ to the defendant's wife or servant or to hand it to him in a sealed envelope without telling him what the envelope contains (*Heath v White* (1844) 2 Dow & L 40; *Banque Russe et Française v Clark* [1894] WN 203, CA). However, it is open to the parties to agree mode of personal service outside the provisions of Ord 10, such as service on the *defendant's* agent (*Kenneth Allison Ltd v A E Limehouse & Co* [1992] 2 AC 105, [1991] 4 All ER 500, HL).

(ii) *On companies.* This is effected by leaving the writ or sending it by post to the registered office.[20] In the case of an overseas company trading in England, the Registrar of Companies holds a list of the names and addresses of persons resident in Great Britain and authorised to accept service of process.[21]

(iii) *On firms.* Where a partnership is sued as a *firm*, service is effected either by personal service on one partner or by leaving the writ at the principal place of business of the partnership within the jurisdiction on any person having at the time of service the control or management of the partnership business there.[22]

(iv) *On bodies corporate.* Service can be validly effected by personal service on the chairman or clerk to the council of a local authority or to a similar officer of other public bodies[23] or by sending it to the registered or principal office of the body in question. In practice, of course, service on such bodies is invariably effected by sending the writ to the solicitor of the body in question.

(v) *Minors.* Service is to be effected on the child's father, guardian or (if he has no father or guardian) upon the person with whom he resides or in whose care he is.[24]

In addition to rules for postal, letter box and personal service described above, RSC Ord 10, r 3 provides that service may be effected in any manner in accordance with terms of a contract between the plaintiff and the defendant which specifies such manner of service in the event of any action in respect of the contract being begun. Consensual service is not, however, restricted to the circumstances envisaged by Ord 10, r 3 and service under an agreement between the parties providing for an alternative method of service is valid and legally effective.

> *Example.* Mr Swann, the plaintiff's agent, visited the defendants' offices to effect personal service of the writ on Mr Hall, a partner in the defendant firm. Mr Swann spoke to Mrs Morgan, Mr Hall's personal assistant, showing her the writ. She consulted Mr Hall, who authorised her to accept the writ. The House of Lords held that Mrs Morgan's acceptance of the writ could not constitute personal service on Mr Hall as the writ had not been handed to or left with him. However, the plaintiffs could rely on the *ad hoc* agreement under which Mr Hall authorised Mrs Morgan to accept service. Adopting the words of Lord Donaldson in the Court of Appeal[25] Lord Bridge said: 'The rules are the servants of the courts and of their customers, not their masters, unless expressed in a wholly mandatory and exclusive fashion which these rules are not. It would be wholly contrary to the spirit of the times that the rules should be construed in a manner which would forbid parties to litigation to act reasonably with a view to eliminating or reducing the acerbities inevitable in litigation, when to do so creates no problems whatsoever for the defendant in terms of deciding precisely when service was effected for the purposes of the Limitation Acts or otherwise.' (*Kenneth Allison Ltd (in liq) v A E Limehouse & Co*[26]).

---

20 Companies Act 1985, s 725.
21 Companies Act 1985, s 695. If no address for service has been filed, the plaintiff may effect service by leaving the writ or sending it to any place of business established by the company in England (s 695(2)).
22 RSC Ord 81, r 3. A writ may also be served by post on a partnership by sending it to the firm at the principal place of business of the partnership within the jurisdiction.
23 RSC Ord 65, r 3.
24 RSC Ord 80, r 16.
25 [1990] 2 All ER 723, at 727.
26 [1992] 2 AC 105, [1991] 4 All ER 500, HL.

There will however still be some cases where personal or postal service is not possible either because the defendant is evading service or because his present whereabouts are unknown. In these circumstances the plaintiff can apply to the master setting out in an affidavit the efforts made to trace the defendant. The master can order that notice of the writ should be effected by some other method, eg by service on a close relative of the defendant or by advertisement. If this order for *substituted service* is complied with, the court deems valid service to have been effected.[27]

Before the master can make an order for substituted service, it must appear to him that 'it is impracticable for any reason' to serve the writ (or any other document for which the order is sought) in the prescribed manner. For the purposes of this rule service of a writ is 'practicable' if it could be effected by using one of the prescribed methods (eg by posting to the defendant's last known address) even though such service would be out of time and therefore serve no useful purpose.[28]

Substituted service will be ordered only where the plaintiff can persuade the master that it is likely to be effective in bringing to the attention of the defendant the fact that the writ has been issued. Where, therefore, the plaintiff has no idea of the whereabouts of the defendant, an order for substituted service will not be made unless:

(i)   the plaintiff's claim is for personal injury arising out of a road traffic accident – in which case service may be effected on the defendant's insurers or the Motor Insurers' Bureau,[29] *or*

(ii) the plaintiff is claiming possession of land in which case the master may permit service by affixing a copy of the writ to some conspicuous part of the land.[30]

(d) Documents to be served with writ

The plaintiff must serve with the writ a form of acknowledgment of service. He should insert on the form the title and number of the action. The form sent contains notes to assist the defendant. A copy of the form and notes is shown on pp 89–92. The plaintiff's solicitor must indorse his name and address on the reverse side of the acknowledgment form.

(e) Validity and renewal of writ

A writ is generally valid for 4 months.[31] If it is not served within that period the plaintiff will have to apply for a renewal. The application is made *ex parte* and the Master or District Judge may extend for a further period of up to 4 months; further applications for renewal may be made thereafter but generally in such a case, the plaintiff will have to consider applying instead for an order of substituted service or for leave to serve out of the jurisdiction. When the writ has been renewed it is stamped showing the period for which the validity has been extended. A defendant who believes the writ should

27 RSC Ord 65, r 4.
28 See, for example, *Paragon Group Ltd v Burnell* [1991] Ch 498, [1991] 2 All ER 388 where the Court of Appeal held (by a majority) that service of a writ was practicable although it would be too late to meet the parties' contractual deadline for the notification of claims. Lloyd LJ said (at 392C): '. . . the question is whether it is practicable to serve the writ, not whether it is practicable to serve it in time'.
29 See *Gurtner v Circuit* [1968] 2 QB 587, [1968] 1 All ER 328, CA.
30 RSC Ord 10, r 4 and see also Ord 113, p 165 post.
31 RSC Ord 6, r 8(1)(b).

not have been extended must file an acknowledgment of service (see p 88, below) and apply for the order extending validity to be discharged and for the writ to be set aside (see RSC Order 12, rule 8(1)). In practice such an application is usually made by the defendant when the limitation period has expired so that no new action could be brought against him.

Example 1. The plaintiff was injured in March 1961. In December 1963 his solicitors issues a writ but took no steps to effect service while they were negotiating with the defendants' insurers. Those negotiations broke down in September 1964. In January 1965 the plaintiffs obtained an order for the renewal of the writ. The defendants applied to discharge the order and to set the writ aside. Megaw J held that in the absence of *exceptional circumstances* leave should not be granted to renew a writ when a fresh writ would be met with a defence under the Limitation Act (*Heaven v Road and Rail Wagons Ltd*[32]).

Example 2. In 1977 the plaintiff bank brought an Admiralty action in rem against a ship, *The Myrto*, to enforce mortgages which had been granted to them over the vessel as security for substantial advances. A dispute then arose between the bank and 165 cargo owners. In 1980 the bank brought proceedings against the major cargo-owner in the belief that the remaining cargo-owners would accept the decision on that case without the necessity for further actions being brought. In 1982, however, they took the precaution of issuing an 'omnibus' writ against the remaining 164 cargo owners but delayed service. After the expiry of the limitation period the bank obtained orders extending the writ. The House of Lords held that the plaintiffs did *not* have to show 'exceptional circumstances' to justify the renewal. The plaintiffs had to show a 'good reason' for their failure to serve while the writ was valid and in then deciding whether to set aside the extension the court had to consider whether the hardship to the plaintiffs if the extension was set aside would outweigh the hardship to the defendants if the extension stood. On the facts the good reason for allowing the extension to stand was the saving of unnecessary proceedings and costs achieved by the delay without any prejudice to the defendants (*Kleinwort Benson Ltd v Barbrak Ltd, The Myrto (No 3)*[33]).

Although the court is entitled to consider the 'balance of hardship' between the parties in deciding whether to permit an extension of validity, hardship cannot, of itself, constitute good reason for doing so.

Example 3. Towards the end of 1979 the plaintiff contracted dermatitis which he alleged was as a result of his skin coming into contact with paraffin and oil whilst working for the defendants as a machine operator. On 4 October 1982 his solicitors obtained a legal aid certificate, which was extended on 26 November 1982 to cover the issue but not service of the writ alleging negligence by the defendants. The writ was issued on 29 November 1982, just within the limitation period. On 9 November 1983, shortly before the expiry of the (then) 12 month period of validity the writ's validity was extended for a further period of 12 months. Only in December 1983, after a favourable expert's report and counsel's opinion, did the plaintiff's solicitors obtain the removal of the restriction against service on the legal aid certificate. When the plaintiff served the writ in April 1984 the defendants successfully applied to have the *ex parte* order discharged and service of the writ set aside on the ground that the plaintiff had failed to show good reason for the extension. The House of Lords held that whilst the court is entitled to take delays caused by the operation of the legal aid system into account in deciding whether a good reason for extension is shown, on the facts the failure to serve the writ in this case was not directly caused by the operation of the legal aid system as the plaintiff's solicitors could have taken the necessary steps to remove the restriction on the certificate before the expiry of the original period of validity. Further, the first instance judge did not err by failing

32 [1965] 2 QB 355, [1965] 2 All ER 409.
33 [1987] AC 597, [1987] 2 All ER 289, HL.

to take account of the balance of hardship between the parties. The *Kleinwort Benson* case showed that it was a proper matter for consideration but '. . . [t]his House was not saying that balance of hardship could of itself constitute good reason for extending the validity of a writ. What it was saying was that, where there were matters which could, potentially at least, constitute good reason for extension, balance of hardship might be a relevant consideration. . .' (*Waddon v Whitecroft-Scovill Ltd*).[34]

It will be appreciated that the question of renewing a writ is critically important where both the limitation period and the period of validity of the writ have expired at the date of the application. Where the relevant period of limitation is still current, the plaintiff may overcome a refusal of an extension by issuing fresh proceedings. Similarly, where the limitation period has expired but an extension is refused before the expiry of the original period of validity, the plaintiff has the remaining period of validity in which to effect good service.[35]

(f) Service on parties domiciled abroad
Where the plaintiff's claim is brought against a person or company domiciled abroad two questions will arise:

(i)   whether the English court will entertain proceedings if the person or company is present within the jurisdiction; and
(ii) whether the court will allow its process to be served abroad if the person or company is not present within the jurisdiction.

The answer to these questions varies according to whether or not the action falls under the provisions of the Civil Jurisdiction and Judgments Acts 1982 and 1991 which respectively implement in the UK the Brussels and Lugano Conventions on jurisdiction and enforcement of judgments in civil matters. The Brussels Convention covers EC countries whereas the Lugano convention extends to EFTA (European Free Trade Association) Member States, such as Austria, Norway and Switzerland. The position can be summarised as follows:

(a)   *Defendants domiciled in a contracting state*
      Where the defendant is domiciled[36] in a contracting EC or EFTA state (e g France or Iceland) then
      (i)   The basic rule is that proceedings can only be brought against him in that state and the English court will have no jurisdiction – even though he may be temporarily living in England or carries on business here.[37]

---

34 [1988] 1 All ER 996, HL. See also *Easy v Universal Anchorage Co* [1974] 2 All ER 1105, CA (negotiations for settlement held not to afford any excuse for failing to serve a writ in time or to renew it).

35 See *Kleinwort Benson Ltd v Barbrak Ltd, The Myrto (No 3)* [1987] 2 All ER 289, per Lord Brandon at 294h.

36 For these purposes, an individual is 'domiciled' here if he is resident and has a substantial connection with the UK. The latter is presumed by three months' residence (CJJA 1982, ss 41–46). A company is domiciled in the country where it was incorporated and has its registered office, or where its central management and control is exercised (CJJA 1982, s 42).

37 Civil Jurisdiction and Judgments Act 1982, Sch 1, art 2; Civil Jurisdiction and Judgments Act 1991, Sch 1, art 2. But note that the mandatory effect of art 2 does not require the English courts to hear and determine proceedings on the basis of the defendant's English domicile where the only conflict of jurisdiction is between courts of a single convention country and those of a non-convention country. Accordingly, the court had jurisdiction to stay or dismiss proceedings against an English domiciled company on the ground of *forum non conveniens* where it considered the Argentine courts to be more appropriate to decide the issues: *Re Harrods (Buenos Aires) Ltd* [1992] Ch 72, [1991] 4 All ER 334, CA.

(ii)   An exception is made in the case of disputes concerning title to land and tenancies: proceedings must usually be brought in the member state where the land in question is situated.[38]

(iii) Further exceptions are made in the case of certain proceedings where process can be issued in the English courts and served abroad.[39] These cases are listed in articles 5–15 of the above Conventions and include claims arising out of breach of a contract to be performed in England and actions in tort where the harmful event occurred here. Similar provisions apply to allocate jurisdiction where the defendant is domiciled in a different part of the UK, ie Scotland or Northern Ireland.[40]

Note that where proceedings are to be commenced in England and served on a defendant outside the jurisdiction under the above provisions the writ must be indorsed with a statement that the court has jurisdiction under the relevant Act and that there are no proceedings pending in Scotland, Northern Ireland or any other convention country.[41] In these cases no leave to issue or serve is necessary.

(b) *Defendants domiciled in other states*
Where the proposed defendant is not domiciled in an EC or EFTA State (eg a person domiciled in the United States of America) the 1982 and 1991 Acts do not apply and a completely different set of rules has to be understood:

(i)   The basic rule is that he can be sued if he is present within the jurisdiction for the purpose of service. If he is so present the court will have jurisdiction over him even though his presence may be purely temporary and the English court will have jurisdiction notwithstanding that the subject matter of the dispute is entirely foreign.[42] The court may, however, stay or dismiss such proceedings on the grounds of *forum non conveniens* if the courts of another country are more appropriate to decide the issues.

(ii)   Conversely, where the proposed defendant is abroad the English court has no jurisdiction over him.

(iii) A limited number of exceptions to rule (ii) is made by RSC Order 11. This provides that the court may give leave for proceedings to be served abroad provided two conditions are satisfied:

(a) the claim falls within one or more of the categories set out in Order 11, rule 1(1) (eg actions brought against a person domiciled within the jurisdiction, actions founded on a tort committed within the jurisdiction, actions relating to the enforcement of contracts made within the jurisdiction, actions for breach of contract occurring within the jurisdiction, actions against another proper party to the action where one defendant has been duly served); and

---

38 Civil Jurisdiction and Judgments Act 1982, Sch 1, art 16; Civil Jurisdiction and Judgments Act 1991, Sch 1, art 16.
39 RSC Ord 11, r 1(2).
40 See Sch 4 to the Civil Jurisdiction and Judgments Act 1982.
41 RSC Ord 6, r 7.
42 *Watkins v North American Land and Timber Co Ltd* (1904) 20 TLR 534, HL.

(b) the case is a proper one for service outside the jurisdiction.[43]
An application for leave to issue the writ[44] and serve it out of the
jurisdiction is made by the plaintiff ex parte to the master supported
by an affidavit setting out (i) the nature of the case in sufficient detail
to show it falls within rule 1(1); (ii) the deponent's belief that the
plaintiff has a good cause of action; (iii) in what country and place
the defendant is or probably may be found.[45]

ACKNOWLEDGMENT OF SERVICE

The defendant is obliged to return the completed forms of acknowledgment
of service to the court office from which the writ has been issued within the
time limited for doing so. That time period is defined by RSC Ord 12, r 5
and is normally 14 days after service of the writ[46] (calculated by including
the day of service). The court clerk receiving the acknowledgment form
stamps it with the date of receipt, enters details in the Cause Book and sends
stamped copies to each party. These will be photocopies produced in the
court office. The acknowledgment of service form enables the defendant to
place himself on the court record and gives the court and the plaintiff
certain information about his intentions.

The defendant is required to state specifically whether or not he intends
to defend the action; if he does not so intend, the plaintiff will be entitled to
enter judgment against him under RSC Ord 13. Since in the case of a
liquidated claim (i e for a debt or sum due under a contract) the judgment
would be enforceable straightaway, the defendant is specifically asked
whether he wishes to apply for a stay of execution: if he does, the court clerk
entering details of the acknowledgment of service in the Cause Book will
make a note to that effect. The plaintiff may still enter judgment but
execution cannot issue for 14 days from the date on which the acknowledgment of service was received at the court office. If within that period of 14
days the defendant issues a summons for a stay under RSC Ord 47, r 1
(accompanied by an affidavit of means) execution cannot issue until that
summons has been heard.

Although where a writ is issued out of a district registry, the acknowledgment
forms must be returned to that registry, the defendant may apply under RSC
Ord 4, r 5(3) for a transfer to London or some other registry. If the defendant
does not reside or carry on business within the area of the registry and the
cause of action did not arise there, the procedure is very simple. The defendant
states in the acknowledgment form that he objects to the cause continuing in
the registry and the district judge is bound to order a transfer unless, within 8
days of the date the acknowledgment of service is received, the plaintiff objects.
If the plaintiff does so object or the defendant resides within the area or the
cause of action arose within the area, transfer is not automatic but is determined
by the district judge at a hearing at which the parties attend.

---

43 See RSC Ord 11, r 4(2) and *The Hagen* [1908] P 189, CA and *Société Générale de Paris v Dreyfus
Bros* (1885) 29 Ch D 239.
44 See RSC Ord 6, r 7.
45 RSC Ord 11, r 4(1).
46 RSC Ord 12, r 5. Acknowledgment of a writ served out of the jurisdiction (but within
European territory) without leave must take place within 21 days of service (RSC Ord 11,
r 1(3)(a)); where service out of the jurisdiction is made with leave, the order granting leave
must limit a time within which the defendant must acknowledge service (Ord 11, r 4(4)).

Acknowledgment of Service of Writ of Summons (Queen's Bench)	**IN THE HIGH COURT OF JUSTICE**

IN THE HIGH COURT OF JUSTICE

Queen's Bench Division   1993.— H.—No. 267

GUILDFORD DISTRICT REGISTRY

The adjacent heading should be completed by the Plaintiff

Between

ALBERT HIGGINS   Plaintiff

AND

THE GOLDEN GRIFFIN RESTAURANT
(a firm)   Defendant

If you intend to instruct a Solicitor to act for you, give him this form IMMEDIATELY. Please complete in black ink.

IMPORTANT. Read the accompanying directions and notes for guidance carefully before completing this form. If any information required is omitted or given wrongly, THIS FORM MAY HAVE TO BE RETURNED. Delay may result in judgment being entered against a Defendant whereby he or his solicitor may have to pay the costs of applying to set it aside.

See Notes 1, 3, 4 and 5

1   State the full name of the Defendant by whom or on whose behalf the service of the Writ is being acknowledged. Tai-Wah LAM and John NG trading as "The Golden Griffin Restaurant"

2   State whether the Defendant intends to contest the proceedings (*tick appropriate box*)   ☐ yes   ☑ no

See Direction 3

3   If the claim against the Defendant is for a debt or liquidated demand, AND he does not intend to contest the proceedings, state if the Defendant intends to apply for a stay of execution against any judgment entered by the Plaintiff (*tick box*)   ☑ yes

See Direction 4

4   If the Writ of Summons was issued out of a District Registry and

    (*a*)   the Defendant's residence, place of business or registered office (if a limited company) is NOT within the district of that District Registry AND

    (*b*)   there is no indorsement on the Writ that the Plaintiff's cause of action arose wholly or in part within that district,

state if the Defendant applies for the transfer of the action (*tick box*) ☐ yes

If YES, state—   ☐   to the Royal Courts of Justice, London:
(*tick appropriate box*)   OR
                                ☐   to the*   District Registry

*State which Registry

Service of the Writ is acknowledged accordingly

(*Signed*)   Chitty & Co

†[Solicitor][~~Agent for~~] for the defendants   ]

Address for service (*See notes overleaf*)

65 Victoria Road, Aldershot, Hants.

†*Where words appear between square brackets, delete if inapplicable. Insert "Defendant in Person" if appropriate*

Please complete overleaf

Indorsement by Plaintiff's solicitor (or by Plaintiff if suing in person) of his name address and reference, if any, in the box below.

BULLEN AND LEAKE
213 UNION STREET
ALDERSHOT
HANTS

Notes as to Address for Service

Solicitor. Where the Defendant is represented by a Solicitor, state the Solicitor's place of business in England or Wales. If the Solicitor is the Agent of another Solicitor, state the name and the place of business of the Solicitor for whom he is acting.

Defendant in person. Where the Defendant is acting in person, he must give his residence OR, if he does not reside in England or Wales, he must give an address in England or Wales where communications for him should be sent. In the case of a limited company, "residence" means its registered or principal office.

OYEZ The Solicitors' Law Stationery Society Ltd. Oyez House, 7 Spa Road, London SE16 3QQ   10 92 F23306
5044213
· · · · ·

High Court E22 (PR)

Acknowledgment
of Service
of Writ
of Summons
(Queen's Bench)
(O. 12, r. 3)

Directions for Acknowledgment of Service

1. The accompanying form of **ACKNOWLEDGMENT OF SERVICE** should be detached and completed by a Solicitor acting on behalf of the Defendant or by the Defendant if acting in person. After completion it must be delivered or sent by post to the Central Office, Royal Courts of Justice, Strand, London WC2A 2LL.

2. A Defendant who states in his Acknowledgment of Service that he intends to contest the proceedings **MUST ALSO SERVE A DEFENCE** on the Solicitor for the Plaintiff (or on the Plaintiff if acting in person).

If a Statement of Claim is indorsed on the Writ (i.e. the words "Statement of Claim" appear at the top of the back of the first page), the Defence must be served within 14 days after the time for acknowledging service of the Writ, unless in the meantime a summons for judgment is served on the Defendant.

If a Statement of Claim is not indorsed on the Writ, the Defence need not be served until 14 days after a Statement of Claim has been served on the Defendant. If the Defendant fails to serve his defence within the appropriate time, the Plaintiff may enter judgment against him without further notice.

3. **A STAY OF EXECUTION** against the Defendant's goods may be applied for where the Defendant is unable to pay the money for which any judgment is entered. If a Defendant to an action for a debt or liquidated demand (i.e. a fixed sum) who does not intend to contest the proceedings states, in answer to Question 3 in the Acknowledgment of Service, that he intends to apply for a stay, execution will be stayed for 14 days after his Acknowledgment, but he must, within that time, **ISSUE A SUMMONS** for a stay of execution, supported by an affidavit of his means. The affidavit should state any offer which the Defendant desires to make for payment of the money by instalments or otherwise.

4. **IF THE WRIT IS ISSUED OUT OF A DISTRICT REGISTRY** but the Defendant does not reside or carry on business within the district of the registry and the writ is not indorsed with a statement that the Plaintiff's cause of action arose in that district, the Defendant may, in answer to Question 4 in the Acknowledgment of Service, apply for the transfer of the action to some other District Registry or to the Royal Courts of Justice.

See over for Notes for Guidance

Notes for Guidance

1. Each Defendant (if there are more than one) is required to complete an Acknowledgment of Service and return it to the appropriate Court Office.

*Not applicable if the Defendant is a Company served at its Registered Office.

*[2. For the purpose of calculating the period of 14 days for acknowledging service, a writ served on the Defendant personally is treated as having been served on the day it was delivered to him and a writ served by post or by insertion through the Defendant's letter box is treated as having been served on the seventh day after the date of posting or insertion unless the contrary is shown.]

3. Where the Defendant is sued in a name different from his own, the form must be completed by him with the addition in paragraph 1 of the words "sued as (*the name stated on the Writ of Summons*)".

4. Where the Defendant is a **FIRM** and a Solicitor is not instructed, the form must be completed by a **PARTNER** by name, with the addition in paragraph 1 of the description "partner in the firm (....)" after his name.

5. Where the Defendant is sued as an individual **TRADING IN A NAME OTHER THAN HIS OWN**, the form must be completed by him with the addition in paragraph 1 of the description "trading as (..............................)" after his name.

6. Where the Defendant is a **LIMITED COMPANY** the form must be completed by a Solicitor or by someone authorised to act on behalf of the Company, but the Company can take no further step in the proceedings without a Solicitor acting on its behalf.

7. Where the Defendant is a **MINOR** or a **MENTAL** Patient, the form must be completed by a Solicitor acting for a guardian *ad litem*.

8. A Defendant acting in person may obtain help in completing the form either at the Central Office of the Royal Courts of Justice or at any District Registry of the High Court or at any Citizens' Advice Bureau.

9. A Defendant who is NOT a Limited Company or a Corporation may be entitled to Legal Aid. Information about the Legal Aid Scheme may be obtained from any Citizens' Advice Bureau and from most firms of Solicitors.

10. These notes deal only with the more usual cases. In case of difficulty a Defendant in person should refer to paragraphs 8 and 9 above.

A limited company may acknowledge service by any person duly authorised to act on its behalf (for example, a director or the company secretary); any subsequent steps in the action must however be conducted by a solicitor instructed by the company.[47] Where proceedings are issued against a firm, service must be acknowledged by the partners in their own names and not in the firm name.[48] Where such proceedings are served on a person who disputes he was a partner in the firm at the relevant time, he may state on the form of acknowledgment that the point is in issue:[49] either side can then apply to the court to determine this specific issue or they can allow the proceedings to continue to trial on a defence specifically raising the issue of the defendant's status.

JUDGMENT IN DEFAULT OF ACKNOWLEDGMENT OF SERVICE

As stated above, the rules usually require the acknowledgment of service to be delivered within 14 days after service of the writ. This does not mean that an acknowledgment cannot be delivered thereafter but it does mean that once 14 days have elapsed, the plaintiff may enter *judgment in default*. Until such judgment is entered, the defendant is free to deliver his acknowledgment notwithstanding the 14 day period has expired. In order to avoid default judgment the defendant must in the acknowledgment state his intention to defend the proceedings, because strictly the defendant's 'default' under RSC Ord 13 is his failure to give notice of intention to defend the claim. Where there is no such notice after the expiry of the 14 day period judgment is entered by the plaintiff obtaining a sealed judgment at the court office. This is purely an administrative act; there is no appearance involved before any judge or master. The plaintiff's solicitor takes to the court office the original writ, an affidavit verifying service, and two completed judgment forms. The court clerk checks the Cause Book and certifies that no acknowledgment has been filed; the forms are then presented for sealing and the judgment is recorded in the Cause Book. Default judgment under this rule is available for cases of claims for (i) liquidated sums, such as debts; (ii) damages; (iii) detention of goods; and (iv) possession of land. The judgment will either be:

(a) *final judgment*, where the claim is liquidated (i e for a fixed or agreed sum, e g £10,000 debt) or for possession of land, or

(b) *interlocutory judgment*, where the amount of damages to be awarded has to be decided by the court (e g damages for negligence[50] or nuisance or trespass). In this case the damages will be assessed by the master (or district judge) and the defendant must be notified and may attend to argue the question of quantum of damages (although he may not dispute his *liability*).[51]

The above procedures relate to actions in which the remedy sought by the plaintiff is the payment of *money* (e g debt or damages). Special rules

---

47 RSC Ord 12, r 1(2).
48 RSC Ord 81, r 4.
49 RSC Ord 81, r 4(2).
50 Note that in county court proceedings claims in negligence for the cost of repairs to a vehicle or property accidentally damaged on or near a highway are treated as liquidated demands: CCR Ord 1, r 11.
51 See RSC Ord 37 for the procedure to be followed.

apply to claims for the detention of goods in which the plaintiff is claiming an order for the delivery of the goods in question.[52]

Equitable claims

Default judgment under RSC Ord 13 is not available for claims for equitable remedies.[53] The reason is that these remedies (e g specific performance or injunctions) are not available as of right but are *discretionary*. This means that even if it is assumed that the plaintiff would be able to establish the defendant's liability, it does not necessarily follow that the plaintiff would succeed in obtaining the equitable relief sought. It would therefore not be right to allow the plaintiff to enter judgment for an equitable remedy in default of notice of intention to defend without the court first being satisfied that it is a proper case to exercise its discretion in the plaintiff's favour.

> *Example.* P Ltd manufacture specialised safety flooring for use in gymnasiums, schools, playgrounds etc. P Ltd's director conceives of means of substantially improving the machinery currently available for the production of such flooring and engages D Ltd to design and produce a machine for them embodying his ideas. Some time after the machine is delivered and installed at P Ltd's premises, they learn that D Ltd are sending circulars to their competitors advertising a machine based on P's idea. P Ltd considers that this constitutes a breach of confidence. A writ is issued in the Chancery Division on 3 July 1992 seeking a permanent injunction. The writ is posted to D Ltd on the same day. On 27 July no acknowledgment of service has been received at the court office. Although the time limited for acknowledging service has expired, P Ltd may *not* enter judgment in default under RSC Order 13 for the injunction claimed.

The correct procedure in the above case is for the plaintiff to proceed as if the defendant *had* given notice of intention to defend by serving on the defendant a statement of claim. If the defendant fails to serve a defence within the time limited for doing so the plaintiff may then apply for judgment in default of pleading under RSC Ord 19. If, as here, an equitable remedy is claimed the plaintiff must apply by notice of motion.[54]

Applications for final judgment in default of defence are often made in the Chancery Division in cases where the plaintiff is seeking a permanent injunction. The application is made by motion to a judge. The notice of motion must be served on the defendant not less than 2 clear days before the hearing. The plaintiff's solicitor must lodge at the Chancery Chambers:

(1) Two plain copies of the writ.
(2) Two copies of the statement of claim; one copy is to be indorsed with a certificate signed by the solicitor that no defence has been served.
(3) Duplicate notice of intention to defend *or* certificate that no notice of intention to defend has been filed.
(4) Affidavit of service of statement of claim (unless indorsed on writ).

---

52 RSC Ord 13, r 3. Under this rule the plaintiff may enter interlocutory judgment for the value of the goods to be assessed, or may apply by summons for final judgment for an order for delivery of the specified goods where the defendant is not to have the alternative of paying their assessed value.
53 RSC Ord 13, r 6.
54 RSC Ord 19, r 7. If an injunction is sought the application is by notice of motion in the Chancery Division or summons in the Queen's Bench Division and the application is heard by a judge. Other interlocutory applications are made by summons to a master.

(5) Two plain copies of the notice of motion showing a date of service at least 14 clear days after the statement of claim was served.
(6) Two copies of the proposed order ('minutes of judgment').
(7) Certificate of counsel that the application is not likely to exceed 10 minutes if the motion is to be listed as 'short'.

In addition the applicant will have to prove service of the notice of motion if the defendant does not appear.

Under this procedure the court (a judge in the case of an injunction) has the benefit of seeing the plaintiff's statement of claim before deciding whether the grant of an equitable remedy is appropriate. If the defendant does serve a defence within the prescribed time the plaintiff may *not* obtain judgment in default under RSC Ord 19. Instead, it may be open to the plaintiff to show that the defence served does not raise a triable issue so as to justify an application for *summary judgment* under RSC Ord 14. For the purposes of such an application, service of a defence by the defendant is treated as notice of intention to defend as required by Ord 14.

Mixed claims

It may be that the plaintiff's writ includes a claim for more than one remedy. Provided each remedy falls within the categories of claim for which Ord 13 judgment is available (eg a claim for possession of land and a debt of £10,000) the plaintiff may enter default judgment in the manner prescribed for each respective remedy.[55] But where there is no notice of intention to defend and the plaintiff claims an equitable remedy as part of the relief sought (eg an injunction to restrain a nuisance and damages), he may *not* enter interlocutory judgment for damages if, under the RSC Ord 19 procedure described above, he intends to pursue the claim for an injunction. In other words, the two remedies cannot be 'severed'. Instead, the plaintiff must choose either to proceed to serve a statement of claim and seek to obtain judgment in default of defence in respect of both remedies under Ord 19 or abandon the claim for an injunction and enter interlocutory judgment for damages only under Ord 13.

In addition to the above special procedures there are certain cases in which leave to enter Ord 13 default judgment is needed. Leave must be obtained in proceedings against the Crown, or if the defendant is any other State,[56] or where the writ was served out of the jurisdiction without leave or within the jurisdiction on a defendant domiciled in an EC or EFTA Convention country.[57]

At first sight it might appear that the acknowledgment of service stage is a pointless formality inasmuch as all the defendant has to do is to complete a simple form. In practice a total of about 140,000 such judgments are entered in each year. It therefore seems that the system effectively provides a method of enabling plaintiffs to obtain (usually in simple debt collection cases) a speedy default judgment.

INTEREST

Section 35A of the Supreme Court Act 1981 provides:

55 RSC Ord 13, r 5.
56 RSC Ord 13, r 7A.
57 RSC Ord 13, r 7B.

'Subject to the rules of court, in proceedings (whenever instituted) before the High Court for the recovery of a debt or damages there may be included in any sum for which judgment is given simple interest at such rate as the court thinks fit or as rules of court may provide, on all or any part of the debt or damages in respect of which judgment is given, or payment is made before judgment, for all or any part of the period between the date when the cause of action arose and –

(a) in the case of any sum paid before judgment, the date of the payment; and
(b) in the case of the sum for which judgment is given, the date of the judgment.'

RSC Ord 13, r 1 enables the plaintiff signing judgment in default for a liquidated sum to include statutory interest down to the date of judgment. In order to obtain such interest the following conditions[58] must be satisfied:

(i) the plaintiff must have indorsed a claim for interest on the writ. Such an indorsement might read as follows:
'The Plaintiff's claim is for the sum of £20,000 and £1200 being interest thereon claimed pursuant to section 35A of the Supreme Court Act 1981 at the rate of 12% per annum from 1 February 1992 to the date hereof and further interest at the aforesaid rate (being £6.66p per day) to judgment or sooner payment.'

(ii) in order to be able to *sign* a judgment for interest the claim must be limited to interest at the rate currently awarded under the Judgments Act 1838 on judgment debts (ie the sums due between judgment and execution or payment). The rate is currently 8%. If the plaintiff wishes to obtain interest at a higher rate he will sign judgment for the principal sum and interest to be assessed. There will then be a hearing before the master at which he will have to justify his claim for a higher level of interest.[59]

Note that alternatively interest may be due under the Bills of Exchange Act or under the specific terms of a contract between the parties or under the Solicitors Act in respect of an outstanding bill of costs. In such a case the writ should set out precisely under what power the interest is claimed, the amount due at the date of the writ and the daily rate.

SETTING ASIDE DEFAULT JUDGMENTS

It frequently happens that a defendant against whom judgment has been entered in default will wish to have the judgment set aside, in other words to be allowed to dispute the claim. He may apply to the master by summons (under RSC Ord 13, r 9)[60] for an order setting the judgment aside and for leave to deliver an acknowledgment of service. Where the default judgment was obtained *irregularly* (eg without leave in a case where leave is required, or before the expiry of the time limited for acknowledging service) the defendant is entitled to have the judgment set aside as of right. Where judgment is *regular* it is standard practice to file an affidavit stating why judgment was allowed to be entered (eg mistake, delay etc) and showing that the defendant has a prima facie defence to the action or there is some triable issue (otherwise it would be a pointless exercise to set the judgment

---

58 See *Practice Direction* [1983] 1 All ER 934, sub nom *Practice Note* [1983] 1 WLR 377.
59 See *Tate and Lyle Food and Distribution Ltd v Greater London Council* [1981] 3 All ER 716, [1982] 1 WLR 149 for the circumstances in which a higher rate may be awarded.
60 The summons must be served on the defendant not less than two clear days before the return day.

aside). In *Evans v Bartlem*[61] (where the defendant had allowed judgment to be entered in default of acknowledgment for what was in effect a gaming debt and then applied to set the judgment aside), Lord Atkin explained the true position and at the same time formulated the classic statement of the basic principle of procedural law, namely that a failure to follow the rules of procedure is not to debar a defendant from seeking judgment on the merits:

> 'The principle obviously is that unless and until the Court has pronounced a judgment upon the merits or by consent, it is to have the power to revoke the expression of its coercive power where that has only been obtained by a failure to follow any of the rules of procedure.'

The form of summons and affidavit which would be used in a typical case are set out on pp 100 and 101. It is good practice for the defendant to exhibit to the affidavit a draft of the defence he proposes to serve if the judgment is set aside.

The power to set aside judgments under RSC Ord 13, r 9 is usually exercised on the application of the defendant, but the court has power to set aside or vary any judgment of its own motion. There are also circumstances where the plaintiff is *required* to set aside a default judgment which he has already obtained. This occurs where, after default judgment has been entered, the copy of the writ sent by post to the defendant is returned to the plaintiff undelivered. The plaintiff must then make a request to the court office for the judgment to be set aside on the ground that the writ has not been duly served.[62] As the request operates in the defendant's favour, the procedure is administrative and no hearing is necessary. Upon the plaintiff producing an affidavit stating the relevant facts to the office in which it was entered the judgment is routinely set aside.[63] Where, however, there may be reasons for allowing the default judgment to stand, notwithstanding the return of the 'undelivered' writ (such as where it is believed that the defendant is deliberately evading service), the plaintiff may instead of requesting that the judgment be set aside apply *ex parte* to the court for directions.[64]

ACKNOWLEDGMENT UNDER PROTEST

Where an acknowledgment of service is returned by the defendant it does *not* prejudice his right to dispute the validity or service of the writ (e g on the grounds that the writ has been renewed after a relevant period of limitation has expired or that it has been served more than 4 months from the date of issue). RSC Ord 12, r 7 provides that:

> 'The acknowledgment by a defendant of service of a writ shall not be treated as a waiver by him of any irregularity in the writ or service thereof or in any order giving leave to serve the writ out of the jurisdiction or extending the validity of the writ for the purpose of service.'

Where the defendant wishes to raise such an issue, he should return the acknowledgment of service in the usual way and then, within the time

---

61 [1937] AC 473 at 480. See also *Alpine Bulk Transport Co Inc v Saudi Eagle Shipping Co Inc, The Saudi Eagle* [1986] 2 Lloyds Rep 221 regarding the exercise of the court's discretion to set judgment aside.
62 RSC Ord 13, r 7(3).
63 RSC Ord 13, r 7(4).
64 RSC Ord 13, r 7(3)(b).

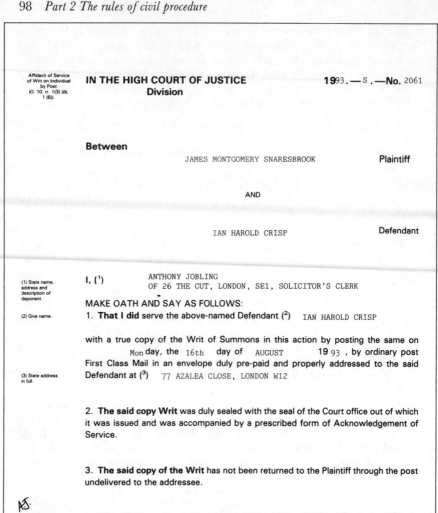

IN THE HIGH COURT OF JUSTICE
Division

19 93 .— S .—No. 2061

Between

JAMES MONTGOMERY SNARESBROOK

Plaintiff

AND

IAN HAROLD CRISP

Defendant

(1) State name,
address and
description of
deponent.

I, (¹)   ANTHONY JOBLING
OF 26 THE CUT, LONDON, SE1, SOLICITOR'S CLERK

(2) Give name.

MAKE OATH AND SAY AS FOLLOWS:

1. **That I did** serve the above-named Defendant (²)   IAN HAROLD CRISP

with a true copy of the Writ of Summons in this action by posting the same on
Mon day, the 16th day of AUGUST   19 93 , by ordinary post
First Class Mail in an envelope duly pre-paid and properly addressed to the said

(3) State address
in full.

Defendant at (³)   77 AZALEA CLOSE, LONDON W12

2. **The said copy Writ** was duly sealed with the seal of the Court office out of which
it was issued and was accompanied by a prescribed form of Acknowledgement of
Service.

3. **The said copy of the Writ** has not been returned to the Plaintiff through the post
undelivered to the addressee.

A.J.

(4) In the case of
posting by the Plaintiff's
Solicitor or any
employee in his firm.

(5) Delete
whichever is
inapplicable.

4. [That in my opinion] [(⁴) In the opinion of the Plaintiff] (⁵) the said Writ of
Summons so posted to the Defendant will have come to his knowledge within seven
days after the said date of posting thereof.

SWORN at   Cheapside
in the City of London
the   6thday of September   19 93

Anthony Jobling

Before me,

Marmaduke Sweet

A Commissioner for Oaths/Solicitor

This affidavit is filed on behalf of the Plaintiff

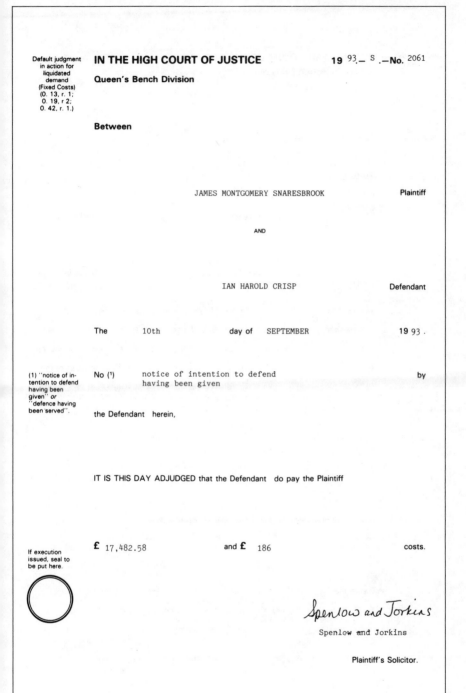

Default judgment in action for liquidated demand (Fixed Costs) (O. 13, r. 1; O. 19, r 2; O. 42, r. 1.)

IN THE HIGH COURT OF JUSTICE

19 93 .— S .—No. 2061

Queen's Bench Division

Between

JAMES MONTGOMERY SNARESBROOK — Plaintiff

AND

IAN HAROLD CRISP — Defendant

The   10th   day of   SEPTEMBER   19 93 .

(1) "notice of intention to defend having been given" or "defence having been served".

No (¹)   notice of intention to defend having been given   by

the Defendant herein,

IT IS THIS DAY ADJUDGED that the Defendant   do pay the Plaintiff

If execution issued, seal to be put here.

£ 17,482.58   and £   186   costs.

Spenlow and Jorkins

Spenlow and Jorkins

Plaintiff's Solicitor.

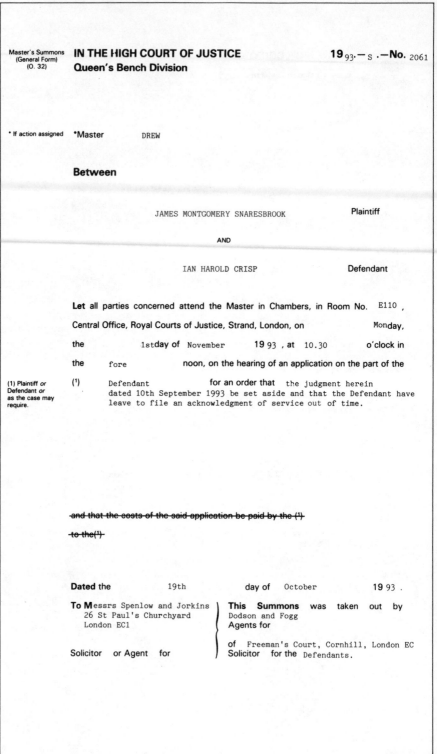

Master's Summons
(General Form)
(O. 32)

IN THE HIGH COURT OF JUSTICE
Queen's Bench Division

19 93 .— s .—**No.** 2061

* If action assigned   *Master   DREW

Between

JAMES MONTGOMERY SNARESBROOK   Plaintiff

AND

IAN HAROLD CRISP   Defendant

Let all parties concerned attend the Master in Chambers, in Room No.   E110 ,

Central Office, Royal Courts of Justice, Strand, London, on   Monday,

the   1st day of November   19 93 , at 10.30   o'clock in

the   fore   noon, on the hearing of an application on the part of the

(1) Plaintiff *or*
Defendant *or*
as the case may
require.

(¹)   Defendant   for an order that the judgment herein
          dated 10th September 1993 be set aside and that the Defendant have
          leave to file an acknowledgment of service out of time.

~~and that the costs of the said application be paid by the (¹)~~

~~to the(¹)~~

Dated the   19th   day of October   19 93 .

To Messrs Spenlow and Jorkins
        26 St Paul's Churchyard
        London EC1

Solicitor   or Agent   for

This   Summons was taken out by
Dodson and Fogg
Agents for

of Freeman's Court, Cornhill, London EC
Solicitor for the Defendants.

In the High Court of Justice   1993-S-No. 2061

Queen's Bench Division

Between:

James Montgomery Snaresbrook   Plaintiff

and

Ian Harold Crisp   Defendant

I, Peter Roger Snow, of 21, Ruislip Avenue, in the London Borough of Hounslow, Legal Executive, make oath and say as follows:-

1. I am a Legal Executive in the employ of Dodson and Fogg, Solicitors for the above-mentioned Defendants and have the conduct of this case under the supervision of my principal.

2. On the 20th day of August,1993, I received from my clients a copy of the writ of summons which they had received on 18th August.

3. On the 22nd day of August I went on my annual leave. Unfortunately I forgot to mention to my court clerk the necessity of filing an acknowledgment of service by the 2nd day of September. On the 6th day of September I returned from my holidays and owing to pressure of work the question of filing the acknowledgment was overlooked.

4. On the 4th day of October 1993 I received a copy of the judgment in default of acknowledgment of service herein.

5. I am informed by the Defendant that he has a valid defence to this claim inasmuch as the goods delivered did not accord to specification.

6. In the circumstances I respectfully apply to this Honourable Court that the judgment herein be set aside and that the Defendants have leave to enter an acknowledgment of service out of time.

Sworn at Ealing
this 15th day of October 1993   Peter Roger Snow

Commissioner of Oaths
    Nicholas Nickleby

This affidavit is filed on behalf of the Defendants.

limit for service of a defence (or such other period as may be ordered on an application to extend made within that period) issue a summons to set aside the writ or service.[65]

STAY OF PROCEEDINGS PENDING ARBITRATION

By section 4 of the Arbitration Act 1950 any party to a contract which provides for disputes to be settled by arbitration and against whom legal proceedings have been commenced may before delivery of any pleadings[66] or taking any other steps in the proceedings apply to the court for a stay pending the reference of the matter to an arbitrator. The power to grant a stay is however discretionary and would normally be refused if it would cause injustice (eg where the plaintiff could obtain legal aid for court proceedings but not for arbitration) or where issues of honesty are involved.

INTERLOCUTORY APPLICATIONS

It may have by this point become apparent that the Rules of the Supreme Court 1965 (and the County Court Rules 1981) provide a detailed framework for the conduct of litigation, designed to minimise the complexity and expense of litigation and to encourage the settlement of the dispute wherever possible. Frequently, a procedure contained in a particular rule requires the party in whose favour it operates to make an application to the court. Alternatively, the relevant rule may provide that a party takes specified action *automatically* at a particular stage in the proceedings and an application to the court by the opposite party becomes necessary to complain of the other's failure to do so.

In either type of case, the matter has to be brought before the court for adjudication in what are called *interlocutory* proceedings, which usually do not dispose of the substantive dispute between the parties, but settle the 'dispute within a dispute' which has arisen. The general rule in such proceedings is that evidence is given in written statements made under oath, called affidavits.

> *Example 1.* The plaintiff delivered goods to the defendant under a contract of sale but a year after delivery the defendant refused to pay the price alleging the goods were defective. The plaintiff denies this, and relies on the defendant's failure to complain earlier. As we shall see (p 149, post) RSC Ord 14 provides a procedure under which P can obtain summary judgment (ie judgment without a full trial) on the grounds that D can have no triable defence to the claim for the price. P must apply by serving a summons (which gives D advance notice of the application) which is heard by (or 'returnable before') the Master or District Judge who will decide whether summary judgment can be ordered after first hearing representations by the parties and reading their affidavits.
>
> *Example 2.* Several weeks after pleadings have closed in a personal injury action the plaintiff has failed without explanation to serve on the defendant a list of relevant documents which are in his possession. RSC Ord 24, r 1 provides that by this stage of the proceedings there 'shall . . . be discovery by the parties of the action'. D will therefore have to make an application by summons to a Master or District Judge seeking an *order* that P serves within so many days a list as required

---

65 RSC Ord 12, r 8.
66 For this purpose acknowledging service does *not* count as delivery of pleadings or taking a step in the proceedings.

OUTLINE OF
COUNTY COURT PROCEDURE

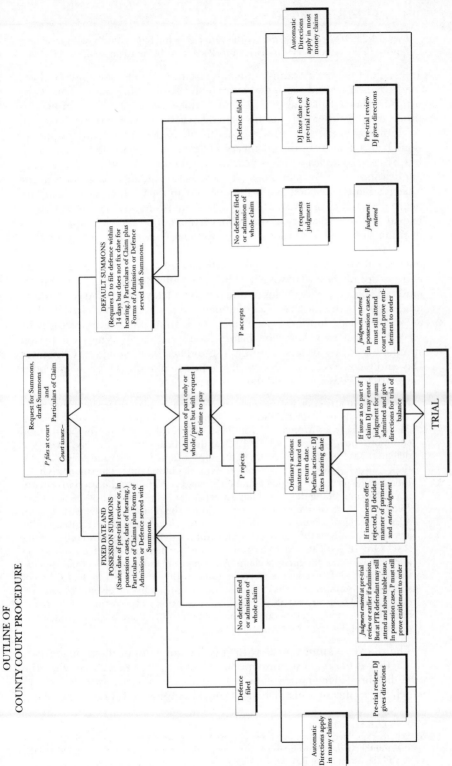

Request for Summons, draft Summons and Particulars of Claim

P files at court

Court issues:-

DEFAULT SUMMONS (Requires D to file defence within 14 days but does not fix date for hearing.) Particulars of Claim plus Forms of Admission or Defence served with Summons.

FIXED DATE AND POSSESSION SUMMONS (States date of pre-trial review or, in possession cases, date of hearing.) Particulars of Claims plus Forms of Admission or Defence served with Summons.

Automatic Directions apply in most money claims

Defence filed

DJ fixes date of pre-trial review

Pre-trial review DJ gives directions

No defence filed or admission of whole claim

P requests judgment

Judgment entered

Admission of part only or whole/part but with request for time to pay

P accepts

Judgment entered In possession cases, P must still attend court and prove entitlement to order

P rejects

Ordinary actions: matters heard on return date. Default actions: DJ fixes hearing date

If issue as to part of claim DJ may enter judgment for sum admitted and give directions for trial of balance

If instalments offer rejected, DJ decides manner of payment and *enters judgment*

No defence filed or admission of whole claim

Judgment entered at pre-trial review or earlier if admission. But at PTR defendant may still attend and show triable issue. In possession cases, P must still prove entitlement to order

Defence filed

Automatic Directions apply in many claims

Pre-trial review: DJ gives directions

TRIAL

by Ord 24. If the Master makes the order P is likely to comply with it since a failure to do so may eventually lead to P's action being dismissed.

In each of the above examples the interlocutory applications involved are made by issuing and serving a *summons* on the opposing party. This is the usual method of making *inter partes* interlocutory applications in actions proceeding in either the Queen's Bench Division or the Chancery Division. An important exception to this general rule is that interlocutory applications before a *judge* in the Chancery Division are not made by summons, but by *notice of motion* which is heard in open court. All other interlocutory applications made by summons (ie those before judges and masters in the Queen's Bench Division and before masters in the Chancery Division) are heard privately in *chambers*. Masters in both divisions have extensive powers to deal with interlocutory business but certain matters, such as applications in either division for interlocutory injunctions,[67] must be heard by a judge. The service of the summons or notice of motion puts the opposite party on notice that an application is to be made and informs him of the date, time and nature of the order sought. The rule under which an application is made will often specify the minimum number of days or 'clear days'[68] which must elapse between the service of notice and the 'return day'. In default of any specified period for a particular application, the summons must be served at least two clear days before the return day.[69] Where the period specified is 7 days or less, Saturdays, Sundays, bank holidays, Christmas Day and Good Friday are *excluded* from the calculation; where the period is longer than 7 days, weekend days etc are *included*.[70]

> *Example 1.* In an action for the recovery of a debt the plaintiff wishes to apply for summary judgment against the plaintiff and an appointment for hearing before a Master is made for Monday 27 July 1992. RSC Ord 14, r 2(3) provides that the summons must be served at least 10 clear days' before the return day, giving the defendant at least 10 days' notice of the application. The relevant period is more than 7 days so weekends etc are included in calculating time. The summons must therefore be served on the defendant on Thursday 16 July at the latest in order to allow 10 intervening days (including weekends) before the day of the hearing.
> *Example 2.* In an action for breach of contract the plaintiff's statement of claim alleges breach of a contract 'made in early 1991'. The plaintiff has refused to give any more details of the alleged contract and the defendant seeks an order under RSC Ord 18, r 12 that the plaintiff provides further and better particulars of allegations in the statement of claim. An appointment for hearing of the application is fixed by D's solicitors for Wednesday 8 July 1992. Ord 18, r 12 does not specify a minimum period of notice so the plaintiff must be given 2 clear days' notice. Weekends are excluded from the calculation as the period is less than 7 days. In order to give proper notice the summons must therefore be served on the plaintiff no later than Friday 3 July.

The above examples deal with interlocutory applications made *inter partes,* that is to say, in the presence of the other party, or at least when the other has been given notice of the hearing. However, circumstances exist in which the applicant is justified in making his application *ex parte,* or without

---

67 RSC Ord 32, rr 11, 14.
68 Where a specified number of 'clear days'' notice of an application must be given, at least that number of days must intervene between the day on which the notice is served and the day of the hearing: see RSC Ord 3, r 2(4).
69 RSC Ord 32, r 3.
70 RSC Ord 3, r 2(5).

telling the party who may be affected by the order sought. This may arise, firstly, where the nature of the application itself creates practical obstacles to the service of notice.

> *Example.* In a writ action arising from a road accident the plaintiff finds he is unable to trace the defendant to effect personal or postal service but knows the name of the defendant's insurance company. An application for an order under RSC Ord 65, r 4 for *substituted service* on the insurance company must be made to the Master *ex parte*, since the plaintiff's difficulty in serving the writ would apply equally to service of a summons giving notice of the application.

Secondly, there are cases where the rules of court or the courts themselves have recognised that a party to an action is justified in applying for an interlocutory order without telling the other party of his intention to do so. This may be because an order is required *urgently* and there is no time to serve a summons on the other party or give them notice, or because the application is deliberately made *secretly* in order to avoid the danger that the other party would take action aimed at defeating the order sought.[71] Obviously, orders made on *ex parte* applications conflict with the basic principle of justice that orders should not be made against a party without giving him the opportunity to be heard. For this reason such orders are provisional only (they take effect until the matter is argued fully on an *inter partes* basis) and are warranted only as an exception to the general principle.

> *Example.* The applicants, who were the administrative receivers of a company in voluntary liquidation, obtained on an *ex parte* application an order under the Insolvency Act 1986 that the respondent, the company's liquidator, should transfer company records and money to them. Hoffmann J held that there was nothing to preclude an *inter partes* hearing and the order should not have been obtained on an *ex parte* application. The Judge held that two conditions must be satisfied before an order should be obtained in such a way: (1) that the applicant was likely to suffer injustice if the respondent was served with notice of the application (either because of the delay this would cause or because of action the respondent or other person might take before the order was made); (2) that the respondent could be compensated for any damage he might suffer as a result of the order being made by the applicant undertaking to the court to provide such compensation if ordered to do so *or* (if he could not be so compensated) that the risk of such damage to the respondent was clearly outweighed by the risk of injustice to the applicant if the *ex parte* order were not made. Per Hoffmann J: 'There is, I think, a tendency among applicants to think that a calculation of the balance of advantage and disadvantage in accordance with the second condition is sufficient to justify an *ex parte* order. In my view, this attitude should be discouraged. One does not reach any balancing of advantage and disadvantage unless the first condition has been satisfied. The principle *audi alterem partem* does not yield to a mere utilitarian calculation. It can be displaced only by invoking the overriding principle of justice which enables the court to act at once when it appears likely that otherwise injustice will be caused.' (*In re First Express Ltd*[72].)

---

71 Obvious examples of these include *Anton Piller orders* and *Mareva* injunctions: see post pp 244–262.
72 [1992] BCLC 824.

SKILLS PRACTICE NOTE

Making an application in Chambers before a master (or district judge) involves a very specialised form of advocacy. You usually have only a limited time to get your points across and yet at the same time you have to make those points crystal clear. We set out below some ideas which you may find helpful.

(1) It is essential that you have a good understanding of the *whole* case and not just the particular matters in dispute in the application. Masters have a tendency to ask questions which seem outside the area of the particular interlocutory application. We suggest that your preparation for the hearing should include:
   (i)   a review of the pleadings to date;
   (ii) preparing a chronology of the steps in the action from issue of the writ to date (noting all the orders that have been made so far and whether or not they have been complied with);
   (iii) preparing a chronology including the key events and correspondence in the substantive claim (e g date of contract, date of delivery, date of first complaint or whatever);
   (iv) checking that you understand the way in which the amount of any damages has been calculated and also checking that you understand any argument being advanced against that calculation.
   It may well be that at the hearing 90% or more of these matters are never mentioned but if you do understand the whole case thoroughly it will give you confidence and authority when you come to argue the particular point in issue at the chambers hearing.

(2) So far as the particular interlocutory dispute is concerned you should:
   (i) have a written chronology of all the relevant dates. (For example if the application is to set aside a default judgment, you should have a timetable showing date of issue of writ, date of service, date the time for acknowledgment of service expired, date defendant became aware of the judgment etc.);
   (ii) have read and flagged the relevant passages in the White Book (or Green Book). It is not enough simply to read the relevant Order; you also need to read carefully the notes which accompany it. Almost certainly you will need to look at more than one Order. For example, suppose you are applying for disclosure of documents, you will find that the *power* to make orders for discovery is set out in Order 24 but the *procedure* is set out in Order 32. You will almost always need to consult:

Order 32	(applications and proceedings in chambers)
Order 41	(affidavits)
Order 42	(which deals with the form of interlocutory orders)
Order 62, rule 3	(which deals with the orders for costs likely to be made at the interlocutory hearing);

(iii) have a very clear idea of the order you want the master to make. If you are making the application, draft out on a sheet of paper the order you propose. Don't forget the question of time periods. For example, if you are applying for an order that the Defendant serve further and better particulars you will need to specify a period for compliance (eg 'within 14 days'); if there is a history of procedural default you may want an 'unless order' (eg 'unless the Defendant serve further and better particulars . . . within 14 days he be debarred from defending this action');

(iv) work out in advance what order for costs the master is likely to make. Note that Order 62, rule 8(2) enables the master to make an order that one party pays the costs incurred in the interlocutory dispute straight away and not, as more usually happens, at the conclusion of the case. Such an order will only be made if you ask for it. Remember also that counsel's fees for attendance before a master or district judge will not be allowed unless the application is certified "fit for counsel".

(3) A contested interlocutory hearing typically follows this pattern:

(i) counsel for the applicant hands the summons and a bundle of the affidavits and exhibits to the master;

(ii) counsel then outlines *very briefly* the nature of the application. An opening speech is not made but if the case is complicated it is very sensible to summarise in a few sentences what the master is going to be asked to decide and then to give him the key dates to write down;

(iii) the affidavits are then read in the order in which they have been sworn. Each counsel reads the affidavits filed on behalf of his side. Quite often the master will wish to read the affidavits himself. (Usually there are one or two paragraphs which are particularly important. You will want to make sure that the master has taken in those important passages. Advocates develop their own formula for politely making sure that this has happened; for example, you can say 'Of course, Master, we rely heavily on the passage in paragraph 5 of Mr Smith's affidavit dealing with . . .');

(iv) once the evidence is read the applicant's counsel summarises briefly why he says he is entitled to the order sought;

(v) the other side then explains why they say the order should not be made (or at least, if it is made, why it should only be made in a modified form);

(vi) if the master agrees with the party opposing the application, he will ask the applicant's counsel if he wishes to reply;

(vii) the master then gives a reasoned judgment and writes his order in note form on the summons. This indorsement forms the basis for the order subsequently drawn up (ie typed out by the applicant's solicitors and sealed);

(viii) the party who has won asks for costs and a certificate for counsel. (If the other side is legally aided they also will require a certificate for counsel.)

(4) In chambers applications before a district judge the procedure is basically the same except that the judge will often have had an opportunity to read the papers in advance.

IMPORTANT NOTE

Remember always that however much the law and procedure seems to be on your side, the court always wants to know where the merits lie. Experienced advocates understand this and manage to get across in their submissions that the order they are seeking is fair and reasonable and in the interests of justice.

Chapter 3

Starting county court proceedings

PROCESS IN THE COUNTY COURT

Note: while reading this chapter please look at the forms set out on pp 114 to 125.

The County Court Rules[1] distinguish between:

(a) *default actions*, where the only relief claimed is the payment of money. Such an action may be for a *liquidated* sum (eg a debt, the price of goods sold and delivered or any other case where the precise amount due can be determined by arithmetical calculation) or for an *unliquidated* sum (eg damages for personal injuries or for non-delivery of goods or any other case where the court has to decide how much should be awarded as compensation); and

(b) *fixed date actions* in which a claim for relief other than payment of money is made (eg a possession order, recovery of goods, an injunction to restrain a nuisance).

The importance of the distinction is that in a *default action* the defendant is at risk if he fails to file a defence within 14 days of service at the court office; if he files a defence, the case proceeds to trial but if he fails to do so the plaintiff may *sign judgment* against him.[2] If the claim is liquidated, the judgment will be for the amount claimed together with interest to the date of judgment; if the claim is unliquidated, the judgment is for damages to be assessed.[3] In a *fixed date action*, the summons states the date upon which the district judge will give directions for trial[4] (except in the case of a *possession action* where the date of hearing is set out on the summons). In a fixed date action there is no automatic judgment in default so that, although the rules require the defendant to file a defence within 14 days, if he does not do so the plaintiff will still have to *attend on the return day and prove his case* by evidence. (Where a default judgment is entered the court has power to set it aside on the application of the defendant.[5])

---

1 See CCR Ord 3, r 2.
2 CCR Ord 9, r 6(1)(1A).
3 CCR Ord 9, r 6(2).
4 CCR Ord 9, r 4A.
5 CCR Ord 37, r 4. The same principles apply as in the High Court. The judge should give reasons for setting aside the judgment.

Actions are commenced in the county court by the plaintiff submitting at the court office:

(a) Two copies of a *request for a summons* (sometimes called a *praecipe*) setting out the names and status of the parties and showing how the court has jurisdiction. The form varies according to the nature of the case. (See p 114, post.)

(b) Copies of *particulars of claim*. This document is exactly the same as the *statement of claim* in High Court proceedings, i e it is the initial pleading. Accordingly the drafting of such particulars is considered in the section on pleadings, post, p 126. One copy is lodged at court; the other copy is served on the defendants.[6] (See p 118, post.)

The court staff then:

(a) Prepare a *plaint note* which is given to the plaintiff and is a receipt for the fees paid by him and in the case of a fixed date action sets out the date of hearing or pre-trial review and in the case of default summons sets out in what circumstances he can sign judgment in default of a defence. (See p 123.)

(b) Prepare a summons to the defendant (unless already done by the plaintiff's solicitor) (see p 116.)

(c) Annex to each copy of the summons a copy of the particulars of claim and a form of admission, defence and counterclaim. This is a standard form which may be used by the defendant to state whether or not he intends to defend the action and, if so, the grounds of his defence (see pp 119 to 122).

Service of the summons and particulars can be effected personally in the manner described under the service of a writ issued out of the High Court. However, in practice, service in the county court is normally effected either

(a) by the court sending the summons by post to the defendant's residence or, if he owns a business, to his place of business;[7] *or*

(b) by the bailiff delivering the summons to any person over 16 at the defendant's residence or, if he owns a business, at his place of business;[7] *or*

(c) in personal injury claims by the plaintiff's solicitor sending a copy of the summons by post to the defendant's residence etc.[8]

Where personal service or service by post is not effective, the district judge may direct that service shall be effected by sending the documents by post to the defendant's last address, by advertisement or by such other means as is likely to give him notice of the action.[9]

---

6 See CCR Ord 3, r 3. Note that in the case of organisations such as finance companies which issue large numbers of debt summonses every week, they may use the Summons Production Centre at Northampton which operates a computerised system into which the plaintiffs input the relevant data. Although such summonses are issued by the centre, the summons carries the name of the appropriate county court which will hear the case and all subsequent steps (including delivery of a defence) are taken at that court (see CCR Ord 2, rr 6 to 12).

7 CCR Ord 7, r 10.

8 CCR Ord 7, r 10A.

9 CCR Ord 7, r 8.

It is vitally important to note that whether the plaintiff is signing judgment in a *default action* or proceeding to prove his claim in *fixed date action*, he must be able to prove service. The novice attending the hearing of an ordinary action at the county court may find (to his relief) that the defendant has not appeared but, though he may be armed with all the evidence needed to prove his case, it will be to no avail if he cannot satisfy the court as to service.[10]

Many actions in the county courts are brought in circumstances where there is no defence to the claim but, because the defendant is in financial difficulties, he cannot afford to pay the sum due. For this reason, as stated above, the rules provide that the defendant is to be sent with the summons two separate reply documents. The first document is to be used where the defendant admits the claim in full and makes an offer to pay; the completed form is then returned *directly* to the plaintiff who may accept or reject the payment proposals. If rejected, the matter is resolved on the return day or, in the case of a default summons, at a disposal day notified to both parties by the district judge. The second document is for use by a defendant who does not fully admit the claim and is divided into four parts:

(1) A form of partial admission.
(2) A form of defence. The defendant is invited to set out the nature of his case. If he is acting by solicitor, this form will not be used but he will deliver a formal pleading.
(3) A form of counterclaim.
(4) A note that if he disputes the claim, he may ask that the matter should go to arbitration. If the sum claimed in the case does not exceed £1000 the action will be automatically referred to arbitration upon the receipt by the court of a defence.[11] Arbitration is intended as a quick and informal method of disposing of a case. It should be noted that once proceedings are referred to arbitration no solicitor's charges are allowed except the fixed costs stated on the summons.[12] This means in practice that the parties will not recover the solicitor's costs even if they are successful. The terms of reference[13] for the arbitration are as follows:
    (1) The arbitrator shall appoint a date for the preliminary consideration of the dispute and ways of resolving it, unless the size or nature of the claim or other circumstances make such a course undesirable or unnecessary.
    (2) At or after the preliminary appointment, if there is one, the arbitrator shall fix a date for the dispute to be heard (unless the parties consent to his deciding it on the statements and documents submitted to him) and shall give such directions

10 One can check whether there has been service by seeing from the *praecipe* whether postal service has been requested; of so, the court staff will know whether the documents have been returned by the post office; in other cases one should ask to see the bailiff's indorsement on the summons. See County Courts Act 1984, s 133(1). As to proof of service by the plaintiff's solicitor in personal injury cases, see CCR Ord 7, r 10A(4).
11 CCR Ord 19, r 2(3).
12 CCR Ord 19, r 6(1). The costs of enforcing the award and such costs as are certified by the arbitrator to have been incurred through the unreasonable conduct of the opposite party may also be awarded. Note the parties may apply to the district judge for the reference to be rescinded on the grounds for example of the complexity of the issues or because a charge of fraud has been raised.
13 CCR Ord 19, r 2(5)(a).

regarding the steps to be taken before and at the hearing as may appear to him to be necessary or desirable. Where the district judge is the arbitrator, he shall have the same powers on the preliminary appointment as he has under Order 17 on a pre-trial review.

(3) Any hearing shall be informal and the strict rules of evidence shall not apply.

(4) At the hearing the arbitrator may adopt any method of procedure which he may consider to be convenient and to afford a fair and equal opportunity to each party to present his case.

(5) If any party does not appear at the arbitration, the arbitrator may make an award on hearing any other party to the proceedings who may be present.

(6) Where an award has been given in the absence of a party, the arbitrator shall have power, on that party's application, to set the award aside and to order a fresh hearing as if the award were a judgment and the application were made pursuant to Order 37, rule 2.

(7) With the consent of the parties and at any time before giving his decision and either before or after the hearing, the arbitrator may consult any expert or call for an expert report on any matter in dispute or invite an expert to attend the hearing as assessor.

(8) Subject to the provisions of Order 19, rule 6, in respect of claims involving £1000 or less, the costs of the action up to and including the entry of judgment shall be in the discretion of the arbitrator to be exercised in the same manner as the discretion of the court under the provisions of the County Court Rules.

Appendix

Easyrider Garages carry on business as second-hand car dealers. On 21 August 1992 James Smith buys a Ford Cortina from them for £8650. James pays by cheque. Next day the car breaks down on the motorway when the engine seizes up because of lack of oil. James believes there was a serious oil leak which had not been repaired and which caused the breakdown. He stops payment of the cheque. Easyrider Garages now commence proceedings against him. Set out on the following pages are:

1. Request for Default Summons (Form N201, Ord 3, r 3(1))
2. Notes accompanying Form N201
3. Default Summons (Form N1, Ord 3, r 3(2)(b))
4. Notes on back of summons Form N1
5. Defence and Counterclaim (Form N9B, Ord 9, r 2)
6. Form of Admission and Statement of Means (Form N9A, Ord 9, r 2)
7. Plaint note (given to Plaintiff when he files the Request for a Default Summons). This has a form which can be used to apply for judgment if the Defendant admits all of part of the claim (Form 205A, Ord 3, r 3(2); Ord 9, r 3, 6(1)).

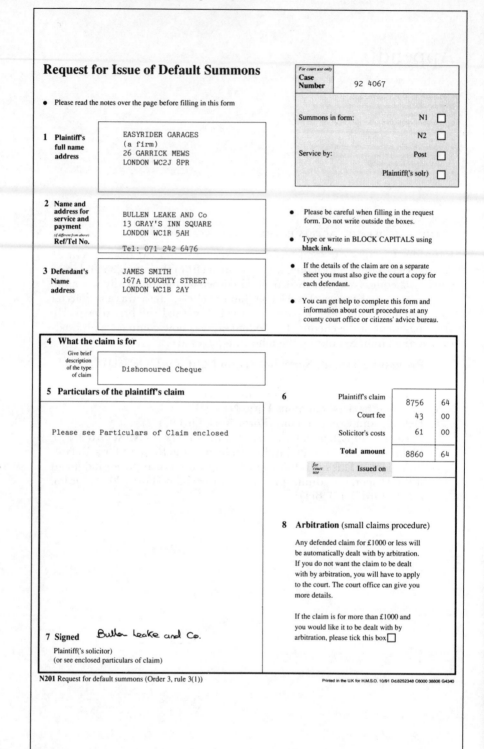

Request for Issue of Default Summons

- Please read the notes over the page before filling in this form

Summons in form: N1 ☐

N2 ☐

Service by: Post ☐

Plaintiff('s solr) ☐

1 Plaintiff's full name address

EASYRIDER GARAGES
(a firm)
26 GARRICK MEWS
LONDON WC2J 8PR

2 Name and address for service and payment *(if different from above)* **Ref/Tel No.**

BULLEN LEAKE AND Co
13 GRAY'S INN SQUARE
LONDON WC1R 5AH

Tel: 071 242 6476

- Please be careful when filling in the request form. Do not write outside the boxes.

- Type or write in BLOCK CAPITALS using black ink.

3 Defendant's Name address

JAMES SMITH
167A DOUGHTY STREET
LONDON WC1B 2AY

- If the details of the claim are on a separate sheet you must also give the court a copy for each defendant.

- You can get help to complete this form and information about court procedures at any county court office or citizens' advice bureau.

4 What the claim is for

Give brief description of the type of claim

Dishonoured Cheque

5 Particulars of the plaintiff's claim

Please see Particulars of Claim enclosed

6

Plaintiff's claim	8756	64
Court fee	43	00
Solicitor's costs	61	00
Total amount	8860	64
for court use Issued on		

8 Arbitration (small claims procedure)

Any defended claim for £1000 or less will be automatically dealt with by arbitration. If you do not want the claim to be dealt with by arbitration, you will have to apply to the court. The court office can give you more details.

If the claim is for more than £1000 and you would like it to be dealt with by arbitration, please tick this box ☐

7 Signed   *Bullen Leake and Co.*

Plaintiff('s solicitor)
(or see enclosed particulars of claim)

N201 Request for default summons (Order 3, rule 3(1))

Printed in the U.K for H.M.S.O. 10/91 Dd.8252348 C6000 38806 G4340

Notes

1 Plaintiff *the person making the claim*
Fill in the plaintiff's full name and address or place of business. If the plaintiff is:

- a **company registered under the Companies Act 1985,** give the address of the registered office and describe it as such.
- **a person trading in a name other than his own,** give his own name followed by the words 'trading as' and the name under which he trades.
- **two or more co-partners suing in the name of their firm,** 'A Firm'.
- **an assignee,** say so and give the name, address and occupation of the assignor.
- **a minor required to sue by next friend,** state this, and give the full names, address or place of business, and occupation of next friend. You will also need to complete and send in Form N235 (which you can get from the court office).
- **suing in a representative capacity,** say in what capacity.

2 Address for service and payment
If this request is completed by a solicitor or by your legal department, the name, address and reference of the solicitor or legal department should be in Box 2. The court will use this address for sending documents to you (service). (If the address is the same as shown at Box 1, please write 'as above' in Box 2).

- **A plaintiff who is not represented by a solicitor or legal department must not use Box 2** except for an address to which payment may be made. In this case you must delete the word 'service' in the title to Box (2).

3 Defendant *the person against whom the claim is made*
Fill in the defendant's surname and (where known) his or her initials or names in full. **It is essential that the defendant should be identified as fully and as accurately as possible.** Also give the defendant's address or place of business (if the owner of a business). Say whether defendant is male or female and, if under 18, state 'minor'. If the defendant is:

- a **company registered under the Companies Act 1985,** the address given can be the registered office of the company (you must describe it as such) or its place of business. If the summons is not sent to the registered office, there is a risk that it will not come to the notice of an appropriate person in the company. As a result, the court may be asked to set aside any judgment or order that has been made. **For fixed amount cases only** - Bear in mind that if the company you are suing defends the case, the case will automatically be transferred to his local court. If the registered office and place of business are not in the same court area, you may decide to choose the address which is most convenient to you.
- **a person trading in a name other than his own** who is sued under that name, add 'A Trading Name'.
- **two or more co-partners** sued in the name of their firm, add 'A Firm'.
- **sued in a representative capacity,** say in what capacity.

4 What the claim is for
Put a brief description of your claim in the box (eg price of goods sold and delivered, work done, money due under an agreement).

5 Particulars of your claim
Give a brief statement of the facts of your claim and the amount for which you are suing. Include any relevant dates and sufficient details so that the defendant understands what your claim is for. He is entitled to ask for further details. If there is not enough space or the details of your claim are too complicated, you should enclose a separate sheet for the court and a copy for each defendant. The court can help you in setting out your particulars of claim.

6 Amount claimed
Fill in the total amount you are claiming. The court fee and solicitor's costs are based on this and you should enter these too. A leaflet setting out the current fees is available from the court

7 Signature
The person filling in the form should sign and date it, unless enclosing separate details of claim (in which case the enclosed sheets should be signed).

8 Arbitration (small claims procedure)
Any defended claim for £1000 or less will be automatically dealt with by arbitration (small claims procedure). If the claim is for more than £1000 and you would like it to be dealt with by arbitration, you may include such a request in your particulars of claim. (Solicitor's costs and the grounds for setting aside an arbitrator's award are strictly limited.)

9 Personal injury claims
In these cases you must include a medical report for the court and for each defendant. If you are also claiming special damages (eg loss of income, medical expenses etc) an up to date statement, to include details of loss of any future expenses or losses, must also be included for the court and for each defendant. If you cannot provide these you should apply to the court for directions.

10 Unliquidated claims for more than £5000
If your claim is not for a fixed amount and you expect to recover more than £5000 (excluding interest and costs), you must state this in your particulars of claim.

11 Where to send the summons
- **If the summons is for a fixed amount,**
  you can ask any county court in England and Wales to issue the summons but you will usually choose your local court or the court for the area where the defendant lives or carries on business. Bear in mind that if the person you are suing defends the case, the case will automatically be transferred to the defendant's local court.
- **For a personal injury or other unliquidated claim,**
  you may prefer to choose the court where the cause of action arose. The case will not be automatically transferred if a defence is filed.

To be completed by the court	
Served on:	
By posting on:	
Officer:	

Further information on how to issue a default summons and what happens after issue can be obtained from any county court office.

In the Westminster County Court   Case No 92 4067

Between:

EASYRIDER GARAGES
(a firm)   <u>Plaintiffs</u>

and

JAMES SMITH   <u>Defendant</u>

Particulars of Claim

1. The plaintiffs are the payees of a cheque for £8650 dated 21 August 1992 and drawn by the Defendant on the Midland Bank plc, Mile End Road, London E9.
2. On 22 August 1992 the Plaintiffs duly presented the said cheque for payment but payment was countermanded by the Defendant.
3. The Plaintiffs further claim interest pursuant to section 57(1) of the Bills of Exchange Act 1882, alternatively pursuant to section 69 of the County Courts Act 1984 at the rate of 15% per annum until judgment or sooner payment or at such rate and for such period as the court thinks fit.

<u>Particulars</u>

Principal sum	£8650.00p
Interest at 15% (3.55 per day) from 22 August 1992 to the date hereof	<u>£ 106.64p</u>
	£8756.64p

And the Plaintiff claims:

   1 £8650.00p
   2 Interest as aforesaid in the sum of £106.64 and continuing at the daily rate of £3.55p per day until judgment or sooner payment
   3 Costs

Dated this 20th day of September 1992

                Bullen Leake & Co
                13 Gray's Inn Square
                London WC2J 8PR
                Solicitors to the Plaintiffs who will accept service of all proceedings on behalf of the Plaintiffs

To the Court and
To the Defendant

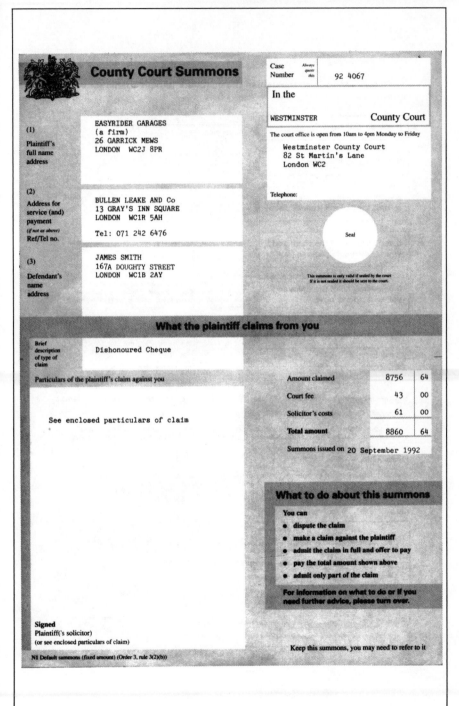

County Court Summons

| Case Number | *Always quote this* | 92 4067 |

In the

WESTMINSTER **County Court**

The court office is open from 10am to 4pm Monday to Friday

Westminster County Court
82 St Martin's Lane
London WC2

Telephone:

Seal

This summons is only valid if sealed by the court
If it is not sealed it should be sent to the court.

(1)
Plaintiff's full name address

EASYRIDER GARAGES
(a firm)
26 GARRICK MEWS
LONDON   WC2J 8PR

(2)
Address for service (and) payment
(if not as above)
Ref/Tel no.

BULLEN LEAKE AND Co
13 GRAY'S INN SQUARE
LONDON   WC1R 5AH

Tel: 071 242 6476

(3)
Defendant's name address

JAMES SMITH
167A DOUGHTY STREET
LONDON   WC1B 2AY

What the plaintiff claims from you

Brief description of type of claim

Dishonoured Cheque

Particulars of the plaintiff's claim against you

See enclosed particulars of claim

Amount claimed	8756	64
Court fee	43	00
Solicitor's costs	61	00
Total amount	8860	64

Summons issued on 20 September 1992

What to do about this summons

You can
- **dispute the claim**
- **make a claim against the plaintiff**
- **admit the claim in full and offer to pay**
- **pay the total amount shown above**
- **admit only part of the claim**

For information on what to do or if you need further advice, please turn over.

Signed
Plaintiff('s solicitor)
(or see enclosed particulars of claim)

Keep this summons, you may need to refer to it

N1 Default summons (fixed amount) (Order 3, rule 3(2)(b))

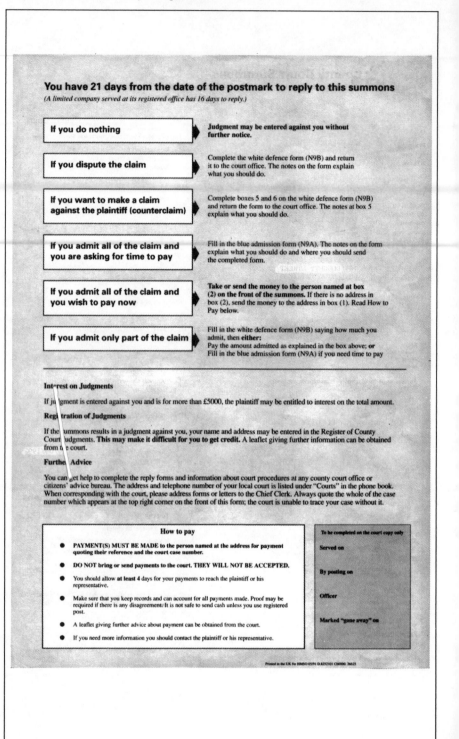

You have 21 days from the date of the postmark to reply to this summons

(A limited company served at its registered office has 16 days to reply.)

If you do nothing	Judgment may be entered against you without further notice.
If you dispute the claim	Complete the white defence form (N9B) and return it to the court office. The notes on the form explain what you should do.
If you want to make a claim against the plaintiff (counterclaim)	Complete boxes 5 and 6 on the white defence form (N9B) and return the form to the court office. The notes at box 5 explain what you should do.
If you admit all of the claim and you are asking for time to pay	Fill in the blue admission form (N9A). The notes on the form explain what you should do and where you should send the completed form.
If you admit all of the claim and you wish to pay now	Take or send the money to the person named at box (2) on the front of the summons. If there is no address in box (2), send the money to the address in box (1). Read How to Pay below.
If you admit only part of the claim	Fill in the white defence form (N9B) saying how much you admit, then **either:** Pay the amount admitted as explained in the box above; **or** Fill in the blue admission form (N9A) if you need time to pay

Interest on Judgments

If judgment is entered against you and is for more than £5000, the plaintiff may be entitled to interest on the total amount.

Registration of Judgments

If the summons results in a judgment against you, your name and address may be entered in the Register of County Court Judgments. **This may make it difficult for you to get credit.** A leaflet giving further information can be obtained from the court.

Further Advice

You can get help to complete the reply forms and information about court procedures at any county court office or citizens' advice bureau. The address and telephone number of your local court is listed under "Courts" in the phone book. When corresponding with the court, please address forms or letters to the Chief Clerk. Always quote the whole of the case number which appears at the top right corner on the front of this form; the court is unable to trace your case without it.

How to pay	To be completed on the court copy only
● **PAYMENT(S) MUST BE MADE to the person named at the address for payment** quoting their reference and the court case number.	Served on
● DO NOT bring or send payments to the court. THEY WILL NOT BE ACCEPTED.	
● You should allow **at least 4** days for your payments to reach the plaintiff or his representative.	By posting on
● Make sure that you keep records and can account for all payments made. Proof may be required if there is any disagreement. It is not safe to send cash unless you use registered post.	Officer
● A leaflet giving further advice about payment can be obtained from the court.	Marked "gone away" on
● If you need more information you should contact the plaintiff or his representative.	

Printed in the UK for HMSO 05/91 D.8292101 C66000 36623

Defence and Counterclaim

When to fill in this form

- Only fill in this form if you wish to dispute all or part of the claim **and/or** make a claim against the plaintiff (counterclaim).

How to fill in this form

- Please check that the correct case details are shown on this form. You must ensure that all the boxes at the top right of this form are completed. You can obtain the correct names and numbers from the summons. The court cannot trace your case without this information.

- Follow the instructions given in each section. Tick the correct boxes and give the other details asked for.

- If you wish only to make a claim against the plaintiff (counterclaim) go to section 5.

- Complete and sign section 6 before returning this form.

Where to send this form

- Send or take this form immediately to the court office at the address shown above.

- If you admit part of the claim and you are asking for time to pay, you will also need to fill in the blue admission form (N9A) and send **both** reply forms to the court.

- Keep the summons and a copy of this defence; you may need them.

Legal Aid

- You may be entitled to legal aid. Ask about the legal aid scheme at any county court office, citizen's advice bureau, legal advice centre or firm of solicitors displaying this legal aid sign.

What happens next

- If you complete box 3 on this form, the court will ask the plaintiff to confirm that he has received payment. If he tells the court that you have not paid, the court will tell you what you should do.

- If you complete box 4 or 5, the court will tell you what you should do.

- If the summons is not from your local county court, it will automatically be transferred to your local court.

1 How much of the claim do you dispute?

☑ I dispute the full amount claimed *(go to section 2)*

or

☑ I admit the amount of **£ 5860** and I dispute the balance

If you dispute only part of the claim you must **either:**

- pay the amount admitted to the person named at the address for payment in box (2) on the front of the summons or if there is no address in box (2), send the money to the address in box (1) (see How to Pay on the back of the summons). Then send this defence to the court.

or

- complete the blue admission form and send it to the court with this defence.

Tick whichever applies

☐ I paid the amount admitted on [   ]

or

☐ I enclose the completed form of admission

(go to section 2)

N9B Form of defence and counterclaim to accompany Form N1 (Order 9, rule 2)

In the

Westminster **County Court**

| Case Number | *Always quote this* | 92 4067 |

| Plaintiff *(including ref.)* | EASYRIDER GARAGES |

| Defendant | JAMES SMITH |

The court office is open from 10am to 4pm Monday to Friday

Westminster County Court
82 St Martin's Lane
London WC2

2 Arbitration under the small claims procedure

- This involves an informal hearing taking place in private instead of a formal trial held in public.

- If you defend a claim for £1000 or less it will be referred to arbitration automatically unless you apply to the court. Your local court office can give you more details.

- The decision of the arbitrator is final. There are only very limited circumstances in which the court can set aside an arbitration decision.

- **If the claim is for more than £1000 it can still go to arbitration if:**
  (a) You and the plaintiff agree. (He may indicate his agreement in his particulars of claim.) **or**
  (b) The court orders it (where only one party applies)

  ☑ Tick here if the claim is for more than £1000 and you would like it to be dealt with in this way.

  (go on to section 3)

3 Do you dispute this claim because you have already paid it? *Tick whichever applies*

☑ No *(go to section 4)*

☐ Yes I paid **£** [   ] to the plaintiff

on [   ] *(before the summons was issued)*

Give details of where and how you paid it in the box below *(then go to section 6)*

MCR 253VK94048 5/91

Case No. [92 4067]

4 If you dispute the claim for reasons other than payment, what are your reasons?

Use the box below to give full details. *(If you need to continue on a separate sheet, put the case number in the top right hand corner.)*

I bought a Ford Cortina from Mr Fagin of Easyrider Garages for £8650 but it broke down the next day so I stopped the cheque. It cost me £2500 to get it put right (new engine) and I can produce bills to prove it. I was without a car for 3 weeks.

5 If you wish to make a claim against the plaintiff (counterclaim)

If your claim is for a specific sum of money, how much are you claiming?   [£3000]

- If your claim against the plaintiff is for more than the plaintiff's claim against you, you may have to pay a fee. Ask at your local court office whether a fee is payable.

- You may not be able to make a counterclaim where the plaintiff is the Crown (e.g. a Government Department). Ask at your local county court office for further information.

What are your reasons for making the counterclaim?

- Use the box opposite to give full details. *(If you need to continue on a separate sheet, put the case number in the top right hand corner.)*

(go on to section 6)

This is what it cost me to put the car right and I want to claim for loss of use.

6   Signed
(To be signed by you or by your solicitor)   James Smith

Position *(firm or company)* [   ]

Give an address to which notices about this case can be sent to you   16A Doughty Street London

Postcode WC1B 2AY

Dated   30th Sept 92

Admission

When to fill in this form

- Only fill in this form if you are admitting all or some of the claim **and** you are asking for time to pay
- If you are disputing the claim or you wish to pay the amount claimed, read the back of the summons

How to fill in this form

- Tick the correct boxes and give as much information as you can. **Then sign and date the form.**
- Make your offer of payment in box 11 on the back of this form. **If you make no offer the plaintiff will decide how you should pay.**
- You can get help to complete this form at **any** county court office or citizens' advice bureau.

Where to send this form

- **If you admit the claim in full**
  Send the completed form to the address shown at box (2) on the front of the summons. If there is no address in box (2) send the form to the address in box (1).
- **If you admit only part of the claim**
  Send the form **to the court** at the address given on the summons, together with the white defence form (N9B).

What happens next

- **If you admit the claim in full and offer to pay**
  If the plaintiff accepts your offer, judgement will be entered and you will be sent an order telling you how and when to pay. If the plaintiff does **not** accept your offer, the court will fix a rate of payment based on the details you have given in this form and the plaintiff's comments. Judgement will be entered and you will be sent an order telling you how and when to pay.
- **If you admit only part of the claim**
  The court will tell you what to do next.

How much of the claim do you admit?

- [ ] I admit the full amount claimed as shown on the summons **or**
- [ ] I admit the amount of £ 5 8 6 0

1 Personal details

Surname	SMITH
Forename	JAMES

[✓] Mr [ ] Mrs [ ] Miss [ ] Ms

[ ] Married [ ] Single [ ] Other *(specify)*

Age 30

Address 167A DOUGHTY STREET LONDON

Postcode WC1B 2AY

In the

WESTMINSTER **County Court**

Case Number *Always quote this* 92 4067

Plaintiff *(including ref.)* EASYRIDER GARAGES

Defendant JAMES SMITH

2 Dependants *(people you look after financially)*

Number of children in each age group

under 11 **2**   11-15 [ ]   16-17 [ ]   18 & over [ ]

Other dependants *(give details)*

3 Employment

[ ] I am employed as a SCHOOL TEACHER

My employer is TOWER HAMLETS

Jobs other than main job *(give details)*

[ ] I am self employed as a

Annual turnover is...................... £

- [ ] I am not in arrears with my national insurance contributions, income tax and VAT
- [ ] I am in arrears and I owe.......... £

Give details of:
(a) contracts and other work in hand
(b) any sums due for work done

[ ] I have been unemployed for   years   months

[ ] I am a pensioner

4 Bank account and savings

[ ] I have a bank account

- [ ] The account is in credit by .... £ 4367
- [ ] The account is overdrawn by.... £

[ ] I have a savings or building society account

The amount in the account is .... £

5 Property

I live in
[ ] my own property [ ] lodgings
[ ] jointly owned property [ ] council property
[✓] rented property

N9A Form of admission and statement of means to accompany Form N1 (Order 9, rule 2)

MCX 600288/K041142 11/91

6 Income

My usual take home pay *(including overtime, commission, bonuses etc)*	£ 1250	per month
Income support	£	per
Child benefit(s)	£	per
Other state benefit(s)	£	per
My pension(s)	£	per
Others living in my home give me	£	per
Other income *(give details below)*		
	£	per
	£	per
	£	per
Total income	£ 1250	per month

8 Priority debts *(This section is for arrears only. Do not include regular expenses listed in box 7.)*

Rent arrears	£ 126	per month
Mortgage arrears	£	per
Community charge arrears	£	per
Water charges arrears	£	per
Fuel debts: Gas	£	per
Electricity	£	per
Other	£	per
Maintenance arrears	£	per
Others *(give details below)*		
	£	per
	£	per
Total priority debts	£ 126	per month

7 Expenses

(Do not include any payments made by other members of the household out of their own income)

I have regular expenses as follows:

Mortgage *(including second mortgage)*	£	per
Rent	£ 620	per month
Community charge	£ 20	per month
Gas	£ 9	per month
Electricity	£ 20	per month
Water charges	£ 9	per month
TV rental and licence	£ 40	per
HP repayments	£ 160	per
Mail order	£ 15	per
Housekeeping, food, school meals	£ 400	per month
Travelling expenses	£	per
Children's clothing	£	per
Maintenance payments	£ 80	per month
Others *(not court orders or credit debts listed in boxes 9 and 10)*		
	£	per
	£	per
	£	per
Total expenses	£ 1373	per month

9 Court orders

Court Case No.	£	per
Total court order instalments	£	per

Of the payments above, I am behind with payments to *(please list)*

10 Credit debts

Loans and credit card debts *(please list)*

Barclaycard	£ 143	per month
	£	per
	£	per

Of the payments above, I am behind with payments to *(please list)*

Barclaycard

11 Do you wish to make an offer of payment?

- *If you take away the totals of boxes, 7, 8 and 9 and the payments you are making in box 10 from the total in box 6 you will get some idea of the sort of sum you should offer. The offer you make should be one you can afford.*

☐ I can pay the amount admitted on [   ]
or
☐ I can pay by monthly instalments of   £ 500

12 Declaration   I declare that the details I have given above are true to the best of my knowledge

Signed	*James Smith*	Dated	30th Sept 92

Position *(firm or company)*

N. 205A

Plaint Note (default summons) and Request for judgment
Order 3, rule 3(2)(d)(i), Order 9, rules 3, 6(1)
[*Introduced* 1991]

Notice of Issue of Default Summons – fixed amount
To the plaintiff('s solicitor)

> BULLEN LEAKE AND CO
> 13 GRAY'S INN SQUARE
> LONDON WC2J 8PR

Your summons was issued today. The defendant has 14 days from the date of service to reply to the summons. If the date of postal service is not shown on this form you will be sent a separate notice of service (Form N222).

The defendant may either
- **Pay** you your total claim.
- **Dispute the whole claim.** The court will send you a copy of the defence and tell you what to do next.
- **Admit that all the money is owed.** The defendant will send you form of admission N9A. You may then ask the court to send the defendant an order to pay you the money owed by completing the request for judgment below and returning it to the court.
- **Admit that only part of your claim is owed.** The court will send you a copy of the reply and tell you what you do next.
- **Not reply at all.** You should wait 14 days from the date of service. You may then ask the court to send the defendant an order to pay you the money owed by completing the request for judgment below and returning it to the court.

In the	WESTMINSTER
	County Court

The court office at
  82 ST MARTINS LANE
  LONDON WC2
**is open between 10am & 4pm
Monday to Friday**

Case Number	*Always quote this*	92 4067

Plaintiff *(including ref.)*
  EASYRIDER GARAGES

Defendant(s) JAMES SMITH

Issue date	20.9.92
Date of postal service	
Issue fee	£ 43.00

**For further information please
turn over**

Request for Judgment

● *Tick and complete either A or B. Make sure that all the case details are given and that the judgment details at C are completed. Remember to sign and date the form. Your signature certifies that the information you have given is correct.*

● *If the defendant has given an address on the form of admission to which correspondence should be sent, which is different from the address shown on the summons, you will need to tell the court.*

A ☐ **The defendant has not replied to my summons**
　　Complete all the judgment details at C. Decide how and when you want the defendant to pay. You can ask for the judgment to be paid by instalments or in one payment.

B ☐ **The defendant admits that all the money is owed**
　　Tick only **one** box below and return the completed slip to the court.

☐ **I accept the defendant's proposal for payment**
　　Complete all the judgment details at C. Say how the defendant intends to pay. The court will send the defendant an order to pay. You will also be sent a copy.

☐ **The defendant has not made any proposal for payment**
　　Complete all the judgment details at C. Say how you want the defendant to pay. You can ask for the judgment to be paid by instalments or in one payment. The court will send the defendant an order to pay. You will also be sent a copy.

☐ **I do NOT accept the defendant's proposal for payment**
　　Complete all the judgment details at C and say how you want the defendants to pay.
　　Give your reasons for objecting to the defendant's offer of payment in the section overleaf. Return this slip to the court **together with the defendant's admission N9A** (or a copy). The court will fix a rate of payment and send the defendant an order to pay. You will also be sent a copy.

I certify that the information given is correct
Signed .... **Dated** ....

In the	WESTMINSTER
	County Court

Case Number	*Always quote this*	92 4067

Plaintiff *(including ref.)*
　　EASYRIDER GARAGES

Defendant　JAMES SMITH

Plaintiff's Ref

C Judgment details

I would like the judgment to be paid
☐ (forthwith) *only tick this box if you intend to enforce the order right away*
☐ (by instalments of £　　per month)
☐ (in full by　　　　)

Amount of claim as stated in summons
(including interest at date of issue) ....

Interest since date of summons (if any) ....
Period .... Rate ...... %

Court fees shown on summons ....
Solicitor's costs (if any) on issuing summons

　　　　　　　　　　　Sub Total　......

Solicitor's costs (if any) on entering judgment

　　　　　　　　　　　Sub Total　......

Deduct amount (if any) paid since issue

　　　　　Amount payable by defendant

—————————————— **Further Information** ——————————————

- The summons must be served within 4 months of the date of issue (or 6 months if leave to serve out of the jurisdiction is granted under Order 8, rule 2). In exceptional circumstances you may apply for this time to be extended provided that you do so before the summons expires.

- If the defendant does not reply to the summons or if he delivers an admission without an offer of payment you may ask for judgment. If you do not ask for judgment within 12 months of the date of service the action will be struck out. It cannot be reinstated.

- You may be entitled to interest if judgment is entered against the defendant and your claim is for more than £5000.

- You should keep a record of any payments you receive from the defendant. If there is a hearing or you wish to take steps to enforce the judgment you will need to satisfy the court about the balance outstanding. You should give the defendant a receipt and payment in cash should always be acknowledged. You should tell the defendant how much he owes if he asks.

- **You must inform the court IMMEDIATELY if you receive any payment before a hearing date or after you have sent a request for enforcement to the court.**

Objections to the defendant's proposal for payment | **Case Number** |

Pleadings

In both High Court and county court actions, the parties are required to set out in writing the factual bases of their respective cases in formal pleadings. The principal purposes of such pleadings are:

 (*a*) to clarify the matters in dispute between the parties so that the court can readily understand what are the real issues in the case;
 (*b*) to enable both sides to know in advance the allegations being made against them so that they will not be taken by surprise at the trial.

The basic pleadings which the rules require to be exchanged are:

 (1) A *statement of claim* by the plaintiff setting out the basis of his claim. In the High Court, the rules require that this document should be served within 14 days of the defendant delivering an acknowledgment of service to the court office stating his intention to defend the action,[1] although in practice the time is frequently extended by agreement between the parties. Sometimes the plaintiff will choose to serve the statement of claim together with the writ rather than waiting until the notice of intention to defend is delivered; instead of serving a separate document, the statement of claim may be indorsed on the back of the writ of summons (see p 77, ante). Where the statement of claim is set out on the back of the writ it is called a 'specially indorsed writ'. This practice was formerly used only in straightforward cases (for example, claims for debts or for the price of goods sold or services rendered); now however it is commonly employed wherever it is clear that an acknowledgement of service will be filed. In the county court, the pleading is called the *particulars of claim*. The rules require that it be delivered to the court office with the praecipe and served with the summons.
 (2) A *defence* in which the defendant is required to state in terms the grounds upon which he resists the plaintiff's claim. In the High Court, the defence should be served within 14 days of service of the statement of claim;[2] in the county court, the rules require a defence to be filed at the court within 14 days of service of the summons.[3]

1 RSC Ord 18, rule 1.
2 Ibid, rule 2.
3 CCR Ord 9, rule 2(6).

The drafting of pleadings is one of the most important functions of counsel. Although under the modern system the aim is for pleadings to be simple and clear, there is still a considerable art in drafting and the discussion below can only be a very rough guide.

DRAFTING THE STATEMENT OF CLAIM

The *statement* (or *particulars*) *of claim* should set out every fact which must be proved by the evidence at the trial if the plaintiff is to succeed in his claim. Before we consider the rules to be applied, it would be helpful to look at three very simple examples:

Contract

You are instructed by Albert and Eliza Doolittle who run a business known as Covent Garden Florists. On 1 September 1989 they bought a second-hand Ford lorry from Easyrider Garages Ltd. of Ealing for £12,000. Three weeks later the lorry seized up on the motorway. Repairs to make it serviceable cost £3000. Whilst it was under repair Albert was forced to hire another lorry for £3000.

In the Brentford County Court	Case No 92/2345

Between:

Covent Garden Florists (a firm)	Plaintiffs
and	
Easyrider Garages Limited	Defendants

Particulars of Claim

1. The Defendants carry on business as dealers in motor vehicles at 25A Lancaster Road, Ealing, London W5.
2. By an agreement in writing dated 1st September 1991 the Defendants sold and delivered to the Plaintiffs a Ford motor lorry registration number C 831 MAA for the sum of £12,000.
3. The following were inter alia implied terms of the said contract of sale:
   (*a*) that the said lorry should be of merchantable quality;
   (*b*) that the said lorry should be reasonably fit for its purpose.
4. In breach of the aforesaid terms the said lorry was not of merchantable quality nor fit for purpose at the date of delivery in that there was a serious oil leak from the sump and the cylinders were glazed and worn so that the engine seized up after 500 miles.
5. By reason of the matters aforesaid the plaintiff has incurred loss and expense and suffered damage.

Particulars of Loss and Expense

Cost of repairs	£3000
Hire of alternative transport from 21st September to 30th November 1991	£3000

5. The Plaintiff claims interest upon such damages as may be awarded pursuant to section 69 of the County Courts Act 1984 to be assessed.

And the Plaintiffs claim damages and interest

(Signature)

Served, etc

It can be seen in this very simple example that most statements of claim for breach of contract will set out:

1. the *details* of the *contract*, i e date, whether it was written or oral and the gist of the contract (e g employment, sale of goods, carriage, etc);
2. any *term* which it is alleged has been broken by the defendants;
3. the *relevant breach*;
4. an *allegation of damage* together with detailed particulars;
5. a *claim for interest*.

Tort

On 21 August 1991 John Smith, an accountant, is driving out of Chancery Lane when he collides with a lorry being driven west along Holborn. The accident was seen by a number of eyewitnesses who confirm the lights in Holborn were red. The driver apologised profusely to John and said 'I can't think why I missed the lights. I must have been asleep'. John sustained rather serious fractures of the femur of his left leg. He was detained in hospital for six weeks and was unable to go back to work for four months. During the period off work he received £1800 sickness benefit.

In the Westminster County Court   Case No 92/1657

Between:

John Smith   Plaintiffs
and
Mammoth Law Book Publishing Company Limited   Defendants

Particulars of Claim

1. On 21st August 1991 at the junction of Chancery Lane and High Holborn, London WC1 a collision occurred between a Sunbeam Alpine sports car owned and driven by the Plaintiff and a Ford lorry owned by the Defendants and driven by their servant one Smee.
2. The said collision was caused by the negligent driving and/or management of the said lorry by the Defendants' said servant.

Particulars of Negligence

The Defendants' said servant:

(*a*) Failed to stop at the traffic lights in Holborn which were red against him.
(*b*) Drove across Chancery Lane when by reason of traffic emerging therefrom it was unsafe so to do.
(*c*) Failed to notice and/or heed the presence and proximity of the Plaintiff's motor car emerging from Chancery Lane.

On 3rd October 1991 the said Smee was convicted at the Bow Street Magistrates' Court of driving the said lorry on the occasion above referred to without due care and attention contrary to section 3 of the Road Traffic Act 1988. The said conviction is pleaded as relevant to the issue of the negligence of the Defendants' servant.

3. By reason of the Defendants' said negligence the Plaintiff sustained personal injuries and has been put to loss and expense.

Particulars

The Plaintiff who is 28 years of age sustained a crack fracture of the left femur. He was detained in hospital for 3 weeks and immobilised in plaster for 6 weeks. Thereafter he underwent physiotherapy. He was off work for 4 months. The

Plaintiff's left leg has been shortened by ¼″ and he has a permanent limp. He experiences aching and discomfort in the knee. (A medical report and statement of special damages are served herewith pursuant to CCR Order 6 rule 1(5).)

And the Plaintiff claims damages and interest pursuant to section 69 of the County Courts Act 1984 to be assessed.

(Signature)

Served, etc

Statement of Special Damage

Cost of repairs to motor car	£2412.40p
Net loss of earnings from 21st August 1991 until 1st January 1992 (19 weeks at £267 per week)	£5073.00p
	£7485.40p

[During the period 21st August 1991 to 1st January 1992 the plaintiff was in receipt of sickness benefit]

It will be noted that in this typical personal injury pleading, the structure is very simple:

(1) A *neutral statement* that a collision has occurred setting out the date and place and persons involved.
(2) An *allegation of negligence* by the defendants followed by detailed particulars of what it is alleged they have done wrong. Where one intends to rely at the trial on a conviction as evidence in the case under section 11 of the Civil Evidence Act 1968 it must be pleaded in the statement of particulars of claim.
(3) An *allegation of damage* caused by that negligence resulting in personal injuries and loss and expense (called 'special damages'). RSC Order 18, r 12(1A) and CCR Order 6, r 1(5) require that a medical report and statement of special damages be served together with the pleading. RSC Order 18, r 12 is so important that it is set out below:

'(1A) Subject to paragraph (1B), a plaintiff in an action for personal injuries shall serve with his statement of claim–
    (a) a medical report, and
    (b) a statement of the special damages claimed.
(1B) Where the documents to which paragraph (1A) applies are not served with the statement of claim, the Court may–
    (a) specify the period of time within which they are to be provided, or
    (b) make such other order as it thinks fit (including an order dispensing with the requirements of paragraph (1A) or staying the proceedings).
(1C) For the purposes of this rule–
    'medical report' means a report substantiating all the personal injuries alleged in the statement of claim which the plaintiff proposes to adduce in evidence as part of his case at the trial;
    'a statement of the special damages claimed' means a statement giving full particulars of the special damages claimed for expenses

and losses already incurred and an estimate of any future expenses and losses (including loss of earnings and of pension rights).'

The provisions of CCR Order 6, r 1(5) to (7) are identical to the High Court rules. A number of points arising from these rules need to be considered. The requirement that a medical report should be served with the statement of claim means that it is not strictly necessary to provide particulars of injuries in the body of the pleading itself; nevertheless, it remains good practice to do so. The particulars should give details of the plaintiff's age, the injury sustained, the treatment he received and finally the extent of his disability at the date of the pleading. It will sometimes happen that the plaintiff's solicitor, although wishing to serve the pleading without delay, will not yet have a medical report (or, at least, a report sufficiently comprehensive to be served). In such a case, he may apply by summons (or notice of application) for leave to serve the statement of claim and for a direction specifying the period in which the report is to be served. Note that the statement of special damage must set out both past and future loss and expense; future loss would seem to include both an estimate of continuing loss of earnings *and* any assertion of handicap on the labour market (which is of course unquantifiable). Note also that, although the responsibility of ascertaining the sum which must be deducted and paid to the DSS in respect of state benefit lies on the defendant under the Social Security Administration Act 1992, it is proper to alert the defendants to the matter by a reference such as appears in the pleading above.

(4)   A *prayer for damages*. Note that a claim for interest must be specifically pleaded (RSC Ord 18, r 8(4)).

Possession

Mr Peter Grimes has let two rooms on the first floor of his house at 23 Jubilee Road, Kennington to a student called Jonah Stevenson. Peter lives on the premises so Jonah is not a protected tenant under the Rent Acts. Peter now wants to sell the house and has given Jonah notice to quit. Jonah has promised to go but he still has not left.

In the Lambeth County Court   Case No 92/126

Between:

Peter Grimes   Plaintiffs
and
Jonah Stevenson   Defendants

Particulars of Claim

1. The Plaintiff is the freehold owner of certain premises known as 23 Jubilee Road, Kennington, London SE1 and at all material times has resided therein.
2. On or about 1st October 1990 the Plaintiff let two rooms on the first floor of the said premises to the Defendant as a weekly tenant at a rent of £40 per week.
3. By notice in writing served 7th January 1992 the Plaintiff required the Defendant to quit the said premises on 7th February 1992 (or at the end of the period of his tenancy which should expire next after 4 weeks from the date of service of the said notice).
4. Since the expiry of the said notice and consequent determination of the

Defendant's tenancy, the Defendant has remained in possession of the said rooms as a trespasser therein.

5. The net annual value for rating of the premises of which the said rooms form part is £250.

And the Plaintiff claims:

1. Possession of the said premises.
2. Mesne profits at the rate of £120 per week from the 7th day of February 1992 to judgment.
3. Costs.

(Signature)

Dated etc

In this basic example of a claim by a landlord for possession it can be seen that the pleading is built up out of the following allegations:

(1) The plaintiff's status – ie his ownership of the house and the fact that he is a resident landlord so the tenant is not protected by the Rent Acts.
(2) The letting – date, period and rent.
(3) The termination of the letting.
(4) The defendant is still in occupation.
(5) The value of the premises – this is necessary to establish the jurisdiction of the county court.

From these illustrations it is hoped that the reader will have gathered the basic idea behind pleadings. The draft must set out in numbered paragraphs the matters of fact which have to be proved before the plaintiff can ask the court for the relief claimed in his prayer. Nothing more than those statements of fact should be pleaded so, for example, in the possession case, it is not relevant that Peter wants to sell the house or that Jonah has promised to leave. Again the plaintiff must not plead the evidence by which he intends to prove the facts alleged so, in the road accident case, the reports of eyewitnesses and the admissions of the defendants' driver although they will be crucial evidence at the trial are not pleaded. It should, however, be noted that it is not generally enough to make a bare allegation of misconduct or damage against the defendant. The defendant is entitled to know precisely the case he has to answer: therefore, wherever the pleading contains an allegation of negligence, breach of duty, fraud, breach of trust, justification of a libel, personal injuries or special damage, the draftsman must set out detailed particulars of the allegation. A claim for aggravated or exemplary damages must contain particulars showing why it is alleged the plaintiff is entitled to such relief.

In addition to these rules, a certain style has developed which has become standard practice. The most important stylistic rules are:

(1) plead chronologically;
(2) the parties are always referred to as 'the Plaintiff' or 'the Defendant';
(3) figures and sums must be set out in arabic numerals.

The important and overriding stylistic principle is of course that the pleading should be simple.

DRAFTING THE DEFENCE

The defence should set out clearly the answers made by the defendant to every material allegation in the statement of claim. It is sensible to begin by considering each paragraph of the statement of claim. The defendant may then take one of three possible steps in respect to each allegation:

(1) He may *admit* the allegation, i e he may concede that the particular point is not in dispute. This relieves the plaintiff from the necessity of producing any evidence to prove the particular point at the trial.
(2) He may *deny* the allegation. This not only means the plaintiff will be required to prove the allegation at the hearing but puts him on notice that the defendant intends to put forward a contrary case. The defendant must go on to set out the nature of that case; it is not sufficient for him merely to deny the allegation without stating what he says the true position is.
(3) He may require the other side to prove an allegation without specifically denying it; this is effected by employing the phrase 'the Defendant does not admit . . .'. This formula is used to deal with matters which are essential elements in the plaintiff's case but upon which the defendant has insufficient information to make any affirmative response.

We set out below the form of defence which might be anticipated in the road traffic case discussed above; notice that the neutral facts of the collision are *admitted*, the allegation of negligence is *denied* (and the defendants' contrary case is set out and *particularised*), while the allegations of injury and loss are *not admitted* so that the plaintiff will have to prove these matters strictly.

In the Westminster County Court   Case No 92/1657

Between:

John Smith   Plaintiffs
and
Mammoth Law Book Publishing Company Limited   Defendants

Defence

---

1. Paragraph 1 of the Statement of Claim is admitted.
2. It is admitted that the Defendants' said servant Smee was convicted as alleged in paragraph 2, but it is denied that the Defendants their servants or agents were negligent as alleged therein or at all.
3. The said collision was caused wholly by or contributed to by the Plaintiff.

Particulars of Negligence

The Plaintiff:

(a) Emerged from Chancery Lane into Holborn when the traffic signal was showing amber against him.
(b) Failed to look right before entering Holborn and/or notice the presence and proximity of the Defendants' vehicle in Holborn.
(c) Drove at too fast a speed.

4. It is not admitted that the Plaintiff sustained injuries or was put to loss as alleged in paragraph 3 of the Statement of Claim or at all.
5. Save as is herebefore expressly admitted, the Defendants deny each and every allegation contained in the Statement of Claim as if the same were here set out and specifically traversed.

(Signature of Counsel)

Served, etc

The reader will notice that paragraph 5 contains a 'blanket' denial of the allegations in the Statement of Claim – strictly in a good pleading this should not be necessary since every point should have been covered. However the formula is commonly used since it protects the draftsman to a certain extent if he has omitted to plead to some minor point.[4] In complex cases involving many points of complaint (e g a building dispute) one party may annex to his pleadings a schedule[5] setting out in columns the items involved and his complaints and then require the other side to complete a third column showing his answer to the complaints. Generally a fourth column is left blank for the use of the trial judge.

COUNTERCLAIM

It very often happens that the defendant not only wishes to defend the claim made by the plaintiff but also desires to bring a cross-action against him. Thus, for example, in our road traffic case, the defendants would almost certainly wish to bring a claim against the plaintiff for the cost of repairs to their lorry. It would in theory be possible for them to bring a completely separate action and apply for the cases to be heard together but in practice, in order to save expense and time, the defendant raises his cross-action by adding a *counterclaim* to his defence as follows:

Counterclaim

6. The Defendants repeat paragraphs 1–3 of the Defence.
7. By reason of the Plaintiff's negligence as aforesaid the Defendants have incurred loss and expense.

Particulars

Cost of repairs to lorry	£906.74p
Hire of alternative vehicle for 2 weeks	£200.00p
	Total £1106.74p

And the Defendants counterclaim against the Plaintiff damages and interest pursuant to section 69 of the County Courts Act 1984 to be assessed.

(Signature)

Served, etc

Where the counterclaim arises directly out of the facts constituting the claim it may also be a *defence* to the claim: for example, if P sues for the price of goods sold and delivered, D may be able to set up a counterclaim for damages for breach of condition as to merchantable quality which will reduce or extinguish P's claim. Such a counterclaim is termed a *set-off*. Where a counterclaim may amount to a defence and so be set-off, it is important to plead it as such since this has an important effect on the costs. The basic rule is that if P wins his claim and D wins the counterclaim each is

---

4 Note RSC Ord 18, r 13(1): '. . . any allegation of fact made by a party in his pleading is deemed to be admitted by the opposite party unless it is traversed by that party in his pleading . . .'. Note also r 13(3) prohibits the use of a general traverse without more. See on the question of the use of the general traverse Lord Denning's dicta in *Warner v Sampson* [1959] 1 QB 297, at 310.
5 Called a Scott Schedule. See p 336 post.

awarded costs, so, for example, P gets £600 costs on the claim and D gets £300 on the counterclaim – net result D pays £300 costs. If however the counterclaim also acts as a set-off and so is a *defence* to the action, P's claim will be *dismissed* (if it does not exceed the counterclaim) and P will be ordered to pay *all* D's costs. When the defendant wishes to make it clear that his counterclaim is to be treated as a set-off he will normally add a paragraph as follows at the conclusion of the defence and before the counterclaim:

'Further or in the alternative, the Defendant is entitled to set-off such damages as he may be awarded upon his counterclaim in extinction or diminution of the plaintiff's claim.'

There are three important instances where the draftsman will plead a set-off:

(i) where P sues for the price of goods sold and delivered, D can set-off damages for breach of warranty (see section 53 of the Sale of Goods Act 1979 – the effect is that the price is abated pro rata);

(ii) where P sues for the price of work done and materials supplied D can set-off damages for defective workmanship and materials (see *Hanak v Green*);[6]

(iii) where P sues for rent, his tenant can set-off the cost of making good the premises if P is in breach of covenant to repair (see *British Anzani (Felixtowe) v International Marine Management (UK) Ltd*).[7]

The above is not an exhaustive list; there are other cases where, because e g the defendant's counterclaim arises out of the same contract as the plaintiff's claim, the courts may permit him to set-off his claim; this concept of 'equitable set-off' is discussed in the leading case of *Hanak v Green* (supra).

The common feature of claims by way of set-off is that they arise from the same transactions as the plaintiff's claim. The only exception to this is where the plaintiff owes the defendant a specific sum of money; even if this arises from a totally separate contract, the defendant will be allowed to set it off against the plaintiff's claim.

REPLY AND DEFENCE TO COUNTERCLAIM

Where the defence does *not* contain a counterclaim, the plaintiff does not usually have to serve any further pleading. There is an implied joinder of issue (see RSC Ord 18, r 14(1)). But where a counterclaim is served on the plaintiff he must within 14 days serve a defence to the counterclaim.[8]

Where the defence raises an issue which is a good answer to the plaintiff's claim as it stands so that the plaintiff cannot succeed unless he raises another matter in answer it will be necessary for him to file a *reply*.[9]

6 [1958] 2 QB 9, [1958] 2 All ER 141, CA.
7 [1980] QB 137, [1979] 2 All ER 1063.
8 RSC Ord 18, r 3(2). In county court cases a defence to counterclaim is usually served unless the counterclaim is in effect nothing more than the converse of the claim, e g an allegation of contributory negligence and damage.
9 Strictly speaking there is no provision in the County Court Rules for the plaintiff to file a reply; sometimes however this is done simply so that the pleadings will accurately reflect the issues between the parties.

Example 1. D provides a reference for P which is highly damaging. P issues a writ for defamation and serves a statement of claim setting out the circumstances of the case and the libel. D serves a defence claiming privilege – on the grounds he was furnishing a reference. In order to answer the claim of privilege P will have to serve a reply alleging malice.

Example 2. D Ltd, a trade association, use the services of an independent contractor, A, for the production of their 1992 members directory and catalogue. A is provided with accommodation at their offices and places an order for the printing of the catalogue with P Ltd. The proofs are totally unacceptable and D Ltd dismiss A and refuse to accept an invoice submitted to them by the printers. P Ltd sue D Ltd upon the invoice and D Ltd serve a defence (a) denying that A was acting as their agent in placing the order in question and (b) in the alternative alleging breaches of contract (if there is in fact a contract between them).

We set out below the form of pleading which would be used in the second example:

Reply

1. The Plaintiffs do not admit the matters set out in paragraphs 1 to 10 of the Defence herein and join issue with the Defendants upon their Defence.
2. At all material times up to and including the date of the agreement alleged in paragraph 1 of the Statement of Claim the Defendants held out Mr Antrobus to the Plaintiffs as their agent duly authorised to transact business on their behalf in that:
   (a) they permitted him to use their headed writing paper;
   (b) they permitted him to carry business cards showing him to be their 'Design Supervisor';
   (c) on 6th June 1992 their managing director (Mr Smith), in conversation with the plaintiffs' purchasing manager (Mr Jones), described Mr Antrobus as 'our leading designer'.
3. If (which is not admitted) Mr Antrobus did not in fact have authority to enter into the said agreement on behalf of the Defendants, the Plaintiffs were none-theless induced by reason of the matters aforesaid to enter into the agreement referred to in paragraph 1 of the Statement of Claim in the belief that Mr Antrobus had said authority.
4. In the premises the Defendants are estopped from denying that Mr Antrobus had authority to enter into the said agreement on their behalf.

AMENDMENT OF WRIT AND PLEADINGS

At almost any stage in an action one side or other may realise that they need to alter the writ or the pleadings so as to enable them to deal with a new point which has emerged or to correct a mistake. The most common examples of amendment are:

(1) where the plaintiff wishes to add another person as defendant; for instance, in the example of the reply discussed above the plaintiff would certainly wish to add the agent as a second defendant (if he is worth suing) and plead breach of warranty of authority by him; it will be necessary in such a case to amend the writ by altering the title of the action and the general indorsement; the statement of claim will, of course, also have to be amended;
(2) where the plaintiff wishes to plead his case in an alternative

manner, eg if he wishes to add an allegation of breach of statutory duty to a claim based on negligence; again it is necessary to amend both the general indorsement of the writ and the statement of claim;

(3) where either side wish to alter or add to detailed statements in the pleadings, eg the calculations of special damage; here no question of amending the writ arises (unless the statement of claim has been indorsed on the writ).

The basic rule is that the party wishing to amend *requires leave* so to do but there are some circumstances in which amendments to the writ and pleadings may be made *without* the leave of the court.

1. Amendment with leave

A party seeking to amend must first obtain the leave of the court by issuing a summons returnable before a master[10] and annex to the summons a copy of the proposed amended pleading. Leave will normally be granted to make the proposed amendment on terms that the party wishing to amend pays the costs of and occasioned by the amendment. Thus CCR Ord 15, r 6 expressly provides that 'no cause or matter shall be defeated by reason of the misjoinder or non joinder of any party' and goes on to give wide power to permit the addition or substitution of parties; similarly RSC Ord 20, r 5 provides that the court 'may at any stage of the proceedings allow the plaintiff to amend his writ, or any party to amend the pleadings, on such terms as to costs or otherwise as may be just'. An amendment will only be refused if the other side can show prejudice, eg it raises an issue upon which they can no longer hope to obtain evidence although such evidence would have been available if the issue had been pleaded at the correct time. The basic principle was expressed thus by Brett MR:

> 'however negligent or careless may have been the first omission, and, however late the proposed amendment, the amendment should be allowed if it can be made without injustice to the other side. There is no injustice if the other side can be compensated by costs'.[11]

Where the amendment in question involves the addition of a new party as co-plaintiff, leave will be refused if that person could no longer sue because the limitation period has expired. This is because section

---

10 See RSC Ord 20. Application can be made to the district judge in the county court or reserved to the trial judge, after amended pleadings have been informally exchanged. The judge will normally allow the informal amendment: CCR Ord 15, rr 1–2.

11 *Clarapede & Co v Commercial Union Association* (1883) 32 WR 262 at 263. But see also *Ketteman v Hansel Properties Ltd* [1987] AC 189, [1988] 1 All ER 38, where the House of Lords, by a majority, held that whether leave to amend should be granted was in the judge's discretion according to the justice of the case and there was no rule of practice of invariably granting leave upon terms as to the payment of costs. Their Lordships were upholding a refusal of leave to amend the defence at the end of the trial to raise for the first time a procedural limitation defence which could have been raised earlier. Per Lord Griffiths: (at 62b) 'There is a clear difference between allowing amendments to clarify the issues in dispute and those that permit a distinct defence to be raised for the first time'; and (at 62d) '. . . justice cannot always be measured in terms of money and in my view a judge is entitled to weigh in the balance the strain the litigation imposes on litigants, particularly if they are personal litigants rather than business corporations, the anxieties occasioned by facing new issues, the raising of false hopes and the legitimate expectation that the trial will determine the issues one way or the other'.

35 of the Limitation Act 1980 provides that no new claim shall be made in the course of action if that claim as a separate action would be statute-barred.

> *Example.* An action was begun against certain insurers to recover insurance monies. After the limitation period had expired, it was realised that the plaintiffs had no right to sue on the contract of insurance because they had only been acting as agents in concluding the contract: their principals should have sued in their own name. An application to add the principals as co-plaintiffs was refused because any claim by them would have been statute barred.[12]

Similarly where the plaintiffs add a new party as defendant after the limitation period has expired, that defendant will be entitled to have the amendment set aside.[13]

> *Example.* In December 1990 the plaintiffs bring proceedings against the manufacturers of certain machinery delivered in January 1985 in defective condition. The manufacturers deliver a defence in February 1991 blaming the consulting engineers employed by the plaintiffs to design the machine. In March 1991 the plaintiffs obtain leave to amend the writ to add the engineers as second defendants. The second defendants are entitled to have the amended writ set aside.

There are, however, a limited number of exceptions to this general rule:

(i) in personal injury cases, an amendment may be made to add a party where the court would have exercised its powers under section 33 of the Limitation Act 1980 to permit a separate action to continue notwithstanding the expiry of the limitation period (see p 70 ante);[14]

(ii) in a number of cases where for technical reasons the claim cannot be determined unless an additional party is made a co-plaintiff or co-defendant (eg where the action is based on a joint contract it must be brought by or against all the joint parties).[15]

In addition, under section 35 of the Limitation Act and RSC Ord 20, r 5 the court is given power to amend the writ in three other cases when the limitation period has expired but no question of adding a new party arises:

(*a*) where there has been a mistake as to the correct name of a party (but nobody has been misled as to who was being sued) and the application is to *substitute* the name of the correct party;[16]

---

12 *Mabro v Eagle Star and British Dominions Insurance Co Ltd* [1932] 1 KB 485, CA.

13 See *Liff v Peasley* [1980] 1 All ER 623, [1980] 1 WLR 781.

14 Limitation Act 1980, s 35(3) and RSC Ord 15, r 6(5)(b). On the question of whether an application under s 33 to override the limitation period must be made *before* seeking leave to amend so as to add the relevant party the authorities are inconclusive. The position appears to be that an application under Ord 15, r 6(5)(b) to add a party cannot be made unless an application under s 33 to disapply the limitation period is made before or at the same time as the application for leave to amend: see *Howe v David Brown Tractors (Retail) Ltd* [1991] 4 All ER 30, CA. But see also *Kennett v Brown* [1988] 2 All ER 600, CA, where the first defendant raised a statute-barred claim by serving a contribution notice on the second defendant. The Court of Appeal held that any application under s 33 to disapply the ordinary limitation period was to be made at the time the limitation issue was raised by the second defendant.

15 Limitation Act 1980, s 35(5) and (6); RSC Ord 15, r 6(6).

16 Limitation Act 1980, s 35(6)(a); RSC Ord 20, r 5(3). For an example of an amendment permitted under this rule see *Evans Construction Co Ltd v Charrington & Co Ltd* [1983] QB 810, [1983] 1 All ER 310, CA.

(*b*) to alter the capacity in which a person sues (eg to show he sues as trustee and not in his personal capacity);[17]

(*c*) to allege a new cause of action arising out of the same facts as were originally pleaded (eg to add a claim for breach of statutory duty in a claim originally pleaded on the basis of negligence).[18]

A similar problem may arise where an application is made after the limitation period has expired to amend the defence:[19]

> *Example 1.* An accident occurred in 1961 when the plaintiff was working on a site at Dagenham and a brick fell and hit him on the head. He sued the site owners and the main contractors. In 1964 the defendants applied after the limitation period had expired to amend their defence to allege contributory negligence by the plaintiff in failing to wear a safety helmet. The plaintiff opposed the application on the grounds that if it had been set out in the original defence served he would have been able to have amended the writ to add a claim against his employers for failing to supply a helmet but that claim was now statute barred. The Court of Appeal allowed the defendants to make the amendment because it did not *directly* blame a third party; (it was also pointed out that it did not raise any matter unknown to the plaintiff when he originally decided who should be blamed for the accident).[20]
>
> *Example 2.* After the expiry of the limitation period the defendants to a personal injury claim received a medical report on the plaintiff which suggested that his disability was caused not by the original injury but by subsequent negligent medical treatment. Although the plaintiff could no longer sue the hospital, the defendants were given leave to amend their defence to plead *novus actus interveniens* because they were not responsible for the delay in obtaining medical reports.[21]

The principle which seems to emerge from these cases is that where the proposed amendment places blame on a third party who cannot be sued because of the expiry of the limitation period the court will refuse leave to amend unless the defendant shows that he is not at fault in not previously realising that the third party was to blame (or possibly that the plaintiff is equally to blame).

2. Amendment without leave

(a) *The writ.* If the plaintiff realises he has made mistakes in drafting the writ he is entitled to amend *once* without obtaining leave *provided* the writ has *not* been served (see Ord 20, r 1). This useful rule even enables, for example, the plaintiff to add new parties or new causes of action which should have been included in the original writ.

Where a party objects to an amendment made without leave by his opponent, he may apply to the court within 14 days of service on him for an order disallowing the amendment (RSC Ord 20, r 4). The court will disallow the amendment if it is satisfied that an application for leave to make the amendment would have been refused.

Practice on amendments to writ without leave

Amendments made without leave are effected by producing the original writ at the Action Department, with the amendments shown clearly in red,

17 Ibid, s 35(7); RSC Ord 20, r 5(4).
18 Ibid, s 35(5)(a); RSC Ord 20, r 5(5).
19 See *Steward v North Metropolitan Tramways Co* (1886) 16 QBD 556, CA.
20 *Turner v Ford Motor Co* [1965] 2 All ER 583, [1965] 1 WLR 948, CA.
21 *Weait v Jayanbee Joinery Ltd* [1963] 1 QB 239, [1962] 2 All ER 568, CA.

and headed 'Amended the ____ day of ____ 199__ pursuant to RSC Order 20, rule 1'. Where the amendment is made before service, the writ must be served as the original writ, but where the writ has been served, the amended writ must be served on all parties, unless the court directs otherwise.

Once the writ has been served, however, only minor mistakes and omissions may be corrected without leave. In particular the plaintiff will have to make application if his amendment involves:

   (i) the addition, omission or substitution of a party to the action or an alteration in a party's capacity; or

  (ii) the addition or substitution of a new cause of action.

(b) *Pleadings*. A party may amend any pleading *once* before pleadings are deemed to be closed (RSC Ord 20, r 3). The amended pleading must be served on the opposite party. Although there is no requirement under r 3 for obtaining leave where the desired amendment consists of the addition or substitution of new parties, causes of action etc, such amendments will inevitably also involve amendment of the writ, so the court's leave will in practice be required. Note that the opportunity for amending a pleading without leave must be deployed before the close of pleadings. There is therefore more time under this rule for amending the statement of claim than for amending a defence or reply.

Practice on amendments to pleadings without leave
Pleadings amended under Ord 20, r 3 must:

   (a) be indorsed with a statement to that effect, with the date of the amendment; and

   (b) show the amendments clearly in red ink;[22] and

   (c) be served on the opposite party.

Amendments to pleadings without leave under Ord 20, r 3 may be disallowed on application to the court within 14 days of service, if the court is satisfied that leave would not have been given for the amendment.

Right of opponent to make consequential amendments
Where an amended statement of claim or defence is served under r 3 the opposite party may serve an amended defence or reply and the time for service of the amended (or original) defence or reply is extended to 14 days after the service of the amended statement of claim or defence (rr 3(2) and (3)). As with amendments made with leave, the right of the other party to make consequential amendments in response to amendments made without leave is limited to those which relate to the first party's amendments and does not entitle the responding party, without express leave, to introduce any amendments that he chooses or those relating to allegations which are not affected by the first party's amendments.[23] Where a party served with an amended pleading does not amend his own pleading he is taken to rely on his unamended pleading in answer to the amended pleading (r 3(6)).

---

22 For the second and any subsequent amendments (which will require leave) the colours to be used are green, violet and yellow respectively.
23 *Squire v Squire* [1972] Ch 391, [1972] 1 All ER 891, CA.

REQUEST FOR FURTHER AND BETTER PARTICULARS

It may well happen that the party upon whom a pleading has been served will feel that it gives him insufficient information to enable him to answer the case or prepare his own case for trial. Consider, for example, the statement of claim set out below:

Statement of Claim
---

1. On the 1st day of August 1990 the Defendants agreed to sell and deliver a combine harvester to the Plaintiffs for £14,000.
2. It was a term of the said contract that the said harvester should be of excellent quality.
3. In breach of this term the harvester when delivered was defective and is not worth £14,000 so that the Plaintiffs have suffered loss.

And the Plaintiffs claim damages.

Clearly the defendant will want a great deal more information than is set out in this pleading. He will therefore send a letter to the plaintiffs' solicitors asking for them to provide further and better particulars[24] of the statement of claim. He will enclose with his letter a request set out in a formal document. This is done because the request and answer become part of the pleadings at the trial. We set out below a request for particulars which would be appropriate in the case above:

In the High Court of Justice   1991–A–No 206

Queen's Bench Division

Between:

Albert Higgins and Co   Plaintiffs
(a firm)
and
Mammoth Motor Sales Limited   Defendants

Request for Further and
Better Particulars of the
Statement of Claim

Under Paragraph 1

Of 'agreed to sell' state whether the alleged agreement was oral or in writing; if oral, state the date, time and place thereof, between whom made and the words alleged to have constituted the agreement; if in writing, identify every relevant document.

Under Paragraph 2

Of 'a term' state whether the alleged term was express or implied and if implied, state all matters which will be relied upon at the trial hereof in support of the Plaintiffs' contention that the said term should be implied into the alleged agreement.

Under Paragraph 3

Of 'defective' state each and every item which is alleged to have been defective and the nature of the alleged defect.

---

24 He must also serve a defence in outline since it is not normally a sufficient ground for delaying the defence that the defendant has sought further and better particulars of the statement of claim.

Of 'loss' state precisely what loss it is alleged the plaintiffs' have sustained.

(*Signature*)

Served, etc

Usually the other side will answer such a request without any formal order but if the request is refused or not sufficiently answered the party seeking particulars can apply by a summons to the master for an order that the other party do give the particulars sought within so many days.[25] The answers to the request should be drafted so as to set out paragraph by paragraph firstly the request and secondly the further and better particulars given. It should however be pointed out that the scope of particulars is limited: particulars may not be sought in order to discover the evidence which the other side will call at the trial. Indeed since each draftsman is under an obligation to his client to leave as much ground open for manoeuvre at the trial as possible, the pleadings as traditionally drafted sometimes told one little more than the very basic issues in dispute. The practice was well described in the Justice Report 'Going to Law':[26]

> 'these issues will still resemble an abstract diagram more than a detailed map of the areas of disputes since one of the principal duties which the pleaders on both sides owe their clients is to keep open for them the widest possible area for manoeuvre at the trial, while scattering as many hurdles as possible into the manoeuvering area of the opposition. Pleading therefore resembles nothing so much as naval warfare before the advent of radar, when each side made blind forays into the sea area of the other, while giving away as little as possible about the disposition of his own forces'.

It may well be that the introduction of the right to serve interrogatories without leave and the new procedure for exchanging statements of oral evidence will lead to a more open form of pleading.

The practice as to the service of request for further and better particulars in the county court is the same as in the High Court: orders for particulars will usually be made at the pre-trial review.

STRIKING OUT WRIT OR PLEADINGS

RSC Ord 18, r 19 enables the defendant[27] to apply by summons to the master for an order striking out the indorsement of the writ or the statement of claim (or part thereof) on the grounds that:

(i) on the face of the pleadings it is clear there is no reasonable cause of action (eg where a claim for defamation specifically pleaded that the words in question had been spoken by a judge in court) or

---

25 If the particulars are still not given, one applies for a final order from the master, ie that 'unless the particulars are delivered by . . . the Plaintiff's claim be struck out (*or the* Defendant be debarred from defending the action)'. In *Samuels v Linzi Dresses Ltd* [1981] QB 115, [1980] 1 All ER 803, CA the Court of Appeal held that the court could extend time even after the period prescribed in the 'unless order' had expired. However, it was made clear that such an extension would be exceptional; per Roskill LJ: 'To say that there is jurisdiction to extend the time where an "unless order" has been made and not complied with is not to suggest, let this be absolutely plain, that relief should be automatically granted to parties who have failed to comply with the orders of the court otherwise than on stringent terms either as to payment of costs or as to bringing money into court or the like.'

26 Stevens, 1974, para 50.

27 Or, in respect of a defence and counterclaim, the plaintiff. The equivalent procedure in the county court is set out at CCR Ord 13, r 5.

defence (e g where the defendant's pleading in answer to a claim for breach of contract merely asserts that the defendant regrets entering into the agreement);

(ii) the claim is scandalous, frivolous or vexatious (e g where the plaintiff is seeking to have re-litigated a matter already determined by the court[28]);

(iii) part of the pleading raises a point which would prejudice, embarrass or delay the fair trial of the action;

(iv) the pleading is otherwise an abuse of the process of the court.

If the application falls within the last three categories set out above, the applicant will produce affidavit evidence to support his contention.[29] If a pleading is struck out under this rule the court may also stay or dismiss the action or enter judgment (as the case may be) unless the defect in the pleading can be cured by an amendment. Pleadings are usually only struck out under Ord 18, r 19 in 'plain and obvious' cases. However an application to strike out may be coupled with an application under Order 14A (see below); in such a case the court would be entitled to strike out even if the determination of the question of law required long and serious argument.

DEFAULT OF DEFENCE

In the High Court when the defendant fails to deliver a defence within the time prescribed (i e 14 days after the time limited for acknowledging service of the writ or 14 days after service of the statement of claim whichever is later), the plaintiff may sign judgment in default.[30] This will be a final judgment in the case of a liquidated claim but interlocutory (e g for damages to be assessed) in other cases. Such a judgment will be set aside if the defendant subsequently applies by summons and shows by affidavit that there is a triable issue. In the county court, we have already seen that the plaintiff is entitled to a default judgment if no defence is served (see p 109, ante).

---

28 As in *Asher v Secretary of State for the Environment* [1974] Ch 208, [1974] 2 All ER 156, CA, where the Clay Cross councillors having failed in an appeal to the High Court against a surcharge by the district auditor commenced fresh proceedings seeking a declaration that the audit had been unlawful.

29 No evidence is admissible on an application that a pleading discloses no reasonable cause of action or defence. The deficiency must be evident from the face of the pleading in question: RSC Ord 18, r 19(2).

30 RSC Ord 19, rr 2–7. If the claim is for delivery up of specific goods or possession of land or an injunction or some other order (other than payment of money) the plaintiff will have to apply by summons for the order he seeks. The rules differ slightly according to the nature of the relief sought: see Ord 19 rules 4 to 7.

Appendix

This book contains a number of pleadings which can be used as basic precedents. The beginner will be tempted to consult the precedent books such as *Bullen and Leake and Jacobs* and *Atkins Court Forms before* drafting his pleadings. This can lead him into error because he may attempt to distort the facts of his case so as to fit one of the model precedents. The correct way to use a precedent book is to make a rough draft first and then check it against the examples in the books. Used in this way such books are of invaluable assistance.

The most important thing for the student is to learn the *structure* of the basic pleadings: the more complex pleading can almost always be built up from that structure. For that reason throughout this book only the most simple pleadings have been employed: together they should be sufficient for the student to discover the essential framework.

List of precedents

1. Negligence – running down case
2. Factory accident
3. Occupier's liability
4. Fatal accident claim
5. Nuisance – claim for injunction
6. Contract – simple breach – claim for damage
7. Contract – breach – claim for injunction
8. Contract – misrepresentation – claim for rescission
9. Claim for account
10. Landlord and tenant – claim against non-protected tenant
11. Claim against a protected tenant
12. Claim on unpaid cheque

1. *Negligence – road traffic*

   (1) On or about the   day of   199   at (*state vicinity*) in the County of   a collision occurred between a motor car owned and driven by the Plaintiff and a   driven by the Defendant (*or* by the Defendant's servant X).

   (2) The said collision was caused by the negligent driving and/or management of the said   by the Defendant (*or* by the Defendant's said servant) in that (*set out detailed Particulars of Negligence*).

(3) By reason of the Defendant's said negligence the Plaintiff sustained injuries and has been put to loss and expense (*set out Particulars of Injuries detailing (a) age plus injuries (b) treatment (c) extent of disability, and annex medical report to pleading. Set out Statement of Special Damage to be annexed to the pleading*).

And the Plaintiff claims damages and interest pursuant to section 35A of the Supreme Court Act 1981 (or s 69 of the County Courts Act 1984).

2. *Factory accident*

(1) The Plaintiff was at all material times employed by the Defendants as (*job*) at their premises at   in the County of   to which the provisions of the Factories Act 1961 (*or the Construction (Working Places) Regulations 1966 or whatever*) applied.

(2) On the   day of   199   the Plaintiff whilst so employed by the Defendants at their said premises was injured when (*set out basic details of accident*).

(3) The matters aforesaid were caused by the negligence and/or breach of statutory duty of the Defendants, their servants or agents in that:

(*set out in detail particulars of negligence and particulars of every statutory provision or regulation alleged to have been broken identifying the same specifically*).

(4) By reason of the Defendants' said negligence and/or breach of statutory duty the Plaintiff sustained injuries and has been put to loss and expense.

(*Set out particulars of injuries and annex medical report and statement of special damage.*)

And the Plaintiff claims damages (and interest pursuant to . . .).

3. *Occupier's liability case*

(1) The Defendants at all material times were the occupiers of premises at (*address*).

(2) On the (*date*) the Plaintiff whilst a visitor at the said premises within the meaning of the Occupiers' Liability Act 1957 was injured when he (*state what occurred*).

(3) The matters aforesaid were caused by the negligence of the Defendants their servants or agents in that (*set out particulars*).

(4) By reason of the matters aforesaid the Plaintiff has sustained injuries and been put to loss and expense.

(*Set out particulars of injuries and annex medical report and statement of special damage.*)

And the Plaintiff claims damages (and interest . . .).

4. *Fatal accident claims*

(1) The Plaintiff is the widow and administratrix (*or* the Plaintiffs are the executors) of the estate of A.B. deceased and brings this action on behalf of the dependants of the deceased under the Fatal Accidents Act 1976 and on behalf of the estate under the Law Reform (Miscellaneous Provisions) Act 1934. Letters of Administration (*or* Probate) were granted to the Plaintiff(s) out of the Principal Registry on (*date*).

(2) (*Set out neutral facts of accident.*)

(3) (*Allege negligence and/or breach of duty as appropriate and particulars.*)

(4) By reason of the matters aforesaid the deceased sustained injuries from which he died on (*date*).

(5) Particulars pursuant to the Fatal Accidents Act are as follows:

    (*a*) The names and dates of birth of the persons for whose benefit this action is brought are

    (*b*) The nature of the claim is that:

The deceased was aged   at the time of his death and was earning £   per week net. The plaintiff received from him the sum of £ for housekeeping and for her own benefit. In addition the deceased discharged the rent of £   per week on the family house at (*address*) and the local tax thereon which averaged £   per year and clothed and supported the said children. The plaintiff and the children of the deceased were wholly dependent upon him for support and by his death have lost the means of support and thereby suffered loss and damage.

(6) Further, by reason of the matters aforesaid, the expectation of life of the deceased was shortened and his estate has thereby suffered loss and damage. In addition, funeral expenses have been incurred amounting to £   .

    And the Plaintiff claims

    (1) Under the Fatal Accidents Act 1976, damages for the aforesaid dependants.

    (2) Under the Law Reform (Miscellaneous Provisions) Act 1934, damages for the benefit of the estate.

    (3) Interest pursuant to section 35A of the Supreme Court Act 1981.

5. *Claim for nuisance*

(1) The Plaintiff is and at all material times has been the owner and occupier of a dwellinghouse and premises known as (*address*).

(2) Since about the month of June 1990 the Defendant who is the tenant of premises adjoining the Plaintiff's garden has caused offensive and noxious smells to emanate from his premises into the Plaintiff's said garden and house by reason of pigs and goats which he has kept in his said premises. (*Where appropriate set out detailed particulars.*)

(3) By reason of the matters aforesaid, the Plaintiff has suffered in the enjoyment of his house and garden and thereby suffered damage.

(4) The Defendant intends, unless restrained from so doing by order of this Honourable Court, to continue the said nuisance.

    And the Plaintiff claims:

    (1) An injunction restraining the Defendant by himself, his servants or agents or otherwise howsoever from continuing or repeating the said nuisance.

    (2) Damages (*limited to £*   ).

6. *Contract – breach*

(1) On the   day of   199   (*or* by a contract in writing dated *or whatever*) the Defendants agreed to (*nature of obligation*) for the Plaintiff at a price of £   (*or whatever consideration was given*).

(2) It was an express (*and/or* implied) term of the said agreement that (*set out term*).

(3) On (*date*), in breach of the said term the Defendants (*set out specific breach*).

(4) By reason of the matters aforesaid the Plaintiff has suffered damage (*set out particulars*).

And the Plaintiff claims damages and interest (*pursuant to the SC Act or at the rate prescribed in the contract*).

7. Contract – Claim for injunction

Set out paragraphs 1–4 as above and then add:

(5) The Defendant intends, unless restrained from so doing by this Honourable Court, to repeat (*or* continue) to (*detail*) in breach of his obligations under the said agreement.

And the Plaintiff claims:

(1) Damages

(2) An injunction to restrain the Defendant by himself, his servants or agents or otherwise howsoever from (*detail precisely the conduct complained of*).

8. Contract – misrepresentation

(1) On [*date*] the Defendants by their servant or agent one   orally represented to the Plaintiff that (*set out gist of representation*).

(2) On [*date*] in reliance upon the aforesaid representation, the plaintiff agreed to purchase from the Defendants (*or whatever*) the said   and paid to the Defendants the sum of £   being the price thereof.

(3) The said representation was false in that (*set out why it is alleged the statement was untrue*).

(4) So soon as he discovered the representation was false the Plaintiff by letter dated   (*or whatever*) rescinded the said agreement but the Defendants have refused to repay the said sum of £   .

(5) By reason of the matters aforesaid the Plaintiff has suffered loss and damage (*set out particulars of special damage*).

And the Plaintiff claims:

(1) The rescission of the said agreement, the return to him of all sums paid thereunder, an indemnity in the sum of £   , interest on such sum(s) pursuant to section 35A of the Supreme Court Act 1981, and all proper consequential directions.

(2) Further or alternatively, damages.

9. Claim for an account

Where it is not certain what sum is due from the Defendant (e g between partners in a business or where a salesman is suing for commission or an author for royalties) the court will order an account to be taken which involves the Defendant delivering a draft account upon which the Plaintiff, having obtained discovery, can examine him. (See RSC Ord 43; CCR Ord 6, rule 2.)

(1) By an agreement in writing dated the   day of   199   the Plaintiff undertook to promote the Defendants' products at shops

and other business establishments within 10 miles of   (*or whatever*).

(2) The following were inter alia express terms of the said agreement:

    (*a*) That the Plaintiff should be entitled to receive commission at the rate of 12 per cent on the value of all orders placed by customers introduced by him.

    (*b*) That on the 31st day of December in each year the Defendants should prepare a statement of account showing the value of each and every order placed by such customers and the amount due to the Plaintiff thereon.

(3) In breach of the aforesaid terms the Defendants have failed to prepare such accounts for the year ending the 31st day of December 199 or pay to the Plaintiff the commission due thereon.

And the Plaintiff claims:

(1) That an account may be taken of all orders placed by such customers with the Defendants during the year ending the 31st day of December 199 .

(2) That the Defendants may be ordered to pay to him the sum found due to him on the taking of such account together with interest pursuant to section 35A of the Supreme Court Act 1981 at such rate and for such period as this Honourable Court may think fit.

10. *Landlord and tenant – tenant not protected – residential landlord*

(1) The Plaintiff is the owner and entitled to possession of the premises known as and situated at (*address*) at which the Plaintiff resides.

(2) On or about the   day of   198 the Plaintiff let (*details of rooms occupied*) at the said premises to the Defendant on a weekly tenancy at a rent of £   per week.

(3) By notice in writing served the (*date*) the Plaintiff required the Defendant to render up possession of the said premises on (*date*) or at the expiry of the week of his tenancy which should end next after four weeks from the service of the said notice upon him.

(4) Since (*date of expiry*) the Defendant has remained in possession of the said rooms (*or whatever*) as a trespasser thereon.

(5) At (*date of expiry of notice*) the Defendant was in arrears of rent to the extent of £   .

(6) The net annual value for rating of the said premises is £   .

And the Plaintiff claims:

(1) Possession of the said premises.

(2) £   arrears of rent.

(3) Mesne profits from (*date of expiry of notice*) at the rate of £   until possession is delivered up.

(4) Costs.

11. *Landlord and tenant – protected tenant – arrears of rent and nuisance and premises required by landlord for his own use*

(1) The Plaintiff is the owner of and entitled to possession of the premises known as and situated at (*address*).

(2) On or about the   day of   198 the Plaintiff let (*details or 'the whole of'*) the said premises to the Defendant on a weekly tenancy at a rate of £   per week.

(3) The provisions of the Rent Act 1977 apply to the said premises.

(4) By notice in writing served the (*date*) the Plaintiff required the Defendant to render up possession of the said premises on (*date, then complete as in paragraph 3 of precedent No 10*).

(5) Since the expiry of the said notice the Defendant has remained in occupation of the said premises as a statutory tenant therein.

(6) The said rent is £   in arrear at the date hereof.

(7) The Defendant has been guilty of conduct which is a nuisance or annoyance to adjoining occupiers in that:
(*set out Particulars of each matter complained of*).

(8) The said premises are reasonably required by the Plaintiff as a residence for himself.

(9) The net annual value for rating of the said premises is £   .

And the Plaintiff claims:

(1) Possession of the said premises pursuant to Cases 1, 2 and 9 of Schedule 15 to the Rent Act 1977.

(2) £   arrears of rent.

(3) Mesne profits at the rate of £   from the date hereof until possession is delivered up.

(4) Costs.

12. *Claim on an unpaid cheque*

(1) The Plaintiff is the payee of a cheque for £   dated the   day of 199   drawn by the Defendant on (*bank*).

(2) The said cheque was duly presented for payment on the   day of 199   but payment was refused on the orders of the Defendant (*or the said cheque was dishonoured*).

(3) *In cases of dishonour.* Notice of dishonour was given to the Defendant by letter dated the   day of   but the Defendant has failed to pay the said sum.

(4) In the premises the Plaintiff is entitled to the sum of £(*amount of cheque*) and the further sum of £   being interest pursuant to section 57(1) of the Bills of Exchange Act 1882 at the rate of 15% from (*date of presentment*) to date and continuing at the aforesaid rate at £   per day until judgment or sooner payment.

And the Plaintiff claims:

(1) The sum of £   .

(2) Interest at the rate of   from the date of presentment to the date hereof.

(3) Such further interest thereafter as this Honourable Court shall think fit.

Summary proceedings, interim payments and security

SUMMARY JUDGMENT

The minimum period which can elapse between the issue of a High Court writ and setting an action down for trial is in the order of six months. In practice the process of exchanging pleadings and lists of documents almost always takes much longer. Even after an action is set down there may well be considerable delay before it is heard. The reality of the situation is that an ordinary Queen's Bench action takes about two years to come to trial so that a successful plaintiff may well be kept out of his money for a substantial time and, although he may eventually be awarded interest on his judgment, that is often inadequate compensation particularly, for example, to a small business with cash flow problems. It is of course right that a real dispute should be adjudicated upon after careful discovery and examination of oral evidence. It would however be outrageous if an unscrupulous defendant could exploit the procedure of the court by serving a defence and thereby automatically obtaining a year or more of grace before judgment. RSC Ord 14 provides a means of preventing a defendant taking advantage of the delay inherent in the procedure before a case comes for trial by providing that, if the plaintiff can prove to the master (or district judge) that there can be no defence to his action, he shall have judgment forthwith. This *summary* judgment effectively denies the defendant the chance of testing the plaintiff's case by discovery and oral evidence and therefore will only be granted where the plaintiff is able to show an *unanswerable* case; it is not enough for a plaintiff to show that he has a strong case or that he is likely to succeed, he will only obtain judgment if he can show that he is bound to succeed.

PRACTICE ON ORDER 14 APPLICATION

The plaintiff may apply for summary judgment at any stage after the defendant has filed an acknowledgment of service stating his intention to defend provided the statement of claim has been served. If, of course, no notice of intention to defend has been given the plaintiff will sign a default judgment (see p 93, ante). The plaintiff who is considering applying under Order 14 will probably indorse the statement of claim on the back of the writ of summons (see p 77, ante). This may be a full pleading or, as frequently happens where the action is for a liquidated sum, merely a

STAGES IN QUEEN'S BENCH ACTIONS

Pre-trial discovery
and views ———————— **CAUSE OF ACTION**

——————————————— Time fixed by statute

Urgent ex parte injunctions
(including Mareva and Anton
Piller applications) —————————

ISSUE OF WRIT

Applications to amend writ,
extend time for service, orders ——————————————— Writ must be served
for substituted service   within 4 months

SERVICE OF WRIT

Applications for injunctions ——————

——————— Acknowledgements of Service must
          be returned within 14 days

D can acknowledge service under protest
and apply to set writ aside ——————

——————— If notice of intention to defend not given
          P can sign judgment: if notice given
          P must serve statement of claim
          within 14 days

Application under Order 14 ———— **STATEMENT OF CLAIM**

——————— If no statement of claim served
          D can apply to strike out: if served,
          D must serve defence within 14 days

Request for further and
better particulars at ————————— **DEFENCE**
any stage from now on

——————— If no defence served
          P can enter judgment

——————— Where defence contains a
CLOSE OF PLEADINGS —— counterclaim or raises new
          issues, P must serve further
          pleading and the time for close
          of pleadings is postponed

Discovery ———— Lists must be served within
          14 days of close of pleadings

Applications for lists to be
verified by affidavit and ——————
for discovery

——————— If summons not taken out by P
          within one month of close of
SUMMONS FOR pleadings, D can take out
DIRECTIONS ISSUED —— summons himself or apply to
except in personal strike out for want of
injury cases prosecution

In theory, all interlocutory
applications should be made ———— **SUMMONS HEARD** ———— Master fixes time for
at this stage   setting down

**EXCHANGE OF WITNESS
STATEMENTS AND EXPERT REPORTS**

ACTION SET DOWN

TRIAL

Note 1: This basic table is intended to be a reminder of the overall stages of the action. In practice, the rigid time periods prescribed by the rules are invariably waived by the parties once notice to defend has been given. Notice that the left hand column gives only a very general idea as to when certain ancillary proceedings occur.

Note 2: In personal injury actions no summons for directions need be issued: Ord 25, r 8 provides a timetable to be followed under which witness statements and expert reports are exchanged within 14 weeks of close of pleadings and the action is to be set down within 6 months.

statement of the amount due by reference to an invoice (see example, p 79, ante). Provided these two conditions are satisfied, i e a notice of intention to defend has been given by the defendant and the plaintiff has served his statement of claim, he can issue in the Action Department in London or at the local district registry a summons requiring the defendant to attend before the master (or district judge) and show that there is a triable defence to the plaintiff's claim.[1] The summons must be served on the defendant 10 clear days before the return date.[2] Service can be effected by post on the defendant's solicitors or, if he has no solicitors, at his usual or last known address. The plaintiff must serve with the summons an affidavit (*a*) verifying his claim (this is often done by simply deposing that the matters set out in the statement of claim are true) and (*b*) asserting that there is no defence to the claim.[3] Although as a general rule hearsay evidence is not permitted in contested proceedings, there is an exception in the case of an Order 14 affidavit: the court has the power to act on statements of information in the affidavit provided the deponent sets out clearly the source of his information (see p 154, post).[4] If the defendant appears on the return day he can oppose the application either by pointing to a procedural irregularity (e g short service) or on the merits or, indeed, on both grounds. If in fact he does wish to defend on the merits, he should serve the plaintiff with an affidavit setting out his case 3 clear days before the return day. Formerly it was a common practice for the defendant to hand in an affidavit at the hearing – which frequently forced the plaintiff to ask for an adjournment to consider the evidence; nowadays the summons served on the defendant expressly directs him to serve his affidavit 3 clear days in advance so that if he fails to do so and the plaintiff requires an adjournment, the defendant will be ordered to pay the costs incurred.[5] The plaintiff on receipt of the defendant's affidavit may serve an affidavit in reply. If this affidavit simply contests the evidence of the defendant, it may only serve to prove that there is indeed an issue to be tried between the parties so that summary judgment is inappropriate. It is however worth serving an affidavit in reply where the plaintiff has evidence (usually correspondence) which effectively destroys the defendant's case or goes so near revealing it to be a sham that the master will impose conditions on granting leave to defend (see below). Indeed, the experienced practitioner usually looks upon the affidavit in reply as the means of casting sufficient doubt on the defendant's case to obtain an order for payment into court as a condition of granting leave to defend; if the defendant's case is indeed spurious it is unlikely that he will continue to defend once he has parted with his money. If the defendant fails to appear at the hearing, the master may give judgment forthwith provided the plaintiff's own pleading is in order, the affidavit proves his case and he can prove

1 In London, if the matter is unlikely to be contested the summons is assigned to the 'Solicitors' List' which is heard by the master between 10.30 am and noon. Where a contest is likely, the summons will be assigned either to 'Counsels' List' at noon (if it is not expected to take more than 20 minutes), or else a special appointment for counsel is taken out.
2 RSC Ord 14, r 2(3). In this case one counts intervening weekends and holidays in calculating the period but discounts the day of service and the day on which the summons is due to be heard (ie the 'return day').
3 Solicitors often employ a standard form of affidavit for this purpose which can be purchased at a law stationers. Such standard forms are however inappropriate in cases where the claim involves any degree of complexity.
4 RSC Ord 14, r 2(2).
5 *Practice Direction* [1970] 1 All ER 343, [1970] 1 WLR 258.

service of the summons and the affidavit on the defendant. It should be noted that if the plaintiff thinks the defendant may not appear he must attend with an affidavit or some other evidence of service.[6] If the defendant appears at the hearing (or exceptionally writes to the court) the master will have to consider on the arguments addressed to him whether to grant judgment.[7] Before discussing this matter it may be convenient to summarise in tabular form the practice up to the hearing.

PRELIMINARY STEPS IN ORDER 14 PROCEDURE

(1) P issues and serves writ (usually indorsed with statement of claim).

(2) D delivers an acknowledgment of service stating his intention to defend.

(3) P serves statement of claim (if not already indorsed on writ).

(4) P issues summons at Action Department or district registry.

(5) P serves summons and affidavit of merits on D. Service can be by post. 10 clear days (weekdays and holidays count) must elapse before return date.

(6) D may serve affidavit in reply. If it is not served 3 clear days (weekends and holidays do *not* count) before the hearing, P can apply for adjournment and costs.

(7) P may prepare affidavit in reply.

(8) If no affidavit is received by P from D, P should prepare an affidavit of service to put in at hearing in case D does not appear.

Note: (a) D may use Order 14 proceedings to obtain summary judgment on a *counter-claim.*[8]

(b) P may employ Order 14 proceedings in respect of *part only* of his claim.[9]

(c) P may obtain judgment against *one* or more defendants: if he does so and executes it will *not* prevent him pursuing his claim against the co-defendants even if they are jointly liable[10] (except where they have been sued in the alternative).[11]

---

6 Under s 7 of the Interpretation Act 1978 service by post is deemed to have been effected by properly addressing, prepaying and posting a letter containing the document and, unless the contrary is proved, to have been effected at the time at which the letter would be delivered in the ordinary course of post. The court today normally reckons that a first-class letter will be delivered on the day following posting.

7 Under RSC Ord 14 r 4(1) the defendant may show cause 'by affidavit *or otherwise* to the satisfaction of the court'.

8 RSC Ord 14, r 5(1). Summary judgment may also be obtained on a counterclaim brought under Ord 15, r 3 against another defendant: see RSC Ord 15, r 3(5A), reversing *C E Heath plc v Ceram Holding Co* [1989] 1 All ER 203, CA.

9 RSC Ord 14, r 1(1).

10 Ibid, r 8(1) which provides: 'Where on an application under rule 1 the plaintiff obtains judgment . . . against any defendant, he may proceed with the action . . . against any other defendant'. Section 3 of the Civil Liability (Contribution) Act 1978 provides: 'Judgment recovered against any person liable in respect of any debt or damage shall not be a bar to an action, or to the continuance of an action against any other person who is (apart from any such bar) jointly liable with him in respect of the same debt or damage.'

11 Where P sues D1 and D2 in the alternative (for example, on the basis D1 is either personally liable on a contract or was acting as agent for D2) a judgment against one operates as a bar against proceedings continuing against the other: see *Scarf v Jardine* (1882) 7 App Cas 345, HL. D retired from a partnership which continued to trade in the firm name and gave no notice of D's retirement. P sold and delivered goods to the new firm and

Summons
under Order 14
for Whole Claim

IN THE HIGH COURT OF JUSTICE
Queen's Bench Division

19 92 .— G.—No. 2934

Master DREW   Master in Chambers

Between

Plaintiff

GRAND ORIENTAL CARPET COMPANY LIMITED

AND

ALI BABA (MALE) (Trading as "Magic Floors Inc")

Defendant

Let all parties concerned attend the Master in Chambers, in Room No. E102 ,
Central Office, Royal Courts of Justice, Strand, London, on   Thursday,
the   17th   **day of** DECEMBER   19 92 , **at**   10.30   o'clock in
the   forenoon on the hearing of an application on the part of the Plaintiff for final

(1) The Defendant
(or if against one
or some of several
Defendants insert
names).

judgment in this action against(¹) the Defendant

(2) Or as the case
may be, setting
out the nature of
the claim.

for the amount claimed in the statement of claim with interest, if any (²)

and costs.

Take Notice that a party intending to oppose this application or to apply for a stay of
execution should send to the opposite party or his solicitor, to reach him not less than
three days before the date above-mentioned, a copy of any affidavit intended to be
used.

Dated the   2nd   **day of**   December   19 92

This Summons was taken out by Snell, Son and Hanbury
of   10 New Square, Gray's Inn, WC1

[Agent for   ]
of

Solicitor for the Plaintiff

To M essrs Street, Winfield and Salmond
    1 Crown Office Row, Temple, EC4
Solicitor or Agent for the Defendant

Filed on behalf of   : Plaintiffs
Name of Deponent : P.A. Fotheringay
No. of Affidavit   : 1st
Date Affidavit sworn: 2.12.92

Affidavit on
Application
under Order 14,
Rule 2, by or on
behalf of Plaintiff.

IN THE HIGH COURT OF JUSTICE
Queen's Bench Division

19 92.— G.—No. 2934

District Registry

Between

GRAND ORIENTAL CARPET COMPANY LIMITED   **Plaintiff**

AND

ALI BABA (MALE) (Trading as "Magic Floors Inc")   **Defendant**

(1) "the above-
named Plaintiff",
or as may be.

I, Percival Archibald Fotheringay

of Pinewood House, Haslemere in the County of Surrey

(¹) Company Director

MAKE OATH AND SAY AS FOLLOWS:—

(2) Is *or* are.
(3) Was *or* were.
(4) Me *or* the
above-named
Plaintiff *or as the
case may be*.

1. The Defendant
   (²) is , and (³) was at the commencement of this action, justly and truly
   indebted to (⁴) the above named plaintiff
   in the sum of £ 25,000 being the price of goods sold and
   delivered by the Plaintiff to the Defendant

The particulars of the said claim appear by the statement of claim in this action.

~~2. It is within my own knowledge that the said debt was incurred and is still due and owing as aforesaid.~~

or

(5) State source
of information.

[2. I am informed by (⁵) one Joseph Smith

(6) State grounds
of belief.

and I verily believe (⁶) on the basis of information supplied
to me by him as the sales manager having charge of this transaction

that the said debt was incurred and is still due and owing as aforesaid.]

3. I verily believe that there is no defence to this action ~~[except as to the amount of the damages claimed].~~

(7) Delete if
sworn by
Plaintiff.

[4. I am duly authorised by the Plaintiff to make this affidavit. (⁷)]

Sworn at Fleet Street EC4

the 2nd day of December 19 92,

Before me, Nathaniel Wilkins

P. A. Fotheringay

A Commissioner for Oaths

This affidavit is filed on behalf of the Plaintiff

THE HEARING OF THE SUMMONS

(a) Technical objections

As indicated above the defendant may oppose summary judgment either on the grounds that the case does not fall within the scope of the order or because of a procedural irregularity committed by the plaintiff in making his application. The following cases do *not* fall within the provisions of Order 14:

(i) Claims for libel, slander, malicious prosecution or false imprisonment.

(ii) Actions for the specific performance or rescission of a contract for the sale of land or grant or assignment of a lease or for the forfeiture or return of a deposit in connection with such matters. But note there is an equivalent procedure in the Chancery Division under Order 86 which deals with these matters (see below).

(iii) Actions not begun by *writ*.

(iv) Admiralty actions *in rem*.

Where the defendant makes a technical objection on the basis of some irregularity to procedure (for example, that there has been short service or the affidavit does not verify the claim) the master may adjourn the hearing or give the plaintiff leave to amend or file a further affidavit instead of dismissing the summons.

(b) Defence on the merits

The corollary of the rule that the plaintiff must prove that he has an unanswerable case is that the defendant in order to succeed need show no more than a 'triable issue': he need do no more than in the words of the order show '*that there is an issue or question in dispute which ought to be tried*' (Ord 14, r 3(1)). It is not of course sufficient for the defendant to depose to his belief that he has a good defence to the action. He must set out in his affidavit the nature of his defence. It is a very good rule in practice to exhibit to the affidavit a draft defence settled by counsel showing precisely the defendant's contentions. If the defendant shows a triable issue then the master will *either* give unconditional leave to defend and order that the costs of the application should be in cause (i e be paid after the trial by the unsuccessful party) *or*, if he considers the plaintiff knew all the time that there was a triable issue, dismiss the summons and order the plaintiff to pay the costs forthwith.

(c) Disposal of case on point of law

For the purposes of Ord 14, r 3 a 'triable issue' usually involves an arguable dispute of fact. Sometimes the issue may involve disputes of fact *and* law. Where the only triable issue is a point of law or involves the construction of a document the court may proceed under Order 14A there and then to hear the parties' arguments and determine the point of law in question, giving judgment accordingly. This should be done, however, only in clear cases

---

successfully sued the firm to recover the price. When the judgment was unsatisfied, he sought to sue D as a former partner (who would have been liable to P on the basis of estoppel). Held: P was precluded from continuing this action because the claims against the new partnership and the former partner were in the alternative and once the plaintiff had elected to sue and take judgment against the partnership, he would not be allowed to pursue the alternative claim. See also *Morel Bros & Co Ltd v Earl of Westmoreland* [1903] 1 KB 64.

where the triable issue of law is 'suitable for determination without a full trial of the action' and when the master's decision on the point of law 'will finally determine (subject only to any possible appeal) the entire cause of matter or any claim or issue therein'.[12] The reasoning behind this new procedure was explained in *R G Carter Ltd v Clarke*:[13]

> 'If a judge is satisfied that there are no issues of fact between the parties, it would be pointless for him to give leave to defend on the basis that there was a triable issue of law. The only result would be that another judge would have to consider the same arguments and decide that issue one way or another . . . But it is quite different if the issue of law is not decisive of all the issues between the parties or, if decisive of part of the plaintiff's claim or of some of those issues, is of such a character as would not justify its being determined as a preliminary point, because little or no savings in costs would ensue. It is an a fortiori case if the answer to the question of law is in any way dependent on undecided issues of fact.'[14]

The procedure under Order 14A differs in one important respect from other applications for summary judgment in that the decision is conclusive against the plaintiff if the court rejects his argument.

(d) Counterclaim and set-off

A counterclaim is a cross-action by the defendant against the plaintiff. It need *not* be connected with the plaintiff's claim in any way.

> *Example.* P sells goods to the value of £10,000 to D. D refuses to pay on the basis of defects in some machinery purchased earlier from P which have now come to light and will cost £11,000 to repair.

In such a case the defendant will not have a defence as such to the plaintiff's claim but it would clearly be unjust that the plaintiff should obtain his money when he may owe the defendant more than the amount of the claim. Accordingly the practice in such cases is for the master to give judgment for the plaintiff on his claim with costs but order that execution of the judgment be stayed pending the trial of the counterclaim. In determining whether a stay will be granted in Order 14 proceedings the extent to which the counterclaim is linked with the claim is one (but not the only) relevant factor. The court may also take into account the strength of the counterclaim and the ability of the plaintiff to satisfy any judgment on the counterclaim.[15]

There will also, however, be cases where the counterclaim is so closely linked to the plaintiff's claim that it provides a *defence* to the claim.

> *Example.* P sells goods to the value of £10,000 to D. They are seriously defective on delivery and D incurs expenses of £2000 in putting them right.

In such a case section 53(1) of the Sale of Goods Act 1979 provides:

> 'Where there is a breach of warranty by the seller, or where the buyer elects (or is compelled) . . . to treat any breach of condition on the part of the seller as a breach of warranty, the buyer . . . may . . . set up against the seller the breach of warranty in diminution or extinction of the price.'

---

12 RSC Ord 14A, r 1(1).
13 [1990] 2 All ER 209, CA. See also *Home and Overseas Insurance Co Ltd v Mentor Insurance Co (UK) Ltd (in liquidation)* [1989] 3 All ER 74, CA per Parker LJ at 77 and *British and Commonwealth Holdings plc v Quadrex Holdings Inc* [1989] QB 842, [1989] 3 All ER 492, CA.
14 Ibid, per Lord Donaldson MR at 213g.
15 *Drake and Fletcher Ltd v Batchelor* [1986] LS Gaz R 1232.

Where a counterclaim arising out of the same transaction as the claim can thus be used as a defence to the action it is termed a *set-off*.[16]

Where a *set-off* is relied upon in an Order 14 application it will count as a *defence* and therefore unconditional leave to defend must be given with an order that costs should be in cause (or, if the plaintiff knew full well of the matters giving rise to the set-off, eg by letters of complaint, the summons will be dismissed with costs).

(e) Special rules concerning cheques

To the above rule concerning set-offs there is a most important exception in the case of bills of exchange, cheques and promissory notes. For commercial reasons our courts treat such documents as equivalent to cash so that in an action for dishonour there are only a limited number of defences available. In particular, it is not a defence to show that the defendant has a valid set-off arising out of the transaction for which the cheque was drawn as payment nor will execution be stayed because of a counterclaim.

> *Example 1.* The plaintiff undertook repair work on the defendants' ship and agreed the repairs would be completed by a certain date. The defendants paid for part of the price of the work by way of a bill of exchange accepted by them before the work was completed. Completion of the repairs was delayed and the defendants were unable to use the vessel on a profitable voyage. They therefore refused to honour the bill of exchange. The plaintiff sued under the Bills of Exchange Act and sought judgment under Order 14. The defendant claimed that execution of any judgment should be stayed pending the trial of their counterclaim for damages for delay in carrying out the repairs. The Court of Appeal upheld an order for immediate judgment without a stay of execution. Roxburgh LJ said that although generally a counterclaim arising out of the same transaction is a good defence to a summons under Order 14, in cases under the Bills of Exchange Act 'a rule more favourable to the plaintiff has in general prevailed; the court treating the execution of a bill of exchange either as analogous to a payment of cash, or as amounting to an independent contract within the wider contract in pursuance of which it was executed and not dependent as regards its enforcement on due performance of the latter' (*James Lamont & Co Ltd v Hyland Ltd*[17]).
>
> *Example 2.* An Italian company entered into a sole distribution agreement with an English company. The Italians sold goods to the English company on the basis of payment by bills of exchange. A dispute arose which led the Italians to terminate the contract and set up another distribution company in England. The English company gave instructions that five bills of exchange then outstanding should be dishonoured. In Order 14 proceedings brought by the Italian company the English company sought to set up a counterclaim for damages for breach of the

16 See p 133, ante. It must be remembered that it is important to plead a set-off wherever this is possible because of the effect this has on the order for costs. If the matter proceeds to trial and both parties are held entitled to succeed the order will be:
Judgment on claim and counterclaim:
    Order: Judgment for P for £15,000 and costs.
               Judgment for D for £15,000 on counterclaim and costs of counterclaim.
    Note: Costs on the claim may be £5000 but will usually be much lower on the counterclaim: say £1500. The net result is that although the defendant owes the plaintiff nothing he may have to pay him £3500 costs. He may be able to persuade the judge to make no order for costs but he certainly will not recover his costs.
Judgment where counterclaim can be set-off
    Order: P's claim dismissed with costs.
    Note: Because the counterclaim was now a defence to the claim, P failed to recover any sum and D became entitled to £5000 as his costs.
17 [1950] 1 KB 585, [1950] 1 All ER 341, CA.

sole distribution agreement. The Court of Appeal held that there should be immediate judgment for the Italian company with no stay of execution. Per Sir Eric Sachs: 'the bona fide holder for value of a bill of exchange is entitled, save in truly exceptional circumstances, on its maturity to have it treated as cash, so that in an action upon it the Court will refuse to regard either as a defence or as grounds for a stay of execution any set off, legal or equitable, or any counterclaim, whether arising on the particular transaction upon which its bill of exchange came into existence, or, a fortiori, arising in any other way. This rule of practice is thus, in effect, pay up on the bill of exchange first and pursue claims later. . . . In my judgment, the Courts should be careful not to whittle away the rule of practice by introducing unnecessary exceptions to it under the influence of sympathy-evoking stories, and should have due regard to the maxim that hard cases can make bad law. Indeed, in these days of increasing international interdependence and increasing need to foster liquidity of resources, the rule may be said to be of special importance to the business community. Pleas to leave in Court large sums to deteriorate in value while official referee scale proceedings are fought out may well to that community seem rather divorced from business realities, and should perhaps be examined with considerable caution' (*Cebora SNC v SIP (Industrial Products) Ltd*[18]).

Example 3. D buys a motor car from P and pays him by a cheque for £8700. Whilst D is driving home he notices serious defects in the vehicle and telephones his bank to stop the cheque. If he immediately notifies the seller that he is rejecting the vehicle he *may* obtain leave to defend a claim by the seller for dishonour on the basis that the cheque was given for a consideration which has wholly failed. He is not, however, entitled to leave to defend an action on the cheque if he decides to keep the car and counterclaim for the cost of repairs.[19]

The Court of Appeal have consistently held that, apart from quite exceptional cases where for instance the bill of exchange is alleged to be fraudulent or given for a consideration which has wholly failed, the court will not entertain a defence or stay judgment in an action for its dishonour. Per Lord Denning MR in *Fielding and Platt Ltd v Najjar*:[20]

'We have repeatedly said in this court that a bill of exchange or a promissory note is to be treated as cash. It is to be honoured unless there is some good reason to the contrary.'

A 'good reason' for this purpose will only exist if there is an arguable case that delivery of the bill of exchange *itself* was induced by fraud or misrepresentation[21] or the transaction for which the bill was given is tainted with illegality or there has been a total failure of consideration.[22] Further, even if the case falls within the above exceptional categories, an arguable defence will arise only *as between the immediate parties to the cheque or bill of exchange*. It is

18 [1976] 1 Lloyd's Rep 271, at 279.
19 See on this point *Goode, Commercial Law* p 475 et seq.
20 [1969] 2 All ER 150, at 152.
21 *Clovertogs v Jean Scenes Ltd* [1982] Com LR 88 (where cheques were handed over on the strength of a misrepresentation that certain goods had been inspected in Korea). But see also *Famous Ltd v Ge Im Ex Italia SRL* (1987) Times, 3 August, CA, where May, LJ, who was also a member of the Court of Appeal in the *Clovertogs* case, said: 'Although I was a party to [the *Clovertogs*] decision, I have no recollection of it . . . Suffice it to say that on its face I find it a surprising decision, save to the extent that it was decided upon its own facts . . .'
22 Or a partial failure when the damages are liquidated: see *Nova (Jersey) Knit Ltd v Kammgarn Spinnerei GmbH* [1977] 2 All ER 463, [1977] 1 WLR, 713, HL. Per Lord Wilberforce at 469: 'I take it to be clear law that unliquidated cross-claims cannot be relied on by way of extinguishing set-off against a claim on a bill of exchange. As between immediate parties, a partial failure of consideration may be relied on as a pro tanto defence, but only when the amount involved is ascertained and liquidated.'.

in the nature of bills of exchange that, being negotiable and treated by the courts as cash, they frequently are sold for cash or *discounted* through banks. A *holder in due course* of bills can not be held answerable for the fraud of the drawer or the failure of the consideration for which the bill was given, so on an action by such a holder for dishonour the defendant may not rely on the above exceptional grounds as justifying leave to defend or a stay of execution.[23]

(f) Leave to defend although no clear defence shown

Order 14, rule 3(1) provides that leave to defend shall be given either if the defendant shows a triable issue of the claim or if he satisfies the court '*that there ought for some other reason to be a trial of that claim*'. This clearly means that there will be circumstances in which summary judgment will be refused notwithstanding that there appears to be no defence. Although this is obviously a residual power intended to prevent injustice and may in the future be employed in diverse circumstances, it would seem that it is primarily aimed at the case where the facts upon which the plaintiff relies are not within the knowledge of the defendant so that fairness requires that he should be able to test the plaintiff's case by discovery and cross-examination.

> *Example*. H sold a farmhouse to P which was occupied by H's wife W. P sued W for possession. Three days after the sale W's solicitors registered a class F land charge which was ineffective to protect her rights of occupation against purchasers prior to registration. P applied under Order 14 for possession on the basis that until registration occurred the wife had no rights against a purchaser for value unless the sale was a pure sham. Megarry J rejected W's contention that the sale was a sham but although she could show no other arguable defence refused summary judgment (*Miles v Bull*[24]).

The learned judge explained his decision as follows:

> 'the defendant can obtain leave to defend if . . . the defendant satisfies the court "that there is an issue or question to dispute which ought to be tried or that there ought for some other reason to be a trial". These last words seem to me to be very wide. They also seem to me to have special significance where (as here) most of all the relevant facts are under the control of the plaintiff and the defendant would have to seek to elicit by discovery, interrogatories and cross-examination those which will aid her. If the defendant cannot point to a specific issue which ought to be tried, but nevertheless satisfies the court that there are circumstances that ought to be investigated, then I think those concluding words are invoked. There are cases when the plaintiff ought to be put to strict proof of his claim, and exposed to the full investigation possible at a trial; and in such cases it would, in my judgment, be wrong to enter summary judgment for the plaintiff.'

Other circumstances which might afford 'some other reason for trial' would be where the defendant was unable to get in touch with an important

---

23 See *Jade International Steel Stahl und Eisen GmbH & Co KG v Robert Nicholas (Steels) Ltd* [1978] QB 917 [1978] 3 All ER 104, CA, where the Court of Appeal upheld summary judgment in favour of a holder in due course. In that case P sold a quantity of steel to D who as payment accepted a bill of exchange drawn by P. P endorsed the bill over to their bankers. D complained at the quality of the steel and ordered the bill to be dishonoured. P's bank eventually indorsed the bill back to P. D was refused leave to defend because P (although originally one of the contracting parties) was now suing as *holder* so D was not entitled to raise a set-off to defeat the Ord 14 application.

24 [1969] 1 QB 258, [1968] 3 All ER 632.

witness who might be able to provide him with material for a defence; or, if
the claim was of a highly technical or complicated nature which could only
be understood if oral evidence was given; or if the plaintiff's case showed he
had acted harshly or unconscionably so that if he was to get judgment at all
it should be in the full light of publicity.[25]

(g) Conditional leave to defend

It has already been stated that it is sufficient for a defendant to show 'a
triable issue' to be granted leave to defend. In the early cases it appeared
that the master was not to enter into any sort of detailed examination of the
merits. Thus in *Jacobs v Booth's Distillery Co*,[26] Lord James of Hereford said:

> 'The view which I think ought to be taken of Order XIV is that the tribunal to
> which the application is made should simply determine "Is there a triable issue to
> go before a jury or a court?" It is not for that tribunal to enter into the merits of the
> case at all.'

Despite this dicta it is now the established practice that the master looks
beyond the mere assertion of facts entitling leave to defend and considers
the merits to the extent that if the defence seems improbable the defendant
will only be permitted to defend on, for example, payment into court of part
or the whole of the amount claimed. This practice was expressly approved
by Devlin J in *Fieldrank Ltd v Stein*[27] where he says at 682:

> 'The broad principle, which is founded on *Jacobs v Booth's Distillery Co* is summa-
> rised on p 266 of the *Annual Practice* (1962 edn) in the following terms: "The
> principle on which the court acts is that where the defendant can show by
> affidavit that there is a bona fide triable issue, he is to be allowed to defend as to
> that issue without condition." If that principle were mandatory, then the con-
> cession by counsel for the plaintiffs that there is here a triable issue would mean at
> once that the appeal ought to be allowed; but counsel for the plaintiffs has drawn
> our attention to some comments that have been made on *Jacobs v Booth's Distillery
> Co* in the [*Annual Practice*]. It is suggested [there] that possibly the case, if it is
> closely examined, does not go as far as it has hitherto been thought to go; and . . .
> the learned editors of the *Annual Practice* have [noted]:
>> "The condition of payment into court, or giving security, is nowadays more
>> often imposed than formerly, and not only where the defendant consents but
>> also where there is a good ground in the evidence for believing that the defence
>> set up a sham defence and the master 'is prepared very nearly to give judgment
>> for the plaintiff'."
> . . . I should be very glad to see some relaxation of the strict rule in *Jacobs v Booth's
> Distillery Co*. I think that any judge who has sat in chambers in RSC Order 14
> summonses has had the experience of a case in which, although he cannot say for
> certain that there is not a triable issue, nevertheless he is left with a real doubt
> about the defendant's good faith, and would like to protect the plaintiff, especially
> if there is not grave hardship on the defendant in being made to pay money into
> court. I should be prepared to accept that there has been a tendency in the last
> few years to use this condition more often than it has been used in the past, and I
> think that that is a good tendency.'

The general form of order in such a case is that the defendant is to bring
into court within a specified time a sum representing the whole or part of the

25 See: *Bank für Gemeinwirtschaft v City of London Garages Ltd* [1971] 1 All ER 541, [1971] 1 WLR
   149, CA per Cairns LJ.
26 (1901) 85 LT 262, HL.
27 [1961] 3 All ER 681n.

claim as security to abide the event and in default the plaintiff is to have leave to sign final judgment for such sum. It is important to note that the plaintiff is secured by such an order against the eventual bankruptcy of the defendant (see *Re Ford, ex p Trustee*).[28]

A problem arises when the defendant contends that because of lack of funds he cannot comply with an order requiring payment into court as a condition of his obtaining leave to defend.

> *Example:* P purchased a Rolls Royce car from D for £21,500. It turned out that the car had been stolen and P sued D to recover the purchase price as damages for breach of warranty of title. P issued a summons under Order 14 and D sought leave to defend on the grounds that he was a mere agent and not a party to the contract of sale. He was granted leave to defend on condition that he brought into court the sum of £12,000 within 28 days. He appealed against the order on the grounds that he was unemployed, was living on supplementary benefit and had no assets. There was however evidence that he had been engaged in buying and selling cars on a cash basis (*M V Yorke Motors v Edwards*[29]).

In the House of Lords, Lord Diplock set out the basic principle as follows at 1027:

> 'If the sum ordered to be paid as a condition of granting leave to defend is one which the defendant would never be able to pay, then that would be a wrongful exercise of discretion, because it would be tantamount to giving judgment for the plaintiff notwithstanding the court's opinion that there was an issue or question in dispute which ought to be tried'.

His lordship approved the following submissions as to the proper approach in such cases:

> '(i)   Where a defendant seeks to avoid or limit a financial condition by reason of his own impecuniosity the onus is upon the defendant to put sufficient and proper evidence before the court. He should make full and frank disclosure.
>
> (ii) It is not sufficient for a legally aided defendant to rely on there being a legal aid certificate. A legally aided defendant with a nil contribution may be able to pay or raise substantial sums.[30]
>
> (iii) A defendant cannot complain because a financial condition is difficult for him to fulfil. He can complain only when a financial condition is imposed which it is impossible for him to fulfil and that impossibility was known or should have been known to the court by reason of the evidence placed before it.'

It may be convenient to summarise at this stage the various orders above discussed:

---

28 [1900] 2 QB 211.
29 [1982] 1 All ER 1024, [1982] 1 WLR 444, HL.
30 Per Brandon LJ in the Court of Appeal at 1028 'The fact that the man has no capital of his own does not mean that he cannot raise any capital; he may have friends, he may have business associates, he may have relatives, all of whom can help him in his hour of need.'

(*a*) If D shows case not under Order 14, or clear triable issue or set-off known to P	summons dismissed with costs
(*b*) If D shows technical defect	adjournment and leave to amend or file fresh evidence but P to pay D costs thrown away *or* summons dismissed with costs
(*c*) If D shows triable issue or set-off which P would not necessarily anticipate	unconditional leave to defend and costs in cause
(*d*) If D shows triable issue or set-off but his defence arouses suspicion	leave to defend on payment into court of whole or part of claim in *x* days to abide event with costs in cause; in default, final judgment and costs
(*e*) If D shows circumstances which although not a defence warrant putting the plaintiff's case to the test of discovery, inter-rogatories and cross-examination	unconditional leave to defend, costs in cause
(*f*) If D shows a valid counterclaim (which does not arise out of the claim and so is not also a set-off)	judgment for P with costs, execution stayed until trial of counterclaim *unless* claim is for dishonoured cheque or bill of exchange
(*g*) If D shows no triable issue, set-off or counter-claim	judgment for P with costs

Notes: (1) As this is a chambers summons counsel must obtain a direction that the case is 'fit for counsel' before his fees will be allowed on taxation.
(2) If the case is one where there is no defence as to liability but the plaintiff is claiming unliquidated damages[31] the order is for final judgment on liability with damages to be assessed under Order 37.

Summary judgment in fraud cases

Until 1992 an application under Order 14 could not be made where the action *included* a claim based on an allegation of fraud. This restriction has now been removed. Nevertheless where the plaintiff's claim necessarily

31 *Associated Bulk Carriers v Koch Shipping Inc, The Fuohsan Maru* [1978] 2 All ER 254, CA. Note the plaintiff can apply for an interim payment pending the assessment (see p 167, post).

involves an allegation of fraud it seems likely that the court will require the clearest evidence if it is to give judgment without permitting the defendant to give oral evidence. One type of case where such judgment would be appropriate would be where the defendant has been convicted in criminal proceedings; in such a case the plaintiff will plead the conviction in the statement of claim and the burden of proving that it was incorrect will rest on the defendant: see Civil Evidence Act 1968, section 11 (discussed at p 129, ante).

DIRECTIONS AS TO FURTHER CONDUCT OF PROCEEDINGS

If leave is granted to defend the master must proceed to give directions as to the future conduct of the action.[32] Normally he will fix a time scale for service of defence, reply and discovery. It should be noted that the normal time limit for service of defence is automatically suspended if the plaintiff serves a summons under Order 14. If the master gives no specific direction, the defence must be served 14 days after the making of the order.[33]

TRANSFER TO COUNTY COURT

It frequently happens that, having given leave to defend, the master directs that the case be transferred to the appropriate county court for trial. If the master does not give a direction for transfer immediately, he *must* order that a statement of the value of the action be lodged and a copy served on every other party; unless such statement is lodged within the time allowed, the action is automatically transferred to a county court (Ord 14, r 6(3)). The idea behind this rule is that the court should be able to determine whether the action is suitable for trial in the High Court under the criteria set out in Article 7(5) of the Jurisdiction Order 1991 (see p 47, ante).

INJUNCTIONS

An application for a final injunction (as opposed to an interlocutory injunction) may be made under Order 14 by a summons to the defendant to appear before a judge in chambers (instead of the master).

> *Example.* Shell-Mex granted the defendants a licence to operate for one year a filling station on a forecourt owned by Shell. At the expiry of the licence the defendants refused to leave. Lord Denning MR in the Court of Appeal referred to a note in the 1970 *Practice* to the effect that a claim for an injunction was by its nature not appropriate for Order 14 proceedings since the master had no power to grant an injunction except by consent. He said: 'It is true that a master has no power to grant an injunction, but the judge has ample power. I see no reason whatever why a plaintiff cannot go straight to the judge and ask for summary judgment under RSC Order 14 for an injunction'. (*Shell-Mex and BP Ltd v Manchester Garages Ltd*[34].)

---

32 RSC Ord 14, r 6. Note that if instead of giving leave to defend the master dismisses the summons he may not give directions as to the further conduct of the action leaving the plaintiff to issue a separate summons for directions.
33 RSC Ord 18, r 2(2).
34 [1971] 1 All ER 841, at 843.

CHANCERY PRACTICE

In addition to the general power under Order 14 (which applies to actions commenced by writ in the Chancery Division in the same way as it does to proceedings in the Queen's Bench Division), Order 86 empowers the Chancery Division to give summary judgment where an action is commenced by writ indorsed with a claim for specific performance or rescission of an agreement, whether in writing or not, for the sale, purchase or exchange of property or for the grant of assignment of a lease. The Order also includes a claim for the forfeiture or return of any deposit under such an agreement. The rule is similar to Order 14 procedure in that judgment is granted on the basis of affidavit evidence verifying the claim and alleging that there is no defence to the action. It differs from Order 14 procedure in that:

(a) no statement of claim need be served
(b) acknowledgement of service need not have been filed
(c) the summons is returnable in 4 clear days from service.

It should be noted that the plaintiff must attach to his summons full minutes of the order to which he claims to be entitled.

APPEALS IN ORDER 14 PROCEEDINGS

Either party may appeal to the judge in chambers from any order made by a master (or district judge in actions proceeding in a district registry) on a summons under Order 14.[35] The notice of appeal must be issued out of the Action Department of the Central Office within 5 days of the order[36] and served on the respondent 2 clear days[37] before the return date. The appeal involves a complete *rehearing* of the summons; either party may put in new evidence (subject to the other side's right to an adjournment if taken by surprise). If the judge grants unconditional leave to defend, the plaintiff can appeal against this decision to the Court of Appeal if, but only if, he obtains leave to appeal either from the judge or from the Court of Appeal.[38] The reason for this restriction is that in the ordinary case, if the judge thinks there is a triable issue, the parties should get on with their action rather than spend further time debating that issue; it is therefore only in exceptional cases that the plaintiff is likely to obtain leave to appeal. On the other hand, if the judge *refuses* unconditional leave to defend, ie he gives judgment for the plaintiff or imposes conditions on the defendant's right to defend (or upholds orders to this effect by the master), the defendant can appeal of right to the Court of Appeal.[39]

SUMMARY JUDGMENT IN THE COUNTY COURT

Order 9, r 14 of the County Court Rules provides that in default actions where the claim exceeds the automatic arbitration limit of £1000[40] and

35 RSC Ord 58, r 1(1). See p 337, post, where the form of notice of appeal is set out.
36 Ibid, r 1(3). 7 days if the appeal is from the decision of a district judge (Ord 58, r 3). If the appeal is to be heard by a judge in the provinces the notice is issued out of the district registry of the trial centre where the judge will hear the appeal.
37 3 if a district registry case.
38 Supreme Court Act 1981, s 18(1)(h).
39 Ibid, s 18(2)(a). It would appear the plaintiff if dissatisfied by an order giving the defendant conditional leave to defend can also appeal of right to the Court of Appeal; see *Gordon v Cradock* [1964] 1 QB 503, [1963] 2 All ER 121, CA.
40 CCR Ord 9, r 14(1A).

where the defendant has delivered a defence (so there can be no judgment signed in default):

> the plaintiff may apply to the court for judgment against the defendant on the ground that, notwithstanding the delivery of that document, the defendant has no defence to the claim or to a particular part of the claim.

The application is made by the plaintiff issuing a notice in the following form:

[title of action]

I wish to apply for judgment against the defendant for the sum of £1800 claimed in the Particulars of Claim and interest at 15% from 1st December 1991 on the grounds that the defendant has no defence to the claim

Signed:

Address for Service: Dated:

(This section to be completed by the Court)

To the Plaintiff/Defendant

Take notice that this application will be heard by the district judge at The Law Courts, Apple Market, Kingston-upon-Thames on Wednesday 5th August 1992 at 10.30 o'clock.

If you do not attend the court will make such order as it thinks fit.

If a date has been fixed for the pre-trial review, the application will be heard on that day. The application must be supported by an affidavit verifying the plaintiff's claim and deposing to his belief that there is no defence. Since a form of defence will have been filed, the affidavit should set out shortly why it is contended that the statements set out in that document do not constitute a defence or why it is claimed they are incorrect. The affidavit should exhibit any documents relied upon as demonstrating that the defence is not true. The notice of application and affidavit in support must be served not less than 7 days before the day fixed for the hearing of the application.[41] The district judge in determining the application applies the same principles as would be applied in the High Court upon an application under RSC Ord 14 (and so can give conditional leave to defend).

SQUATTERS

Special problems arise in utilising the ordinary procedure for recovery of land where the identity of the persons in occupation are not known to the owner. To meet this difficulty and to provide a speedy alternative to Order 14 where it is beyond doubt the occupants have no existing licence to occupy the land special procedures have been created by RSC Ord 113 and CCR Ord 24.[42] The rules in the county court (which apply where the rateable value of the premises does not exceed £1000) are to all intents and purposes identical to the provisions of the corresponding rules in the High

41 CCR Ord 9, r 14(3).
42 The procedure should be adopted in cases where it can be shown that there is no real defence to a claim for possession: *Filemart Ltd v Avery* [1989] 2 EGLR 177, CA.

Court. Since most such actions are commenced in the county court we shall describe the procedure under Order 24 here. The stages in the action are:

(*a*) The applicant issues an *originating application* seeking recovery of possession on the grounds that he is entitled to possession and that the persons in occupation of the premises are not tenants or tenants holding over after the termination of a tenancy and have entered or remained in occupation without licence or consent.

(*b*) He files an affidavit in support stating (i) his interest in the land (ii) the circumstances in which the land has been occupied without licence or consent and in which his claim to possession arises and (iii) if it be the case, that he is unaware of the identity of some of the occupants.

(*c*) Notice of the date of hearing, a copy of the application and the affidavit are served on the persons named by (i) personal delivery or (ii) by an officer of the court leaving the documents at or posting them to the premises or (iii) by serving a solicitor instructed to accept service by the respondent or (iv) in such other manner as the court may direct.

(*d*) If there are persons in occupation who are not identified a copy of the originating application and of the affidavit in support and unless the court directs otherwise a notice telling them of the date of hearing and of their rights to be made parties to the application are inserted through the letter box in a sealed envelope addressed to 'the occupiers'. Further copies are affixed to the main door or to stakes placed in the ground or other conspicuous part of the premises.

The hearing of the application must be not less than 5 clear days after the date of service. At the hearing, if the applicant proves his title as absolute owner of the land (usually by production of a land certificate which will be conclusive proof of his title) and his intention to regain possession, the onus then falls on the respondent to prove either a tenancy or a licence which has not been determined (see *Portland Management Ltd v Harte*[43]). If the defendant succeeds in establishing an arguable defence the judge will normally give directions for pleadings and discovery as if the application had begun as a normal action. We set out below the forms which would be used in a typical case where the identity of some of the occupants was not known.

In the Westminster County Court   No 91.263

In the Matter of Premises known
as 501A Greek Street, London W1.

       Between:

              Charles Henry Dickens   Applicant
                   and
              Susie Wong (Spinster)   Respondent

The applicant Charles Henry Dickens of 36 Doughty Street, London WC1, hereby applies to the Court for an Order for recovery of possession of all the premises known as and situated at 501A Greek Street, London W1 on the ground that he is entitled to possession and that the persons in occupation of the premises

---

43 [1977] QB 306, [1976] 1 All ER 225, CA.

not being tenants or tenants holding over after the termination of a tenancy are in occupation without licence or consent. The person in occupation who is intended to be served personally with this application is Miss Susie Wong. There are other persons in occupation whose names are not known to the applicant.

Dated the   *Dodson and Fogg*
1st day of July 1991   Solicitors for the Applicant
                                            Address for service

---

In the Westminster County Court   No 91.263

In the Matter of Premises known
as 501A Greek Street, London W1

         Between:

                     Charles Henry Dickens   <u>Applicant</u>
                             and
                     Susie Wong (Spinster)   <u>Respondent</u>

I, Charles Henry Dickens, of 36 Doughty Street, London WC1, journalist, make oath and say as follows:

(1) I am the freehold owner of the premises situated at and known as 501A Greek Street, London W1 which is a first floor flat formerly occupied by me as my residence. There is now produced and shown to me marked 'CHD 1' a copy of the entry in HM Land Registry under title No LN 526357 showing my title to the said premises.

(2) In May 1990 I left the premises for an extensive stay in Italy. When I returned to this country on the 6th day of June 1991 I went immediately to the said premises to find that the locks on the outer door had been changed. It appeared that the premises were inhabited and I saw a notice on the bell push 'Miss Susie Wong – professional model'. I immediately contacted the police and when I returned with a uniformed constable a man of about 30 years of age opened the door and said 'I am the tenant here – clear off'. He said he paid his rent to a Mr. William Sikes. He refused to give his name. I have returned on a number of occasions to the premises but on each such occasion have seen the said man who has refused to disclose his identity.

(3) The persons now in occupation are there without my licence or consent and I respectfully apply to this Honourable Court for an order pursuant to Order 24 of the County Court Rules 1981 for an order requiring them to deliver up possession of the said premises forthwith.

Sworn at 26 Cheapside, London EC2   } *Charles Dickens*
this 23rd day of July 1991
Before me,
Marmaduke Smiles
      Marmaduke Smiles LLB
      A Commissioner of Oaths

INTERIM PAYMENTS

An order for interim payment (i e payment on account of damages likely to be awarded on final judgment) may be made in the High Court or county court[44]

---

44 CCR Ord 13, r 12. Note the damages or sum claimed in the action must exceed £1000 (r 12(1)). The notice of application and affidavit in support must be served not less than 7 days before the hearing of the application. The High Court rules are applied to the procedure and govern the principles applied.

wherever it appears virtually certain that the plaintiff will succeed at the trial.

> *Example.* P is a passenger in a motor car which, whilst being driven by D, collides with a tree. P receives such serious injuries that, although his solicitors have issued a writ, they are reluctant to settle the claim until the true extent of his permanent disability is revealed. His doctors say that a final prognosis cannot be given for at least a year. In this case P's solicitors can apply for an interim payment on account of the damages he is eventually bound to recover.

The power of the High Court to award an interim payment is derived from section 32(5) of the Supreme Court Act 1981 and is set out in Ord 29 rr 9–17. The basic procedure is as follows:

(1) After the time for acknowledgment of service has expired the plaintiff issues a summons applying for an interim order. This summons must be served 10 clear days before the return date.

(2) The plaintiff serves at the same time an affidavit which (*a*) verifies in detail the special damage (eg loss of wages) to date (*b*) exhibits any relevant documents (such as medical reports) and (*c*) if the claim arises under the Fatal Accidents Act sets out the statutory particulars of dependency.

(3) At the hearing of the summons the master may make an interim award provided (*a*) the defendant admits liability or (*b*) the plaintiff has obtained judgment for damages to be assessed or (*c*) if it is clear that the plaintiff would obtain judgment for substantial damages if the action proceeded to trial. The award must not exceed a reasonable proportion of the damages which in the opinion of the court are likely to be recovered by the plaintiff after taking into account any reduction for contributory negligence or for a set off or counterclaim.[45] In personal injury cases interim payments can be ordered only where the defendant is (*a*) insured in respect of the claim or (*b*) a public authority or (*c*) a person whose means and resources are such as to enable him to make an interim payment.[46] In such cases the interim award, if made, will cover special damage incurred to the date of the application and a sum to pay for necessary future medical expenses and the cost of convalescence.[47]

Although interim awards were originally introduced to deal with

---

45 RSC Ord 29, r 11. In *Shanning International Ltd v George Wimpey International Ltd* [1988] 3 All ER 475, CA, the Court of Appeal held that the court must approach the making of an interim payment order in two stages. Per Glidewell LJ (at p 482): 'I agree with the judge that it was correct for him to consider the matter arising on the application for an interim payment in two stages. The first stage was to answer the question, was he satisfied that, if the action proceeded to trial, the plaintiff would obtain judgment for a substantial sum? . . . In my judgment, on the wording of the rule it is inescapable that, at stage 1, the likelihood of a set-off or other defence succeeding must be considered by the court. If, but only if, the court is satisfied at stage 1, then it proceeds to consider at stage 2 whether, in its discretion, it should order an interim payment and, if so, of what amount. At that stage the rules again require the court to take any set-off claimed by the defendant into account or any counterclaim arising out of some other transaction and not available as a defence, and, in an application under r 11, any alleged contributory negligence.'

46 RSC Ord 29, r 11(2).

47 In awarding interim payments against general damages in personal injury cases there is a tendency for the courts to require the plaintiff to establish some need for the money. In other cases, there is no such requirement: see *Schott Kem Ltd v Bentley* [1991] 1 QB 61, [1990] 3 All ER 850, CA.

the problem of accident victims who might have to wait substantial periods before the final resolution of their claim, the power to make such awards has been extended to *all* actions claiming 'damages, debt or other sum'. Thus, for example, an application for an interim award can be made in commercial actions where it is clear that a substantial sum is due but the quantum has to be assessed. In a claim for possession of land, an interim award may be made in respect of the defendant's use and occupation of the land.[48]

(4) At the eventual trial the court (which must not be told of the interim award until it has ruled on liability and quantum) may make appropriate orders adjusting payment between defendants and even ordering repayment by the plaintiff in the rare case where the interim award was too high.[49]

It was stated above that the plaintiff does not need to obtain judgment against a defendant or an admission of liability from him in order to apply for an interim payment. RSC Ord 29, r 11(1)(c) provides that an interim payment can be ordered where the court is satisfied:

'that, if the action proceeded to trial, the plaintiff would obtain judgment for substantial damages against the respondent or, where there are two or more defendants, against any of them.'

The language adopted in this rule raises the question whether, in an action against two or more defendants, it is sufficient for the plaintiff merely to show that he is likely to succeed ultimately against *one or other* of them to justify an interim payment order against any defendant of the plaintiff's choice. The problem is particularly significant where the plaintiff claims against multiple defendants in the *alternative*.

Example. Following a burglary at their shop premises, RB Ltd made an insurance claim for over £74,000. The underwriters refused to accept liability, saying that no valid policy had been effected because the insurance brokers had exceeded their authority by failing to include in the policy standard terms, such as the installation of an alarm system. RB Ltd therefore commenced proceedings against the underwriters for payment under the policy and in the alternative against the brokers for their failure to procure a valid policy. The master refused an application for summary judgment under RSC Order 14 but the brokers were ordered to make an interim payment of £50,000 to RB Ltd. The Court of Appeal held that the order should not have been made as RB Ltd had not proved the likelihood of success against any particular defendant to the necessary standard (*Ricci Burns Ltd v Toole*[50]). Per Ralph Gibson LJ:

'. . . where the application is made against more than one defendant the terms of r 11(1)(c), "where there are two or more defendants, against any [one] of them", do not on their true construction permit an order to be made against one or other of two defendants on the ground that the court is satisfied that the plaintiff will succeed against one or other of them. Proof of success to the necessary standard against any defendant is required before an order can be made against him.'[51]

---

48 RSC Ord 29, r 12(b).
49 RSC Ord 29, r 17. Where a repayment is ordered under r 17, the court has power to order the plaintiff to repay the sum with interest: *Mercers Co v New Hampshire Insurance Co* [1991] 4 All ER 542, Phillips J.
50 [1989] 3 All ER 478.
51 Ibid, at 485g.

The prospect of success against another defendant was not, however, irrelevant to the question of whether an interim payment should be ordered:

> 'Although an order cannot be made against one defendant merely because the plaintiff shows that he will recover either against that defendant or some other defendant, nevertheless the fact that if the plaintiff should fail against the defendant against whom the order is sought he will succeed against another solvent defendant would, in my view, be a relevant fact to be taken into account in balancing all the facts on the particular application. It would be relevant to the plaintiff's ability to repay in the event of his failing at trial against the defendant ordered to make the payment.'[52]

Interim payments on applications for summary judgment

As illustrated by the *Ricci Burns* case above, a plaintiff often combines an application for summary judgment under RSC Ord 14 with a request for an interim payment. If interlocutory judgment is obtained under Order 14, with damages to be assessed, the master can proceed to order the defendant to make an interim payment on the ground that judgment has been obtained against him. But where the plaintiff does not obtain summary judgment, because the defendant raises a triable defence, the master can nevertheless order the defendant to make an interim payment on the ground that the plaintiff would obtain substantial damages against him. The Court of Appeal in *Ricci Burns* considered that there was no inconsistency in a master finding that there was a triable defence justifying an order for unconditional leave to defend under Order 14 but nonetheless making an order for an interim payment. However, in *British and Commonwealth Holdings plc v Quadrex Holdings Inc*[53] a differently constituted Court of Appeal disagreed, holding that an interim payment could be ordered only where the master had sufficient doubts about the genuineness of the defence as to give *conditional* leave to defend. Per Browne-Wilkinson V-C:[54]

> 'For myself, I find it an impossible concept that the same court can be simultaneously "satisfied" that the plaintiff *will* succeed at trial and at the same time consider that the defendant has an arguable defence sufficient to warrant unconditional leave to defend. If there is a distinction between the two concepts which I have failed to detect, such distinction must in my judgment be the result of "an uncommon nicety of approach" which the requirements of certainty in the law would make it undesirable to recognise. In my judgment, therefore, it is impossible to make an order for interim payment where unconditional leave to defend has been given.'

The position therefore seems to be that where applications are made for summary judgment and an interim payment the court may well grant conditional leave and order an interim payment but only in the most exceptional case (if at all) would it be right to grant unconditional leave to defend and at the same time make an order for an interim payment.

SECURITY FOR COSTS

We have seen above how a plaintiff who considers there is no credible defence to the action is able to issue a summons under Order 14 which may

52 Ibid, at 486b.
53 [1989] QB 842, [1989] 3 All ER 492, CA.
54 Ibid, at 511a.

either result in his obtaining judgment or at least obtaining an order for a sum to be paid into court. We have now to consider the position where the defendant feels that he has a strong case but is concerned that if the action proceeds to trial and he then wins the plaintiff will not be able to pay the costs awarded against him. The basic rule is that there is nothing the defendant can do in these circumstances: the impecuniosity of the plaintiff is *not* in itself sufficient grounds for an order that he gives security for costs.[55] However in the following circumstances the court *may* on application by the defendant order security:[56]

(1) Where the plaintiff is ordinarily resident outside the United Kingdom[57] and has no substantial property in this country.
(2) Where the plaintiff is a limited company and 'it appears by credible testimony that there is reason to believe that the company will be unable to pay the costs of the defendant if successful in his defence'.[58]

Even though the above conditions are satisfied it does not automatically follow that security will be ordered. In the leading case *Sir Lindsay Parkinson & Co Ltd v Triplan Ltd*[59] the Court of Appeal held that in exercising its discretion the court should take into account the following matters:

(1) Whether the plaintiff's claim is bona fide.
(2) Whether he had a reasonably good prospect of success.
(3) Whether there is an admission by the defendants on the pleadings or elsewhere that money is due.
(4) Whether there is a substantial payment into court (so that the question becomes whether the plaintiff has reasonable prospects of succeeding in recovering more than the payment-in).
(5) Whether the application for security is being used oppressively, e g so as to stifle a genuine claim.
(6) Whether the plaintiff's want of means has been brought about by any conduct of the defendants.
(7) The stage of the proceedings at which the application is made: it should generally be made as early as possible.

Another relevant factor would be the existence of a co-plaintiff within the jurisdiction who would be able to meet an award of costs.[60]

It should be noted that security for costs may be ordered against a legally aided person in exceptional circumstances.[61]

An application for security for costs is made in the High Court by

---

55 Except on appeal to the Court of Appeal: see p 344, post.
56 Ord 23 also provides for security against a nominal plaintiff or a plaintiff who deliberately mis-states his address on the writ or who has changed his address to evade the consequences of the litigation.
57 RSC Ord 23, r 1(1)(a). However the court will take into account the substantial and improved rights available to a defendant for enforcing an order for costs in a convention territory under the Civil Jurisdiction and Judgments Act 1982: see *Porzelack KG v Porzelack (UK) Ltd* [1987] 1 All ER 1074, Chancery Division; and *De Bry v Fitzgerald* [1990] 1 All ER 560, CA. Further, ease of enforcement against a plaintiff resident in a non-convention territory may be a sufficient ground for denying an order for security for costs: *Thune v London Properties Ltd* [1990] 1 All ER 972, CA.
58 Companies Act 1985, s 726.
59 [1973] QB 609, [1973] 2 All ER 273, CA.
60 See *Slazengers Ltd v Seaspeed Ferries International Ltd* [1987] 3 All ER 967, CA.
61 See *Conway v George Wimpey & Co Ltd* [1951] 1 All ER 56, CA and *Jackson v John Dickinson & Co (Bolton) Ltd* [1952] 1 All ER 104, CA.

summons to the master or district judge with an affidavit in support. The defendant should exhibit to his affidavit in support of the application a draft bill showing the recoverable costs to date and give an estimate of the amount such costs are likely to have reached by the conclusion of the trial.[62] The court has an unrestricted discretion as to the amount of security and will order such amount as the court thinks just in all the circumstances of the case. In so doing, it is relevant to take into account the possibility that the case may be settled, and to make an arbitrary discount of the estimated future costs, based on the court's view of all the circumstances.[63] The form of order is that the action be stayed unless security be given within a specified period. In the county court, the application is on notice to the district judge; the same principles are applied as in the High Court.[64]

---

62 *T Sloyan & Sons (Builders) Ltd v Brothers of Christian Instruction* [1974] 3 All ER 715.
63 *Procon (GB) Ltd v Provincial Building Co Ltd* [1984] 2 All ER 368, CA.
64 See CCR Ord 13, r 8.

Chapter 6

Injunctions

(The beginner is advised to read through the examples appended at the end of this chapter before studying the text.)

An injunction is an order of the court restraining[1] the defendant from continuing in a course of wrongful conduct (eg publishing a libel) or requiring[2] him to take certain measures to abate a wrong which he has created (eg an order to a landlord who has wrongfully evicted his tenant by changing the locks requiring him to give the tenant free access to the premises by delivering up the new keys). In exceptional cases an injunction will be granted to prevent the commission of a threatened wrong although no actual wrong has yet been committed (eg a proposed infringement of copyright): this is known as a *quia timet* injunction. In all cases an applicant must be able show that the conduct complained of is *unlawful*. It is not enough that the defendant's actions are harmful to the person seeking the injunction.

> *Example.* The publishers of the *Daily Mail* sued IM Ltd who were proposing to arrange for advertising leaflets to be placed in the newspapers by retail newsagents. In support of their claim for an interlocutory injunction the plaintiffs said that the defendants' conduct would damage their goodwill and argued that whether or not they had a cause of action an injunction could be granted under the Supreme Court Act 1981, s 37 when it was just and convenient to do so. Hoffmann J *held* that an injunction could not be granted because a claim for an injunction to restrain damage to the plaintiff's property or goodwill had to be based on a cause of action and there was no such cause of action (*Associated Newspapers Group plc v Insert Media Ltd*[3]).

Injunctions were developed by the Court of Chancery as a discretionary remedy to supplement the inadequate relief granted by the common law courts; two important characteristics of the modern law reveal the historical origin of the remedy, namely:

(*a*) that the grant of an injunction is discretionary and being an equitable remedy will be refused if damages would be an adequate remedy, and

(*b*) the enforcement of the court's order is generally by imprisonment or

---

1 Called a *prohibitory* injunction.
2 Called a *mandatory* injunction.
3 [1988] 2 All ER 420. See also *Siskina v Distos Cia Naviera SA* [1979] AC 210, [1977] 3 All ER 803, CA.

fine for contempt, ie the court acts against the person in default rather than his property.

An injunction may be the substantive relief required in an action, ie the *final* order in the case after the trial of the action. Often however, the court will be asked to grant an *interlocutory* injunction to cover the period between the issue of proceedings and the trial of the action. This chapter is primarily concerned with the procedure by which such interlocutory relief can be obtained. It should be noted that in many cases (especially in the Chancery Division) the action terminates with the decision as to interlocutory relief because the parties are content to accept this interim decision as representing the likely result of the trial.

APPLICATIONS IN THE QUEEN'S BENCH DIVISION

An application for an interlocutory injunction in proceedings in the Queen's Bench Division is brought by a summons to the defendant requiring him to attend before a *judge in chambers* and setting out the terms of the order sought. The summons must be served not less than 2 clear days before the date for hearing (ie the 'return day').[4] The plaintiff must prepare an affidavit verifying the matters which he alleges are grounds for granting an injunction. The affidavit may contain hearsay evidence provided the deponent states the source of the information.[5] The affidavit should be served at the same time as the summons; later service may result in the defendant applying for an adjournment to put in his own evidence. The plaintiff's solicitors should also prepare and if possible serve with the summons a draft of the order which the judge will be asked to make. If, as will frequently be the case, the defendant fails to attend at the hearing of the summons, the court will proceed in his absence[6] provided the plaintiff can prove service. For this reason it is a sensible course for the plaintiff's solicitor to have an affidavit of service sworn by the process server and available at the hearing whenever it is not certain that the defendant will attend. If the defendant wishes to dispute the facts alleged in the plaintiff's affidavit he will put an affidavit in reply. However the court at this stage is not primarily concerned with resolving disputes as to the evidence or conflicting issues of fact. At the most it will determine only the limited issues which are relevant in deciding whether to make an interim order. After the hearing in chambers is concluded, the plaintiff's solicitor will draw up the order[7] and the parties will file their affidavits at the Central Office.

APPLICATIONS IN THE CHANCERY DIVISION

By contrast with the privacy of proceedings in the Queen's Bench Division, applications for injunctions in the Chancery Division are heard in open court. The plaintiff issues a *notice of motion* informing the defendant that the

---

4 RSC Ord 32, r 4(2). In calculating '2 clear days' exclude day of service, return day, Saturdays, Sundays and bank holidays: see Ord 3, r 2(4),(5).
5 RSC Ord 41, r 5(2).
6 RSC Ord 32, r 5.
7 See RSC Order 42, r 5. The judge will correct the draft order and then initial it. The plaintiff's solicitor takes the draft and the summons and two copies of the drawn-up order to the court office where the order is checked and one copy is sealed. Note in the case of an injunction it is necessary to set out a penal notice (see p 185, post).

court will be moved by counsel for an interlocutory injunction in the terms specified in the notice. The notice must again be served two clear days before the motion is heard. The affidavits to be used ought to be filed at court before the hearing of the motion (although in practice it frequently happens that the parties because of lack of time are unable to do this and give an undertaking to file).

As stated above the application is heard in open court (unless the court directs otherwise). The procedure which is followed at the Royal Courts of Justice in London may at first sight appear rather bewildering (at least to non-Chancery practitioners) and so it seems worthwhile to explain it here. (It should be noted that this procedure applies not only to applications in the Chancery Division for injunctions but wherever an application for an interlocutory order has to be made to a judge.) All the *motions* are listed to be taken by one of the Chancery Judges and all counsel who have an application have to be in court at 10.30 am. The judge starts by going through the list of motions and asking counsel:–

(i)   whether the motion is 'effective' (contested) or 'ineffective' (ie the parties have agreed terms);
(ii) the estimated length of time of the motion if it is 'effective'.

The judge will hear the 'ineffective' motions first but before he does so he will indicate the order in which he proposes to take the 'effective' motions.

When an effective motion is called on the procedure is as follows:–

(1) The applicant's counsel opens his case.
(2) The affidavit evidence is read over by each counsel in turn in the order in which the affidavits were sworn.
(3) Counsel for the applicant makes his submissions.
(4) Counsel for the respondent replies.
(5) Counsel for the applicant answers the respondent's submissions.

If the hearing of an effective motion is likely to take over two hours (ie because the evidence is complex) the motion will be stood over to be listed on a specific day when there will be time to hear it. This is called a 'motion by order'. Normally this is done on the defendant undertaking to preserve the status quo until the motion can be disposed of. If the defendant is not prepared to give such undertakings, the plaintiff moves the court ex parte for a decision whether an injunction should be granted (or continue) pending the hearing of the contested motion. Although in theory this application is ex parte some judges permit the defendant's counsel (who is of course present) to address them. Note that where a hearing is adjourned it is good practice to prepare and file a paginated bundle containing all the evidence which the judge will be able to see in advance.

APPLICATIONS IN THE COUNTY COURT

The county court has jurisdiction to make any order, including the grant of an injunction, 'which could be made by the High Court if the proceedings were in the High Court'.[8]

---

8 County Courts Act 1984, s 38(1), as amended by the Courts and Legal Services Act 1990, s 3.

The procedure in the county court so far as interlocutory relief is concerned is that the plaintiff must serve on the defendant and file at court, not less than 2 clear days before hearing, a notice that the plaintiff intends to apply for an injunction, together with a draft order and an affidavit setting out the grounds for making the application.[9] If the application has to be made ex parte, the affidavit must also explain the reasons for so doing.[10] If the judge grants the order, he may sign the order as settled or with such alteration as he thinks proper. The application must be in the prescribed form (CC Form N16A) and the order will be drawn up following another prescribed form (N16). The form of application (together with the form used when no injunction is granted because the defendant gives undertakings to the court) are set out at pp 194–195, post.

THE PRINCIPLES UPON WHICH THE COURT ACTS

The problem which the court faces when asked for interlocutory relief is that it must make a decision affecting the rights of the parties without the opportunity of a full investigation of the disputed issues in the action. The traditional approach was for the court to determine two matters:

(*a*) whether the plaintiff could show a prima facie case, (ie that on the affidavit evidence he would be more likely than not to succeed at the trial); and

(*b*) if so, whether he could prove that the damage he would suffer if an injunction was refused would outweigh the nuisance and inconvenience and possible loss of income to the defendant in having his activities temporarily restricted.

If he could prove *both* these points, he would obtain an injunction restraining the defendants until the trial of the action when the rights of the parties would be finally decided. The essential feature of this approach was that the court attempted to predict the eventual outcome of the case. However in *American Cyanamid Co v Ethicon Ltd*,[11] the House of Lords stated that it was *not* necessary for the plaintiff to establish a prima facie case to succeed; it was sufficient that there was a serious issue to be tried. Their lordships held that the court should not embark on any sort of review of the evidence. Thus Lord Diplock at 510 pointed out:

'It is no part of the court's function at this stage of the litigation to try to resolve conflicts of evidence on affidavit as to facts on which the claims of either party may ultimately depend nor to decide difficult questions of law which call for detailed argument or mature considerations. These are matters to be dealt with at the trial.'

In the *American Cyanamid* case the plaintiffs applied for an interim injunction to restrain the defendants from acts allegedly infringing their patent on a special sort of surgical stitch which would dissolve and be absorbed into the body. The Court of Appeal held that the plaintiffs had failed to show a

---

9 CCR Ord 13, rr 1 and 6(3). It is important when applying for an injunction in the County Court to check that all the requirements of CCR Ord 13, r 6 have been complied with. We have set out the text of the rule in the example at p 193, post.
10 Ibid, r 6(3A).
11 [1975] AC 396, [1975] 1 All ER 504.

prima facie case that the patent would be infringed and refused the application. The House of Lords unanimously reversed this decision because, as stated above, they held that the appellants did *not* have to show a prima facie case that they would win the eventual trial of the action in order to be granted relief; they had merely to show that there was a *serious question to be tried* between themselves and the defendant (in the sense that his claim was not frivolous or vexatious). Once this was established the court had then to consider whether the balance of convenience lay in favour of granting or refusing interlocutory relief.

The correct approach appears to be for the court to consider the following questions:

(1) Has the plaintiff shown a serious question to be tried?
(2) If so, has he also shown that, if he is not granted an injunction at this stage, an award of damages at the trial will *not* be adequate compensation? Such an award of damages is not an adequate remedy if the harm suffered by the plaintiff is not financial loss (eg claims for nuisance by noise) or, though financial, is not capable of precise calculation (eg loss of profit in running a business). Damages are also not an adequate remedy where, although the loss is capable of precise calculation, it is unlikely that the defendant would have the means to pay. (If the plaintiff is unable to establish the inadequacy of damages on at least one of the above grounds an injunction will be refused.)
(3) If both conditions are satisfied the court then looks at the defendant's position and asks whether, if he eventually wins, damages will adequately compensate him for any loss he may suffer by reason of the injunction. If so, the injunction should be granted.
(4) If, however, it appears that damages will not compensate him, the court should then compare the likely hardship to the plaintiff and defendant and see where the balance of convenience lies, ie who is likely to suffer the greater hardship. This may first involve considering the *extent* to which the potential loss to each party is incapable of being compensated in damages. If all else is equal the court should generally lean to preserving the status quo but it may at this stage be proper to take into account the relative strength of each party's case. Lord Diplock however emphasised this 'should be done only where it is apparent on the facts disclosed by evidence as to which there is no credible dispute that the strength of one party's case is disproportionate to that of the other party. The court is not justified in embarking on anything resembling a trial of the action on conflicting affidavits in order to evaluate the strength of either party's case.'.

It may be helpful at this stage to consider two cases which show how the guidelines formulated by Lord Diplock in the *American Cyanamid* case are applied.

Example 1. A firm of solicitors in Walthamstow employed a young legal executive under a written contract which provided that after he left their employment he should not be employed 'in the legal profession' in the area for a period of five years. Some time after he had left their employment he obtained work in the area with another firm of solicitors. His former employers issued a writ claiming damages and an injunction and sought an interim injunction restraining him from working in the district until the trial of the action. The Court of Appeal refused an interlocutory injunction. Browne LJ approached the case by saying (1) that the plaintiffs' case showed a serious question to be tried but (2) since they failed to provide any evidence of likely damage, interlocutory relief should be refused. Sir John Pennycuick went further and analysed the defendant's position and pointed out that 'the possible inconvenience to the plaintiffs in that they might lose a few clients appears to be much less than the certain inconvenience to the defendant of being prevented from continuing his present employment in Walthamstow' (*Fellowes & Son v Fisher*[12]).

Example 2. A firm of estate agents in Islington who had acted for property developers in the area were picketed by a group of social workers complaining at the tactics allegedly used by the developers and their agents. The plaintiffs issued a writ for nuisance and conspiracy. They alleged in the statement of claim that 'the said picketing has been carried out in such a manner as substantially to interfere with the plaintiff's enjoyment of the said premises and the conduct of their said business and so as to intimidate or deter persons wishing to transact business with the plaintiffs.' The Court of Appeal approved the granting of an interlocutory injunction. Orr LJ after holding that there was a serious question to be tried went on to say: 'The next question to be asked is whether, if the plaintiffs were to succeed at the trial, they would be adequately compensated for the interim continuance of the defendants' activities. In my judgment, the answer is that they plainly would not because such continuance might well cause very serious damage to their business, and the judge was entitled, on this issue, to have regard to any doubts he might feel as to the defendants' ability to satisfy any award of damages made against them. . . . The next question to be asked is the converse question whether if the defendants were to succeed at the trial they would be adequately compensated for the interim restriction on their activities which the grant of an interlocutory injunction would have imposed. I have no doubt that they would be, since the only restriction imposed by the injunction would be in respect of activities in front of the plaintiffs' premises, leaving the defendants free to conduct their campaign by lawful means elsewhere, . . . It followed the balance of convenience lay in granting the interlocutory relief' (*Hubbard v Pitt*[13]).

The important point to note about the principles in the *American Cyanamid* case is that they provide that the court should *not* normally consider the likely prospects of success in the action in determining whether or not to grant interlocutory relief. The advantage of the decision is that it relieves the court from the burden of considering the evidence and making a provisional assessment. In practice, however, it has been found that a rigid adherence to the *American Cyanamid* approach is capable of working injustice and so a number of authorities have indicated where a different approach should be followed:–

(i)   *No serious question to be tried.* If it is obvious from the beginning that the plaintiff is unlikely to succeed in his claim, the court will not grant him interlocutory relief: this means that care must be taken in drafting the plaintiff's affidavit to see that the evidence if accepted at the trial would entitle him to relief (see *Re Lord Cable, Garratt v Waters*[14]). This approach is, in substance, no more than an application of the first *Cyanamid* question (no interlocutory injunction in the absence of a serious question to be tried).

12 [1975] 2 All ER 829 at 844.
13 [1975] 3 All ER 1 at 20. But see also *Cambridge Nutrition Ltd v BBC* [1990] 3 All ER 523, CA where it was held that the BBC would not be compensated by an eventual award of damages in respect of the permanent loss of its right to transmit a programme on a topic of public interest in the form and at the time of its choice.
14 [1976] 3 All ER 417, [1977] 1 WLR 7.

(ii) *Interlocutory injunction contrary to the public interest.* If to grant an injunction before the trial would be contrary to the public interest, it will be refused. Thus the court will not ordinarily restrain the publication of an alleged libel where the defendant pleads justification (ie that the statement is not defamatory because it is true) (see *Bestobell Paints v Bigg*[15] where the defendant who was aggrieved at the results of painting his house with a particular brand of paint erected a hoarding beside the house advertising that the paint used was provided by the plaintiffs). The same principle may also apply where the cause of action against the defendant is framed as a breach of confidence.[16] But where the defendant is subject to a valid *contractual* obligation not to disclose confidential information, the public interest lies in upholding the plaintiff's contractual rights in preference to freedom of expression.[17]

(iii) *Injunctions against public authorities.* Interlocutory injunctions may be obtained against public authorities, including the Crown,[18] but in assessing the 'balance of convenience' the interests of the public in general may be taken into account.[19] Where the validity of a law is in question, the applicant will usually need to show a very strong prima facie case for an injunction, but it seems that this is not an absolute rule.[20]

(iv) *Facts and law clear.* Where the relevant facts are not contested and the law is clear, the court can and should grant or refuse relief by deciding whether or not the plaintiff will succeed at the trial. This will apply to some cases where the plaintiff is claiming an injunction to enforce a restrictive covenant which is clearly valid (see *Office Overload Ltd v Gunn*[21]). However the former practice of treating all actions to enforce restrictive covenants as an exception to the *American Cyanamid* approach was heavily criticised by the Court of Appeal in *Lawrence David Ltd v Ashton*.[22] Balcombe LJ said:

'. . . both counsel appear to have been of the view that [the *Cyanamid*] approach is not relevant where an interlocutory injunction is sought to

---

15 [1975] FSR 421. The principle that the public interest lies in permitting the publication of an alleged libel (unless clearly untrue) is long established: see for example *Bonnard v Perryman* [1891] 2 Ch 269, CA.
16 *Woodward v Hutchins* [1977] 2 All ER 751, [1977] 1 WLR 760, CA, but there may be a competing public interest, such as that of national security, which justifies that grant of an injunction: see *A-G v Guardian Newspapers Ltd* [1987] 3 All ER 316, HL (the *Spycatcher* case).
17 See, for example, *A-G v Barker* [1990] 3 All ER 257, CA, per Lord Donaldson of Lymington MR (at 261d): 'I cannot believe that there is a foreign country which would regard the sanctity of contract as not being of enormous importance and central to the necessities of a democratic society.'
18 See *Factortame Ltd v Secretary of State for Transport (No 2)* [1991] 1 All ER 70, HL.
19 See *Smith v Inner London Education Authority* [1978] 1 All ER 411, CA.
20 *Factortame Ltd v Secretary of State for Transport (No 2)* per Lord Goff of Chieveley at 120g: 'I cannot dismiss from my mind the possibility (no doubt remote) that such a party may suffer such serious and irreparable harm in the event of the law being enforced against him that it may be just or convenient to restrain its enforcement by an interim injunction even though so heavy a burden has not been discharged by him. In the end, the matter is one for the discretion of the court, taking into account all the circumstances of the case. Even so, the court should not restrain a public authority by interim injunction from enforcing an apparently authentic law unless it is satisfied . . . that the challenge to the validity of the law is, prima facie, so firmly based as to justify so exceptional a course being taken.'
21 [1977] FSR 39, CA.
22 [1991] 1 All ER 385, [1989] ICR 123.

enforce a contractual obligation in restraint of trade. We were told that this is a view widely held in the profession. If so, it is time that the profession is disabused.'[23]

(v) *Mandatory injunctions.* Interlocutory mandatory injunctions, ie orders which in substance require the defendant to take positive steps pending trial, usually carry a higher risk of injustice to the defendant if subsequently shown to have been wrongly granted. Accordingly, the court requires a 'high degree of assurance' that the plaintiff's claim will succeed at trial.[24] But if, exceptionally, the potential injustice to the plaintiff of refusing the order is greater than the risk of injustice in granting it, a mandatory injunction will be granted even though the plaintiff has not established a high degree of assurance that he will succeed at trial.

Example. The plaintiff company sought an interlocutory mandatory injunction to compel the defendant, a film distribution company, to deliver films in accordance with a contract between them. Hoffmann J granted an interlocutory injunction even though it was mandatory in substance because delivery of the films to the plaintiff would cause no uncompensatable loss to the defendant but a failure to deliver the films would prevent the plaintiff from further distributing the films in Italy, causing loss which might be very difficult to quantify. Further, as the process of distribution had already been set in motion, permitting an interruption to the status quo carried a much greater risk of injustice than if the injunction was granted but the plaintiff did not succeed at trial (*Films Rover International Ltd and others v Cannon Film Sales Ltd*[25]).

The major criticism which has been levelled at the *American Cyanamid* decision is that before this rule was promulgated in many cases (including a substantial number of leading authorities) the litigation did not continue to trial because the parties were content to accept a provisional decision on the merits by the judge hearing the interlocutory application. Thus in *Fellowes v Fisher* Sir John Pennycuick pointed out (at 843):

'By far the most serious difficulty, to my mind, lies in the requirement that the prospects of success in the action have apparently to be disregarded except as a last resort when the balance of convenience is otherwise even. In many classes of cases, in particular those depending in whole or in great part on the construction of a written instrument, the prospect of success is a matter within the competence of the judge who hears the interlocutory application and represents a factor which can hardly be disregarded in determining whether or not it is just to give interlocutory relief. Indeed many cases of this kind never get beyond the interlocutory stage, the parties being content to accept the judge's decision as a sufficient indication of the probable upshot of the action. . . . There is also a class where immediate judicial interference is essential, eg to take two examples at random, trespass or the internal affairs of a company, and in which the court could not do justice without to some extent considering the probable upshot of the action if it ever came to be fought out, or in other words, the merits.'

In *NWL Ltd v Woods*,[26] the House of Lords made it clear that the *American Cyanamid* case was not to be applied where, even though the evidence was disputed, the parties accepted that the interlocutory decision would be

---

23 Ibid, at [1991] 1 All ER 392f, [1989] ICR 131D.
24 See *Shepherd Homes Ltd v Sandham* [1971] Ch 340, [1970] 3 All ER 402, Megarry J and *Locabail International Finance Ltd v Agroexport, The Sea Hawk* [1986] 1 All ER 901, [1986] 1 WLR 657, CA.
25 [1986] 3 All ER 772.
26 [1979] 3 All ER 614, [1979] 1 WLR 1294, HL.

effective to determine the dispute between them. That case concerned an attempt to prevent trade unions 'blacking' ships whose crews were paid substandard wages; the case concerned section 17 of the Trade Union and Labour Relations Act 1974 which was enacted expressly to prevent the *American Cyanamid* decision being applied to claims for injunctions in trade disputes:

> 'It is hereby declared for the avoidance of doubt that where an application is made to a court pending the trial of an action for an interlocutory injunction and the party against whom the injunction is sought claims that he acted in contemplation or furtherance of a trade dispute, the court shall, in exercising its discretion whether or not to grant the injunction, *have regard to the likelihood of the party succeeding at the trial of the action in establishing* [that he was acting in contemplation or furtherance of a trade dispute].'

Lord Diplock observed that this section was not strictly necessary because the *American Cyanamid* decision did not apply to cases such as trade disputes where everyone realised that the action would not continue after the court had decided whether or not to grant interlocutory relief:

> 'Where . . . the grant or refusal of the interlocutory injunction will have the practical effect of putting an end to the action because the harm that will have been already caused to the losing party by its grant or refusal is complete and of a kind for which money cannot constitute any worthwhile recompense, the degree of likelihood that the plaintiff would have succeeded in establishing his right to an injunction if the action had gone to trial is a factor to be brought into the balance by the judge in weighing the risks that injustice may result from his deciding the application one way rather than the other.'

Although it should be noted that Lord Diplock describes this consideration as 'a factor' in reality it will usually be the decisive factor where the interlocutory decision will determine the dispute between the parties. Some care must be taken, however, before concluding that a case is one in which the grant or refusal of an interlocutory injunction will 'have the practical effect of putting an end to the action'. If either party will pursue the matter to trial in order to demonstrate that the interlocutory decision was 'wrong', the case does not properly fall within the *NWL v Woods* category.[27] On this point, actions to enforce restrictive covenants against former employees again raise special difficulties. Such covenants frequently operate only for a relatively short period after termination of the contract and will have expired before the full trial of the action. The outcome of the trial therefore serves only to settle the question of any damages payable to the plaintiff in respect of an interlocutory injunction being wrongly refused or to the defendant on the plaintiff's undertaking where the court concludes that the defendant was wrongly restrained during the currency of the covenant. Whilst either party is theoretically at liberty to pursue the matter to trial on the question of damages, the courts have shown a tendency to regard them as unlikely to do so and to treat such cases as falling within the *NWL v Woods* category by looking at the plaintiff's prospects of success on the merits.[28] The following example gives

27 See, for example, *Cambridge Nutrition Ltd v BBC* [1990] 3 All ER 523 CA, per Ralph Gibson LJ at 539h.
28 See *Lawrence David Ltd v Ashton* [1991] 1 All ER 385 at 395j, [1989] ICR 123 at 135A, CA, per Balcombe LJ and *Lansing Linde Ltd v Kerr* [1991] 1 All ER 418 at 424d, [1991] ICR 428 at 435H, CA, per Staughton LJ. But see also *Dairy Crest Ltd v Pigott* [1989] ICR 92, CA, where Balcombe LJ considered that a claim for interlocutory relief in relation to a two year restrictive covenant fell outside the *NWL v Woods* exception in circumstances where directions for a speedy trial were appropriate.

an illustration of the sort of other circumstances in which the grant or refusal of an injunction at the interlocutory stage effectively disposes of the action.

> *Example.* Shareholders in GNR plc wanted to remove the directors of the company at the next general meeting scheduled for 13 September. The directors entered into a contract with M Inc which provided, *inter alia*, for a number of shares in GNR to be issued and received by M Inc before that date. This would have effectively given M Inc control over GNR plc and it was known that M Inc would then keep the existing directors in power. Certain shareholders in GNR plc applied for an interlocutory injunction restraining the company from proceeding with the deal before first receiving the shareholders' approval at the next general meeting. The Court of Appeal held that whether the injunction was granted or refused the decision was 'highly likely' to determine the issue: if granted, the shareholders would have achieved their objective and 'the possibility of proceeding to trial for damages is but a pale shadow of the real claim'; if refused, the deal would proceed and it would not be possible to unscramble it. Since the interlocutory decision would be tantamount to giving judgment the Court of Appeal therefore considered the prospects of the shareholders succeeding on the merits (*Cayne v Global Natural Resources plc*[29]).

Where it is clear that the decision at the interlocutory stage will effectively resolve the dispute between the parties (because neither will continue to trial) the court is of course being asked to decide the matter without hearing the witnesses give evidence. In effect this is very like an application for summary judgment so the plaintiff must have very convincing proof of his case.

UNDERTAKING AS TO DAMAGES

Where an interlocutory injunction is granted it is the inevitable practice of the courts to extract from the applicant an undertaking to compensate the other party for any loss he may sustain in consequence of the injunction if it eventually appears at the trial that the applicant was not entitled to the relief sought. Where an interlocutory injunction is sought on behalf of the Crown in order to enforce the law in the manner prescribed by statute, an undertaking in damages is unlikely to be required unless the defendant shows special reasons why justice requires it.[30] Interlocutory injunctions may similarly be granted to other public authorities acting in pursuance of their law enforcement functions without the need to enter into an undertaking in damages.[31]

In some cases, the potentially enormous liability in damages to the defendant which the plaintiff may incur on his undertaking may deter the plaintiff from seeking an interlocutory injunction pending the main trial of the action. Instead, he may choose to tolerate the defendant's conduct until the trial and, if successful, obtain a final injunction and damages for the intervening period during which the defendant continued to commit the wrongful acts. In this way, the plaintiff does not enter an undertaking in

29 [1984] 1 All ER 225, CA.
30 *F Hoffmann-La Roche & Co AG v Secretary of State for Trade and Industry* [1975] AC 295, [1974] 2 All ER 1128, HL. See also *Director General of Fair Trading v Tobyward Ltd* [1989] 2 All ER 266, Ch D (no undertaking in damages required where an interlocutory injunction was the only prescribed method of enforcing the Control of Misleading Advertisement Regulations 1988).
31 See *Kirklees Metropolitan Borough Council v Wickes Building Supplies Ltd* [1993] AC 227, [1992] 3 All ER 717, HL.

damages and bears no risk of paying damages to the defendant in the event that he loses at trial. Whilst this may make good sense for the plaintiff, it creates a dilemma for the defendant. If he continues the activity in question and loses at trial, he will be liable in damages to the plaintiff. But without the protection of the plaintiff's undertaking in damages, any voluntary discontinuance[32] is at his own risk. When this situation arose in *Blue Town Investments Ltd v Higgs & Hill plc*[33] Sir Nicolas Browne-Wilkinson V-C ordered the plaintiffs' claim to be struck out as vexatious, unless they were prepared to apply for an interlocutory injunction until trial accompanied by an undertaking to compensate the defendants in damages. This decision may, however, be exceptional in that the judge considered the plaintiffs' case to be tenuous and their chances of success 'minimal'. In a similar case in which the owners of a site on an industrial estate applied for a final injunction against a religious charity, restraining them from constructing a mosque on the estate allegedly in breach of covenant, Hoffmann J refused to strike out the claim on the grounds that the plaintiffs had not also applied for an interlocutory injunction. The learned judge said:[34]

'The mere existence of the claim to an injunction constitutes no interference with the defendant's liberty. The uncertainty which it creates is no more than a necessary consequence of the existence of a claim which has not yet been adjudicated. If the defendants are confident of their case, they are free to ignore the claim at their own risk . . .'

COSTS

The normal order for costs will be as follows:

(*a*) If the application for an injunction succeeds, costs will be *in cause*, so that whichever party wins at the conclusion of the case will obtain the costs he has incurred in applying for or opposing the interlocutory injunction.

(*b*) If the application is refused it will not necessarily follow that the applicant will be ordered to pay the costs. Where for instance the balance of convenience is nearly even, the right order would be costs in cause.

Where an application for an injunction is made to a county court judge by counsel the costs of his attendance will only be allowed if he applies and the judge certifies the case as fit for counsel.[35]

URGENT CASES

There will be cases where the need for an injunction is so urgent that the applicant will have already sustained irreparable harm if he has to wait for the other side to be served with notice of his application. In such exceptional

32 The situation here should not be confused with the case where the plaintiff *does* apply for an interlocutory injunction, but the defendant voluntarily undertakes to cease the activity complained of until trial. In the latter case the plaintiff enters into a *cross-undertaking* to compensate the defendant for any loss unnecessarily suffered by the defendant in the event that the plaintiff loses at trial.
33 [1990] 2 All ER 897, Ch D.
34 *Oxy Electric Ltd v Zainuddin* [1990] 2 All ER 902 at 906d, Ch D.
35 See CCR Ord 38, r 8(1).

cases both the High Court and the county court will grant temporary orders on an ex parte application by the plaintiff (i e without notice being given to the defendant). Indeed such relief may be granted notwithstanding the writ or originating summons or county court summons has not been issued. The plaintiff will present the court[36] with an affidavit as to the merits of his case and if he is successful the court will issue an injunction effective for a short period (usually five days to a week) during which the plaintiff must serve notice on the defendant of his intention to apply at the expiry of the injunction that it should be continued to trial. The plaintiff will be required to give the usual undertaking to compensate the defendant if it transpires he was not entitled to the relief sought and to issue and serve the writ or other process forthwith. Frequently the order gives the defendant liberty to apply to the court on, for instance, one day's notice to discharge the injunction. It must be emphasised that ex parte injunctions are for cases of real urgency where there has been a true impossibility of giving notice of the application. In less urgent cases, the plaintiff may apply to the court for leave to issue a summons or notice of motion with *short notice* (i e less than two clear days). The first illustration at the end of this chapter shows how an application is made for an ex parte order.

INJUNCTIONS TO ASSIST EXECUTION

An injunction may be granted to restrain the defendant from disposing of his assets in such a way as to defeat any award the plaintiff is likely to obtain if he is successful in the action. Orders of this sort are called *Mareva injunctions* after the name of the case in which the principles were first formulated.[37] This important topic is considered separately in Chapter 10, to which the reader should refer.

SETTLEMENT OF INTERLOCUTORY PROCEEDINGS

Where the defendant is prepared to agree to the terms of the proposed injunction or offers to accept modified terms the usual practice is for him to offer *undertakings* to the court which does not then proceed to issue a formal injunction. An undertaking can be enforced in exactly the same method as an injunction: it merely means (*a*) that normally the court does not have to investigate the matters at all and (*b*) that there is no order which has to be served on the defendant.

In the county court the undertaking is reduced to writing on a formal court document and the court may require the defendant to sign it[38] (for an example see p 195).

Sometimes the parties will agree at the hearing of the interlocutory application on terms intended to settle the whole of the action. In these circumstances in the Queen's Bench Division and county court the parties normally draw up terms of final judgment including the appropriate permanent injunction. In the Chancery Division the common practice is to

---

36 In extreme cases where the court is not sitting, application may be made to a judge at his home. The plaintiff's solicitors should telephone to the Royal Courts of Justice who will be able to put them in touch with a judge available for the hearing of urgent applications.
37 *Mareva Cia Naviera SA v International Bulkcarriers SA* [1980] 1 All ER 213, [1975] 2 Lloyds Rep 509, CA.
38 CCR Ord 29, r 1A.

stay further proceedings in the action on terms set out in a schedule annexed to the order. This form of order (known as a *Tomlin Order* from the judge who formulated the order) is set out as follows: 'The plaintiff and the defendant having agreed to the terms set forth in the schedule hereto, it is ordered that all further proceedings in this action be stayed, except for the purpose of carrying such terms into effect. Liberty to apply as to carrying such terms into effect.'

ENFORCEMENT OF INJUNCTIONS

As soon as possible after the injunction has been granted the applicant should obtain a sealed copy of the order[39] and effect personal service on the defendant. The order *must* be indorsed with a *penal notice* warning the defendant that he is liable to be committed to prison if he disobeys the order. The form of indorsement (where the injunction restrains the defendant from certain conduct) would be as follows:

'If you, the within-named Joseph Soap disobey this order, you will be liable to process of execution for the purpose of compelling you to obey the same.'[40]

The order duly indorsed with the penal notice must be served personally on the defendant. If the defendant is in breach of the terms of an injunction or his undertaking to the court, the plaintiff will then apply by *notice of motion* for an order that he be committed to prison for contempt.

The procedure is regulated by RSC Order 45, rules 5 to 8 and Order 52, rule 4. The notice of motion must state clearly the breach alleged and be served personally on the defendant two clear days before the hearing (a specimen motion is set out at page 192, post). In the county court, Order 29, rule 1(4) provides that the court shall issue a notice addressed to the defendant requiring him to attend and show cause why an order of attachment (ie committal) should not be made. Once again there must be personal service not later than two clear days before the hearing. At the hearing the applicant will have to prove:

(1) *Service of the injunction together with the penal notice* (although, in the case of prohibitory injunctions, it is sufficient to prove the defendant's presence when the order was made or that he has been notified of the order[41] and in all cases the court may dispense with service where it is just so to do[42]).

(2) *Breach* of the injunction or undertaking (this is proved by affidavit evidence).

(3) *Service* of the *notice of motion* and the *affidavits* on the defendant. This is particularly important because frequently the defendant will not

---

39 The procedure in the Queen's Bench Division is that the judge indorses the draft order or returns the summons indorsed with a short note of his decision and the plaintiff's solicitors prepare a formal order (as set out in the example at p 189) and take it (together with a copy for filing) to the Central Office or district registry. In the county court, the order is drawn up by the court itself and issued on application by the plaintiff.

40 If the order is mandatory, the notice begins 'If you . . . neglect to obey this order by the time limited within . . .' In the county court the penal notice reads 'If you do not obey this order you will be guilty of contempt of court and you may be sent to prison': Ord 29, r 1(3), Form N16.

41 RSC Ord 45, r 7(6).

42 Ibid, r 7(7). In the county court strict service of the order need only be proved if the defendant fails to appear: Ord 29, r 1(6) and (7).

attend at the application and no order can be made unless it is proved that he has had notice of the application and a copy of the affidavit. For this reason the plaintiff should *always* prepare an *affidavit of service* of the motion and affidavit of merits. The affidavits of service of the original order and the notice of motion must be sworn by the persons who effected service and must state how they identified the defendant.

If the court finds that the defendant is in breach of the injunction (or his undertaking) it may commit him to prison forthwith for his contempt. More commonly if the defendant offers suitable apologies the court will suspend the committal order so long as he thereafter complies with the terms of the injunction or original undertaking together with any new undertakings required by the court. The costs of the hearing will be awarded to the successful applicant.[43]

Example 1 – Injunction in Queen's Bench Division. In September 1990 Miss Henrietta Carlova (the internationally renowned soprano) agreed to appear at the Metropolitan Opera House for the 1990/1 Winter Season. On 1 November after a furious quarrel with the artistic director she stormed out of rehearsals for 'La Boheme', which was to be the first production of the new season. On 5 November the London evening newspapers carried a story that she intended to open in a production of the 'Marriage of Figaro' at a rival theatre on the following Wednesday. The Opera House consulted their solicitors who explained that although the courts will not enforce a contract of service by injunction (ie will not *force* an employee to work for his employer) they will enforce reasonable restrictions on the employee's right to work for rival concerns (see *Lumley v Wagner*[44]). In the present case Miss Carlova's contract contained a clause prohibiting her appearing for any other companies during the winter season. Her solicitors therefore instructed counsel to settle as a matter or urgency a writ and an affidavit of merits. As soon as these documents were prepared they applied ex parte to a Queen's Bench judge in chambers for an interlocutory injunction.

The general indorsement of the writ read: 'The plaintiffs' claim is for damages for breach of a written contract dated the 23rd day of September 1990 whereby the defendant agreed to perform at the plaintiff's Opera House during the Winter Season 1990–91 and for an injunction restraining the defendant from appearing at any other establishment in breach of the terms of the said contract.' The affidavit is set out at page 188. Note that it contains statements of hearsay evidence (paragraphs 3 and 4). These are permissible because the application is for interlocutory relief. Note also how the relevant documents (ie the written agreement and the newspaper cutting) are exhibited to the affidavit.

The judge decided that there were urgent reasons for preserving the status quo until Miss Carlova could be heard. Accordingly, he granted an injunction but:

(1) obtained an undertaking from the plaintiffs that they would issue the writ and serve it and a statement of claim forthwith,
(2) obtained an undertaking from the plaintiffs to compensate the defendant if it eventually transpired that the injunction should not have been granted,
(3) ordered that the injunction was to remain in force for only 8 days (if the plaintiffs wish it continued thereafter they should serve a summons on the

43 The order will be either for the costs to be taxed and paid forthwith or for the costs to be the applicant's 'in any event', ie payable by the opposing party in the ultimate settlement of costs after the action has been heard. See *Allied Collection Agencies Ltd v Wood* [1981] 3 All ER 176.
44 (1852) 1 De GM & G 604.

defendant returnable on or before the day on which the injunction would expire),

(4) gave the defendant leave to apply on one day's notice to discharge the injunction if she was so advised.

The order is set out in document No 2 (p 189). Note that it is indorsed with a *penal notice* warning the defendant of the consequences of disobeying the order of the court. Document No 3 (p 190) shows the summons served at the same time as the injunction telling the defendant of the next hearing of the matter. Document No 1 (the affidavit of merits) would be served at the same time since the plaintiffs would use that again at the hearing of the summons. Document No 4 (p 191) shows the statement of claim seeking a permanent injunction and damages.

To the plaintiffs' consternation Miss Carlova not only tore up the order when she was served but announced her intention of appearing the next day at the Empire Theatre. And indeed the very next evening she appeared in the first night of 'The Marriage of Figaro'. In these circumstances the plaintiffs had no option but to apply by *notice of motion* (document No 5; p 192) to commit her for breach of the injunction. At the hearing they would produce:

(*a*) an affidavit deposing to the service of the injunction (duly indorsed with the penal notice) on her,

(*b*) an affidavit as to the breach by her of the injunction,

(*c*) an affidavit proving service of the notice of motion.

It would certainly be likely that for so flagrant a breach of the court's order Miss Carlova would find herself committed to prison. Her only chance of avoiding such a fate would be to apologise abjectly and promise henceforth to obey the order.

In the High Court of Justice

Queen's Bench Division

1990-T.No. 1067
1. Plaintiffs
2. J.S. Tooth
3. 1st
4. 6.11.90

Between:

THE METROPOLITAN OPERA COMPANY
LIMITED   Plaintiffs

and

HENRIETTA CARLOVA   Defendant

_____

I, Jeremy Sebastian Tooth, of 24a South Audley Street, London W1, a director of the Plaintiff Company, make oath and say as follows:

1.   I am the principal casting director at the Metropolitan Opera House and as such responsible for the engagement of artists.

2.   On the 23rd day of September, 1990, the Defendant entered into a written agreement with the Plaintiffs to appear in the Winter Season productions at the Opera House. There is now produced and shown to be marked "JST 1" a true copy of the said agreement.

3.   I am informed by M. Serge Stroganoff, the artistic director of the company's current production of the opera "La Boheme", and verily believe to be true, that after a rehearsal of the said opera on the 1st day of November, 1990 the Defendant left the Opera House stating that she had no intention of working with sub-standard performers. I am further informed by him and verily believe to be true that the Defendant has failed to appear at all subsequent rehearsals at the theatre.

4.   There is now produced and shown to me marked "JST 2" an extract from the "Evening News" dated the 5th day of November, 1990, containing an item indicating that the Defendant intends appearing at the Empire Theatre's current season.

5.   On the 6th day of November, 1990, I spoke to the Defendant on the telephone and asked her if this item was true. She said "I can do what I like" and after uttering certain words of abuse replaced the receiver.

6.   I verily believe that the Defendant will appear at the said Theatre in breach of the terms of her agreement with the Plaintiffs unless restrained by order of this Honourable Court from so doing.

Sworn at Holborn

this 6th day of November 1990   Jeremy S. Tooth
before me

          Marmaduke Sweet
A Commissioner of Oaths

This affidavit is filed on behalf of the Plaintiffs

In the High Court of Justice   1990-T.No. 106

Queen's Bench Division

Between:

THE METROPOLITAN OPERA COMPANY   Plaintiffs
LIMITED

and

HENRIETTA CARLOVA   Defendant

The Hon. Mr. Justice Strawberry in Chambers

UPON HEARING Counsel for the Plaintiffs

ex parte

AND UPON READING the affidavit of Jeremy Sebastian Tooth filed the 7th day of November 1990.

AND UPON THE PLAINTIFFS by their Counsel undertaking to issue and serve a writ forthwith upon the Defendant and undertaking to abide by any order this Court may make as to damages in case this Court shall hereafter be of opinion that the Defendant shall have sustained any by reason of this Order which the Plaintiffs ought to pay,

IT IS ORDERED THAT the Defendant be restrained and an injunction is hereby granted restraining her from appearing as a performer at the Empire Theatre, Haymarket, London W1 or at any other opera house, theatre, concert hall or public or private entertainment whatsoever until after the hearing of a summons returnable on the 16th day of November, 1990 next or until further order.

Liberty for the Defendant to apply to discharge this order on 1 day's notice.

Dated the 8th day of November, 1990

IMPORTANT NOTICE

If you the within named HENRIETTA CARLOVA disobey this Order, you may be held to be in contempt of Court and liable to imprisonment.

Judge's Summons
(General Form)
(O. 32)

IN THE HIGH COURT OF JUSTICE   19 90 .— T .—**No.** 106
Queen's Bench Division

Between

THE ROYAL METROPOLITAN OPERA COMPANY LIMITED   Plaintiff

AND

HENRIETTA CARLOVA   Defendant

(1) 'Judge in Chambers, Central Office' or 'Judge in Court' as the case may be.

Let all parties concerned attend the (¹) Judge in Chambers, Room 206
Royal Courts of Justice, Strand, London, on   Thurs **day, the** 18th
day of   November   **19** 90, **at**   10.30   **o'clock in the** fore **noon,**

(2) Plaintiff or Defendant or as the case may require.

on the hearing of an application on the part of (²) the Plaintiffs

for an order that the injunction granted the 8th day of November,
1990 by the Hon. Mr. Justice Strawberry whereby the
Defendant was restrained from appearing or performing
at the Empire Theatre, Haymarket, London W11 or at any
opera house, theatre, concert hall of other public or
private entertainment in the British Isles until the
hearing of this summons be continued until the trial
hereof or further order.

and that the costs of the said application be paid by the (²) Defendant
to the (²) Plaintiffs

Dated the   8th   **day of**   November   19 90 .

To M iss Henrietta Carlova
   Hilton Hotel
   Park Lane
   London W1

This Summons was taken out by
                   Dodson and Fogg
Agent for

of Cornhill, London EC3
Solicitor for the Plaintiffs

Solicitor   or Agent for

In the High Court of Justice   1990-T.No. 106

Queen's Bench Division

(Writ issued the 8th day of November 1990

Between:

THE METROPOLITAN OPERA COMPANY LIMITED	Plaintiffs
and	
HENRIETTA CARLOVA	Defendant

Statement of Claim

1. By a contract in writing dated 23rd September 1990 the Defendant agreed to appear at the Plaintiffs' Opera House, Bow Street, London WC1 during the Winter Season 1990-1991. The Plaintiffs will refer to the said contract at the trial for its full terms and effect.

2. It was expressly provided by the said contract as follows:-

      (a) by clause xi thereof that the Defendant should attend punctually at all rehearsals and performances;

      (b) by clause xiv thereof that during the currency of the said agreement she should not appear at any other opera house, theatre, concert hall or place of public entertainment without the prior consent in writing of the Plaintiffs.

3. In breach of the terms referred to in paragraph 2(a) hereof the Defendant has failed to attend at rehearsals and performances at the Plaintiffs theatre since 1st November 1990.

4. By reason of the matters aforesaid the Plaintiffs have suffered damage.

5. Further the Defendant threatens and intends in breach of the term referred to in paragraph 2(b) hereof to appear at performances at the Empire Theatre, Haymarket, London W1 commencing 8th November 1990 unless restrained by order of this Honourable Court from so doing.

And the Plaintiffs claim:

    1. An injunction to restrain the Defendant from appearing at any opera house, theatre, concert hall or place of public entertainment (other than the Plaintiff's opera house at Bow Street) without the prior consent of the Plaintiffs in writing until 31st March 1991.

    2. Damages.

                               Robert Jordan

Served etc.

In the High Court of Justice   1990-T.No. 106

Queen's Bench Division

        Between:

THE METROPOLITAN OPERA COMPANY   Plaintiffs
LIMITED

and

HENRIETTA CARLOVA   Defendant

In the Matter of an Application on behalf of
the Plaintiffs against the Defendant for an
Order of Committal.

Notice of Motion

TAKE NOTICE that this Court will be moved before one of the Judges of the High Court
sitting at the Royal Courts of Justice, Strand, London WC1, on Monday the 15th day
of November,1990 at 10.30 o'clock in the forenoon or as soon thereafter as counsel
can be heard by counsel on behalf of the Plaintiffs for an order:

1.   That the Defendant be committed to one of Her Majesty's Prisons for
    her contempt of court in appearing at the Empire Theatre, London W1
    on the 9th day of November 1990 in breach of the injunction made by
    the order of the Honourable Mr. Justice Strawberry, dated the 8th day
    of November 1990.

2.   That the said Defendant do pay to the Plaintiffs their costs of and
    incidental to this application and the order to be made thereon.

3.   That such further or other order may be made as to the Court shall
    seem proper.

AND FURTHER TAKE NOTICE that the applicants herein, the said Plaintiffs, intend to
read and use in support of the application the affidavit of Benjamin Hutchinson sworn
the 10th day of November 1990 and the exhibits thereto, a true copy of which
affidavit is served together with this Notice of Motion.

Dated the -10th day of November 1990

To: Miss Henrietta Carlova   Dodson and Fogg
of   Freeman's Court
Hilton Hotel   Cornhill
Park Lane   London EC3
London W1   Solicitors for the
                                 Plaintiffs

Example 2 – Injunction in county court. In February 1993 Mrs Smith was distressed to find that her next door neighbours had built a lean-to garage against the flank wall of her house. The wall and area beside it were clearly within her property so that the neighbours had no right to do this. When she complains she is told the structure is only temporary and that next week the neighbours propose to build a brick structure using her wall as one side of the garage! Mrs Smith will apply for (1) a prohibitory injunction to prevent her neighbours building the permanent structure and (2) a mandatory injunction instructing them to take down the temporary garage. She will claim the above orders in her particulars of claim as final injunctions to be granted after the trial of the action but she will also apply for interlocutory injunctions to cover the period before trial. The relevant procedure is set out in CCR Ord 13, r 6 which provides:–

'6–(1) An application for the grant of an injunction may be made by any party to an action or matter before or after the trial or hearing, whether or not a claim for the injunction was included in that party's particulars of claim, originating application, petition, counterclaim or third party notice, as the case may be.

(2) Except where the district judge has power under Order 21, rule 5 or otherwise to hear and determine the proceedings in which the application is made, the application shall be made to the judge and rule 1(6) shall not apply.

(3) The application shall be made in the appropriate prescribed form and shall–
   (a) state the terms of the injunction applied for; and
   (b) be supported by an affidavit in which the grounds for making the application are set out,
and a copy of the affidavit and a copy of the application shall be served on the party against whom the injunction is sought not less than 2 days before the hearing of the application.

(3A) Where an order is sought ex parte before a copy of the application has been served on the other party, the affidavit shall explain why the application is so made and a copy of any order made ex parte shall be served with the application and affidavit in accordance with paragraph (3).

(4) An application may not be made before the issue of the summons, originating application or petition by which the action or matter is to be commenced except where the case is one of urgency, and in that case–
   (a) the affidavit in support of the application shall show that the action or matter is one which the court to which the application is made has jurisdiction to hear and determine, and
   (b) the injunction applied for shall, if granted, be on terms providing for the issue of the summons, originating application or petition in the court granting the application and on such terms, if any, as the court thinks fit.

(4A) Paragraph (4)(a) and (b) shall apply, with the necessary modifications, where an application for an injunction is made by a defendant in a case of urgency before issuing a counterclaim or cross-application.

(5) Unless otherwise directed, every application not made ex parte shall be made in open court.

(6) Except where the case is one of urgency, a draft of the injunction shall be prepared beforehand by the party making an application to the judge under paragraph (1) and, if the application is granted, the draft shall be submitted to the judge by whom the application was heard and shall be settled by him.

(7) The injunction, when settled, shall be forwarded to the proper office for filing.'

Application for Injunction (General Form)

In the

EDMONTON **County Court**

Between

PEGGY BROWN

☑ Plaintiff
☐ Applicant
☐ Petitioner
(Tick whichever applies)

and

JOHN CLARK

☑ Defendant
☐ Respondent

Case No. ~~Always quote this~~ 93 356

Plaintiff's Ref.

Defendant's Ref.

Notes on completion

Tick whichever box applies

(1) Enter the full name of the person making the application

(2) Enter the full name of the person the injunction is to be directed to

(3) Set out here the proposed restraining orders (If the defendant is a limited company delete the wording in brackets and insert "Whether by its servants, agents, officers or otherwise")

(4) Set out here any proposed mandatory orders requiring acts to be done

(5) Set out here any further terms asked for including provision for costs

(6) Enter the names of all persons who have sworn affidavits in support of this application

(7) Enter the names and addresses of all persons upon whom it is intended to serve this application

(8) Enter the full name and address for service and delete as required

☑ By application in pending proceedings

☐ In the matter of the Domestic Violence and Matrimonial Proceedings Act 1976

Seal

The Plaintiff ~~(Applicant/Petitioner)~~ (1)   PEGGY BROWN

applies to the court for an injunction order in the following terms:

That the Defendant~~(Respondent)~~ (2)   JOHN CLARK

be forbidden (whether by himself or by instructing or encouraging any other person (3)

from carrying out any building works within 15 feet of the west flank wall of her house at 50 Bishops Avenue, London N15 (other than dismantling the existing structure thereon) until trial or further order

And that the Defendant(Respondent) (4)

within 2 weeks of service of this order upon him do remove the structure abutting or resting against the flank wall of 50 Bishops Avenue aforesaid

And that (5)

the Defendant do pay the costs of this application

The grounds of this application are set out in the sworn statement(s)

of (6)   Peggy Brown and Ian Timothy Daniels

This (these) sworn statement(s) is (are) served with this application.

This application is to be served upon (7)

John Clark, 52 Bishops Avenue, London N15

This application is filed by (8)   Clerk and Lindsell

(the Solicitors for) the Plaintiff~~(Applicant/Petitioner)~~

whose address for service is 26 High Street, Edmonton N18 2XT

Signed   Clerk and Lindsell   **Dated** 03/02/1993

This section to be completed by the court

* Name and address of the person application is directed to

To *   John Clark
of   52 Bishops Avenue, London N15

This application will be heard by the ~~(District)~~ Judge

at   the Court House, 59 Fore Street, Upper Edmonton, London N18 2NT

on   Monday   **the** 8th **day of** February   **199** 3 **at** 10.30 **o'clock**

If you do not attend at the time shown the court may make an injunction order in your absence

If you do not understand anything in this order you should go to a Solicitor, Legal Advice Centre or a Citizens' Advice Bureau

The court office at   59 Fore Street, Upper Edmonton, London N18 2NT

is open between 10 am and 4 pm Mon - Fri. When corresponding with the court, please address all forms and letters to the Chief Clerk and quote the case number.

N16A General form of application for injunction Order 13, rule 6(3), Order 47, rule 8(2) .

MCR 073947/1/K94973 360 3/91 DTPS

General Form of Undertaking

In the

EDMONTON **County Court**

Case No *Always quote this*	93 356
Plaintiff's Ref	
Defendant's Ref	

Between PEGGY BROWN _____ Plaintiff
Applicant
Petitioner

and JOHN CLARK _____ Defendant
Respondent

This form is to be used only for an undertaking not for an injunction

On the 8TH **day of** February 1993 ,

(1) JOHN CLARK

[appeared in person] [was represented by ~~Solicitor~~ / Counsel]

(1) Name of the person giving undertaking

and gave an undertaking to the Court promising (2)

(2) Set out terms of undertaking

not to carry out any building works within 15 feet
of the west flank wall of 50 Bishops Avenue, London N15
(other than dismantling the existing structure thereon)

(3) Give the date and time or event when the undertaking will expire

(4) The judge may direct that the party who gives the undertaking shall personally sign the statement overleaf

And to be bound by these promises until (3) the trial of this action

The Court explained to (1) JOHN CLARK

the meaning of his undertaking and the consequences of failing to keep his promises,

And the Court accepted his undertaking (4) [and *if so ordered* directed that

(1) should sign the statement overleaf] .

And the Court ordered that (5)

(5) Set out any other directions given by the court

the Defendant do serve a defence with 14 days hereof

(6) Address of the person giving undertaking

Dated 8th February 1993

To (1)
of (6)

JOHN CLARK
52 Bishops Avenue
London N15

Important Notice

- You may be sent to prison for contempt of court if you break the promises that you have given to the Court.

- If you do not understand anything in this document you should go to a Solicitor, Legal Advice Centre or a Citizens' Advice Bureau

Seal

The Court Office at

is open from 10 am to 4 pm. When corresponding with the court, address all forms and letters to the Chief Clerk and quote the case number

N117   General form of undertaking Order 29, rule 1(a)

Chapter 7

Third party procedure

DEFENDANT'S RIGHT TO BRING IN THIRD PARTIES

Where a defendant wishes to claim that a person not a party to the proceedings should be responsible in whole or in part for any damages he may have to pay the plaintiff he will issue a *third party notice* which has the effect of enabling the issues between the defendant and the third party to be determined in the action proceeding between the plaintiff and the defendant.

> *Example 1.* P is a passenger in a car driven by T which is involved in a collision with a lorry driven by D. P sues D for damages for personal injuries. D can join T as a third party and claim contribution under the Civil Liability (Contribution) Act 1978.[1]
>
> *Example 2.* Thomas enters into a hire purchase agreement with Paramount Finance Company. His uncle, Donald, signs a guarantee. Thomas defaults in payment and the company sue Donald on the guarantee. Donald can join Thomas as a third party and claim indemnity.
>
> *Example 3.* Paul is injured whilst working a machine at Dickson's factory and brings an action claiming damages. Dickson can join the Thompson Engineering Co. who made the machine and claim damages for breach of the conditions as to fitness for purpose implied by the Sale of Goods Act.
>
> *Example 4.* David buys a second-hand car from Terry. In fact the car had originally been obtained by a rogue from Peter's garage and sold by him to Terry. Peter sues David for specific recovery of the vehicle. David can join Terry as third party and claim damages for breach of condition as to title since a common question in respect of the subject matter of both claims arises, namely did Terry have good title to pass to David.

It can be seen from the above examples that there are basically four cases where a third party notice may be issued, namely:[2]

(1) Where the defendant claims *contribution*.
(2) Where he claims an *indemnity*.

---

1 Section 1(1) provides '. . . any person liable in respect of any damage suffered by another person may recover contribution from any other person liable in respect of the same damage (whether jointly with him or otherwise)', section 2(1) provides 'in any proceedings for contribution under section 1 above the amount of the contribution recoverable from any person shall be such as may be found by the court to be just and equitable having regard to the extent of that person's responsibility for the damage in question'.
2 See RSC Ord 16, r 1; CCR Ord 12.

(3) Where he claims against the third party *substantially the same relief* in respect of the *same subject matter* as the plaintiff claims against him.

(4) Where he requires that any *question* or *issue* relating to or connected with the original subject matter of the action should be determined not only as between himself and the plaintiff but between either or both of them and a third party.

In theory in each of the above cases it would be possible to permit the defendant to bring a separate action against the third party but the issue of a third party notice saves time, expense and the possibility of the courts coming to a different conclusion on the same point.

THIRD PARTY NOTICE PROCEDURE

Example. D Copperfield Ltd is a company which operates a fleet of lorries in West London. On 12 August 1991 their managing director, Mr Green, visits the garage premises of Easy Rider Garages in Chiswick and sees a lorry for sale at £10,000. He is told by the salesman that the lorry is in excellent condition. He then agrees to take the lorry and finance is arranged by way of hire purchase agreement with the Universal Finance Company. The lorry develops serious defects and the purchasers stop paying the instalments. The finance company sue in the High Court for the return of the lorry and a minimum payment under the contract or damages for breach of contract. The purchasers wish to join the garage to claim either an indemnity if they have to return the lorry or else damages for the cost of repairs.

The procedure to be followed is set out in RSC Order 16. The first step is for the defendant to issue a third party notice; the procedure for issue and service is the same as in the case of a writ except that where the defendant has already been served a defence, he must obtain leave by applying ex parte to a master with an affidavit setting out the nature of the case, the stage which it has reached, the basis of his claim against the third party and the name and address of the person to whom the notice is to be issued. The form of notice is set out below:

Royal Arms

In the High Court of Justice   1991–U–No 2067

Queen's Bench Division

Between:

Universal Finance Company Limited	Plaintiffs
and	
David Copperfield Limited	Defendants
and	
Easy Rider Garages (a firm)	Third Party

Third Party Notice

Issued pursuant to the order of Master Cooper dated the 23rd day of January 1992.

To Easy Rider Garages of 206 High Street, Chiswick, London W7.

TAKE NOTICE that this action has been brought by the Plaintiffs against the

Defendants. In it the Plaintiffs claim the sum of £8,569 being the balance of the hire charges and interest outstanding on a Ford motor lorry registration number 'A 12 AMO' or the return of the said vehicle and damages as appears from the Writ of Summons a copy whereof is served herewith together with a copy of the Statement of Claim.

The Defendants claim against you to be indemnified against the Plaintiff's claim and the costs of this action alternatively the following relief or remedy namely damages on the grounds that they were induced to hire purchase the said vehicle by negligent mis-statements as to its condition or quality by your servant or agent and/or that the vehicle is defective and unroadworthy in breach of a warranty collateral to the contract of hire purchase.

AND TAKE NOTICE that within 14 days after service of this notice on you, counting the day of service, you must acknowledge service and state in your acknowledgment whether you intend to contest the proceedings. If you fail to do so, or if your acknowledgment does not state your intention to contest the proceedings, you will be deemed to admit the plaintiff's claim against the defendant and the defendant's claim against you and your liability to indemnify the defendant or in damages and will be bound by any judgment or decision given in the action and the judgment may be enforced against you in accordance with Order 16 of the Rules of the Supreme Court.

Dated . . . . Signed

Solicitors of the Defendants

Important

Directions for Acknowledgment of Service are given with the accompanying form.

Once the third party has filed an acknowledgment of service, the defendant must issue a summons for 'third party directions'. This is served on the plaintiff and the third party and enables the master

(a) to consider whether the third party notice should stand, ie whether the case is appropriate for third party proceedings,

(b) to give directions as to the future conduct of the case. This will often involve an order that the defendant serves a detailed statement of his claim on the third party since the third party notice will generally only contain a short outline of the case analogous to the general indorsement on a writ.

We set out below the typical wording of a summons for third party directions which will indicate the sort of orders which will be requested:

Let all parties concerned attend the Master in Chambers in Room No 207 at the Central Office, Royal Courts of Justice on Thursday the 21st day of January 1993 at 11 o'clock in the forenoon for an order for third party directions, as follows:

1. That the Defendants serve a statement of their claim on the Third Party within 28 days from this date.
2. That the Third Party plead thereto within 14 days of service.
3. That the Defendants and Third Party do respectively exchange lists of documents within 14 days after these pleadings are closed and that there be inspection of documents within 7 days thereafter.
4. And that the said Third Party by at liberty to appear at the trial of this action and take such part as the Judge shall direct, and be bound by the result of the trial,

And that the question of the liability of the said Third Party to indemnify the

Defendants and the said Defendants' claim for damages be tried at the trial of this action, but subsequent thereto.

5. And that the costs of this application be costs in the cause and in the Third Party proceedings.

The practice in the County Court is set out in CCR Order 12 and follows the High Court procedure. A notice[3] is issued requiring the third party (*a*) to deliver to the court two copies of the defence to the third party claim within 14 days and (*b*) to attend at a pre-trial review at which directions for the further conduct of the action will be given. The defendant must obtain leave from the district judge to issue the third party notice in a fixed date action or in a default action where a day has been fixed for the pre-trial review or hearing or where the automatic directions apply and the pleadings are deemed to be closed.

CONTRIBUTION NOTICE

We have dealt so far with the situation where a defendant seeks an indemnity, contribution, etc from a person who is *not* already a party to the proceedings. We have now to consider the position where one defendant seeks an indemnity or contribution from another defendant.

Example 1. P is a passenger in a van driven by D1 which collides with a car driven by D2. P sues both D1 and D2. D2 wishes to claim contribution from D1.

Example 2. An opera house sue one of their singers who has taken a post at another opera company in breach of her contract. They also sue the other company for inducing a breach of contract. That company wish to claim indemnity from the singer on the basis that by her contract she expressly warranted that 'no other company has any enforceable rights to my services during currency of this agreement'.

In the first example above, D1 and D2 are sued as tortfeasors liable in respect of the same damage so that the court has a statutory power to apportion liability between them without the necessity of either side filing any notice.[4] If however either party wishes to obtain discovery from the other or administer interrogatories then he will have to issue a formal notice and take out a summons for third party directions.

In the second example given above, the opera company will only be able to claim indemnity if they have issued a notice of contribution upon the singer and taken out a summons for direction.[5] The form of notice reads as follows:

To the Defendant A B of (address).

Take notice that the Defendant C D claims against you to be indemnified against the Plaintiff's claim and to the costs of this action on the ground that . . .

INTERPLEADER SUMMONS

Where a defendant is sued by a plaintiff claiming property held by the defendant in which the defendant has no interest but which is also claimed

---

3 Form N15.

4 Civil Liability (Contribution) Act 1978, s 2(1). It is customary to serve an informal notice of intention to ask the court for an order apportioning liability: *Clayson v Rolls Royce Ltd* [1951] 1 KB 746, [1950] 2 All ER 884, CA.

5 See RSC Ord 16, r 8; CCR Ord 12, r 5.

by a third party, the defendant may take out and serve a summons[6] on both claimants for an order that the issue as to ownership be decided between them.

> *Example.* A buys a car from a rogue R who has obtained it by a trick from the original owner O. The car is seized by the police in connection with proceedings against R. Now A has brought an action against the police claiming delivery. O has also intimated a claim.

The interpleader summons must be supported by an affidavit stating (*a*) that the defendant claims no interest in the subject matter in dispute except his charges and costs; (*b*) that he does not collude with either claimant and (*c*) that he is willing to pay or transfer the subject matter into court or dispose of it as the court directs. The effect of the summons is of course that the party interpleading drops out and the action proceeds as between the two claimants.[7]

---

6 RSC Ord 17; CCR Ord 33. If neither claimant has brought proceedings, the person holding the disputed property may issue an originating summons for the same purpose. The rule applies equally to debts where there are two claimants.

7 The problem of rival claimants to goods can easily arise where either sheriff's officers or the bailiffs of a county court enter premises to seize goods by way of execution. As to the special rules in such circumstances: see RSC Ord 17, rr 2, 4, 6 and CCR Ord 33.

Chapter 8

Disclosure of evidence

A party to litigation is entitled to know in advance the allegations which he will have to meet at the trial; the function of *pleadings* is to set out clearly what these allegations are. A party is also entitled to see all the documentary evidence which is held by his opponent – even if the opposite party does not intend to use it at the trial; this process is known as *discovery of documents*. In addition, it has long been the rule that each party is entitled to see well in advance of the trial statements of the *expert evidence* which is to be called. Until recently, however, there was no obligation on any party to disclose in advance the evidence which would be given at the hearing. Sometimes, of course, such evidence would be revealed in interlocutory proceedings (eg the affidavits filed on applications for an injunction or summary judgment). In some (rare) cases it was possible to obtain answers on affidavit in response to specific written questions (called *interrogatories*). The absence of any general obligation to disclose witness statements in advance of the trial was unsatisfactory for a number of reasons and from the late 1970s the practice grew up in the Commercial Court and before the Official Referees (where sometimes huge sums of money were at stake and the oral evidence would often be very complicated) of the judges encouraging the parties to agree to exchange witness statements before the trial. This practice proved so successful that it was gradually extended to the Chancery and then the Queen's Bench Division and the county courts. It has also become compulsory rather than dependent upon the consent of the parties. The present procedure is set out in RSC Ord 38, r 2A and CCR Ord 20, r 12A which provide that in most cases the parties shall disclose in advance written statements of the oral evidence which they intend to lead at the trial.

This chapter is concerned with the extent to which one party can compel the other to reveal his evidence – the process originally developed in the Court of Chancery and known as *discovery*. We shall see that the position can be summarised as follows:

(1) The parties are compelled to disclose all *documentary* evidence.
(2) *Expert* evidence which is to be used at the trial must be revealed to the other side.
(3) One party can *cross-examine* the other before the trial by means of *interrogatories*.
(4) The parties will be required to *exchange their witnesses' statements* as a

pre-condition to leading the evidence contained in them where disclosure will assist to dispose fairly of the action and save costs.

We shall also consider the extent to which information can be obtained before the action is begun and the circumstances in which it can be obtained from non-parties.

PRE-ACTION DISCOVERY

As a general rule the courts will not intervene to assist a person who wants to discover information in order to bring proceedings.

> *Example*. A collision occurs in which one driver sustains injuries and suffers amnesia. He cannot obtain an order against the other driver or witnesses to the accident requiring them to set out their recollection of the incident in order for him to decide whether it is worth suing the other driver.

There are three exceptions to this basic proposition, each designed to prevent injustice to a person who may have a valid claim.

(1) *Documents in personal injury and fatal accident cases.* Section 33(2) of the Supreme Court Act 1981 empowers the court to order disclosure of relevant documents by any person who is 'likely to be a party to subsequent proceedings in that court in which a claim in respect of personal injuries to a person, or in respect of a person's death is likely to be made'. The procedure is governed by Ord 24, r 7A. The applicant issues an *originating summons* applying for an order that the respondent discloses the relevant documents to his legal and medical advisers.[1] This summons must be supported by an affidavit explaining the circumstances in which it is said the respondent is likely to be a party to the eventual action, setting out the reasons why the documents in question are relevant at this stage and deposing to the applicant's belief that the respondent has the documents in his possession, custody or power.[2] Section 52(2) of the County Courts Act 1984 enables the County Court to make similar orders.

> *Example 1.* Mrs Dunning went into Liverpool Royal Infirmary for a minor ailment but whilst there developed very serious symptoms and left hospital considerably disabled. She believed her condition was the result of negligent treatment. An independent report obtained by her solicitors stated that the hospital was probably not at fault but regretted that the hospital had failed to provide copies of the notes of her treatment. The doctor concluded 'As an independent medical witness it is my opinion that this failure to reveal the hospital notes has unreasonably prolonged the litigation in this patient's case . . . It is my opinion that once these notes have been made available and their contents explained in lay terms to the plaintiffs their minds will be set at rest.' Mrs Dunning's solicitors then made an application under Ord 24, r 7A for disclosure of the hospital records. The hospital opposed the application on the grounds that in view of the doctor's report it could not be said the records were needed for a claim which was *likely* to be made. Lord Denning MR (at 457) said that 'we should construe "likely to be made" as meaning "may" or "may well be made" dependant on the outcome of the discovery'. James LJ at 460 said that section 33(2) 'covers both the situation in

---

1 Note that *before* making an application to the court the party seeking the information should write to the proposed respondent setting out the nature of his allegations and the reason for supposing the documents in question are relevant to his claim: *Shaw v Vauxhall Motors Ltd* [1974] 1 WLR 1035.

2 The applicant generally pays the costs in such cases even if an order is made.

which without sight of the documents in question the intending plaintiff may have ample evidence on which to found a claim, and also the situation in which the documents are evidence essential to the claim or are evidence without which the claim is not so strong'. He went on to say that in view of the medical expert's qualification of his view with the comment that the absence of hospital notes made his task difficult 'it leaves open the possibility that the notes . . . may add to the existing evidence to support Mrs Dunning's allegation . . . I would construe "likely" there as meaning "a reasonable prospect"' (*Dunning v United Liverpool Hospital's Board of Governors*[3]).

Example 2. In 1961 and 1965 H underwent unsuccessful eye operations which left her eye painful and partly closed. In 1987 she was advised that a claim might be possible against the health authority and applied under section 33(2) of the Supreme Court Act 1981 for pre-action disclosure of the medical records relating to her treatment. The health authority argued that the order should not be made because they intended to rely on a defence under the Limitation Act 1980 which would probably succeed, whilst it was argued on H's behalf that the prospects of success of a defence based on limitation should be disregarded. The Court of Appeal held that the order for pre-action disclosure should be granted because, although the limitation defence had a strong prospect of succeeding, the pre-action disclosure might reveal facts relevant to the argument – e g as to why the court should exercise its powers to allow the action to proceed under s 33 Limitation Act 1980 (*Harris v Newcastle Health Authority*[4]).

It should be noted that the section does not enable the court to order the production of documents for which the respondent could claim privilege. 'Privilege' in this context usually either means 'legal professional privilege' or 'public interest immunity' (see pp 210–217, post). An example of a case where this latter head of privilege was unsuccessfully raised is *Campbell v Tameside Metropolitan Borough Council*:[5]

A schoolteacher was attacked at school by an eleven-year-old pupil and sustained serious injuries. Her legal advisers believed she might have had a claim against her employers for negligence in failing to transfer this child to a special school for maladjusted children. Before deciding whether or not to bring proceedings they wished to see whether the reports of other teachers and educational psychologists on the child showed him to be of so violent a disposition that he would be a danger at an ordinary school. They therefore issued an originating summons seeking an order for disclosure under section 33(2) of the Supreme Court Act. The local authority opposed the application on the ground that such confidential reports were privileged because disclosure would be contrary to the public interest. The Court of Appeal rejected this argument and ordered disclosure.

(2) *Pre-action inspection of property.* By section 33(1) of the Supreme Court Act 1981 the High Court[6] has power to make orders for:

'(*a*) the inspection, photographing, preservation, custody and detention of property which appears to the court to be property which may become the subject matter of subsequent proceedings, or as to which any question may arise in any such proceedings, and

3 [1973] 2 All ER 454, CA. *Note:* James LJ also said (at p 460): 'In order to take advantage of the section the applicant for relief must disclose the nature of the claim he intends to make and show not only the intention of making it but also that there is a reasonable basis for making it. Ill founded, irresponsible and speculative allegations or allegations based merely on hope would not provide a reasonable basis for an intended claim in subsequent proceedings.'
4 [1989] 2 All ER 273, CA.
5 [1982] QB 1065, [1982] 2 All ER 791, CA.
6 The County Court has the same power under County Courts Act 1984, s 52(1).

(*b*) the taking of samples of any such property as is mentioned in paragraph (*a*) and the carrying out of any experiment on or with any such property.'

The expression property 'includes any land, chattel or other corporeal property of any description'.[7]

Example. P is injured when he catches his hand in a press at work. In order to decide whether there has been a breach of the Factory Acts his solicitors can apply to the court for an order enabling them to inspect the machine before they finally decide whether or not to issue a writ.

The procedure is governed by Ord 29, r 7A. The applicant issues[8] and serves an originating summons accompanied by an affidavit showing how his claim falls within the order. If an order is made the defendant is nonetheless entitled to the costs of and incidental to the application and of complying with the order.[9] The High Court procedure is followed where the application is made in the county court.[10]

In one important respect the requirements of s 33(2) for an application for pre-action discovery of documents differ from those under s 33(1) for inspection of property; in the former case, but not the latter, proceedings in respect of personal injury or a person's death must be contemplated. Since all documents (eg letters, books, video tapes and computer disks) are also *property*, the question arises whether it it open to a prospective plaintiff in an action other than for personal injury to apply to the court before the commencement of proceedings for an order under s 33(1) to inspect such documents on the basis that they also constitute 'property', under that subsection. An application in these circumstances was unsuccessfully attempted in *Huddlestone v Control Risks Information Services Ltd*:[11]

The president and chairman of the Anti-Apartheid Movement feared that they would be defamed in a document to be provided for sale by the defendant, Control Risks Information Services Ltd, and described as 'a study of the activities of anti-apartheid groups in Europe, their relationship with terrorist groups and their intentions'. They therefore applied under the RSC Ord 29, r 7A for an order for pre-action production and inspection of the study as 'property' within the meaning of s 33(1) of the Supreme Court Act 1981. Hoffmann J held that whilst a written instrument or other object carrying information could be 'property' under s 33(1) as well as a 'document' under s 33(2), which category it fell into depended on whether the question which arose was concerned with the *medium*, ie the physical object carrying the information or with the *message*, ie the information which the object conveyed. Where the question relates to the actual physical object, the application is to inspect property under s 33(1), but where the information conveyed by the object is sought, the application is for discovery and is available only in the more limited circumstances under s 33(2). Accordingly, because the plaintiffs were concerned with whether the defendant's study contained defamatory words the application related to the information or 'message' and could be brought only under s 33(2). Since, the plaintiffs' claim was not in respect of personal injury the court had no jurisdiction under s 33 to order pre-action inspection of the defendant's study.

7 Section 35(5).
8 The applicant will of course have first written to the other side explaining what inspection is sought and requesting it should be given without the necessity of application to the court.
9 RSC Ord 62, r 6(9).
10 CCR Ord 13, r 7(1)(g).
11 [1987] 2 All ER 1035, QBD.

(3) *Discovery against persons who have facilitated the wrong in question.* To the general rule stated earlier in this chapter that the court will not compel an innocent party to disclose information which would assist a prospective litigant in determining whether or not to bring an action, there is an exception where that person though innocent has in some way facilitated or become 'mixed up' in the wrong in question. This exception was laid down by the House of Lords in *Norwich Pharmacal Co v Customs and Excise Comrs*[12] where the facts were:

> The Plaintiffs owned a patent for the production and sale of a chemical fertiliser. Every importer of chemicals into the United Kingdom is required to identify the substances imported to the Customs. The Excise statistics for 1969–1970 showed 30 consignments of this chemical fertiliser had been imported into the country by persons other than the plaintiffs in breach of the plaintiffs' monopoly. The Customs refused to disclose the identity of the importers.
>
> The House of Lords held that an *action for discovery* lay to compel the Commissioners to disclose the information. Although they had committed no tort themselves, without customs' clearance the fertiliser could not have been brought into the country and so they had unwittingly facilitated the breach of the plaintiffs' patent. Lord Reid (at 948) explained the principle to be applied as follows:
>> 'if through no fault of his own a person gets mixed up in the tortious acts of others so as to facilitate their wrongdoing he may incur no personal liability but he comes under a duty to assist the person who has been wronged by giving him full information and disclosing the identity of the wrongdoers. I do not think it matters whether he became so mixed up by voluntary action on his part or because it was his duty to do what he did. It may be that if this causes him expense the person seeking the information ought to reimburse him. But justice requires that he should co-operate in righting the wrong if he unwittingly facilitated its perpetration'.

The important point to note is that the plaintiff must prove the defendant has in some way *facilitated* the wrong in question.[13] That would seem to cover the case where A lends B his car and B (who is uninsured) is involved in an accident. It is an open question whether there would be an order in the case below:

> Farmer Giles lets some close friends camp at the bottom of his meadow for their summer holiday. Next door to the meadow is the country home of Sir Roderick Murgatroyd who at the material time had himself gone abroad on holiday. Unbeknown to Giles, his friends trespass on Sir Roderick's land causing extensive damage. When Sir Roderick returns from holiday he demands to know the identity of the campers. Giles refuses to tell him.

In the *Norwich Pharmacal* case the person who is required to provide the information is not himself guilty of any wrongdoing. Where the person is himself a wrongdoer, he is *a fortiori* under a duty to inform the plaintiff of the identity of those also concerned. This duty is however subject to his right to claim privilege against disclosure (eg on the grounds of self-incrimination or under s 10 of the Contempt of Court Act 1981).

12 [1974] AC 133, [1973] 2 All ER 943.
13 Where a defendant has been required to make disclosure, an order may also be issued against his servants or agents so where a polytechnic was ordered to disclose the identity of persons who had prevented a student attending classes, a further order was made requiring lecturers to identify the persons in question: *Harrington v North London Polytechnic* [1984] 3 All ER 666, CA.

Example 1. P had exclusive rights to gather shellfish in tidal waters near Hunstanton in Norfolk. P had seen three boats illegally fishing the area in question and was able to identify the owners of two of the boats in question. P brought proceedings against those owners (who were either themselves wrongdoers or facilitating a wrong by allowing their boats to be used by the wrongdoers). He then applied successfully by notice of motion for an order requiring them to disclose the identity of the persons aboard the vessels and of the owner of the third boat (*Loose v Williamson*[14]).

Example 2. During a national steel strike confidential documents belonging to BSC were copied and given to Granada Television who used them in a television programme. BSC issued proceedings against Granada and applied by notice of motion for an order that Granada should reveal the identity of the person who had provided the documents. *Held*, Granada would have been under a duty to disclose the identity of the wrongdoer even if they had been involved through no fault of their own; having used the documents for their own purposes knowing they had been so removed, they were themselves wrongdoers and *a fortiori* compellable to make such disclosure (*British Steel Corpn v Granada Television Ltd*[15]).

After the decision in the *British Steel* case, the Contempt of Court Act 1981 was passed which provides an important restriction on the grant of *Norwich Pharmacal* and similar orders. Section 10 provides:–

'No court may require a person to disclose, nor is any person guilty of contempt of court for refusing to disclose, the source of information contained in a publication for which he is responsible, unless it be established to the satisfaction of the court that disclosure is necessary in the interests of justice or national security or for the prevention of disorder or crime.'

The effect of this provision is that journalists' sources of information are generally protected from disclosure but the court may require the source to be identified if the privilege from disclosure is overridden by one of the four matters specifically listed in the section.

Example. X Ltd prepared a business plan for the purpose of obtaining a substantial bank loan to raise additional capital. An employee stole a copy of the plan and informed a journalist of its contents. The journalist checked certain matters with X Ltd who then realised their plan had been 'leaked'. They applied for an order for disclosure of the identity of the disloyal employee who had stolen the copy of the plan. The House of Lords held that it was necessary to order disclosure in the interests of justice. Per Lord Bridge:

'The importance to the plaintiffs of obtaining disclosure lies in the threat of severe damage to their business, and consequentially to the livelihood of their employees, which would arise from disclosure of the information contained in their corporate plan while their refinancing negotiations are still continuing. This threat, accurately described by Lord Donaldson MR as "ticking away beneath them like a time bomb", can only be defused if they can identify the source either as himself the thief of the stolen copy of the plan or as a means to lead to the identification of the thief and thus put themselves in a position to institute proceedings for the recovery of the missing document. The importance of protecting the source on the other hand is much diminished by the source's complicity, at the very least, in a gross breach of confidentiality which is not counterbalanced by any legitimate interest which publication of the information was calculated to serve. Disclosure in the interests of justice is, on this view of the balance, clearly of preponderating importance so as to override

14   [1978] 3 All ER 89, [1978] 1 WLR 639.
15   [1981] AC 1096, HL.

the policy underlying the statutory protection of sources and the test of necessity for disclosure is satisfied' (*X Ltd v Morgan–Grampian (Publishers) Ltd*[16]).

The procedure which was adopted in the *Norwich Pharmacal* case by the plaintiffs was based on the old Chancery action of discovery. A writ or originating summons is issued seeking an order 'that the defendants disclose the following documents . . .' More usually the order is sought in the context of existing proceedings where one wrongdoer or potential wrongdoer has been identified. The procedure is then by notice of motion (ChD) or summons (QBD) in those proceedings. Another area where *Norwich Pharmacal* type orders are sought is where a Mareva injunction has been issued. This is discussed at p 244, below).

ANTON PILLER ORDERS

There will be cases where it is obvious, because the defendant is involved in some type of fraud, that he would not obey the rules relating to discovery and, indeed, that he would almost certainly destroy or get rid of any incriminating documents or property. In such cases the court will make ex parte orders against the defendant requiring him to permit the plaintiff to search for and if necessary seize the evidence which would otherwise be destroyed. The principles governing the grant of *Anton Piller* orders are discussed fully in Chapter 10.

DISCOVERY BETWEEN PARTIES AFTER ACTION COMMENCED

(a) Inspection of documents referred to in pleadings etc
If any document is referred to in one party's pleadings or affidavits, his opponent may serve notice on him requiring him within 4 days of receipt of the notice to notify him of a time within 7 days when he will provide facilities for inspection of the document.[17] Thus, if for example, a pleading refers to 'an agreement in writing dated . . .' the other side can inspect that document without waiting for the formal discovery which occurs after the pleadings are closed. Indeed the order effectively enables inspection before the other party settles any pleading in reply. If inspection is not forthcoming the applicant can issue an interlocutory summons to a master for an order.

(b) Automatic discovery by list
In actions commenced by writ in the High Court each party is required within 14 days of the close of pleadings[18] to send the other party a list of all documents relating to matters in question in the action which are or have been in his possession, custody or power. The list is divided into two schedules; the first schedule sets out details of all documents which the party has at present in his possession and is subdivided into a list of documents he is willing to disclose and those for which he claims privilege; the second schedule describes the material documents which were formerly

16 [1991] 1 AC 1, [1990] 2 All ER 1, HL.
17 RSC Ord 24, r 10; CCR Ord 14, r 4; see County Court Form N266.
18 See RSC Ord 24, r 2 and Ord 25, r 8(1)(a); close of pleadings is defined by RSC Ord 18, r 20 as occurring 14 days after service of reply or defence to counterclaim or if neither such reply nor defence to counterclaim is served, as the expiration of 14 days after service of the defence.

in his possession stating when they were last in his possession, what became of them and in whose possession they now are. The list must conclude with a notice stating a place and time within 7 days of service of the list at which the documents may be inspected.[19] It is important to notice that the exchange of lists and inspection of disclosed documents takes place without any specific order of the court, the process occurs automatically at the close of pleadings.[20]

(c) Orders of discovery

The process of automatic discovery by exchange of lists does not apply in the following cases:

(1) Third party procedure.
(2) Originating summons procedure (where frequently there will be no dispute on evidence).
(3) To *defendants* in personal injury cases where liability is admitted or where the claim arises out of a road accident (since there are generally *no* relevant documents).[21]
(4) Certain county court proceedings.[22]

In all the above cases however, the parties may serve on the other side a request either for delivery of a list of all material documents or for discovery of specific documents, and, in default, apply to the court.[23]

(d) What documents are to be disclosed

There is an important difference between discovery and inspection in that on discovery one is notifying the other side of the *existence* of the document in question whilst at inspection one is *showing* the document to the other side. It should be noted that all relevant documents must be disclosed on discovery even though inspection will be refused on a claim for privilege:

> 'The rule as to the discovery of documents is the exact contrary to that as to inspection – you must disclose every document you have in your possession, whether you are bound to produce it or not.'[24]

The documents which must be disclosed are all documents 'relating to any matter in question . . . in the action'. This expression covers not only documents which are direct evidence of the facts in issue or which one intends to use at the trial but every document which contains information which may enable one's opponent to advance his own case or damage one's own case or which 'may fairly lead him to a train of inquiry which may have

19 The above paragraph paraphrases the provisions of RSC Ord 24, rr 1, 2, 5 and 9.
20 The standard form used is set out, ante.
21 RSC Ord 25, r 8(1)(a); the plaintiff in such cases is only required to make disclosure of documents relating to special damage (eg loss of earnings).
22 See CCR Ord 17, r 11. The automatic directions which apply in default and fixed date actions require discovery within 28 days of the close of pleadings. Automatic discovery does not occur if the proceedings fall in one of the excluded categories under r 17(1) (eg possession actions) but where such actions are defended discovery will almost invariably be ordered at the pre-trial review.
23 In the High Court the application is by summons to the master under Ord 24, r 3. In the county court the procedure, which is governed by Ord 14, rr 1 and 2, is by application to the district judge.
24 *Gardner v Irvin* (1878) 4 Ex D 49, CA.

either of these two consequences'.[25] The exact limit of this rule has however never been defined.

> *Example.* A (a rogue) sues B on an oral contract. In particulars of his pleading he sets out the precise date and time and place of the alleged agreement. B has in his possession his passport which shows he was out of the country at the relevant time. Is B bound to disclose this document?

One would have thought the answer to the above problem was clearly in the affirmative, even though the disclosure would enable A to trim his account in advance of the trial to meet the new evidence. However in *Britten v F H Pilcher & Sons*[26] (where insurers in a workman's claim for personal injuries did not disclose the existence of a statement headed 'for company's solicitors' and made by the plaintiff himself immediately after the accident and produced it at the trial to rebut his sworn evidence) Thesiger J said (at 493):

> 'The difficulty that I feel in saying that this document ought to have been disclosed . . . is that this is the sort of document that is prepared . . . in many cases of mining accidents, in many cases of railway accidents and in very many industrial injury cases where it is to the advantage of a potential defendant and employer to ascertain as quickly as possible what the various witnesses in and about the place can tell them as to how the accident happened. I have nowhere previously . . . heard it suggested that all documents obtained under a heading like this from the various witnesses ought to be disclosed to a plaintiff in order that he can avoid calling witnesses without giving them the opportunity of trimming the evidence they propose to give to the more contemporary document.'

(e) Failure to make discovery

A party who fails to serve a list as required by the rules may be ordered to do so under Order 24, r 3, but suppose one party suspects the other has not revealed a relevant document in his possession. In such a case he may serve a notice requiring that party to verify his list by affidavit.[27] The affidavit must be served within 14 days. Alternatively (or if the procedure above has failed to produce disclosure of the document) he can apply to the master with an affidavit setting out why he believes his opponent has the document in question. The other side will be ordered to file an affidavit dealing specifically with the allegation. This affidavit is regarded as conclusive.[28] Where a dispute arises as to whether the existence of documents should be *disclosed* the burden is upon the party objecting to disclosure of the documents to satisfy the court that discovery in *not* necessary for disposing fairly of the action or saving costs.[29]

---

25 *Compagnie Financière Et Commerciale Du Pacifique v Peruvian Guano Co* (1882) 11 QBD 55, CA.
26 [1969] 1 All ER 491. This case is actually reported because the unsuccessful plaintiffs resisted an order for costs on the grounds that if the document had been disclosed they might have decided not to continue the case. Such statements from witnesses will normally be covered by legal professional privilege which protects them from inspection but not disclosure. Any such privilege may have to be waived, however, upon an order under RSC Ord 38, r 2A that the parties exchange statements of oral testimony on which they intend to rely at the trial (see below p 291).
27 See RSC Ord 24, r 2(7).
28 See Ord 24, r 7. In *Lonrho plc v Fayed (No 3)* (1993) Times, 24 June, the Court of Appeal held that such an affidavit was conclusive and could not be controverted by a further affidavit or by cross-examination.
29 See *Dolling-Baker v Merrett* [1991] 2 All ER 890, CA.

(f) Inspection

This crucial stage of the action is described in the *Justice Report* on *Going to Law*[30] as follows:

> '"Inspection" is a lengthy meeting between representatives of both firms of solicitors at which each inspects the documents in the possession of the other. All this is painstaking and important work, on which success or failure at the trial may depend. It requires many hours of undisturbed concentration, the writing of a good many letters, and much time on the Xerox machine.'

The reason of course why this stage is of such immense importance is that the most telling evidence at the trial is often not what the parties say in the witness box but what contemporary documents show they said and did at the time when the cause of action arose. It is significant that the compilers of the Justice Report found that settlements of actions are most commonly effected at the time of compilation of lists of inspection:

> 'Because of the mounting expenses of this phase of the proceedings often reflected in requests from the solicitors to their clients for the payment of more money on account of costs, it is a phase when many actions are settled – especially if the collection of documents for discovery shows that they will not help one's client's case, and more favourable terms of settlement can therefore be expected if the other side has not yet had a chance to see them. But there are other reasons too; inspection of documents is often the first real chance that each side has to assess the true strength of the other's case, and it provides the only occasion before the trial itself when the solicitors are bound to meet, and can casually talk about settlement, without being suspected of weakness by being the first to ask for a meeting.'

(g) Documents privileged from inspection

Although the general rule is that each party is bound to show the other side all material documents in his possession the courts have held that the public interest requires that there should be exceptions where there are factors outweighing this general rule. The exceptional categories in which privilege from production may arise are: (i) communications between legal advisers and client or third party (legal professional privilege); (ii) documents which may expose a party to criminal proceedings; and (iii) documents coming into existence as a part of 'without prejudice' communications. It should be noted that where a dispute arises as to whether a document disclosed in a party's list should be inspected by the other side, the burden is on the party seeking inspection to show that its inspection is necessary for disposing fairly of the case or saving costs.[31] Even where it is so shown, it remains open to the party objecting to inspection to argue that the document is privileged.

(i) *Legal professional privilege.* The most important ground of privilege in practice is that which protects from inspection any direct communication between a party and his legal advisers. This covers communications before any litigation has begun or was even contemplated. It extends to communications between employers and salaried solicitors employed directly by them (eg the legal departments of ministries and large companies). The

---

30 Stevens 1974, p 14.
31 *Dolling-Baker v Merrett* [1991] 2 All ER 890, CA. Note, however, that in county court proceedings the burden is on the person objecting to inspection to show that inspection is not necessary either for disposing fairly of the action or for saving costs: see CCR Ord 14, r 8(1).

reason for this privilege is that the courts consider they have an overriding obligation to ensure full and candid disclosure by clients to their legal advisers which would not be possible unless the clients were aware that their confidences could not be broken. In *Ventouris v Mountain (The Italia Express)*[32] the basis of the privilege was explained in the following terms:

'The doctrine of legal professional privilege is rooted in the public interest, which requires that hopeless and exaggerated claims and unsound and spurious defences be so far as possible discouraged, and civil disputes so far as possible settled without resort to judicial decision. To this end it is necessary that actual and potential litigants, be they claimants or respondents, should be free to unburden themselves without reserve to their legal advisers, and their legal advisers be free to give honest and candid advice on a sound factual basis, without fear that these communications may be relied on by an opposing party . . .'

Documents are also privileged if they are prepared by a third party for submission to the litigant's solicitor in order to enable him to advise his client (eg expert reports in a factory accident). Legal professional privilege does *not* apply to documents which were *obtained* by a party's solicitors for the purposes of the litigation but which were not *created* for that purpose.

Example. A ship was destroyed in an explosion. The shipowner sued the insurance underwriters for the value of the ship. The underwriters claimed the ship had been deliberately destroyed so as to obtain the insurance monies. They obtained from a third party documents tending to show this was the case. The shipowner applied for inspection of these documents but the insurers objected on the grounds that, since they came into their possession in the course of preparing their case, the documents were covered by legal professional privilege. The Court of Appeal held the documents were not privileged from inspection. Per Bingham LJ:

'The courts must not in any way encroach on the right of a litigant or potential litigant to seek and obtain legal advice on his prospects and the conduct of proceedings under the seal of confidence or on the right of such a litigant and his legal adviser to prepare for and conduct his case without, directly or indirectly, revealing the effect of that advice. In recognition of these rights, perhaps generously interpreted, proofs of witnesses, whether factual or expert, and communications with potential witnesses, have been held immune from production. But it is hard to see how these rights are infringed if a party is obliged to produce an original document which was in existence before litigation was in the air, and which a litigant or his legal adviser has obtained from a third party for purposes of the litigation, but which the third party could himself be compelled to produce at the trial without any possible ground for objection.' (*Ventouris v Mountain (The Italia Express)*[33]).

Even if it is established that one of the reasons a document came into existence was that it should be used by a solicitor for the purposes of conducting litigation, it still does not necessarily follow that it is covered by legal professional privilege. So for example if it was contemplated that it should initially be used for some other purpose the privilege may not attach to it.

Example 1. A member of a trade union who thought that he had been unjustly dismissed by his employers furnished the union authorities with information in

32 [1991] 3 All ER 472, CA per Bingham LJ at 475g.
33 [1991] 3 All ER 472, CA. Similarly, where non-privileged documents are copied for the purposes of obtaining legal advice no privilege will attach to the copies: see *Dubai Bank Ltd v Galadari* [1990] Ch 98, [1989] 3 All ER 769, CA.

writing as to the facts of the case in order to satisfy them it was proper for them to instruct a solicitor on his behalf. His employers obtained discovery of this document on the ground that the immediate purpose of the document was not its reference to a solicitor but merely to the trade union committee.[34]

Example 2. Purchase tax was assessed on the basis of the wholesale value of amusement machines manufactured and sold by A. The Commissioners of Customs and Excise obtained substantial documentary evidence from A's customers on which they based their assessment of value for tax purposes. A challenged the assessment and demanded production of the evidence collected from his customers. The Commissioners claimed privilege on the ground that they had expected the assessment to be challenged and knew when they collected the information that they would probably be passing it to their legal advisers. The claim for privilege failed on the basis that the *immediate* purpose of the document was not its reference to a solicitor but merely to provide the Commissioners with the information for making an assessment.[35]

A limit is however placed on this rule where an intermediary receives a document which he will transmit at once to legal advisers without acting on it himself; in such a case the document remains privileged. Thus an accident claim form sent to insurers is privileged.[36] Similarly it is submitted that an accident report sent to a trade union officer for immediate despatch to the trade union's legal department or solicitors would be protected.

The fourth point of importance so far as this aspect of privilege is concerned is that where the report in question has been prepared for more than one reason, it will only be protected by privilege if the dominant reason was so that it could be referred to solicitors to assist them in prosecuting or handling a potential claim.

Example. A workman was fatally injured in an accident on the railway. Two days later a report was prepared incorporating statements of witnesses. This was sent to the safety inspectorate to assist them in their investigation of the accident. The report was headed with a statement that it would be finally sent to the Board's solicitors for the purpose of enabling them to advise the Board. The workman's widow sued under the Fatal Accidents Acts and sought discovery of the report. The Board refused to disclose it on the grounds that since one of the reasons why it was prepared was to assist their solicitors in dealing with any claim, it was protected by privilege. The House of Lords ordered disclosure on the grounds the privilege only applied when its reference to legal advisers was the dominant purpose of the person who made the report.[37]

(ii) *Privilege against self-incrimination.* Where the production of documents might expose the producing party to criminal prosecution or any penalty[38]

---

34 *Jones v Great Central Rly Co* [1910] AC 4, HL.

35 *Alfred Compton Amusement Machines Ltd v Customs and Excise Comrs (No 2)* [1974] AC 405, [1973] 2 All ER 1169, HL. Note an alternative claim based on Crown Privilege succeeded.

36 *Westminster Airways Ltd v Kuwait Oil Co Ltd* [1951] 1 KB 134, [1950] 2 All ER 596, CA.

37 *Waugh v British Railways Board* [1980] AC 521, [1979] 2 All ER 1169, HL. Note this decision should prevent the use of this claim of privilege for most accident reports: per Lord Edmund-Davies at 544 'the test of dominance will, as I think, be difficult to satisfy when inquiries are instituted and reports produced automatically whenever any mishap occurs, whatever its nature, its gravity, or even its triviality'.

38 Under the Civil Evidence Act 1968, s 14(1) any right to privilege in civil proceedings on the grounds of self-incrimination is limited to the production of documents which 'would tend to expose that [party] to proceedings for an offence or for the recovery of any penalty'. For this purpose a 'penalty' includes a fine imposed by the court for a civil contempt: see *Bhimji v Chatwani (No 3)* [1992] 4 All ER 912, per Knox J.

he may claim privilege in respect of those documents.[39] Privilege from production of documents or furnishing information on the grounds of self-incrimination has, however, been widely eroded by statute. For example, the privilege has been removed in respect of criminal liability under the Theft Act 1968 which may arise from civil proceedings for recovery of any property[40] and in relation to intellectual property actions where production might expose the defendant to prosecution for related offences.[41] The extent of the exceptions to privilege on the ground of self-incrimination has increasingly led to judicial criticism. In *AT & T Istel Ltd v Tully*.[42] Lord Griffiths said (at 533):

> 'I can for myself see no argument in favour of the privilege against producing a document the contents of which may go to show that the holder has committed a criminal offence. The contents of the document will speak for itself and there is no risk of the false confession which underlies the privilege against having to answer questions that may incriminate the speaker. The rule may once have been justified by the fear that without it an accused might be tortured into production of documents but those days are surely past and this consideration cannot apply in the context of a civil action. I therefore associate myself with Lord Templeman when he says . . .:
>
>> "I regard the privilege against self-incrimination exercisable in civil proceedings as an archaic and unjustifiable survival from the past when the court directs the production of relevant documents and requires the defendant to specify his dealings with the plaintiff's property or money."'

In the *Tully* case the House of Lords held that there was no absolute privilege against answering self-incriminating questions in civil proceedings and the courts could order disclosure where the relevant prosecuting authorities gave an unequivocal undertaking not to use the material disclosed in criminal proceedings.

(iii) *'Without prejudice' communications.* Letters passing between solicitors in an attempt to settle a case are privileged from production in court if written without prejudice to their clients' claims. Usually, this form of privilege is achieved by marking the letters with the words 'without prejudice' but even in the absence of these words the courts may be prepared to infer that the

---

39 For the basis of this ground of privilege and other 'rights of silence' see *Smith v Director of Serious Fraud Office* [1992] 3 All ER 456, HL per Lord Mustill at 463–464.

40 See Theft Act 1968, s 31. But note, however, that s 31 removes privilege only in respect of self-incrimination of offences 'under' the Theft Act 1968 and does not extend, eg, to offences of conspiracy to defraud either at common law or under the Criminal Law Act 1977. Further, s 31 applies only to proceedings 'for the recovery of any property' etc and not to claims for damages: see *Sociedade Nacional de Combustiveis de Angola UEE v Lundqvist* [1991] 2 QB 310, [1990] 3 All ER 283, CA; *Tate Access Floors Inc v Boswell* [1991] Ch 512, [1990] 3 All ER 303, CA.

41 Supreme Court Act 1981, s 72. Privilege has also been held to be impliedly removed in relation to questioning under a statute such as the Companies Act 1985 or the Insolvency Act 1986: see *Re London United Investments plc* [1992] Ch 578, [1992] 2 All ER 842, CA (no privilege on examination by inspectors appointed by Department of Trade and Industry under s 432 of the Companies Act 1985); *Bank of England v Riley* [1992] Ch 475, [1992] 1 All ER 769, CA (no privilege on examination under the Banking Act 1987); *Bishopsgate Investment Management Ltd v Maxwell* [1993] Ch 1, [1992] 2 All ER 856, CA (person examined by office-holders of a company under ss 235 and 236 of the Companies Act 1985 not entitled to rely on privilege against self-incrimination).

42 [1993] AC 45, [1992] 3 All ER 523, HL.

negotiations were conducted on such a basis.[43] Such correspondence will appear in the section of the List of Documents which sets out material for which privilege is claimed. The privilege may attach not only to correspondence itself but to other documents which come into existence in pursuance of without prejudice discussions.[44] The rule also prevents one party to litigation seeking disclosure of documents which have passed between the other parties in the course of negotiations for settlement:

> *Example.* A dispute arose between main contractors on a very large building development and subcontractors as to the amount due to the subcontractors. The main contractors would not pay because the surveyors for the site owner would not accept the validity of the claims. Eventually the main contractors brought Official Referee proceedings against the subcontractors and the site owners in which the critical issue was the value to be placed on the subcontractors' work. By the time of completion there were many other disputes between the site owners and the main contractors. Eventually they settled *all* their disputes on the basis of a payment of £1.2 million by the site owners to the main contractors. The main contractors refused to tell the subcontractors what value in the overall settlement had been placed on the subcontractors' claim. The subcontractors took out a summons for specific discovery of the correspondence between the site owners and the main contractors; the main contractors claimed such documents would be inadmissible evidence in the Official Referee's case and were immune from discovery as being 'without prejudice' documents. The House of Lords upheld the claim to privilege: per Lord Griffiths:
>
> > 'I have come to the conclusion that the wiser course is to protect without prejudice communications between parties to litigation from production to other parties in the same litigation. In multi-party litigation it is not an infrequent experience that one party takes up an unreasonably intransigent attitude that makes it extremely difficult to settle with him. In such circumstances it would, I think, place a serious fetter on negotiations between other parties if they knew that everything that passed between them would ultimately have to be revealed to the one obdurate litigant. What would in fact happen would be that nothing would be put on paper, but this itself is a recipe for disaster in difficult negotiations which are far better spelt out with precision in writing.
> >
> > If the party who obtains discovery of the without prejudice correspondence can make no use of it at trial it can be of only very limited value to him. It may give some insight into his opponent's general approach to the issues in the case but in most cases this is likely to be of marginal significance and will probably be revealed to him in direct negotiations in any event. In my view, this advantage does not outweigh the damage that would be done to the conduct of settlement negotiations if solicitors thought that what was said and written between them would become common currency available to all other parties to the litigation. In my view, the general public policy that applies to protect genuine negotiations from being admissible in evidence should also be extended to protect those negotiations from being discoverable to third parties.' (*Rush & Tompkins Ltd v Greater London Council*[45]).

---

43 See *Rush & Tompkins Ltd v Greater London Council* [1988] 3 All ER 737, HL, per Lord Griffiths at 740b.

44 See, for example, *Rabin v Mendoza & Co* [1954] 1 All ER 247, CA, where, in pursuance of without prejudice discussions, the defendant surveyors obtained a report from another surveyor on the prospects of obtaining insurance cover for the plaintiff's potential claims. In subsequent proceedings the plaintiff's attempt to obtain discovery of the report failed on the grounds that it came into being as a result of without prejudice negotiations and was therefore privileged from production.

45 [1989] AC 1280, [1988] 3 All ER 737, HL.

Negofiations between parties which begin on a 'without prejudice' basis remain so unless the party seeking to change that basis shows that it is 'brought home and made absolutely clear' to the other party that the without prejudice basis of the negotiations is being changed.[46]

(h) Disclosure of public documents

The basic rule that any document which is relevant to the litigation must be disclosed applies even though the document in question emanates from a government department or local authority or some other public body. The courts will, however, refuse to order disclosure where they are satisfied that to order production would be contrary to the public interest.

> *Example.* In 1939 a new submarine 'Thetis' was lost at sea while engaged in a trial dive. The widow of one of the sailors who died sued the shipbuilders alleging negligent design of the vessel. The shipbuilders were instructed by the Admiralty to refuse discovery of the plans of the vessel and this objection was upheld by the House of Lords. Per Viscount Simon LC: 'The principle to be applied in every case is that documents otherwise relevant and liable to production must not be produced if the public interest requires that they should be withheld. This test may be found to be satisfied either (a) by having regard to the contents of the particular document or (b) by the fact that the document belongs to a class which, on grounds of public interest, must as a class be withheld from production.' The Lord Chancellor went on to indicate the cases where such a claim could not properly be made: 'It is not a sufficient ground that the documents are "State documents" or "official" or are marked "confidential". It would not be a good ground that production might involve the department or the government in parliamentary discussion or in public criticism, or might necessitate the attendance as witnesses or otherwise of officials who have pressing duties elsewhere. Neither would it be a good ground that production might tend to expose a want of efficiency in the administration or tend to lay the department open to claims for compensation. In a word, it is not enough that the minister of the department does not want to have the documents produced. The minister . . . ought not to take the responsibility of withholding production except in cases when the public interest would otherwise be damnified, for example where disclosure would be injurious to national defence, or to good diplomatic relations, or where the practice of keeping a class of documents secret is necessary for the proper functioning of the public service' (*Duncan v Cammell Laird & Co Ltd*[47]).

Where a claim for 'public interest immunity' is made the minister concerned provides a certificate explaining why the documents should not be revealed. The court may accept this statement as showing a sufficient reason for refusing disclosure but it has the right to inspect the document to determine whether the plea for immunity is well founded:

> 'A claim made by a minister on the basis that the disclosure of the contents would be prejudicial to the public interest must receive the greatest weight: but . . . the minister should go as far as he properly can without prejudicing the public interest in saying why the contents require protection. In such cases it would be rare indeed for the court to override the minister but it has the legal power to do so, first inspecting the document itself and then, if it thinks proper to do so, ordering its production.'[48]

---

46 *Cheddar Valley Engineering Ltd v Chaddlewood Homes Ltd* [1992] 4 All ER 942.
47 [1942] AC 624.
48 Per Lord Upjohn: *Conway v Rimmer* [1968] AC 910 at 993, [1968] 1 All ER 874 at 914, (reports on probationary constable not covered by privilege).

Where the claim is made by a local authority or police force or similar body the point is taken by delivering an affidavit from a senior official. In practice the objection seems to be taken in two different types of case:

(1) *where the documents contain information provided in confidence.* In such a case the mere fact that the information was supplied in confidential circumstances is not sufficient reason for refusing disclosure; it is necessary in order to resist disclosure to show that the harm which would be caused to the public service by disclosure outweighs the harm to the administration of justice in concealing from the court relevant information. Thus the courts have ordered disclosure of reports on probationary police officers[49] and disturbed children at school[50] but refused to order disclosure of the identity of persons giving information to the Customs[51] or the police[52] or the NSPCC.[53] Essentially in such cases the court has to balance competing claims.

(2) *where the documents might reveal the formulation of public policy.* It is on this basis that, for example, cabinet minutes are always said to be privileged. Thus per Lord Reid in *Conway v Rimmer* (at 952):

> 'I do not doubt that there are certain classes of documents which ought not to be disclosed whatever their content might be. Virtually everyone agrees that Cabinet minutes and the like ought not to be disclosed until such time as they are only of historical interest. . . . The business of government is difficult enough as it is, and no government could contemplate with equanimity the inner workings of the government machine being exposed to the gaze of those ready to criticize without adequate knowledge of the background and perhaps with some axe to grind. And that must, in my view, also apply to all documents concerned with policy making within departments including, it may be, minutes and the like by quite junior officials and correspondence with outside bodies. Further it may be that deliberations about a particular case require protection as much as deliberation about policy. I do not think it is possible to limit such documents by any definition. But there seems to me to be a wide difference between such documents and routine reports.'

In *Burmah Oil Co Ltd v Governor & Co of the Bank of England*[54] the plaintiffs sought discovery of documents which they believed would show the Government had induced the defendants to pressurise them into selling their shares at an unconscionable price. The House of Lords considered the documents and then refused to order disclosure because they contained nothing of relevance to the case. It seems implicit in the decision that if the documents had advanced the plaintiff's case disclosure would have been

---

49 *Conway v Rimmer* [1968] AC 910, [1968] 1 All ER 874, HL.
50 *Campbell v Tameside Metropolitan Borough Council* [1982] QB 1065, [1982] 2 All ER 791, CA.
51 *Alfred Compton Amusement Machines Ltd v Customs and Excise Comrs (No 2)* [1974] AC 405, [1973] 2 All ER 1169, HL.
52 Note in proceedings against the police public interest immunity extends to statements taken by the officers investigating the complaint (including the complainant's own statement) and to the transcripts of disciplinary proceedings: see *Makanjuola v Metropolitan Police Comr* [1992] 3 All ER 617, CA. Note the immunity prevents a police officer obtaining production of police files for the purpose of proceedings before industrial tribunals even though information in such files was directly relevant to the issues between her and the police authority: see *Halford v Sharples* [1992] 3 All ER 624, CA. Immunity has been held *not* to apply, however, to statements made during the course of a police *discrimination grievance procedure:* see *Metropolitan Police Comr v Locker* [1993] ICR 440, [1993] IRLR 319, per Knox J.
53 *D v NSPCC* [1978] AC 171, [1977] 1 All ER 589, HL.
54 [1980] AC 1090, [1979] 3 All ER 700 HL.

ordered notwithstanding the claim for privilege. In other words even though the documents relate to the formulation of policy, the courts will still order disclosure if they are of opinion that the reasons advanced for keeping the contents of the documents secret are outweighed in the particular case by the need to see justice is done.

DISCOVERY BETWEEN CO-DEFENDANTS

RSC Ord 24, r 6 provides that a defendant is entitled to receive a copy of any list served by any other defendant on the plaintiff. In the county court, the automatic directions under Ord 17, r 11(5) provide for each party to serve a list of documents on *all* other parties.[55]

DISCOVERY AGAINST NON-PARTIES

The basic rule is that the parties to an action have no right to compel persons not parties to disclose relevant documents in their possession. They can issue a *subpoena duces tecum* requiring the non-party to attend at the trial with the relevant document but they are not entitled to inspect it before the trial. To this general rule are four exceptions:

(i) In personal injury and fatal accident cases, a party to the action can apply for an order that a person who is not a party (eg a hospital authority) disclose relevant documents. The application is made by summons served on
   (*a*) the person holding the documents, and
   (*b*) on all other parties to the action.
Note this procedure can only be adopted *after* an action has begun (see s 34(2) of the Supreme Court Act 1981; RSC Ord 24, r 7A(2); County Court Act 1984, s 53(2).

(ii) A similar application can be made to inspect property held by a person who is not a party to an action (see s 34(3) of the Supreme Court Act 1981; RSC Ord 29, r 7A(2); County Court Act 1984, s 53(3).

(iii) It may be that an application could be made under the principle in the *Norwich Pharmacal* case (see page 205, ante) for an order against a person not a party but who facilitated the commission of the alleged wrong by the defendant.

(iv) Either party may apply ex parte to the master for an order that a bank not a party to the action be required to permit him to inspect entries in its books and take copies – s 7 of the Bankers' Books Evidence Act 1879. If the account in question has been held at any time by the other party a summons will be issued so he can attend at the hearing of the application.

MEDICAL EXAMINATION OF THE PLAINTIFF

Although nothing in the rules provides for the compulsory medical examination of the plaintiff in a personal injury case (or other case where his health or life expectancy would be relevant) the courts will refuse to allow the plaintiff to continue his case if he will not agree to a reasonable request for

---

55 Where there is no automatic discovery an application would be made under CCR Ord 14, r 1.

medical examination. In *Edmeades v Thames Board Mills Ltd*[56] Lord Denning (at 129) (after quoting from the Winn Committee on Personal Injuries Litigation[57] where the committee recommended a rule that the plaintiff should be required to submit to medical examination but felt legislation would be necessary to create such a rule) said:

> 'I do not think legislation is necessary. This court has ample jurisdiction to grant a stay whenever it is just and reasonable so to do. It can, therefore, order a stay if the conduct of the plaintiff in refusing a reasonable request is such as to prevent the just determination of the cause.'

A request for examination would not be reasonable if it involved the plaintiff undergoing tests which would cause injury or serious discomfort.[58] The plaintiff is not entitled to stipulate the conditions under which he will undergo examination. Thus he has no right to object to the defendants' choice of consultant[59] nor to insist on his own doctor's attendance at the examination.[60] He is *not* entitled to insist that the defendants should provide his solicitors with a copy of the report made by their consultant[61] although (as will be seen later) he will usually receive a copy in due course if the defendants intend to rely upon the report at the trial.

INSPECTION OF PROPERTY

Either party can apply at any stage in an action for an order permitting him to inspect premises or property in the possession of another party.[62] The order may authorise him to draw plans, take samples, etc as may be necessary.

EXPERT EVIDENCE

A report from an expert concerning the subject matter of the action and commissioned when proceedings were contemplated or after they had commenced is clearly a privileged document and inspection of it will not be ordered.

> *Example.* Before P's solicitors issued a writ for damages for personal injuries they permitted the defendant's insurers to arrange for their doctors to examine P but omitted to take an undertaking from the insurers that copies of the medical reports would be sent to them. After the action was commenced they applied for an order against the defendants requiring them to provide copies of the reports. The order was refused on the ground that the reports were privileged. Per Roskill LJ: 'so long as we have an adversary system, a party is entitled not to produce documents which are properly protected by privilege if it is not to his advantage to produce them and even though their production might assist his adversary if his adversary or his solicitor were aware of their contents or might lead the court to a different conclusion from that to which the court would come in ignorance of

56 [1969] 2 QB 67, [1969] 2 All ER 127, CA.
57 Cmnd 3691 of 1968 at para 312.
58 See *Aspinall v Sterling Mansell Ltd* [1981] 3 All ER 866 and *Prescott v Bulldog Tools* [1981] 3 All ER 869.
59 *Starr v National Coal Board* [1977] 1 All ER 243, [1977] 1 WLR 63, CA. In theory he could object if he could prove the consultant selected would not produce a fair report; in practice it would be impossible to show this.
60 *Hall v Avon Health Authority* [1980] 1 All ER 516, [1980] 1 WLR 481, CA.
61 *Megarity v D J Ryan & Sons Ltd* [1980] 2 All ER 832, [1980] 1 WLR 1237, CA.
62 RSC Ord 29, r 2; CCR Ord 13, r 7.

their existence. Some may regret this; but the law always has allowed it and it is not for us to change the law in this respect.'[63]

This rule if unmodified would cause very great inconvenience in practice since by its very nature opinion evidence requires reflection and careful study by the opposing advocates and experts. Indeed it would be a great injustice if an advocate was forced to cross-examine on a complex statement of expert opinion without the opportunity of digesting it and seeking advice from his own experts. For this reason Parliament has enacted that the courts shall have power to compel the disclosure of opinion evidence *which is to be put in at the trial.*[64]

'Notwithstanding any enactment or rule of law by virtue of which documents prepared for the purpose of pending or contemplated civil proceedings are . . . privileged . . . provisions may be made by rules of court in any civil proceedings to direct . . . that the parties . . . shall each . . . disclose to the other . . . in the form of one or more expert reports the expert evidence . . . which he proposes to adduce as part of his case at the trial. . . .'[65]

The sanction behind the court's order is that a party will not be permitted to call expert evidence which has not been disclosed.

The basic rule applied in the High Court is that expert evidence can only be called either by agreement or by leave of the court (RSC Ord 38, r 36(1)); normally leave will be granted only on the basis that the evidence is disclosed to the other side (RSC Ord 38, r 37(1)). The High Court rules are expressly applied to county court procedure by CCR Ord 20, r 28. This basic principle that there must be disclosure of expert evidence is so important that we set out below the relevant text of Ord 38, r 37(1):

'. . . where in any cause or matter an application is made under rule 36(1) in respect of oral expert evidence, then, unless the Court considers that there are special reasons for not doing so, it shall direct that the substance of the evidence be disclosed in the form of a written report or reports to such other parties and within such period as the Court may specify.'

In *Naylor v Preston Area Health Authority*[66] (which was a case under the old rules) the following statement of principle was made by Sir John Donaldson MR (which is applicable to the current rules):

'The exercise of discretion has to be approached on the basis of the philosophy that the basic objective is always the achievement of true justice, which takes account of time, money and what can only be described as the anguish of uncertainty, as well as of a just outcome. It has to be exercised on the basis that the procedure of the courts must be, and is, intended to achieve the resolution of disputes by a variety of methods, of which a resolution by judgment is but one, and probably the least desirable. Accordingly, anything which enables the parties to appreciate the true strength or weakness of their positions at the earliest possible moment and at the same time enables them to enter on fully informed and realistic discussions designed to achieve a consensual resolution of the dispute is very much in the public interest.'

---

63 *Causton v Mann Egerton (Johnsons) Ltd* [1974] 1 All ER 453, at 460.
64 *Note* the eventual evidence may be *oral:* the section requires that the report on which oral evidence will be based should be submitted to the other side. *Note* also the rule does *not* apply to opinion evidence which one party has obtained (such as a medical report unfavourable to his case) which he does *not* propose to call.
65 Civil Evidence Act 1972, s 2(3).
66 [1987] 2 All ER 353, CA.

In *Naylor* (which was a medical negligence case) the Court of Appeal identified the sort of circumstances which might justify non-disclosure as including:

(i)   cases where the particulars of negligence were too vague for the defendants' expert to be able to deal with them (in such a case there would be an order for sequential exchange, ie the plaintiff would reveal his report first and the defendants would subsequently serve a report in response);

(ii) cases where disclosure may enable the plaintiff or his experts to trim their evidence;

(iii) some cases where there is evidence which shows that the plaintiff's alleged disability is non-existent or exaggerated, or is due to an undisclosed pre-existing medical condition.

Although the principles on which the court decides whether there should be disclosure of expert evidence are clear, the procedural rules are a little complicated because sometimes the disclosure is made without application and sometimes there may have to be an application. The procedure is summarised below:

(i) High Court: personal injury cases
In personal injury cases the plaintiff will have served a medical report with the statement of claim (see RSC Ord 18, r 12(1A) discussed at p 129 ante). Thereafter the procedure is governed by the automatic directions set out in RSC Ord 25, r 8 which provide:

'(1)(*b*) subject to paragraph (2) where any party intends to place reliance at the trial on expert evidence, he shall, within 10 weeks, disclose the substance of that evidence to the other parties in the form of a written report, which shall be agreed if possible;

(*c*) unless such reports are agreed, the parties shall be at liberty to call as expert witnesses those witnesses the substance of whose evidence has been disclosed in accordance with the preceding sub-paragraph, except that the number of expert witnesses shall be limited in any case to two medical experts and one expert of any other kind . . .

(2) Where paragraph 1(*b*) applies to more than one party the reports shall be disclosed by mutual exchange, medical for medical and non-medical for non-medical, within the time provided or as soon thereafter as the reports on each side are available.

(3) Nothing in paragraph (1) shall prevent any party to an action to which this rule applies from applying to the Court for such further or different directions or orders as may, in the circumstances, be appropriate or prevent the making of an order for the transfer of the proceedings to a county court.'

If a party does not wish to disclose his report or wishes disclosure to be sequential, he will issue a summons under RSC Ord 38, r 36 for the court to give specific directions.

(ii) County court: personal injuries
Again normally the plaintiff's report will have been served with the particulars of claim. The county court automatic directions are contained in CCR Ord 17, r 11 and provide:

'(3) When the pleadings are deemed to be closed the following directions shall take effect –

... (*b*) except with the leave of the court or where all parties agree –
  (i) no expert evidence may be adduced at the trial unless the substance of that evidence has been disclosed to the other parties in the form of a written report within 10 weeks; and
  (ii) subject to paragraph (7), the number of expert witnesses of any kind shall be limited to two ...
(7) In an action for personal injuries –
  (*a*) the number of expert witnesses shall be limited in any case to two medical experts and one expert of any other kind;
  (*b*) nothing in paragraph (3) shall require a party to produce a further medical report if he proposes to rely at the trial only on the report provided pursuant to Order 6, rule 1(5) or (6) but, where a further report is disclosed, that report shall be accompanied by an amended statement of the special damages claimed, if appropriate.'

(iii) *High Court: other cases*
In other cases (including medical negligence cases) the parties either agree between themselves or else a summons is taken out under RSC Ord 38, r 36(1) for specific directions.

(iv) *County courts: other cases*
In the county courts the automatic directions apply to many types of case. Where they do apply the position is as follows:

'(3) When the pleadings are deemed to be closed the following directions shall take effect –
... (*b*) except with the leave of the court or where all parties agree –
  (i) no expert evidence may be adduced at the trial unless the substance of that evidence has been disclosed to the other parties in the form of a written report within 10 weeks; and
  (ii) ... the number of expert witnesses of any kind shall be limited to two.'

If a party does not wish to disclose his report or the automatic directions do not apply (eg in possession actions) then an application is made to the district judge for a specific order.

It is to be noted that disclosure should ordinarily be 'mutual',[67] ie one party is not entitled to delay obtaining his report until after he has seen the report of the other side's expert. There will, however, be exceptional cases where such a course would be proper.[68]

MEETING OF EXPERTS

In building cases the Official Referees have for many years directed that the expert witnesses should meet on a without prejudice basis before the trial to see what facts can be agreed or to identify what are the real matters in

---

67 Other than in personal injuries cases in which the plaintiff serves a copy of a medical report with the statement of claim under RSC Ord 18, r 12(1A), where disclosure of the defendant's medical evidence will inevitably be sequential.
68 See *Kirkup v Bristol Rail Engineering Ltd* [1983] 1 All ER 855, [1983] 1 WLR 190 per Croom-Johnson J at 194: 'in a proper case it may well be permissible to order one party to disclose his report first, so that the expert consulted by the other party may address his mind specifically to the points made in it. Although to do this may be said, in one sense, to give the latter party an advantage, it may do much towards crystallising the issues and may lead to an earlier and fairer settlement of the action.'

dispute. This sensible practice (which of course saves time and costs) is now applied by RSC Ord 38, r 38 to all types of case:

> 'In any cause or matter the Court may, if it thinks fit, direct that there be a meeting "without prejudice" of such experts within such periods before or after the disclosure of their reports as the Court may specify, for the purpose of identifying those parts of their evidence which are in issue. Where such a meeting takes place the experts may prepare a joint statement indicating those parts of their evidence on which they are, and those on which they are not, in agreement.'

ADMISSIONS AND INTERROGATORIES

The effect of the rules discussed above is that each side is normally fully aware of the documentary and expert evidence which will be adduced at the trial. There are however circumstances where one party needs to know *in advance* what his opponent will say on certain points in order to prepare his own case properly or to save costs. Where the information sought will form part of the oral evidence called on behalf of the opponent normally it will be made available in advance to the other party under the procedure for the mutual exchange of witness statements under RSC Ord 38, r 2A and CCR Ord 20, r 12A (discussed below). This exchange of witness statements, however, tends to take place in the last few weeks before the hearing, but it will often be the case that one party needs to know at a much earlier stage what his opponent is saying about a specific matter. In such a case a party may serve on the other side *interrogatories* or questions relating to any matter in question between the parties which are necessary for disposing fairly of the action or for saving costs.[69]

> *Example.* You are instructed by 'Claude et Cie of Clapham' (a firm of ladies' hairdressers) who are being sued by a former client in respect of negligent permanent waving which is alleged to have caused hair loss and irritation. A medical report (dated 12 months after the treatment) says that the plaintiff suffered itchiness after the permanent waving and treated her hair with 'a number of concoctions privately purchased but they failed to improve matters and the condition deteriorated'.

In the above example it is clearly of vital importance to know precisely what preparations the plaintiff put on her hair after she found her scalp was itchy (a normal consequence of permanent waving). It may be that armed with this information it will be possible to show that her condition is not attributable in any way to the defendant's conduct.

In such a case the defendant may (without making an application for an order[70]) serve interrogatories consisting of a number of questions usually drafted by counsel designed to extract precise information as to the matters in question and which the plaintiff is required to answer on oath within 28 days of service.[71] In the present case the interrogatories might begin as follows:

> (1) Did you tell Doctor - - - - - that you had applied 'a number of concoctions' to your hair after the permanent wave treatment the subject of this action or some other words to that effect?

69 RSC Ord 26, r 1.
70 RSC Ord 26, r 1; CCR Ord 14, r 11 – the practice and principles are the same in the County Court.
71 RSC Ord 26, r 2.

(2) If yes, what was the proprietary name of each concoction purchased and on how many occasions was each such concoction applied and with what results?

Interrogatories may be served without order in this way on two occasions[72] but the party on whom they are served may within 14 days of service apply to the court for them to be varied or withdrawn.[73] In deciding whether interrogatories should be allowed the court must apply RSC Ord 26, r 1(1) which provides:

'A party to any cause or matter may in accordance with the following provisions of this Order serve on any other party interrogatories relating to any matter in question between the applicant and that other party in the cause or matter which are necessary either –
(a) for disposing fairly of the cause or matter, or
(b) saving costs.'

Until the last ten years practitioners very seldom served interrogatories perhaps because the courts tended to give a restrictive interpretation to the words of this Order. The modern approach of the courts[74] which recognises that a matter may be fairly disposed of and costs saved by settlement has led to a different attitude and this, together with the new rules permitting the service of interrogatories without order, makes it likely that such pre-trial questioning will become a standard practice in civil litigation.

The limits on this procedure are at the moment uncertain but the following points can be made:

(1) Interrogatories will usually not be allowed if the answers to the questions raised can be provided by further and better particulars of the pleadings or by admissions or discovery. Thus RSC Ord 26, r 4(2) provides:

'(2) In deciding whether to give leave to serve interrogatories, the Court shall take into account any offer made by the party to be interrogated to give particulars, make admissions or produce documents relating to any matter in question and whether or not interrogatories without order have been administered.'

(2) Interrogatories will not be allowed to enable a party to frame a new case against the defendant, ie a case which he has not already pleaded. Nor will interrogatories be allowed if the only purpose is to discover how the defendant proposes to prove his case at the trial, eg the identity of the witnesses he proposes to call. Such interrogatories are an example of 'fishing interrogatories'.

(3) The other party may object to answering interrogatories on the grounds of *privilege*. The categories of privilege applicable to discovery of documents applies also to interrogatories; the interrogated party may state his objection on the grounds of privilege on oath in his answer.[75]

---

72 RSC Ord 26, r 3(1). Note however that interrogatories without order may not be served on the Crown: RSC Ord 26, r 3(3).
73 RSC Ord 26, r 3(2).
74 As stated in the context of discovery by Sir John Donaldson MR in *Naylor v Preston Area Health Authority*, see p 219, ante.
75 RSC Ord 26, r 5(1).

NOTICE TO ADMIT FACTS

Although interrogatories can be employed to obtain specific admissions from the other side this can also and sometimes more conveniently be done by serving on the other side a *notice to admit facts*. The procedure is set out in RSC Ord 27, r 2:

'A party to a cause or matter may not later than 21 days after the cause or matter is set down for trial serve on any other party a notice requiring him to admit, for the purpose of that cause or matter only, the facts specified in the notice.'

If the other party does not admit the facts in question but they are proven at the trial, RSC Ord 62, r 6(7) provides that the cost of proving such facts shall be borne by him even if he wins the substantial action. When therefore a notice to admit evokes no response or no specific admission, one can either proceed at once to apply for interrogatories or simply set in hand the preparation of evidence to cover the matters in question in the confident knowledge that win or lose one's opponent will pay the costs of proving these matters.

In cases where interrogatories without order cannot be served (such as where they have already been served on two previous occasions or where the other party is the Crown) a party may apply to the court for an order giving him leave to serve interrogatories.[76] The application is made to a master by summons which must be accompanied by a copy of the proposed interrogatories.[77]

In conclusion we set out below two cases which illustrate how interrogatories are used:

Example 1. P who has just alighted from a stationary omnibus was knocked down and injured by a motor car as she was coming from behind the omnibus. She sustained concussion and had no clear recollection of the accident. The master and the judge held that interrogatories were not proper in 'running down cases'. The Court of Appeal reversed this decision and ordered the defendant to answer precise interrogatories designed to show his course prior to the accident and the position of his vehicle at the moment of impact. Per Scrutton LJ: 'In most accident cases both parties are able to call witnesses, and therefore to interrogate upon small questions of fact relating to the details of the accident cannot be necessary for the fair trial of the action, and interrogatories should not be allowed. Nor should interrogatories be allowed for 'fishing purposes'[78] or to obtain the names of the opponent's witnesses. These considerations are probably sufficient to disentitle the party to interrogate in most accident cases. But there should be no other fetter' (*Griebart v Morris*[79]).

Example 2. The following interrogatories were permitted in a case of medical negligence: '(1) Were any, and if so how many, swabs removed from the deceased prior to the conclusion of the said operation? If yes, on whose instructions were they removed and what became of them? (2) Did you or some other, and what, person purport to remove the swabs from the deceased's abdomen? Whose duty do you allege it was to remove the swabs from the deceased's abdomen? If the said swabs were removed by some person other than you, on whose instructions were they acting? (3) Was a swab measuring 10 by 8 inches left in the deceased's

76 RSC Ord 26, r 1(2).
77 RSC Ord 26, r 4(1).
78 I e trying to build up a case when one does not have the basic evidence oneself to establish a prima facie case – see *Rofe v Kevorkian* [1936] 2 All ER 1334, CA.
79 [1920] 1 KB 659 at 666.

abdomen? If yes, how, and in what way do you say it came to be left there?'
(*Mahon v Osborne*[80]).

EXCHANGE OF NON-EXPERT WITNESS STATEMENTS

One of the most important developments in the rules of court towards
greater openness in the conduct of civil litigation is the *automatic* requirement that the parties exchange written statements of the oral evidence they
intend to adduce at the trial. This procedure is discussed in Chapter 13
Preparing for Trial (see pp 291–293, post).

80 [1939] 2 KB 14, [1939] 1 All ER 535, CA.

SKILLS PRACTICE NOTE

The Expert Witness

In a very large number of cases a successful outcome depends on expert evidence. For example, a building dispute will often turn upon the evidence of a surveyor, an application to fix the rent of a new tenancy will involve the expert opinion of a valuer, the quantum in a personal injury claim will be determined on the basis of the assessment of disability by a consultant. The litigation lawyer is constantly seeking advice from experts in fields in which he may have no knowledge himself, yet he is responsible for judging the validity of the experts' opinions and presenting the evidence in a way in which it can be understood by the court. This often involves very considerable skill on the part of the lawyer. The following suggestions may be helpful:

(1) *Choose the best expert your client can afford*

You may not always be able to use the first expert who reports (eg the surgeon at the local hospital who operated on your client may not be the person to provide the medical report you are going to use at the trial; your client's local accountant may not have the experience of litigation to provide the evidence you will need at the trial). You may need to seek help from colleagues (including counsel) as to a suitable expert. In personal injury cases, APIL (the Association of Personal Injury Lawyers) is able to provide valuable assistance.

(2) *Don't let your expert baffle you*

If you do not understand what your expert is saying there is little chance you will be able to prepare the case properly or accurately assess your client's chances of success. Expert witnesses have a tendency to talk in jargon; sometimes the jargon conceals the fact that they are not answering the question. You need to make the ground rules clear to the expert from the beginning: explain that you are not an expert and, more importantly, neither will the judge be – so the expert has got to be able to make you understand what he is saying. A sensible technique is to go through the expert's report once it arrives highlighting everything you do not understand. Then when you meet the expert get him to expand and if necessary re-write those passages so the meaning is clear to a layman. Before you send the report to the other side what the expert is saying should be crystal clear. Never forget that a diagram or a picture (or indeed a videotape) may be worth pages of explanation.

(3) *Insist on mutual exchange*

There are rare cases where the court will order that your report should be served before the other side serve their report but do not agree to such a course unless there are very good reasons for doing so. The reason, of course, is that if you provide your report first the other side's expert may be tempted to provide a report tearing it to pieces rather than a statement of his own opinion uninfluenced by his position as being 'employed' by the other side. (In personal injury cases, of course, the plaintiff has to provide his report first but if the medical evidence is disputed this will normally be supplemented by much more detailed reports which should be mutually exchanged.)

(4) *Why are the other side wrong?*

Your expert must be able to explain why the other side's expert has reached a different conclusion and why he says that conclusion is wrong. You must understand his reasons before you can make an assessment of whether your expert's view is likely to be accepted by the court. *Your* decision on this matter will be critical in deciding whether to settle the case and, if so, on what terms.

(5) *Your expert should meet the other side*

The rules now specifically provide for the court to order meetings between experts so they can agree facts and limit the issues. You should take advantage of this procedure. You must ensure *before* the meeting that your expert knows exactly what points he proposes to make when he meets the other side. Remember that the other side's expert will be reporting back on his assessment of your expert's views and this may be of great importance in achieving settlement.

If the case proceeds to court remember to obtain a fixture if possible: you cannot expect your expert to make himself available without adequate warning. The expert may suggest that he need only attend for the time needed for him to give evidence. This may well be a mistake. You need your expert present to hear the witnesses as to fact and to listen to the other side's expert. Before the case you will need your expert to plan out with you (or counsel if you are not conducting the case) the lines of cross-examination to be employed against the other side's expert (and often the other side's witnesses).

Library

You should build up your own library of books or pamphlets which will help you prepare expert evidence. In common law practice you will need access to:

(1) diagrams showing the bones in the body and the movements of the various joints. In addition you will need a medical dictionary;

(2) a simple book demonstrating the workings of the various parts of a motor car. In specific cases this can be supplemented by the detailed books available at any public library describing particular models;

(3) a simple book describing (with ample diagrams) how a house is built including the structure of the roof and the different systems of damp-proofing;

(4) a guide to the layout of accountants' reports and in particular an explanation of how to read balance sheets and profit and loss accounts.

Chapter 9

Evidence

Once discovery has been completed the parties must put their minds to how they will prove their case in court. In a case of any substance the papers will be sent to counsel to provide an advice on evidence. In minor cases, especially in the county court, the parties cannot afford such luxury although in those very cases, because frequently the defendant does not appear and so the rules of evidence are rigidly applied against the plaintiff, it is of vital importance to be able to produce admissible evidence which will prove every essential allegation in the pleadings. In this chapter we shall discuss the problems of evidence which most frequently give trouble in the preparation of a case. At the end of the chapter we shall consider how counsel would write an advice on evidence in two typical cases.

DOCUMENTARY EVIDENCE

The 'best evidence' rule (which at one time was applied strictly by the courts) meant that when a document was put in as evidence the original had to be produced. In recent years the courts have adopted a different approach; the modern attitude to the rule is set out by Lloyd LJ in *R v Governor of Pentonville Prison, ex p Osman:*[1]

'. . . this court would be more than happy to say goodbye to the best evidence rule. We accept that it served an important purpose in the days of parchment and quill pens. But, since the invention of carbon paper and, still more, the photocopier and the telefacsimile machine, that purpose has largely gone. Where there is an allegation of forgery the court will attach little, if any, weight to anything other than the original; so also if the copy produced in court is illegible. But to maintain a general exclusionary rule for these limited purposes is, in our view, hardly justifiable . . . But, although the little loved best evidence rule has been dying for some time, the recent authorities suggest that it is still not quite dead. Thus in *Kajala v Noble* (1982) 75 Cr App Rep 149 at 152 Ackner LJ said:
    "The old rule, that a party must produce the best evidence that the nature of the case will allow, and that any less good evidence is to be excluded, has gone by the board long ago. The only remaining instance of it is that, if an original document is available in one's hands, one must produce it; that one cannot give secondary evidence by producing a copy."
In *R v Wayte* (1982) 76 Cr App Rep 110 at 116 Beldam J said:
    "First, there are no degrees of secondary evidence. The mere fact that it is easy

1 [1989] 3 All ER 701 at page 728.

to construct a false document by photocopying techniques does not render the photocopy inadmissible. Moreover, it is now well established that any application of the best evidence rule is confined to cases in which it can be shown that the party has the original and could produce it but does not."

What is meant by a party having a document available in his hands? We would say that it means a party who has the original of a document with him in court, or could have it in court without any difficulty. In such a case, if he refuses to produce the original and can give no reasonable explanation, the court would infer the worst. The copy should be excluded. If, in taking that view, we are cutting down still further what remains of the best evidence rule, we are content.'

The rule therefore survives in civil litigation to the limited extent that if the original document is available it must be produced.[2] If it is *not* available then the court will admit secondary evidence (eg a copy of sworn testimony as to the contents of the original document) if:

(i) The party wishing to produce the document shows that the original could not reasonably be provided. One example would be where the document has been destroyed or has been lost (and all reasonable steps to find it have been unsuccessful). Note that (unless the other side agree to the production of a copy) this involves calling evidence as to the destruction or loss of the document. Such evidence could be by sworn testimony or where the destruction or loss is not likely to be contested, by affidavit.[3]

(ii) The original *is in the possession of the opposing party* and he has been served with *notice to produce* that original at the trial, but has failed to do so. In the High Court, where there has been discovery by list each party is deemed to have been served with notice requiring him to produce all documents he has listed as being in his possession.[4] In all other High Court cases and *in all county court actions* each party must serve on the other a specific notice to produce any original documents held by the other side which he wishes to put in as part of his case.[5] The practice followed is that when counsel comes to the stage in his case where he wishes to put in the original document, he 'calls for its production'. If his opponent does not then produce the original, counsel may at once prove its contents by, for example, producing a copy and calling evidence to show this corresponds with the original.

If the original document is in the possession of a person who is not party to the action, he must be served with a *subpoena duces tecum*;[6] if he fails to produce it, secondary evidence does *not* become admissible – the remedy is to enforce the subpoena against him.[7]

Assuming that one can produce all the original documents necessary in one's case (or will be able to put in secondary evidence under the above

2 An exception applies in the case of bank records which are admitted provided the person taking the copy attends or swears an affidavit verifying the copy – Bankers' Books Evidence Act 1879, ss 4–5.

3 One must send a copy of the affidavit and notice of intention to use it to the other side, see RSC Ord 38, r 2; CCR Ord 20, r 7.

4 See RSC Ord 27, r 4(3).

5 RSC Ord 27, r 5(4); CCR Ord 20, r 3(4).

6 I e an order of the court directing him to produce the relevant documents.

7 If a person under subpoena lawfully refuses to produce the original document, secondary evidence may then be given.

rules) a question still remains as to how one proves the documents are authentic.

> *Example 1.* In order to succeed in an action A needs to produce a lease made in 1960 and an assignment of that lease in 1963. All the parties to the lease and assignment are now dead.
> *Example 2.* B wishes to produce a series of letters which he says were written to him by the defendant. What happens if the defendant does not appear at the trial? What would happen if the letters were written not by the defendant but by his predecessor-in-title who is now dead?

Clearly great expense would be caused if in the above cases the authenticity of the document had to be strictly proved. Of course there will be some cases where this is necessary (ie where it is suggested that the document is a forgery) but generally since there is likely to be no dispute about the matters the rules provide:

(*a*) that in High Court actions *where a list of documents is served*, the party on whom the list if served is deemed to admit the authenticity of the original documents set out in the list (and also that all copies mentioned therein are true copies) unless he serves a counter-notice to the effect that he challenges their authenticity;[8]

(*b*) in county court cases where a document is produced from proper custody, it is admitted without further proof if in the opinion of the court it appears genuine and no objection is taken to its admission.[9]

Where, in the above cases a counter-notice is served or objection taken, the authenticity of the document must then be strictly proved. If its authenticity is so proved, the party challenging it will normally be required to pay the costs occasioned by proving this item even if he succeeds overall in the case. It should be noted that certain documents are deemed to be authentic without any notice having been served.[10]

ATTENDANCE OF WITNESSES

Each party must arrange to secure the attendance of all his witnesses (together with all relevant documents) at court. If there is the slightest doubt about the willingness of the witness to attend, an application should be made for an order requiring his attendance at the trial.

In the High Court[11] the procedure is governed by Order 38, rule 14. The party wishing to secure the attendance of the witness fills in an application

---

8 RSC Ord 27, r 4. The counter-notice is to be served before the expiry of 21 days from the date of inspection or after the time limited for inspection has expired. Where no list of documents has been served, the party wishing to rely on a particular document may serve a *notice to admit* requiring the other side to serve a counter-notice if the authenticity of the document is challenged: RSC Ord 27, r 5.

9 CCR Ord 20, r 11. Note that in county court cases where it is thought there may be a dispute as to the authenticity of a document, the party seeking to rely on it can serve a *notice to admit* which requires the other side to state whether the document is challenged: CCR Ord 20, r 3(1).

10 Public documents (such as entries in public registers) are deemed to be authentic and copies duly certified by the officer in charge of the register or record are admitted without his attendance in court. Thus copy marriage certificates, records of convictions, copy entries in rent registers, adjudications of rent tribunals, land certificates, etc generally require no proof of authenticity. See on this point *Cross on Evidence* (7th edn, p 572 etc).

11 The relevant procedure in the county court is set out in CCR Ord 20, r 12.

Subpoena Duces
Tecum at Sittings
of High Court
(O. 38, r. 14)

IN THE HIGH COURT OF JUSTICE 19 91 — F . —**No.** 8651

QUEEN'S BENCH **Division**

Between

JAMES FRY Plaintiff

AND

RALPH TROTT Defendant

Elizabeth the Second, by the Grace of God, of the United Kingdom of Great Britain and Northern Ireland and of Our other realms and territories Queen, Head of the Commonwealth, Defender of the Faith,

(1) Here give name
of witness.

To (¹)

JOSEPHINE LAM of 13 REEF GARDENS, LONDON W4

WE COMMAND YOU to attend at the Sittings of the Queen's Bench
                          Division of Our High Court of Justice at the Royal Courts of Justice, Strand, London, on the day fixed for the trial of the above-named cause, notice of which will be given to you, and from day to day thereafter until the end of the trial, to give

(2) "Plaintiff" or
"Defendant".

evidence on behalf of the (²) Plaintiff

(3) Here describe
the documents or
things to be
produced.

AND WE ALSO COMMAND YOU to bring with you and produce at the place aforesaid on the day notified to you (³) all original orders and invoices relating to transactions conducted with your customers and suppliers by the Defendant in this action on your behalf while employed by you between 11 March 1991 and 10 September 1991.

Witness, The Rt Hon Lord Mackay of Clashfern

Lord High Chancellor of Great Britain,

the   24th   day of   June   1993.

form (called a *praecipe*) which he delivers to the Central Office.[12] If the case is to be heard in open court the order called a *subpoena ad testificandum* (or, if only the production of a document is required, called a *subpoena duces tecum*) is issued of right. If the matter is proceeding in chambers, the applicant will have to obtain leave from the master and so should swear an affidavit setting out his reasons for requiring the subpoena. The subpoena may be served anywhere in the United Kingdom.[13] It is sealed like a writ and must be served personally within 12 weeks of its issue and not less than 4 days (or such period as the court may fix) before the day on which the witness' attendance is required.[14] When service is effected the witness must be given conduct money (ie a sufficient sum to defray his expenses in coming to, attending at and returning from court).[15] Disobedience of a subpoena is punishable as contempt of court.[16] We reproduce an example of a *subpoena duces tecum* on p 231.

In the county court the procedure is set out in CCR Order 20, rule 12. An application is made at the court office for the issue of a *witness summons*. This application must be made not less than seven days before the hearing date (unless the district judge otherwise directs). The witness summons must be *served* not less than four days before the hearing (again, unless the district judge allows shorter service). The witness summons is usually served personally (although the rule permits postal service – in which case it is deemed to have been served on the seventh day after posting unless the contrary is shown). The witness must be paid a prescribed sum (at the moment £6 for police officers and £8.50 for anyone else) together with a 'sum reasonably sufficient to cover his expenses in travelling to and from court'.

It should be noted that if either party wishes to produce evidence of entries in a banker's ledger (and this frequently happens when there is a dispute as to whether sums were paid some considerable time ago) he can obtain an order for him to inspect the books under section 7 of the Bankers' Books Evidence Act 1879 and take a copy rather than issuing a subpoena to the bank requiring an officer to attend.

WITNESSES UNABLE TO ATTEND COURT

What is the position if a crucial witness is unable to attend court? We shall see below that in some circumstances the court will receive a statement made by the witness pursuant to the Civil Evidence Act 1968 but this course necessarily means that the other side will not have the opportunity of cross-examining the witness and therefore is not satisfactory where the evidence is important and very much contested.

> *Example 1.* In a probate action it was highly relevant to ascertain the state of the deceased's mental health immediately prior to the execution of the will. The only relevant witness was an old lady who had been a friend of the deceased but was now bedridden and could not attend the court to give evidence.
>
> *Example 2.* O sues T for possession of certain property which O has just bought

---

12 Or appropriate district registry.
13 Supreme Court Act 1981, s 36(1).
14 RSC Ord 38, r 17.
15 Supreme Court Act 1981, s 36(4).
16 If the witness is in Scotland or Northern Ireland a certificate of default is transmitted to the Court of Session or High Court in Belfast who will then punish the contempt.

and in which T is living. T claims to be a tenant. O has a statement from his predecessor in title W saying he had never granted T any tenancy.

(a) Witness in England or Wales

In the High Court[17] the party desiring to call the evidence applies on notice to the master for an order that an examiner be appointed to take the sworn evidence of the witness in the form of a deposition. The application should be accompanied by an affidavit setting out the reasons why the application is made, e g that the witness is too old or infirm to attend court, or might die before the trial or intends to leave the country before the trial. The examiner appoints the date and place for the examination and both parties attend by counsel and proceed respectively to examine and cross-examine the witness whose answers are recorded by the examiner in a deposition.

Frequently in practice in lieu of a deposition the parties agree that a shorthand transcript should be taken. Where an objection is taken to a question, the objection is noted but the question and answer are recorded leaving the trial judge to decide whether to uphold the objection and strike out the testimony or to overrule it.

(b) Witness abroad

As a general rule it is today far less expensive to pay the air fare of a witness abroad to England than arrange for this examination overseas. The following methods[18] are however available if the party desiring to call the witness can prove that it is not practicable to bring the witness to this country:

(i) *Letters of request.* The English court issues a request to the judicial authorities abroad to arrange for the attendance of the witness and his answers to be recorded either to viva voce questioning or to a set of prepared interrogatories. This method is available for all countries.[19]

(ii) *Convention countries.* Various countries[20] have agreed that evidence can be taken before a British Consul. This procedure is generally however only available where the witness is willing to give evidence. In other cases letters of request should be issued. Other countries will permit the English court to nominate a *special examiner* to record the evidence of willing witnesses.[21]

One of the basic rules of evidence is that no evidence should be given which cannot be tested by cross-examination. Suppose P (who has no recollection of an accident) wishes to prove that D drove past a red traffic light:

(a) P can call W to say he saw D go past the light *but*

---

17 RSC Ord 39, r 1. The equivalent procedure in the county court is set out in CCR Ord 20, r 13. Often the district judge will act as examiner.
18 See RSC Ord 39, rr 2 and 3. Note the county court cannot deal with the above matters so that where a witness in a county court action is abroad application has to be made to the High Court: County Courts Act 1984, s 56.
19 This is the method generally employed for witnesses in Eire and in Commonwealth countries.
20 Eg France, Italy, Belgium, Netherlands, Germany.
21 Eg the United States of America.

(*b*) P cannot give evidence to the effect that W had told him that he had seen D go past the light *nor*

(*c*) can P put in a written statement by W to that effect.

In the second and third examples it would be unfair that the court should hear this damning testimony when D cannot cross-examine W. This principle of the law of evidence, which is called '*the hearsay rule*', can be roughly formulated as follows:

> No witness is allowed to give evidence in court by reference to what he has been told by somebody else about the matters in question or by producing an account of those matters written by somebody else.

This rule was sensible where the tribunal of fact consisted of a jury who might not have had the intelligence to realise the risks of accepting evidence which had not been subjected to the test of cross-examination. The rule could however work considerable injustice. Suppose the person who could give direct evidence was dead or could not be traced or was overseas (but the value of the claim could not justify paying his passage to England or issuing letters of request). Again, suppose the witness would have no recollection of the matters any longer so that his attendance at court would be a waste of time (e g a clerk who prepared a formal delivery note). To deal with these problems the Civil Evidence Act 1968[22] provided that hearsay evidence should be admissible subject to certain safeguards:

> 'In any civil proceedings a statement made, whether orally or in a document or otherwise, by any person . . . shall, subject to this section and to rules of court, be admissible as evidence of any fact stated therein of which direct oral evidence by him would be admissible.'[23]

This section amongst other things means that a party can choose to present evidence at court by submitting a written statement without calling as a witness the person who made it. This can be of great practical advantage in preparing a case.

The procedure is set out in RSC Order 38, rule 20 et seq.[24] Any party wishing to put in hearsay evidence should serve on every other party a notice to that effect not later than 21 days from the date of setting down.[25] The notice must contain:[26]

(*a*) details of the date, time and place and circumstances in which the statement was made,

(*b*) the name of the person who made it,

22 Replacing and extending the scope of earlier statutes.
23 Section 2(1). This section also provides an exception to another rule of evidence namely that a person called in court is not allowed to give evidence of earlier consistent oral statements made by him, i e cannot say 'what I am saying is true because I have said it before'. Such evidence is in limited circumstances admissible – see s 2(2) and s 3.
24 In the county court the procedure (which is substantially identical) is governed by CCR Ord 20, rr 14–26. The notice of intention to put in hearsay evidence is to be served not less than 14 clear days before the date fixed for the hearing and the counter-notice within 7 days of service of the notice. The time limits do not apply where no defence has been served although late service of the notice may cause the other side to apply for an adjournment of the hearing.
25 See RSC Ord 38, r 21. In the case of an originating summons in the Chancery Division, notice must be served not later than 21 days from the date when the summons was 'adjourned into court' (see 329, post).
26 RSC Ord 38, r 22. See notice at p 242, post.

(*c*) if oral, the substance of what was said; if in writing, a copy thereof, must be supplied,

(*d*) if the statement is to be submitted because the maker is dead, unfit by reason of his bodily or mental condition to attend as a witness, overseas, unable to be found or identified despite the exercise of reasonable diligence, or cannot reasonably be expected to have any recollection of matters relevant to the accuracy or otherwise of the statement, then the notice must contain a statement to that effect specifying the reason relied on.[27]

Upon receipt of the notice the other parties have 21 days in which to serve a counter-notice.[28] They *must* do this if they are attacking the credibility of the maker of the statement.[29] If the applicant is not relying on any of the reasons set out in paragraph (*d*) above, the service of the counter-notice prevents his using the hearsay evidence at the trial. If he is relying on one of those reasons, he must apply to the master for a determination of the issue whether that reason is made out.[30] If it is, he can submit the hearsay evidence *of right*.

Example. P sued D for damages for injuries after she was run over by a bus owned by D. D served notice under RSC Order 38, rule 21 of intention to put in a written statement by an eye-witness to the effect that 'the pedestrian walked straight out into the road without looking in either direction'. D stated in the notice that the eye-witness who was Jamaican had returned home. P served a counter-notice and the issue then arose whether D could prove the witness was overseas and if so whether the court could nevertheless refuse to admit this damning evidence in the absence of the maker. Finer J. held (1) that the issue of fact was to be determined on a balance of probabilities and (2) that once any of the stated conditions was proven (e g that the witness was overseas) the court had no discretionary power to refuse to admit the statement.[31]

A statement may be admitted under the Civil Evidence Act 1968 notwithstanding a failure to follow the above rules.[32] In particular, notices under the Act are frequently served long after the 21 day period from setting down has elapsed. The courts almost invariably treat such notices as valid unless the other side can show that they are prejudiced or that there has

---

27 RSC Ord 38, r 25; Civil Evidence Act 1968, s 8(2)(*b*).
28 RSC Ord 38, r 26.
29 RSC Ord 38, r 30.
30 RSC Ord 38, r 27.
31 *Rasool v West Midlands Passenger Transport Executive* [1974] 3 All ER 638. The procedure is summarised by Finer J (at 641) as follows: 'Now the short effect of all these complicated provisions seems to be as follows: that the system of adducing a written statement in evidence without calling the maker involves the service by the party wishing to take that course on the other parties of a notice in the prescribed form. A party receiving such a notice who objects to the proposal to put in the statement can, by an appropriate counter-notice, require the witness to be called, failing which the statement (subject to an overriding discretion which the court has to admit it under rule 29) will be excluded. This right of objection, however, is modified in the case where the stated reason for desiring to put the statement in evidence without calling the witness is one or other of the five reasons mentioned in section 8(2)(*b*) of the 1968 Act and rule 25. In such a case the objecting party must, despite the assertion in the notice that the witness cannot or should not be called because he is dead, or beyond the seas, or as the case may be, state in his counter-notice that the witness can or should be called. This raises the issue as to the truth or validity of the reason relied on, and that issue will be determined . . . under the procedure laid-down by rule 27.'
32 Civil Evidence Act 1968, s 8(3)(*a*). RSC Ord 38, r 29. CCR Ord 20, r 20.

been a deliberate breach of the rules by the party seeking to put in the evidence.[33]

COMPUTER STATEMENTS

Increasingly evidence is produced to the court in the form of computer statements or 'print-outs'. Such evidence is often agreed but in the absence of agreement it may be admitted under section 5 of the Civil Evidence Act 1968 provided the following conditions are satisfied:

(*a*) the computer has been regularly used to store or process information over a period which includes the date when the 'print-out' was made;

(*b*) during such period information of the kind contained in the print-out (or of a kind from which such information is derived) has been regularly supplied to the computer;

(*c*) the computer has been operating properly throughout such period (or, if not, such malfunction as has occurred would not have affected the accuracy of the material contained in the 'print-out');

(*d*) the information contained in the 'print-out' reproduces or is derived from information supplied to the computer in the ordinary course of its activities.

There are potentially three witnesses who can attest to the fact that these conditions are satisfied:–

(i) the person who was managing the business whose activities are recorded by the computer: he would be expected to be aware of any errors produced in the supply of information;

(ii) the person responsible for overseeing the input of information to the computer;

(iii) the person responsible for the 'hardware' and programming of the computer.

RSC Order 38, rule 24 provides that a Civil Evidence Act notice must be served in respect of such computer statements identifying each of its three persons referred to above and confirming that the computer has been working properly during the relevant period. The other party is entitled to give notice under rule 26 requiring the attendance of any of these named persons at the hearing for cross-examination.

---

33 *Ford (an infant) v Lewis* [1971] 2 All ER 983, [1971] 1 WLR 623, CA (deliberate decision not to serve Civil Evidence Act notice because counsel believed the other side might adjust their case to meet this evidence – application to admit hearsay refused). See also *Rover International Ltd v Cannon Film Sales Ltd (No 2)* [1987] 3 All ER 986, [1987] 1 WLR 1597, Harman J.

SKILLS PRACTICE NOTE

Advice on Evidence

After the pleadings have been exchanged and discovery has taken place, counsel may be asked to advise on evidence. He will be sent all the proofs of evidence taken by his solicitors, the correspondence, the documents disclosed by his side on discovery and copies of the documents disclosed by the other side. In order to advise on evidence counsel should go through each allegation in the pleadings which is disputed and ask himself how he can prove each such matter. The process is vividly described in a report by *Justice, Going to Law*[34] at paragraph 59:

'To write a useful advice on evidence, counsel has to rehearse in his mind's eye every possible scenario for the trial. Who will make the opening speech? What documents will have to be handed to the judge? Will the witnesses have to have a bundle of correspondence to refer to? Whose job will it be to prepare these? What are the issues as defined by the pleadings? For each of these, which party has the burden of proving it? What admissible evidence is there to prove it? Do the statements of the various witnesses cover not only what they have to prove, but also the matters on which they are likely to be cross-examined? Are any documents still missing? Above all, what could go wrong during the performance, and what contingency plans need to be made to cover such eventualities.'

Although it is impossible to set out here every matter which has to be considered in writing an advice on evidence, it is probably a sensible rule to commence by listing each of the separate issues in the trial and then taking each issue separately consider the following:

(a) The *burden of proof*.

(b) What evidence is available to prove the particular issue. If a statement has been taken, does it need to be supplemented: will the witness attend voluntarily or should a subpoena or witness summons be issued: will the witness need to refer to some documents, if so can they be agreed or will this witness or someone else need to produce them?

(c) Are any *witnesses unavailable*? If so notices must be served under the *Civil Evidence Act*. Similarly, is it a case where although a witness is available he would have no present recollection of matters set out in a document or his evidence is unlikely to be contradicted? In both cases it would again be right to serve notices under the Act.

(d) Are there any *original* or *copy documents* which need to be put in as evidence? If so, who has them? If the originals are in one's own possession is it necessary to serve notice to admit? It should be remembered that this will frequently be necessary in county court actions. If they are in the possession of the other side, is notice to produce necessary? If they are in the possession of a third party a *subpoena duces tecum* may be necessary.

(e) Are there matters which the other side will probably *admit* if a *notice to admit facts* is served (see p 224).

In almost any case of complexity it is necessary for the plaintiff to prepare copies of a *bundle of documents* which can be used by the judge, counsel and the witnesses. In order to show how any advice is prepared in practice we

34 Report of Justice Committee.

shall conclude this section by considering two specimen cases. Note how frequently in practice is it necessary to use the provisions of the Civil Evidence Act if matters cannot be agreed.

EXAMPLES OF ADVISING ON EVIDENCE

A POSSESSION ACTION

On 1st December 1992 P let an upstairs room in his house to D at a rent of £60 per week. The terms of the tenancy were set out in a written agreement. On 20th April 1993 P's solicitors served notice to quit on D. Since P actually lived at the house, the tenancy is not an assured tenancy under the Housing Act 1988. On 10th September 1992 arrears of rent amounted to £136. P issued a summons for possession in the local county court. No defence has been filed.

Advice on Evidence
 (1) In this case the plaintiff must prove (a) the creation of the tenancy; (b) service of the notice to quit; (c) that the notice is effective; (d) the amount of arrears outstanding; and (e) that the defendants are still in occupation.
 (2) The Plaintiff can himself give evidence to prove the tenancy. He must produce his copy of the tenancy agreement and notice to admit should be served on the defendant. He must give evidence that he (the plaintiff) lives at the premises as his residence.
 (3) Those instructing me should have available at the hearing a witness who can speak as to the date of posting the notice to quit and produce the appropriate post office advice of recorded delivery. That witness should also be able to produce a copy of the notice to quit. Notice to produce the original should be sent to the defendant.
 (4) The plaintiff must give oral evidence of the rent in arrears to the date of the hearing and confirm the defendant is still in occupation. The plaintiff should produce his record of payments. It would be sensible to have copies available of the relevant pages. Notice should be served on the defendant to produce his Rent Book at the hearing which should confirm the plaintiff's calculations.

A MOTOR ACCIDENT CASE

On 6 June 1993 a collision occurred on the M3 motorway when a lorry owned by D pulled across into the path of a motor car driven by P. P claims that the lorry gave no warning whatsoever of its intention to change lane. P sustained a serious fracture of the leg which has left him with considerable disabilities. He was off work for 6 months. Repairs to his vehicle cost £2450. The scene was witnessed by an American tourist W who has written to P's solicitors from New York a detailed explanation of the incident exonerating P. The position of the vehicles after the accident was taken down by the police who interviewed D's driver under caution. No criminal charges were however brought against D's driver. P issued proceedings in the county court.

Advice on Evidence
 (1) P will have to prove (a) the collision was caused by D's negligence and (b) that as a result thereof he has sustained injuries to the extent alleged and (c) financial loss as alleged.
 (2) On the issue of liability, P must give oral evidence in accordance with his proof. It is essential to have available an agreed plan and photographs of the locus in quo to which P can refer. The statement of the witness W is admissible under the Civil Evidence Act 1968. A copy of the statement and details of when and by whom it was made must be sent to the defendant's solicitors with notice of our intention to put in the statement as evidence

without calling the maker on the grounds that he is beyond the seas. The notice must be served not later than 14 days before the hearing. The notes of the officer who prepared the police report and took the oral statement from the defendant's driver should also be sent to the defendant's solicitors if that has not happened already. The police notes are receivable in evidence under CCR Ord 17, r 11(3): please check that the contents of those notes are agreed. If not, issue a witness summons to ensure the attendance of the officer at court.

(3) So far as the medical evidence is concerned, those instructing me must obtain an up-to-date medical report setting out the extent of the plaintiff's present disabilities and the prognosis. There must be mutual exchange with the defendant of the medical evidence which will be presented at the trial. I would hope that the various reports disclosed can be put in as an agreed bundle.

(4) So far as repair costs are concerned, please serve a notice to admit that the repairs were carried out and the charges made as shown on the invoice and receipt. The notice is served under CCR Ord 20, r 2. If these matters cannot be admitted then:

   (*a*) Issue a witness summons to secure the attendance of a representative of the garage who has direct knowledge of the repairs carried out and can produce the estimate, invoice and receipt for payment.

   (*b*) The Plaintiff can give evidence that the repairs are all attributable to the accident.

   The insurance company's claims assessor who inspected the vehicle must state that in his expert opinion the cost of repairs was fair and reasonable. A copy of his report must be sent to the defendant's solicitors under CCR Ord 17, r 11(3). This should be accompanied by a notice that we propose to adduce this evidence by putting in his report under section 1(1) of the Civil Evidence Act 1972 unless a counter-notice is served: see CCR Ord 20, r 26.

(5) Please prepare an up to date Schedule of Special Damage for the trial. So far as loss of earnings are concerned serve upon the defendants' solicitors a statement from P's employers setting out his total *net* loss of earnings. Notice should accompany these statements of our intention to adduce the same under the Civil Evidence Act 1968. We should obtain a certificate of total benefit (CRV 100) from the DSS so that we know how much of any award will be subject to the claw-back provisions. This certificate will not, however, be put in as evidence.

SKILLS PRACTICE NOTE

Example of Civil Evidence Act Notice
and Notices to Produce and Admit Documents

Problem:

On 20 January 1992 Lady Bracknell (who owns a small villa in France) writes to Mr Worthing (a public relations consultant) agreeing to let him her villa for 7 months (March – September 1992) at a rental of £2000 per month. The letter stipulates that in no circumstances is Worthing to sublet the villa. In September, Lady Bracknell visits the villa and finds it occupied by a Mme Marie-Laure Peloux who tells her that she has been paying Worthing £5000 per month since June. Lady Bracknell has written to Worthing (who is now back in London) but has received no reply. She now consults you.

Question:

Worthing seems to be in breach of contract but is Lady Bracknell entitled to damages? In civil litigation, the problem which faces the practitioner is frequently not whether there is a cause of action but what damages his client is entitled to recover. You should consult one of the standard works such as *McGregor on Damages*, 15th edition para 1421 to make sure you know how much your client could recover before sending a letter before action or issuing a writ. You would find that although damages in contract are normally intended to place the parties in the same position as if the contract had been properly performed, a plaintiff may be entitled to recover as damages the *profit* which has been made by a defendant from a deliberate breach of contract or trespass (see *Penarth Dock Engineering Co v Pounds* [1963] 1 Lloyds Rep 359).

Never start proceedings without having first worked out precisely what you are claiming and making sure that you are entitled to it.

Problem continued:

After the letter before action is ignored you issue a writ with a statement of claim specially indorsed (do not forget to claim interest). The writ is served on 1 December 1992. Worthing fails to file an acknowledgement of service and on 23 December you enter judgment in default under RSC Ord 13, r 2. Note the claim is *unliquidated* (i e the amount of damage cannot be calculated by reference to the contract alone; this means that you will have to *prove* the profit Worthing made). Therefore the judgment is for damages to be assessed.

Remember that you cannot obtain a default judgment for a specific sum except in cases of debt or where the amount due can be calculated precisely from the terms of the contract (e g rent or the price of goods delivered).

Problem continued:

Since damages have to be assessed you will take out an appointment for the assessment before a Master (under RSC Ord 37, r 1). It is possible the assessment might be transferred to a county court but more likely it will be heard by the Master. At an assessment of damages the plaintiff has to prove the damages exactly as she would have done at the trial. What do you have to prove in this case?

Answer:

You have to prove:

1. That the premises were let at £2000 per month.

2. That in the four months from June to September Worthing received £5000 per month (ie £20,000) in total from Mme Peloux.

The profit he has made from his breach of contract is therefore £20,000 less £8,000 = £12,000.

Note:

(i) You should prepare a calculation showing the profit each month and the interest on that profit at the judgment debt rate to the date of the assessment.

(ii) You do *not* have to prove at the assessment that Worthing is in breach of contract. This has already been determined by the default judgment (in other words, having let judgment be entered in default, Worthing will not now be allowed to contest the fact that he is in breach of contract).

Problem:

How are you going to prove the damages? [Assume Worthing may not turn up so you will be put by the Master to strict proof of your case.]

Answer:

(a) Lady Bracknell will give oral evidence (she must prove the amount of the contractual rent). She sensibly kept a copy of the letter she sent to Worthing but the original is of course held by Worthing. She will be allowed to produce the copy in evidence provided *notice to produce* the original has been served on Worthing. [Note: a notice to produce is *not* necessary where the other side have served a list in which the existence of the document is disclosed but on an assessment of damages and in many cases in the county court there will *not* have been discovery by list. In the example below you will see the notice also requires Worthing to produce any other documents he holds which may be relevant to the issues on the assessment.]

Always check whether you need to serve a Notice to Produce. Do not work on the basis the judge will let you produce a copy when such a notice has not been served.

(b) Mme Peloux is anxious to help but reluctant to come all the way from Paris and has sent a letter to you confirming the amount she received from Worthing. Since she is abroad you will be able to put in this letter provided you have served a Civil Evidence Act notice within 21 days after the date when the appointment was taken out.

If a witness is abroad the simple way of putting in their evidence is by serving a Civil Evidence Act notice. The cost is minimal but unless the notice has been served there may be a gap in your evidence and you may lose the case.

The notices which would be used in this case are reproduced below:–

In the High Court of Justice   1992–B–No. 2571

Queen's Bench Division

Between:

                The Right Honourable Augusta,   Plaintiff
                         Lady Bracknell

                              - and -

                         Ernest Worthing   Defendant

                    Notice to Produce Documents

TAKE NOTICE that you are hereby required to produce and show to the Court at the hearing of the assessment of damages herein all books, papers, letters, copies of letters and other writings and documents in your custody, possession or power relating to the matters in question in the said assessment and in particular:–

(1) the letter dated 20th January 1992 written by the plaintiff to you setting out the terms of the tenancy agreement in respect of Villa Catalan, Bandol, Var, France.

(2) all correspondence between you and Mme Marie-Laure Peloux concerning her occupation of the said premises and payments made by her to you in respect thereof.

Dated 21st January 1993

Spenlow and Jorkins
18 St Paul's Churchyard
London EC1 2BX

Solicitors for the plaintiff

To the Defendant and to

Dodson and Fogg
Freemans Court
Cornhill EC2 1XV
his solicitors

In the High Court of Justice   1992–B–No. 2571
Queen's Bench Division

Between:

The Right Honourable Augusta,   Plaintiff
Lady Bracknell

- and -

Ernest Worthing   Defendant

Notice under the Civil Evidence Act 1968

TAKE NOTICE that at the hearing of the assessment of damages herein the Plaintiff desires to give in evidence the statement made in the following document namely a letter by Mme Marie-Laure Peloux dated 16 December 1992. A copy of the document is annexed hereto.

And FURTHER TAKE NOTICE that the particulars of the said document are as follows:

that it was written:

(1) by Mme Marie-Laure Peloux
(2) to the Plaintiff's solicitor, Mr Stephen Spenlow
(3) on 16th December 1992
(4) at 217 Rue de l'Universitaire, Paris, 6e
(5) in the following circumstances, namely to confirm that she rented the Plaintiff's villa at Bandol in the South of France from the Defendant between June/September 1992 at a rent of £5000 per month.

And FURTHER TAKE NOTICE that the said Mme Marie-Laure Peloux should not be called as a witness because she is beyond the seas.

Dated 21st January 1993

Spenlow and Jorkins
18 St Paul's Churchyard
London EC1 2BX

Solicitors for the plaintiff

To the Defendant and to Messrs
Dodson and Fogg, his solicitors

<u>COPY</u>

217 Rue de l'Universitaire
Paris 6e

16th December 1992

Dear Mr Spenlow

I am writing to confirm the dreadful circumstances in which the rogue Worthing let me into Lady Bracknell's beautiful villa in Bandol. The letting was for 4 months from June to September this year at a rental of £5000 (English pounds) per month. Imagine my horror when dear Lady Bracknell arrived in September and told me the villain had no right to let the villa! By then, of course, I had paid all the rent.

Please give my regards to your charming client.

Yours sincerely

Marie-Laure Peloux

Chapter 10

Mareva injunctions and Anton Piller orders

MAREVA INJUNCTIONS

A Mareva injunction is an order of the court restraining the defendant from disposing of assets held by him in such a way as to defeat an award the plaintiff is likely to obtain if he is successful in the action. In order to understand the present form of the Mareva injunction it is necessary to know a little of the history of this procedure.

Pre 1975

Until 1975 it was thought that our courts had no power to intervene to prevent a defendant using his *own* property as he wished before there was a judgment of the court against him: the leading case which seemed to establish this proposition was *Lister & Co v Stubbs*:[1]

> S bought goods as agent for L and took a secret commission from the suppliers – thereby defrauding his principal. L sued to recover the commission. Before the action came to trial L applied for an injunction restraining S from dealing with the investments he had purchased with the commission. The Court of Appeal held that no injunction could be granted; per Cotton LJ: 'I know of no case where, because it was highly probable that if the action were brought to a hearing the plaintiff could establish that a debt was due from the defendant, the defendant has been ordered to give security until that [debt] has been established by the judgment or decree.'

This rule never applied where the plaintiff was claiming that the monies or assets in question belonged to him; so, for example, if he alleged that a fund was held on trust for him, the court would in an appropriate case restrain the defendant from using that fund until the issues in dispute had been decided. The rule did mean, however, that in ordinary debt and contract cases the courts would not freeze the defendant's assets unless and until there was a judgment against him.

The Mareva case[2]

> Shipowners (P) chartered a vessel to the defendants who in turn granted a sub-charter to the Government of India. The sub-charterers used the vessel for a voyage carrying fertilizer from Bordeaux to ports in India and paid the hire under

1 (1890) 45 Ch D 1, CA.
2 *Mareva Cia Naviera SA v International Bulk Carriers SA* [1975] 2 Lloyds Rep 509, CA also reported [1980] 1 All ER 213n.

the sub-charter into the defendants' bank in London. The defendant charterers failed to pay the instalments of hire due from them to the shipowners. The charterparty gave the English courts jurisdiction. The shipowners obtained an injunction *ex parte* to restrain the defendants removing from the jurisdiction the funds which had been deposited with their bankers. The Court of Appeal held that there was power to grant such an injunction provided (i) there was evidence of a debt due and owing; (ii) there was also evidence of assets within the jurisdiction; and (iii) there was a real danger that the defendants might deal with those assets so as to defeat any judgment obtained against them.

In *Nippon Yusen Kaisha v Karageorgis*[3] the power to make such orders was justified by Lord Denning MR as follows:

'We are told that . . . [it] has never been the practice of the English courts to seize assets of a defendant in advance of judgment, or to restrain the disposal of them. . . . It seems to me that the time has come when we should revise our practice. There is no reason why the High Court . . . should not make an order such as is asked for here. It is warranted by [section 37(1) of the Supreme Court Act 1981] which says the High Court may grant a mandamus or injunction or appoint a receiver by an interlocutory order in all cases in which it appears to the court to be just or convenient so to do.'

The Pertamina case[4]

In the *Mareva* case the right of the plaintiffs to be paid was unarguable; they would have been bound to have obtained summary judgment under RSC Order 14; they needed an injunction because they believed that the defendants' assets would have been removed from the jurisdiction before the summons for judgment could be heard. In the *Pertamina* case the Court of Appeal was faced with a case where the merits were not so clear cut:

The plaintiffs brought proceedings for damages for repudiation by the defendants of an agreement to charter oil tankers. The defendants had collected at the docks in Liverpool the component parts of a fertilizer plant they intended to build in Indonesia. The plaintiffs obtained an *ex parte* injunction in the Commercial Court to restrain the defendants removing this machinery out of the jurisdiction. The defendants applied successfully to the court for the injunction to be discharged. They argued that the agreement had been fraudulently negotiated between their own agent and the plaintiffs and put in evidence to that effect. The plaintiffs appealed to the Court of Appeal. The Court of Appeal held (1) that since the defence (ie the question of corruption) was so clearly raised in the evidence it would be wrong to grant an injunction; (2) a Mareva injunction should in any event not be granted where the assets in question are of little practical value by way of execution and the real reason the plaintiffs have obtained the injunction is to embarrass the defendants and put pressure on them to settle.

In the *Pertamina* case Lord Denning MR considered the plaintiffs did not need to prove that they would be bound to obtain summary judgment:

'I would not myself limit the discretion of the court to cases so plain that the plaintiff can get judgment under RSC Ord 14. We have all had experience of summonses under RSC Ord 14. The defendant may put in an affidavit putting forward a specious defence sufficient to get him leave to defend, conditional or unconditional. But when the case actually comes to the court for trial, he throws

---

3 [1975] 3 All ER 282, [1975] 1 WLR 1093, CA, a similar case where charterers failed to pay hire charges but had substantial funds in banks in London.
4 *Rasu Maratima SA v Perusahaan Pertambangan Minyak Dan Gas Bumi Negara (Pertamina)* [1978] QB 644, [1977] 3 All ER 324, CA.

his hand in. It is then seen that the affidavit was simply filed in order to gain time. So under this new procedure a defendant may put forward a specious defence just so as to remove his assets from the jurisdiction. The weakness of the defence may not appear until later. So I would hold that an order restraining removal of assets can be made whenever the plaintiff can show that he has a "good arguable case".[5]

This decision, that the plaintiff need only show a 'good arguable case', greatly extended the scope of the remedy; it has meant that instead of being confined to the comparatively rare case where the claim was demonstrably unanswerable it can be used wherever there is clear evidence in support of the plaintiff's claim.

The Siskina case[6]

The plaintiff must show that his substantive claim is justiciable by the English courts:

Saudi cargo owners sued Greek shipowners in Cyprus on bills of lading issued in Italy and sought an order from the English courts freezing substantial insurance monies held on behalf of the defendants in London. The House of Lords held that no order could be made because the substantive claim by the cargo owners could never have been heard by the English courts.

There is an exception to this rule: section 25 of the Civil Jurisdiction and Judgments Act 1982 in effect provides that a Mareva injunction may be granted where litigation has been begun (or is about to be begun) in another EC or EFTA[7] country against a defendant domiciled in an EC or EFTA country.

Assets outside the jurisdiction

As a general principle, there must be assets within the jurisdiction over which the Mareva injunction can take effect. Exceptionally however, there may be special circumstances which justify the making of an order in respect of assets *outside* the jurisdiction of the English courts.[8] Such 'worldwide' Mareva injunctions are rarely granted and cannot be obtained when there are sufficient assets within the jurisdiction to satisfy the plaintiff's claim. The difficulties associated with the granting of worldwide Mareva injunctions were considered by the Court of Appeal in *Derby & Co Ltd v Weldon (No 2)*.[9] One major difficulty faced by the courts is how such an order could be *enforced* given the assets are legally beyond the reach of the English courts. Lord Donaldson MR said:[10]

I find it difficult to believe that . . . the words 'cannot be enforced' . . . [mean] 'cannot be specifically enforced'. That that is not the true test is clear, because it is

5 Ibid. [1977] 3 All ER at 334.
6 *Siskina v Distos Cia Naviera SA* [1979] AC 210, [1977] 3 All ER 803, HL.
7 See Civil Jurisdiction and Judgments Act 1991, Schedule 2, para 12(a), which, implementing the Lugano Convention of 1988, extends the scope of s 25 of the Act of 1981 to EFTA countries.
8 Note that judgments may be enforced against assets situated in EC or EFTA states by virtue of the Civil Jurisdiction and Judgments Acts of 1982 and 1991. A plaintiff seeking a Mareva injunction against such assets will therefore have to establish that the defendant is likely to deal with the assets in such a way as to avoid the reciprocal enforcement provisions: see *Montecchi v Shimco Ltd* [1979] 1 WLR 1180, CA.
9 [1989] 1 All ER 1002, CA.
10 Ibid, at 1010f.

not uncommon for a court to order the disclosure of information which exists only in the mind of an individual. If he is unusually obdurate the order is unenforceable in the sense that the information will not be disclosed . . . [I]n the context of the grant of a Mareva injunction, I think that a sufficient sanction exists in the fact that, in the event of disobedience, the court could bar the defendant's right to defend. This is not a consequence which they could contemplate lightly as they would become fugitives from a final judgment given against them without their explanations having been heard and which might well be enforced against them by other courts.

A further problem recognised by the Court of Appeal was that of the position of third parties, such as foreign banks with no branch in or any other connection with England. Such third parties, who are not subject to the jurisdiction of the English courts, 'may take, and have indeed taken, offence at being, as they see it, "ordered about" by the English courts' when served with copies of Mareva injunctions issued in England. Lord Donaldson's solution was that a proviso in the following terms should be included in any order having extra-territorial effect:

> PROVIDED THAT, in so far as this order purports to have any extra-territorial effect, no person shall be affected thereby or concerned with the terms thereof until it shall be declared enforceable or be enforced by a foreign court and then it shall only affect them to the extent of such declaration or enforcement UNLESS they are (a) a person to whom this order is addressed or an officer of or an agent appointed by a power of attorney of such a person or (b) persons who are subject to the jurisdiction of this court and (i) have been given written notice of this order at their residence or place of business within the jurisdiction, and (ii) are able to prevent acts or omissions outside the jurisdiction of this court which assist in the breach of the terms of this order.[11]

HOW IS A MAREVA INJUNCTION OBTAINED?

An application for a Mareva injunction must be made in the High Court; the county courts have no power to make such an order.[12] Invariably, the application will be made *ex parte* (for to give the defendant notice would be self-defeating). In *Third Chandris Shipping Corpn v Unimarine SA*[13] the following guidelines were laid down by Lord Denning MR:

> '(i) The plaintiff should make full and frank disclosure of all matters in his knowledge which are material for the judge to know: . . . (ii) The plaintiff should give particulars of his claim against the defendant, stating the ground of his claim and the amount thereof, and fairly stating the points made against it by the defendant. (iii) The plaintiff should give some grounds for believing that the defendants have assets here . . . In most cases the plaintiff will not know the extent of the assets. He will only have indications of them. The existence of a bank account in England is enough, whether it is in overdraft or not. (iv) The plaintiff should give some grounds for believing that there is a risk of the assets being removed[14] before the judgment or award is satisfied. The mere fact that the defendant is abroad is not by itself sufficient . . . (v) The plaintiffs must, or course,

11 Ibid, at 1013a.
12 County Courts Remedies Regulations 1991; the High Court and County Courts Jurisdiction Order 1991, art 3.
13 [1979] QB 645, [1979] 2 All ER 972, CA (at 984g). The judgment of Mustill J at first instance (at 974) should be read for a valuable account of the development in practice of the Mareva injunction.
14 Or dealt with so as to defeat the ends of justice – see *Z Ltd v A-Z and AA-LL* [1982] QB 558, CA.

give an undertaking in damages, in case they fail in their claim or the injunction turns out to be unjustified. In a suitable case this should be supported by a bond or security: and the injunction only granted on it being given, or undertaken to be given.'

In practice the plaintiff's advisers will take the following steps:

(1) A writ usually indorsed with a statement of claim will be drafted ready for issue. The statement of claim must set out clearly and precisely the substantive relief which is claimed.

(2) An affidavit is prepared which must (i) depose to facts showing a good arguable case against the defendant: relevant documentation will inevitably be exhibited to prove the case (it should be stated that the defendant is resident within the jurisdiction or the claim is triable here); (ii) identify specific assets (such as bank accounts) which the plaintiff wants frozen – if no specific fund can be identified there must be evidence from which the court can infer that such funds do exist; (iii) there must be evidence from which the court can conclude that the defendant will dissipate or remove such assets from the jurisdiction if an order is not granted.

(3) A draft order is prepared. The original form of Mareva injunction froze a specific asset such as a fund held by the defendant's bankers; however, the practice quickly developed of framing the order so as to prevent the defendant from using *any* of his assets within the jurisdiction save to the extent any given fund exceeded the amount of the claim. It is this form of order which is now invariably used. The draft order will frequently contain interrogatories designed to discover the whereabouts of specific property; such an order (which is seldom made *ex parte*) is appropriate where the plaintiff is claiming that his own property is being held by the defendant or where there is clear evidence of trickiness on the part of the defendant or where it is necessary for 'the proper and effective exercise' of the jurisdiction (eg to prevent an excessive sum being frozen because of the wide scope of the order).[15]

At the hearing (which is in Chambers) the judge may accept that there is a good arguable case that a debt is due and owing and be prepared to infer that there are funds within the jurisdiction but he may nevertheless be uncertain whether the defendant is likely to dispose of his assets so as to defeat the claim. In such a case the plaintiff's counsel may need to argue that the misconduct of the defendant in relation to the substantive claim justifies the inference that he would attempt to defeat the claim by disposing of his assets. In the *Third Chandris* case Lawton LJ said:[16]

'There must be facts from which the Commercial Court,[17] like a prudent, sensible commercial man, can properly infer a danger of default if assets are removed from the jurisdiction. For commercial men, when assessing risks, there is no commercial equivalent of the Criminal Records Office or Ruff's Guide to the Turf. What they have to do is find out all they can about the party with whom they are

15 See *A v C* [1981] QB 956n, [1980] 2 All ER 347; *A J Bekhor v Bilton* [1981] QB 923, [1981] 2 All ER 565, CA.
16 [1979] 2 All ER 972, CA at 987b.
17 Although the Lord Justice refers throughout this passage to the judges of the Commercial Court, other judges of the High Court are also likely to have sufficient experience to make the assessments of risk of the kind described.

dealing, including origins, business domicile, length of time in business, assets and the like; and they will probably be wary of the appearances of wealth which are not backed by known assets. In my judgment the Commercial Court should approve applications for Mareva injunctions in the same way. Its judges have special experience of commercial cases and they can be expected to identify likely debt dodgers as well as, probably better than, most businessmen. They should not expect to be given proof of previous defaults or specific incidents of commercial malpractice. Further they should remember that affidavits asserting belief in, or the fear of, likely default have no probative value unless the sources and grounds thereof are set out: see RSC Ord 41, r 5(2). In my judgment an affidavit in support of a Mareva injunction should give enough particulars of the plaintiff's case to enable the court to assess its strength and should set out what enquiries have been made about the defendant's business and what information has been revealed, including that relating to its size, origins, business domicile, the location of known assets and the circumstances in which the dispute has arisen. These facts should enable a commercial judge to infer whether there is likely to be any real risk of default. Default is most unlikely if the defendant is a long-established, well-known foreign corporation or is known to have substantial assets in countries where English judgments can easily be enforced . . . But if nothing can be found out about the defendant, that by itself may be enough to justify a Mareva injunction.'

APPLICATION TO DISCHARGE OR VARY

Once the order has been served the defendants have the right to apply to the court that it should be varied or set aside. The following arguments may be put forward:

(i)   the plaintiff's case is itself based on trickiness or fraud (as was alleged in the *Pertamina* case) so that it would be inequitable to grant relief;

(ii) there is no real risk of default.

An illustration of such an application is *The Niedersachen*:[18]

The plaintiffs purchased a ship from a German company and, having paid over the purchase price, then applied successfully *ex parte* that part of the price should be frozen because of a claim for breach of warranty in respect of defects in the vessel. The *ex parte* injunction was set aside by the Court of Appeal because the plaintiffs had failed to establish in the light of evidence as to the good reputation and status of the sellers that they would fail to honour a judgment.

Another ground upon which the court will discharge a Mareva injunction (indeed without considering the merits) is if it can be shown that the plaintiffs misstated some material matter in their *ex parte* application.[19] It is for this reason that very great care must be taken in preparing the affidavit to make sure that all relevant matters (including the defendant's response to any claim) are set out.

EFFECT OF A MAREVA INJUNCTION

A Mareva injunction does not place the plaintiff in the position of a secured creditor; if for instance, a receiver claims the frozen fund under a debenture

---

18 *Ninemia Maritime Corp v Trave Schiffahrtsgesellschaft mbH & Co KG, The Niedersachen* [1983] 1 All ER 398, CA.
19 See *Brinks–MAT Ltd v Elcombe* [1988] 1 WLR 1350, CA and *Ali and Fahd Shobokshi Group Ltd v Moneim* [1989] 1 WLR 710.

or charge it must be released.[20] Since the plaintiff has no priority over other creditors, the defendant (who disputes the plaintiff's substantive claim) may be permitted by the court to pay out of the frozen funds other creditors whose debts fall due in the ordinary course of business.[21]

MAREVA AFTER JUDGMENT

Once a Mareva injunction has been granted, the Court may well continue it after judgment (whether at trial or on an Order 14 application or in default).[22] Even if no Mareva injunction has been granted, there will be some cases where the defendant's evidence at trial indicates so clearly his dishonesty that the Court may make an immediate Mareva injunction after giving judgment.[23]

The following Practice Note illustrates the procedures involved in an application for a typical Mareva injunction.

20 See *Cretanor Maritime* case [1978] 3 All ER 164, CA.
21 See *Iraqi Ministry of Defence v Arcepy Shipping Co SA, The Angel Bell* [1981] QB 65, [1980] 1 All ER 480.
22 See *Stewart Chartering Ltd v C and O Managements SA* [1980] 1 WLR 460.
23 See *Orwell Steel Ltd v Asphalt and Tarmac (UK) Ltd* [1984] 1 WLR 1097.

SKILLS PRACTICE NOTE

Application for Mareva injunction

The background
We act for Mr Raj Patel who on 15 March 1993 lent £30,000 to Mr Mohammed
Khan who needed to finance the purchase of a food store. Mr Patel agreed to
make the loan during a telephone call from Mr Khan and the money was
subsequently handed to Mr Khan in the form of cash at Mr Patel's home in
Barchester. Under their agreement the loan was repayable on 30 June 1993 with
interest payable at the rate of 30% per annum. In May 1993 Mr Patel discovered
that the sale of the store had in fact fallen through but was unable to contact Mr
Khan who has returned to Pakistan to attend to 'urgent family commitments'.
Mr Patel has not been paid the money and the whole amount together with
interest remains outstanding. Mr Patel has consulted us after seeing Mr Khan
recently in the High Street at Oxbridge. When tackled about the money on this
occasion Mr Khan told Mr Patel that the money would be repaid after the sale of
his Indian restaurant in December 1993. Mr Patel no longer trusts Mr Khan and
is very concerned that the money may never be repaid and in particular that any
attempt to recover the sum outstanding through legal means is likely to result in
Mr Khan disappearing again together with the money he is owed.

Is there a case for a Mareva injunction?
We should apply for a Mareva injunction only if the facts of the case justify the
making of an order. Before proceeding further we must therefore decide whether
each of the essential conditions set out below can be met:

(1) *Is there a good arguable case?* Although the application will be *ex parte* this must
be established in the light of any matters of which we are aware and which
support the *defendant's* case; it should be noted that any failure to include such
matters in the plaintiff's affidavit will result in the Mareva injunction being
discharged without regard to the substantive merits of the case.
(2) *Is D resident or is the claim triable within the jurisdiction?* The defendant is now
present in England but even if he is not resident here the English courts
clearly have jurisdiction over this dispute.
(3) *Is there evidence that the defendant has assets within the jurisdiction?* There is evidence
that the defendant owns assets in the form of an Indian restaurant and it is
also possible to infer the existence of a bank account in the name of the
defendant or the restaurant itself.
(4) *Is there evidence that the defendant is likely to dispose of his assets?* It will usually be
sufficient to rely on some evidence of misconduct or default by the defendant
from which the likelihood of disposal of assets may be inferred. In this case we
should rely on the defendant's bad faith in holding on to the money after the
purchase of the food store had fallen through. We should also refer to the
defendant's disappearance to Pakistan.

Preparing the documents required
Once we have decided that the case is appropriate for an application for a Mareva
injunction we must prepare the necessary documentation as follows:

(a) *A draft statement of claim.* Although the application for the injunction will be
made *ex parte*, we must be prepared to issue a writ to be served together with a
statement of claim as soon as the injunction is obtained. On the face of it the
case appears to amount to a simple action for a debt. If, however, there is any
suggestion of a more complicated contract, for example that the money was
lent as part of a partnership venture, the full circumstances must be
discovered from Mr Patel and pleaded in the statement of claim. It should be
remembered that if a Mareva injunction is obtained on the basis of

incomplete facts this will lead to an application by the defendant to discharge the order as soon as the incomplete affidavit or inaccurate statement of claim is served.
(b) *A draft order.* The order must specify the assets which are to be frozen by the injunction. It should also include any ancillary orders which are needed such as interrogatories designed to discover the existence and whereabouts of the defendant's assets such as bank account details etc.
(c) *A draft affidavit.* The application must be supported by the plaintiff's affidavit setting out fully all those matters justifying the grant of a Mareva injunction together with any matters known to the applicant which support the defendant's side of the dispute. In this case the affidavit will need to cover all those matters relating to (i) the debt; (ii) the defendant's default; (iii) the existence of known assets within the jurisdiction (eg the defendant's Indian restaurant); and (iv) the evidence of the defendant's default and misconduct suggesting he may remove or dispose of his assets before any judgment could be executed. A draft affidavit and order which would be used in this case are set out below.

AFFIDAVIT

(a) *Draft affidavit*

I, Raj Patel, of 36 Sunnybrook Road, Barchester, Barsetshire, Property Consultant make oath and say as follows:

1. In March 1993 the Defendant (whom I have known socially for about three years) telephoned me at home and asked me whether I would be prepared to advance him by way of loan the sum of £30000. He told me he needed this money as bridging finance for the purchase by him of a food store business in Barsetshire. He told me that the money would be repaid not later than 30 June 1993 and that he would pay interest at 30% per annum.
2. I agreed to make the advance to the Defendant and on 15 March he came to my home where I paid him in cash the sum of £30000. There is now produced and shown to me and marked 'RP1' a receipt signed by the Defendant acknowledging the said loan.
3. The monies were not repaid on 30 June and indeed the whole sum and interest remains outstanding. From about May 1993 I have tried to get in touch with the Defendant because I had been told by Mr Singh the owner of the food store business that the sale had fallen through. Although I telephoned repeatedly to the Defendant's flat I was always told that he had returned to Pakistan because of urgent family commitments.
4. Last week I saw the Defendant in Oxbridge High Street and I tackled him concerning repayment. He said: 'Do not worry, I cannot pay you now but you will get paid as soon as we sell the Indus Valley Restaurant. The sale should go through in December.'
5. I believe the Defendant is the owner of the aforesaid restaurant which he purchased from his brother last year. I also believe that he has one or more accounts at the Barchester High Street branch of the Midland Bank.
6. Although I am aware that the Defendant rents a flat at Paramount Court, Barchester, I believe he is not permanently settled in this country and further that there is a strong likelihood that after the sale of the restaurant he will return to Pakistan.
7. I further believe in view of his behaviour as aforesaid that he is likely to transfer out of the jurisdiction or otherwise dispose of his assets in order to defeat any judgment I may obtain.
8. I confirm that the sum now outstanding under the loan agreement is £34615 as at the date of this affidavit. I am informed by my solicitors and believe that the costs of these proceedings will not be less than £5000.

9. In the circumstances I respectfully ask the Court to make an order in the terms of the draft now produced and shown to me marked 'RP2'.

Sworn etc . . .

(*b*) *Checklist for affidavit*
Make sure the draft affidavit clearly shows the following:

(1) a good arguable case;
(2) any evidence or arguments on which the defendant may rely;
(3) the claim is justiciable in England and Wales;
(4) the defendant has assets within the jurisdiction;
(5) evidence of misconduct which justifies an inference that the defendant would remove or dispose of the assets.

ORDER

(*a*) *Draft Order*

In the High Court of Justice
Queen's Bench Division
The Hon Mr Justice . . . .   In Chambers

Between:

Raj Patel   Plaintiff

and
Mohammed Khan   Defendant

UPON hearing Counsel for the Plaintiff and upon reading the draft Affidavit of Raj Patel sworn herein on
AND upon the Plaintiff by his Counsel undertaking:

(1) Forthwith to issue a Writ of Summons in the form of the draft produced to the Court and initialled by the Judge and to serve the same on the Defendant as soon as is reasonably practicable thereafter.
(2) Forthwith to swear and file an Affidavit in the form of the draft initialled by the Judge.
(3) Forthwith to give notice of the terms of this Order to the Defendant by telephone and of the telephone number of a representative of the Plaintiff's Solicitors to whom any notice of an application to set aside or vary this Order may be given out of office hours.
(4) Forthwith to serve copies of this Order and the said affidavit and the exhibits thereto on the Defendant as soon as is reasonably practicable.
(5) To abide by an order which the Court may make as to damages in case this Court is hereafter of the opinion that the Defendant or any other person served with notice of this Order have suffered any by reason of this Order which the Plaintiff ought to pay.
(6) To pay the reasonable costs and expenses incurred by any third party to whom notice of the terms of this Order has been given, in ascertaining whether any assets to which this Order applies are within their control and in complying with this Order and to indemnify any such person against all liabilities which may flow from such compliance.
(7) To serve a copy of this Order upon any third party to whom the Plaintiff gives notice of this Order.
(8) To notify the Defendant and any Third Party to whom notice of this Order is given by the Plaintiffs or their Solicitors of their right to apply to the Court on notice to vary or set aside this Order in so far as it may affect them.

IT IS ORDERED THAT:

1. The Defendant be restrained and an injunction is hereby granted restraining him until trial or further order, whether by himself, his servants, agents or otherwise howsoever, from removing from the jurisdiction, disposing of, mortgaging, assigning, charging or otherwise dealing with any of his assets within the jurisdiction (including but not limited to (1) his interest in the property and business carried on at Indus Valley Restaurant, Station Road, Barchester or the proceeds of sale thereof and (2) all monies standing to his credit on any account in his name or in the name of Indus Valley Restaurant at Midland Bank plc, Barchester High Street branch, Barchester) save insofar as the unencumbered value of those assets exceeds £39000.

2. Notwithstanding paragraph 1 hereof, the Defendant shall be entitled to draw and expend from a bank account or other source (the identity of which shall first be notified to the Plaintiff's Solicitors):

   (a) a sum not exceeding £150 per week for ordinary living expenses;
   (b) a sum not exceeding £1000 in order to obtain legal advice and representation for the purpose of defending these proceedings;
   (c) such further sum or sums, if any, as the Plaintiff's Solicitors may from time to time agree in writing.

   Provided, however, that nothing in sub-paragraph (a), (b) or (c) of this paragraph shall impose any obligation on any third party to enquire into the purpose for which any sum drawn by the Defendant thereunder is in fact required or used.

3. The Defendant does within 7 days of service upon him of this Order make and serve upon the Plaintiff's Solicitor an Affidavit setting out:

   (a) full particulars of what has become of the sum of £30000 paid to him by the Plaintiff on 15 March 1993 and if the same or any part thereof was paid into any bank, building society or other savings account identifying the same and exhibiting statements of such account or accounts from payment-in to date and if the same or any part thereof was paid over to any third party identifying the person or persons to whom the same was paid, stating the consideration therefor and exhibiting any receipt or other document evidencing such payment;
   (b) full details of all his assets within the jurisdiction (save insofar as individual assets have a value of less than £500) including the location of such assets and of any documents of title or ownership relating thereto. Without prejudice to the generality of the foregoing the Defendant is to state whether and if so when and to whom the aforesaid Indus Valley Restaurant business was sold and if so what has become of the proceeds of sale and if not whether a contract for sale has been concluded and if so the date for completion and the identity of the Solicitors acting and is to identify all bank, building society, savings and other accounts held in his name (whether absolutely or jointly with others) or otherwise on his behalf and is to specify the amounts standing in each account.

4. Nothing in this Order shall prevent any Bank from exercising any rights of set-off it may have in respect of facilities afforded by such Bank prior to the date of this Order.

5. Liberty to the Defendant or any other person affected by this Order to apply on notice to the Plaintiff's Solicitors to set aside or vary this Order.

6. Costs reserved.

(*b*) *Checklist for Order*

Check that the draft Order contains the following:

(1) any necessary undertakings to the Court;

(2) specifies any particular assets within the jurisdiction believed to be the defendant's and which are required to be frozen;
(3) appropriate interrogatories designed to discover the whereabouts of other assets or a means of monitoring the movement of such assets (e g whether and to what extent the defendant's interest in the restaurant is subject to any charges; or, if it has not yet been sold, whether any deposit was paid and to what stage the sale has progressed).

ANTON PILLER ORDERS

In exceptional cases the High Court has the power to make an order that the defendant permits the plaintiff to search his premises and seize evidence which would otherwise be destroyed. In the leading case (from which the order takes its name) the facts were as follows:

> The plaintiffs, a German company, owned the copyright over a design for a frequencies convertor (part of a computer). They learnt that the defendants, who were their agents in England, were about to supply copies of drawings of the convertor to a rival concern. They applied, *ex parte*, for an injunction requiring the defendants to permit the plaintiffs' representatives (together with their solicitor) to enter the defendant's premises and to inspect all documents and files relating to the manufacture and supply of the frequency convertor and to remove and retain relevant documents.

The lower court refused to make such an order but the Court of Appeal granted the relief sought. Ormrod LJ set out the circumstances in which such orders could be made:

> There are three essential pre-conditions for the making of such an order . . . First, there must be an extremely strong prima facie case. Secondly, the damage, potential or actual, must be very serious for the plaintiff. Thirdly, there must be clear evidence that the defendants have in their possession incriminating documents or things, and that there is a real possibility that they may destroy such material before any application inter partes can be made.[24]

Anton Piller orders are not confined to cases where the defendant is alleged to be in possession of incriminating documents; such orders can be made where there is evidence that the defendant has property belonging to the plaintiff (or over which he has property rights) and that the defendant would destroy such property rather than deliver it up.[25]

The procedure is exceptional in that after an *ex parte* application, of which the defendant will know nothing, an order is made requiring him to give access to his premises and open his files to a party with whom he is in dispute. In the early 1980s the order was frequently sought by the large City firms of solicitors whose clients' rights were being infringed by defendants in a relatively modest way of business. The courts gradually came to realise that the order which was intended to defeat injustice could be itself an instrument of oppression.[26] In recent years the trend has been to restrict the granting of such orders to very clear cases and to provide strict safeguards.

24 *Anton Piller KG v Manufacturing Processes Ltd* [1976] Ch 55, [1976] 1 All ER 779, CA.
25 See *CBS (UK) Ltd v Lambert* [1983] Ch 37, [1982] 3 All ER 237, CA.
26 See *Columbia Picture Industries Inc v Robinson* [1987] Ch 38, [1986] 3 All ER 338, Ch D. Injustice was particularly likely to result after the development of the practice of adding a Mareva injunction to the Anton Piller order: this could effectively close down the defendant's business.

In *Lock International plc v Beswick*[27] Hoffmann J pointed out[28] that the courts will not normally assume that persons directed to preserve property will disobey its orders so as to justify the making of a full Anton Piller order:

'Even in cases in which the plaintiff has strong evidence that an employee has taken what is undoubtedly specific confidential information, such as a list of customers, the court must employ a graduated response. To borrow a useful concept from the jurisprudence of the European Community, there must be *proportionality* between the perceived threat to the plaintiff's rights and the remedy granted. The fact that there is overwhelming evidence that the defendant has behaved wrongfully in his commercial relationships does not necessarily justify an Anton Piller order. People whose commercial morality allows them to take a list of the customers with whom they were in contact while employed will not necessarily disobey an order of the court requiring them to deliver it up. Not everyone who is misusing confidential information will destroy documents in the face of a court order requiring him to preserve them.

    In many cases it will therefore be sufficient to make an order for delivery up of the plaintiff's documents to his solicitor or, in cases in which the documents belong to the defendant but may provide evidence against him, an order that he preserves the documents pending further order, or allows the plaintiff's solicitor to make copies. The more intrusive orders allowing searches of premises or vehicles require a careful balancing of, on the one hand, the plaintiff's right to recover his property or to preserve important evidence against, on the other hand, violation of the privacy of a defendant who has had no opportunity to put his side of the case. It is not merely that the defendant may be innocent. The making of an intrusive order *ex parte* even against a guilty defendant is contrary to normal principles of justice and can only be done when there is a paramount need to prevent a denial of justice to the plaintiff. The absolute extremity of the court's powers is to permit a search of a defendant's dwelling house, with the humiliation and family distress which that frequently involves.'

PROCEDURE

As indicated above, the application will be made *ex parte* and in chambers. The plaintiff's solicitor prepares:

(i)   A *writ* which should (if time permits) be indorsed with a statement of claim settled by counsel setting out precise details of the substantive claim against the defendant. If possible the writ should be issued; if that is not possible an undertaking is given to the court to issue as soon as the court office is open.

(ii)   An *affidavit* which must (a) show that there is very clear evidence to justify the plaintiff's substantive claim; (b) also show that the potential or actual damage which the plaintiff will suffer if an order is not made will be very serious; and (c) justify the assertion that the defendant is likely to destroy or dispose of the property in question if a simple order for delivery-up or retention is made.

(iii) A *draft order*. The specimen provided in the notes to RSC Order 72 in the Supreme Court Practice[29] should be followed but amended to take into account current developments in practice.[30] A worked-out specimen order is provided at the end of this chapter.

27 [1989] 3 All ER 373, [1989] 1 WLR 1268, Ch D.
28 Ibid, at 1279.
29 See *Supreme Court Practice* 1993, volume 1 pp 1260–1.
30 Such as the proposals by Sir Donald Nicholls V-C in *Universal Thermosensors Ltd v Hibben* [1992] 3 All ER 257, Ch D.

THE ORDER

The courts require substantial undertakings to be given by the plaintiff in addition to the usual undertaking to pay damages if it transpires the order should not have been made. We set out below the undertakings which are typically required:

(i) *that the order should be served and execution supervised by an independent solicitor*[31] who should report back to the court. It is desirable that the order should be served and executed by a solicitor who is not a member of the firm acting for the plaintiff. He should be an experienced solicitor having some familiarity with the workings of Anton Piller orders. He should prepare a written report on what occurred when the order was executed; a copy of his report should be served on the defendant and presented to the court at an inter partes hearing preferably before the judge who made the order.

(ii) *the order should provide for the defendant to have the right to obtain legal advice.*[32] The order will normally contain a term to the effect that the solicitor serving the order should explain fairly and in everyday language to the person served the meaning and effect of the order and his right to obtain legal advice before compliance with the order provided such advice is obtained speedily. Such a provision is, of course, meaningless unless such advice is available and therefore the order will normally also provide that it is to be served only at a time when the defendant will be able to obtain legal advice.

(iii) *that the order will provide for the solicitor supervising execution to list all documents taken.* In general such a list should be prepared at the premises being searched before they are removed and the defendant should be given an opportunity to check the list.

APPLICATION BY DEFENDANT

If, having obtained legal advice, the defendant comes to the conclusion that the order should not have been made,[33] what is he to do? In theory he can refuse to comply and apply at once to the judge who made the order for it to be discharged but in taking such a course he runs the risk of being in contempt of court:

'[The defendants] could if they had wished have refused immediate compliance and instead have made an urgent application to have the order set aside . . . However, I must emphasise . . . that defendants who take this line do so very much at their peril. If they succeed in getting the order discharged, all well and good. But, if they fail they will render themselves liable to penalties for contempt of court. If they fail and there is any reason to believe that, in the period between the time when the order has been served on them and the time when they eventually comply with the order, they had taken steps which were inconsistent with the order, they had, for example, destroyed any records, the consequence to them would be of the utmost gravity.'[34]

31 See *Universal Thermosensors* case, loc cit.
32 See *Bhimji v Chatwani* [1991] 1 All ER 705.
33 Eg because of material non-disclosure by the plaintiff in the affidavit used to obtain the order (see *Arab Monetary Fund v Hashim* [1989] 3 All ER 466, Ch D) or because the documents sought would incriminate the defendant in a charge of conspiracy to defraud (see *Tate Access Floors Inc v Boswell* [1991] Ch 512, [1990] 3 All ER 303, Ch D).
34 *WEA Records Ltd v Visions Channel 4 Ltd* [1983] 2 All ER 589, CA at 592f per Sir John Donaldson MR.

The prudent course will almost always be to obey the order; complaints that it should not have been made can be reserved to the eventual trial of the action (and found an application for damages to be awarded against the plaintiff[35]). In very rare cases, where, for example, it is considered that it is essential that the plaintiff should not be allowed to see the documents in question, so that an application for discharge should be made before compliance, the defendant's solicitor should arrange for specific steps to be taken to ensure no material is lost or destroyed before the hearing to discharge.[36]

---

35 See *Dormeuil Frères SA v Nicolian International (Textiles) Ltd* [1988] 3 All ER 197, Ch D.
36 See further on this point *Bhimji v Chatwani* [1991] 1 All ER 705, per Scott J at p 713f: 'when a committal application is made something more to justify an order under it must be shown than a mere technical breach of the obligation to allow entry forthwith'.

SKILLS PRACTICE NOTE

<u>Application for Anton Piller order</u>

The background

We have been instructed by Law Computers Ltd, which specialises in supplying computers and appropriate software to solicitors for use in conveyancing, maintaining accounts and similar purposes. On 1 April 1987 Law Computers Ltd employed Oliver Twist as its sales manager. Under his written contract Twist agreed:

(1) after termination of his employment not to use or disclose any confidential information obtained during his employment; and

(2) not for a period of 1 year after termination of his employment to carry on or work in any business carried on within a radius of 50 miles of his place of work concerned with the sale or hire of computer equipment and software to members of the legal profession.

On 21 November 1992 Twist left following a row with Michael White, the managing director of Law Computers Ltd. Mr White has now heard that Twist is to start work next week with Juradata Ltd, Law Computers' principal competitor. On checking, Mr White also discovered that confidential price lists, customer discounts and business projections were missing from the offices at which Twist had been based. Mr White immediately telephoned Twist, who quickly became abusive and denied all knowledge of the missing documents saying: 'Even if I had them, you'll never get your hands on them.'

These matters are of particular concern to Law Computers Ltd which has reached a delicate stage in negotiations with a publishing company over a proposed takeover of Law Computers' business. It is therefore essential that steps are taken to pre-empt any action by Twist which would damage the company or prejudice the negotiations.

Is there a case for an Anton Piller order?

An Anton Piller order is obtained *ex parte* and can be made only when there is a paramount need to prevent a denial of justice to the plaintiff. Otherwise, the plaintiff should make an application on notice.[37] Before applying for an Anton Piller order we must be sure of the following matters:

(1) *There is an extremely strong prima facie case.* It is questionable whether there is such a strong case in relation to the non-competition covenant, which is arguably void as being in restraint of trade. The case based on misuse of confidential information is stronger, however, and would give rise to a claim for breach of the implied duty of fidelity even in the absence of an express term protecting use or disclosure of trade secrets.

(2) *The actual or potential damage is very serious for P.* In this case the loss to the plaintiff company may go beyond the usual damage which they may suffer from the misuse of their trade secrets. The proposed deal with the publishing company to take-over Law Computers Ltd may be called off with inestimable loss thereby caused to the plaintiff.

(3) *There is clear evidence of incriminating material in the possession of the defendant and a real possibility that it will be destroyed if notice of the application is given.* There is no direct evidence that Twist has taken the missing documents but the inferen-

---

37 Under RSC Ord 29, r 2 where proceedings have been commenced or under RSC Ord 29, r 7A(1) where an order is required before the commencement of the action.

ces that he *has* done so and would destroy them if given the opportunity are strengthened by his abusive attitude and the words spoken to Mr White when questioned about the missing material. This should therefore be stressed in the affidavit in support of the application.

A draft Statement of Claim and Order to be used in this case are set out below:

To be indorsed on writ

Statement of Claim

1. The Plaintiffs are a company carrying on business at Unit 66 Marketsdowne Industrial Estate, Basildon, Essex and engaged inter alia in selling and hiring computer equipment and software for use by solicitors and conveyancers.
2. By a contract in writing dated 1 April 1987 the Plaintiffs employed the Defendant as their regional sales manager based at the said address.
3. It was expressly provided by the said contract as follows:

   (a) By clause 8 thereof that at all times after the termination of his employment the Defendant should keep secret and not use any confidential information obtained by him during his employment;
   (b) By clause 9 thereof that the Defendant should not for a period of 12 months after the termination of his employment carry on or work in any business carried on within 50 miles of the said Plaintiff address concerned with the sale or hire of computer equipment and software to members of the legal profession.

4. On 21 November 1992 the Defendant's employment with the Plaintiffs was determined.
5. The Defendant has removed from the Plaintiffs' premises documents containing confidential price lists, details of customer discounts and projections and plans prepared for the Plaintiff company's future trading (as itemised in the Schedule hereto).
6. The Defendant intends unless restrained by order of this Honourable Court from so doing to reveal confidential information (including the information contained in the aforesaid documents) to third persons whereby the Plaintiffs will suffer damage.
7. Further, the Defendant threatens and intends unless restrained by order of this Honourable Court from so doing to take employment with Juradata Limited at 101 Temple Passage, London EC4 which business is directly concerned with the sale and hire of computer equipment and software to members of the legal profession.

And the Plaintiffs claim:

(1) An order for the delivery up of all documents taken by the Defendant from the Plaintiffs' premises;
(2) An injunction to restrain the Defendant from revealing confidential information concerning the Plaintiffs' business to any third parties;
(3) An injunction to restrain the Defendant until 20 November 1993 from carrying on or working for any business within 50 miles of the Plaintiffs' said address concerned with the sale or hire of computer equipment to members of the legal profession.

Schedule

[list documents taken]

In the High Court of Justice
Queen's Bench Division
The Hon Mr Justice   In Chambers

Between:

Law Computers Limited   Plaintiffs

and

Oliver Twist   Defendant

Order

UPON hearing Counsel for the Plaintiffs and upon reading the affidavit of Michael White sworn   day of December 1992

AND upon the Plaintiffs by their Counsel undertaking:

(1) Forthwith to issue a Writ of Summons claiming relief similar to or connected with that hereinafter granted.
(2) At the time of the execution of this order or as soon as possible thereafter to serve upon the Defendant by a Solicitor of the Supreme Court the writ and copies of this Order and the said affidavit and the exhibits thereto.
(3) To abide by any order which the Court may make as to damages in case the Court is hereafter of the opinion that the Defendant shall have sustained any damages by reason of this Order which the Plaintiffs ought to pay.
(4) To abide by any order this Court may make as to damages if it shall consider that any innocent party, other than the Defendant, shall have sustained any damages by reason of this Order which the Plaintiffs ought to pay.

And the Solicitors for the Plaintiffs by Counsel for the Plaintiffs (being their Counsel for this purpose) undertaking:

(1) To serve this Order by a solicitor of the Supreme Court.
(2) To offer to explain fairly and in everyday language to the person or persons served with this Order its meaning and effect and to advise the person on whom the same is served of his right to obtain legal advice before complying with this Order provided that such advice is obtained forthwith.
(3) To retain in their safe custody until further order all articles and documents taken or delivered to them pursuant to this Order.
(4) To answer forthwith any query made by the Defendant as to whether any particular document or article is within the scope of this Order.
(5) To make a list of all such articles and documents obtained as a result of this Order prior to removal of any such articles or documents into their safe custody and to provide the Defendant or the persons served with this Order a copy thereof prior to such removal.
(6) To return the originals of all documents obtained as a result of this Order within 2 working days of removal of the same.
(7) Where ownership of any articles obtained as a result of this Order is disputed to deliver up any such articles to the custody of the Solicitors acting on behalf of the Defendant within 2 working days of receipt of an undertaking in writing from the Defendant's Solicitors to retain the same in safe custody and produce the same, if required by the Court.

IT IS ORDERED:

1. That the Defendant be restrained until after the hearing of a summons returnable on 21 day of December 1992 or further order in the meantime

whether by himself his servants or agents or otherwise howsoever from doing the following acts or any of them, that is to say:

   (a) disclosing to any person or using any confidential information obtained by him during his employment with the Plaintiffs including details of prices, customer discounts and trading projections and plans;

   (b) carrying on or working in any business carried on within 50 miles of Unit 66 Marketsdowne Industrial Estate, Basildon, Essex concerned with the sale or hire of computer equipment and software to barristers, solicitors, conveyancers or other persons employed in the legal profession;

   (c) directly or indirectly informing or notifying, otherwise than for the purpose of seeking legal advice, any person company or firm of these proceedings or of the provisions of this Order.

2. That the Defendant does forthwith disclose to the person serving this Order the whereabouts of all documents removed by him from the Plaintiffs' premises.

3. That the Defendant does forthwith deliver to the Plaintiffs' Solicitors all such documents as are referred to in paragraph 2 of this Order which are in his possession custody or power.

4. That the Defendant by himself or by any person appearing to be in control of the premises hereinafter mentioned do permit the person serving this Order upon them and such other person duly authorised by the Plaintiffs (such persons not to exceed 3 in number altogether) to enter forthwith at any time between 8 o'clock in the morning and 7 o'clock in the evening the premises known as 23 Acacia Avenue Middletown and any other premises or vehicles to the extent that any of the said premises or vehicles are in the power, possession, occupation or control of the Defendant for the purpose of looking for and taking into the custody of the Plaintiffs' Solicitors all such documents.

5. That within 7 days of service of this Order the Defendant does make and serve on the Plaintiff's Solicitors an Affidavit setting out all the information to be disclosed under paragraph 2.

6. Liberty to the Defendant and to any Third Party affected by this Order to apply to vary or discharge this Order upon giving notice to the Plaintiffs' Solicitors of their intention to do so.

7. Costs reserved.

Dated this   day of   19 .

_____

Chapter 11

Payment into court and infant settlements

PAYMENT INTO COURT

Once the pleadings are closed and discovery has taken place it may well be that the defendant will wish to make an offer of settlement to the plaintiff. In considering that offer the plaintiff will obviously take into account not only the value of his claim and his likely chance of success but also the amount he has already incurred in costs due to his solicitor. Suppose he decides not to accept the defendant's offer but to let the matter continue to trial. If he eventually is awarded only the amount offered by the defendant or a lesser sum, it would be unfair that the defendant should be liable for the costs incurred after his offer was refused. In order to solve this problem the courts permit a defendant to make a formal offer by paying the amount offered to the court to hold until either the plaintiff accepts the sum in question or the matter goes to trial. If the plaintiff does not accept the sum offered but at the end of the trial only recovers that amount or a lesser sum, the court will order that the plaintiff is only to have the costs of the action to the date of payment-in and that he is to pay the costs incurred by the defendant thereafter.

> *Example.* P sustains a serious injury as a result of D's negligence. Counsel advised him he is likely to recover total damages in the region of £70,000. After the summons for directions D pays into court £60,000. At that stage P's costs would tax at about £5000. P can accept the payment into court and at once tax his costs – so the *total* sum received will be £65,000 although of course, he will pay £5000 to his solicitors. Assume P refuses the offer and fights the case but is awarded only £55,000. Although he has won the action, the order for costs will be P's costs to the date of payment into court (ie £5000) but he will have to bear his own costs thereafter (£10,000) *and* pay the taxed costs incurred by the defendant from the date of payment in (also £10,000) and, in addition, pay his own solicitor £5000. The net result is that he finishes with £35,000 whilst he would have had £60,000 clear if he had accepted the payment into court. Only £5000 of the shortfall is attributable to the amount of *damages* recovered in each case.

The High Court procedure for making and accepting a payment into court is set out in RSC Order 22 and can be summarised as follows.

(1) At any time after the writ is served a defendant may make payment into court.

(2) He calculates an amount to include interest (whether under section

35A Supreme Court Act 1981 or Bills of Exchange Act 1882 or under a contract).[1]

(3) He prepares a form of 'notice of payment into court'; in a simple case it would set out the title of the action and then read: 'Take notice that the Defendant has paid £   into court. The said £   is in satisfaction of all the causes of action in respect of which the plaintiff claims and interest thereon and after taking into account and satisfying the above-named defendant's cause of action for damages in respect of which he counterclaims'.[2]

(4) In actions for personal injuries which occurred on or after 1 January 1989 the Social Security Act 1989 entitles the Department of Social Security to recoup from any payment of damages any 'relevant benefits' (such as sickness benefit or invalidity benefit) which have been received by the plaintiff. Where the Act applies the *defendant* is required to deduct the gross amount of any such benefits and pay it to the Secretary of State. The notice of payment into court will therefore include a statement in the following terms: 'The defendant has withheld from this payment the sum of £   in accordance with section 93 of the Social Security Administration Act 1992'.[3]

(5) The defendant pays in the sum offered by producing cash, a cheque made payable to the Accountant General of the Supreme Court or a banker's draft at the Court Funds Office, 22 Kingsway, London WC2B 6LE or at district registry.[4] The form of notice is then duly stamped and receipted and the payment is recorded in the court ledgers.

(6) The notice of payment-in must then be served on the plaintiff and every other defendant.[5]

(7) Within 3 working days of receiving notice of payment-in the plaintiff must send an acknowledgment of its receipt to the defendant.[6]

(8) Within 21 days of the date of receipt of the notice of payment into court, the plaintiff may give notice to the defendant that he accepts the payment into court,[7] and arrange for the monies to be paid out to his solicitor (who will have to retain them in a legal aid case to deal with the Law Society's first charge on all sums recovered by an assisted person). The defendant must also pay the plaintiff's costs of the action incurred up to the time the notice of acceptance was given.[8] Once the plaintiff has accepted a payment into court all further proceedings in respect of the cause of action are stayed

---

1 RSC Ord 22, r 1(8).
2 The relevant form is Form No 23 of the General Forms set out as Appendix A to the RSC. The form makes provision for payment in to satisfy separate causes of action and for apportionment between them.
3 The operation of these 'clawback' provisions is outlined below at p 267.
4 Court Funds Rules 1987, r 16.
5 RSC Ord 22, r 1(2).
6 Ibid.
7 RSC Ord 22, r 3(1).
8 RSC Ord 62, r 5(4). Note, however, that the plaintiff is not automatically entitled to recover from the paying-in defendant the costs of pursuing the action against other defendants; the words 'his costs of the action' in rule 5(4) refer to his costs of the action as against that specific defendant: see *QBE Insurance (UK) Ltd v Mediterranean Insurance and Reinsurance Co Ltd* [1992] 1 All ER 12, per Webster J.

against the defendant who has paid into court and all other defendants sued jointly with him or in the alternative to him.[9]

(9) After 21 days have elapsed from the date of payment-in the plaintiff may still accept the payment into court but he must obtain leave to do so and will usually be ordered to pay the costs incurred by the defendant since the date of payment-in.

(10) The defendant may increase the amount of his payment into court at any time. He must serve a notice of increase on the plaintiff or any co-defendant.[10]

(11) The monies paid into court will carry no interest if accepted within the 21 days limited for acceptance.[11] Thereafter, the sum will be placed in an interest bearing 'basic account'.[12] Where money is paid out under a judgment or where leave is obtained to take money paid-in out of court after the 21 day period the court must also make a direction dealing with the accrued interest. Normally, the court will direct that (i) interest accruing between the date of payment in and the judgment or order for payment out is paid to the party who made the payment in and (ii) interest accruing subsequently is paid proportionately to the party to whom the payment out is made.[13]

(12) The plaintiff cannot take out a payment into court once the trial of the action has effectively started unless the defendant consents.[14]

(13) The defendant may pay money into court or increase the sum paid in even after the trial has begun which the plaintiff may accept within two days or up to the moment when the judge commences his judgment.[15] If the plaintiff chooses to accept monies paid in or increased after the trial has begun, the question of costs is at large.[16]

(14) The fact of payment into court is not to be disclosed to the judge until he has given judgment.[17]

(15) A defendant may not withdraw a payment into court without the leave of the court.[18]

(16) As stated above, where the sum eventually awarded to a plaintiff who has not accepted the payment into court is no more than the amount paid in by the defendant, the plaintiff will be entitled to his costs to the date of payment in but he will be required to pay the costs incurred thereafter by the defendant.[19]

(17) When two or more defendants are sued in the same action, and one makes a payment into court which the plaintiff wishes to accept,

9 RSC Ord 22, r 3(4) and (5).
10 RSC Ord 22, r 1(3).
11 Court Funds Rules 1987, r 32(4).
12 Ibid, rr 28, 31(1).
13 QBD *Practice Direction* [1988] 3 All ER 896.
14 RSC Ord 22, r 3(1).
15 RSC Ord 22, rr 1(1), 3(2), (3).
16 RSC Ord 22, r 4(3).
17 RSC Ord 22, r 7.
18 RSC Ord 22, r 1(3). Leave will be granted only where it is justified by a sufficient change of circumstances since the payment in: see *W A Sherratt Ltd v John Bromley (Church Stretton) Ltd* [1985] QB 1038, [1985] 1 All ER 216, CA.
19 RSC Ord 62, r 9(1)(b) in fact merely provides: 'The court in exercising its discretion as to costs shall take into account . . . any payment of money into court and the amount of such payment. . .'. See *Brown v New Empress Saloons Ltd* [1937] 2 All ER 133, CA. As to the position where the difference is very small, see *Tingay v Harris* [1967] 2 QB 327, CA.

special rules apply. Where the claim in question is *joint* or *alternative* only (but not *several*): (i) the action is stayed against the defendant whose payment in has been accepted and against the all the other defendants;[20] the plaintiff will therefore require leave to proceed with the action against the remaining defendants; and (ii) no money in court may be paid out to the plaintiff without an order of the court (which must also deal with the question of costs) unless all the other defendants consent in writing to the payment out.[21]

(18) Where there has been a payment into court the plaintiff becomes a secured creditor to the extent of the money paid in.[22]

It will be noted that once 21 days has elapsed from the date the plaintiff received notice of payment-in he will only be entitled to accept the offer by issuing a summons for leave to take the monies paid-in out of court; once the trial has begun, he cannot apply for leave unless the defendant agrees.

Example 1. P sued D for damages in respect of an eye injury sustained at work. D raised an allegation of substantial contributory negligence by P in not wearing goggles. D in due course paid £5500 into court. At the trial it became clear that P was not likely to succeed and he applied to take the monies paid in out of court. The Court of Appeal held that the trial judge is not to know that monies have been paid into court so an application for leave to take out cannot be made to him unless the defendant consents. The Court also pointed out there is a distinction between an application to take out made at the trial and an application made *before* the trial begins; where an application is made by summons before the trial the master has a discretion whether or not to permit payment-out. Per Lord Denning MR: 'If the chances of success or failure – or of greater or less damages – are substantially the same as they were at the time of the payment into court, the master may allow the payment out to the plaintiff, but he will usually allow it only on the terms that the plaintiff pays all the costs from the date of the payment into Court. If the chances have substantially altered, then the master should not allow the plaintiff to take the payment out: for the simple reason that it would be unfair to hold the defendant to a sum which he offered in different circumstances . . . I think the defendant should indicate to the master the circumstances which have altered the position, such as a decision of the courts which have changed the way in which damages are to be assessed, or the discovery of further evidence or information affecting the chances. But I do not think the defendant should be required to state circumstances which, if disclosed to the plaintiff at this stage, would affect the conduct of the case at the trial as, for instance, by making the plaintiff aware of the questions which he might be asked in cross-examination.'[23]

Example 2. On 1 May 1988 *The Sunday Times* published an article entitled 'The SAS in the Dock'. P considered she had been libelled in the article which stated amongst other things that she had lied to Thames Television in a programme about the shooting in Gibraltar of three members of the IRA and that she earned her living by running in partnership with well known criminals an escort agency in Spain for rich Arabs. In January 1989 P issued a writ for libel against D Ltd, the publishers of *The Sunday Times*. In their defence, D Ltd denied the words published were defamatory and raised a defence of fair comment. In June 1989 D Ltd gave notice of payment into court in respect of the claim and two months later gave notice of further payment in. In September 1989 D Ltd obtained leave to amend its defence so as to plead justification in lieu of fair comment, and later

20 RSC Ord 22, r 3(4).
21 See RSC Ord 22, r 4(1); (2). See also *Scania (GB) Ltd v Andrews* [1992] 3 All ER 143, CA.
22 See *W A Sherratt Ltd v John Bromley (Church Stretton) Ltd* [1985] QB 1038, [1985] 1 All ER 216, CA.
23 *Gaskins v British Aluminium Co Ltd* [1976] QB 524, [1976] 1 All ER 208 at 211, CA.

obtained further leave from the Court of Appeal to amend its defence. At a further application in June 1990, D Ltd obtained an extension of time for serving Civil Evidence Act notices but at the same time the judge granted P an extension of time for accepting the money paid into court. On D Ltd's appeal the Court of Appeal held that the judge had been wrong to extend the time because there had been a substantial alteration of the risks. Per Neill LJ:

> 'In many cases I accept that a mere change of plea may not alter the risks to any appreciable extent, but in this case it seems to me that the introduction of a plea of justification was an important factor. *A fortiori* the risks were again substantially altered when the Court of Appeal allowed further amendment and then again when the notices under the Civil Evidence Act 1968 were allowed out of time.'[24]

A defendant who has made a payment into court may wish to withdraw the payment because, for example, he discovers fresh evidence or there is a new judicial decision which materially affects the likely outcome of the action. In such a case the leave of the court must first be obtained before the payment-in can be withdrawn. The court has power to permit a defendant to withdraw money paid into court even before the expiry of the period of 21 days limited for acceptance of the payment-in without leave, provided the defendant can establish a 'good reason'.

> *Example.* Following expert advice in a claim for defective building work D paid money into court on 18 November 1985. On 20 November a second expert advised D that P's claim was wrongly inflated by double counting which had not been identified by the first expert. When, on 28 November, D served a summons on P giving notice of an application to withdraw the payment-in P gave notice of acceptance of the payment-in. The Official Referee held that, on the facts, D had not shown good reason to withdraw the payment-in as the information on which he relied had always been available to him. However, the Court held that it had a discretion to allow the defendant to withdraw a payment-in within the period of 21 days limited for acceptance, even where the payment-in was 'accepted' before the defendant's summons to withdraw the payment is heard.[25]

RECOUPMENT OF STATE BENEFITS

Until recently, where damages were to be assessed in a personal injury claim, either the full or partial amount of most state benefits received by the plaintiff had to be deducted from the amount of damages payable by the defendant. The effect of this system was that a part of the plaintiff's loss caused by the defendant was borne by the taxpayer. In relation to injuries which occurred on or after 1 January 1989 however, what is now the Social Security Administration Act 1992 provides that in claims arising from an accident, injury or disease suffered by the plaintiff the 'compensator' must, before making any payment of damages, obtain from the Secretary of State a certificate of total benefit. The certificate shows the gross amount of the *relevant benefits*[26] paid or likely to be paid to the 'victim' in the period of five years from the date of the injury or until final settlement of the claim if sooner (the *relevant period*).[27] The sum stated in the certificate is then payable

---

24 *Proetta v Times Newspapers Ltd* [1991] 4 All ER 46, CA.
25 See *Manku v Seehra* [1986] CILL 224, [1986] NLJ Rep 236, Judge Newey QC.
26 The relevant benefits are set out in the Social Security (Recoupment) Regulations 1990 and include, *inter alia:* unemployment benefit, family credit, income support, invalidity pension and allowance, mobility allowance, disablement benefit and allowance, sickness benefit and statutory sick-pay.
27 Social Security Administration Act 1992, s 81(1).

by the compensator to the Secretary of State.[28] The effect of these recoupment or 'clawback' provisions is that a greater part of the cost of compensating the plaintiff for personal injuries is borne by the defendant (or his insurers) who is to blame for the plaintiff's injuries.

The basic principle is contained in section 82 which provides:

'82(1) A person (the 'compensator') making a compensation payment, whether on behalf of himself or another, in consequence of an accident, injury or disease suffered by another person (the 'victim') shall not do so until the Secretary of State has furnished him with a certificate of total benefit and shall then –

(a) deduct from the payment an amount, determined in accordance with the certificate of total benefit, equal to the gross amount of any relevant benefits paid or likely to be paid to or for the victim during the relevant period in respect of that accident, injury or disease;

(b) pay to the Secretary of State an amount equal to that which is required to be so deducted; and

(c) furnish the person to whom the compensation payment is or, apart from this section, would have been made (the 'intended recipient') with a certificate of deduction.

(2) Any right of the intended recipient to receive the compensation payment in question shall be regarded as satisfied to the extent of the amount certified in the certificate of deduction.'

Payments into court in personal injury actions are formal offers of settlement which may, if accepted, result in the payment of compensation. They are, therefore, affected by the above recoupment provisions. The Social Security Administration Act 1992, section 93(2) provides:

'Where a party to an action makes a payment into court, which had it been paid directly to the other party, would have constituted a compensation payment, the making of that payment shall be regarded for the purposes of the recoupment provisions as the making of a compensation payment . . .'

The procedure to be followed in the case of payments into court which are affected by the recoupment provisions is summarised below:

(1) A defendant who is considering making a payment-in in a personal injury case should first obtain and complete an application form (Form CRU4) for a certificate of total benefit from the Compensation Recovery Unit of the DSS at Newcastle.[29]

(2) A Certificate of Total Benefit (Form CRU100) will be returned to the defendant indicating the amount of relevant benefits received by the plaintiff.

(3) Before making any payment-in the defendant should withhold from the amount to be paid into court an amount equal to the total benefits shown on the certificate from the day following the date of the accident to the date of the payment-in.[30] Upon making the payment-in the defendant must furnish the court with a certificate showing the amount so withheld.[31]

---

28 Social Security Administration Act 1992, s 82(1)(b).
29 The application form is obtained by forwarding a completed Form CRU1 to the Compensation Recovery Unit.
30 Social Security Administration Act 1992, s 93(2)(a).
31 Ibid, s 93(3)(a).

(4) If the payment-in is accepted, the defendant then furnishes the plaintiff[32] with a certificate of deduction showing the amount withheld and must pay the amount deducted to the Secretary of State.[33]

(5) The amount of the payment-in is treated as increased by the amount certified as withheld[34] and, if the payment-in is accepted, the plaintiff's entitlement to compensation is regarded as satisfied to the extent of the amount certified in addition to the sum paid out of court.[35]

(6) The defendant may make a payment into court *before* obtaining a certificate of total benefit,[36] but he must apply for a certificate no later than the day on which the payment-in is made[37] and he remains liable to pay the amount of total benefit shown on the subsequent certificate whether or not he has deducted a corresponding amount from the sum he paid into court.[38]

NON-MONETARY OFFERS

RSC Ord 22, r 1 applies only to 'any action for a debt or damages' and provides only for the payment into court of 'a sum of money in satisfaction of the cause of action'. The question therefore arises as to whether a defendant to proceedings in which the plaintiff claims some other remedy, such as an injunction or possession of land, can similarly make a formal non-monetary offer of settlement which will protect his position as to costs. The same question also arises where the plaintiff is claiming a debt or damages but the defendant nevertheless wishes to offer a non-monetary settlement.

> *Example.* H brought proceedings against W, his wife, claiming a share of the matrimonial home. In a letter marked 'without prejudice' W offered to transfer another house worth £12,000 to H in exchange for his agreement to vacate the matrimonial home. H refused and the trial judge awarded H £10,000 from the sale of the matrimonial home, but made no order as to costs. The Court of Appeal held that a payment into court was not appropriate, but, as H had recovered an amount smaller than that offered by W, the letter protected her position as to costs from the date of the offer.[39]

The principle formulated by the Court of Appeal in the *Calderbank* case forms the basis of RSC Ord 22, r 14. It provides:

'(1) A party to proceedings may at any time make a written offer to any other party to those proceedings which is expressed to be 'without prejudice save as to costs' and which relates to any issue in the proceedings.

(2) Where an offer is made under paragraph (1), the fact that such an offer has been made shall not be communicated to the Court until the question of costs falls to be decided.'

The effect of the above rule is that the principle that communications marked 'without prejudice' are inadmissible against the writer on the

32 Ibid, s 82(1)(c).
33 Ibid, s 82(1)(b); s 93(2)(b).
34 Ibid, s 93(3)(b).
35 Ibid, s 82(2).
36 Ibid, s 93(2)(a)(ii).
37 Ibid, s 93(4)(a).
38 Ibid, s 93(4)(b).
39 *Calderbank v Calderbank* [1976] Fam 93, [1975] 3 All ER 333, CA.

grounds of privilege has been qualified to the limited extent that the court may take account of offers marked 'without prejudice save as to costs', but, as with payments into court, only after the questions of liability and quantum have been decided. The court may not, however, take account of any such written offer under Ord 22, r 14 in exercising its discretion as to costs in any case where the defendant could have protected his position as to costs by means of proper payment into court.[40] It should also be noted that where a written offer is made under Ord 22, r 14 the question of costs is a matter for the discretion of the trial judge and the court will not usurp that discretion by directing, in advance of the trial, that a written offer will be treated as equivalent to a payment into court.[41]

COUNTY COURT PROCEDURE

The procedure in the county court is substantially similar to that followed in the High Court.[42] It should be noted that where an action is brought on behalf of minors, a payment-in cannot be accepted without the approval of the court under RSC Ord 80, r 10.

CONTRIBUTION NOTICE

So far we have been considering the position as between plaintiff and defendant, but there will be cases where one defendant will wish to preserve his position as regards the costs he may have to pay his co-defendants as a third party.

> *Example 1.* P, a passenger is D1's car is injured when it is in collision with a lorry owned and driven by D2. P sues both drivers.
> *Example 2.* P sues D as shopkeeper for damages in breach of warranty in respect of certain defective goods. D issues third party proceedings against the manufacturer T who decides in his defence that D is partly responsible for the matters in question because of his negligent storage of the goods.

In both the above cases the court will have to determine not only the issue between the plaintiff and the defendant(s) but also the extent to which each of the co-defendants (or the defendant and the third party) should contribute towards the judgment and what orders as to costs should be made as between themselves. RSC Ord 16, r 10 provides that a third party or joint tortfeasor may make a written offer, without prejudice to his defence, to another party to contribute to a specified extent to the debt or damages

---

40 RSC Ord 62, r 9(1)(d).
41 See *Corby District Council v Holst & Co Ltd* [1985] 1 All ER 321, CA.
42 The procedure is set out in CCR Ord 11 which also deals with payment into court of the *whole* sum claimed and costs of summons (cf procedure on payment-in of whole sum claimed on writ where only fixed costs are payable RSC Ord 6, r 2) and payments into court of a sum on *account* of admitted liability for the whole or part. Where a payment in is made in the county court of a lesser sum in *satisfaction* of the plaintiff's claim (i e as an officer of settlement) care must be taken to see that the notice submitted to the court on payment-in specifies this; if it is not so specified it is deemed to be 'on account' so that the plaintiff can take the sum out and continue with his action for the balance (CCR Ord 11, r 1(2)). If payment-in is made within 14 days of service of a summons for a liquidated sum one should include the fixed costs appropriate to the amount paid in: if this is done the plaintiff will generally not be entitled to any other costs if he accepts the payment-in (see CCR Ord 11, r 3(4)). In other cases r 3(5) specifically provides for orders as to costs where the payment-in is accepted.

for which they may both be liable. Such an offer is known as an 'offer of contribution'. There is no prescribed form but the notice generally is set out with the title of action and such words as:

> 'Take notice that I the above-named First Defendant pursuant to Order 16, rule 10 offer to make contribution as to – per cent of the damages and taxed costs which may be awarded to the plaintiff in this action and for which we jointly stand liable.'

If this offer is rejected the trial judge will have to determine the issues as between the co-defendants[43] and decide the extent of their respective contributions inter se. Once he has made this determination (but *not* before) the notice will be brought to his attention and he will take the offer into account in determining the order for costs as between the co-defendants.[44] In the county court, an offer of contribution is made under CCR Ord 12, r 7.

INFANT SETTLEMENTS

Where an action is brought on behalf of a minor (or any other person who is under a disability) the defendant will wish to be certain that any settlement entered into with the minor's next friend shall be binding on the minor when he attains his majority. The next friend also may wish to be certain that any compromise he agrees cannot at a later date give rise to a claim against him by the minor and to be relieved of the responsibility of looking after the money recovered during his minority. The rules[45] therefore provide that:

(*a*) before proceedings are commenced the approval of the court can be sought for any proposed settlement by issuing and serving an *originating summons* on the proposed defendants;

(*b*) after proceedings are commenced, the approval of the court *must* be obtained by an *interlocutory summons* served on the defendants.

The parties duly attend before the master who considers:

(i) The question of liability. In accident cases, each party puts his version of the facts before the master and indicates the evidence in support of his version of the case. Counsel's advice on liability should be put in. The master should then be able to have an opinion of the minor's likely chances of success if the action was fought and whether any allowance should be made for contributory negligence.

(ii) The master must then consider the question of quantum.[46] In personal injury cases he should be shown the medical reports on both sides. An up-to-date report must be available. In fatal accident claims he should be told how the dependency is calculated and the apportionment between the widow and the children.

---

43 Or defendant and third parties.

44 See *Clarke v ER Wright & Son* [1957] 3 All ER 486, [1957] 1 WLR 1191, CA and *Bragg v Crosville Motor Services Ltd* [1959] 1 All ER 613, [1959] 1 WLR 324, CA.

45 RSC Ord 80, rr 10 and 11. The equivalent procedure in the county court is governed by CCR Ord 10, r 10.

46 In modern times because of the rapid decrease in the value of money he will wish to know what factor in the proposed figure represents interest from the date of the writ or of the death.

The summons must *not* disclose the amount offered as the master must approach the matter with a fresh mind. If he feels the sum offered is not enough (and this is quite often the case) he may adjourn the summons for the parties to continue negotiating. If he approves the settlement, he will go on to give directions as to how the damages should be dealt with.[47] This will usually involve the fund being placed in the special reserve account established under the Court Funds Rules 1987. The master will complete Form 212 requiring the Investment Manager to invest the funds along the lines set out by the master. The minor may apply through his parent to the master or district judge during his minority for sums to be paid out for clothing, education, holidays, etc. Once he attains the age of eighteen he is entitled to payment out to him of the balance of the fund and interest.

In infant settlement cases the student must know the relevant provisions as to costs. Where a minor wishes to accept a *payment into court* by the defendant and the master approves the proposal unless the Court otherwise orders the order for costs will be:

(*a*) That the costs which the minor is to pay his own solicitor are to be taxed by the taxing officer. Such a taxation is on the indemnity basis ie all costs are to be paid except insofar as such costs are of an unreasonable amount or have been unreasonably incurred.[48]

(*b*) That the costs which the defendant is to pay are to be taxed on the *standard basis* to the date of payment into court. On such a taxation the court orders payment of a reasonable amount in respect of costs reasonably incurred.[49]

There almost always will be a difference between the solicitor and client costs and the costs the defendant has to pay (see p 313, post). In practice, however, most solicitors acting for a minor agree to waive their additional costs so there will be only one taxation on a standard basis.

47 RSC Ord 80, r 12; CCR Ord 10, r 11.
48 See RSC Ord 62, rr 12(2) and 16.
49 RSC Ord 62, rr 12(1) and 16.

Chapter 12

Striking out for want of prosecution

The Supreme Court Rules provide a timetable for the parties to follow from the moment the writ is served to the time when the action is set down for trial. In practice this timetable is never followed; almost always the solicitors on both sides, themselves harassed by the pressure of other work or simply the problems of preparing the evidence in the action, will extend each other's time for taking the necessary steps in prosecuting the action. Without this relaxation of the rules it would be impossible for most litigation to be undertaken. However it sometimes happens that the plaintiff's solicitor (who of course is the person who has the power under the rules to force the defendant to proceed expeditiously and the duty to issue the summons for directions and to set down) will allow a substantial time to elapse while the action 'goes to sleep'. In these circumstances the defendant may apply for a summons to the master for an order that the action be struck out.[1] In order to succeed in his application he must show:

(a) prolonged delay by the plaintiff,
(b) which is inexcusable,[2]
(c) and which causes prejudice to the defendant,[3]
(d) the limitation period has expired.[4]

1 This application can be brought if P fails to deliver a statement of claim (RSC Ord 19, r 1), fails to make discovery (RSC Ord 24, r 16), fails to comply with any order of the master as to the conduct of the suit, fails to take out a summons for direction (RSC Ord 25, r 1(4)), and fails to set down for trial (RSC Ord 34, r 2). In addition, the court may dismiss an action for want of prosecution under its inherent jurisdiction: see *Costellow v Somerset County Council* [1993] 1 All ER 952, CA per Sir Thomas Bingham MR at 959d. The county court has similar powers by virtue of County Courts Act 1984, s 76. See *Kirkpatrick v Salvation Army Trustee Co Ltd* [1969] 1 All ER 388, [1968] 1 WLR 1955, CA. The application should be made at first instance to the district judge from whom appeal will be to the judge. Note also that under CCR Ord 17, r 11(9), in cases where automatic directions apply, a county court action will be *automatically* struck out if the plaintiff does not, within 15 months of the close of pleadings, request the court to fix a day for the hearing of the action. This important provision is considered more fully in the main text below.
2 The plaintiff should file an affidavit setting out his reasons for the delay.
3 Usually the prejudice suffered by the defendant is that as a result of the plaintiff's delay a fair trial of the action is no longer possible.
4 See *Birkett v James* [1978] AC 297, [1977] 2 All ER 801, HL. See also *Tolley v Morris* [1979] 1 All ER 71, [1979] 1 WLR 205, CA; affd [1979] 2 All ER 561, [1979] 1 WLR 592, HL: (plaintiff as a minor was entitled to the extended limitation period prescribed by s 28 Limitation Act 1980; therefore, despite culpable delay, no order to strike out).

The principles have been described by Lord Denning MR in the following trenchant phrases:[5]

> 'The delay of justice is a denial of justice. Magna Carta will have none of it. "To no one will we deny or delay right of justice." All through the years men have protested at the law's delay and counted it as a grievous wrong, hard to bear. Shakespeare ranks it among the whips and scorns of time. Dickens tells us how it exhausts finances, patience, courage, hope. To put right this wrong, we will in this court do all in our power to enforce expedition: and, if need be, we will strike out actions when there has been excessive delay. . . . The principle upon which we go is clear: when the delay is prolonged and inexcusable, and is such as to go grave injustice to one side or the other or both, the court may in its discretion dismiss the action straightaway, leaving the plaintiff to his remedy against his own solicitor who has brought him to this plight.'

(i) Inordinate and inexcusable delay

As stated by Lord Denning, the plaintiff's delay must be prolonged or inordinate before the court can consider dismissing the action. Since the delay in question is in *prosecuting* the action the question arises whether delay on the part of the plaintiff *before* issuing proceedings can be taken into account in deciding whether there has been an inordinate delay in prosecuting the action once it has been commenced:

> *Example.* In December 1978 a lorry driven by D Ltd's employee crashed into a bridge owned by P (the Department of Transport), causing extensive damage. Shortly afterwards P informed D Ltd that it intended making a claim in respect of the damage but did not issue a writ until 30 May 1984, six months before the expiry of the limitation period, and did not serve the writ until 19 March 1985, three months after the limitation period expired. The statement of claim was not served until 23 September 1985. D Ltd took out a summons for directions because the P had failed to do so. At the hearing of the summons on 8 July 1986 P was ordered, *inter alia*, to set the action down for trial within 28 days. P failed to do so and in April 1987 D Ltd applied to have the action struck out for want of prosecution. The House of Lords held (i) P could not be penalised for delay occurring between the accrual of the cause of action and the issue of proceedings within the limitation period; but (ii) where there had been a long delay before the issue of the writ D had only to show something *more than minimal* additional prejudice attributable to the post-writ delay to justify striking out. Since, on the facts, D could show only *minimal* prejudice as a result of P's delay after issuing proceedings the action would not be struck out.[6]

The position is different in cases where the plaintiff is guilty of delay *after* the issue of proceedings but claims that he should not be penalised for the delay because it occurred *before* the expiry of the relevant limitation period

---

5 *Allen v Sir Alfred McAlpine & Sons Ltd* [1968] 2 QB 229 at 245–6, [1968] 1 All ER 543, at 546–7. The action arose out of a fatal accident in 1959. Pleadings were delivered in 1961. No further action was taken until 1967 when the defendant applied to strike the action out.

6 *Department of Transport v Chris Smaller (Transport) Ltd* [1989] AC 1197, [1989] 1 All ER 897, HL. See also *William C Parker Ltd v F J Ham & Son Ltd* [1972] 3 All ER 1051 at 1055, [1972] 1 WLR 1583 at 1588, where it was argued that since the plaintiff had 6 years to bring his claim, delay in issuing the writ was totally irrelevant. The court held that although such delay in itself could not give rise to a right to strike out, it was relevant in considering whether delay after the issue of the writ was inordinate and inexcusable, i e if one leaves the issue of proceedings to the last moment, one should then pursue the suit with expedition and further delay is normally inexcusable. See also *Biss v Lambeth, Southwark and Lewisham Area Health Authority* [1978] 2 All ER 125, [1978] 1 WLR 382, CA.

and therefore during a period when it remained open to him to commence an action:

> *Example.* In February 1983 the plaintiffs purchased a bungalow in reliance on a structural report provided to them by the defendants, a firm of surveyors. Shortly afterwards defects in the bungalow became apparent which the plaintiffs considered ought to have been disclosed by the defendants' report. On 22 May 1984 the plaintiffs issued writ against *inter alia* the defendants alleging negligence. The action proceeded to the point at which defences were served but thereafter the plaintiffs took no further steps until they issued a notice of intention to proceed under RSC Ord 3, r 6 on 6 May 1988. A further such notice was served on 17 February 1989 followed by a summons for directions issued by the plaintiffs a month later. In November 1989 (several months after the expiry of the limitation period) the defendants applied to have the action dismissed for want of prosecution. It was argued on behalf of the plaintiffs that the court should ignore that part of the period of inordinate and inexcusable delay which had occurred while the limitation period was still running, because a plaintiff who caused substantial prejudice by delaying the issue of the writ to the eleventh hour would otherwise be in a better position than these plaintiffs, who had begun their action expeditiously. The Court of Appeal rejected this submission and held that the action should be dismissed for want of prosecution on account of the plaintiffs' inordinate delay before, as well as after, the expiry of the limitation period. Per Slade LJ: '. . . I can find no support for the proposition that time elapsed *after the issue of a writ but before the expiration of the limitation period* cannot constitute inordinate delay for the relevant purpose. The late issue of a writ is one thing; by itself it cannot be regarded as culpable. The casual and dilatory conduct of proceedings in breach of the rules, after a writ has been issued, is another thing. If a person who claims to have a cause of action chooses to take advantage of the process of the court by issuing a writ at whatever time during the limitation period, he has, in the words of Lord Diplock ([1977] 2 All ER 801 at 809, [1978] AC 297 at 323), "a corresponding right to continue to prosecute it to trial and judgment *so long as he does so with reasonable diligence*" (my emphasis).[7]

(ii) Prejudice to the defendant

It should be noted that the power to strike out is generally exercised because the delay has caused prejudice:[8] as time goes on memories will fade, witnesses may die or disappear and so it may become impossible for the court to reach a fair conclusion on the issues. Where, however, the case is not one where the court is going to be asked to determine disputed issues on the basis of oral testimony, it may be that although the defendant can prove inordinate and inexcusable delay on the part of the plaintiff, he will be unable to prove that he is prejudiced by the delay and in consequence the action will not be dismissed.

> *Example.* In 1963 D failed to deliver certain goods to P Co. In 1967 P Co issued a writ and the parties exchanged pleadings – D denying liability. No further steps were taken by P Co: they failed to make discovery, they failed to take out a

7 *Rath v CS Lawrence & Partners (a firm)* [1991] 3 All ER 679, CA at 688h. See also *Trill v Sacher* [1993] 1 All ER 961, CA.

8 Even where the plaintiff has been guilty of inordinate, inexcusable and prejudicial delay the court has no discretion to strike out an action for want of prosecution where the defendant has induced the plaintiff to believe that the action would nevertheless proceed to trial: see *Reynolds v British Leyland Ltd* [1991] 2 All ER 243, CA. But note that where after a long delay the plaintiff serves notice of intention to proceed under RSC Ord 3, r 6 the defendant's failure to seek dismissal of the action within the period of one month's notice provided for by that rule is not, of itself, sufficient to prevent the defendant applying to have the action dismissed: see *Trill v Sacher* [1993] 1 All ER 961, CA.

summons for directions, they in fact did nothing. In 1972 D applied for the action to be dismissed for want of prosecution. P Co admitted that there had been inordinate and inexcusable delay after the pleadings had closed but claimed that since all the relevant evidence was totally contained in contemporary documents, the delay had not prejudiced the defendants. The Court of Appeal accepted this contention. Per Buckley LJ: 'The question to which the court must address its mind is whether that delay which is properly described as "inordinate and inexcusable" has given rise to circumstances in which it is possible that a fair trial may be impossible or that the defendant may be seriously prejudiced. If the facts are such that no additional prejudice to the defendant has arisen as the result of delay after the end of that period in which delay can be said to be excusable, it cannot be right, in my judgment, for the court to dismiss the action under this rule.'[9]

In most cases the prejudice caused to a defendant as a result of an inordinate delay by the plaintiff in prosecuting the action is the risk that a fair trial is no longer possible. Other forms of prejudice to the defendant may, however, be sufficient to justify striking out of the action. Examples of such prejudice include anxiety suffered by nurses whose professional competence remained in question during the plaintiff's delay,[10] and prejudice caused by proceedings hanging over a professional man.[11] Such cases are, however, exceptional and the courts are slow to accept prejudice other than to a fair trial of the action as grounds for striking out. In *Department of Transport v Chris Smaller (Transport) Ltd*[12] Lord Griffiths said:

'I would, however, express a note of caution against allowing the mere fact of the anxiety that accompanies any litigation being regarded as of itself a sufficient prejudice to justify striking out an action. Counsel for the defendants did not seek to argue that the anxiety occasioned by the extra 13 months in this case should be regarded as a sufficient ground of prejudice to justify making a striking out order. There are, however, passages in some of the judgments that suggest that the mere sword of Damocles, hanging for an unnecessary period, might be a sufficient reason of itself to strike out. On this aspect I repeat the note of caution I expressed in the Court of Appeal in *Eagil Trust Co Ltd v Pigott-Brown* [1985] 3 All ER 119 at 124, where I said:

"Any action is bound to cause anxiety, but it would as a general rule be an exceptional case where that sort of anxiety alone would found a sufficient ground for striking out in the absence of evidence of any particular prejudice. *Biss*'s case is an example of such an exceptional case, the action hanging over for 11½ years, with professional reputations at stake."'

There is one rare but important exception to the rule that the defendant must show prejudice. If he can show that the delay by the plaintiff had been *deliberate* the court may strike out the action without considering the question of prejudice, on the grounds that the plaintiff's conduct is an abuse of the process of the court.

Example. D, a minority shareholder in a company run by P, wished to expose misapplication of company funds by P. D published a circular letter alleging

---

9 *William C Parker Ltd v F J Ham & Son Ltd* [1972] 3 All ER 1051 at 1055, [1972] 1 WLR 1583 at 1588, CA. For another example of inordinate and inexcusable delay which did not give rise to a substantial risk that a fair trial would not be possible nor caused any other serious prejudice to the defendants see *Trill v Sacher* [1993] 1 All ER 961, CA.
10 See *Biss v Lambeth Southwark and Lewisham Area Health Authority* [1978] 2 All ER 125, [1978] 1 WLR 382, CA.
11 *Haynes v Atkins* (1983) Times, 12 October, CA.
12 [1989] AC 1197, [1989] 1 All ER 897, HL; the other four judges agreed with Lord Griffiths.

fraud by P. P issued a writ for libel and obtained an interlocutory injunction prohibiting D repeating the alleged libel until the trial. Having successfully silenced D, P took no real action in the next five years to bring the case to trial. The Court of Appeal held that P's action should be struck out. Per Lord Denning MR: '[the plaintiff] has made default time after time. He failed to give proper discovery. He failed to deliver a proper defence, He failed to set the action down for trial. It is obvious that he was not at all keen that the action should come to trial. It would suit him well if it dragged on for ever. So long as he could prolong the proceedings he could always say – as he so often did – "These matters are sub judice, so they cannot be discussed." All things considered, it must have been plain to [him] that his best strategy was to conduct this action as if it were a war of attrition. If he fought it long enough, he might be able to break [the defendant's] nerve, exhaust his limited resources, make him give up trying, so that the case would never come to trial. . . . To my mind his action was an abuse of the process of the court. His defaults . . . were "intentional and contumelious". . . . Where the court meets with such abuse, it has the means to cope with it. It will strike out the action. . . .'[13]

(iii) The limitation period must have expired[14]

Except in cases of *deliberate* default (considered above), the court will not strike out an action for want of prosecution during the currency of the relevant limitation period as it would be a pointless exercise; the plaintiff would issue fresh proceedings – so prolonging the delay and causing the defendant even greater prejudice. Usually, there is unlikely to be any difficulty in determining whether, for the purposes of an application to strike out, a fresh action would be statute-barred. But sometimes there may be a dispute between the parties as to whether a new action would be time-barred: the plaintiff arguing that it would not, so that the present action should not be dismissed; the defendant maintaining that it would not be pointless to dismiss the present action, because any new action commenced by the plaintiff would be brought out of time. In *Barclays Bank plc v Miller and another*[15] the Court of Appeal considered this question. The court concluded that where it was open to doubt and serious argument whether the cause of action would be time-barred if a fresh writ were issued:

'it may well be that the interests of justice are best served by dismissing the action for want of prosecution, leaving it to the plaintiff, if he chooses to do so and if he has the funds, to start a fresh action. The alternative is that masters, and judges on appeal and even this court, may become embroiled, on an application to dismiss for want of prosecution, in long and elaborate arguments as to whether some future action, if it were brought, would be time-barred. There is a good deal to be said for the view that masters should not have that task forced on them when the problem may never arise, and if it does arise, could perhaps more conveniently be considered in another way.'[16]

(iv) Application to extend time limit

It sometimes happens that at the hearing of the defendant's summons to dismiss for want of prosecution the plaintiff makes an application under

---

13 *Wallersteiner v Moir* [1974] 3 All ER 217 at 231. The principle in this case applies even if the limitation period is still running.
14 Note that once an action has been struck out for want of prosecution and the limitation period has expired the plaintiff cannot issue a new writ and apply under s 33 of the Limitation Act 1980 for the action to be allowed to proceed: see *Walkley v Precision Forgings Ltd* [1979] 2 All ER 548, [1979] 1 WLR 606, HL (discussed at p 71, ante).
15 [1990] 1 All ER 1040, CA.
16 Ibid, per Staughton LJ at 1044a.

RSC Ord 3, r 5 for an extension of time to remedy his failure to take the step in the action which prompted the defendant's application. Earlier authorities[17] suggested that in such circumstances the application for an extension of time should be heard *first*, so that if the plaintiff fails to satisfy the court that time should be extended, the defendant's application to dismiss becomes a mere formality and must succeed. In *Costellow v Somerset County Council*[18] the Court of Appeal gave guidance as to the correct approach in such cases. Sir Thomas Bingham MR said:[19]

'The resolution of problems such as the present cannot in my view be governed by a single universally applicable rule of thumb. A rigid, mechanistic approach is inappropriate. Where, as here, the defendant seeks to dismiss and the plaintiff seeks an extension of time, there can be no general rule that the plaintiff's application should be heard first, with dismissal of his action as an inevitable consequence if he fails to show a good reason for his procedural default. In the great mass of cases, it is appropriate for the court to hear both summonses together, since, in considering what justice requires, the court is concerned to do justice to both parties, the plaintiff as well as the defendant, and the case is best viewed in the round. In the present case, there was before the district judge no application by the plaintiff for an extension, although there was before the judge. It is in my view of little or no significance whether the plaintiff makes such an application or not: if he does not, the court considering the defendant's application to dismiss will inevitably consider the plaintiff's position, and, if the court refuses to dismiss, it has power to grant the plaintiff any necessary extension whether separate application is made or not.'

Where there has been inexcusable delay but the court decides not to strike the action out it may instead prescribe strict time limits for the future conduct of the action and further order that the action should stand dismissed for failure to comply with these conditions.[20] Once an action stands dismissed for failure to comply with such an order a new action may be dismissed as an abuse of process even though the limitation period has not expired.

Example. In 1978 P issued a writ claiming damages for a breach of contract which had occurred during that year. P delayed taking any steps after pleadings had been delivered and in March 1980 the master ordered that the action be struck out unless P served a summons for directions by 1 April 1980. The action was struck out because of P's failure to comply with this order. P then issued a new writ (the limitation period not having expired). The Court of Appeal ordered the second action to be struck out as an abuse of the process of the court. Per Dunn LJ: 'This is a case in which the necessity for maintaining the principle that orders are made to be complied with should be upheld, and in the absence of any explanation as to why the order was not complied with in the previous action or any assurance as to the conduct of this action I would strike out this present action. . .'[21]

---

17 See *Price v Dannimac Ltd* (1990) Independent, 3 August, CA; but cf *Erskine Communications Ltd v Worthington* (1991) Times, 8 July, CA.
18 [1993] 1 All ER 952, CA.
19 Ibid, at 959h.
20 *Pryer v Smith* [1977] 1 All ER 218, [1977] 1 WLR 425, CA. Note in exceptional cases the court may extend the prescribed periods even though there has been a failure to comply with the 'unless order' see *Samuels v Linzi Dresses Ltd* [1981] QB 115, [1980] 1 All ER 803, CA; also *Re Jokai Tea Holdings Ltd* [1993] 1 All ER 630, CA and *Grand Metropolitan Nominee (No 2) Co Ltd v Evans* [1993] 1 All ER 642, CA.
21 *Janov v Morris* [1981] 3 All ER 780 at 785, [1981] 1 WLR 1389 at 1395, CA.

AUTOMATIC DISMISSAL IN THE COUNTY COURT

As we have seen above, where in High Court or county court proceedings the defendant considers that the plaintiff is guilty of inordinate, inexcusable and prejudicial delay in the conduct of the litigation, he may apply by summons for the action to be struck out. At the hearing of the application it is open to the plaintiff to argue that the action should not be dismissed, because, for example, no substantial prejudice has been suffered by the defendant. It is particularly important for the plaintiff to have one last opportunity of proceeding with his claim where the relevant limitation period has expired because in such a case the dismissal of the action will have the effect of permanently depriving the plaintiff of a remedy. In county court proceedings, however, any action to which automatic directions apply, will be *automatically* struck out if the plaintiff makes no application to the court to fix a date for the hearing of the action within 15 months of the day on which pleadings are deemed to be closed. CCR Ord 17, r 11 provides:

'(3) When the pleadings are deemed to be closed, the following directions shall take effect –. . .
    (*d*) unless a day has already been fixed, the plaintiff shall within 6 months request the proper office to fix a day for the hearing. . .
(9) If no request is made pursuant to paragraph (3)(*d*) within 15 months of the day on which pleadings are deemed to be closed (or within 9 months after the expiry of any period fixed by the court for making such a request), the action shall be automatically struck out.'

It is not completely clear whether, once an action has been struck out under these automatic directions, the plaintiff will be able to have the action reinstated.

Example. An accident occurred in February 1990. The plaintiff's solicitor issued proceedings in the county court and the case progressed with reasonable speed at first. Under the rules an application to fix a hearing date should have been made by 22 March 1993. The solicitor who had the conduct of the case was ill in hospital from 26 January to 1 April 1993. When he returned to work, he found that the action had been automatically struck out.

It would seem likely that in such a case the plaintiff's solicitor could apply for an extension of time in which to fix a hearing date; CCR Ord 13, r 4 provides:

'(1) Except as otherwise provided, the period within which a person is required or authorised by these rules . . . to do any act in any proceedings may be extended or abridged . . . by the court on the application of any party.
(2) Any such period may be extended by the court although the application for extension is not made until after the expiration of the period.'

It would therefore seem that an application to extend time can be made even after an action has been struck out. In *R v Bloomsbury County Court, ex p Villerwest Ltd*[22] Lord Denning MR said:

---

22 [1976] 1 All ER 897 at 900, where a judge had extended time for payment of rent notwithstanding there had been a failure to comply with a final order. See also *Samuels v Linzi Dresses Ltd* [1981] QB 115, [1980] 1 All ER 803, CA (ante).

'It seems . . . to be suggested that if a condition is not fulfilled the action ceases to exist, as though no extension of time can be granted. I do not agree with that line of reasoning. Even though the action may be said to cease to exist, the court always has power to bring it to life again by extending the time.'

Chapter 13

Preparing for trial

THE SUMMONS FOR DIRECTIONS

In actions begun by writ in the High Court (except personal injury claims, Chancery actions where the only matters to be determined are mode of trial and the time for setting down and specialist actions) the plaintiff is bound to issue a summons within one month of the close of pleadings[1] requiring the defendants to attend an appointment[2] before the master[3] at which he will give directions as to the future conduct of the case. The standard form of summons (see p 282) lists the following numbered paragraphs which the master may be asked to consider at this stage:

(1)   That the action be consolidated with other pending cases (see p 51).

(2)   For an order that *the case be heard by an official referee* rather than by the judge. This would be appropriate for example in a building dispute where the case involved consideration of many small detailed points. The parties may also agree for the matter to be tried by a master.

(3)   That the *action be transferred to the county court*. The plaintiff is required under RSC Order 25, rule 6(2A) to lodge at court and serve on every other party not later than the day before the hearing of the summons for directions a statement of the value of the action. Put shortly, the purpose of this procedure is to ensure that in the ordinary way actions with a value of less than £25,000 are transferred to the County Court.

(4)–(5)   Application for *leave to amend the writ or pleadings* (see pp 135–139, ante).

---

1   RSC Ord 25, r 1. The pleadings are deemed to be closed 14 days after the defence is served unless a reply or defence to counterclaim has to be served in which case the close of pleadings occurs 14 days after service of those documents (see RSC Ord 18, r 20). Where, as is often the case, the parties agree that discovery should be postponed, the date for issue of the summons for directions is extended to 14 days after the date agreed for discovery to take place (see Ord 25, r 1(3)). If the plaintiff fails to issue the summons for directions, the defendant may do so himself or apply for the action to be dismissed for want of prosecution (RSC Ord 25, r 1(4)).

2   The summons is returnable in not less than 14 days from the date of *issue*.

3   Or district judge; in commercial list cases, the summons and all interlocutory applications are heard by the Commercial Judge. See RSC Ord 72, r 2.

Summons for
Directions,
pursuant to
Order 25

IN THE HIGH COURT OF JUSTICE   19   .—   .—No.

Division

Master   Master in Chambers.

Between

                                                            Plaintiff

AND

                                                            Defendant

Let all parties attend the Master in Chambers in Room No.   Royal Courts
of Justice, Strand, London WC2A 2LL, on   day, the   day of
                    19   , at   o'clock in the   noon on
the hearing of an application for directions in this action:

1. This action be consolidated with action(s) 19   ,   , No.   ,
    and 19   ,   , No.   and that this action [action
    19   ,   , No.   ] be the leading action.

2. The action be transferred to an Official Referee, and that the costs of this application
    be costs in the cause.

3. The action be transferred to   County
    Court under section 40 of the County Courts Act 1984, and that the costs of the
    action, including this application, be in the discretion of the County Court.

4. The Plaintiff have leave to amend the writ of Summons as shown in the document
    initialled by the Master and that service of the writ and the Defendant's acknowledg-
    ment of service do stand and that the costs incurred and thrown away by the
    amendment be the Defendant's costs in any event.

5. [The Plaintiff have leave to amend the Statement of Claim] [The Defendant have
    leave to amend the Defence (and Counterclaim)] [The Plaintiff have leave to
    amend the Reply (and Defence to Counterclaim)] as shown in the document initialled
    by the Master, and to re-serve the amended pleading within
    days and that the opposite party have leave to serve an amended consequential
    pleading, if so advised within   days thereafter and that the costs of
    and occasioned and thrown away by the amendments be the Defendant's [the
    Plaintiff's] in any event.

6. [The Plaintiff serve on the Defendant] [The Defendant serve on the Plaintiff] within
              days the Further and Better Particulars of his pleading specified in the
    document initialled by the Master.

7. The Plaintiff within   days serve on the Defendant and the Defendant
    within   days serve on the Plaintiff a list of documents (and file an
    affidavit verifying such list) [limited to the documents relating to the special damages
    claimed] (¹).

(1) Or as may be.

8. There be inspection of the documents within   days of the service of
    the lists (and filing of the affidavits).

9. The [Plaintiff] [Defendant] retain and preserve pending the trial of the action [and upon   days notice give inspection of] the subject matter of the action ([2])

(2) Or describe the property in question.

to the Defendant (Plaintiff) and to his legal advisers (and experts).

10. ([3]).

(3) Set out fully and precisely any other directions intended to be applied for (e.g. adducing expert evidence, etc.).

11. Trial. Place: —   Mode: —
      Listing Category: —A or B or C.
      [Estimated length: —   To be set down within   days
      [and to be listed with and tried immediately after (before) action 19
      No.   ].]

12. The costs of this application be costs in the cause.

Dated the   day of   19   .

To Messrs

of

Solicitors for the Defendant(s) .

This Summons was issued by

of

Solicitors for the Plaintiff(s)
Solicitor's Reference

(6)   Applications for further and better particulars of pleadings (see pp 140–141, ante).

(7)–(8)   The master in cases where there is no automatic discovery may be asked to order *discovery*; in other cases he may be asked to resolve disputes concerning discovery, e g an application by one party that the other disclose a document not shown on his list or for an order for inspection of a document claimed to be privileged (see pp 209–217, ante).

(9)   An application may be made for the *custody and inspection* of property pending the trial (see p 218, ante).

(10)   The master may be asked to give leave to call expert advice and for directions as to disclosure (see p 218, ante).

(11)   The master will normally be asked to give directions that signed statements of witnesses of fact be cross-served by a stated date and that copies of those statements be lodged with the court together with the pleadings upon setting down for trial (see p 291, post).

(12)   A space is left on the form for the plaintiff to insert any other direction he may wish the master to deal with. Thus for example, the master may deal at this stage with an application for interrogatories, for evidence to be taken by an examiner, for statements to be admitted at the trial under the provisions of the Civil Evidence Act 1968 and indeed with any other interlocutory matter.

(13)   That directions should be given as to the mode of trial (i e with or without jury) and the *place* at which it is to be heard and for the *setting down* of the action. The parties are required to give a time estimate and indication of the completing of the action. The three categories for the purpose of listing are: (a) cases of great substance or great difficulty or of public importance; (b) cases of substance or difficulty; (c) other cases.

The practice is for the plaintiff to strike out on his summons the paragraph *number* of any matters which he does not wish the master to deal with. The defendant not less than 7 days before the hearing of the summons gives notice of all other matters which he may wish should be dealt with at the summons.

It will be appreciated that the purpose of the summons for directions is two-fold:

(a) It enables the court to deal at one and the same time with all interlocutory matters in dispute thus saving the costs of numerous applications. Indeed RSC Order 25, rule 7 provides that it is the duty of the parties so far as is practicable to make all interlocutory applications at this stage; the sanction for issuing a separate summons being in theory an order for costs.

(b) It should provide a 'stock-taking' process at which the master can consider whether the case is ready for trial and check that consideration has been given to the provision of all evidence (and e g plans, photographs) which could assist the court.

In practice the position is very different. When a serious dispute arises as to interlocutory matters, the parties generally brief counsel to attend the master on a straightforward interlocutory summons raising that point and nothing else[4] so that, unless there is agreement between the parties it is *not* the general rule that the matters set out above are decided at one time on the summons for directions. Normally on the summons for directions the parties are obtaining the official sanction of the court to courses they have already chosen. The position as it used to be was accurately described by the Justice Committee in *Going to Law* as follows:[5]

> 'Instead of the "stock-taking" which the summons for directions was designed to achieve, it is more often a two-minute formality, in which two very junior clerks from the respective firms of solicitors appear before the master, themselves knowing little if anything about the case, and with no authority to agree any orders which might provoke a sense of urgency, or involve extra expense, in the pursuit of the litigation. The master too, is under pressure: although he will be handed the pleadings at the hearing, he will not have seen them before and will certainly not have time to read them in detail. Nine times out of ten, he will be asked only to make an agreed order for "trial by judge alone at [London], set down for forty-two days after inspection, costs in cause". He initials the form, the two clerks disappear, the next pair take their place. Even if he had wanted to, he could not have made any order which was not asked for by at least one of the parties.'

Although the attitude of the court to management of cases has changed since the Civil Justice Review (and in particular the masters take a robust view on the desirability of transfer to the county court) it is still true that the procedure does not enable the court to spend time on any sort of detailed review of the case.

It follows therefore that the primary use of the summons for directions today is in practice to obtain the order of the master as to the place and mode of trial. So far as the place of trial is concerned, the court considers the convenience of the parties and their witnesses and the date at which the trial can take place.[6] The normal method of trial is by judge alone except for cases falling within section 69 of the Supreme Court Act 1981 which provides:

> 'Where, on the application of any party to an action to be tried in the Queen's Bench Division of the High Court, the court is satisfied that there is in issue–
>
> (a) a charge of fraud against the party; or
> (b) a claim in respect of libel, slander, malicious prosecution, or false imprisonment is in issue,
> (c) any question or issue of a kind prescribed for the purposes of this paragraph,
>
> the action shall be ordered to be tried with a jury unless the court is of opinion that the trial requires any prolonged examination of documents or accounts or any scientific or local investigation which cannot conveniently be made with a jury.'

Although this section goes on to preserve the inherent discretion of the court

---

4 Alternatively counsel may attend at an adjourned hearing of the summons for directions again to argue this specific point.

5 Op cit, para 55.

6 See RSC Ord 33, r 1. The Queen's Bench judges sit at 'trial centres' to hear actions at Birmingham, Lincoln, Nottingham, Oxford, Stafford, Warwick, Leeds, Newcastle upon Tyne, Sheffield, Teeside, Carlisle, Liverpool, Manchester, Preston, Norwich, Chelmsford, Lewes, Caernavon, Cardiff, Chester, Mold, Swansea, Bristol, Exeter, Truro and Winchester. Chancery actions may be heard at Birmingham, Bristol, Cardiff, Leeds, Liverpool, Manchester, Newcastle upon Tyne and Preston.

to order trial by jury in other cases, jury trial is in fact confined today to cases falling within the section.[7]

If the action is to be tried in the Queen's Bench Division in London the master must assign the case to the appropriate list of actions (usually the Non-Jury List).[8] The master must also direct the period within which the case is to be *set down* for trial.

AUTOMATIC DIRECTIONS IN PERSONAL INJURY CASES

It has been pointed out above that in many cases the summons for directions is a formality rather than a review of the procedural matters outstanding in the case. In personal injury actions this was so much the case that the Rule Committee decided to substitute for the summons for directions a timetable which in the ordinary case the parties would follow without resort to the court for directions. Order 25, rule 8 provides that in personal injury cases[9] the parties shall comply with the following directions:–

(1) within 14 days of the close of pleadings[10] each party[11] serves the other with a List of Documents; inspection of the documents is to take place 7 days thereafter;

(2) within 14 weeks of the close of pleadings each party must serve written statements of the oral evidence which it is proposed to adduce at the trial;

(3) within 14 weeks of the close of pleadings there is to be mutual exchange of expert reports; each party is to have leave to call two medical experts and one expert of any other kind at the trial provided their reports have been disclosed;

(4) photographs, sketch plans and police accident reports shall be receivable in evidence at the trial and shall be agreed if possible;

(5) within 6 months of the close of pleadings the action is to be set down either in London or, if proceeding in a district registry, at the appropriate trial centre. The action is to be set down for trial by 'Judge alone: Category B'. The court is to be notified, on setting down, of the estimated length of trial.

It will be appreciated that the purpose of these automatic directions is that a straightforward action can proceed from the pleadings stage to setting down without the necessity of any application by summons for directions to

---

7 See *Ward v James* [1966] 1 QB 273, [1965] 1 All ER 563 (jury trial not appropriate in personal injury cases) and *Williams v Beesley* [1973] 3 All ER 144, [1973] 1 WLR 1295 (House of Lords held jury trial not to be ordered in action involving allegations of negligence by solicitor's articled clerk). See also *H v Ministry of Defence* [1991] 2 QB 103, [1991] 2 All ER 834 – jury trial not appropriate to determine quantum even in exceptional personal injury cases. Jury trial may be appropriate if there was a case for exemplary damages.

8 The seven separate lists of Queen's Bench action are – Jury List, Non-Jury List, Short Cause List (ie actions likely to take less than 4 hours), Commercial List, Arbitration Case List, Admiralty List and Crown Office List (dealing with applications for judicial review, etc).

9 This expression includes claims arising out of a death (RSC Ord 1, r 4) but does not include claims alleging negligent medical treatment.

10 See RSC Ord 18, r 20. This occurs at the expiration of 14 days after the defence or if a reply or defence to counterclaim is served, 14 days thereafter.

11 Except in road accident cases where only the plaintiff serves a List verifying the special damage claimed.

the court. Of course, there will be many cases where because the automatic directions are not appropriate (eg different directions are required as to disclosure of expert reports) or because they have not been complied with (eg failure by one side to make discovery) alternative directions will be needed. In such a case a summons for specific directions is issued:

> 'Nothing . . . shall prevent any party to an action to which this rule applies from applying to the Court for such further or different directions or orders as may, in the circumstances, be appropriate.'[12]

STANDARD DIRECTIONS IN CHANCERY ACTIONS

Order 25, rule 9 provides that in Chancery actions the parties may dispense with the summons for directions where they are agreed that the action should be tried by judge alone and set down within six months and they also agree that no other directions are required.

SETTING DOWN FOR TRIAL

An action in the Queen's Bench Division is set down by the plaintiff's solicitors delivering a request that the action be set down and by lodging with the court[13] two bundles each comprising top copies of the following documents:

(i) the writ;
(ii) the pleadings including any request or order for particulars and the particulars given (in personal injury cases there will be an up to date schedule of special damage);
(iii) all orders made in the course of the action;
(iv) all notices of issue and amendment of Legal Aid certificates;
(v) a statement of the value of the action (ie usually this will be that it exceeds £25,000); in personal injury cases, it must not be worth less than £50,000;
(vi) a note of the estimated length of trial and of the list in which the action is to be included.

One of the two bundles is used by the judge at the trial; the other bundle is stamped to show the appropriate fee on setting down has been paid and is retained by the court officers as the official record. The names, addresses and telephone numbers of the parties' solicitors (or the parties themselves if they are appearing in person) must be indorsed on the record bundle.

The plaintiff must notify all other parties within twenty-four hours that he has set down the action for trial. An action set down in the non-jury list is initially put into a general list of actions pending where it waits its turn for hearing. Either party may however apply to the Clerk of the Lists for a fixed date for hearing (in which case the action is removed from the general list

---

12 RSC Ord 25, r 8(3).
13 See RSC Ord 34, r 3. If the trial is to be in the Queen's Bench Division in London the documents are delivered or posted to the Head Clerk, Crown Office and Associates Department (Room W11), Central Office. In the Chancery Division, they are lodged at the Chancery Chambers Room 813–814 Thomas More Building. If the trial is to be out of London, they are lodged with the district judge for the district where the trial is to be held.

since it has become a fixture).[14] Such an application should be made where, for example, witnesses from overseas or experts are to be called so that it is desirable that they should have advance notice of a fixed date when the action will be tried.

How does the solicitor tell when an action in the general list is likely to come on for trial? He will be able to get rough guidance from the court as to the position of the action in the general list but in practice well before the action could come on both solicitors will have warned the clerk to counsel briefed in the action. Eventually (and this may well not be for many months) the clerks will find the case appears in the daily bulletin issued by the court showing the sittings arranged for the next day and the actions fixed for hearing or which are likely to be heard within the next week. The actual list of actions for each day's sittings is compiled the previous afternoon by the Clerk of the Lists. For this reason as soon as a case appears in the warned list counsel's clerks attend each day before the Clerk of the Lists to check whether or not the action in which they are involved is to be listed for hearing next day. If, as often happens, counsel briefed will not be available, the clerks will wish the case not to be listed the next day and will seek to persuade the Clerk of the Lists to put the action over. Normally they will succeed on a first or second occasion but eventually they will be forced to accept the decision of the Clerk of the Lists. If counsel is still unavailable, this will result in the brief being *returned*, i e given to another member of the bar who will have to prepare the brief hurriedly for the trial and who will not have had any opportunity of seeing the client in conference. Not unnaturally this causes intense resentment on the part of the client as well as distress and embarrassment to the instructing solicitor. The only method of avoiding a last minute transfer is to apply for a fixture.[15]

Where a case has been assigned a fixed date or is currently listed in the week's list any party may apply to the judge in charge of the non-jury list to vacate the date or stand the case out. Such applications, unless supported by very convincing explanations, inevitably incur considerable judicial displeasure and are by no means automatically granted. Since one can therefore expect the hearing to be a difficult task in persuasion for the advocate it is *vital* to note that the proper procedure for lodging any documents including affidavits before the application is to be heard is as follows: such papers must be lodged with the Clerk of the Lists (Room W11) (or the officer in charge of listing at trial centres out of London) by 1.00 pm on the day before the application is made.

---

14 In actions ordered to be tried outside London, the plaintiff's solicitor must file a certificate of readiness stating whether the orders made on the summons for directions have been complied with, the estimated length of trial, a statement that the plaintiff is ready for the action to be brought to trial, names and addresses and telephone numbers of the solicitors and of any party in person and a statement that he has given each defendant 7 days' notice of his intention to file the certificate. The district judge then marks the action as ready for trial and informs the parties of the likely date of trial. The parties may apply for a fixed date or for the case not to be tried before a certain date.

15 This should ensure that if the brief has to be returned it is referred to the barrister who will in fact appear in reasonable time for preparation. In practice this does not always work because counsel's clerk will keep the brief until the last moment in the hope that counsel will be free.

CIRCUMSTANCES WHICH MAY ARISE ON A PRE-TRIAL REVIEW IN AN ACTION

Circumstances	How to be dealt with	Relevant provision in rules
1. Defendant files defence and appears.	Unless defendant withdraws defence or defence is struck out, district judge gives directions for trial and fixes date of hearing, or, if appropriate, refers to arbitration or for inquiry or report.	Ord 17, rr 1 and 9. Ord 19, rr 2 and 7.
2. Defendant files defence but does not appear.	(a) District judge may strike out defence and give judgment (interlocutory unless plaintiff ready to prove damages). (b) Plaintiff may elect to prove his claim and get judgment. (c) Otherwise, directions for trial and adjourn.	Ord 13, r 5; Ord 17, rr 4 and 7. Ord 17, r 8. See 1.
3. Defendant does not file defence or appear.	(a) District judge may direct defendant to file defence with judgment in default. (b) District judge may enter judgment (interlocutory unless plaintiff ready to prove damages).	Ord 9, r 11 (1); Ord 13, r 2 (2); Ord 17, r 4; Ord 22, r 5. Ord 17, r 7.
4. Defendant does not file a defence but appears.	(a) If defendant seems to have a defence, he may be ordered to file one with judgment in default. (b) By consent of parties and if district judge (having jurisdiction) agrees, appointment may be treated as trial of action (and adjourned into court) or, where appropriate, as arbitration. (c) If defendant admits claim (or part which plaintiff accepts), district judge may enter judgment and make any necessary instalment order.	See 3 (a). Ord 17, r 6.
5. Defendant files an admission but there is a dispute – (a) as to mode of payment. (b) as to quantum.	(a) District judge makes order for payment. (b) (i) If defendant does not appear, plaintiff may elect to prove his damages and get judgment. (ii) In any case, treat as a defended action unless defence as to quantum is struck out.	Ord 17, r 6. Ord 17, r 8. See 1 and 2 (a).

COUNTY COURT

In the county court (as we have seen earlier see p 109) there are two different types of action:–

- (i) *default actions* where the *only* relief sought is the payment of money (e g a debt, the price of goods sold) or damages (e g claim for breach of contract or for damages for personal injuries);
- (ii) *fixed date actions* where there is a claim for some relief other than just the payment of money (e g a claim for trespass and nuisance where an injunction is sought).

In both default and fixed date actions, once a defence has been filed there will have to be a hearing. The rules in force until recently provided that in such cases there would generally be a *pre-trial review* at which the district judge would give directions on matters such as discovery, exchange of expert reports and for obtaining a hearing date. CCR Order 17, rule 11(3) now provides that in most contested actions (unless the parties want a specific direction or order from the district judge) the following automatic directions shall take effect once the pleadings are deemed to be closed:–

'(*a*) there shall be discovery of documents within 28 days and inspection within 7 days thereafter [discovery is to be by serving a list of documents];
(*b*) except with the leave of the court or where all parties agree–
  (i) no expert evidence may be adduced at the trial unless the substance of that evidence has been disclosed to the other parties in form of a written report within 10 weeks;
  (ii) [except in personal injury cases] the number of expert witnesses of any kind shall be limited to two; [in personal injury cases, the parties may each call two medical experts and one expert of any kind] and
  (iii) any party who intends to place reliance at the trial on any other oral evidence shall, within 10 weeks, serve on the other parties written statements of all such oral evidence which he intends to adduce;
(*c*) photographs and sketch plans and, in an action for personal injuries, the contents of any police accident report book shall be receivable in evidence at the trial and shall be agreed if possible;
(*d*) unless a day has already been fixed, the plaintiff shall within 6 months request the proper offices to fix a day for the hearing . . .'

It will be seen that in effect Order 17, rule 11(3) lays down a timetable which the parties are to follow and which runs from close of pleadings; the timetable prescribes:–

- (1) discovery by lists within 10 days;
- (2) expert reports to be exchanged within 10 weeks;
- (3) witness statements to be exchanged within 10 weeks;
- (4) a date to be fixed for the hearing within 6 months.

There are some actions to which these automatic directions do not apply; in such a case there will be a *pre-trial review*. The most important exceptions are:–

- (i) possession and rent actions
- (ii) consumer credit cases
- (iii) actions for the delivery up of goods.

When the plaintiff applies for a hearing date he must file a note (usually agreed between the parties) of the estimated length of trial and the number of witnesses to be called.

EXCHANGE OF WITNESS STATEMENTS

The Civil Justice Review (Cmnd 394 of 1988) recommended that in all cases in the High Court and in the county court, the parties should be required to exchange statements of evidence by the witnesses they proposed to call:–

> '[para 229] General pre-trial exchange of witness statements would advance three main objectives. It should provide the basis for earlier, better informed settlements. It should improve pre-trial preparation. And it should shorten trials by helping to identify issues and reduce the need to take oral evidence.
> [para 230] It is proposed that it should not be permissible, without the special leave of the court or agreement of other parties, to call a witness whose statement has not previously been served on other parties. This system has been in force in the Chancery Division, the Commercial Court, the Admiralty Court and for official referees' business since 1986, where it applies to particular cases in which the court so directs.'

In both High Court and the county court the rules now provide for mutual exchange of witness statements:

> 'At the summons for directions in an action commenced by writ the Court shall direct every party to serve on the other parties, within 14 weeks (or such other period as the Court may specify) of the hearing of the summons and on such terms as the Court may specify, written statements of the oral evidence which the party intends to adduce on any issues of fact to be decided at the trial. The Court may give a direction to any party under this paragraph at any other stage of such an action and at any stage of any other cause or matter.' (RSC Order 38, rule 2A(2))

The equivalent provision in the County Court Rules is Order 20, rule 12A which is in identical terms except that the period normally to be prescribed is 10 instead of 14 weeks.

The sanction to ensure compliance with the order is set out in Order 38, rule 2A(10):

> 'Where a party fails to comply with a direction for the exchange of witness statements he shall not be entitled to adduce evidence to which the direction related without the leave of the Court.'

Certain other provisions of the new rules should be noted:–

(1) the statement is to be dated and signed by the intended witness and must include a statement by him that the contents are true to the best of his knowledge and belief;

(2) every witness must identify any documents referred to in the statement; the other side are entitled to inspection of such documents (if they have not already obtained copies) by serving a notice under RSC Order 24, rule 10 (CCR Order 14, rule 4);

(3) statements are to be exchanged simultaneously by the parties.

It will sometimes happen that a party wishes to call a witness who is not prepared to make a statement; in such a case, that party should refer the matter to the Court which may direct that the name of the witness and a statement of the nature of the evidence which it is expected that the witness will give should be provided to the other side.

We shall discuss in the next chapter the use which can be made of such statements at the trial; at this stage it is sufficient to note that at the trial the court may direct that the witness statement shall stand as the evidence in chief of the witness. Where the party proposing to call the witness changes his mind, no other party may put the statement in at the trial (unless he serves a Civil Evidence Act notice).

One curious provision that should be noted is in paragraph (2) of the RSC Ord 38, rule 2A:

> 'Order 3, rule 5(3) shall not apply to any period specified by the Court under this paragraph.'

Order 3, rule 5(3) provides:–

> 'The period within which a person is required by these rules, or by any order or direction, to serve . . . any document may be extended by consent (given in writing) without an order of the Court being made for that purpose.'

The effect of this provision appears to be that the parties cannot themselves extend the period for compliance with a direction to exchange witness statements.

The new rules provide for the Court to direct either that there should be no disclosure at all or that disclosure should be limited. It may be that in a case involving fraud or misconduct the court might direct that there should be no disclosure to prevent a dishonest party being able later to trim his evidence. However, it is important to note that there is no general rule that disclosure is not to take place where the credibility of witnesses is in issue. In *Mercer v Chief Constable of Lancashire*[16] the Court of Appeal upheld the decision of Steyn J that disclosure of witness statements should be made in two particular cases involving allegations of false imprisonment and malicious prosecution. Steyn J said (see 508):–

> 'Some on this circuit may wistfully think of the joys of advocacy in an erstwhile system which enabled the advocate to play his cards very close to his chest. But I believe Ord 38, r 2A has proved a most useful innovation which, to the great benefit of parties and the administration of justice, has been accommodated in our adversarial system. . . Counsel for the defendants submits that claims in respect of fraud, libel, malicious prosecution and false imprisonment, even if not tried by a jury, ought to be regarded as a special class of business falling outside Ord 38, r 2A. He is undoubtedly right in saying that, initially, after the introduction of the new system, the practice in the Commercial Court was to treat fraud cases as falling into a separate category. . . But fraud cases are now commonplace in the Commercial Court, and it is now common practice to order such an exchange even in fraud cases. It is noteworthy that the recently published Commercial Court guide contains no restriction in respect of fraud cases as a class of business, and it explicitly recognises that the fact that credibility is in issue is no good reason why such an order should [not] be made. But I accept, of course, that there may be good reasons in a particular fraud case not to order an exchange. My view is that a similar approach should follow in relation to the litigation involved in the two matters before me, namely false imprisonment and malicious prosecution. Such cases fall within the language of the rule, and there is no reason why, *as a class of business*, such cases should be treated as falling outside that rule. Of course there may be good reasons in a particular case where such an order should not be made.'

It is worth noting that the court has power to order that witness statements should be served sequentially; in some cases where credibility is in issue this may be the appropriate order. Thus in *Mercer v Chief Constable of Lancashire*, Lord Donaldson MR said at p 511:–

16 [1991] 2 All ER 504.

'The normal rule should be that the exchange of witness statements shall be simultaneous. This is, I think, inherent in the concept of an "exchange" of witnesses statements, but in any event flows from the fact that what is involved is a process of discovery and not of pleading and the undesirability of either party being in a position to seek some tactical advantage by delaying service of its witness statements until it has been served with witness statements by the other side. But if either party shows any reluctance to "come clean" the district judge has the power to order that the exchange of witness statements be wholly or partially sequential [Ord 38, r 2A(3)] thereby tying the party down to a particular case [see Ord 38, r 2A(7)] before the other party has to prepare his own witness statements.'

SKILLS PRACTICE NOTE

Preparing Witness Statements

The importance of the preparation of witness statements cannot be exaggerated. For that reason we set out below the relevant passage from the current Commercial Court Guide. Although this reflects the particular practice in the Commercial Court it provides a very useful explanation which can usefully be followed (with suitable modification) in any action in the High Court or the County Court.

One particular matter should be mentioned at this stage and that is the involvement of counsel in the preparation of such statements. Generally speaking counsel is not entitled to see in advance the witnesses who are to be called at the trial except for his client (or in the case of a company the officer of the company who instructs his solicitor) and expert witness. The Code of Conduct of the Bar provides as follows:–

'CONTACT WITH WITNESSES

Save in exceptional circumstances and subject to paragraphs 607.2 and 609 a barrister in independent practice must not discuss a case in which he may expect to examine any witness:

    (a) with or in the presence of potential witnesses other than the lay client character witnesses or expert witnesses;

    (b) with the lay client character witnesses or expert witnesses in the absence of his professional client or his representative.

In a civil case a practising barrister may in the presence of his professional client or his representative discuss the case with a potential witness if he considers that the interests of his lay client so require and after he has been supplied with a proper proof of evidence of that potential witness prepared by the witness himself or by his professional client or by a third party.

A practising barrister must not when interviewing a witness out of Court:

    (a) place a witness who is being interviewed under any pressure to provide other than a truthful account of his evidence;

    (b) rehearse practise or coach a witness in relation to his evidence or the way in which he should give it.'

We would suggest that as a general rule counsel should not be asked to draft the statement of the client. A statement should be prepared which can then be discussed and amended as appropriate in conference.

The witness statements of other witnesses should be submitted to counsel and he can of course be asked to point out passages which need clarification and to draw attention to matters which have been omitted and ought to be covered.

EXTRACT FROM COMMERCIAL COURT GUIDE

EXCHANGE OF EVIDENCE: FACTUAL WITNESSES

The standard direction is that the statements shall be signed by the witnesses; this has the advantage that each witness is required to lend his personal credit to the statement. It is also possible for the Court to order that the statement be put in the form of an affidavit. The party's representatives should be aware of the impropriety of serving a statement known to be false or of allowing a witness to sign a statement which the witness does not in all respects actually believe to be true. Quite apart from matters of propriety, service of such a statement will merely lead to that witness, and even that party's case, being discredited.

The statement should, in the words of the rule, be 'oral evidence which the party intends to lead' from that witness at the trial. It should not include inadmissible or irrelevant evidence. It should represent the whole truth of the witness's evidence on the points covered. It should, save for formal matters, be expressed in the witness's own words, not those of the lawyer. Where the witness is not fluent enough in English to give his evidence in English, the signed statement should be in the witness's own language and a translation provided. The rules of any relevant professional body regarding the drafting of statements should be observed.

The standard directions [may] include a direction that *unless otherwise ordered* the statement shall stand as the evidence in chief of the witness. This does not fetter in any way the discretion open to the Judge at the trial as to the amount of oral evidence that he permits to be led from the witness. What is then appropriate will depend upon the circumstances in each case. The main object is to avoid time-consuming oral examinations in chief where they are not strictly necessary in the interests of justice. In many cases there will be matters arising from statements or other evidence which, subject to O.38, r 2A(5)(a), have to be covered; the witness may between the time of signing his statement and being called as a witness at the trial have a different recollection of matters included in his statement. Where there is a contested conversation, meeting or series of events, it may be better for the relevant witnesses to give their evidence in chief on those points orally in the traditional way; but even in such cases it may be better to let the witness's unaided recollection be tested in cross-examination. The fact that a witness's credit is challenged is not normally a reason for not putting his statement in chief (and still less a reason for not making an order under r 2A in the first place).

Parties are reminded that under r 2A(10) any party failing to comply with a direction given under r 2A(2) is not to be entitled to adduce evidence to which the direction related without the leave of the Court.

The exchange of statements can facilitate the making of an order under O.38, r 3 for evidence of particular facts to be given in a particular way.

Unlike experts' reports, witness statements are not normally read by the Judge in advance without an express invitation to do so. There may be an objection to admissibility or the witness may never be called. Accordingly if parties wish the Judge to read witness statements in advance, they should make that clear at the time of providing the trial documents to the Court. Where there is to be an objection to admissibility or relevance, the objection should if possible be communicated to the other party before the time that the trial documents are prepared so that it may be resolved by agreement and/or taken into account in the preparation of the bundles. However it should be remembered that it will rarely be necessary to remove the parts objected to physically from the bundle; some annotation of the objection will normally suffice. Where a party has decided not to call a witness whose statement has been exchanged, that fact should be taken into account in making up the trial bundles.

Exceptionally there are cases where relevant matters about which evidence can properly be given continue to occur after the time of the exchange of statements; such matters should if possible be dealt with by agreement and if necessary the summons for directions must be restored. There may be other exceptional cases where issues of credit arise from the exchanged statements which may either involve the calling of additional evidence or, very exceptionally, the non-disclosure of such additional evidence. How such situations are best dealt with must depend upon the circumstances but it must be remembered that at some stage the party adducing the additional evidence will require the leave of the Court.

THE COURT BUNDLE

In the High Court proceedings the plaintiff's solicitor is required under Order 34, rule 10 to prepare a bundle of documents which must be lodged with the court prior to trial. The court bundle (which must be paginated) comprises:–

(1) witness statements which have been exchanged;
(2) expert reports;
(3) documents relied upon by either party (which should be placed in chronological order).

The defendant must notify the plaintiff's solicitor 14 days before the date fixed for trial of the documents he wishes included; if there is no fixed date, he must notify the plaintiff's solicitor within three weeks of receiving notice the case has entered the warned list.

The idea is that the trial judge should be able to read in advance both the pleadings bundle (which will already have been lodged when the case was set down) and a 'court bundle' containing the evidence. In many cases the parties will add in the court bundle:–

(i)   a summary of the issues involved;
(ii) a summary of any propositions of law to be advanced together with a list of the authorities to be cited; and
(iii) a chronology of relevant events.

Where possible the summary of issues and chronology should be agreed. It should be noted that the court may direct such summaries to be lodged; this may be ordered at the summons for directions or later on application by either party (see Order 25, rule 3(2) and Order 34, rule 10(3)).

The court bundle must be lodged:–

(i) 14 days before the date fixed for trial
(ii) where no date has been fixed, but the action is in the Warned List of cases which will be taken for trial, at least 2 clear days before the date when the action is likely to be called on.

In the Queen's Bench Division two bundles are required; they will be lodged in London at the office of the Clerk of the Lists (Room W11). In the Chancery Division only one bundle is required; it is lodged with the Clerk of Lists (Room 812), Chancery Chambers.

In the County Court, Order 17, rule 12 provides that a court bundle must be prepared:–

(i) in personal injury actions and other actions where automatic directions apply
(ii) in actions where there has been a pre-trial review.

(In effect the court bundle has to be prepared except in possession and rent actions, some consumer credit cases and actions for delivery up of goods; even in these cases the court will direct a bundle to be prepared if there is likely to be a contested hearing involving substantial issues.) Order 17, rule 12 provides that:–

'(2) At least 14 days before the day fixed for the hearing the defendant shall inform the plaintiff of the documents which he wishes to have included in the [court] bundle. . .

(3) At least 7 days before the day fixed for the hearing the plaintiff shall file one copy of a paginated and indexed bundle comprising the documents on which either of the parties intends to rely or which either party wishes to have before the court at the hearing together with two copies of each of the following documents–

(a) any request for particulars and the particulars given and any answer to interrogatories,

(b) witness statements which have been exchanged, and expert reports which have been disclosed, together with an indication of whether the contents of such documents are agreed,

(c) the requisite legal aid documents [all notices of issue and amendment of Legal Aid Certificates].'

It will be appreciated that the County Court will already have its own bundle of the pleadings lodged and all interlocutory orders.

SKILLS PRACTICE NOTE

Preparation of bundles for trial

The smooth running of your case will depend on your preparing suitable bundles for use in the hearing. Again we have set out below the suggestions in the Commercial Court Guide which can be adopted and modified to suit any particular case. Do remember that because the other side agree a document should go into the agreed bundle that does not mean they agree its authenticity or that it is admissible evidence of the facts stated therein. Always check you can prove the document and prove any statements in it.

EXTRACT FROM COMMERCIAL COURT GUIDE

DOCUMENTS

16.1 The efficient preparation of documents for the use on any hearing is a very important part of commercial litigation. This applies both to summonses and to trials. To this end:

(a) Bundles should be paginated, fully legible and of a convenient size.

(b) Bundles should have an identification and be labelled on their exterior with the short title of the action and a description of their contents.

(c) Bundles of correspondence and similar documents should be arranged chronologically; for bundles not being arranged chronologically, indices and dividers (or flags) are normally appropriate and documents should always bear their date on the first page.

(d) Where a bundle is made up from documents originating from more than one source, as for example a sequence from the exhibits to more than one affidavit or from the discovery of more than one party, the individual copy documents used should, unless this is clearly unnecessary, have on them an indication of their origin.

(e) Where a document needs to be transcribed to make it fully legible or to be translated, the transcription or translation should be clearly marked and identified and adjacent to the original document.

(f) All bundles should be suitably secured having regard to the use that will have to be made of them. Bundles for use by counsel and the Court at a trial are usually best placed in lever-arched files so that additions and rearrangements can be made as the need arises; but such bundles are less easy for witnesses to use than ordinary ring binders.

(g) For the trial a handy sized core bundle should (unless clearly unnecessary) also be provided containing the really important documents upon which the case will turn or to which repeated reference will have to be made. The documents in this bundle should normally be paginated but should also bear the reference to where they may be found in the main bundles. The bundles supplied to the Court should be contained in a loose-leaf file which can easily have further documents added to it if wished.

(h) Bundles and their pagination should be agreed in sufficient time before any hearing for counsel to be able to prepare for the hearing by reference to that pagination and to include it in their skeleton arguments. For summonses this should be at the latest two clear days before the hearing. For trials the latest time should ordinarily be about three weeks before the fixed date and the standard direction reflects this. Where oral witnesses are to be called at the trial, an appropriate set of bundles must also be provided for use in the witness-box.

16.2 A common error is to copy for the trial or other hearing far more documents than can reasonably be thought to be relevant or necessary. Copying costs are often a considerable cause of expense to the litigants. Accordingly consideration must always be given to what documents are and are not relevant and necessary and only those that are included. It is recognised that a balance has to be struck between the cost of selecting documents for exclusion and the savings in having only the relevant documents but, in cases where the Court is of the opinion that costs have been wasted by the copying of unnecessary documents, the Court will have no hesitation in making a special order for costs against the relevant person.

16.3 The preparation of bundles of documents for trials and other hearings requires a high level of co-operation between the practitioners concerned. It is their duty to give this co-operation, and this is what ordinarily occurs. The unnecessary copying or duplication of documents or bundles, as will occur if there is a lack of co-operation, must be avoided. Where a party fails to co-operate and costs are thrown away the person responsible must expect to have to bear them.

16.4 In the ordinary course it is the responsibility of the plaintiff or applicant to prepare the bundles for the trial or other hearing. Where documents are required from other parties as well for inclusion in the bundles (*eg* composite bundles prepared in accordance with paragraph 16.1 (c) or (d) above), legible copies of those documents must ordinarily be supplied to the applicant at the latest four clear days before the return date of the summons, or to the plaintiff at the latest five weeks before the trial date. Where documents from the defendant or respondent are to be separately bundled, that party must prepare its own bundles unless it has, not later than the times previously stated, supplied legible copies to the plaintiff or applicant. The party preparing the bundles should, as a matter or course, provide the other parties in the trial or hearing with a set of the bundles within the timescale set out in paragraph 16.1 (h) above and any additional copies may be provided on request. The cost of any bundles supplied should be paid for by the party receiving them.

16.5 Doubt sometimes arises concerning the status of documents in an agreed bundle. When bundles are agreed, the parties should also settle–

(a) whether they are doing no more than agree the composition and pagination of the bundles,

(b) whether they are also agreeing the authenticity of the documents even if any of them were not disclosed on discovery,

(c) whether they are also agreeing that any documents may be treated as evidence of the facts stated in them even though not covered by any Civil Evidence Act notice.

As a matter of good practice a party should always expressly make it clear if he disputes the authenticity of a document (see paragraph 11.4 above) or if he is expecting an agreement to waive the strict requirements of the Civil Evidence Acts.

Chapter 14

The trial

The rules of court were originally drafted when civil cases were frequently tried by jury; in modern times (except for some defamation cases) trial is by a judge alone. Accordingly in this chapter we shall deal only with trial by a judge.

It should be noted that in the county court the district judge will have the power to try the following cases:

(a) any action where the defendant has admitted the claim or fails to appear at the hearing;
(b) any action where the sum claimed (or the value of the goods in question) does not exceed £5000;
(c) claims for possession by mortgagees (eg building societies and banks);
(d) by leave of the judge and with the consent of the parties, any other action or matter.[1]

FAILURE OF ONE PARTY TO APPEAR

On rare occasions in the High Court but frequently in the county court, the plaintiff attends on the day appointed for the hearing only to find that the defendant has not appeared. If the defendant has not supplied any satisfactory explanation of his absence to the court, the plaintiff will be entitled to prove his case and obtain judgment.[2] If the case is proceeding in the county court and no defence or form of admission has been received, the plaintiff will have to prove service on the defendant.[3] It is worth noting that the plaintiff who has to prove his case in the absence of the defendant is held strictly to the rules of evidence: matters which might be admitted for the sake of convenience if the defendant were present will have to be strictly

1 CCR Ord 25, r 5(1).
2 RSC Ord 35, r 1; CCR Ord 21, r 3.
3 Service in the county court is usually effected in the first instance by the court bailiff who indorses details of service on the court copy of the summons. This indorsement is in itself sufficient proof of service – County Courts Act 1984, s 133. If therefore the defendant does not appear one should check with the court staff to see the indorsement on the copy summons. If the bailiff is unable to effect service, the district judge will send notice of non-service on the plaintiff's solicitors who must then arrange service themselves. Such service is proved by affidavit.

proved. Thus, for example, the plaintiff's witnesses must not give hearsay evidence (unless the requisite notices under the Civil Evidence Act have been served) nor will the court permit the production of copies of original documents in the defendant's possession (unless notice to produce has been served).[4] In county court actions where a money judgment is obtained in the absence of the defendant no fee is normally allowed for counsel's attendance unless the defendant has filed a defence to the action.[5] Normally however in such a case in any event one asks the judge hearing the case to 'assess' the costs which the defendant is to pay to save, in what is probably a relatively small claim, the extra costs and bother of a taxation.[6] Even where the plaintiff obtains judgment in the absence of the defendant his problems may not be over because the defendant may apply to have the judgment set aside.[7] The application to set aside would be accompanied by an affidavit explaining the absence of the defendant and setting out the nature of his defence. If this is credible the judgment will normally be set aside on terms that the defendant pay the costs thrown away; if the merits of the defence are not convincing, a condition may be imposed that the defendant pays the amount of the judgment into court.

When the plaintiff fails to attend at the hearing of an action in the High Court the defendant may apply for judgment for dismissing the claim with costs;[8] in the county court, he should apply for the action to be struck out.[9] It should be noted that if the plaintiff has some reasonable excuse for his failure to attend, then the court will on application set aside the judgment[10] or restore the action.[11]

APPLICATION FOR AN ADJOURNMENT

It frequently happens that when an action is about to be heard one side wishes the case to be adjourned. An adjournment will only be granted in such circumstances either by consent or because the party seeking the adjournment can show compelling reasons why the action should not proceed to trial.[12] The applicant will inevitably be ordered to pay the costs thrown away 'in any event' (i e whether he wins or loses the action). Where the application is made by the defendant and there is reason to believe that he is merely stalling for time the plaintiff should ask the judge to make it a

4 Thus, for example, in a possession action the plaintiff may find himself wholly unable to prove the contents of the notice to quit since the copy retained by his solicitor will be inadmissible unless notice to produce the original has been served.

5 CCR Ord 38, r 8(2). Note this only applies to *money* claims. Counsel's attendance is always a proper item where some other relief is sought, eg a possession action.

6 CCR Ord 38, r 19. The costs to be allowed are set out in Appendix C, CCR 1981.

7 RSC Ord 35, r 2. The application is to be made by summons to attend the judge issued (unless time is extended) within 7 days of the trial. In the county court a similar application may be made under CCR Ord 37, r 2. In this case no period is limited for service of the notice of application but the defendant must proceed with expedition once he has notice of the judgment.

8 RSC Ord 35, r 1; *Armour v Bate* [1891] 2 QB 233, CA.

9 CCR Ord 21, r 1(1).

10 RSC Ord 35, r 2(1); the application should be made within 7 days but may be made later with leave.

11 CCR Ord 21, r 1(3).

12 For example the absence through ill health of a crucial witness. See *Dick v Piller* [1943] KB 497, [1943] 1 All ER 627, CA – refusal of adjournment although evidence defendant unwell: new trial ordered by Court of Appeal. See also *Grimshaw v Dunbar* [1953] 1 QB 408 at 415, [1953] All ER 350 at 353, CA and *Maxwell v Keun* [1928] 1 KB 645, CA.

condition of the granting of an adjournment that the defendant pay into court within a stated number of days the whole or part of the sum claimed and that in default there should be judgment entered for the plaintiff with costs.

OFFERS OF SETTLEMENT

When a man knows that his action is about to be tried 'it concentrates his mind wonderfully' so that at the court door the most intransigent litigants begin to appreciate the merits of the case on the other side. Regrettably under our present system of procedure it is frequently only at this stage that counsel meet each other and discuss the terms of settlement. Accordingly a very large number of actions are settled in the rushed atmosphere outside the court – possibly with the judge sending out messages to the helpless advocates that unless some progress towards settlement is reported he intends to come into court and start the case. Despite the pressure on the advocates it is extremely important that settlements made at court should be clearly understood by the parties themselves before they are accepted and that the eventual order should effectively realise the intention of both parties. There are two[13] different methods which are commonly employed where the parties have come to terms:

(1) Counsel draft out the proposed order of the court which is headed 'by consent',[14] approved by the judge and made an order of the court which can be enforced like any other judgment.

(2) Counsel agree that the action be dismissed on the terms of settlement endorsed on their briefs. This order is useful where the parties do not wish publicity to be given to the agreed terms but it has the serious disadvantage that if either party does not comply with the terms of settlement a new action will have to be brought to enforce the agreement – as if it were a contract.[15]

The advocate, in considering any proposed terms of settlement, should be careful to check that the proposed order includes such terms as to costs as will properly safeguard his client. In cases where the plaintiff is legally aided it must be remembered that the Board has a charge on any sum or property recovered or preserved so that when the defendant has agreed to judgment in a specific sum and to pay costs, the plaintiff will only receive the amount awarded on judgment after his solicitors have made a deduction of the difference between the costs incurred by the legal aid authority and the costs it will receive from the defendant.[16] Again terms of settlement however apparently attractive are worthless if there is little chance of execution succeeding: for this reason where a defendant offers terms but the

13 A third method employed in the Chancery Division is the Tomlin Order whereby proceedings are stayed on the terms set out in a schedule with liberty to the parties to apply as to the enforcement of the terms. See p 184, ante.

14 Except in county court possession cases where the practice has developed of omitting such words because some local authorities will not rehouse a tenant who has vacated by consent.

15 See *Green v Rozen* [1955] 2 All ER 797, [1955] 1 WLR 741. See generally on this topic Foskett, *The Law and Practice of Compromise* (3rd edn, 1991) Sweet and Maxwell 1985.

16 Legal Aid Act 1988, s 16(6). Solicitors, counsel and judges sometimes erroneously suppose that the Legal Aid Board has a discretion to waive the charge and settlements are made on this assumption. In fact where the charge applies it has statutory force and cannot be waived even if it produces severe hardship.

plaintiff is doubtful as to his willingness to pay, it is worthwhile obtaining security for payment (eg by the defendant consenting to the registration of a charge on land owned by him to secure the payment of the judgment debt).

OPENING SPEECH

The hearing of the case begins with an opening speech by counsel for the plaintiffs.[17] Normally, the judge will have read the pleadings and the court bundle (comprising the witness statements, the experts' reports and the correspondence which the parties wish to put before the court). In making his opening speech therefore the advocate needs to bear in mind that the judge may already have acquired a considerable understanding of the issues involved.

In making his opening speech counsel will usually adopt the following procedure:

(a) He sets out in chronological order the events which give rise to the case. Where (for example, in most contract cases) much of the evidence is contained in correspondence and other documents, counsel will pause in the chronology whenever he comes to a document in the court bundle which is of importance and which can then be referred to. In complex cases it is now common to provide a written summary of the opening including a chronology which refers to the relevant pages in the court bundle.

(b) He then takes the judge through the pleadings, summarising the formal parts of the pleading but pointing out carefully the paragraphs which show the real issues between the parties. Again in complex cases it is sensible to prepare and, if possible, agree with the other side a written statement of the questions which it seems the judge will have to decide.

(c) He then refers the judge to the correspondence which is agreed. The plaintiff's solicitor will have included in the court bundle all the relevant letters which have not been marked 'without prejudice'. The value of a clear letter before action becomes apparent at this stage because the judge then has a written summary setting out the plaintiff's case in much greater detail than the formalised pleadings.

Once the opening is concluded, the plaintiff proceeds at once to call his evidence; under our system the defendant does not have the right to address the court at this stage of the proceedings.

EXAMINATION-IN-CHIEF

The plaintiff's counsel calls his witnesses in turn and examines them *in chief* from the proofs of evidence which have been prepared by his solicitor. Since *examination-in-chief* is designed to elicit evidence favourable to one's own case, two important restrictions are placed on the advocate:

17 Exceptionally, where the onus of proof lies on the defence, counsel for the defendants opens the case – eg where a bailee is sued for the loss of a chattel belonging to the plaintiff so that to escape liability he must prove the loss occurred without negligence on his part. See RSC Ord 35, r 7 and *Mills v Barber* (1836) 1 M & W 425.

(i)   He must not ask *leading questions* on contentious matters. A question is leading if it is so framed as to suggest a particular answer.

(ii) *He must not contradict the testimony* of his own witness by reference to his proof of evidence or to any prior inconsistent statement. Thus if the witness says something different from what is contained in counsel's proof of evidence, he must accept the answer given, and is not allowed to refer him to what he said when the proof was taken.[18] It must be understood that counsel will normally not have spoken to any witness other than his own client or an expert and so it is by no means uncommon for him to be faced with an answer at variance with his proof.

There will be cases where the trial judge will direct that the witness statements which have been exchanged before the trial should stand as the evidence-in-chief; such a direction would not seem appropriate, however, where there are substantial issues of credibility. In *Mercer v Chief Constable of Lancashire*[19] Lord Donaldson MR gave the following guidance:–

> 'In the late 1950s the Restrictive Practices Court, in the exercise of its inherent jurisdiction to control its own procedures, began to direct the exchange of witnesses' proofs of evidence. The witnesses concerned were experts in accountancy and economics and were giving opinion evidence. Their proofs were mammoth documents and it was an obvious waste of time to examine them in chief when all parties were in possession of the proofs. The practice was therefore for the witness to take the oath, to be asked to identify his proof and to state whether he wished to add to, vary or subtract from it. He was then tendered for cross-examination. This was obviously a sensible innovation and the only problem was that, as I know to my cost, counsel appearing for the respondent Registrar of Restrictive Trading Agreements could not be expected to cross-examine a series of expert witnesses about extremely complex matters for day after day for weeks on end. There had therefore to be periodic adjournments. Nevertheless much time was saved and no injustice was done, at least on that account.
>
> Where witness statements have been exchanged, time and therefore expense will always be saved if this procedure is adopted. However injustice may be done. It is one thing to use this procedure with expert witnesses giving opinion evidence. It is another to use it with witnesses giving evidence as to matters of fact. It is one thing to use it in a trial before a judge alone. It is another to use it in a trial before a judge and jury, since a jury may be more able to absorb evidence presented to it orally rather than in written form.

18 Although it is open to counsel to apply to the judge at the conclusion of examination-in-chief to put in the conflicting statement under s 2(2) of the Civil Evidence Act 1968, which provides that:

> 'Where in any civil proceedings a party desiring to give a statement in evidence by virtue of this section has called or intends to call as a witness in the proceedings the person by whom the statement was made, the statement (*a*) shall not be given in evidence by virtue of this section on behalf of that party without leave of the court; and (*b*) without prejudice to paragraph (*a*) above shall not be given in evidence by virtue of this section on behalf of that party before the conclusion of the examination-in-chief of the person by whom it was made, except –
>
> (i)   where before that person is called the court allows evidence of the making of the statement to be given on behalf of that party by some other person; or
>
> (ii) in so far as the court allows the person by whom the statement was made to narrate it in the course of his examination-in-chief on the ground that to prevent him from doing so would adversely affect the intelligibility of his evidence.'

In practice where the situation arises the party calling the witness will not normally have served the notices required by the rules and thus the Act itself provides that the statement will only be admitted if the court gives leave.

19 [1991] 2 All ER 504. CA at 507.

Order 38, r 2A(5)(*b*) provides that the court may, on such terms as it thinks fit, direct that the statement served, or part of it, shall stand as the evidence-in-chief of the witness or part of such evidence. In exercising this jurisdiction it should never be forgotten that how evidence is presented at the trial is very much a matter for the trial judge and I do not understand the rule to be intended to empower the court at a hearing for directions before some other judge to fetter the trial judge's discretion in any way. All that the rule authorises is a decision in principle which will stand unless and until varied by the trial judge. If no order is made, the trial judge can still direct that the statements stand as the witness's evidence-in-chief. If such an order is made, he can depart from it if it seems to him desirable to do so.

That said, there will be many cases in which it will be right to make such an order, but it will be more appropriate in the case of expert witnesses than in the case of witnesses as to fact and, other things being equal, it will be more appropriate in the case of a trial by judge alone than in a trial by judge and jury. But perhaps the most important factor of all will be the extent to which the evidence of a particular witness is likely to be controversial and his credibility in issue. If so, the way in which he responds to oral examination-in-chief may be of great importance. Against this background it is wrong in principle to make a general order applying to all witness statements which may be exchanged pursuant to an order under Ord 38 r 2A without regard to whether the witness is an expert giving opinion evidence or a witness as to matters of fact and without regard to the extent to which the witness's evidence is likely to be controversial and go to the heart of the dispute.'

CROSS-EXAMINATION AND RE-EXAMINATION

Once the *examination in chief* of a witness has been concluded, counsel for the opposing party will *cross-examine* the witness in an attempt to discredit the answers he has given or to elicit testimony favourable to his own client. He is entitled to ask as many leading questions as he chooses and of course can refer the witness to any contradictory statement he has made.

In cross-examination the defendant's counsel must put to each witness the points where his evidence will be challenged when the defendant and his witness give evidence. When the cross-examination is concluded, the plaintiff's advocate has the right to re-examine his witness on matters arising out of the cross-examination. In re-examination, he is not allowed to ask leading questions or refer to earlier statements of the witness (except to the extent they have been introduced in evidence by cross-examination).

Where the witness produces a document or plan or photograph or other object as original evidence it becomes an *exhibit* in the case and is marked and kept by the associate.[20]

THE JUDGE'S ROLE

Although the judge can and will ask questions of the witnesses it is a basic characteristic of our system that the introduction and testing of testimony is principally the function of counsel and not of the court. The role of the judge in our system has been explained by Denning LJ (as he then was)[21] as follows:

---

20 RSC Ord 35, r 11. The plaintiff's exhibits are normally marked P1, P2, P3, etc. In the county court, the exhibits are kept by the clerk of the court.
21 *Jones v National Coal Board* [1957] 2 QB 55 at 63–64. In that case the Court of Appeal allowed a re-trial because of persistent interruptions of counsel's cross-examination.

'If a judge, said Lord Greene, should himself conduct the examination of witnesses, "he so to speak, descends into the arena and is liable to have his vision clouded by the dust of conflict": see *Yuill v Yuill*[22] . . . [He] must keep his vision unclouded. It is all very well to paint justice blind, but she does better without a bandage around her eyes. She should be blind indeed to favour or prejudice, but clear to see which way lies the truth: and the less dust there is about the better . . . [The] judge is not allowed in a civil dispute to call a witness whom he thinks might throw some light on the facts. He must rest content with the witnesses called by the parties: see *Re Enoch and Zaretsky, Bock & Co's Arbitration*.[23] So also it is for the advocates, each in his turn, to examine the witnesses, and not for the judge to take it on himself lest by so doing he appear to favour one side or the other . . . And it is for the advocate to state his case as fairly and strongly as he can, without undue interruption, lest the sequence of his argument be lost . . . The judge's part in all this is to hearken to the evidence, only himself asking questions of witnesses when it is necessary to clear up any point that has been overlooked or left obscure; to see that the advocates behave themselves seemly and keep to the rules laid down by law; to exclude irrelevancies and discourage repetition; to make sure by wise intervention that he follows the points that the advocates are making and can assess their worth; and at the end to make up his mind where the truth lies. If he goes beyond this, he drops the mantle of a judge and assumes the robe of an advocate; and the change does not become him well. Lord Chancellor Bacon spoke right when he said that:[24] "Patience and gravity of hearing is an essential part of justice; and an over-speaking judge is no well-tuned cymbal".'

SUBMISSION OF NO CASE AND NON SUIT

In criminal trials, it often happens that at the conclusion of the case for the prosecution, counsel for the defence will submit that there is 'no case to answer' either in the sense that the prosecution have failed to call any evidence to prove an essential ingredient of the offence charged or on the ground that the prosecution evidence is so weak or has been so discredited by cross-examination that no reasonable jury could convict. If this submission succeeds, the accused is entitled to be acquitted and no appeal will lie from the ruling.

In civil cases, it is also possible for counsel for the defendant to make such a submission to the judge sitting alone. However if the judge rules in favour of the submission and gives judgment dismissing the plaintiff's claim, the plaintiff can appeal. If the plaintiff succeeds in the Court of Appeal, the defendant will doubtless ask for the matter to be remitted for the trial judge to hear the defence evidence. This means that a great deal of costs will have been incurred and time wasted because of the initial wrong ruling. To prevent this happening, civil judges normally refuse to rule on a submission of no case unless the defendant agrees to stand by the submission and call no evidence in the event of the submission being rejected.[25]

Submissions of no case can (subject to the above-mentioned condition that the defendant must elect to call no evidence) be made in either the High Court or county court. If the submission succeeds the defendant is entitled to have judgment entered dismissing the claim and the matter can never be litigated again. In the county court, where litigants frequently appear in person, the plaintiff may well fail on a technical ground, for

22 [1945] P 15 at 20, CA.
23 [1910] 1 KB 327, CA.
24 *Essays on Counsels Civil and Moral*: 'Of Judicature'.
25 See *Alexander v Rayson* [1936] 1 KB 169, CA.

example because he has produced no admissible evidence to prove an essential point (e g he only has a copy notice to quit and no notice to produce has been given). In such a case the court instead of dismissing the claim may *non suit* the plaintiff which has the effect of striking out the case but preserving the plaintiff's right to have the matter heard again when his tackle is in order.[26] It should be noted that there is no power to *non suit* a plaintiff in High Court proceedings.

DEFENCE CASE, VIEWS AND CLOSING SPEECHES

Counsel for the defendant has the right if he is calling evidence to open his case.[27] In the county court this right is seldom exercised – possibly because if counsel elects to open the defence case he is not entitled to make a closing speech except with leave of the court. The defence evidence is presented in exactly the same manner as the plaintiff's evidence and is subject to the same rules.

It may happen at any stage in the trial and frequently at the conclusion of the evidence that the judge will wish to review the scene of the events in question.[28] If the view involves any display of machinery or reconstruction of the events the parties and their legal representatives should attend; if the view only involves visual observation of a public place, the judge may attend alone but he should state that he has done so before delivering judgment so that the parties may point out to him any changes in the *locus in quo* or other material differences between the conditions at the time of the view and the trial of the action.[29] Once the evidence is concluded counsel for the defendant addresses the court. Counsel for the plaintiff then summarises his submissions and answers his opponent's arguments – unless the judge has already decided to find for him on all points – in which case he will indicate that counsel need not trouble to address him.[30] It would be impossible to set out here all the matters which should be borne in mind by the advocate in

26 CCR Ord 21, r 2. Where the evidence has not been completed the plaintiff may claim to be non-suited of right but thereafter the matter is for the court's discretion. See *Clack v Arthur's Engineering Ltd* [1959] 2 QB 211, [1959] 2 All ER 503, CA.
27 RSC Ord 35, r 7(4).
28 The power of the court to inspect any place or thing with respect to which any question arises in the cause or matter is set out in RSC Ord 35, r 8 and CCR Ord 21, r 6. Note that in the county court the expenses of such a view are to be paid *in the first instance* by the party on whose application the inspection is made or ordered, or if made or ordered without application, by the plaintiff, but are subsequently borne by the unsuccessful party unless the judge otherwise orders.
29 See *Salsbury v Woodland* [1970] 1 QB 324, [1969] 3 All ER 863 where the principles are discussed. Per Sachs LJ at 879: 'Knowing how plans and photographs may give an incomplete impression of a place, it may, indeed, often be wise to go and have a look in order to get a first-hand impression of the locality as a whole – to obtain a clearer and three-dimensional picture, so that, in effect the evidence falls into place. It must be remembered that all he is doing is to appreciate the evidence already given in the light of a static background. Such visits by judges alone have a long history. . . . Widgery LJ has . . . mentioned the visit paid by Lord Goddard to Euston Station – and there can be but few who had more practical experience of such matters, both as a "circuiteer" and as a judge. He gave no advance notice of his going to Euston Station. . . . It is, of course, wise, when practicable, to give advance notice of a visit. It is wise if there has been a visit before closing speeches, to inform counsel of that; but it is not always practicable; and it would be no credit to the law if judges were not allowed to visit public places without an expensive legal panoply accompanying them.'
30 If the defendant chooses to call no evidence the plaintiff's counsel addresses the judge first and the defendant's counsel has the last word: see RSC Ord 35, r 7(3).

addressing the court but perhaps the following suggestions may prove helpful:

(a) The novice often irritates the court by not understanding how a legal argument should be advanced – for example, the advocate should never state his own personal opinion on any matter: therefore it is unprofessional to say 'I think' – one should always use the expression 'in my submission' or 'I submit . . .'.

(b) Again you should learn the correct method of referring to a law report: 'I would refer your Lordship to *X and X* reported in the second volume of the Queen's Bench Reports for 1963 at page 206 as authority for the proposition that . . .' It is quite pointless for the advocate to read a report unless he has first told the judge what legal proposition he claims can be derived from it. Some judges dislike reference to current textbooks; however, the most conservative judge will be prepared to listen if the textbook is properly introduced into the speech by the advocate '*adopting* the argument of the learned author at page . . .'

(c) It is often helpful to begin by telling the judge the facts which you invite him to find proved and then to go on to explain why you say he should do so. As a case is heard, it often becomes clear that the decision will turn upon the judge's opinion on a quite limited point in the evidence (for example, what was said on a particular day at a particular time or whether any signal was given by a motorist before executing a particular manoeuvre). Where the judge is faced with a conflict of evidence on the critical point it may be useful to incorporate in your speech reference to:–

    (i) the probabilities (independent of the recollection of the witnesses) that such events occurred as you suggest. The more improbable the other side's version of the critical facts, the less likely it is that their witness's recollection is correct.

    (ii) whether the account given by the witness is consistent or inconsistent with the facts which are not in dispute (eg the correspondence which resulted from a particular conversation or the position at which vehicles ended up after a collision).

Of course, you will often also want to address the judge on the credibility of the witness as appeared from his answers in cross-examination and his demeanour in the witness box.

(d) Almost invariably the judge will need to hear argument on the question of damage. If damages are not agreed you must be able to show what *evidence* proves your contentions. You will often need to refer to an accurate legal statement of the principles which you contend entitle your client to the amount claimed; you will frequently need to have a photocopy with you of the relevant passages in such textbooks as *McGregor on Damages* (15th edn) (Sweet and Maxwell). In personal injury cases there was once a firm practice that counsel should never state the precise amount he wished the judge to award as damages for pain and suffering; the rule is no longer rigidly applied. Counsel will invariably refer the court to awards which he says are relevant as set out in *Kemp & Kemp: Quantum of Damages in Personal Injury and Fatal Accident Cases*[31] or *Current Law* or in the *Times* reports.

31 1975, Sweet & Maxwell.

Of course in all cases where there has been a payment into court, care must be taken by the advocate not to mention this matter to the judge.

JUDGMENT

In every civil case the judge is bound to deliver a reasoned judgment setting out his findings of fact on the evidence and his conclusions thereon. Where he is uncertain as to where the truth lies on any issue he must find against the party bearing the onus of proof since that party will have failed to establish the matter on a balance of probabilities.[32] The judge will normally give an opinion on every issue which would be relevant in the event of appeal succeeding against any one of his findings (for example, in a personal injury case, if he finds against the plaintiff on the issue of liability he will nevertheless give his decision on quantum to save the expense of a re-trial if the Court of Appeal uphold an appeal on the question of liability). The judgment in the High Court is transcribed by an official short-hand reporter (or tape-recorded): in the county court, where such facilities are not available, it is the duty of counsel on both sides to take a full note of the judgment since this will be the only record available to the Court of Appeal.[33]

At the conclusion of the oral judgment, counsel for the successful party asks formally for

(a) judgment[34] (e g 'judgment for the plaintiff for £2000' or 'that there be judgment for the defendant and the claim be dismissed'),
(b) interest, if appropriate (see below), and
(c) costs.

We shall discuss the appropriate orders as to costs in the next chapter. The rules as to interest deserve attention and are set out below.

INTEREST

In many cases the plaintiff will wish to have added to the judgment a further sum by way of interest to compensate him for being kept out of his money while the action has been proceeding. If he sues under a loan agreement or some other contract which specifies a right to interest, there is no problem: the court simply awards interest as provided in the contract. If he sues for dishonour of a cheque or bill of exchange interest can be claimed under section 57 of the Bills of Exchange Act 1882 and is automatically added to the judgment. In other cases the award of interest is discretionary and is

---

32 It should be remembered that the standard of proof in civil litigation is quite different from the standard in criminal cases; in a civil action it suffices that the judge concludes that the fact to be proved is 'more likely than not', i e is the most likely explanation on a balance of probabilities. In criminal cases the prosecution have to prove their case so as to destroy all rational likelihood of any explanation other than guilt (i e prove its case beyond reasonable doubt).

33 The parties may apply to the judge for leave to tape record the judgment: see s 9 Contempt of Court Act 1981 and *Practice Direction* [1981] 3 All ER 848, [1981] 1 WLR 1526.

34 Note the judgment may be for payment in a foreign currency; see *Miliangos v George Frank (Textiles) Ltd* [1976] AC 443, [1975] 3 All ER 801, HL. Note also that in personal injury cases the courts have power to make provisional awards: see Supreme Court Act 1981, s 32A; County Courts Act, 1984, s 51.

made under section 35A of the Supreme Court Act 1981 (or section 69 of the County Court Act 1984). Section 35 provides:–

> 'Subject to rules of court, in proceedings (whenever instituted) before the High Court for the recovery of a debt or damages there may be included in any sum for which judgment is given simple interest at such rate as the court thinks fit or as rules of court may provide on all or any part of the debt or damages in respect of which judgment is given . . . for all or any part of the period between the date when the cause of action arose and . . . the date of judgment.'

It will be appreciated that the judge has to determine two matters

(i)   the date from which statutory interest should run
(ii) the rate at which it should be awarded.

In commercial cases where large sums are involved the court will consider the rate at which the plaintiff could have borrowed the money of which he has been deprived or which he has had to use to put right damage caused by the defendant's actions.

> *Example.* The defendants' works caused access to the plaintiff's jetty to silt up and the plaintiffs were put to the expense of dredging a channel. They claimed interest on the damages awarded to them. Per Forbes J: 'The correct thing to do is to take the rate at which plaintiffs in general could borrow money. This does not . . . mean that you exclude entirely all attributes of the plaintiff other than that he is a plaintiff. There is evidence here that large public companies of the size and prestige of these plaintiffs could expect to borrow at 1% over MLR [minimum lending rate or bank rate], while for smaller and less prestigious concerns the rate might be as high as 3% over MLR. I think it would always be right to look at the rate at which plaintiffs with the general attributes of the actual plaintiff in the case (though not of course, with any special or peculiar attribute) could borrow money as a guide to the appropriate interest rate.'[34a]

If an award is made at commercial rates the court will specify a starting point which accords with the actual loss sustained by the plaintiff: if the damage occurred gradually the court may award interest at a lower rate until judgment. In simple debt and contract cases the rate is likely to be fixed by reference to the interest rate on judgment debts. After a judgment has been entered interest is automatically added to the judgment debt until payment[35] (which of course may be many months later); section 35A(3) of the Supreme Court Act expressly refers to the rate under the Judgments Act as being appropriate for the award of interest for the period *before* as well as *after* judgment. The interest will run in the case of debt from the date of demand and in the case of a breach of contract from the date when the plaintiff first suffered damage.

In personal injury and fatal accident cases the court must award interest under its general statutory power if the sum awarded exceeds £200 unless there are special reasons justifying the refusal of an award. The principles to be applied when awarding interest in personal injury claims are set out in the decision of the Court of Appeal in *Jefford v Gee*[36] as follows:

(i)   interest on general damages for pain and suffering should be

---

34a *Tate & Lyle Food Distribution v Greater London Council* [1982] 3 All ER 716, [1982] 1 WLR 149.
35 Judgments Act 1838, s 17.
36 [1970] 2 QB 130, [1970] 1 All ER 1202 as modified in *Birkett v Hayes* [1982] 2 All ER 710, [1982] 1 WLR 816.

awarded usually at the rate of 2% from the date of service of the writ until the date of trial

(ii) interest on special damage should be awarded at half the average rate of interest on money in court placed in the Special Account[37] over the period for which interest is awarded[38]

(iii) no interest is to be awarded on that part of general damages which is awarded for loss of future earnings.

DRAWING UP THE JUDGMENT

In proceedings in the Queen's Bench Division the solicitor of the successful party draws up the terms of the judgment on a form purchased from the court and takes this with the writ to the Judgment Department where it is formally sealed.[39] The court itself has a record of this judgment in the form of a certificate drawn up by the associate.[40] In the county court the court staff themselves draw up and issue the record of the judgment. The forms of judgment are set out in the *County Court Practice*.

---

37 See p 272, ante.
38 The relevant rates in recent years are:

From November 1st, 1988	12¼%
From January 1st, 1989	13%
From November 1st, 1989	14¼%
From April 1st, 1991	12%
From October 1st, 1991	10¼%
From February 1st 1993	8%

The current rates will be found in the notes set out under Ord 6, r 2 in the Supreme Court Practice.
39 RSC Ord 42, r 5. The procedure in the Chancery Division is set out at RSC Ord 42, rr 6–7.
40 RSC Ord 35, r 10.

Chapter 15

Costs

SOLICITOR AND OWN CLIENT COSTS

After the case is over each party will have to pay his solicitor's charges. Sometimes the solicitor will present his client with a *gross* sum bill showing in only in the briefest outline what is due. The client, however, is entitled to insist on a detailed bill showing the *profit costs* (ie the solicitor's charges for the work he has done) and *disbursements* (ie the payments to other persons such as counsel and expert witnesses).[1] If the client does not agree with the charges shown on the bill he may ask the court for an order that it be *taxed* (ie that the court should decide whether the amounts charged are proper).[2] The taxing master or district judge taxes the bill on an *indemnity basis*[3] under which

> 'all costs shall be allowed except insofar as they are of an unreasonable amount or have been unreasonably incurred'.[4]

The rules provide that such costs shall be presumed:

'(a) to have been reasonably incurred if they were incurred with the express or implied approval of the client, and
(b) to have been reasonable in amount if their amount was expressly or impliedly approved by the client, and
(c) to have been unreasonably incurred if in the circumstances of the case they are of an unusual nature unless the solicitor satisfies the taxing officer that prior to their being incurred he informed his client that they might not be allowed on a taxation of costs inter partes.'[5]

COSTS INTER PARTES

At the conclusion of nearly every case, the court will have to deal with an application by the winner that the costs he has incurred (including costs of interlocutory proceedings which have been 'reserved' to the trial judge) be

---

1 Solicitors Act 1974, s 64(2).
2 Ibid, s 70. The client can demand a taxation of right if he applies within one month of delivery of the bill; thereafter the court may order taxation (but may impose terms); after twelve months taxation will not be ordered except in special circumstances.
3 RSC Ord 62, r 15(2).
4 Ibid, r 12 and any doubts the taxing officer has whether the costs were reasonably incurred or were reasonable in amount are to be resolved in favour of the solicitor.
5 See RSC Ord 62, r 15(2).

paid by the loser. The general rule contained in RSC Order 62, r 3(3) is that costs 'follow the event', i e that the party who wins also obtains an order for costs:

> 'If the Court in the exercise of its discretion sees fit to make any order as to the costs of any proceedings, the Court shall order the costs to follow the event, except when it appears to the Court that in the circumstances of the case some other order should be made as to the whole or any part of the costs.'

This does not mean that the winner will normally recover all the costs which he has paid or will have to pay to his solicitor.

As we have seen above the costs payable to his own solicitor are charged on an *indemnity basis*; however, the costs paid by the loser are calculated in a different way known as the *standard basis*:–

> 'On a taxation of costs on the standard basis there shall be allowed a *reasonable amount in respect of all costs reasonably incurred* and any doubts which the taxing officer may have as to whether the costs were reasonably incurred or were reasonable in amount shall be resolved in favour of the paying party.'[6]

The effect of these provisions is that the winner recovers most but not all of the costs that he has had to pay his solicitor; there is usually a shortfall of about 20%. The position is exactly the same in county court litigation.[7]

What is meant by the expression 'a reasonable amount in respect of all costs reasonably incurred'? In *Francis v Francis and Dickerson*[8] Sachs J set out what has become the accepted approach:–

> 'When considering whether or not an item in a bill is "proper" the correct viewpoint to be adopted by a taxing officer is that of a sensible solicitor sitting in his chair and considering what in the light of his then knowledge is reasonable in the interest of his lay client. . . .
>
> It is wrong for the taxing officer to adopt an attitude akin to a revenue official called upon to apply rigorously one of those Income Tax rules as to expenses which have been judicially described as "jealously restricted" and "notoriously rigid and narrow in their operation". I should add that . . . the lay client in question should be deemed a man of means adequate to bear the expense of litigation out of his own pocket – and by "adequate" I mean neither "barely adequate" nor "super abundant".
>
> It may save misapprehension too, if one remembers that neither in an unassisted case nor in an assisted case has a solicitor any implied authority to take steps which are extravagant or over-cautious.'

INDEMNITY COSTS

In comparatively rare cases (e g where a party is in contempt of court) an order may be made that he should pay his *opponent's* costs on an *indemnity basis* (ie that 'all costs should be allowed except insofar as they are of an unreasonable amount or have been unreasonably incurred').[9] Such taxation affords the innocent party an indemnity against his solicitor and own client costs (except to the extent that those costs were inflated by unusual items authorised by the winner).[10]

6 RSC Ord 62, r 12(1).
7 CCR Ord 38, r 19A.
8 [1956] P 87, [1955] 3 All ER 836. This case concerned the taxation of a bill on what was called the 'common fund basis' which in practice was very similar to the new 'standard basis'.
9 RSC Ord 62, r 12(2).
10 See *EMI Records Ltd v Ian Cameron Wallace Ltd* [1983] Ch 59, [1982] 2 All ER 980, Ch D.

HIGH COURT TAXATION

Whether the costs are to be taxed on a standard basis or on an indemnity basis the taxing officer has to scrutinise a bill of costs drawn up to show the solicitor's direct costs and the uplift for care and conduct of the case (see Ord 62 Appendix 5 – 'The Masters' Practice Notes 1986'). The format and content of a typical bill of costs is described below.

The form of a bill of costs
The full bill of costs is set out in a format prescribed by Appendix 2 to RSC Ord 62. An example of such a bill is set out at the end of this chapter. Typically the bill is drawn up in the following way:

1. It starts with a brief narrative account explaining the nature of the case and the work which has been done.
2. The bill then itemises the specific work done (setting out all the disbursements paid – e g fees to counsel and expert witnesses).
3. Charges are then made:
   Part A: for the direct cost of the work done;
   Part B: for the general care and conduct of the proceedings;
   Part C: to cover travelling and waiting time.

Why should there be Part A costs and in addition a Part B charge for care and conduct? The answer is that it is intended to reflect the imponderable factors such as supervision of staff for which a direct charge cannot be made and also to cover a proper element of commercial profit. In *Johnson v Reed Corrugated Cases Ltd*[11] Evans J explained the calculation of a fee for 'care and conduct':–

> 'I approach the assessment on the following basis. I am advised that the range for normal, i e non-exceptional, cases starts at 50%, which the registrar regarded, rightly in my view, as an appropriate figure for 'run-of-the-mill' cases. The figure increases above 50% so as to reflect a number of possible factors – including the complexity of the case, any particular need for special attention to be paid to it and any additional responsibilities which the solicitor may have undertaken towards the client, and others, depending on the circumstances – but only a small percentage of accident cases results in an allowance over 70%. To justify a figure of 100% or even one closely approaching 100% there must be some factor or combination of factors which mean that the case approaches the exceptional. A figure above 100% would seem to be appropriate only where the individual case, or cases of the particular kind, can properly be regarded as exceptional, and such cases will be rare. I am aware that the figures cannot be precise, but equally in my view the need for consistency and fairness means that some limits, however elastic, should be recognised.'

In practice if a point arises on the assessment of costs, one needs to consult:–

(i) Appendix 2 to RSC Ord 62
(ii) Masters' Practice Notes (reprinted in the Supreme Court Practice 1993 at para 62/A5/6).

COUNTY COURT COSTS

In county courts cases the costs awarded to a successful party will either be

11 [1992] 1 All ER 169.

(*a*) *taxed* – i e a bill will be submitted to the district judge and the unsuc-
    cessful party will be able to challenge items he thinks are unjustified
    or inordinate; or
(*b*) *assessed* – i e at the conclusion of the trial the judge or district judge
    hearing the case will make an immediate assessment based in part on
    fixed tables set out in the *County Court Practice*[12] and in part on his own
    impression of the complexity of the case.

Assessed cost will always be less than the costs which would be awarded on
taxation but in fact successful parties often ask for such an assessment to
save the time and expense of drawing up a bill for taxation, especially where
they are doubtful about the possibilities of eventually recovering the costs
awarded. Thus for example many courts in London have a fixed sum which
will be awarded as assessed costs in simple possession actions to the
plaintiff's solicitor who will ask for such an assessment because he knows he
is unlikely in any event to recover such costs and is more interested in
simply getting an order to evict his tenant.

The amount awarded as costs in the county court will vary according to
the nature of the action and the amount of money or damages involved.
Where the action is for a specific sum of money or damages, the costs
awarded are on a scale governed in the case of a successful plaintiff by the
amount awarded and in the case of a successful defendant by the amount
claimed.[13] The appropriate scales are set out below:

Sum of money	Scale applicable
Exceeding £25 but not exceeding £100	Lower scale
Exceeding £1000 but not exceeding £3000	Scale 1
Exceeding £3000	Scale 2

The above rule is, however, subject to the important exception that where
the claim is for £1000 or less it will be automatically referred to arbitration if
a defence is served; in that event the only costs allowed will be:

(*a*) the costs stated on the summons
(*b*) the costs of enforcing the award
(*c*) such costs as are certified by the arbitrator to have been incurred
    through the unreasonable conduct of the opposite party.[14]

For practical purposes the position is that in claims involving £1000 or less
and nothing else the successful litigant will recover virtually nothing of the
bill he will have to pay his own solicitor. It must be remembered, however,
that if the plaintiff is claiming some other relief as well as the money
claimed, e g possession of land or an injunction, costs will be awarded which
will normally then cover a much greater part of his solicitor's bill.

12 See CCR Ord 38, r 19 and Appendix C to the Rules.
13 The judge may grant a certificate to the effect that the district judge is not to be bound by
   the relevant scale in respect of the taxation or particular items: this is appropriate where
   the nature of the case or the conduct of the action has involved the successful party in
   incurring costs which would not be wholly recoverable on taxation. See CCR Ord 38, r 9.
   The district judge has a power to ignore the scale limitations even if no certificate has been
   granted: Ord 38, r 9(5).
14 CCR Ord 19, r 6.

HIGH COURT COSTS

It has already been explained (p 42 ante) that a plaintiff is required to bring proceedings involving personal injuries under £50,000, Rent Act and Housing Act possession cases, Consumer Credit Act regulated agreements and mortgage repossession actions outside London in a county court. Section 51 of the Supreme Court Act 1981 provides a sanction where proceedings are wrongly commenced in the High Court:–

'(8) Where –
  (*a*) a person has commenced proceedings in the High Court; but
  (*b*) those proceedings should, in the opinion of the court, have been commenced in a county court in accordance with any provision made under section 1 of the Courts and Legal Services Act 1990 or by or under any enactment, the person responsible for determining the amount which is to be awarded to that person by way of costs shall have regard to those circumstances.
  (9) Where, in complying with subsection (8), the responsible person reduces the amount which would otherwise be awarded to the person in question –
  (*a*) the amount of reduction shall not exceed 25%; and
  (*b*) on any taxation of the costs payable by that person to his legal representative, regard shall be had to the amount of the reduction.'

We have also seen that for various reasons plaintiffs frequently bring proceedings in the High Court for claims under £25,000 in value. Where such a case is transferred to the county court, the usual order is that 'the costs of the action be in the discretion of the county court'.[15]

When the plaintiff has properly begun the action in the High Court so as to be able to apply for summary judgement under Order 14, the master may make an order for transfer on giving leave to defend and stipulate that 'costs to be in cause'; this is a direction that the judge in the county court who tries the case shall award High Court costs to the winner up to the date of transfer and county courts costs thereafter.[16]

LEGAL AID CASES

Where a litigant who has been issued with a certificate under the Legal Aid Act 1988 wins he is entitled to the normal order for costs to be taxed on a standard basis against his opponent and in addition, whether he wins or loses, the court will order a special taxation of his own solicitor's costs (called a *legal aid taxation*) so as to determine the amount the solicitor is to recover from the fund. The legal aid taxation is also made on a *standard basis* i e the taxing officer will allow a 'reasonable amount in respect of costs reasonably incurred'. On a legal aid taxation certain items (such as obtaining counsel's opinion for the sole purpose of removing a limitation on a certificate) will be allowed although they may not be chargeable against an unsuccessful opponent.[17] It should be noted that the Law Society have a first charge on any sum awarded to or property recovered or preserved for a successful assisted litigant. This means he will not receive his damages until the costs ordered on the legal aid taxation have been paid.[18]

Where an assisted person is the unsuccessful party to an action only a

---

15 See County Courts Act 1984, s 45.
16 *Simmons & Son Ltd v Wiltshire* [1938] 3 All ER 403, CA.
17 Civil Legal Aid General Regulations 1989, reg 111.
18 Legal Aid Act 1988, s 16; Civil Legal Aid General Regulations 1989, reg 87.

restricted order for costs can be made by the court against *him* (as opposed to the legal aid authority whose position is considered below). This is the effect of section 17(1) of the Legal Aid Act 1988 which provides that:

> 'The liability of a legally assisted party under an order for costs made against him with respect to any proceedings *shall not exceed the amount (if any) which is a reasonable one for him to pay* having regard to all the circumstances, including the *financial resources* of all the parties and their *conduct* in connection with the dispute.'

The effect of this provision can be understood by considering a simple personal injury claim.

> *Example.* P who is privately represented sues D for damages for injuries received in a road accident. P loses. D will have to pay his solicitor £3000 costs but will recover £2500 costs from P. Now assume instead that P is legally aided with a contribution to the fund of £750. The court is bound to consider his means and is most unlikely to order him to pay more than the amount he has already paid to the Legal Aid Board as his contribution towards his own costs. The means that D, though he wins, will still be the worse off by £2250.

If one bears in mind that over 45 per cent of all plaintiffs prosecuting accident claims are legally aided it will be realised that there is often a strong incentive to the defendant to settle however meritorious he may consider his own case.

To a certain extent the harshness of the provision is mitigated by section 18 of the 1988 Act which provides that the court may order the Legal Aid Board to pay the costs of the successful party provided:

(*a*) he is not assisted himself,
(*b*) he did not begin the case,
(*c*) the court has already considered the liability of the assisted litigant to contribute towards the costs,
(*d*) it would be just and equitable to make an order, and
(*e*) the successful party would incur 'severe financial hardship' if an order was not made.

The last condition was considered by the Court of Appeal in the case of *Hanning v Maitland (No 2).*[19]

> In April 1966 the defendant was on a walking tour in Hertfordshire. On a dark, wet night the plaintiff who was a member of a cycling club, rode into him. The plaintiff obtained legal aid and brought an action alleging negligence, i e that the walker should have carried lights or been on the other side of the road. The defendant, who was 54 and of limited income applied for legal aid to defend the case. His application was refused because his savings, though small, took him outside the limit. He won the case but was refused an order for costs against the Legal Aid Fund on the grounds of his own capital. The Court of Appeal reversed this decision and ordered the fund to pay his costs. Lord Denning MR said that the rule that the successful defendant must show 'severe financial hardship' is designed to prevent costs being awarded against the Fund to 'insurance companies, commercial concerns who are in a considerable way of business and wealthy folk who can meet the costs without feeling it'.[20]

19 [1970] 1 QB 580, [1970] 1 All ER 812.
20 Since this decision the door is open for all save insurance companies and very wealthy persons to claim against the Board.

We have already seen (p 133, ante) that where a defendant counterclaims damages which arise out of the same transactions as the plaintiff's claim he may *set-off* the damages he recovers against the plaintiff's claim. If the set-off extinguishes the claim then, since a set-off is in law a complete defence to the claim, the plaintiff's claim will be dismissed and he will be ordered to pay the defendant's costs.

> *Example.* P agrees to service D's machinery and claims £500 being the cost of overhauling the equipment. D refuses to pay on the ground that part of the equipment was wrongly re-fitted and this caused damage to the machine which cost £500 to repair. If D proves his case the order will be: 'Plaintiff's case dismissed: plaintiff to pay defendant's costs.'

Where a successful counterclaim does *not* arise out of the same transaction as the claim it cannot be set-off as a defence so that the order for costs *may* be:

(i) Judgment for P on claim with costs.
(ii) Judgment for D on counterclaim with costs.

In this case the costs of P and D are set off so that D will pay less than if he had not raised the counterclaim but nonetheless there is almost always a substantial balance of costs in favour of the plaintiff (because the defendant is only entitled to recover the costs exclusively referable to the counterclaim, i e only the amount by which the costs of the proceedings have been increased by the counterclaim[21]).

> 'Where a court orders that a claim and counterclaim be dismissed (or allowed) with costs, the rule of taxation is that the claim should be treated as if it stood alone and the counterclaim should bear only the amount by which the costs of the proceedings have been increased by it.'[22]

This rule could produce a very unfair result if it was applied rigidly:

> *Example.* P sues D for damages to his car (£1000) arising out of a collision. D counterclaims for damages caused to his car (also £1000). The judge finds each equally to blame for the accident: if he awards P £500 damages on the claim and costs and D £500 on the counterclaim and costs the net result might be: P recovers £500 plus £500 costs D recovers £500 but only £30 costs (because this is the total sum exclusively referable to the counterclaim).

To prevent such an absurd result D's advocate must ask for a 'special order';[23] on the facts stated above the order would be that D should be awarded the costs of the action.[24]

---

21 See *Medway Oil and Storage Co v Continental Contractors* [1929] AC 88, [1928] All Rep ER 330, HL.
22 *Millican v Tucker* [1980] 1 All ER 1083, [1980] 1 WLR 640, CA per Donaldson LJ at 1086.
23 *Chell Engineering Ltd v Unit Tool and Engineering Co Ltd* [1950] 1 All ER 378, CA per Denning LJ: 'in most of these cases it is desirable that a judge should consider whether a special order should be made as to costs because the issues are often very much interlocked, and the usual order of "judgment for plaintiff on claim with costs and for defendant on counterclaim with costs" does not always give a just result'.
24 Such a 'special order' can only be made between parties: it cannot be made against the Legal Aid Board who have funded an unsuccessful counterclaim: see *Millican v Tucker*, supra.

COSTS AFTER PAYMENT INTO COURT

We have also already discussed the position where a defendant pays money into court as an offer to the plaintiff to settle (see p 263, ante). If the plaintiff does not accept the sum offered but at the end of the trial is awarded no more than the sum paid into court,[25] then the order for costs is:[26]

(i) D to pay P costs to date of payment-in.
(ii) P to pay D's costs thereafter.

As we have already explained, since the bulk of the costs is usually incurred at the trial stage the plaintiff is likely to have his damages reduced so as to pay the balance of costs outstanding to the defendant.

OFFERS WITHOUT PREJUDICE SAVE AS TO COSTS

Where a claim is brought for an injunction or a declaration or some other order where the defendant cannot protect his position by paying into court he can instead make a 'without prejudice' offer to the plaintiff which will not be brought to the attention of the Court until the question of costs arises. Such offers are invariably described as *Calderbank* offers (from the Family Division case where the practice was first considered).[27] This procedure is now expressly sanctioned by RSC Order 22, rule 14.

'(1) A party to proceedings may at any time make a written offer to any other party to those proceedings which is expressed to be "without prejudice save as to costs" and which relates to any issue in the proceedings.
(2) Where an offer is made under paragraph (1) the fact that such an offer has been made shall not be communicated to the Court until the question of costs falls to be decided.'[28]

RSC Order 62, rule 90 specifically provides that such an offer may be taken into account by the court in exercising its discretion as to costs but not if, at the time it was made, the party making it could have protected his position as to costs by means of a payment into court under Order 22. This important limitation that such an offer must not be used as a substitute for payment-in was emphasised by the Court of Appeal in *Cutts v Head*:[29]

'I think it must now be taken to be established that the *Calderbank* formula is not restricted to matrimonial proceedings but is available in all cases where what is in issue is something more than a simple money claim in respect of which a payment into court would be the appropriate way of proceeding. I would only add one word of caution. The qualification imposed on the "Without Prejudice" nature of the *Calderbank* letter is . . . sufficient to enable it to be taken into account on the question of costs but it should not be thought that this involves the consequence that such a letter can now be used as a substitute for payment into court when a payment into court is appropriate. In the case of a simple money claim, a defendant who wishes to avail himself of the protection afforded by an offer must,

25 The test is to look at the sum awarded *after* any set-off has been deducted but *before* any sum due by counterclaim is considered; see *Chell Engineering Ltd v Unit Tool Co* [1950] 1 All ER 378.
26 See Ord 62, r 9; if the difference is so small that the de minimis rule applies, a different order may be appropriate: see *Tingay v Harris* [1967] 2 QB 327, CA.
27 *Calderbank v Calderbank* [1976] Fam 93, [1975] 3 All ER 333, CA.
28 Similar provisions apply in the county court – see CCR Ord 11, r 10. The offer is filed at court in a sealed envelope.
29 [1984] 1 All ER 597, per Oliver LJ.

in the ordinary way, back his offer with cash by making a payment-in and, speaking for myself, I should not, as at present advised be disposed in such a case to treat a *Calderbank* offer as carrying the same consequences as payment-in.'

It should be noted that the effect of a *Calderbank* letter on the eventual order for costs cannot be predicted precisely:–

> 'The question of costs is in the Court's discretion where there has been a payment into court, and where there has been a *Calderbank* offer the latter should not be equated precisely to a payment into Court. A payment into court is usually unambiguous whilst a *Calderbank* offer may not be precisely in the terms of the judgment or order made. Its existence will influence but not govern the exercise of the discretion.'[30]

BULLOCK AND SANDERSON ORDERS

There will be many cases where a plaintiff is placed in a dilemma as to which of two parties should be sued:

> *Example.* P is a passenger in a vehicle driven by D1 which collides with a car driven by D2. D1 and D2 blame each other. At the trial D1 is held to be solely to blame for the accident.

In such circumstances the successful defendant is entitled to look for his costs from the plaintiff since he is blameless and the plaintiff decided to bring the action against him. However, the plaintiff was forced into this action by the intransigence of the unsuccessful defendant in refusing to admit liability and in insisting that the innocent defendant was to blame; it therefore follows that the plaintiff should be indemnified in the costs he has to pay the successful defendant by the unsuccessful defendant. This form of order known as a *Bullock Order*[31] involves an order in the following terms:

(i)   Judgment for P against D1 with costs.
(ii) Claim against D2 dismissed; P to pay D2's costs.
(iii) D1 to pay P costs so paid by P to D2.

This order safeguards the innocent defendant provided the plaintiff has the means to pay. If, however, the plaintiff is insolvent or legally aided in circumstances where the successful defendant will not recover costs from the Legal Aid Board, the defendant may well prefer an order for costs against the unsuccessful defendant directly. This form of order is known as a *Sanderson Order*[32] and involves:

(i) Judgment for P against D1 with costs.
(ii) Claim against D2 dismissed; D1 to pay D2's costs.

INTERLOCUTORY ORDERS

Interlocutory disputes (eg an application for an interim injunction or for security) may involve a great deal of time and effort by a party's legal advisers and make up a substantial element in the costs he will eventually

---

30 *Cook on Costs*, p 175.
31 From the case of *Bullock v London General Omnibus Co* [1907] 1 KB 264, CA where the facts were very similar to those in the example above.
32 From the case of *Sanderson v Blyth Theatre Co* [1903] 2 KB 533, CA, when, confusingly, the order in fact made was a Bullock Order. A *Sanderson Order* is the form of order suggested in the Court of Appeal in that case as more suitable where the plaintiff is unlikely to be able to pay the innocent defendant's costs.

have to pay his solicitors. For that reason it is very important that an appropriate order for costs should be made whenever such an application is made.

The table below (reproduced from Order 62, rule 3(6)) sets out the most common interlocutory orders:–

Term	Effect
'Costs'	(a) Where this order is made in interlocutory proceedings, the party in whose favour it is made shall be entitled to his costs in respect of those proceedings whatever the outcome of the cause or matter in which the proceedings arise; and (b) where this order is made at the conclusion of a cause or matter, the party in whose favour it is made shall be entitled to have his costs taxed forthwith;
'Costs reserved'	(Except in proceedings in the Family Division) the party in whose favour an order for costs is made at the conclusion of the cause or matter in which the proceedings arise shall be entitled to his costs of the proceedings in respect of which this order is made unless the Court orders otherwise;
'Costs in any event'	This order has the same effect as an order for 'costs' made in interlocutory proceedings;
'Costs here and below'	The party in whose favour this order is made shall be entitled not only to his costs in respect of the proceedings in which it is made but also to his costs of the same proceedings in any lower court, save that where such an order is made by the Court of Appeal on an appeal from a Divisional Court the party shall not be entitled by virtue of that order to any costs which he has incurred in any court below the Divisional Court;
'Costs in the cause' or 'costs in application'	The party in whose favour this order is made at the conclusion of the cause or matter in which the proceedings arise shall be entitled to his costs of the proceedings in respect of which such an order is made;
'Plaintiff's costs in the cause' or 'Defendant's costs in the cause'	The plaintiff of defendant, as the case may be shall be entitled to his costs of the proceedings in respect of which such an order is made if judgement is given in his favour in the cause or matter in which the proceedings arise, but he shall not be liable to pay the costs of any other party in respect of those proceedings if judgment is given in favour of any other party or parties in the cause or matter in question;
'Costs thrown away'	Where the proceedings or any part of them have been ineffective or have been subsequently set aside, the party in whose favour this order is made shall be entitled to his costs of those proceedings or that part of the proceedings in respect of which it is made.

WASTED COSTS ORDERS

Order 62, rule 10 provides that where a litigant has acted unreasonably or improperly in respect of some matter in the proceedings, the Court may order that party to bear the costs involved. An example would be where a plaintiff refused to agree to a reasonable request for medical examination thereby forcing the defendants to obtain a court order.

Where costs are unreasonably incurred it is more often because of a mistake by the legal representative than any unreasonableness by the party himself. For example, pressure of work or forgetfulness may mean that one side is unable to proceed with a hearing and the matter has to be adjourned. Section 51 of the Supreme Court Act 1981 provides:–

'(6) In any proceedings . . . the court may disallow, or (as the case may be) order the legal or other representative concerned to meet, the whole of any wasted costs or such part of them as may be determined in accordance with rule of court.

(7) In subsection (6), "wasted costs" means any cost incurred by a party–
(a) as a result of any improper, unreasonable or negligent act or omission on the part of any legal or other representative or any employee of such a representative; or
(b) which, in the light of any such act or omission occurring after they were incurred, the court considers it is unreasonable to expect the party to pay.'

Order 62, rule 11 provides that the court may either make an order on the basis of its own perception of what has occurred or refer the matter to a taxing officer to report before making the order. No order is to be made unless the legal representative concerned has had a reasonable opportunity to appear and show cause why an order should not be made. Such orders can be made both in the High Court and the county court.

IN THE BARNET COUNTY COURT   CASE No 93 1067
BETWEEN

ANNA MADRIGAL   Plaintiff

and

BEAUCHAMP HALCYON   Defendant

BILL OF COSTS of the Plaintiff to be taxed on Scale 2
and paid by the Defendant pursuant to order
dated 1st March 1993

No. 2 A4 Taxation Costs Fronts Oyez Stationery

Taxed Off				Value Added Tax		Disburse-ments		Profit Costs	
			Instructions to commence proceedings against the Defendant for an injunction to restrain him entering the Plaintiff's premises at 28 Barbary Lane, Barnet. The Defendant attended court and consented to a Tomlin Order (including an order for the payment of costs to be taxed on scale 2).						
			The matter was conducted by a solicitor and charged at £40 per hour.						
			20th February 1993						
			1 Summons filed and served by post Paid fee				30	00		
			2 Application for injunction filed Paid fee				30	00		
			3 Affidavit in support filed Paid oath and exhibit				3	75		
			26th February 1993						
			Brief delivered to Counsel						
			1st March 1993						

			4 (a)(i) Attending hearing before Judge
			        with Counsel when Tomlin Order
			        made with costs against Defendant
			        Engaged 5 hours - £200
									200	00

			(ii) Care and conduct 50% - £100						100	00
			(b) Travelling and waiting time 2 hours - £40						40	00
			5 Paid brief fee to Counsel	35	00	200	00		
				35	00	263	75	340	00

No. 2B Taxation Costs Backsheets Oyez Stationery

Taxed Off				Value Added Tax	Disburse- ments	Profit Costs	
		Preparation					
		Part A:					
		(i)	Attendance and correspondence with Plaintiff				
			Personal attendances				
			3 hours 120				
			6 telephone attendances 60				
			2 letters out 20				
			——				
			200				
		(ii)	Defendant's solicitors				
			Telephone attendance				
			(1 hour timed) 40				
			1 letter out 10				
			——				
			50				
		(iii)	Documents Preparation of summons and pleadings, notice of application and affidavit				
			Engaged 6 hours 160				
			Total of items under Part A £410				
		Part B:					
		General care and conduct of proceedings at 60% £246					
		Part C:					
		Travel to inspect premises Engaged 3 hours £120					
		Total of items A, B, C				776	00
		5 Taxation					
		(i) Preparing bill and attending on taxation - 3 hours				120	00
		(ii) Care and conduct at 30%				36	00
		(iii) Travel and waiting 1 hour				40	00
						972	00

No. 2B Taxation Costs Backsheets Oyez Stationery

Taxed Off			Value Added Tax		Disburse-ments		Profit Costs	
		Summary						
		Page 1	35	00	263	75	340	00
		Page 2					972	00
			35	00	263	75	1312	00
		Less Taxed Off	—		—		—	—
		Add VAT on Profit Costs					230	00
		Add disbursements					263	75
		Add VAT on disbursements					35	00
							1840	75
		Add Taxing Fee					143	45
							1984	20

Chapter 16

Originating summons procedure

So far we have discussed proceedings which have been commenced by the issue of a writ out of the High Court or by filing a praecipe for a summons in the county court. The characteristics of such proceedings (technically 'actions') are that (1) the parties exchange pleadings, (2) witnesses are called to give oral evidence at the trial and (3) various default procedures are available. Such procedure tends to be unnecessarily expensive and time-consuming where the principal issue is one of the law or the construction of a written instrument, and where there is no substantial dispute on the facts. In such cases proceedings may be begun by what in the High Court is called an originating summons; its counterpart (though not identical) in the county court is an originating application. RSC Order 5, rule 4(2) provides the basic test as to which cases should be begun by originating summons.

'Proceedings –
(a) in which the sole or principal question at issue is, or is likely to be, one of the construction of an Act or of any instrument made under an Act, or any deed, will, contract or other document, or some other question of the law, or
(b) in which there is unlikely to be any substantial dispute of fact, are appropriate to be begun by originating summons.'

One could add to the above rule a third category – namely cases brought under the provisions of particular statutes (such as the Landlord and Tenant Act 1954 in relation to business tenancies, the Variation of Trusts Act 1958, or applications for inspection of property or documents before proceedings under the Supreme Court Act 1981). It will be appreciated that although the originating summons procedure is used principally in the Chancery Division, it is by no means the only procedure employed in that Division: thus, for example an originating summons would be inappropriate in any case where there was an allegation of dishonest breach of trust, fraud or undue influence.[1] Probate actions must be begun by writ: RSC Order 76, rule 2. Nowadays many actions of a commerial nature are brought in the Chancery Division.

---

1 If proceedings are begun by originating summons which should have been commenced by writ, the court can direct that they shall continue as if begun by writ and the parties may be ordered to exchange pleadings. An affidavit already lodged on behalf of the plaintiff may be and often is ordered to stand as a statement of claim. The position is similar in the county court – see CCR Ord 37, r 5 and notes in *County Court Practice* to Ord 3, r 4.

ORIGINATING SUMMONS PROCEDURE[2]

We shall take as an illustration for this chapter a problem arising out of the provision of a will.

Example. On 31 October 1990, Jeremiah Jarndyce made a will by which he appointed his brothers Sebastian and Nathaniel executors and left his entire estate after payment of debts and tax to them 'in the assured confidence that they will distribute the same amongst societies for the suppression of pornography'. He died on 3 November 1991. Probate was granted on 2 February 1992. Jeremiah left a widow, Florence, but no issue, parent, brother or sister or issue of a brother or sister. (The widow is therefore absolutely entitled to any assets passing on intestacy.)

The problems which face Sebastian and Nathaniel in this case can be summarised as follows:

(1) Do the words 'in the assured confidence' impose a trust which binds the executors or are they merely expressing the testator's hopes as to what will be done?

(2) If they are apt to impose a binding trust, is such trust valid? It will be remembered that a trust for a specific purpose is only valid if the object is 'charitable'. Is the 'suppression of pornography' a charitable purpose? If it is not, then the residuary property will be held by the trustee for the persons entitled to take on an intestacy.

The executors will want to get the court's determination on those questions so that they can be sure of distributing the estate in accordance with the law and without incurring personal risk; they will therefore apply by way of originating summons to the court. We set out below the form of summons. Note that in all Chancery proceedings the title of the action should include a reference to any document which is to be construed. The widow will argue for intestacy; the Attorney-General will argue that the gift is charitable and good in law.

In the High Court of Justice

Chancery Division

In the Matter of the Will dated the 31st day
of October 1990 of Jeremiah Jarndyce, deceased.

Between

(1) Sebastian Jarndyce and
(2) Nathaniel Jarndyce   Plaintiffs

and

(1) Florence Jarndyce (Widow) and
(2) Her Majesty's Attorney-General   Defendants

To Florence Jarndyce of 23 Garden Walk, Aldershot in the County of Hampshire, the widow of the above named Jeremiah Jarndyce deceased (who died on 3 November 1991) and who is beneficially entitled to any assets as to which the said Jeremiah Jarndyce died intestate, and to Her Majesty's Attorney-General:

2 Note: practitioners will find the answer to many procedural points of detail by consulting the Chancery Division Practice Directions (set out in the *Supreme Court Practice* 1993 Vol 2 paras 801–873).

Let the Defendants, within 14 days after service of this summons on them counting the day of service, return the accompanying Acknowledgment of Service to the appropriate Court Office.

By this summons, which is issued on the application of the Plaintiffs Sebastian Jarndyce of 26 Trinity Street, Cambridge and Nathaniel Jarndyce, 10 High Street, Trumpington in the County of Cambridge (who are executors of the Will above mentioned having proved the same in the Principal Registry of the Family Division of this Honourable Court on the 2nd day of February 1992), the Plaintiffs seek the determination of the Court on the following questions and the following relief namely:

1. Whether upon the true construction of the said Will and in the events which have happened the Plaintiffs hold the residuary estate of the above-named Jeremiah Jarndyce
    (a) upon trust to distribute the same amongst societies for the suppression of pornography; or
    (b) upon trust for the First Defendant absolutely; or
    (c) upon some other and if so what trusts.
2. If, and so far as may be necessary, that there may be an order for the administration of the trusts of the said Will by this Honourable Court.
3. That provision may be made for the costs of this application.
4. That such further or other relief may be granted as to this Honourable Court shall seem fit.

If the Defendants do not acknowledge service, such judgment may be given or order made against them or in relation to them as the Court may think just and expedient.

Dated the 3rd Day of June 1992.

Note: This summons may not be served later than 4 calendar months beginning with the above date unless renewed by order of the Court.

This summons was taken out by Tulkington and Co., Solicitors, of 50 Lincoln's Inn Fields, London WC2, Solicitors for the said Plaintiffs whose addresses are stated above.

IMPORTANT

Directions for Acknowledgement of Service are given with the accompanying form.

Once the summons has been drafted the procedure to be followed is:

(1) Three copies of the summons are taken to the Chancery Chambers or one of the Chancery District Registries and sealed, a revenue stamp is affixed to one copy which is retained and the others are returned to the plaintiff.[3] Notice that all persons interested who are not themselves plaintiffs but whom it is desired should be bound by the order of the court should be added as defendants. A guardian ad litem will be appointed to watch over the interests of infant defendants. Where beneficiaries are unborn or unascertained (eg the possible future children or issue of living persons) a representation order is made appointing one of the defendants to represent their interests.[4]

(2) The plaintiff serves the summons in the same manner as a writ.

3　See RSC Ord 7, r 5.
4　If there is a large class of many persons with the same interest it may be appropriate to join one of them only and obtain an order that he or she represent the others pursuant to RSC Ord 15, r 3. The accepted practice is to join all members of a class if they are 5 or fewer in number.

(3) If any defendant wishes to contest or support the summons he must deliver a completed acknowledgment of service to the court office within 14 days of service.[5]

(4) The plaintiff must file at court the affidavits which he intends to use at the hearing. This must be done 'before the expiration of 14 days' after the defendant (or any one defendant if several are named in the summons) acknowledges service.[6] The plaintiff must serve copies of this affidavit evidence on each defendant before the expiration of 14 days after that defendant has filed his acknowledgement of service; there is no reason why he should not do so earlier if he wishes; thus, the affidavits may be served at the same time as the originating summons. In our example, the executors would make an affidavit referring to the will, the probate, the assets of the estate, the state of the deceased's family and any other facts which would be relevant – such as the deceased's connection with anti-pornography campaigns. The probate itself (and the will annexed) is lodged at the court: being technically an order of the court it does not need to be proved. A photostat copy of the will should be lodged in Chambers.

(5) The defendant may if he wishes file affidavit evidence within 28 days of service of the plaintiff's affidavits.[7]

(6) Once the affidavit evidence is lodged the plaintiff takes out a 'notice of appointment'. This requires the parties to attend before a Chancery Master (or district judge) who will give directions for the further conduct of the case. The notice must be issued 'within one month of the expiry of the time within which copies of affidavit evidence may be served'.[8] The notice would read as follows:–

> To [*name of defendant*]
> Take notice that the originating summons issued herein on the 3rd day of June 1993 will be heard by the Master – at Chancery Chambers, Room No– Royal Courts of Justice, Strand, London WC2A 2LL on Friday, the 10th day of October 1993 at 10.30 o'clock. You may attend in person or by your solicitor or counsel. If you fail to attend, such order will be made as the Court may think just and expedient.
>
> [*Signed*]
> [Dated . . . .] Solicitors for the Plaintiff

(7) At the first hearing the master will give directions for the lodging of further evidence, attendance of deponents for cross-examination etc. Although in certain cases he has jurisdiction to make final orders, normally his function is to see the case is properly prepared before it is referred for decision to the judge.

(8) When all is in order, the master will adjourn the summons into the court to be heard by the judge.

---

5 Note that an acknowledgment of service is not required in the case of *ex parte* originating summonses – eg an originating summons for possession of land under RSC Ord 113: see RSC Ord 10, r 5; RSC Ord 7.
6 RSC Ord 28, r 1A(1) and (3).
7 Ibid, r 1A(4).
8 Ibid, r 2(1).

The procedure at the hearing is that the plaintiff opens his case, the affidavits are read, if any deponent has been ordered to attend for cross-examination his evidence is taken, and each defendant addresses the court. On the hearing of an originating summons the plaintiff can normally address the court only once and so he will usually deal with questions of law in his opening (although the judge has a discretion to allow a reply and generally does so on particular points of law and authorities cited by the other side). It should be noted that the common law principle that costs follow the event is seldom applicable to cases brought by originating summons where the question in issue is as to the proper application of a trust fund. Thus, for instance, in the problem above one would expect the costs of the executors to be taxed on an *indemnity basis* and the costs of the defendants to be taxed on a *standard basis*[9] and paid out of the estate: the reason for this is that the parties have really been brought before the court by the testator making a will the effect of which was unclear.

COUNTY COURT PROCEDURE

In the county court, proceedings which would be brought by originating summons in the High Court are brought by way of originating application under CCR Order 3, rule 4. The application differs from an originating summons in that it sets out not only the relief being claimed but also the grounds upon which it is claimed. The facts as set out in the application are not supported by an affidavit. The application is served together with a plaint note and notice of the day upon which the registrar will conduct the pre-trial review. Usually he will direct the respondent to file an answer setting out his case. The evidence when the case comes on for hearing will normally be oral rather than by affidavit. This form of procedure is used in disputes between husband and wife where no divorce proceedings are pending but the court has jurisdiction under the Married Women's Property Act 1882. It is also employed where a business tenant applies for a new tenancy under Part II of the Landlord and Tenant Act 1954.[10] We set out below an illustration of the type of case which might be brought by originating summons. It is important to note that the county court equity jurisdiction is limited by the size of the fund or property concerned.[11]

> *Example.* In 1985 Polly and Tony who were living together but were not married decided to purchase a small garret flat in Bloomsbury. The purchase price was £45,000 of which £40,000 was obtained by way of mortgage and the balance was contributed by each of them in equal shares. In order more easily to obtain a mortgage they decided that the house should be conveyed into Tony's name. Polly has now left Tony but he refuses to give her a half share in the flat. The present value of the flat is £65,000 and the equity is £25,000.

---

9 When costs are granted to a trustee or personal representative they are taxed on a indemnity basis but will be disallowed 'if they were incurred contrary to the duty of the trustee or personal representative as such': RSC Ord 62, r 14(2).

10 A special procedure is set out in CCR Ord 43, rr 6–8. The application must be set out in the prescribed form and an answer must be filed within 14 days of service. See Form N397 for a precedent for such an application and Form N400 for an answer.

11 County Courts Act 1984, s 23. At the present the limit is £30,000.

In the Bloomsbury and Marylebone

No of Application

County Court

In the Matter of Flat 3, 6 Ampton Street
in the London Borough of Camden

Between:

Polly Browne   Applicant

and

Anthony Brockhurst   Respondent

I, Polly Browne of 31 Lamb's Conduit Street, London WC1 the above-named
Applicant, apply to the Court for an order in the following terms:

(1) That it may be declared that the Respondent holds the leasehold premises
     situated at and known as Flat 3, 6 Ampton Street, in the London Borough
     of Camden on trust for himself and for me in equal shares or in such shares
     as this Honourable Court shall determine.
(2) That the Respondent may be ordered to sell the said premises and pay to
     me out of the net proceeds of sale thereof one-half or such other proportion
     as may represent my interest therein.
(3) That the Respondent may be ordered to pay the costs of this application.
(4) That I may be granted such further or other relief as may be just.

The grounds on which I claim to be entitled to this order are as follows:

(1) On the 1st day of September 1985 the Respondent and I purchased a lease
     for 99 years of the aforesaid property for the sum of £45,000 of which
     £40,000 was obtained by way of mortgage with the Sunnyhomes Building
     Society. The Respondent and I each contributed £2500 to make up the
     balance of the purchase price out of our savings.
(2) The said property was conveyed into the sole name of the Respondent.
(3) I cohabited with the Respondent at the above address until April 1993.
     During that period we pooled out resources and the mortgage repayments
     were made out of our joint bank account.
(4) Since we separated the Respondent has refused to acknowledge my inter-
     est in the said property or to compensate me therefor.
(5) These proceedings are brought under section 30 of the Law of Property Act
     1925.

The name and address of the person upon whom it is intended to serve this
application is:

Anthony Brockhurst,
c/o his solicitors, Dodson and Fogg
Freeman's Court, Cornhill, London EC3

The applicant's address for service is:

c/o her solicitors, Evans and Bartlam
5 South Square, Gray's Inn, London WC1

Dated this 12th day of July 1993.

Signed   *Evans and Bartlam*
                           [Solicitors for the Applicant.]

Chapter 17

Official referees' business

High Court cases which involve the detailed analysis of technical evidence are generally heard by an Official Referee. This is the title given to the Circuit Judges nominated by the Lord Chancellor to deal with such claims. In London, the Official Referees sit in St Dunstan's House, Fetter Lane. (The registry is on the third floor.) Proceedings are started by the issue of a writ in the ordinary way but marked 'Official Referees' Business'. The following cases should be commenced in this manner:

(a) disputes relating to construction, building or engineering works;

(b) claims by or against engineers, architects, surveyors and other professional persons such as accountants where detailed evidence has to be considered;

(c) claims by or against local authorities relating to their statutory duties in respect of building operations;

(d) claims in trespass, nuisance and under the strict liability rule in *Rylands v Fletcher* where detailed consideration of evidence either on liability or quantum or both is required;

(e) complicated claims between landlords and tenants concerning repairing covenants;

(f) involved claims concerning the quality of goods sold or work done.

Where a case which falls into one of the above categories is brought in the Queen's Bench Division and it becomes apparent that complex issues of fact arise, the Master may order that it be transferred to an Official Referee. Although a substantial number of the cases before the Official Referees involve large sums of money, the procedure should also be utilised for moderate claims, for example, disputes with builders over renovation or extension works to family houses. There may be substantial advantages to the client in commencing such actions before an Official Referee because he is more likely to make orders for summary judgment or interim payment and speedy trial.

OUTLINE OF PROCEDURE (SEE RSC ORDER 36)

Once a claim is designated 'Official Referees' Business' it is assigned to one of the judges appointed to deal with such cases and interlocutory applications as well as the eventual trial will be heard by him. The course of a typical case might well be as follows:

(i) *The Writ is issued* marked 'Official Referees' Business'. Actions in London are assigned by a 'rota clerk' to one of the Referees; in district registries, the case is assigned to the Circuit Judge dealing with such business.

(ii) *The Writ* (and often the *statement of claim* as well) is *served*; the defendant files an *acknowledgment of service* stating his intention to defend. Frequently the defendant will issue at once third party proceedings (e g to pass the claim onto a sub-contractor). The defendant serves a *defence*.

(iii) Within fourteen days of notice of intention to defend the plaintiff issues '*the first summons*' seeking directions as to the further conduct of the case. (At this stage he may also issue a summons for judgment under Order 14 combined with an application for an interim payment under Order 29 – this will not be heard by the assigned judge but by another Official Referee.) Note in such cases in London the court itself indorses certain standard directions on the RSC Order 14/29 summons. These require service of the summons and evidence in support within 3 days of issue of the summons, the defendant's evidence in reply to be served within 24 days of the issue of the summons and the plaintiff to file at court not less than 2 days before the hearing a paginated bundle of affidavits and exhibits.

(iv) At the hearing of the first summons, the following directions are given:

    (*a*) for the preparation of a Scott Schedule (see below) setting out the respective contentions of each party as to the items of work or whatever are in dispute.

    (*b*) for the trial of liability to be separated from the assessment of damages.

    (*c*) for discovery of documents by list (see p 207, ante).

    (*d*) for exchange of witness statements (see p 291, ante).

    (*e*) for directions as to exchange of expert reports and for a meeting of experts 'without prejudice with a view to agreeing technical facts and narrowing issues' (see p 218, ante).

    (*f*) for inspection, for example, of the building or machinery in question by the experts.

In addition to these directions, the Official Referee will fix at this first summons a date for the hearing of the action. This means the parties are aware at an early stage when the case will be heard and can make preparations (including retaining counsel and experts) accordingly.

(v) Any party who wishes further directions, takes out an *interlocutory summons* for hearing before the Official Referee in charge of the case.

(vi) *Pre-trial conference*: the Official Referees exercise close supervision of the litigation process and frequently set a date at which counsel will report progress and the court can give directions. The plaintiff's counsel will be required to provide before the pre-trial conference a list of issues and proposals as to how the case should be dealt with; the defendant's counsel will then provide comments thereon.

(vii) *The hearing*: in London each Official Referee has a court room provided with large tables for counsel and solicitors (because of the likely bulk of the documents), a witness box in which the witness sits while giving evidence and recording apparatus. Now that parties are usually required to exchange their proofs of evidence in advance, at the hearing, the court sometimes directs that witnesses' statements are to stand as their evidence-in-chief instead of the witnesses being led through their statements. It will be appreciated that the exchange of witness statements and expert reports in advance of the trial increases substantially the chances of the parties reaching a fair settlement of the case.

PLEADINGS

In many building and engineering disputes one or other party will be complaining of a large number of individual defects – for example, in a dispute concerning the renovation of a house there may be five separate matters of complaint relating to the roofing, ten alleged defects in the work to windows and doors, a specific complaint relating to a damp-proof course and so on. These items will be listed in the surveyor's report obtained before proceedings commence. An acceptable method of pleading such a case is to mention the defects by reference to the report in the statement of claim and set out each individual defect in tabular form in a Scott Schedule (called after the Official Referee who devised the system in the 1920s). This Schedule will be completed by the parties so that, for example, it may contain one column identifying the piece of work in question, and setting out the plaintiff's complaints in respect to that item, a second column filled in by the defendant setting out his response (subsequent columns to be completed by other defendants and third parties), and finally a column left blank for the use of the Official Referee. Exactly the same form of pleading and schedule is appropriate in a small building claim proceeding in the county court: we set out below such a pleading in a straightforward building dispute and an extract from a Scott Schedule.

PARTICULARS OF CLAIM

(1) On or about 21st October 1992 the Defendant agreed to carry out certain works of re-roofing and renovation and redecoration at the Plaintiff's house at 21 Barchester Road, Plumstead, Barsetshire for the sum of £30,000. The agreement is evidenced by the Defendant's estimate dated 16th September 1992 and the Plaintiff's instructions to proceed contained in a letter dated 21st October 1992.

(2) It was an express alternatively implied term of the said agreement that the Defendant would carry out the said works with all due care, skill and diligence and complete the same in a good and workmanlike manner and with good and proper materials.

(3) Further it was an express term of the said agreement that such works should be completed by 1st March 1993.

(4) On about 1st November 1992 the Defendant commenced work at the said premises.

(5) Between 1st November 1992 and 28th February 1993 the Plaintiff has paid to the Defendant sums by way of interim payment amounting to £25,000.

(6) The Defendant failed to complete the said works by 1st March 1993 and on 5th March 1993 he ceased work at the said premises.

(7) In breach of the terms referred to in paragraph 2 the Defendant failed to carry out the said work with proper care, skill or diligence or to complete the same in a proper manner or with suitable materials. Particulars of the specific

matters of complaint are set out in the schedule hereto and the report of Messrs Harding and Bold a copy of which is served herewith.

(8) By reason of the matters aforesaid the Plaintiff has been put to loss and expense.

PARTICULARS

Cost of making good defects in roofing	£9567
Cost of making good defects in works of renovation and redecoration and completing same	£8378

(9) Further by reason of the Defendant's failure to complete the said works by 1st March 1993 the Plaintiff has been put to expense and suffered inconvenience.

PARTICULARS

Rental of alternative accommodation until work complete on 12 May 1993	£1500

AND the Plaintiff claims Damages and Interest pursuant to Section 35A of the Supreme Court Act 1981.

EXTRACT FROM SCOTT SCHEDULE

1 No. of Item	2 Plantiffs' complaints	3 Plaintiff's estimate of the cost of remedying the defects complained of	4 Defendant's estimate of the cost of remedying any admitted defects	5 Defendant's observations	6 Column for Official Referee
26	WINDOW IN STUDY The sill and frames are rotted – complete replacement necessary.	£1200	£200	A small area of the sill is rotten – this could be made good.	
27	PAINTWORK IN STUDY Insufficient preparation of surface – paintwork patchy. Re-painting required.	£1000	£120	One small area requires re-touching.	
28	CEILING IN STUDY Cracks have appeared due to inadequate work. Replastering is necessary.	£1400	£320	Cracks are limited to small area in north-west corner: making good only required.	

Note. A Schedule of this sort is a sensible device in any building dispute and could be profitably employed in county court proceedings as well as Official Referee cases. The actual form of the Schedule will vary according to the nature of the dispute.

Chapter 18

Appeal systems

Where any order is made by a master or district judge on any one of the procedural applications discussed in this book or on an application for summary judgment under RSC Ord 14, either party may appeal against his decision to a judge in chambers.

> *Example.* D fails to return an acknowledgment of service giving notice of his intention to defend the action within the prescribed period and P signs judgment in default of appearance under RSC Order 13. D takes out a summons for the judgment to be set aside and for leave to give notice of intention to defend out of time but at the hearing of the application the master refuses to set the judgment aside. D can appeal of right to the judge in chambers.

The procedure is governed by RSC Order 58. The appellant drafts a notice of appeal in the form set out below and takes it to the Action Department at the Law Courts[1] where it is sealed and issued. The notice must be issued within 5 days[2] of the order appealed against and served within 5 days thereafter. It should be noted this notice does *not* state the grounds of appeal since the appeal is by way of a complete rehearing of the case (although the appellant will open the case).

NOTICE OF APPEAL TO JUDGE IN CHAMBERS

In the High Court of Justice   1993–W–No 206

Queen's Bench Division

Between:

John Wellington Wells   Plaintiff

and

St Mary Axe Novelty Company Limited   Defendants

TAKE NOTICE that the above-named Defendants intend to appeal against the decision of Master Cooper given on the 29th day of April, 1993 refusing to set aside the judgment for £16,000 and £186 costs entered herein by the Plaintiffs on

---

1 Or to the district registry or local trial centre if appeal to be heard out of London.
2 Discount the day of the order and Saturdays and Sundays in computing 5 days – see Ord 3, r 2. In the district registry the period is 7 days. Note that the court has power in any event to extend the time.

the 6th day of March 1993 in default of notice of intention to defend and ordering the Defendants to pay the costs of the application.

AND further take notice that you are required to attend before the Judge in Chambers at the Central Office, Royal Courts of Justice, Strand on Friday the 28th day of May, 1993 at 10.30 o'clock in the forenoon, on the hearing of an application by the said Defendants that the said judgment be set aside and that the Defendants be granted unconditional leave to defend this action and that the said order for costs be set aside and the Plaintiffs to pay to the Defendants the costs of this appeal and of the said application.

AND further take notice that it is the intention of the said Defendants to attend by Counsel.

Dated this 4th day of May, 1993

Dodson and Fogg
Solicitors for Defendants

To
    Evans and Bartlam
    10, Holborn Court,
    Gray's Inn,
    Solicitors for the Plaintiff

Either side may ask the judge to consider affidavit evidence not produced to the master although, if notice of this new evidence has not been given in advance, the other side may ask for an adjournment to consider the evidence and for an order for the costs thrown away. The appeal is therefore a complete rehearing so that although the judge 'will of course give the weight it deserves to the previous decision of the master . . . he is in no way bound by it'.[3] The successful party at the hearing must ask for the costs of the appeal and of the appearance below since the appeal costs will not be costs in the cause and neither party will get them unless an order is made. An appeal to the Court of Appeal will lie from the decision of the judge with leave[4] (either from the judge himself or from the Court of Appeal). We set out below the current practice directions.

PRACTICE NOTES

(1) Queen's Bench judge in chambers: inter partes applications and appeals in London

1. All *inter partes* applications and appeals to the Queen's Bench judge in chambers would initially be entered in a general list. They would be listed for hearing in room E101 or some other nominated venue.
2. Any matter which could not be dealt with within 30 minutes would not be taken on the date given for the general list appointment. If the parties agreed that it could not be so disposed of the applicant/appellant had to, as soon as practicable, and in any event not less than 24 hours before the date given, transfer the case to (i) the chambers appeals list, or (ii) for all other than appeals, the special appointments list. If the parties did not so agree, or agreed less than 24 hours before the date given, the parties had to attend on the date given.
3. [This relates to special appointments.]
4. Cases in the chambers appeals list would be listed by the clerk of the lists, room W14 and the parties would be notified by the court of the date on which such appeals would enter the warned list. Cases in the warned list might be listed for hearing at any time on or after that date. Fixtures would only be given in exceptional circumstances.

3 Per Lord Atkin in *Evans v Bartlam* [1937] AC 473 at 478.
4 Supreme Court Act 1981, s 18(1)(h); No leave is required where the defendant wishes to appeal against an order under RSC Ord 14, see s 18(2).

5. The original exhibits to affidavits should be retained by the parties but had to be available for production at the hearing.
6. In order to ensure that a complete set of papers in proper order was available for perusal by the judge before the hearing of such applications and appeals, the parties had to in advance of the hearing (see paragraph 7 below) lodge in room W15 a bundle, properly paged in order of date and indexed, containing copies of the following documents: (i) the notice of appeal or, as the case might be, summons; (ii) the pleadings, if any; (iii) copies of all affidavits, together with copy exhibits, upon which any party intended to rely and (iv) any relevant order made in the action. The bundle should be agreed if possible. In all but simple cases a skeleton argument and, where that would be helpful, a chronology should also be lodged.
7. Where a date for the hearing had been fixed, which would normally be the case for special appointments, the bundle had to be lodged not later than three clear days before the fixed date. For appeals where there was no fixed date for hearing, the bundle had to be lodged not later than 48 hours after the parties had been notified that the case was to appear in the warned list and for cases in the general list, the bundle had to be lodged at least 48 hours before the hearing. Skeleton arguments, with chronology, had to be lodged not later than 24 hours before the hearing.
8. Except with leave of the judge, no document might be adduced in evidence or relied upon unless a copy of it had been included in the bundle referred to at paragraph 6 above. If any party sought to rely upon an affidavit which had not been included in the bundle that party should lodge the original, with copy exhibits, in room W15 in advance of the hearing or with the clerk/associate before the hearing commenced.

July 29, 1993

(2) Appeals at the trial centres out of London

1. To the extent that the business of the courts permits, and subject to the provisions of this direction, judges of the Queen's Bench Division will sit in chambers at any place where sittings of the High Court are held, as well as in London, to deal with any business which may be dealt with by a judge of the Queen's Bench Division in chambers except any business which may from time to time be notified.
2. Where a party desires that a matter be heard before a judge in chambers outside London, the notice of an appeal or summons shall bear the title of the district registry in which the action is proceeding but shall be issued in the district registry at the place at which it is to be heard.
3. Before a party issues a judge's summons or a notice of appeal in a district registry, he should enquire at the registry whether the state of business will permit the matter to be heard there and it is proper to be so heard.
4. A judge's summons or notice of appeal issued in a district registry may be transferred for hearing to a judge in chambers sitting in London or at another place outside London on the application of a party made to the judge or by the court of its own motion, and such a summons or notice issued in the Central Office may similarly be transferred for hearing to a place outside London. Before a transfer to a place outside London is ordered, the court will require to be informed, from enquiries made by the parties or the court officers, whether the matter can conveniently be taken there.
5. In cases not specifically provided for, the practice of the Central Office as to district registry appeals shall be followed as nearly as circumstances permit.

(3) Documents to be lodged at trial centre

(1) In order to ensure that a complete set of papers in proper order is available for perusal by the judge before hearing such appeals, the parties must in advance of the hearing lodge in the civil listing office of the trial centre

concerned a bundle properly paged in order of date and indexed, containing copies of the following documents: (i) the notice of appeal; (ii) the pleadings (if any); (iii) copies of all affidavits (together with exhibits thereto) upon which any party intends to rely; (iv) any relevant order made in the action; (v) notes (if any) of reasons given by the district judge, prepared by the district judge, counsel or solicitors.

The bundle should be agreed. The original of all affidavits intended to be relied on should be bespoken or produced at the hearing and all exhibits thereto should be available.

(2)   Where a date for hearing has been fixed, the bundle must be lodged not later than three clear days before the fixed date. For appeals where there is no fixed date for the hearing, the bundle must be lodged not later than 24 hours after the parties have been notified that the case is to appear in the warned list or, if that is not possible, it must be lodged as soon as practicable thereafter.

(3)   Except with leave of the judge, no document may be adduced in evidence or relied on unless a copy of it has been lodged and the original bespoken as aforesaid.

(4)   In cases of complexity a skeleton argument or, where that would be helpful, a chronology should be lodged at the same time as the bundle.

[1991] 1 All ER 1056

APPEALS TO COUNTY COURT JUDGE

In the county court appeal lies to the judge under CCR Order 13, rule 1(10) from any decision of the district judge on an interlocutory order by filing and serving a notice of application within 5 days after the date of the order appealed from. The principles discussed above apply equally in the county court. Under CCR Order 37, rule 6 an appeal lies to a judge against any final order or judgment by the district judge[5] by notice served within 14 days after the day on which the order or judgment was given. An example of such an appeal would be from a district judge's decision on quantum in a personal injury case where the defendant had admitted liability so quantum fell to be considered by the district judge. The judge may make any of the following orders:

(a)   he may set aside or vary the judgment, or

(b)   he may give some other judgment having heard the appeal, or

(c)   he may remit the action to the registrar for retrial or further consideration, or

(d)   he may order a new trial to take place before himself or another judge of the court on a day to be fixed.[6]

APPEALS TO THE COURT OF APPEAL

Appeal lies to the Court of Appeal from the High Court and the county court. In some circumstances it is necessary for the proposed appellant to obtain leave to appeal, thus:

(1)   where the appeal is from a consent order or against the exercise of the

---

5   It should be remembered that the district judge has extensive jurisdiction over minor claims – see p 41, ante.

6   CCR Ord 37, r 6(1).

judge's discretion as to costs, leave must be obtained from the trial judge;[7]

(2) where the appeal is from the decision of a county court judge on a claim where the amount involved does not exceed £5000, leave must be obtained from the judge or the Court of Appeal. In equity proceedings leave is required if the value of the fund does not exceed £15,000. In mortgage actions, leave is required where the amount owing does not exceed £15,000;[8]

(3) where an appeal is from the decision of a county court judge hearing an appeal from the district judge, leave must be obtained from the county court judge or the Court of Appeal;[9]

(4) where the appeal is from an interlocutory order, leave must be given either by the judge who made the order or by the Court of Appeal.[10] Leave is not required when the appeal is against a refusal to grant unconditional leave to defend or against the grant or refusal of an interlocutory injunction.

Where in cases (2) (3) and (4) above leave is refused by the judge, the application for leave to appeal can then be renewed ex parte before a single judge of the Court of Appeal; no appeal will lie from his decision.[11] Note that applications for leave to appeal are normally decided in the first instance by a single Lord Justice reading the papers, but if he refuses leave the application may be renewed in open court.[12]

It should also be noted that in the county court (but *not* in the High Court) either party can apply to the judge for a new trial if there has been a serious irregularity at the original hearing or if there is fresh evidence. The procedure is governed by CCR Order 37.

Where a party desires to appeal he must draft and serve on the respondent a notice of appeal 'within 4 weeks from the date on which the judgment or order of the court below was signed, entered or otherwise perfected'.[13] If the notice is not served in time an application for leave to serve out of time is made to the Registrar of the Civil Division of the Court of Appeal. The Court has indicated that only in exceptional cases will such

---

7 Supreme Court Act 1981, s 18(1)(f). Where it is contended that the judge has applied the wrong principles of law in deciding the question of costs, so that the Court of Appeal is being asked to do more than review the exercise of discretion, leave is not required: see *Scherer v Counting Instruments Ltd* [1986] 2 All ER 529 and *Bankamerica Finance Ltd v Nock* [1988] AC 1002, [1988] 1 All ER 81, HL. As to the procedure where the appellant appeals against a court order on the *Scherer* grounds; see *Marshall v Levine* [1985] 2 All ER 177, CA. If the application for leave is not made at the original hearing the party desiring leave should ask the judge's clerk to arrange for the matter to be listed before the judge and give notice of the day fixed to the other parties.

8 County Courts Act 1984, s 77 and County Courts Appeal Order 1991 (SI 1991/1877).

9 Ibid.

10 Supreme Court Act 1981, s 18(1)(h). The test whether an order is interlocutory or final is determined by considering whether the order sought from the Court of Appeal would have the effect of continuing the litigation. Order 59 rule 1A(3) provides a basic definition of a trial order: 'A judgment or order shall be treated as final if the entire cause or matter would (subject only to any possible appeal) have been finally determined whichever way the court below had decided the issues before it.' Note that where a split trial is ordered the decision at the end of one part of the trial is treated as a final judgment. Note also Order 59 rule 1A paragraph 6 which contains a comprehensive list of orders regarded as interlocutory.

11 See Supreme Court Act 1981, s 54(6).

12 RSC Ord 59, r 14(7).

13 Ord 59, r 4. The court has power to extend the time on application under Ord 3, r 5. The court below may also extend the time period before it has elapsed Ord 59, r 15.

leave be granted. An appeal will lie from the decision of the Registrar to the single Judge.[14]

The notice of appeal will follow the form set out below.

In the Court of Appeal   Plaint No. 92 0356

On appeal from the Clerkenwell County Court

Between:

	Martha Bardell	Plaintiff
	(Widow)	
	and	
	Samuel Pickwick	Defendant

Notice of Appeal

TAKE NOTICE that the Court of Appeal will be moved so soon as counsel can be heard on behalf of the above-named Defendant by way of appeal from the whole of the judgment and order of His Honour Judge Barker given on the 4th day of December 1992 (whereby it was adjudged and ordered that the Defendant should deliver up possession of the first and second floors at 32 Goswell Street, London EC2 to the Plaintiff on the 3rd day of January 1993) for an order that the said judgment and order may be set aside and that the Plaintiff may be ordered to pay to the Defendant his costs of this action and of this appeal to be taxed or in the alternative that a new trial may be ordered.

AND FURTHER TAKE NOTICE that the grounds of this appeal are:

(1) The learned judge wrongly permitted the Plaintiff to amend her pleadings at the trial so as to allege that the said premises were not protected under the provisions of the Rent Act 1977 and thereafter wrongly refused the Defendant an adjournment.

(2) The learned judge wrongly admitted in evidence the testimony of one Jackson to the effect that he had been informed by a person not called as a witness that the notice to quit had been served on the Defendant before the 1st day of October 1992.

(3) The learned judge improperly interrupted the Defendant's evidence-in-chief to indicate his disbelief of the Defendant's testimony and impatience at the amount of time the evidence was taking.

(4) The learned judge erred in law and fact in holding that the Plaintiff was resident at the said premises.

AND FURTHER TAKE NOTICE that the Defendant proposes to apply to set down this appeal in the County Courts Final List.

Dated the 30th day of December 1992

To the above-named Plaintiff and to	*Parker and Co.* of
Messrs. Dodson and Fogg, her solicitors	2 Holborn Court,
and to the Registrar of the Clerkenwell	Gray's Inn.
County Court	Solicitors for the Defendant.

NOTE

No notice as to the date on which this appeal will be in the list for hearing will be given: it is the duty of solicitors to keep themselves informed as to the state of the lists. A respondent intending to appear in person should inform the Registrar of

14 On an appeal from the Registrar the single Judge considers the matter de novo and is not bound by the Registrar's decision on matters involving the exercise of discretion: see *CM Van Stillevoldt BV v EL Carriers Inc* [1983] 1 All ER 699, [1983] 1 WLR 207, CA.

Civil Appeals, Civil Appeals Office, Royal Courts of Justice, Strand, London WC2 of that fact and give his address; if he does so, he will be notified at the address he has given of the date when the appeal is expected to be heard.

PROCEDURE ON APPEAL TO COURT OF APPEAL

The procedure to be followed is set out below:

(1) The notice of appeal must be served on every party affected within the prescribed period of 4 weeks. In cases where an application for leave is required the notice of appeal may be served within 7 days after the date when leave is granted.[15] In county court cases, a copy must be sent to the county court district judge. Ordinary service (ie by leaving the notice at the respondent's address or sending it by post) is sufficient.

(2) Within 7 days after service, the appellant must 'set down' the appeal. This is done by producing and depositing at the Civil Appeals office the judgment of the court below two copies of the notice of appeal.[16]

(3) The court then sets down the appeal for hearing in the relevant group of appeals (eg the Queen's Bench Division Interlocutory List, and Queen's Bench Division Final List, the County Court Interlocutory List, the County Court Final List). The Registrar notifies the appellant of the CA reference number and the date when the appeal will be added to the List of Forthcoming Appeals.

(4) Within 4 days of notification from the Registrar the appellant must give notice thereof to all the parties.[17]

(5) The respondent must within 21 days of service of the notice of appeal serve a 'respondent's notice' if he wishes to contend that the judgment below should be affirmed on other grounds than those appearing in the judgment or that it should be varied (either in any event or only on the appeal being allowed).[18]

(6) The respondent must within 4 days of service of his notice, lodge two copies at the court.[19]

(7) Some time after the appeal is set down it will appear in the 'List of Forthcoming Appeals' which is printed in the Daily Cause List. The appellant, not more than 14 days after the appeal first appears in the List, must lodge[20] three copies of the following documents:
(*a*) The notice of appeal.
(*b*) The respondent's notice, if any.
(*c*) Any supplementary notice.
(*d*) The judgment or order of the court below.
(*e*) The pleadings (including further and better particulars).
(*f*) In High Court appeals, so much of the shorthand note of the judgment and so much of the note of the evidence as is relevant.

---

15 RSC Ord 59, r 4(3).
16 Ibid.
17 Ibid, r 5(4).
18 Ibid, r 6(3).
19 Ibid, r 6(4).
20 As to the form of the bundle to be lodged see the detailed notes in *Practice Note* [1983] 2 All ER 416, CA.

In county court appeals, a note of the judgment (usually prepared by counsel who have a duty to take down the oral judgment and submit it to the county court judge for his approval).[21] If any passage of evidence is relevant counsel will normally submit a copy of their notes to the county court judge and request him to approve the note or furnish a copy of his own note on the point.

(g) The list of exhibits.

(h) Such affidavits or exhibits as are relevant to the appeal. At the same time, time estimates signed by the appellant's counsel are lodged.

(8) After the documents have been lodged the Registrar is empowered to give 'such directions in relation to the documents to be produced at the appeal and the manner in which they are to be presented and as to other matters incidental to the conduct of the appeal as appear adapted to secure the just, expeditious and economical disposal of the appeal'.[22]

(9) After the court bundle and time estimates have been delivered a date for hearing is fixed; short cases are not fixed but entered in a 'short warned list'.

(10) Not less than 2 weeks before the date for hearing skeleton arguments must be sent to the other side and three copies lodged at the Civil Appeals Office. Where the appeal is in the 'short warned list' the copies are to be lodged 10 days before the case is 'on call'.

The current Practice Directions relating to the preparation and presentation of appeals are set out in the Supreme Court Practice 1993, pp 978–988. The Court expects all advocates appearing before it to be thoroughly familiar with those directions.

Where an appeal is taken there are a number of points which may arise for decision before the appeal can be heard:

(1) *Stay of execution:* the appellant may apply on notice to the judge at first instance for a stay pending the determination of the appeal; if this is refused he may make application to the Court of Appeal.[23] Where the judgment is for payment of money, the general principle is that a stay will not be granted unless the appellant is able to produce evidence to show that if the damages are paid there is no reasonable possibility of getting them back if the appeal succeeds.

(2) *Security of costs:* the respondent may apply to the Court of Appeal in *special circumstances* for an order requiring the appellant to provide security for the costs of the appeal. Security might be ordered if the appellant was ordinarily resident abroad and had no property in the jurisdiction *or* was an insolvent company or in the other circumstances laid down in RSC Order 23, rule 1.[24] It would also probably be ordered even where the appellant was legally aided[25] if it could be shown that he had not the means to pay the costs ordered below.

(3) *Fresh evidence:* if the appellant desires to place new evidence before the

---

21 In theory an advocate in the county court can ask the judge to make a specific note on any point of law under s 80 of the County Courts Act 1984 but this is seldom done in practice.
22 RSC Ord 59, r 9(3).
23 See RSC Ord 59, rr 13 and 19(5).
24 RSC Ord 59, r 10(5).
25 See *Bampton v Cook* [1954] 1 All ER 457; *Wyld v Silver (No 2)* [1962] 2 All ER 809.

Court of Appeal he must apply on notice for leave to do so before the appeal comes on for hearing. If the appeal is from a decision of the county court this application[26] will not normally be entertained unless he has applied to the trial judge for a new trial and been refused.[27] Leave will only be granted by the Court of Appeal where there has been a hearing on the merits if 'special grounds' are shown. In practice this means the following conditions must be satisfied: 'first, it must be shown that the evidence could not have been obtained with reasonable diligence for use at the trial; secondly, the evidence must be such that, if given, it would probably have an important influence on the result of the case, though it need not be decisive; thirdly, the evidence must be such as is presumably to be believed, or, in other words, it must be apparently credible though it need not be incontrovertible'.[28]

The appeal will come on for hearing before three Lords Justices of Appeal sitting at the Royal Courts of Justice.[29] Counsel must leave a list of authorities with the Chief Usher not later than 4 pm on the day before the hearing. A copy of the list of authorities is sent by hand or fax to counsel on the other side. At the beginning of the appeal the presiding Lord Justice will indicate to counsel the papers which the court has considered. Counsel for the appellant will then begin at once his argument referring as he does so to the skeleton argument he has provided. It should be carefully noted that the appellant will not be permitted to raise any point in the Court of Appeal which was not taken below unless the court 'is in possession of all the material necessary to enable it to dispose of the matter finally, without injustice to the other party, and without recourse to a further hearing below'.[30] The Court of Appeal has power to make any order that could have been made by the court below so that, if it decides to allow an appeal, it will generally endeavour to determine all the issues then arising between the parties. Where however the appeal is allowed because of a substantial miscarriage of justice in the court below or because of new evidence then the court will order a re-trial.[31]

APPEAL TO THE HOUSE OF LORDS

An appeal will lie from any decision of the Court of Appeal to the House of Lords if leave is granted by the Court of Appeal or by the House on a petition lodged within one month of the decision of the court.[32] An appeal will also lie to the House of Lords from the decision of a single judge of the High Court if with the consent of the parties he certifies that a point of law of public importance is involved relating either to a point of construction or to

26 RSC Ord 59, r 10(2).
27 CCR Ord 37, r 1.
28 Per Denning LJ in *Ladd v Marshall* [1954] 1 WLR 1489 at 1491. See also *Langdale v Danby* [1982] 3 All ER 129, [1982] 1 WLR 1123, HL where the House of Lords held that a defendant appealing to the Court of Appeal against summary judgment entered under Ord 14 or 86 had to show 'special grounds' to justify the reception of further evidence.
29 Two Lords Justices instead of three may determine interlocutory appeals.
30 Per Widgery LJ in *Wilson v Liverpool City Council* [1971] 1 All ER 628 at 633.
31 Note: where a litigant in a county court desires a new trial on the ground, for example, of new evidence he should apply under CCR Ord 37, r 1 to the county court judge for new trial and only if the application is refused appeal to the Court of Appeal.
32 Administration of Justice (Appeals) Act 1934, s 1.

a point of law upon which there is binding authority in the Court of Appeal *and* the House then grants leave to appeal.[33]

REFERENCE TO THE EUROPEAN COURT OF JUSTICE[34]

Where a question arises in a case before either the High Court or the county court as to the validity or interpretation of any acts of the institutions of the EC or as to the interpretation of the Treaties and a ruling on that question is necessary to determine that case the court *may*[35] refer the question to the European Court for a preliminary ruling. The rules as to the circumstances where such a reference should be made have been formulated by the Court of Appeal in its decision in *H P Bulmer Ltd v J Bollinger SA*:[36]

> Producers of champagne in France brought proceedings in the Chancery Division to prohibit English cider manufacturers marketing their product as 'Champagne perry'. They claimed this infringed a community regulation dealing with the application of geographical descriptions. The issue was whether the regulation applied to wine only or to all forms of drink. The manufacturers applied for the judge to refer this question to the European Court. The judge refused on the ground that such a reference was not necessary in order to enable him to give judgment.

The Court of Appeal upheld his decision and ruled:

(*a*) That before a reference was made it had to be shown that a ruling on the point of law was *necessary* to enable the English court to give judgment. It would only be necessary if (i) the facts of the case had been determined and it was clear that the point had to be decided in order to give judgment and (ii) the point of law was not already covered by clear authority or so straightforward that the English court could readily decide the matter itself.

(*b*) Even if such a ruling was necessary the court should still consider whether to save time and cost it should not exercise its discretion to rule on the matter itself. Only points of real difficulty and importance should be referred to the European Court.

The European Court has held that a reference is not necessary where the point has already been decided in a previous case or is so obvious as to leave no scope for argument.[37]

---

33 Administration of Justice Act 1969, ss 12 et seq.
34 Article 117 of the Treaty of Rome; RSC Ord 114; CCR Ord 19, r 3.
35 Except in the case of the House of Lords which being the final court of appeal *must* make a reference if the determination of the point of law is necessary.
36 [1974] Ch 401, [1974] 2 All ER 1226. See also *Application Des Gaz SA v Falks Veritas Ltd* [1974] Ch 381, [1974] 3 All ER 51.
37 See Medhurst *Brief Guide to EC Law* (1990) Blackwell, p 42.

Chapter 19

Enforcement of judgments

When judgment has been delivered the layman is apt to assume that the case is then effectively finished; in fact, nothing could be further from the truth, for the judgment does nothing more than declare the respective rights of the parties and says nothing about how the order of the court is to be executed. After the judgment has been delivered the successful party must then consider how his judgment is to be enforced. This chapter deals with the means by which the courts will assist a successful litigant to realise the fruits of his victory.

DISPOSAL OF PROPERTY BEFORE JUDGMENT

It is of little value to a plaintiff to succeed in his claim if the defendant has lost or disposed of all his property before trial in such a manner that it is no longer amenable to the enforcement procedure. The student should there-fore remember the following methods of freezing the defendant's assets:

(1) An application under Order 14 is often made with the express purpose of obtaining an order that the defendant shall only be permitted to defend if he pays the whole or part of the claim into court to abide the event. Once this has been done the plaintiff is in the position of a secured creditor (see p 161, ante).

(2) Where the plaintiff can show that the defendant is withdrawing his assets from the jurisdiction or disposing of them with intent to evade judgment the court will grant a Mareva injunction to restrain him even though the rights of the parties have not been finally determined.[1] Note that the plaintiff who has obtained an order freezing the defendant's assets pending the trial does *not* have any rights in preference to other creditors over those assets.[2]

(3) Where the plaintiff has an interest in a fund held by the defendant (e g partnership property) he may apply by summons or motion for the appointment of a receiver (i e an independent person appointed to manage the property pending the trial under the supervision of the court).[3]

1 *Mareva Cia Naviera SA v International Bulk Carriers SA, The Mareva* [1980] 1 All ER 213n, CA: see p 244, ante.
2 *Cretanor Maritime Co Ltd v Irish Marine Management Ltd* [1978] 3 All ER 164, [1978] 1 WLR 966, CA.
3 RSC Ord 30, r 1; CCR Ord 32, r 1.

(4) Where the plaintiff is suing to enforce any interest on land he should register a 'notice of pending action' at the Land Registry so that if the owner sells the land before the case has been decided the purchaser will be bound by the claim.[4]

INSTALMENT ORDERS

A High Court money judgment normally takes effect from the day on which it is pronounced[5] but the court has the power on the application of the defendant to stay execution of the judgment on terms that he pays the judgment debt by such instalments as the court deems appropriate.[6] This application can be made immediately after judgment[7] to the trial judge or subsequently by summons to a master. Where the application is made by summons it should be supported by an affidavit containing a complete and accurate account of the defendant's income and assets and should set out his proposals for payment. The court will examine the debtor as to his means in order to determine whether an instalment order should be made at all (it clearly would not be made if he had ample assets to enable him to pay the debt at once) and, if so, how much he should be ordered to pay in each instalment. The order of the court typically runs:

'. . . stay of execution so long as the defendant pays the judgment debt and costs by instalments at the rate of £— per month, the first instalment to commence on the — day of — 199–, provided that if he should make default in the payment of the said instalments or any part thereof on the due date, the stay be forthwith removed in respect of the whole outstanding balance at the time of such default and the plaintiff be then at liberty forthwith to issue execution by writ of *fi fa* on the said judgment and costs'.

The county court is given express power to make an instalment order on the application of either party[8] and stay all execution until default occurs.[9]

EFFECT ON THE BANKRUPTCY OF JUDGMENT DEBTOR

The successful litigant remains at risk that the debtor will become bankrupt before he has actually completed the process of enforcing the judgment. Once a petition has been presented the Bankruptcy Court will normally stay any execution or other legal process against the property of the debtor;[10] the judgment creditor will not be allowed to proceed to execution but must prove in the debtor's bankruptcy and take a proportionate share

---

4 Land Charges Act 1972, section 5 (Note also section 6 – registration of writs and orders affecting land issued after judgment.)
5 RSC Ord 42, r 3.
6 Execution Act 1844, s 61; RSC Ord 47, r 1. In formal terms the court stays execution against the debtor's *goods* but since every other form of order for execution requires leave of the court it can effectively protect the judgment debtor so long as he complies with the order of the court.
7 Note that a defendant who admits the plaintiff's claim may indicate this on the form of acknowledgment of service. If he does so he may indicate that he intends to apply for a stay of execution. The clerk recording the acknowledgement makes a special entry to this effect in the cause book (Ord 12, r 4). The plaintiff may still sign judgment but execution cannot issue if within 14 days of the acknowledgment of service the defendant issues a summons applying for a stay (Ord 13, r 8).
8 County Courts Act 1984, s 71(1).
9 Ibid, s 88.
10 Insolvency Act 1986, s 285(1).

with the other creditors. Even if execution has taken place the judgment creditor will not be entitled to the sum recovered unless the execution has been 'completed':–

'(1) . . . where the creditor of any person who is adjudged bankrupt has, before the commencement of the bankruptcy –
(a) issued execution against the goods or land of that person, or
(b) attached a debt due to that person from another person,
that creditor is not entitled, as against the official receiver or trustee of the bankrupt's estate, to retain the benefit of the execution or attachment, or any sums paid to avoid it, unless the execution or attachment was completed, or the sums were paid, before the commencement of the bankruptcy. . . .

(5) For the purposes of this section –
(a) an execution against goods is completed by seizure and sale or by the making of a charging order under Section 1 of the Charging Orders Act 1979;
(b) an execution against land is completed by seizure, by the appointment of a receiver, or by the making of a charging order under that section;
(c) an attachment of a debt is completed by the receipt of the debt.'[11]

Similarly, section 183 of the Insolvency Act 1986 provides that the creditor of a company cannot retain the benefit of an execution unless it is complete before the commencement of the winding up (or, if the judgment creditor had notice of a meeting at which a resolution for voluntary winding up was to be proposed, the date of such notice).[12] The position has been summarised by Pennycuick J as follows:

'The basic scheme of these provisions is that unsecured creditors rank pari passu, and that an execution creditor who has not completed execution at the commencement of the [winding-up proceedings] is for this purpose in the same position as any other unsecured creditor.'[13]

The moral, of course, is that the judgment creditor should proceed speedily to enforce his judgment if there is the slightest risk of the insolvency of the debtor.

DISCOVERY IN AID OF EXECUTION

The judgment creditor may have little or no knowledge of the income or capital of the debtor. Since the methods of enforcement differ according to the nature of the asset in question it will be necessary for him to discover something about the debtor's financial position if he is to choose the appropriate remedy. This of course can be done informally (eg by the employment of an inquiry agent), but in addition the rules provide for the debtor to be summoned for an examination as to his means before an officer of the court.[14] In the High Court, the creditor applies ex parte on affidavit to the master for an order requiring the attendance of the debtor. He then obtains a date for the hearing which is indorsed on the order together with a penal notice warning the debtor that he is liable to be committed for

---

11 Insolvency Act 1986, s 346.
12 Ibid, s 183(2). Note also the power in section 126 to stay any execution which is proceeding.
13 *Re Redman (Builders) Ltd* [1964] 1 All ER 851 at 855.
14 RSC Ord 48, r 1; CCR Ord 25, r 3. Note the examination of a debtor under a High Court judgment may be undertaken by an officer of the local county court at the request of the master.

contempt if he fails to attend. The order must then be served personally (i e in the same manner as a writ) and the debtor must be tendered a sum sufficient to cover the cost of his attendance. The procedure in the county court follows the same broad lines except that the application commences by filing a request for an order for oral examination.[15] When the debtor appears the creditor is entitled to conduct the most exhaustive inquiry into his means and assets:

> 'As I understand the rule, the examination is to be "as to whether any and what debts are owing to the judgment debtor" . . . Any question, therefore, fairly pertinent to the subject matter of the inquiry, which means put with a view to ascertain as far as possible, by discovery from a reluctant defendant, what debts are owing to him, ought to be answered by the defendant . . . he must answer all questions fairly directed to ascertain from him what amount of debts are due, from whom due, and to give all necessary particulars to enable the plaintiffs to recover under a garnishee order.'[16]

THE METHODS AVAILABLE FOR ENFORCING A MONEY JUDGMENT

Before we consider in detail the procedure adopted in the case of the different methods of execution open to the judgment creditor it may be convenient to set out in tabular form the complete range of remedies.

15 Form N37.
16 Per Sir George Jessel MR in *Republic of Costa Rica v Strousberg* (1880) 16 Ch D 8, CA. And see per James LJ at 12: 'The examination is not only intended to be an examination, but to be a cross-examination, and that of the severest kind.'

METHODS OF ENFORCEMENT

Asset	*Method*	*High Court*	*County Court*
(1) Goods, leases, cheques	Seizure and sale	Writ of fi fa, RSC Ord 46–47	Warrant of execution, CCR Ord 26, r 1
(2) Land, stocks and shares	Register charge and obtain order and sale	Charging Orders Act 1979; RSC Ord 50	CCR Ord 31
(3) Bank accounts and other debts due to judgment debtor	Garnishee order	Attachment RSC Ord 49	CCR Ord 30
(4) Sums due at future date e g rent, royalties on book, reversionary interest under trust, and insurance policies	Appointment of receiver	RSC Ord 51	CCR Ord 32
(5) Salary	Instalment order followed by attachment of earnings if debtor defaults	Transfer to county court	Attachment of Earnings Act 1971, s 24 CCR Ord 27
(6) Debtor runs a business and debt exceeds £750	Statutory demand and bankruptcy petition	Insolvency Act 1986, ss 268–272	Out of London certain county courts have bankruptcy jurisdiction
(7) Debtor is a limited company and debt exceeds £750	Serve statutory demand and present petition to wind-up company	Insolvency Act 1986, ss 122–123	Where share capital does not exceed £120,000 Insolvency Act 1986, s 117(2)

EXECUTION AGAINST CHATTELS

The courts provide the means by which a judgment creditor can obtain the seizure and sale of chattels owned by the debtor so as to satisfy the judgment. Although in theory an effective remedy, in practice as we shall see the creditor may find this method of enforcement fails because the assets in question are the property of someone other than the debtor.

Example. D, an allegedly impecunious plumber against whom judgment for £6000 has been entered, runs a Jaguar motor car, has two colour television sets and a cabin cruiser.

The practice in respect of a High Court judgment[17] is that the creditor applies for a writ of fieri facias (fi fa) by delivering a formal request (praecipe) at the court together with office copies of the judgment and certificate for costs in the action, pays the appropriate fee and submits a copy of the writ of fi fa. The writ is then sealed and delivered to the under-sheriff of the county (bailiwick) where the assets are to be found. The form of writ is shown on p 353. It will be noted that the writ is a command to the sheriff to seize and sell sufficient of the debtor's goods to discharge his own costs and the judgment debt and costs. The writ is executed by the sheriff's officers.[18]

Section 15 of the Courts and Legal Services Act 1990 provides that the following goods are exempt from seizure:

(i)   such tools, books, vehicles and other items of equipment as are necessary to the defendant for use personally or in his job or business;

(ii) such clothing, bedding, furniture, household equipment and provisions as are necessary for satisfying the basic domestic needs of the defendant and his family.

The Lord Chancellor's Department, has issued the following guidance to bailiffs[19] (which would seem to be equally applicable to execution by the sheriff's officers):

'Necessary items
An item should be regarded as necessary if it is so essential that without it there would be no way a defendant could continue his/her existing job or business.

Motor vehicles
It should be the exception rather than the rule that a defendant is allowed to retain a motor vehicle as a *necessary* item. It is for the defendant to satisfy the bailiff where it is claimed that a vehicle is necessary to allow him/her to continue his/her job or business. The fact that a defendant claims to need a vehicle to get to and from his/her place of work should not by itself be considered grounds to exempt the vehicle. The bailiff must be satisfied that no reasonable alternative is available.

Household items
Items such as stereo equipment, televisions, videos or microwave ovens where there is also a conventional cooker, are *not* considered to be necessary for satisfying the basic needs of the defendant and his/her family.'

A more important restriction in practice is that it may transpire that no goods worth seizing are found on the premises[20] or that goods apparently belonging to the debtor are claimed by someone else. In the example above it may be that the car and the cabin cruiser are being bought on hire purchase whilst the colour television sets may belong to rental companies. Clearly in such cases the property cannot be seized. What is the position

---

17 RSC Ord 46, r 6.
18 The officers may enter the debtor's house provided they do not break any outer doors. They do not have to remove the goods at once: instead they may enter into 'walking possession' of the goods in which case the debtor will sign an agreement that in consideration of the bailiff not removing the goods he will not dispose of the goods or permit them to be removed from the premises. See *Abingdon RDC v O'Gorman* [1968] 3 All ER 79 at 81.
19 Court Users Guide 1991, Appendix 3.
20 This is particularly the case where county court bailiffs are seeking to execute a warrant of execution; there is a substantial risk in such a case that the creditor will be faced with a 'nil return'.

Writ of
Fieri Facias
(O. 45, r. 12)

IN THE HIGH COURT OF JUSTICE   19 90 .— M .—**High Court No.** 2075

Queen's Bench **Division**   **County Court Plaint No.**

[(On transfer from   County Court)]

Between

Murdstone and Grinby (Blackfriars) Ltd   **Plaintiff**

AND

Wilkins Micawber   **Defendant**

ELIZABETH THE SECOND, by the Grace of God, of the United Kingdom of Great Britain, Northern Ireland and of Our other realms and territories Queen, Head of the Commonwealth, Defender of the Faith.

To the sheriff of the County of Kent   greeting:

Whereas in the above-named action it was on the   10th day of

(1) "adjudged" or "ordered".

November   , 19 92 (1)   in this Court [or in the
                                County Court under plaint No.   ]

(2) Name of Defendant.
(3) Name of Plaintiff.

that the Defendant (2) Wilkins Micawber

do pay the Plaintiff (3)   Murdstone and Grinby (Blackfriars) Limited

£ 14,000   [and £   [costs] [costs to be taxed, which costs have been taxed and allowed at £5,000   as appears by the certificate of the taxing officer dated the   15th   day of

April   1993]]:

WE COMMAND YOU that of the goods, chattels and other property of (2) the

said Wilkins Micawber

(4) The words in this set of square brackets are to be omitted where the judgment or order is for less than £600 and does not entitle the Plaintiff to costs against the person against whom the writ is issued.

in your county authorised by law to be seized in execution you cause to be made the sum[s] of £ 19,000   (4) [and £8.40   for costs of execution] and also interest on £4,000   at the rate of (5) £ 10 per cent per annum from the   10th   day of November   , 19 92 ,

(5) Insert the appropriate rate of interest at date of entry of judgment.

until payment (4) [together with sheriff's poundage, officers' fees, costs of levying and all other legal, incidental expenses] and that immediately after execution of this writ you pay (3) the said Murdstone and Grinby (Blackfriars) Limited

(6) "judgment" or "order".

in pursuance of the said (6)   judgment   the amount levied in respect of the said sum and interest.

AND WE ALSO COMMAND YOU that you indorse on this writ immediately after execution thereof a statement of the manner in which you have executed it and send a copy of the statement to (3) the said Murdstone and Grinby (Blackfriars) Limited

Witness   Rt Hon Lord Hailsham of St Marylebone

Lord High Chancellor of Great Britain,

the   20th day of September   , 19 93 .

where a claim is made by a third party to goods found in the debtor's possession but the judgment creditor insists the goods really belong to the debtor and so should be seized? In such a case the sheriff retains possession and issues an interpleader summons so that both claimants can be brought before the court which can determine their respective rights.[21] In the case of a claim by the debtor's wife the creditor is often well advised to dispute the claim because the assertion is easily made but often is untrue or incapable of proof.

Where the value of the goods exceeds £20 the sheriff must sell them by public auction unless either party applies to the court for an order permitting sale under private contract.[22] During this period the judgment debtor may apply by summons pursuant to Order 47, rule 1 to the court for an order staying the execution.

It can be seen from the illustration above that execution against goods may not be an effective remedy. However, there is one case where the issue of a writ of fi fa is likely to be very effective; that is when the writ is issued against a person running a business. The reason is that the service of such a writ carries with it the possibility of subsequent bankruptcy: section 26 of the Insolvency Act 1986 provides that a debtor is deemed unable to pay his debts if execution issued in respect of a judgment debt has been returned unsatisfied in whole or in part.

The rules above stated apply equally to the enforcement by the county court of a warrant of execution.[23] However, it is unlikely that the county court machinery will be used for execution against goods. Where the amount of the judgment debt is £5000 or more execution against goods must be by the High Court writ of fi fa (*even though the judgment was entered in county court proceedings*).[24] If the amount is less than £2000 the judgment creditor has to use the county court procedure whereby a warrant of execution is enforced by the bailiffs.[25] In practice, whilst the sheriff's officers enforce a High Court writ with considerable vigour, the County Court bailiffs tend to be less efficient so that it is likely that enforcement of judgments of £2000 or more but less than £5000 will be enforced in the High Court (although there is a concurrent county court jurisdiction).

CHARGING ORDER ON LAND OR SECURITIES

The High Court and, where the judgment debt does not exceed £5000, the county courts are given power under the Charging Orders Act 1979 to impose a charge on any freehold or leasehold land owned by a judgment debtor so as to provide security for payment of the judgment debt. This can be a very effective remedy but before it can be employed the creditor has to obtain prima facie proof of the ownership of the land in question. Since 1990 the Land Register has been open to the public and the authority of the registered proprietor has not been required for a search. The application for a search is made on LR Form 109 – see SI 1990/1361. The creditor applies[26]

21 RSC Ord 17, see p 199, ante.
22 See RSC Ord 47, r 6 and County Court Act 1984, ss 97, 98.
23 The judgment creditors produce the plaint note and an application for a warrant: see County Courts Act 1984, s 85 and CCR Ord 26, r 1 and Forms N42(C) and N323. No sale is allowed until 5 days have elapsed from the date of seizure: County Courts Act 1984, s 93.
24 High Court and County Courts Jurisdiction Order 1991, art 8(1)(a).
25 Ibid, art 8(1)(b).
26 RSC Ord 50, r 1.

ex parte by affidavit setting out the amount of the judgment unpaid, the name of the judgment debtor and any creditor the applicant can identify, the land proposed to be charged and verifying that the land is beneficially owned by the debtor.[27] The master will make an *order nisi*, i e an order that the land is to stand charged until the hearing on notice of the application. The effect of the order is that the creditor may register the charge[28] (or in the case of registered land, lodge a caution[29]) so that any person dealing with the land thereafter can only take subject to the creditor's rights to enforce his security. In very urgent cases where it is thought that the debtor might attempt to dispose of the land before registration, the master may grant an injunction restraining dealings with the land. Once the order is made a copy stating the date and time of further consideration of the matter must be served on the debtor. Generally this order must be served at least 7 days before the appointment. At the subsequent hearing the master 'shall either make the order absolute, with or without modifications, or discharge it'.[30]

Section 1(5) of the Land Charges Act provides that:

'. . . in deciding whether to make a charging order the Court shall consider all the circumstances of the case, and, in particular any evidence before it as to –
   (a) the personal circumstances of the debtor, and
   (b) whether any other creditor of the debtor would be likely to be unduly prejudiced by the making of the order.'

In *Roberts Petroleum Ltd v Bernard Kenny Ltd*[31] Lord Brandon set out the principles to be applied by the court:

'(1) The question whether a charging order nisi should not be made absolute is one for the discretion of the court.
 (2) The burden of showing cause why a charging order should not be made absolute is on the judgment debtor.
 (3) For the purpose of the exercise of the court's discretion there is, in general at any rate, no material difference between the making absolute of a charging order nisi on the one hand and a garnishee order nisi on the other.
 (4) In exercising its discretion the court has both the right and duty to take into account all the circumstances of any particular case, whether such circumstances arose before or after the making of the order nisi.
 (5) The court should so exercise its discretion as to equity, so far as possible, to all the various parties involved, that is to say the judgment debtor, the judgment creditor and all other unsecured creditors.'

An order will not be made absolute if it transpires that the judgment debtor is insolvent *and* that a scheme of arrangement has been entered into by the main body of creditors which has a reasonable prospect of success.[32] Again where a resolution for winding up a company or a winding-up order is made after the charging order nisi but before the hearing of the application to make it absolute, a charging order should *not* be made.[33]

---

27 If the debtor is a joint tenant, e g he owns the house jointly with his wife, the order will charge his interest under the trust for sale.
28 Land Charges Act 1972, s 6.
29 Land Registration Act 1925, s 59(3).
30 RSC Ord 50, r 3(1). Note, however, that the burden of showing cause why a charging order *nisi* should not be made absolute is on the judgment debtor: see *Supreme Court Practice 1993* para 50/1–9/10.
31 [1982] 1 All ER 685, CA; [1983] 2 AC 192, [1983] 1 All ER 564, HL.
32 See *Rainbow v Moorgate Properties Ltd* [1975] 2 All ER 821, [1975] 1 WLR 788, CA.
33 *Roberts Petroleum Ltd v Bernard Kenny Ltd* [1983] 2 AC 192, [1983] 1 All ER 564, HL.

The effect of such an order when registered is that it inhibits any dealings with the property by the debtor. This in itself may be sufficient incentive to the debtor to pay off the debt. It must however be noted that:

(a) If the debtor becomes bankrupt the creditor is secured. This is because once a charging order is made, execution against the land is deemed to have been completed.

(b) If the creditor wishes to enforce the charge he must apply for an order for sale under RSC Order 88 (or CCR Ord 31, r 4) as if he was a mortgagee of the land. Presumably the court hearing an application under RSC Order 88 for sale of a house will consider the wide powers granted to it under section 36(2) of the Administration of Justice Act 1970 to adjourn the proceedings or stay or suspend its order if it appears that the debtor is likely within a reasonable time to pay any of the sum secured by the charge.

It may be convenient to set out these complex provisions in summary form:

(1) Creditor (C) files an affidavit ex parte asking for (*a*) charging order and possibly (*b*) injunction.

(2) Order nisi. Register at once. Serve order.

(3) Appointment for further consideration. Order absolute.

(4) Subsequently C can apply for an order for sale.

The procedure in the county court is effectively the same save that there is no order nisi stage: see CCR Order 31. The procedure in respect of securities (i e stocks and shares) which is substantially the same is set out in RSC Order 50 and CCR Order 31. As to the procedure in respect of charging a partner's interest in partnership property and profits – see RSC Order 81, rule 10.

Example. Murdstone and Grinby Ltd obtain judgment for £2000 against Micawber. They issue a writ of fi fa but the sheriff is unable to seize any goods worth selling. They now learn that Micawber owns a house in Canterbury. It appears that he is about to sell the house in order to stave off his creditors who are threatening to serve a bankruptcy notice. We set out opposite the form of affidavit which could be used on an ex parte application to impose a charge on the land and for an injunction to restrain the sale.

In the High Court of Justice   1990-M-No.2075

Queen's Bench Division

       Between

Murdstone and Grinby
(Blackfriars)Limited   Plaintiffs
and
Wilkins Micawber   Defendant

I, Samuel Jackson of 236 City Road, London EC1, a clerk in the employ of Dodson and
Fogg, Freeman's Court, Cornhill, London EC3, Solicitors for the Plaintiffs therein,
make oath and say as follows:

(1) Subject to the supervision of my principals, I have the conduct of this
action on behalf of the Plaintiffs.

(2) On the 10th day of November 1992 it was adjudged by this Honourable
Court that the Defendant do pay the Plaintiffs the sum of £14000 and
costs to be taxed, which costs have been taxed and allowed at £5000 as
appears by the certificate of the taxing officer dated the 15th day of April
1993. The said judgment remains wholly unsatisfied.

(3) The above named Plaintiff is entitled to enforce the judgment.

(4) On the 20th day of September 1993 the Plaintiffs sued out a writ of fieri
facias directed to the Sheriff of the County of Kent for having execution of
the said judgment. From a copy of the indorsement made by the Sheriff on
the said writ, showing the manner in which he executed it, dated the 12th
day of October 1993 and now produced and shown to me marked 'S.J.1' it
appears that the Defendant has no property available for execution under
the said writ.

(5) Upon his oral examination in these proceedings the defendant admitted that
he was the owner of the freehold interest in the house and premises
situated at 26 St. Alphege's Lane, Canterbury in the County of Kent. I
have caused a search to be made in HM Land Registry against the title
number of the said premises and such search revealed a charge against the
said property in the name of Friendly Homes Building Society to secure
the sum of £5000. A copy of the said entry is now produced and shown to
me marked 'S.J.2'.

(6) I am informed by Mr Edward Murdstone a director of the Plaintiff
Company and verily believed to be true that the Defendant has already
instructed estate agents to offer the said premises for sale and that unless
he is restrained from so doing by order of his Honourable Court intends to
sell or otherwise dispose of the said premises so that the Plaintiffs lose
the benefit of their judgment herein.

(7) At the date hereof the Plaintiff is, I am informed by him, unaware of any
other creditors of the Defendant save for the said Building Society.

(8) In the circumstances, I respectfully request that an order be made
imposing a charge on the said house and premises of the judgment debtor
and that an injunction do issue meanwhile restraining the Defendant by
himself, his servants or agents, howsoever, from selling or otherwise
disposing of the said house and premises.

Sworn etc.

GARNISHEE ORDERS

Suppose the judgment creditor knows that the judgment debtor is owed money by a third party; in such a case it is obviously an effective method of execution to obtain an order from the court diverting the payment from the judgment debtor to the judgment creditor. This process is known as *attachment* and the order is known as a *garnishee order*. It is most commonly used in order to obtain money standing to the credit of a debtor in his bank account.[34] It can also be a very effective means of execution where the creditor knows that a solicitor is holding monies in a client account for the debtor, eg upon the sale of a house.

The procedure followed in the High Court can be summarised as follows:

(1) The creditor applies ex parte by affidavit for an order addressed to the third party (called a garnishee) forbidding him from paying the debt over to the judgment debtor and requiring him to attend before the master to show cause why the monies should not be paid to the judgment creditor. This order is called a *garnishee order nisi*. The application is made ex parte to prevent the debtor having the time to obtain payment to himself and thus frustrate the procedure.

(2) The order is drawn up (see form at end of this section) and served on the garnishee and on the judgment debtor at least 7 days before the time appointed for the further consideration of the matter.

(3) At the hearing if the court is satisfied that the garnishee is indebted to the judgment debtor and no other persons have prior claims to the monies, it will order the garnishee to pay over the debt to the judgment creditor. This is called a *garnishee order absolute*.[35]

A similar procedure is available in the county court for the enforcement of both county court and High Court judgments.[36]

We conclude this section by setting out (*a*) the form of order which is drawn up by the creditor's solicitors once the order nisi has been made and (*b*) the form or order when the order is made absolute:

(a) Order nisi

In the High Court of Justice   1993 M No 2075
Queen's Bench Division

Master Cooper in Chambers
    Between:

Murdstone and Grinby (Blackfriars) Ltd	Judgment Creditors
and	
Wilkins Micawber	Judgment Debtor
and	
Midland Bank Limited	Garnishee

---

34 It will be remembered that a bank is in the position of debtor to its customers who are in credit. Garnishee orders can be made in respect of deposit accounts, post office accounts, trustee savings bank accounts and building society accounts (Supreme Court Act 1981, s 40); orders can also be made in respect of National Savings Accounts (Crown Proceedings Act 1947, s 27 and Supreme Court Act 1981, s 139).

35 The practice described above is set out in RSC Ord 49.

36 The procedure is set out in CCR Ord 30.

Upon reading the affidavit of Benjamin Wickes filed on the 16th day of February 1993

IT IS ORDERED by Master Cooper that all debts due or accruing from the above mentioned garnishee to the above mentioned judgment debtor (in the sum of £19,000) be attached to answer a judgment recovered against the said judgment debtor by the above-named judgment creditor in the High Court of Justice on the 10th day of November 1992, for the sum of £14,000 debt and £5000 costs (together with the costs of the garnishee proceedings) on which judgment the sum of £19,000 remains due and unpaid.

AND IT IS FURTHER ORDERED that the said garnishee attend Master Cooper in Chambers in Room No E102, Central Office, Royal Courts of Justice, Strand, London on Monday the 8th day of March 1993 at half past 10 o'clock in the forenoon, on an application by the said judgment creditor that the said garnishee do pay the said sum to the said judgment debtor, or so much thereof as may be sufficient to satisfy the said judgment, together with the costs of the garnishee proceedings.

DATED the 17th day of February 1993

To the above-named Garnishee

And to the Judgment Debtor

(b) Order absolute

(Title as above)

Upon hearing the solicitors for the judgment creditor and garnishee and upon hearing the judgment debtor in person, and upon reading the affidavit of Benjamin Wickes filed herein and the order to show cause herein dated the 17th day of February 1993, whereby it was ordered that all debts owing or accruing due from the above-named garnishee to the above-named judgment debtor should be attached to answer a judgment recovered against the said judgment debtor by the above-named judgment creditor in the High Court of Justice on the 10th day of November 1992 for the sum of £14,000 debt and £5000 costs (together with the costs of the garnishee proceedings) on which judgment the sum of £19,000 remained due and unpaid.

IT IS ORDERED that the said garnishee (after deducting therefrom £40 for his costs of this application) do forthwith pay[37] to the said judgment creditor £3206 the debt due from the said garnishee to the said judgment debtor. And that the sum of £79.50 the costs of the judgment creditor of this application be added to the judgment debt and be retained out of the money recovered by the said judgment creditor under this order and in priority to the amount of the judgment debt.

Dated the 8th day of March 1993.

EQUITABLE EXECUTION

A receiver may be appointed by way of equitable execution where the debtor will be in receipt of income which cannot conveniently be attached by the usual methods of execution (eg where he receives rent from tenants), so that it is necessary that an independent person collects the income.

Since this is an expensive mode of execution the remedy is discretionary and the court is expressly required 'in determining whether it is just and convenient that the appointment should be made' to 'have regard to the amount claimed by the judgment creditor, to the amount likely to be

---

37 If the garnishee's debt exceeds the judgment debt the order runs '£   being so much of the debt due . . . as is sufficient to satisfy the judgment debt. . . .'

obtained by the receiver, and to the probable costs of his appointment and may direct any inquiry on any of these matters or any other matter before making the appointment'.[38]

The practice is for the creditor to apply by summons or motion for the appointment of a suitable person as receiver. In urgent cases this may be done ex parte.[39] In all cases an affidavit is required setting out the judgment debtor's interest in the property and the fitness of the proposed receiver. It should also show that the creditor has taken all other convenient steps to execute the judgment without success. If the receiver is appointed the court will normally require him to give security for the proper execution of his duties. We set out opposite the form of order drawn up in the High Court where the receiver is to receive income from land held by the debtor. Study this form carefully because it explains precisely how the receiver is to operate.

38 RSC Ord 51, r 1.
39 See RSC Ord 51, r 3 and RSC Ord 30, r 1; CCR Ord 32, r 1.

<u>In the High Court of Justice</u>   <u>1990-M-No.2075</u>
<u>Queen's Bench Division</u>
Master Cooper in Chambers

    Between

Murdstone and Grinby (Blackfriars) Limited	<u>Plaintiffs</u>
and	
Wilkins Micawber	<u>Defendant</u>

Upon hearing the solicitors for the Plaintiffs and the Defendant in person
And upon reading the affidavit of Samuel Jackson sworn the 20th day of April 1993.
   IT IS ORDERED
   (1) that Septimus Wickfield of 30 High Street, Rochester, in the County of Kent, without giving security, be and is hereby appointed to receive the rent, profits and monies receivable in respect of the above-named Defendant's interest in the following premises, namely all that office block known as 25/30 Station Road, Rochester aforesaid.
   (2) that this appointment shall be without prejudice to the rights of any prior incumbrancers upon the said property who may think proper to take possession of or receive the same by virtue of their respective securities or, if any prior incumbrancer is in possession, then without prejudice to such possession.
   (3) That the tenants of premises comprised in the said property do attorn and pay their rents in arrear and growing rents to the receiver.
   (4) That the receiver have liberty, if he shall think proper (but not otherwise), out of the rents, profits and monies to be received by him to keep down the interest upon the prior incumbrances, according to their priorities, and be allowed such payments, if any, in passing his accounts.
   (5) That the receiver shall on the 9th day of September 1993 and at such further and other times as may be ordered by the Master submit his accounts and shall pay into Court the balance or balances appearing due on the accounts so left, or such part thereof as shall be certified as proper to be paid, such sums to be paid in or towards satisfaction of what shall for the time being be due in respect of the judgment given on the 10th day of November 1992 for the sum of £14000 and £5000 costs, making together the sum of £19000.
   AND that the costs of the receiver (including his remuneration) the costs of obtaining his appointment, of completing his security, of passing his accounts and of obtaining his discharge shall not exceed 10 per cent of the amount due under the said judgment or the amount recovered by the receiver, whichever is the less, provided that not less than £500 be allowed unless otherwise ordered. Such costs shall be taxed unless assessed by the Master and shall be primarily payable out of the sums received by the receiver, but if there shall be no sums received or the amount shall be insufficient, then upon the certificate of the Master being given stating the amount of the deficiency, the amount of the deficiency so certified shall be paid by the Defendant to the Plaintiff.
   IT IS ALSO ORDERED that the balance (if any) remaining in the hands of the receiver, after making the several payments aforesaid, shall unless otherwise directed by the Master forthwith be paid by the receiver into court to the credit of this action, subject to further order.
   AND that any of the parties be at liberty to apply to the Master in Chambers as there may be occasion.

Dated the 9th day of June 1993.

ATTACHMENT OF EARNINGS ORDERS

Where a debtor has a regular job but no substantial assets the court will normally order him to pay the judgment debt by weekly or monthly instalments appropriate to his means and liabilities. What happens if he defaults? Formerly the practice was to apply for an order committing him to prison (usually suspended on terms that he paid the remainder of the debt and the arrears by instalments). This procedure has now for all practical purposes been abolished and instead the judgment creditor will apply to the county court for the district in which the debtor resides for an *attachment of earnings order*.[40] Only the debtor's local county court has power to make such an order but that court has power to enforce judgments given in the High Court[41] or any other county court. It is important to note that before an order will be made two conditions must be satisfied:

(1) The debtor must have defaulted in one or more instalments under a judgment ordered to be paid by such instalments.
(2) The debtor must be in employment. This covers the man who regularly subcontracts his labour to one employer (eg lump workers on building sites) but does not cover the man who regularly hires his services to different persons.

The making of an attachment of earnings order is governed by CCR Order 27 which prescribes that the following procedure should be followed:–

(i) The creditor files a request for an attachment of earnings order: see Form N 337 below. He fills in details of the debt and (if known) the name and address of the employers. The creditor or his solicitor must certify that the whole or part of the instalments due have not been paid and set out the balance outstanding.
(ii) The court staff then issue a Notice of Application which is sent to the debtor together with a reply form (embodying a statement of means) which he must complete and return to the court office within 8 days. The Form (N56) is set out at page 364, below. Note the debtor is expressly told that he may apply for a suspended order – i e an order whereby, provided he makes regular payments, his employers will not be contacted.
(iii) Once the reply is received, the court clerk responsible for dealing with attachment of earnings may make an attachment order and at the same time a further order suspending the attachment order. There is no hearing and none of the parties attend court. Notice of the order made is sent to the creditor and debtor; if either of them is not satisfied they may ask for the matter to be referred to the district judge. If the court staff are not satisfied that they have adequate information to make an order, they will send notice to both parties of a date when the application will be heard before the district judge.
(iv) If the debtor fails to comply with a suspended order the creditor can

---

40 Attachment of Earnings Act 1971, s 1; CCR Ord 27.
41 The High Court has no power to make such an order in civil actions as opposed to matrimonial disputes.

N. 337

Request for Attachment of Earnings Order

Order 27, rule 4(1)

[As substituted 1991]

Request for Attachment of Earnings Order

To be completed and signed by the plaintiff or his solicitor and sent to the court with the appropriate fee.

1. Plaintiff's name and address

In the

County Court

Case Number.

2. Name and address for service and payment (if different from above) **Ref/Tel No.**

For court use only

A/E Application no.

Issue date:

Hearing date

on

at   o'clock

at (address)

3. Defendant's name and address

4. Judgment Details:

Court where judgment/order made if not court of issue

I apply for an attachment of earnings order

5. Outstanding debt

Balance due at date of this request* (excluding issue fee but including unsatisfied warrant costs)
*you may also be entitled to interest to date of request where judgment is for over £5000 and is entered on or after 1 July 1991

I certify that the whole or part of any instalments due under the judgment or order have not been paid and the balance now due is as shown.

Signed

Plaintiff (Plaintiff's solicitor)

Issue fee

AMOUNT NOW DUE

Dated

6. Employment Details:
(*Please give as much information as you can— it will help the court to make an order more quickly*)

7. Other details
(*Give any other details about the defendant's circumstances which may be relevant to the application*)

Employer's name and address

Defendant's place of work (*if different from employer's address*)

IMPORTANT
You must inform the court immediately of any payments you receive after you have sent this request to the court.

The defendant is employed as

Works No./Pay Ref.

N. 56

Form for Replying to an Attachment of Earnings application (Statement of means)

Order 27, rule 5(1)

[As amended 1991]

Form for Replying to an Attachment of Earnings Application

- Read the notes on the notice of application before completing this form.
- Tick the correct boxes and give as much information as you can . The court will make an order based on the information you give on this form. You must give full details of your employment and your income and outgoings. Enclose a copy of your most recent pay slip if you can.
- *Make your offer of payment in box 10. You will get some idea of how much to offer by adding up your expenses in boxes 6, 7, 8 and 9 and taking them from your total income (box 5).*
- Send or take this completed and signed form immediately to the court office shown on the notice of application.
- You should keep your copy of the notice of application unless you are making full payment. (This does not apply to maintenance applications).
- For details of where and how to pay see the notice of application.

In the   **County Court**

Case Number   *Always quote this*

Application number

Plaintiff *(including ref.)*

Defendant

1 Personal details

Surname

Forenames

☐ Mr ☐ Mrs ☐ Miss ☐ Ms

☐ Married ☐ Single ☐ Other *(specify)*.

Age

Address

Postcode

2 Dependants *(people you look after financially)*

Number of children in each age group

under 11 ☐ 11–15 ☐ 16–17 ☐

18 & over ☐

Other dependants *(give details)*

3 Employment

I am ☐ employed as a

☐ self employed as a

☐ unemployed

☐ a pensioner

a. employment

My employer is

Employer's address

Address of employer's head office *(if different from above)*

My works number and/or pay reference is

Jobs other than main job *(give details)*

b. self employment

Length of time self employed   year   months

c. unemployment

Length of time unemployed   years   months

Give details of any outstanding interviews

4 Bank account and savings

☐ I have a bank account

   ☐ The account is in credit by .. £ :

   ☐ The account is overdrawn by £ :

☐ I have a savings or building society account

   The amount in the account is .. £ :

5 Income

My usual take home pay (*including overtime, commission, bonuses etc*)	£	: per
My husband's or wife's usual take home pay	£	: per
Income support	£	: per
Child benefit(s)	£	: per
Other state benefit(s)	£	: per
My pension(s)	£	: per
Others living in my home give me	£	: per
Other income (*give details below*)	£	:per
	£	: per
	£	: per
	£	: per
Total income	£	: per

6 Expenses

(*Do not include any payments made by other members of the household out of their own income*)

I have regular expenses as follows:

Mortgage (*including second mortgage*)	£	: per
Rent	£	: per
Community charge	£	: per
Gas	£	: per
Electricity	£	: per
Water charges	£	: per
TV rental and licence	£	: per
HP repayments	£	: per
Mail order	£	: per
Housekeeping, food, school meals	£	: per
Travelling expenses	£	: per
Children's clothing	£	: per
Maintenance payments	£	: per
Others (*not court orders or credit debts listed in boxes 8 and 9*)		
	£	: per
	£	: per
	£	: per
Total expenses	£	: per

7 Priority debts (*This section is for arrears only. Do not include regular expenses listed in box 6.*)

Rent arrears	£	: per
Mortgage arrears	£	: per
Community charge arrears	£	: per
Water charges arrears	£	: per
Fuel debts: Gas	£	: per
Electricity	£	: per
Other	£	: per
Maintenance arrears	£	: per
Others (*give details below*)		
	£	: per
	£	: per
Total priority debts	£	: per

8 Court orders

Court	Case No.	£	: per
Total court order instalments		£	: per

Of the payments above, I am behind with payments to (*please list*)

9 Credit debts

Loans and credit card debts (*please list*)

	£	: per
	£	: per
	£	: per

Of the payments above, I am behind with payments to (*please list*)

10 Offer of Payment

I offer to have £ _____ week/month from my pay _____ deducted

● If you want an opportunity to pay voluntarily without your employer being ordered to make deductions from your pay you should ask for a suspended order. Tick the box below and give your reasons.

☐ I would like a suspended order because

11 Declaration   I declare that the details I have given above are true to the best of my knowledge

Signed _____   Dated _____

apply for the court to send notice of the attachment of earnings order without further notice to the debtor's employers.

It should be noted that very frequently a debtor will fail to return a completed statement of means. The court then issues a notice requiring him to attend court and show cause why he should not be committed to prison for his failure to comply with the directions of the court. In practice such debtors very seldom go to prison; the court will invariably persuade them at the hearing of the good sense of completing the reply. It should be noted also that if the reply is inadequate the court may at once send an order to the employers requiring them to provide information as to salary and other income.

In making an attachment of earnings order the court has to determine:

(i)   *A normal deduction rate* – i e the rate at which the court thinks the debtor's earnings should be used to satisfy the judgment.

(ii) *A protected earnings rate* – a man's income may well fluctuate from week to week according to the availability of overtime, short working, etc. In making the order the court sets a minimum sum necessary to provide for the debtor and his dependants and directs that the order is not to be applied so as to reduce his earnings below that level.

The order when made is addressed to the debtor's employer and requires him on penalty of fine to take all reasonable steps to ensure that the appropriate deduction is made from the debtor's wages and paid to the court. It should be noted that both the debtor and his employer are required to notify the court if his employment ceases. As stated above the order is frequently retained by the court and not served unless the debtor defaults in future payments.

BANKRUPTCY PROCEEDINGS

Bankruptcy is the process by which the court through a receiver takes over the debtor's property and supervises the distribution of his assets amongst his creditors. The primary purpose of the procedure is to ensure that every creditor shall receive a fair share of whatever is available for distribution. It might be thought that such proceedings would be very much a matter of last resort. In fact, since the consequences of bankruptcy proceedings is to stop a debtor carrying on his business, the procedure is often initiated as a very effective means of forcing a recalcitrant debtor to settle with his creditor. Indeed the procedure is so effective that when the judgment debtor is a tradesman or in business it is often quite pointless to employ the methods of execution discussed above because the threat of bankruptcy and the consequential closure of his business will inevitably induce him to pay up if he has funds available.

Although we need not attempt to consider the general law of bankruptcy, it is necessary to have a general knowledge of the use of bankruptcy as a method of execution. A bankruptcy petition can be filed if it can be shown that the debtor appears to be unable to pay a debt; this can be proved only by showing his failure to comply with a *statutory demand* or that execution has been attempted without success. Thus section 268 of the Insolvency Act 1986 provides:–

'. . . the debtor appears to be unable to pay a debt if, but only if, the debt is payable immediately and either –

(*a*) the petitioning creditor to whom the debt is owed has served on the debtor a demand (known as "the statutory demand") in the prescribed form requiring him to pay the debt or to secure or compound for it to the satisfaction of the creditor, at least 3 weeks have elapsed since the demand was served and the demand has been neither complied with nor set aside in accordance with the rules, or

(*b*) execution or other process issued in respect of the debt on a judgment or order of any court in favour of the petitioning creditor, or one or more of the petitioning creditors to whom the debt is owed, has been returned unsatisfied in whole or part.'

The form of statutory demand (which can be purchased at a law stationers) is as set out on pp 368–370. (The form illustrated is that used where there is an existing judgment debt but note that a statutory demand in a slightly different form can be served where there have been no court proceedings; as such it is a substitute for issuing a writ and applying for summary judgment but it must only be used where the fact that there is a debt outstanding is clear beyond dispute.)

As indicated above the normal effect of a statutory demand is that if funds are available to the debtor the creditor will be paid. If payment is not forthcoming, the creditor will have to consider issuing a *bankruptcy petition*. A petition may be issued whenever the debt due to the petitioner exceeds the prescribed minimal level (currently £750). The petition will be presented at the High Court in cases where the debtor resides or carries on business in London; in other cases it will be presented at the appropriate county court having bankruptcy jurisdiction. The court will normally at this stage appoint the Official Receivers to protect the debtor's property prior to the hearing of the petition. Once the bankruptcy order is made the bankrupt must submit a *statement of affairs* to the Official Receiver. The statement is in a prescribed form designed to show details of all other creditors and of the assets held by the bankrupt. If the statement is unsatisfactory the Official Receiver may apply to the court for a *public examination* of the bankrupt at which he can be cross-examined as to his assets. The Official Receiver will normally call a *meeting of creditors* to decide on the appointment of a *trustee in bankruptcy* to be responsible for subsequent control over the bankrupt's property and distribution to the creditors.

WINDING-UP PROCEEDINGS

A limited company cannot be made bankrupt; however a creditor is entitled to petition the court for the company to be wound-up if it can be shown that the company is unable to pay its debts (section 122(1) of the Insolvency Act 1986). Just as in the case of personal insolvency, the Act provides for the service of a statutory demand as *one* of the means by which the solvency of the company can be tested. Section 123 reads as follows:–

'(1) A company is deemed unable to pay its debts –

(*a*) if a creditor (by assignment or otherwise) to whom the company is indebted in a sum exceeding £750 then due has served on the company, by leaving at the company's registered office, a written demand (in the prescribed form) requiring the company to pay the sum so due and the company has for 3 weeks thereafter neglected to pay the sum or to

Form 6.2

Statutory Demand
under section 268(1)(a)
of the Insolvency
Act 1986.
Debt for Liquidated
Sum Payable
Immediately
Following a Judgment
or Order of the Court
(Rule 6.7)

NOTES FOR CREDITOR
- If the Creditor is entitled to the debt by way of assignment, details of the original Creditor and any intermediary assignees should be given in part C on page 3.
- If the amount of debt includes interest not previously notified to the Debtor as included in the Debtor's liability, details should be given, including the grounds upon which interest is charged. The amount of interest must be shown separately.
- Any other charge accruing due from time to time may be claimed. The amount or rate of the charge must be identified and the grounds on which it is claimed must be stated.
- In either case the amount claimed must be limited to that which has accrued due at the date of the Demand.
- If the Creditor holds any security the amount of debt should be the sum the Creditor is prepared to regard as unsecured for the purposes of this Demand. Brief details of the total debt should be included and the nature of the security and the value put upon it by the Creditor, as at the date of the Demand, must be specified.
- Details of the judgment or order should be inserted, including details of the Division of the Court or District Registry and Court reference, where judgment is obtained in the High Court.
- If signatory of the Demand is a solicitor or other agent of the Creditor, the name of his/her firm should be given.

* Delete if signed by the Creditor himself.

WARNING

- This is an **important** document. You should refer to the notes entitled "How to comply with a Statutory Demand or have it set aside".
- If you wish to have this Demand set aside you must make application to do so **within 18 days** from its service on you.
- If you do not apply to set aside **within 18 days** or otherwise deal with this Demand as set out in the notes **within 21 days** after its service on you, you could be made bankrupt and your property and goods taken away from you.
- Please read the Demand and notes carefully. If you are in any doubt about your position you should seek advice **immediately** from a solicitor or your nearest Citizens Advice Bureau.

DEMAND

To   WILKINS MICAWBER

Address   103 Goswell Road
London EC2A 5BR

This Demand is served on you by the Creditor:

Name   MURDSTONE & GRINBY (BLACKFRIARS) LIMITED

Address   3 Puddle Dock
London EC4Y 2AR

The Creditor claims that you owe the sum of £ 19,000
full particulars of which are set out on page 2, and that it is payable immediately and, to the extent of the sum demanded, is unsecured.

By a Judgment /~~Order~~ of the High Court   dated 10th November 1992   /
~~County Court~~ in proceedings entitled
~~(Case)~~ Number 1990 M 2075   between   Murdstone and Grinby
(Blackfriars) Limited   **Plaintiff**
and Wilkins Micawber   **Defendant**
it was adjudged/~~ordered~~ that you pay to the Creditor the sum of £ 14,000
and £ 5,000   for costs.

The Creditor demands that you pay the above debt or secure or compound for it to the Creditor's satisfaction.

~~[The Creditor making this Demand is a Minister of the Crown or a Government Department, and it is intended to present a Bankruptcy Petition in the High Court in London.] [Delete if inappropriate].~~

Signature of individual   Francis Guppy (for Dodson and Fogg)

Name   DODSON AND FOGG
(BLOCK LETTERS)

Date   15th   day of   July   19 93 .

~~*Position with or relationship to Creditor:~~
*I am authorised to make this Demand on the Creditor's behalf.

Address   Freeman's Court
Cornhill
London EC3X 2YV

Tel. No. 071 621 1873   Ref. No. G/93/206

N.B. The person making this Demand must complete the whole of pages 1, 2 and parts A, B and C (as applicable) on page 3.

[P.T.O.

Particulars of Debt
(These particulars must include (a) when the debt was incurred (b) the consideration for the debt (or if there is no consideration the way in which it arose) and (c) the amount due as at the date of this demand).

On the 10th day of November 1992 it was adjuged that the Defendant do pay the Plaintifffs the sum of £14,000 and costs to be taxed which costs have been taxed and allowed at £5,000 as appears by the certificate of the taxing officer dated the 15th day of April 1993. The said judgment remains wholly unsatisfied.

NOTES FOR CREDITOR
- If the Creditor is entitled to the debt by way of assignment, details of the original Creditor and any intermediary assignees should be given in part C on page 3.
- If the amount of debt includes interest not previously notified to the Debtor as included in the Debtor's liability, details should be given, including the grounds upon which interest is charged. The amount of interest must be shown separately.
- Any other charge accruing due from time to time may be claimed. The amount or rate of the charge must be identified and the grounds on which it is claimed must be stated.
- In either case the amount claimed must be limited to that which has accrued due at the date of the Demand.
- If the Creditor holds any security the amount of debt should be the sum the Creditor is prepared to regard as unsecured for the purposes of this Demand. Brief details of the total debt should be included and the nature of the security and the value put upon it by the Creditor, as at the date of the Demand, must be specified.
- If signatory is a solicitor or other agent of the Creditor, the name of his/her firm should be given.

Note:
If space is insufficient continue on page 4 and clearly indicate on this page that you are doing so.

2

Part A

Appropriate Court for Setting Aside Demand

Rule 6.4(2) of the Insolvency Rules 1986 states that the appropriate Court is the Court to which you would have to present your own Bankruptcy Petition in accordance with Rule 6.40(1) and 6.40(2).

Any application by you to set aside this Demand should be made to that Court, or, if this Demand is issued by a Minister of the Crown or a Government Department, you must apply to the High Court to set aside if it is intended to present a Bankruptcy Petition against you in the High Court (see page 1).

In accordance with those rules on present information the appropriate Court is [the High Court of Justice] [~~County Court~~]
(address)

Thomas More Buildings, Royal Courts of Justice, Strand, London WC2A 2LL

Part B

The individual or individuals to whom any communication regarding this Demand may be addressed is/are:

Name .... ~~Dodson and Fogg (solicitors)~~
(BLOCK LETTERS)

Address .... Freeman's Court
                  Cornhill

                  London EC3X 2YV

Telephone Number 071 621 1873

Reference G/93/206

Part C

For completion if the Creditor is entitled to the debt by way of assignment.

	Name	Date(s) of Assignment
Original Creditor		
Assignees	N/A	

How to comply with a Statutory Demand or have it set aside (ACT WITHIN 18 DAYS)

If you wish to avoid a Bankruptcy Petition being presented against you, you must pay the debt shown on page 1, particulars of which are set out on page 2 of this notice, within the period of **21 days** after its service upon you. However, if the Demand follows (includes) a Judgment or Order of a County Court, any payment must be made to that County Court (quoting the Case No.). Alternatively, you can attempt to come to a settlement with the Creditor. To do this you should:

• inform the individual (or one of the individuals) named in Part B above immediately that you are willing and able to offer security for the debt to the Creditor's satisfaction; *or*
• inform the individual (or one of the individuals) named in Part B above immediately that you are willing and able to compound for the debt to the Creditor's satisfaction.

If you dispute the Demand in whole or in part you should:
• contact the individual (or one of the individuals) named in Part B immediately.

If you consider that you have grounds to have this Demand set aside or if you do not quickly receive a satisfactory written reply from the individual named in Part B whom you have contacted you should **apply within 18 days** from the date of service of this Demand on you to the appropriate Court shown in Part A above to have the Demand set aside.

Any application to set aside the Demand (Form 6.4 in Schedule 4 of the Insolvency Rules 1986) should be made within 18 days from the date of service upon you and be supported by an Affidavit (Form 6.5 in Schedule 4 to those Rules) stating the grounds on which the Demand should be set aside. The forms may be obtained from the appropriate Court when you attend to make the application.

> **Remember:** From the date of service on you of this document:
> (a) you have only **18 days** to apply to the Court to have the Demand set aside, and
> (b) you have only **21 days** before the Creditor may present a Bankruptcy Petition.

3

secure or compound for it to the reasonable satisfaction of the creditor, or

(b) if, in England and Wales, execution or other process issued on a judgment decree or order of any court in favour of a creditor of the company is returned unsatisfied in whole or in part, or [paras (c) and (d) relate to Scotland and Northern Ireland]

(e) if it is proved to the satisfaction of the court that the company is unable to pay its debts as they fall due.

(2) A company is also deemed unable to pay its debts if it is proved to the satisfaction of the court that the value of the company's assets is less than the amount of its liabilities, taking into account its contingent and prospective liabilities.'

It will be appreciated that just as in the case of personal insolvency, the statutory demand may be used:

(i) as an alternative to the issue of execution under a judgment debt (eg instead of a writ of fi fa);

(ii) as an alternative to proceedings for recovery of the debt (eg instead of issue of a writ).

It should be noted that the statutory demand must not be used as an alternative to proceedings where the creditor knows there are issues to be tried. If a company is served with a statutory demand in respect of a disputed debt it should inform the creditors' representatives at once and, if they are not prepared to withdraw the notice, it should apply to the Companies Court for an injunction to restrain the issue of a winding-up petition. In *Re a Company (No 0012209 of 1991)*[42] Hoffmann J said at 800:

'It does seem to me that a tendency has developed, possibly since the decision in *Cornhill Insurance plc v Improvement Services Ltd* [1986] 1 WLR 114, to present petitions against solvent companies as a way of putting pressure upon them to make payments of money which is bona fide disputed rather than to invoke the procedures which the rules provide for summary judgment. I do not for a moment wish to detract from anything which was said in the *Cornhill Insurance* case, which indeed followed earlier authority, to the effect that a refusal to pay an indisputable debt is evidence from which the inference may be drawn that the debtor is unable to pay. It was, however, a somewhat unusual case in which it was quite clear that the company in question had no grounds at all for its refusal. Equally it seems to me that if the court comes to the conclusion that a solvent company is not putting forward any defence in good faith and is merely seeking to take for itself credit which it is not allowed under the contract, then the court would not be inclined to restrain presentation of the petition. But, if, as in this case, it appears that the defence has a prospect of success and the company is solvent, then I think that the court should give the company the benefit of the doubt and not do anything which would encourage the use of the Companies Court as an alternative to the RSC Ord 14 procedure.

For those reasons the injunction will go. The basis upon which the injunction is granted is that the [use of a statutory demand] is an abuse of the process of the court. I think that it should be made clear that abuse of the petition procedure in these circumstances is a high risk strategy, and consequently I think the appropriate order is that the petitioner should pay the applicant's costs on an indemnity basis.

If a company fails to comply with a statutory demand properly made (eg where a judgment debt remains unpaid) then the creditor will present a winding-up petition.

42 [1992] 2 All ER 797, Ch D.

The petition is presented by delivering two copies for sealing by a Registrar of the Companies Court. The petition is stamped with a notice stating the time, date and place for the hearing of the petition. An affidavit verifying the petition must be lodged at court. A typical petition is set out on p 373.

Once the petition has been presented, the petitioner must then take the following steps:

(1) Serve the petition at the company's registered office and swear and file at court an affidavit of service.
(2) Cause notice of the petition and the date of hearing and the rights of creditors and contributories to oppose or support the petition to be advertised in the *London Gazette*. The advertisement must appear not less than seven business days before the hearing and not less than seven business days after service.

Before the petition is heard the petitioner must file a certificate at court showing compliance with the rules and a copy of the advertisement.

Any creditor or contributory of the company is entitled to require a copy of the petition from the petitioner. If he desires to appear in support of the proposed order or to oppose it he *must* give notice of his intention to the petitioner and may file an affidavit setting out his reasons. Notice of intention to appear must be served (or posted to reach the petitioner by ordinary post) not later than 4 pm on the day prior to the hearing. The petitioner immediately before the hearing must provide the court with a list showing in prescribed form in columns the following information in respect of each person who has given notice:

(1) his name;
(2) his address;
(3) the name and address of his solicitor;
(4) the amount of debt if he is a creditor;
(5) the number of his shares if he is a contributory;
(6) whether he is opposing or supporting the petition.

If no one has given notice of intention to appear then a form is put in to that effect and the court is told the list is 'negative'.

The effect of a winding-up petition will be to stimulate the debtor into action and frequently the petitioning creditor will agree to an adjournment to see whether funds will be forthcoming. If the debt cannot be paid however then normally the petitioner is entitled to have the company wound-up *ex debito justitiae*. The 'usual' order for costs is that the petitioner, the company, the creditors, and the contributories supporting the petition are given costs to be paid in the first instance out of the company's assets.

Note the procedure set out above is prescribed by Part 4 of the Insolvency Rules 1986.

OTHER METHODS OF ENFORCEMENT

We have discussed above the methods of enforcement applicable to money judgments. It should be remembered that:

(*a*) An order in the form of an injunction is enforced by committal (which is discussed at p 185, *ante*). Such an order can also be enforced

In the High Court of Justice   No 5761 of 1993
Chancery Division
Companies Court

In the Matter of:

West Middlesex Salvage Company Limited

and

In the Matter of the Insolvency Act 1986

To Her Majesty's High Court of Justice
The Petition of OliverTwist of 25 Acacia Gardens, Ealing, London, W5 shows that:

(1) West Middlesex Salvage Company Limited was incorporated on the 20th day of September 1968 under the Companies Act 1948.

(2) The registered office of the Company is at 20 Uxbridge Road, Southall.

(3) The nominal capital of the Company is £100 divided into 100 Ordinary Shares of £1.00 each. The amount of capital paid up or credited as paid up is £98.00p.

(4) The principal objects for which the Company was established are as follows: To carry on the business of salvage and waste paper merchants and other objects stated in the memorandum of association of the Company.

(5) The Company is indebted to the Petitioner in the sum of £75795.21p being as to £65000.00p the amount of a final judgment obtained by the Petitioner against the Company in the High Court of Justice, Queen's Bench Division on 28th May 1993 and as to £10795.21p the costs of obtaining the said judgment, the brief record whereof is 1991 T.No.1465. The judgment debt is in respect of damages awarded to the Petitioner for personal injury sustained by him in the course of his employment.

(6) On 5th August 1993 the Petitioner issued a write of fi.fa. upon the judgment directed to the Sheriff of the County of Middlesex but the Sheriff has returned the same wholly unsatisfied as the Company had no goods upon which execution could be levied.

(7) The Company is unable to pay its debts.

(8) In the circumstances it is just and equitable that the Company should be wound up.

The Petitioner therefore prays as follows:-
(1) That West Middlesex Salvage Company Limited may be wound up by the Court under the provisions of the Insolvency Act 1986 or
(2) that such other order may be made as the Court thinks fit.

Note: It is intended to serve this petition on West Middlesex Salvage Company Limited.

against rich and powerful bodies by writ of sequestration whereby commissioners are appointed to seize the defendants' assets until they have purged their contempt. Thus, for example, in 1973 the property of the AEU was made subject to such a writ by the National Industrial Relations Court for refusal to obey an order of the court.[43]

(*b*) Judgment for possession of land or the specific delivery of goods is enforced by the sheriff or county court bailiffs under writs or warrants of possession or specific delivery.[44]

---

43 *Eckman v Midland Bank Ltd* [1973] QB 519, [1973] 1 All ER 609.
44 See RSC Ord 45, r 3 and 4. CCR Ord 25, rr 16 and 17.

Statutes and Rules

The Civil Evidence Act 1968

Part I

HEARSAY EVIDENCE

1. Hearsay evidence to be admissible only by virtue of this Act and other statutory provisions, or by agreement

(1) In any civil proceedings a statement other than one made by a person while giving oral evidence in those proceedings shall be admissible as evidence of any fact stated therein to the extent that it is so admissible by virtue of any provision of this Part of this Act or by virtue of any other statutory provision or by agreement of the parties, but not otherwise.

(2) In this section 'statutory provision' means any provision contained in, or in an instrument made under, this or any other Act, including any Act passed after this Act.

2. Admissibility of out-of-court statements as evidence of facts stated

(1) In any civil proceedings a statement made, whether orally or in a document or otherwise, by any person, whether called as a witness in those proceedings or not, shall, subject to this section and to rules of court, be admissible as evidence of any fact stated therein of which direct oral evidence by him would be admissible.

(2) Where in any civil proceedings a party desiring to give a statement in evidence by virtue of this section has called or intends to call as a witness in the proceedings the person by whom the statement was made, the statement –

(a) shall not be given in evidence by virtue of this section on behalf of that party without the leave of the court; and

(b) without prejudice to paragraph (a) above, shall not be given in evidence by virtue of this section on behalf of that party before the conclusion of the examination-in-chief of the person by whom it was made, except –

(i) where before that person is called the court allows evidence of the making of the statement to be given on behalf of that party by some other person; or

(ii) in so far as the court allows the person by whom the statement was made to narrate it in the course of his examination-in-chief on the ground that to prevent him from doing so would adversely affect the intelligibility of his evidence.

(3) Where in any civil proceedings a statement which was made otherwise than in a document is admissible by virtue of this section, no evidence other than direct oral evidence by the person who made the statement or any person who heard or otherwise perceived it being made shall be admissible for the purpose of proving it:

Provided that if the statement in question was made by a person while giving oral evidence in some other legal proceedings (whether civil or criminal), it may be proved in any manner authorised by the court.

3. Witness's previous statement, if proved, to be evidence of facts stated

(1) Where in any civil proceedings –

(*a*) a previous inconsistent or contradictory statement made by a person called as a witness in those proceedings is proved by virtue of section 3, 4 or 5 of the Criminal Procedure Act 1865; or

(*b*) a previous statement made by a person called as aforesaid is proved for the purpose of rebutting a suggestion that his evidence has been fabricated,

that statement shall by virtue of this subsection be admissible as evidence of any fact stated therein of which direct oral evidence by him would be admissible.

(2) Nothing in this Act shall affect any of the rules of law relating to the circumstances in which, where a person called as a witness in any civil proceedings is cross-examined on a document used by him to refresh his memory, that document may be made evidence in those proceedings; and where a document or any part of a document is received in evidence in any such proceedings by virtue of any such rule of law, any statement made in that document or part by the person using the document to refresh his memory shall by virtue of this subsection be admissible as evidence of any fact stated therein of which direct oral evidence by him would be admissible.

4. Admissibility of certain records as evidence of facts stated

(1) Without prejudice to section 5 of this Act, in any civil proceedings a statement contained in a document shall, subject to this section and to rules of court, be admissible as evidence of any fact stated therein of which direct oral evidence would be admissible, if the document is, or forms part of, a record compiled by a person acting under a duty from information which was supplied by a person (whether acting under a duty or not) who had, or may reasonably be supposed to have had, personal knowledge of the matters dealt with in that information and which, if not supplied by that person to the compiler of the record directly, was supplied by him to the compiler of the record indirectly through one or more intermediaries each acting under a duty.

(2) Where in any civil proceedings a party desiring to give a statement in evidence by virtue of this section has called or intends to call as a witness in the proceedings the person who originally supplied the information from which the record containing the statement was compiled, the statement –

(*a*) shall not be given in evidence by virtue of this section on behalf of that
party without the leave of the court; and

(*b*) without prejudice to paragraph (*a*) above, shall not without the leave
of the court be given in evidence by virtue of this section on behalf of
that party before the conclusion of the examination-in-chief of the
person who originally supplied the said information.

(3) Any reference in this section to a person acting under a duty includes
a reference to a person acting in the course of any trade, business, profession
or other occupation in which he is engaged or employed or for the purposes
of any paid or unpaid office held by him.

5. Admissibility of statements produced by computers

(1) In any civil proceedings a statement contained in a document produced by a computer shall, subject to rules of court, be admissible as evidence of any fact stated therein of which direct oral evidence would be
admissible, if it is shown that the conditions mentioned in subsection (2)
below are satisfied in relation to the statement and computer in question.

(2) The said conditions are –

(*a*) that the document containing the statement was produced by the
computer during a period over which the computer was used
regularly to store or process information for the purposes of any
activities regularly carried on over that period, whether for profit or
not, by any body, whether corporate or not, or by any individual;

(*b*) that over that period there was regularly supplied to the computer in
the ordinary course of those activities information of the kind contained in the statement or of the kind from which the information so
contained is derived;

(*c*) that throughout the material part of that period the computer was
operating properly or, if not, that any respect in which it was not
operating properly or was out of operation during that part of that
period was not such as to affect the production of the document or the
accuracy of its contents; and

(*d*) that the information contained in the statement reproduces or is
derived from information supplied to the computer in the ordinary
course of those activities.

(3) Where over a period the function of storing or processing information for the purposes of any activities regularly carried on over that period
as mentioned in subsection (2) (*a*) above was regularly performed by
computers, whether –

(*a*) by a combination of computers operating over that period; or

(*b*) by different computers operating in succession over that period; or

(*c*) by different combinations of computers operating in succession over
that period; or

(*d*) in any other manner involving the successive operation over that
period, in whatever order, of one or more computers and one or more
combinations of computers,

all the computers used for that purpose during that period shall be treated for the
purposes of this Part of this Act as constituting a single computer; and references
in this Part of this Act to a computer shall be construed accordingly.

(4) In any civil proceedings where it is desired to give a statement in evidence by virtue of this section, a certificate doing any of the following things, that is to say –

(*a*) identifying the document containing the statement and describing the manner in which it was produced;

(*b*) giving such particulars of any device involved in the production of that document as may be appropriate for the purpose of showing that the document was produced by a computer;

(*c*) dealing with any of the matters to which the conditions mentioned in subsection (2) above relate,

and purporting to be signed by a person occupying a responsible position in relation to the operation of the relevant device or the management of the relevant activities (whichever is appropriate) shall be evidence of any matter stated in the certificate; and for the purposes of this subsection it shall be sufficient for a matter to be stated to the best of the knowledge and belief of the person stating it.

(5) For the purposes of this Part of this Act –

(*a*) information shall be taken to be supplied to a computer if it is supplied thereto in any appropriate form and whether it is so supplied directly or (with or without human intervention) by means of any appropriate equipment;

(*b*) where, in the course of activities carried on by any individual or body, information is supplied with a view to its being stored or processed for the purposes of those activities by a computer operated otherwise than in the course of those activities, that information, if duly supplied to that computer, shall be taken to be supplied to it in the course of those activities;

(*c*) a document shall be taken to have been produced by a computer whether it was produced by it directly or (with or without human intervention) by means of any appropriate equipment.

(6) Subject to subsection (3) above, in this Part of this Act 'computer' means any device for storing and processing information, and any reference to information being derived from other information is a reference to its being derived therefrom by calculation, comparison or any other process.

8. Rules of court

(1) Provision shall be made by rules of court as to the procedure which, subject to any exceptions provided for in the rules, must be followed and the other conditions which, subject as aforesaid, must be fulfilled before a statement can be given in evidence in civil proceedings by virtue of section 2, 4 or 5 of this Act.

(2) Rules of court made in pursuance of subsection (1) above shall in particular, subject to such exceptions (if any) as may be provided for in the rules –

(*a*) require a party to any civil proceedings who desires to give in evidence any such statement as is mentioned in that subsection to give to every other party to the proceedings such notice of his desire to do so and such particulars of or relating to the statement as may be specified in the rules, including particulars of such one or more of the persons connected with the making or recording of the statement or, in the case of a statement falling within section 5 (1) of this Act, such one or more of the persons concerned as mentioned in section 6 (3) (*c*) of this Act as the rules may in any case require; and

(*b*) enable any party who receives such notice as aforesaid by counter-notice to require any person of whom particulars were given with the notice to be called as a witness in the proceedings unless that person is dead, or beyond the seas, or unfit by reason of his bodily or mental condition to attend as a witness, or cannot with reasonable diligence be identified or found, or cannot reasonably be expected (having regard to the time which has elapsed since he was connected or concerned as aforesaid and to all the circumstances) to have any recollection of matters relevant to the accuracy or otherwise of the statement.

(3) Rules of court made in pursuance of subsection (1) above –

(*a*) may confer on the court in any civil proceedings a discretion to allow a statement falling within section 2 (1), 4 (1) or 5 (1) of this Act to be given in evidence notwithstanding that any requirement of the rules affecting the admissibility of that statement has not been complied with, but except in pursuance of paragraph (*b*) below shall not confer on the court a discretion to exclude such a statement where the requirements of the rules affecting its admissibility have been complied with;

(*b*) may confer on the court power, where a party to any civil proceedings has given notice that he desires to give in evidence –

  (i) a statement falling within section 2 (1) of this Act which was made by a person, whether orally or in a document, in the course of giving evidence in some other legal proceedings (whether civil or criminal); or

  (ii) a statement falling within section 4 (1) of this Act which is contained in a record of any direct oral evidence given in some other legal proceedings (whether civil or criminal),

to give directions on the application of any party to the proceedings as to whether, and if so on what conditions, the party desiring to give the statement in evidence will be permitted to do so and (where applicable) as to the manner in which that statement and any other evidence given in those other proceedings is to be proved; and

(*c*) may make different provision for different circumstances, and in particular may make different provision with respect to statements falling within sections 2 (1), 4 (1) and 5 (1) of this Act respectively;

and any discretion conferred on the court by rules of court made as aforesaid may be either a general discretion or a discretion exercisable only in such circumstances as may be specified in the rules.

(4) Rules of court may make provision for preventing a party to any civil proceedings (subject to any exceptions provided for in the rules) from adducing in relation to a person who is not called as a witness in those proceedings any evidence which could otherwise be adduced by him by virtue of section 7 of this Act unless that party has in pursuance of the rules given in respect of that person such a counter-notice as is mentioned in subsection 2 (*b*) above.

(5) In deciding for the purposes of any rules of court made in pursuance of this section whether or not a person is fit to attend as a witness, a court may act on a certificate purporting to be a certificate of a fully registered medical practitioner.

(6) Nothing in the foregoing provisions of this section shall prejudice the generality of section [75 of the County Courts Act 1984], [section 144 of the Magistrates' Courts Act 1980] or any other enactment conferring power to make rules of court; and nothing in [section 75(2) of the County Courts Act 1984] or any other enactment restricting the matters with respect to which rules of court may be made shall prejudice the making of rules of court with respect to any matter mentioned in the foregoing provisions of this section or the operation of any rules of court made with respect to any such matter.

Part II

Miscellaneous General

Convictions, etc. as evidence in civil proceedings
11. Convictions as evidence in civil proceedings
(1) In any civil proceedings the fact that a person has been convicted of an offence by or before any court in the United Kingdom or by a court-martial there or elsewhere shall (subject to subsection (3) below) be admissible in evidence for the purpose of proving, where to do so is relevant to any issue in those proceedings, that he committed that offence, whether he was so convicted upon a plea of guilty or otherwise and whether or not he is a party to the civil proceedings; but no conviction other than a subsisting one shall be admissible in evidence by virtue of this section.

(2) In any civil proceedings in which by virtue of this section a person is proved to have been convicted of an offence by or before any court in the United Kingdom or by a court-martial there or elsewhere –

(*a*) he shall be taken to have committed that offence unless the contrary is proved; and

(*b*) without prejudice to the reception of any other admissible evidence for the purpose of identifying the facts on which the conviction was based, the contents of any document which is admissible as evidence of the conviction, and the contents of the information, complaint, indictment, or charge-sheet on which the person in question was convicted, shall be admissible in evidence for that purpose.

(3) Nothing in this section shall prejudice the operation of section 13 of this Act or any other enactment whereby a conviction or a finding of fact in any criminal proceedings is for the purposes of any other proceedings made conclusive evidence of any fact.

(4) Where in any civil proceedings the contents of any document are admissible in evidence by virtue of subsection (2) above, a copy of that document, or of the material part thereof, purporting to be certified or otherwise authenticated by or on behalf of the court or authority having custody of that document shall be admissible in evidence and shall be taken to be a true copy of that document or part unless the contrary is shown.

(5) Nothing in any of the following enactments, that is to say –

(*a*) [[section 1C] of the Powers of Criminal Courts Act 1973] (under which a conviction leading to discharge is to be disregarded except as therein mentioned);

(*b*) section 9 of the Criminal Justice (Scotland) Act 1949 (which makes similar provision in respect of convictions on indictment in Scotland); and

(*c*) section 8 of the Probation Act (Northern Ireland) 1950 (which corresponds to the said section 12) or any corresponding enactment of the Parliament of Northern Ireland for the time being in force,

shall affect the operation of this section; and for the purposes of this section any order made by a court of summary jurisdiction in Scotland under section 1 or section 2 of the said Act of 1949 shall be treated as a conviction.

(6) In this section 'court-martial' means a court-martial constituted under the Army Act 1955, the Air Force Act 1955 or the Naval Discipline Act 1957 or a disciplinary court constituted under section 50 of the said Act of 1957, and in relation to a court-martial 'conviction', as regards a court-martial constiuted under either of the said Acts of 1955, means a finding of guilty which is, or falls to be treated as, a finding of the court duly confirmed and, as regards a court-martial or disciplinary court constituted under the said Act of 1957, means a finding of guilty which is, or falls to be treated as, the finding of the court, and 'convicted' shall be construed accordingly.

Limitation Act 1980

Actions in respect of wrongs causing personal injuries or death

11. Special time limit for actions in respect of personal injuries

(1) This section applies to any action for damages for negligence, nuisance or breach of duty (whether the duty exists by virtue of a contract or of provision made by or under a statute or independently of any contract or any such provision) where the damages claimed by the plaintiff for the negligence, nuisance or breach of duty consist of or include damages in respect of personal injuries to the plaintiff or any other person.

(2) None of the time limits given in the preceding provisions of this Act shall apply to an action to which this section applies.

(3) An action to which this section applies shall not be brought after the expiration of the period applicable in accordance with subsection (4) or (5) below.

(4) Except where subsection (5) below applies, the period applicable is three years from –

(*a*) the date on which the cause of action accrued; or
(*b*) the date of knowledge (if later) of the person injured.

(5) If the person injured dies before the expiration of the period mentioned in subsection (4) above, the period applicable as respects the cause of action surviving for the benefit of his estate by virtue of section 1 of the Law Reform (Miscellaneous Provisions) Act 1934 shall be three years from –

(*a*) the date of death; or
(*b*) the date of the personal representative's knowledge;

whichever is the later.

(6) For the purposes of this section 'personal representative' includes any person who is or has been a personal representative of the deceased, including an executor who has not proved the will (whether or not he has renounced probate) but not anyone appointed only as a special personal representative in relation to settled land; and regard shall be had to any knowledge acquired by any such person while a personal representative or previously.

(7) If there is more than one personal representative, and their dates of knowledge are different, subsection (5) (*b*) above shall be read as referring to the earliest of those dates.

11A. Actions in respect of defective products

(1) This section shall apply to an action for damages by virtue of any provision of Part I of the Consumer Protection Act 1987.

(2) None of the time limits given in the preceding provisions of this Act shall apply to an action to which this section applies.

(3) An action to which this section applies shall not be brought after the expiration of the period of ten years from the relevant time, within the meaning of section 4 of the said Act of 1987; and this subsection shall operate to extinguish a right of action and shall do so whether or not that right of action had accrued, or time under the following provisions of this Act had begun to run, at the end of the said period of ten years.

(4) Subject to subsection (5) below, an action to which this section applies in which the damages claimed by the plaintiff consist of or include damages in respect of personal injuries to the plaintiff or any other person or loss of or damage to any property, shall not be brought after the expiration of the period of three years from whichever is the later of –

(a) the date on which the cause of action accrued; and
(b) the date of knowledge of the injured person or, in the case of loss of or damage to property, the date of knowledge of the plaintiff or (if earlier) of any person in whom his cause of action was previously vested.

(5) If in a case where the damages claimed by the plaintiff consist of or include damages in respect of personal injuries to the plaintiff or any other person the injured person died before the expiration of the period mentioned in subsection (4) above, that subsection shall have effect as respects the cause of action surviving for the benefit of his estate by virtue of section 1 of the Law Reform (Miscellaneous Provisions) Act 1934 as if for the reference to that period there were substituted a reference to the period of three years from whichever is the later of –

(a) the date of death; and
(b) the date of the personal representative's knowledge.

(6) For the purposes of this section 'personal representative' includes any person who is or has been a personal representative of the deceased, including an executor who has not proved the will (whether or not he has renounced probate) but not anyone appointed only as a special personal representative in relation to settled land; and regard shall be had to any knowledge acquired by any such person while a personal representative or previously.

(7) If there is more than one personal representative and their dates of knowledge are different, subsection (5) (b) above shall be read as referring to the earliest of those dates.

(8) Expressions used in this section or section 14 of this Act and in Part I of the Consumer Protection Act 1987 have the same meanings in this section or that section as in that Part; and section 1 (1) of that Act (Part I to be construed as enacted for the purpose of complying with the product liability Directive) shall apply for the purpose of construing this section and the following provisions of this Act so far as they relate to an action by virtue of any provision of that Part as it applies for the purpose of construing that Part.

12. Special time limit for actions under Fatal Accidents legislation

(1) An action under the Fatal Accidents Act 1976 shall not be brought if the death occurred when the person injured could no longer maintain an action and recover damages in respect of the injury (whether because of a time limit in this Act or in any other Act, or for any other reason).

Where any such action by the injured person would have been barred by the time limit in section 11 [or 11A] of this Act, no account shall be taken of the possibility of that time limit being overridden under section 33 of this Act.

(2) None of the time limits given in the preceding provisions of this Act shall apply to an action under the Fatal Accidents Act 1976, but no such action shall be brought after the expiration of three years from –

> (*a*)   the date of death; or
> (*b*)   the date of knowledge of the person for whose benefit the action is brought;

whichever is the later.

(3) An action under the Fatal Accidents Act 1976 shall be one to which sections 28, 33 and 35 of this Act apply, and the application to any such action of the time limit under subsection (2) above shall be subject to section 39; but otherwise Parts II and III of this Act shall not apply to any such action.

13. Operation of time limit under section 12 in relation to different dependants

(1) Where there is more than one person for whose benefit an action under the Fatal Accidents Act 1976 is brought, section 12 (2) (*b*) of this Act shall be applied separately to each of them.

(2) Subject to subsection (3) below, if by virtue of subsection (1) above the action would be outside the time limit given by section 12 (2) as regards one or more, but not all, of the persons for whose benefit it is brought, the court shall direct that any person as regards whom the action would be outside that limit shall be excluded from those for whom the action is brought.

(3) The court shall not give such a direction if it is shown that if the action were brought exclusively for the benefit of the person in question it would not be defeated by a defence of limitation (whether in consequence of section 28 of this Act or an agreement between the parties not to raise the defence, or otherwise).

14. Definition of date of knowledge for purposes of sections 11 and 12

(1) Subject to subsection (1A) below, in sections 11 and 12 of this Act references to a person's date of knowlege are references to the date on which he first had knowledge of the following facts –

> (*a*)   that the injury in question was significant; and
> (*b*)   that the injury was attributable in whole or in part to the act or omission which is alleged to constitute negligence, nuisance or breach of duty; and
> (*c*)   the identity of the defendant; and
> (*d*)   if it is alleged that the act or omission was that of a person other than

the defendant, the identity of that person and the additional facts supporting the bringing of an action against the defendant;

and knowledge that any acts or omissions did or did not, as a matter of law, involve negligence, nuisance or breach of duty is irrelevant.

(1A) In section 11A of this Act and in section 12 of this Act so far as that section applies to an action by virtue of section 6 (1) (*a*) of the Consumer Protection Act 1987 (death caused by defective product) references to a person's date of knowledge are references to the date on which he first had knowledge of the following facts –

(*a*) such facts about the damage caused by the defect as would lead a reasonable person who had suffered such damage to consider it sufficiently serious to justify his instituting proceedings for damages against a defendant who did not dispute liability and was able to satisfy a judgment; and

(*b*) that the damage was wholly or partly attributable to the facts and circumstances alleged to constitute the defect; and

(*c*) the identity of the defendant;

but, in determining the date on which a person first had such knowledge there shall be disregarded both the extent (if any) of that person's knowledge on any date of whether particular facts or circumstances would or would not, as a matter of law, constitute a defect and, in a case relating to loss of or damage to property, any knowlege which that person had on a date on which he had no right of action by virtue of Part I of that Act in respect of the loss or damage.

(2) For the purposes of this section an injury is significant if the person whose date of knowledge is in question would reasonably have considered it sufficiently serious to justify his instituting proceedings for damages against a defendant who did not dispute liability and was able to satisfy a judgment.

(3) For the purposes of this section a person's knowledge includes knowledge which he might reasonably have been expected to acquire –

(*a*) from facts observable or ascertainable by him; or

(*b*) from facts ascertainable by him with the help of medical or other appropriate expert advice which it is reasonable for him to seek;

but a person shall not be fixed under this subsection with knowledge of a fact ascertainable only with the help of expert advice so long as he has taken all reasonable steps to obtain (and, where appropriate, to act on) that advice.

14A. Special time limit for negligence actions where facts relevant to cause of action are not known at date of accrual

(1) This section applies to any action for damages for negligence, other than one to which section 11 of this Act applies, where the starting date for reckoning the period of limitation under subsection (4) (*b*) below falls after the date on which the cause of action accrued.

(2) Section 2 of this Act shall not apply to an action to which this section applies.

(3) An action to which this section applies shall not be brought after the expiration of the period applicable in accordance with subsection (4) below.

(4) That period is either –

(*a*) six years from the date on which the cause of action accrued; or
(*b*) three years from the starting date as defined by subsection (5) below, if that period expires later than the period mentioned in paragraph (*a*) above.

(5) For the purposes of this section, the starting date for reckoning the period of limitation under subsection (4) (*b*) above is the earliest date on which the plaintiff or any person in whom the cause of action was vested before him first had both the knowledge required for bringing an action for damages in respect of the relevant damage and a right to bring such an action.

(6) In subsection (5) above 'the knowledge required for bringing an action for damages in respect of the relevant damage' means knowledge both –

(*a*) of the material facts about the damage in respect of which damages are claimed; and
(*b*) of the other facts relevant to the current action mentioned in subsection (8) below.

(7) For the purposes of subsection (6) (*a*) above, the material facts about the damage are such facts about the damage as would lead a reasonable person who had suffered such damage to consider it sufficiently serious to justify his instituting proceedings for damages against a defendant who did not dispute liability and was able to satisfy a judgment.

(8) The other facts referred to in subsection (6) (*b*) above are –

(*a*) that the damage was attributable in whole or in part to the act or omission which is alleged to constitute negligence; and
(*b*) the identity of the defendant; and
(*c*) if it is alleged that the act or omission was that of a person other than the defendant, the identity of that person and the additional facts supporting the bringing of an action against the defendant.

(9) Knowledge that any acts or omissions did or did not, as a matter of law, involve negligence is irrelevant for the purposes of subsection (5) above.

(10) For the purposes of this section a person's knowledge includes knowledge which he might reasonably have been expected to acquire –

(*a*) from facts observable or ascertainable by him; or
(*b*) from facts ascertainable by him with the help of appropriate expert advice which it is reasonable for him to seek;

but a person shall not be taken by virtue of this subsection to have knowledge of a fact ascertainable only with the help of expert advice so long as he has taken all reasonable steps to obtain (and, where appropriate, to act on) that advice.

14B. Overriding time limit for negligence actions not involving personal injuries

(1) An action for damages for negligence, other than one to which section 11 of this Act applies, shall not be brought after the expiration of fifteen

years from the date (or, if more than one, from the last of the dates) on which there occurred any act or omission –

(*a*) which is alleged to constitute negligence; and
(*b*) to which the damage in respect of which damages are claimed is alleged to be attributable (in whole or in part).

(2) This section bars the right of action in a case to which subsection (1) above applies notwithstanding that –

(*a*) the cause of action has not yet accrued; or
(*b*) where section 14A of this Act applies to the action, the date which is for the purposes of that section the starting date for reckoning the period mentioned in subsection (4) (*b*) of that section has not yet occurred;

before the end of the period of limitation prescribed by this section.

PART II

EXTENSION OR EXCLUSION OF ORDINARY TIME LIMITS

Disability

28. Extension of limitation period in case of disability

(1) Subject to the following provisions of this section, if on the date when any right of action accrued for which a period of limitation is prescribed by this Act, the person to whom it accrued was under a disability, the action may be brought at any time before the expiration of six years from the date when he ceased to be under a disability or died (whichever first occurred) notwithstanding that the period of limitation has expired.

(2) This section shall not affect any case where the right of action first accrued to some person (not under a disability) through whom the person under a disability claims.

(3) When a right of action which has accrued to a person under a disability accrues, on the death of that person while still under a disability, to another person under a disability, no further extension of time shall be allowed by reason of the disability of the second person.

(4) No action to recover land or money charged on land shall be brought by virtue of this section by any person after the expiration of thirty years from the date on which the right of action accrued to that person or some person through whom he claims.

(4A) If the action is one to which section 4A of this Act applies, subsection (1) above shall have effect as if for the words from 'at any time' to 'occurred' there were substituted the words 'by him at any time before the expiration of three years from the date when he ceased to be under a disability'.

(5) If the action is one to which section 10 of this Act applies, subsection (1) above shall have effect as if for the words 'six years' there were substituted the words 'two years'.

(6) If the action is one to which section 11 or 12 (2) of this Act applies, subsection (1) above shall have effect as if for the words 'six years' there were substituted the words 'three years'.

(7) If the action is one to which section 11A of this Act applies or one by virtue of section 6 (1) (*a*) of the Consumer Protection Act 1987 (death caused by defective product), subsection (1) above –

(*a*) shall not apply to the time limit prescribed by subsection (3) of the said section 11A or to that time limit as applied by virtue of section 12 (1) of this Act; and

(*b*) in relation to any other time limit prescribed by this Act shall have effect as if for the words 'six years' there were substituted the words 'three years'.

28A. Extension for cases where the limitation period is the period under section 14A (4) (*b*)

(1) Subject to subsection (2) below, if in the case of any action for which a period of limitation is prescribed by section 14A of this Act –

(*a*) the period applicable in accordance with subsection (4) of that section is the period mentioned in paragraph (*b*) of that subsection;

(*b*) on the date which is for the purposes of that section the starting date for reckoning that period the person by reference to whose knowledge that date fell to be determined under subsection (5) of that section was under a disability; and

(*c*) section 28 of this Act does not apply to the action;

the action may be brought at any time before the expiration of three years from the date when he ceased to be under a disability or died (whichever first occurred) notwithstanding that the period mentioned above has expired.

(2) An action may not be brought by virtue of subsection (1) above after the end of the period of limitation prescribed by section 14B of this Act.

Fraud, concealment and mistake

32. Postponement of limitation period in case of fraud, concealment or mistake

(1) Subject to subsections (3) and (4A) below, where in the case of any action for which a period of limitation is prescribed by this Act, either –

(*a*) the action is based upon the fraud of the defendant; or

(*b*) any fact relevant to the plaintiff's right of action has been deliberately concealed from him by the defendant; or

(*c*) the action is for relief from the consequences of a mistake;

the period of limitation shall not begin to run until the plaintiff has discovered the fraud, concealment or mistake (as the case may be) or could with reasonable diligence have discovered it.

References in this subsection to the defendant include references to the defendant's agent and to any person through whom the defendant claims and his agent.

(2) For the purposes of subsection (1) above, deliberate commission of a breach of duty in circumstances in which it is unlikely to be discovered for some time amounts to deliberate concealment of the facts involved in that breach of duty.

(3) Nothing in this section shall enable any action –

(*a*) to recover, or recover the value of, any property; or
(*b*) to enforce any charge against, or set aside any transaction affecting, any property;

to be brought against the purchaser of the property or any person claiming through him in any case where the property has been purchased for valuable consideration by an innocent third party since the fraud or concealment or (as the case may be) the transaction in which the mistake was made took place.

(4) A purchaser is an innocent third party for the purposes of this section –

(*a*) in the case of fraud or concealment of any fact relevant to the plaintiff's right of action, if he was not a party to the fraud or (as the case may be) to the concealment of that fact and did not at the time of the purchase know or have reason to believe that the fraud or concealment had taken place; and
(*b*) in the case of mistake, if he did not at the time of the purchase know or have reason to believe that the mistake had been made.

(4A) Subsection (1) above shall not apply in relation to the time limit prescribed by section 11A (3) of this Act or in relation to that time limit as applied by virtue of section 12 (1) of this Act.

(5) Sections 14A and 14B of this Act shall not apply to any action to which subsection (1) (*b*) above applies (and accordingly the period of limitation referred to in that subsection, in any case to which either of those sections would otherwise apply, is the period applicable under section 2 of this Act).

Discretionary exclusion of time limit for actions in respect of personal injuries or death

32A. Discretionary extension of time limit for actions for libel or slander

Where a person to whom a cause of action for libel or slander has accrued has not brought such an action within the period of three years mentioned in section 4A of this Act (or, where applicable, the period allowed by section 28 (1) as modified by section 28 (4A)) because all or any of the facts relevant to that cause of action did not become known to him until after the expiration of that period, such an action –

(*a*) may be brought by him at any time before the expiration of one year from the earliest date on which he knew all the facts relevant to that cause of action; but
(*b*) shall not be so brought without the leave of the High Court.

33. Discretionary exclusion of time limit for actions in respect of personal injuries or death

(1) If it appears to the court that it would be equitable to allow an action to proceed having regard to the degree to which –

(*a*) the provisions of section 11 or 11A or 12 of this Act prejudice the plaintiff or any person whom he represents; and (*b*) any decision of the court under this subsection would prejudice the defendant or any person whom he represents;

the court may direct that those provisions shall not apply to the action, or shall not apply to any specified cause of action to which the action relates.

(1A) The court shall not under this section disapply –

(*a*) subsection (3) of section 11A; or
(*b*) where the damages claimed by the plaintiff are confined to damages for loss of or damage to any property, any other provision in its application to an action by virtue of Part I of the Consumer Protection Act 1987.

(2) The court shall not under this section disapply section 12 (1) except where the reason why the person injured could no longer maintain an action was because of the time limit in section 11 or subsection (4) of section 11A.

If, for example, the person injured could at his death no longer maintain an action under the Fatal Accidents Act 1976 because of the time limit in Article 29 in Schedule 1 to the Carriage by Air Act 1961, the court has no power to direct that section 12 (1) shall not apply.

(3) In acting under this section the court shall have regard to all the circumstances of the case and in particular to –

(*a*) the length of, and the reasons for, the delay on the part of the plaintiff;
(*b*) the extent to which, having regard to the delay, the evidence adduced or likely to be adduced by the plaintiff or the defendant is or is likely to be less cogent than if the action had been brought within the time allowed by section 11, by section 11A or (as the case may be) by section 12;
(*c*) the conduct of the defendant after the cause of action arose, including the extent (if any) to which he responded to requests reasonably made by the plaintiff for information or inspection for the purpose of ascertaining facts which were or might be relevant to the plaintiff's cause of action against the defendant;
(*d*) the duration of any disability of the plaintiff arising after the date of the accrual of the cause of action;
(*e*) the extent to which the plaintiff acted promptly and reasonably once he knew whether or not the act or omission of the defendant, to which the injury was attributable, might be capable at that time of giving rise to an action for damages;
(*f*) the steps, if any, taken by the plaintiff to obtain medical, legal or other expert advice and the nature of any such advice he may have received.

(4) In a case where the person injured died when, because of section 11 or subsection (4) of section 11A, he could no longer maintain an action and recover damages in respect of the injury, the court shall have regard in particular to the length of, and the reasons for, the delay on the part of the deceased.

(5) In a case under subsection (4) above, or any other case where the time limit, or one of the time limits, depends on the date of knowledge of a person other than the plaintiff, subsection (3) above shall have effect with appropriate modifications, and shall have effect in particular as if references to the

plaintiff included references to any person whose date of knowledge is or was relevant in determining a time limit.

(6) A direction by the court disapplying the provisions of section 12 (1) shall operate to disapply the provisions to the same effect in section 1 (1) of the Fatal Accidents Act 1976.

(7) In this section 'the court' means the court in which the action has been brought.

(8) References in this section to section 11 or 11A include references to that section as extended by any of the preceding provisions of this Part of this Act or by any provision of Part III of this Act.

Part III

Miscellaneous and General

35. New claims in pending actions: rules of court

(1) For the purposes of this Act, any new claim made in the course of any action shall be deemed to be a separate action and to have been commenced –

- (a) in the case of a new claim made in or by way of third party proceedings, on the date on which those proceedings were commenced; and
- (b) in the case of any other new claim, on the same date as the original action.

(2) In this section a new claim means any claim by way of set-off or counterclaim, and any claim involving either –

- (a) the addition or substitution of a new cause of action; or
- (b) the addition or substitution of a new party;

and 'third party proceedings' means any proceedings brought in the course of any action by any party to the action against a person not previously a party to the action, other than proceedings brought by joining any such person as defendant to any claim already made in the original action by the party bringing the proceedings.

(3) Except as provided by section 33 of this Act or by rules of court, neither the High Court nor any county court shall allow a new claim within subsection 1 (b) above, other than an original set-off or counterclaim, to be made in the course of any action after the expiry of any time limit under this Act which would affect a new action to enforce that claim.

For the purposes of this subsection, a claim is an original set-off or an original counterclaim if it is a claim made by way of set-off or (as the case may be) by way of counterclaim by a party who has not previously made any claim in the action.

(4) Rules of court may provide for allowing a new claim to which subsection (3) above applies to be made as there mentioned, but only if the conditions specified in subsection (5) below are satisfied, and subject to any further restrictions the rules may impose.

(5) The conditions referred to in subsection (4) above are the following –

- (a) in the case of a claim involving a new cause of action, if the new cause of action arises out of the same facts or substantially the same facts as are already in issue on any claim previously made in the original action; and (*b*) in the case of a claim involving a new party, if the addition or substitution of the new party is necessary for the determination of the original action.

(6) The addition or substitution of a new party shall not be regarded for the purposes of subsection (5) (*b*) above as necessary for the determination of the original action unless either –

(*a*) the new party is substituted for a party whose name was given in any claim made in the original action in mistake for the new party's name; or

(*b*) any claim already made in the original action cannot be maintained by or against an existing party unless the new party is joined or substituted as plaintiff or defendant in that action.

(7) Subject to subsection (4) above, rules of court may provide for allowing a party to any action to claim relief in a new capacity in respect of a new cause of action notwithstanding that he had no title to make that claim at the date of the commencement of the action.

This subsection shall not be taken as prejudicing the power of rules of court to provide for allowing a party to claim relief in a new capacity without adding or substituting a new cause of action.

(8) Subsections (3) to (7) above shall apply in relation to a new claim made in the course of third party proceedings as if those proceedings were the original action, and subject to such other modifications as may be prescribed by rules of court in any case or class of case.

36. Equitable jurisdiction and remedies

(1) The following time limits under this Act, that is to say –

(*a*) the time limit under section 2 for actions founded on tort;

(*aa*) the time limit under section 4A for actions for libel or slander;

(*b*) the time limit under section 5 for actions founded on simple contract;

(*c*) the time limit under section 7 for actions to enforce awards where the submission is not by an instrument under seal;

(*d*) the time limit under section 8 for actions on a specialty;

(*e*) the time limit under section 9 for actions to recover a sum recoverable by virtue of any enactment; and

(*f*) the time limit under section 24 for actions to enforce a judgment;

shall not apply to any claim for specific performance of a contract or for an injunction or for other equitable relief, except in so far as any such time limit may be applied by the court by analogy in like manner as the corresponding time limit under any enactment repealed by the Limitation Act 1939 was applied before 1st July 1940.

(2) Nothing in this Act shall affect any equitable jurisdiction to refuse relief on the ground of acquiescence or otherwise.

County Courts Act 1984

Actions of contract and tort
15. General jurisdiction in actions of contract and tort
(1) Subject to subsection (2), a county court shall have jurisdiction to hear and determine any action founded on contract or tort.

(2) A county court shall not, except as in this Act provided, have jurisdiction to hear and determine –

    (*a*) [. . .]
    (*b*) any action in which the title to any toll, fair, market or franchise is in question; or
    (*c*) any action for libel or slander.

23. Equity jurisdiction
A county court shall have all the jurisdiction of the High Court to hear and determine –

    (*a*) proceedings for the administration of the estate of a deceased person, where the estate does not exceed in amount or value the county court limit [£30,000],
    (*b*) proceedings –
        (i)   for the execution of any trust, or
        (ii) for a declaration that a trust subsists, or
        (iii) under section 1 of the Variation of Trusts Act 1958,
        where the estate or fund subject, or alleged to be subject, to the trust does not exceed in amount or value the county court limit [£30,000];
    (*c*) proceedings for foreclosure or redemption of any mortgage or for enforcing any charge or lien, where the amount owing in respect of the mortgage charge or lien does not exceed the county court limit [£30,000];
    (*d*) proceedings for the specific performance, or for the rectification, delivery up or cancellation, of any agreement for the sale, purchase or lease of any property, where, in the case of a sale or purchase, the purchase money, or in the case of a lease, the value of the property, does not exceed the county court limit [£30,000];
    (*e*) proceedings relating to the maintenance or advancement of a minor,

where the property of the minor does not exceed in amount or value the county court limit;

(*f*) proceedings for the dissolution or winding-up of any partnership (whether or not the existence of the partnership is in dispute), where the whole assets of the partnership do not exceed in amount or value the county court limit [£30,000];

(*g*) proceedings for relief against fraud or mistake where the damage sustained or the estate or fund in respect of which relief is sought does not exceed in amount or value the county court limit [£30,000].

24. Jurisdiction by agreement in certain equity proceedings

(1) If, as respects any proceedings to which this section applies, the parties agree, by a memorandum signed by them or by their respective legal representatives or agents, that a county court specified in the memorandum shall have jurisdiction in the proceedings, that court shall, notwithstanding anything in any enactment, have jurisdiction to hear and determine the proceedings accordingly.

(2) Subject to subsection (3), this section applies to any proceedings in which a county court would have jurisdiction by virtue of –

(*a*) section 113 (3) of the Settled Land Act 1925,

(*b*) section 63A of the Trustee Act 1925,

(*c*) sections 3 (7), 49 (4), 66 (4), 89 (7), 90 (3), 91 (8), 92 (2), 136 (3), 181 (2), 188 (2) of, and paragraph 3A of Part III and paragraph 1 (3A) and (4A) of Part IV of Schedule 1 to, the Law of Property Act 1925,

(*d*) sections 17 (2), 38 (4), 41 (1A) and 43 (4) of the Administration of Estates Act 1925,

(*e*) section 6 (1) of the Leasehold Property (Repairs) Act 1938,

(*f*) sections 1 (6A) and 5 (11) of the Land Charges Act 1972, and

(*g*) sections 23 and 25 of this Act,

but for the limits of the jurisdiction of the court provided in those enactments.

(3) This section does not apply to proceedings under section 1 of the Variation of Trusts Act 1958.

38. Remedies available in county courts

(1) Subject to what follows, in any proceedings in a county court the court may make any order which could be made by the High Court if the proceedings were in the High Court.

(2) Any order made by the county court may be –

(*a*) absolute or conditional;

(*b*) final or interlocutory.

(3) A county court shall not have power –

(*a*) to order mandamus, certiorari or prohibition; or

(*b*) to make any order of a prescribed kind.

(4) Regulations under subsection (3) –

(*a*) may provide for any of their provisions not to apply in such circumstances or descriptions of case as may be specified in the regulations;

(*b*) may provide for the transfer of the proceedings to the High Court for the purpose of enabling an order of a kind prescribed under subsection (3) to be made;

(c) may make such provision with respect to matters of procedure as the Lord Chancellor considers expedient; and

(d) may make provision amending or repealing any provision made by or under any enactment, so far as may be necessary or expedient in consequence of the regulations.

(5) In this section 'prescribed' means prescribed by regulations made by the Lord Chancellor under this section.

(6) The power to make regulations under this section shall be exercised by statutory instrument.

(7) No such statutory instrument shall be made unless a draft of the instrument has been approved by both Houses of Parliament.

Transfer of proceedings
40. Transfer of proceedings to county court

(1) Where the High Court is satisfied that any proceedings before it are required by any provision of a kind mentioned in subsection (8) to be in a county court it shall –

(a) order the transfer of the proceedings to a county court; or

(b) if the court is satisfied that the person bringing the proceedings knew, or ought to have known, of that requirement, order that they be struck out.

(2) Subject to any such provision, the High Court may order the transfer of any proceedings before it to a county court.

(3) An order under this section may be made either on the motion of the High Court itself or on the application of any party to the proceedings.

(4) Proceedings transferred under this section shall be transferred to such county court as the High Court considers appropriate, having taken into account the convenience of the parties and that of any other persons likely to be affected and the state of business in the courts concerned.

(5) The transfer of any proceedings under this section shall not affect any right of appeal from the order directing the transfer.

(6) Where proceedings for the enforcement of any judgment or order of the High Court are transferred under this section –

(a) the judgment or order may be enforced as if it were a judgment or order of a county court; and

(b) subject to subsection (7), it shall be treated as a judgment or order of that court for all purposes.

(7) Where proceedings for the enforcement of any judgment or order of the High Court are transferred under this section –

(a) the powers of any court to set aside, correct, vary or quash a judgment or order of the High Court, and the enactments relating to appeals from such a judgment or order, shall continue to apply; and

(b) the powers of any court to set aside, correct, vary or quash a judgment or order of a county court, and the enactments relating to appeals from such a judgment or order, shall not apply.

(8) The provisions referred to in subsection (1) are any made –

(*a*) under section 1 of the Courts and Legal Services Act 1990; or

(*b*) by or under any other enactment.

(9) This section does not apply to family proceedings within the meaning of Part V of the Matrimonial and Family Proceedings Act 1984.

41. Transfer to High Court by order of High Court

(1) If at any stage in proceedings commenced in a county court or transferred to a county court under section 10, the High Court thinks it desirable that the proceedings, or any part of them, should be heard and determined in the High Court, it may order the transfer to the High Court of the proceedings or, as the case may be, of that part of them.

(2) The power conferred by subsection (1) is without prejudice to section 29 of the Supreme Court Act 1981 (power of High Court to issue prerogative orders) but shall be exercised in relation to family proceedings (within the meaning of Part V of the Matrimonial and Family Proceedings Act 1984) in accordance with any direction given under section 37 of that Act (directions as to distribution and transfer of family business and proceedings).

(3) The power conferred by subsection (1) shall be exercised subject to any provision made –

(*a*) under section 1 of the Courts and Legal Services Act 1990; or

(*b*) by or under any other enactment.

42. Transfer to High Court by order of a county court

(1) Where a county court is satisfied that any proceedings before it are required by any provision of a kind mentioned in subsection (7) to be in the High Court, it shall –

(*a*) order the transfer of the proceedings to the High Court; or

(*b*) if the court is satisfied that the person bringing the proceedings knew, or ought to have known, of that requirement, order that they be struck out.

(2) Subject to any such provision, a county court may order the transfer of any proceedings before it to the High Court.

(3) An order under this section may be made either on the motion of the court itself or on the application of any party to the proceedings.

(4) The transfer of any proceedings under this section shall not affect any right of appeal from the order directing the transfer.

(5) Where the proceedings for the enforcement of any judgment or order of a county court are transferred under this section –

(*a*) the judgment or order may be enforced as if it were a judgment or order of the High Court; and

(*b*) subject to subsection (6), it shall be treated as a judgment or order of that court for all purposes.

(6) Where proceedings for the enforcement of any judgment or order of a county court are transferred under this section –

(*a*) the powers of any court to set aside, correct, vary or quash a judgment or order of a county court, and the enactments relating to appeals from a judgment or order, shall continue to apply; and (*b*) the powers of any court to set aside, correct, vary or quash a judgment or order of the High Court, and the enactments relating to appeals from such a judgment or order, shall not apply.

(7) The provisions referred to in subsection (1) are any made –

(*a*) under section 1 of the Courts and Legal Services Act 1990; or

(*b*) by or under any other enactment.

(8) This section does not apply to family proceedings within the meaning of Part V of the Matrimonial and Family Proceedings Act 1984.

76. Application of practice of High Court

In any case not expressly provided for by or in pursuance of this Act, the general principles of practice in the High Court may be adopted and applied to proceedings in a county court.

High Court and County Courts Jurisdiction Order 1991

Jurisdiction

2.—(1) A county court shall have jurisdiction under –

(*a*) sections 30, 146 and 147 of the Law of Property Act 1925,
(*b*) section 58C of the Trade Marks Act 1938,
(*c*) section 26 of the Arbitration Act 1950,
(*d*) section 63 (2) of the Landlord and Tenant Act 1954,
(*e*) section 28 (3) of the Mines and Quarries (Tips) Act 1969,
(*f*) section 66 of the Taxes Management Act 1970,
(*g*) section 41 of the Administration of Justice Act 1970,
(*h*) section 139 (5) (*b*) of the Consumer Credit Act 1974,
(*i*) section 13 of the Torts (Interference with Goods) Act 1977,
(*j*) section 87 of the Magistrates' Courts Act 1980,
(*k*) sections 19 and 20 of the Local Government Finance Act 1982,
(*l*) section 15, 16, 21, 24 and 139 of the County Courts Act 1984,
(*m*) section 39 (4) of, and paragraph 3 (1) of Schedule 3 to, the Legal Aid Act 1988,
(*n*) sections 99, 102 (5), 114, 195, 204, 230, 231 and 235 (5) of the Copyright, Designs and Patents Act 1988, and
(*o*) section 40 of the Housing Act 1988,

whatever the amount involved in the proceedings and whatever the value of any fund or asset connected with the proceedings.

(2) A county court shall have jurisdiction under –

(*a*) section 10 of the Local Land Charges Act 1975, and
(*b*) section 10(4) of the Rentcharges Act 1977,

where the sum concerned or amount claimed does not exceed £5,000.

(3) A county court shall have jurisdiction under the following provisions of the Law of Property Act 1925 where the capital value of the land or interest in land which is to be dealt with does not exceed £30,000:

(*a*) sections 3, 49, 66, 181, and 188;
(*b*) proviso (iii) to paragraph 3 of Part III of Schedule 1;
(*c*) proviso (v) to paragraph 1 (3) of Part IV of Schedule 1;
(*d*) provisos (iii) and (iv) to paragraph 1 (4) of Part IV of Schedule 1.

(4) A county court shall have jurisdiction under sections 89, 90, 91 and 92 of the Law of Property Act 1925 where the amount owing in respect of the mortgage or charge at the commencement of the proceedings does not exceed £30,000.

(5) A county court shall have jurisdiction under the proviso to section 136 (1) of the Law of Property Act 1925 where the amount or value of the debt or thing in action does not exceed £30,000.

(6) A county court shall have jurisdiction under section 1 (6) of the Land Charges Act 1972 –

(*a*) in the case of a land charge of Class C(i), C(ii) or D(i), if the amount does not exceed £30,000;

(*b*) in the case of a land charge of Class C(iii), if it is for a specified capital sum of money not exceeding £30,000 or, where it is not for a specified capital sum, if the capital value of the land affected does not exceed £30,000;

(*c*) in the case of a land charge of Class A, Class B, Class C(iv), Class D(ii), Class D(iii) or Class E, if the capital value of the land affected does not exceed £30,000;

(*d*) in the case of a land charge of Class F, if the land affected by it is the subject of an order made by the court under section 1 of the Matrimonial Homes Act 1983 or an application for an order under that section relating to that land has been made to the court;

(*e*) in a case where an application under section 23 of the Deeds of Arrangement Act 1914 could be entertained by the court.

(7) A county court shall have jurisdiction under sections 69, 70 and 71 of the Solicitors Act 1974 where a bill of costs relates wholly or partly to contentious business done in a county court and the amount of the bill does not exceed £5,000.

(8) The enactments and statutory instruments listed in the Schedule to this Order are amended as specified therein, being amendments which are consequential on the provisions of this article.

Injunctions
3. The High Court shall have jurisdiction to hear an application for an injunction made in the course of or in anticipation of proceedings in a county court where a county court may not, by virtue of regulations under section 38 (3) (*b*) of the County Courts Act 1984 or otherwise, grant such an injunction.

Allocation – Commencement of proceedings
4. Subject to articles 5 and 6, proceedings in which both the county courts and the High Court have jurisdiction may be commenced either in a county court or in the High Court.

5.—(1) Proceedings in which county courts have jurisdiction and which include a claim for damages in respect of personal injuries shall be commenced in a county court, unless the value of the action is £50,000 or more.

(2) In this article 'personal injuries' means personal injuries to the plaintiff or any other person, and includes disease, impairment of physical or mental condition, and death.

6. Applications under section 19 of the Local Government Finance Act 1982 and appeals under section 20 of that Act shall be commenced in the High Court.

Allocation – Trial

7.—(1) Subject to the following provisions of this article, proceedings in which both the High Court and the county courts have jurisdiction may be tried in the High Court or in a county court.

(2) The following provisions of this article apply to proceedings in which both the High Court and the county courts have jurisdiction, other than proceedings mentioned in section 23, 24 or 32 of the County Courts Act 1984, save that paragraphs (3) and (4) do not apply to proceedings which have no quantifiable value.

(3) An action of which the value is less than £25,000 shall be tried in a county court unless –

> (*a*) a county court, having regard to the criteria set out in sub-paragraphs (*a*) to (*d*) of paragraph (5), considers that it ought to transfer the action to the High Court for trial and the High Court considers that it ought to try the action; or
>
> (*b*) it is commenced in the High Court and the High Court, having regard to the said criteria, considers that it ought to try the action.

(4) An action of which the value is £50,000 or more shall be tried in the High Court unless –

> (*a*) it is commenced in a county court and the county court does not, having regard to the criteria set out in sub-paragraphs (*a*) to (*d*) of paragraph (5), consider that the action ought to be transferred to the High Court for trial; or
>
> (*b*) the High Court, having regard to the said criteria, considers that it ought to transfer the case to a county court for trial.

(5) The High Court and the county courts, when considering whether to exercise their powers under section 40 (2), 41 (1) or 42 (2) of the County Courts Act 1984 (Transfer) shall have regard to the following criteria –

> (*a*) the financial substance of the action, including the value of any counterclaim,
>
> (*b*) whether the action is otherwise important and, in particular, whether it raises questions of importance to persons who are not parties or questions of general public interest,
>
> (*c*) the complexity of the facts, legal issues, remedies or procedures involved, and
>
> (*d*) whether transfer is likely to result in a more speedy trial of the action, but no transfer shall be made on the grounds of sub-paragraph (*d*) alone.

Enforcement

8.—(1) A judgment or order of a county court for the payment of a sum of money which it is sought to enforce wholly or partially by execution against goods –

> (*a*) shall be enforced only in the High Court where the sum which it is sought to enforce is £5,000 or more and the proceedings in which the

judgment or order was obtained did not arise out of an agreement regulated by the Consumer Credit Act 1974;

(*b*) shall be enforced only in a county court where the sum which it is sought to enforce is less than £2,000;

(*c*) in any other case may be enforced in either the High Court or a county court.

(2) Section 85 (1) of the County Court Act 1984 is amended by the insertion, at the beginning of the subsection, of the words 'Subject to article 8 of the High Court and County Courts Jurisdiction Order 1991,'.

Definition of value of action

9.—(1) For the purposes of articles 5 and 7 –

(*a*) the value of an action for a sum of money, whether specified or not, is the amount which the plaintiff or applicant reasonably expects to recover;

(*b*) an action for specified relief other than a sum of money –

    (i) has a value equal to the amount of money which the plaintiff or applicant could reasonably state to be the financial worth of the claim to him, or

    (ii) where there is no such amount, has no quantifiable value;

(*c*) an action which includes more than one claim –

    (i) if one or more of the claims is of a kind specified in paragraph (*b*) (ii), has no quantifiable value;

    (ii) in any other case, has a value which is the aggregate of the value of the claims as determined in accordance with paragraphs (*a*) and (*b*) (i).

(2) In determining the value of an action under paragraph (1), claims for –

(*a*) unspecified further or other relief,

(*b*) interest, other than interest pursuant to a contract, and

(*c*) costs,

shall be disregarded.

(3) In determining the value, under paragraph (1), of an action which is brought by more than one plaintiff or applicant regard shall be had to the aggregate of the expectations or interests of all the plaintiffs or applicants.

(4) In determining the value of an action under paragraph (1) (*a*) –

(*a*) the sum which the plaintiff or applicant reasonably expects to recover shall be reduced by the amount of any debt which he admits that he owes to a defendant in that action and which arises from the circumstances which give rise to the action;

(*b*) no account shall be taken of a possible finding of contributory negligence, except to the extent, if any, that such negligence is admitted;

(*c*) where the plaintiff seeks an award of provisional damages as described in section 32A (2) (*a*) of the Supreme Court Act 1981, no account shall be taken of the possibility of a future application for further damages;

(*d*) the value shall be taken to include sums which, by virtue of section 22 of the Social Security Act 1989, are required to be paid to the Secretary of State.

10. The value of an action shall be determined –

(*a*) for the purposes of article 5, as at the time when the action is commenced, and

(*b*) for the purposes of article 7, as at the time when the value is declared in accordance with rules of court.

Crown proceedings – transitional provisions
11. For a period of two years from the date upon which this Order comes into force no order shall be made transferring proceedings in the High Court to which the Crown is a party to a county court, except –

(*a*) when the proceedings are set down to be tried or heard; or

(*b*) with the consent of the Crown.

Savings
12. This Order shall not apply to:

(*a*) family proceedings within the meaning of Part V of the Matrimonial and Family Proceedings Act 1984;

(*b*) proceedings to which section 27 (1) of the County Courts Act 1984 (Admiralty jurisdiction) applies.

County Court Remedies Regulations 1991

2. In these Regulations, 'prescribed relief' means relief of any of the following kinds –

    (*a*) an order requiring a party to admit any other party to premises for the purpose of inspecting or removing documents or articles which may provide evidence in any proceedings, whether or not the proceedings have been commenced;

    (*b*) an interlocutory injunction –

        (i) restraining a party from removing from the jurisdiction of the High Court assets located within that jurisdiction; or

        (ii) restraining a party from dealing with assets whether located within the jurisdiction of the High Court or not.

3.—(1) Subject to the following provisions of this regulation, a county court shall not grant prescribed relief or vary or revoke an order made by the High Court granting such relief.

    (2) Paragraph (1) shall not apply to –

    (*a*) any county court held by a judge of the Court of Appeal or judge of the High Court sitting as a judge for any county court district;

    (*b*) a patents county court held by a person nominated under section 291 of the Copyright, Designs and Patents Act 1988 to sit as a judge of that court.

    (3) A county court may grant relief of a kind referred to in regulation 2 (*b*) –

    (*a*) when exercising jurisdiction in family proceedings within the meaning of Part V of the Matrimonial and Family Proceedings Act 1984;

    (*b*) for the purpose of making an order for the preservation, custody or detention of property which forms or may form the subject matter of proceedings, or

    (*c*) in aid of execution of a judgment or order made in proceedings in a county court to preserve assets until execution can be levied upon them.

    (4) Paragraph (1) shall not –

    (*a*) affect or modify powers expressly conferred on a county court by or
    under any enactment other than section 38 of the County Courts Act
    1984; or

    (*b*) prevent a county court from varying an order granting prescribed
    relief where all the parties are agreed on the terms of the variation.

4. An application to the High Court for relief of a kind referred to in regulation 2 (*a*) in county court proceedings shall be deemed to include an application for transfer of the proceedings to the High Court.

5.—(1) After an application for prescribed relief has been disposed of by
the High Court, the proceedings shall, unless the High Court orders otherwise, be transferred to a county court if –

    (*a*) they were transferred to the High Court; or

    (*b*) apart from these Regulations, they should have been commenced in a
    county court.

    (2) Where an order is made on ex parte application, the application shall
not be treated as disposed of for the purposes of paragraph (1) until any
application to set aside or vary the order has been heard, or until the expiry
of 28 days (or such other period as the Court may specify) during which no
such application has been made.

County Court Rules 1981

ORDER 1

Computation of time

9.—(1) Any period of time fixed by these rules or by a judgment, order or direction for doing any act shall be reckoned in accordance with the following provisions of this rule.

(2) Where the act is required to be done not less than a specified period before a specified date, the period starts immediately after the date on which the act is done and ends immediately before the specified date [1982].

(3) Where the act is required to be done within a specified period after or from a specified date the period starts immediately after that date.

(4) Where, apart from this paragraph, the period in question being a period of 3 days or less would include a day on which the court office is closed, that day shall be excluded.

(5) Where the time so fixed for doing an act in the court office expires on a day on which the office is closed, and for that reason the act cannot be done on that day, the act shall be in time if done on the next day on which the office is open.

ORDER 4

Venue for Bringing Proceedings

General provisions as to actions

2.—(1) An action may be commenced –

(a) in the court for the district in which the defendant or one of the defendants resides or carries on business.

(b) in the court for the district in which the cause of action wholly or in part arose, or

(c) in the case of a default action, in any county court.

(2) Where the plaintiff sues as assignee, the action shall be commenced only in a court in which the assignor might have commenced the action but for the assignment.

Proceedings relating to land

3. Proceedings –

(*a*) for the recovery of land, or

(*b*) for the foreclosure or redemption of any mortgage or, subject to Order 31, rule 4, for enforcing any charge or lien on land, or

(*c*) for the recovery of moneys secured by a mortgage or charge on land,

may be commenced only in the court for the district in which the land or any part thereof is situated.

ORDER 5

Partner may sue and be sued in firm name

9.—(1) Subject to the provisions of any enactment, any two or more persons claiming to be entitled, or alleged to be liable, as partners in respect of a cause of action and carrying on business within England or Wales may sue or be sued in the name of the firm of which they were partners when the cause of action arose.

(2) Where partners sue or are sued in the name of the firm, the partners shall, on demand made in writing by any other party, forthwith deliver to the party making the demand and file a statement of the names and places of residence of all the persons who were partners in the firm when the cause of action arose.

(3) If the partners fail to comply with such a demand, the court, on application by any other party, may order the partners to furnish him with such a statement and to verify it on oath and may direct that in default –

(*a*) if the partners are plaintiffs, the proceedings be stayed on such terms as the court thinks fit, or

(*b*) if the partners are defendants, they be debarred from defending the action.

(4) When the names and places of residence of the partners have been stated in compliance with a demand or order under this rule, the proceedings shall continue in the name of the firm.

Defendant carrying on business in another name

10.—(1) A person carrying on business in England or Wales in a name other than his own name may be sued –

(*a*) in his own name, followed by the words 'trading as A.B.', or,

(*b*) in his business name, followed by the words '(a trading name)'.

(2) Where a person is sued in his business name in accordance with paragraph (1) (*b*), the provisions of these rules relating to actions against firms shall, subject to the provisions of any enactment, apply as if he were a partner and the name in which he carries on business were the name of his firm.

ORDER 7

Service of Documents

Part I – Generally

General mode of service

1.—(1) Where by virtue of these rules any document is required to be served on any person and no other mode of service is prescribed by any Act or rule, the document may be served –

(*a*) if the person to be served is acting in person, by delivering it to him personally or by delivering it at, or sending it by first-class post to, his address for service or, if he has no address for service –

    (i) by delivering the document at his residence or by sending it by first-class post to his last known residence, or

    (ii) in the case of a proprietor of a business, by delivering the document at his place of business or sending it by first-class post to his last known place of business;

(*b*) if the person to be served is acting by a solicitor –

    (i) by delivering the document at, or sending it by first-class post to, the solicitor's address for service, or

    (ii) where the solicitor's address for service includes a numbered box at a document exchange, by leaving the document at that document exchange or at a document exchange which transmits documents daily to that document exchange.

(2) In this Order 'first-class post' means first-class post which has been pre-paid or in respect of which prepayment is not required.

(3) Any document which is left at a document exchange in accordance with paragraph (1) (*b*) (ii) shall, unless the contrary is proved, be deemed to have been served on the second day on which it is left.

(4) In determining for the purposes of paragraphs (1) (*b*) (ii) and (3) –

(*a*) whether a document exchange transmits documents daily to another document exchange, and

(*b*) the second day after a document is left at a document exchange,

any day on which the court office is closed shall be excluded.

Personal service

2. Where any document is required by an Act or rule to be served personally –

(*a*) service shall be effected by leaving the document with the person to be served;

(*b*) the document may be served by –

    (i) a bailiff of the court or, if the person to be served attends at the office of the court, any other officer of the court; or

    (ii) a party to the proceedings or some person acting as his agent; or

    (iii) the solicitor of a party or a solicitor acting as an agent for such solicitor or some person employed by either solicitor to serve the document;

but service shall not be effected by any person under the age of 16 years.

Days on which no service permitted

3. Without prejudice to Order 40, rule 5 (5), no process shall be served or executed within England or Wales on a Sunday, Good Friday or Christmas Day except, in the case of urgency, with the leave of the court.

Service beyond boundary of district

4.—(1) Any process to be served or executed by the bailiff of any court may be served or executed within a distance of not more than 500 metres beyond the boundary of the district of that court.

(2) Without prejudice to paragraph (1), any process to be served or executed by bailiff may, if the judge or registrar [district judge] of the court from which it issues so directs be served or executed within the district of any other court by the bailiff of the court from which the process issues.

Proof of service or non-service
6.—(1) The person effecting service of any document shall –

(a) if he is an officer of the court, make, sign and file a certificate showing the date, place and mode of service and any conduct money paid or tendered to the person served; and

(b) if he is not an officer of the court, file an affidavit of service.

(2) A bailiff who has failed to effect service of any document to be served by bailiff shall make, sign and file a certificate of non-service showing the reason why service has not been effected, and the proper officer of the bailiff's court shall send notice of non-service to the person at whose instance the document was issued.

Substituted service
8.—(1) If it appears to the court that it is impracticable for any reason to serve a document in any manner prescribed by these rules for the service of that document, the court may, upon an affidavit showing grounds, make an order (in this rule called 'an order for substituted service') giving leave for such steps to be taken as the court directs to bring the document to the notice of the person to be served.

(2) Where a document is to be served by bailiff, the proper officer of the bailiff's court shall, if so requested, take such steps as may be necessary to provide evidence on which an order for substituted service may be made.

PART II—DEFAULT AND FIXED DATE SUMMONSES

Application of Part II
9. Except as otherwise provided, this Part of this Order shall apply to both default and fixed date summonses and 'summons' shall be construed accordingly.

Mode of service
10.—(1) Subject to the provisions of any Act or rule (including the following paragraphs of this rule), service of a summons shall be effected –

(a) by the plaintiff delivering the summons to the defendant personally; or

(b) by an officer of the court sending it by first-class post to the defendant at the address stated in the request for the summons.

(2) Unless the plaintiff or his solicitor otherwise requests, service shall be effected in accordance with paragraph (1) (b).

(3) Where a summons is served in accordance with paragraph (1) (b), the date of service shall, unless the contrary is shown, be deemed to be the seventh day after the date on which the summons was sent to the defendant.

(4) Where a summons has been sent by post under paragraph (1) (b) to the address stated in the request for the summons and has been returned to the court office undelivered, notice of non-service shall be sent pursuant to

rule 6 (2) together with a notice informing the plaintiff that he may request bailiff service at that address and, if such service is requested, it shall be effected by a bailiff of the court –

- (*a*) inserting the summons, enclosed in an envelope addressed to the defendant, through the letterbox at the address stated in the request for the summons, or
- (*b*) delivering the summons to some person, apparently not less than 16 years old, at the address stated in the request for the summons, or
- (*c*) delivering the summons to the defendant personally.

(5) Service of a fixed date summons shall be effected not less than 21 days before the return day; but, without prejudice to the power to abridge that period under Order 13, rule 4, service may be effected at any time before the return day on the plaintiff satisfying the registrar [district judge] by affidavit that the defendant is about to remove from the address stated in the request for the summons.

Service by post by solicitors
10A.—(1) In an action for personal injuries, the summons may be served in accordance with the provisions of this rule by the plaintiff's solicitor sending it by first-class post to the defendant at the address stated in the summons.
(2) Service may be effected under this rule only where the summons has been prepared in accordance with Order 3, rule 3 (1A).
(3) Where a summons is served under this rule –

- (*a*) rules 10 (3) and (4) and 13 and Order 37, rule 3 shall apply, with the necessary modifications, as if the summons had been served by post by an officer of the court;
- (*b*) rules 6 (1) (*b*) and 10 (2) shall not apply, and
- (*c*) it shall be treated, for the purposes of these rules, as if it had been served by an officer of the court.

(4) Where a summons has been served under this rule and the plaintiff applies for judgment under Order 9, rule 6 (1), his request under paragraph (1A) (*a*) of that rule shall be accompanied by an affidavit verifying that service was effected in accordance with this rule and that the summons was not returned undelivered.

Solicitor accepting service
11. Where a defendant's solicitor gives a certificate that he accepts service of the summons on behalf of that defendant and stating an address for service, the summons shall be deemed to have been duly served on that defendant on the date on which the certificate was made.

Presumed service of summons
12. Where a summons has not been served in accordance with these rules but the defendant delivers a defence, admission or counterclaim, the summons shall be deemed, unless the contrary is shown, to have been duly served on him on the date on which the defence, admission or counterclaim was so delivered.

Partners

13.—(1) Subject to the following paragraphs of this rule, where partners are sued in the name of their firm, service of a summons shall be good service on all the partners, whether any of them is out of England and Wales or not, if the summons is –

(*a*) delivered by the plaintiff to a partner personally, or
(*b*) served by an officer of the court sending it by first-class post to the firm at the address stated in the request for the summons.

(2) Where the partnership has to the knowledge of the plaintiff been dissolved before the commencement of the action, the summons shall be served upon every person within England and Wales sought to be made liable.

(3) Rule 10 (2) and (3) shall apply in relation to service by post under paragraph (1) (*b*) as they apply in relation to service under rule 10.

(4) Rule 10 (4) shall apply in relation to service under this rule as it applies in relation to service under rule 10, but with the reference to paragraph (1) (*b*) being read as a reference to the same paragraph in this rule and with the substitution for paragraphs (*b*) and (*c*) of the following paragraphs –

'(*b*) delivering the summons at the principal place of the partnership business within the district within which the summons is to be served to any person having, or appearing to have, at the time of service, the control or management of the business there, or
(*c*) delivering the summons to a partner personally.'

Service on body corporate

14.—(1) Service of a summons on a body corporate may, in cases for which provision is not otherwise made by an enactment, be effected by serving it on the mayor, chairman or president of the body or the chief executive, clerk, secretary, treasurer or other similar officer thereof.

(2) Service of a summons on a company registered in England and Wales may be effected by serving it at the registered office or at any place of business of the company which has some real connection with the cause or matter in issue.

(3) Where a summons has been served under paragraph (2) other than at the registered office, and, after judgment has been entered or given or an order has been made, it appears to the court that the summons did not come to the knowledge of an appropriate person within the company in due time, the court may, upon application or of its own motion, set aside the judgment or order and may give such directions as it thinks fit.

Recovery of land

15.—(1) Where, in the case of a summons for the recovery of land which is to be served by bailiff, the court is of opinion that it is impracticable to serve the summons in accordance with any of the foregoing provisions of this part of this Order, the summons may be served in a manner authorised by this rule.

(2) The summons may be served on any person on the premises who is the husband or wife of the defendant or on any person who has or appears to have the authority of the defendant –

(*a*) to reside or carry on business in the premises or to manage them on behalf of the defendant or to receive any rents or profits of the premises or to pay any outgoings in respect of the premises; or

(*b*) to safeguard or deal with the premises or with the furniture or other goods on the premises,

and service on any such person shall be effected in the manner required by these rules with respect to a fixed date summons.

(3) Paragraph (2) shall apply to a man and woman who are living with each other in the same household as husband and wife as it applies to the parties to a marriage.

(4) Where the premises are vacant or are occupied only by virtue of the presence of furniture or other goods, the summons may be served by affixing it to some conspicuous part of the premises.

(5) Unless the court otherwise orders, service of a summons in accordance with this rule shall be good service on the defendant, but if a claim for the recovery of money is joined with the claim for recovery of land, the court shall order the summons to be marked 'not served' with respect to the money claim unless in special circumstances the court thinks it just to hear and determine both claims.

Notice of service of default summons
21. Where a default summons has been served by a bailiff or other officer of a county court, the proper officer of that court shall send notice of service to the plaintiff.

ORDER 9

ADMISSION, DEFENCE, COUNTERCLAIM AND ANSWER

Application of Order
1. Except as otherwise provided, the provisions of this Order relating to actions shall apply to both default and fixed date actions.

Admission, defence or counterclaim to be delivered
2.—(1) This rule applies where a defendant in any action –

(*a*) admits his liability for the whole or part of the plaintiff's claim;
(*b*) desires time for payment of any sum admitted by him;
(*c*) disputes his liability for the whole or part of the plaintiff's claim, or
(*d*) desires to set up a counterclaim.

(2) In this rule and rules 3 and 6 –

'a request for time for payment' means a request containing a proposal as to the date of payment or, if it is proposed to pay by instalments, the frequency and amount of the instalments;
'admission' and 'a statement of means' means the relevant form appended to the summons completed according to the circumstances of the case;
'defence' includes a counterclaim and means the relevant form appended

to the summons completed according to the circumstances of the case or a defence otherwise than on that form;

'proper officer' does not include the district judge;

and paragraph (1A) of Order 6, rule 1 shall apply, with the necessary modifications, to a defendant making a counterclaim as it applies to a plaintiff.

(3) Except where paragraph (5) (*a*) applies, a defendant in an action for a liquidated sum who –

(*a*) admits his liability for the whole of the plaintiff's claim, and

(*b*) desires time for payment of the sum admitted by him,

shall, within 14 days after the service of the summons on him, deliver to the plaintiff a form of admission together with a statement of his means and a request for time for payment.

(4) The court may at any time allow a defendant to amend or withdraw an admission made by him under this rule on such terms as may be just.

(5) A defendant who admits liability –

(*a*) in an action brought by a plaintiff under disability,

(*b*) in an action for an unliquidated sum, or

(*c*) in an action for a liquidated sum, for part of the plaintiff's claim

shall, within 14 days after the service of the summons on him, –

(i)   deliver at the court office an admission of liability together with, if he so wishes, a request for time for payment and, where such a request is made, a statement of means, and

(ii) if he wishes to defend part of the plaintiff's claim or to make a counterclaim, comply with the requirements of paragraph (6).

(6) A defendant who either –

(*a*) disputes his liability for the whole or part of the plaintiff's claim; or

(*b*) desires to set up a counterclaim

shall, within 14 days after the service of the summons on him, and in addition to any documents he may provide pursuant to paragraph (5), deliver at the court office a defence –

(i)   defending the whole or part of the claim, or, as the case may be,

(ii) making a counterclaim.

(7) On receipt of the admission or defence, the proper officer shall –

(*a*) send a copy to the plaintiff together, in a case to which paragraph (1) of rule 3 relates, with a notice of the requirements of that paragraph; and

(*b*) where the defendant states in his defence that he has paid the amount claimed, request the plaintiff to confirm in writing that he wishes the proceedings to continue.

(8) In an action for a liquidated sum, the proceedings shall be automatically transferred to the defendant's home court if the action was not commenced in that court –

(*a*) except where sub-paragraph (*b*) applies, on the filing of a defence, or (*b*) in a case to which paragraph (7) (*b*) applies, where the plaintiff confirms in writing under that paragraph that he wishes the proceedings to continue.

Admission of part or request for time in default action
3.—(1) Where the defendant admits part of the plaintiff's claim or admits the whole or part of the plaintiff's claim and makes a request for time for payment, the plaintiff may, if he accepts the amount admitted, –

(*a*) in an action to which rule 2 (3) applies, in filing a request in the appropriate form and certifying the terms of the defendant's admission, have judgment entered for the amount so admitted and costs (less any payments made);

(*b*) where the amount admitted is less than the amount claimed and the plaintiff accepts any proposal as to the time of payment, on filing a request in the appropriate form, stating what (if any) payment has been made, have judgment entered for the amount so admitted and costs (less any payments made); or

(*c*) give notice that he accepts the amount so admitted but not the proposal as to time of payment.

(2) A plaintiff's notice under paragraph (1) (*c*) shall be given in the appropriate form and shall –

(*a*) give his reasons for the non-acceptance;
(*b*) state what (if any) payments have been made; and
(*c*) where the defendant sent his admission direct to the plaintiff pursuant to rule 2 (3), be accompanied by a copy of the defendant's admission.

(3) Upon receipt of the plaintiff's notice under paragraph (1) (*c*), the proper officer shall determine the time of payment and enter judgment accordingly.

(4) Any party affected by a judgment entered under paragraph (3) may, within 14 days of service of the judgment on him and giving his reasons, apply on notice for the order as to time of payment to be re-considered and, where such an application is made –

(*a*) the proceedings shall be automatically transferred to the defendant's home court if the judgment or order was not given or made in that court;

(*b*) the proper officer shall fix a day for the hearing of the application before the district judge and give to the plaintiff and the defendant not less than 8 days' notice of the day so fixed.

(5) On hearing an application under paragraph (4), the district judge may confirm the order or set it aside and make such new order as he thinks fit, and the order so made shall be entered in the records of the court.

(6) Where the defendant admits part of the plaintiff's claim and the plaintiff notifies the proper officer that he does not accept the amount admitted,

(*a*) the proceedings shall be automatically transferred to the defendant's home court if the action was not commenced in that court;

(*b*) the proper officer shall fix a day for a pre-trial review or, if he thinks fit, a day for the hearing of the action and give to the plaintiff and defendant not less than 8 days' notice of the day so fixed.

Nothing in sub-paragraph (*b*) shall require the proper officer to fix a day for a pre-trial review in proceedings which are referred to arbitration under Order 19.

(7) Where the action is for unliquidated damages and the defendant delivers an admission of liability for the claim but disputes or does not admit the amount of the plaintiff's damages, then –

(*a*) if the defendant offers to pay in satisfaction of the claim a specific sum which the plaintiff accepts, the provisions of this rule shall apply as if the defendant had admitted part of the plaintiff's claim; and

(*b*) in any other case, the plaintiff may apply to the court for such judgment as he may be entitled to upon the admission, and the court may give such judgment, including interlocutory judgment for damages to be assessed and costs, or make such other order on the application as it thinks just.

(8) Where it appears that the proper officer's notice under rule 2 (7) or the judgment under paragraph (3) above did not come to the knowledge of the party to be served in due time, the district judge may of his own motion or on application set aside the judgment and may give such directions as he thinks fit.

Admission in fixed date action

4.—(1) If within the period of 14 days mentioned in rule 2 the defendant in a fixed date action other than an action for the recovery of land delivers at the court office an admission of the whole or part of the plaintiff's claim, the plaintiff may apply to the court for such judgment as he may be entitled to upon the admission, without waiting for the return day or for the determination of any other question between the parties and the court may give such judgment or make such order on the application as it thinks just.

(2) An application under paragraph (1) shall, if made before the return day, be made on notice to the defendant.

Judgment in default in fixed date action

4A. Where, in a fixed date action to which Order 17, rule 11 applies, the defendant fails to deliver a defence within the period of 14 days mentioned in rule 2, the plaintiff may apply to the court for judgment or directions as to the conduct of the proceedings and the court may, subject to the provisions of these rules, give such judgment or directions on the application as it thinks just.

Defence or counterclaim in default action

5.—(1) Subject to paragraph (2), if –

(*a*) within 14 days after service of the summons upon him, the defendant in a default action delivers at the court office either a defence not accompanied by an admission of any part of the plaintiff's claim or a counterclaim; or

(*b*) in a case to which rule 2 (7) (*b*) applies, after the plaintiff has confirmed that he wishes the proceedings to continue, the proper officer shall –

> (i) fix a day for a pre-trial review or, if he thinks fit, a day for the hearing of the action, and
> (ii) give to all parties not less than 14 days' notice of the day so fixed for the pre-trial review or, in the case of a day for the hearing of the action, not less than 21 days' notice.

(2) Nothing in paragraph (1) shall require the proper officer to fix a day in a case to which Order 17, rule 11 applies.

Judgment in default or on admission in default action
6.—(1) Subject to paragraphs (2), (3) and (4) and rule 7, if the defendant in a default action –

> (a) does not within 14 days after service of the summons on him pay to the plaintiff the total amount of the claim and costs on the summons,
> (b) delivers an admission of the whole of the plaintiff's claim unaccompanied by a counterclaim or a request for time for payment, or
> (c) does not deliver an admission of part of the plaintiff's claim, a defence or counterclaim,

the plaintiff may upon fulfilling the requirements of paragraph (1A) have judgment entered against the defendant for the amount of the claim and costs (less any payments made); and the order shall be for payment forthwith or at such time or times as the plaintiff may specify.

(1A) The requirements are that the plaintiff shall –

> (a) file a request for judgment,
> (b) where the action is for a liquidated sum, certify that the defendant has not sent to him any reply to the summons, and
> (c) state what (if any) payment has been made.

In this paragraph, 'reply to the summons' means –

> (i) a defence,
> (ii) a counterclaim,
> (iii) an admission of the whole of the plaintiff's claim accompanied by a counterclaim or a request for time for payment,
> (iv) an admission of part of the plaintiff's claim,

or any other written reply of a similar kind.

(2) If the plaintiff's claim is for unliquidated damages, any judgment entered under paragraph (1) shall be an interlocutory judgment for damages to be assessed and costs.

(3) Where the defendant is a State as defined in section 14 of the State Immunity Act 1978 –

> (a) the plaintiff may not enter judgment under paragraph (1) without the leave of the judge and RSC Order 13, rule 7A, shall apply to an application for such leave as it applies to an application for leave to enter judgment against a State in the High Court;
> (b) the plaintiff may not enforce a judgment entered pursuant to such leave until two months after a copy of it has been served on the State.

(4) Where an originating process has been served out of England and Wales under Order 8, rule 2 (2) (a) or has been served within England and

Wales on a defendant domiciled in Scotland or Northern Ireland or in any other Convention territory the plaintiff may not enter Judgment under paragraph (1) without the leave of the court and RSC Order 13, rule 7B shall apply to an application for such leave as it applies to an application for leave to enter judgment in the High Court.

Recovery of interest

8.—(1) The sum for which judgment is entered under rule 3 (3) or 6 (1) may include interest to the date of the issue of the summons or, where it is claimed at the same rate in respect of the period down to judgment, to the date of the request for entry of judgment, provided that –

(*a*) particulars of the amount claimed down to issue, rate and period are set out in the particulars of claim; and

(*b*) in the case of interest claimed under section 69 of the Act the rate is not higher than that payable on judgment debts in the High Court at the date of issue of the summons.

(2) Where, in accordance with paragraph (1), the plaintiff requests the entry of judgment for interest in respect of a period subsequent to issue, he shall enter such interest on the appropriate form of request as an additional item, with particulars of the amount, rate and period.

(3) Save as provided by paragraph (1), where a judgment is sought under rule 3 (3) or 6 (1) in respect of a claim which includes a claim for interest, and the plaintiff so requests, the judgment shall, as regards the interest, be an interlocutory judgment for interest to be assessed.

Failure to deliver admission etc. in time

9.—(1) Notwithstanding that the period of 14 days mentioned in rule 2 has expired, a defendant may deliver an admission, defence or counterclaim at any time before the entry of judgment under rule 6 or, in a fixed date action, before the entry of judgment under rule 4A or the return day, whichever is the earlier and if time permits the same procedure shall be followed as if the admission, defence or counterclaim had been delivered within the said period of 14 days.

(2) Notwithstanding that he has failed to deliver a defence, the defendant in a fixed date action may appear on the return day and dispute the plaintiff's claim.

(3) In any case to which paragraph (1) or (2) applies, the court may order the defendant to pay any costs properly incurred in consequence of his delay or failure.

Striking out default action after twelve months

10. Where 12 months have expired from the date of service of a default summons and –

(i) no admission, defence or counterclaim has been delivered and judgment has not been entered against the defendant, or

(ii) an admission has been delivered but no judgment has been entered under rule 6 (1) or, as the circumstances may require, no notice of acceptance or non-acceptance has been received by the proper officer,

the action shall be struck out and no enlargement of the period of 12 months shall be granted under Order 13, rule 4.

Summary judgment where no real defence
14.—(1) This rule applies to any action except –

    (*a*) an action which stands referred to arbitration under Order 19, rule 3;

    (*b*) an action in which a claim is made for possession of land or in which the title to any land is in question;

    (*c*) an action which includes a claim by the plaintiff for libel, slander, malicious prosecution or false imprisonment;

    (*d*) [*Omitted.*]

    (*e*) an Admiralty action *in rem*.

(1A) Without prejudice to rule 11 and Order 13, rule 5, where the defendant in an action to which this rule applies has delivered at the court office a document purporting to be a defence, the plaintiff may apply to the court for judgment against the defendant on the ground that, notwithstanding the delivery of that document, the defendant has no defence to the claim or to a particular part of the claim.

(2) An application under paragraph (1) shall be supported by an affidavit verifying the facts on which the claim or the part of it to which the application relates is based and stating that in the deponent's belief, notwithstanding the document which has been delivered, there is no defence to the claim or that part.

(3) Notice of the application, together with a copy of the affidavit in support and of any exhibits referred to therein, shall be served on the defendant not less than 7 days before the day fixed for the hearing of the application.

(4) Where an application under paragraph (1) is made at a time when a day has been fixed for the pre-trial review of the action, the application shall, unless otherwise directed, be heard on that day, and in any case, if on the hearing of the application the court orders that the defendant do have leave (whether conditional or unconditional) to defend the action with respect to the claim or part of the claim, the court may treat the hearing as a pre-trial review and Order 17 with the necessary modifications shall apply accordingly.

(5) The provisions of the RSC relating to –

    (*a*) showing cause against an application under Order 14 of those rules,

    (*b*) giving the plaintiff judgment or granting the defendant leave to defend on such an application, and

    (*c*) granting summary judgment on a counterclaim,

shall apply in relation to an application under this rule as they apply in relation to an application under the said Order 14.

ORDER 13

APPLICATIONS AND ORDERS IN THE COURSE OF PROCEEDINGS

General provisions
1.—(1) Except as otherwise provided, the following paragraphs of this rule shall have effect in relation to any application authorised by or under any

Act or rule to be made in the course of an action or matter before or after judgment.

(2) Unless allowed or authorised to be made ex parte, the application shall be made on notice, which shall be filed and served on the opposite party not less than two days before the hearing of the application.

(3) Where the application is made ex parte, notice of the application shall be filed a reasonable time before the application is heard, unless the court otherwise directs.

(4) Unless allowed or authorised to be made otherwise, every application shall be heard in chambers.

(5) Where any party to the application fails to attend on the hearing the court may proceed in his absence if, having regard to the nature of the application, the court thinks it expedient to do so.

(6) The jurisdiction of the court to hear and determine the application may be exercised by the registrar and the applicant shall, unless the judge otherwise directs, make the application to the registrar in the first instance.

(7) Where the application is made to the registrar, he may refer to the judge any matter which he thinks should properly be decided by the judge, and the judge may either dispose of the matter or refer it back to the registrar with such directions as he thinks fit.

(8) The court may, as a condition of granting any application, impose such terms and conditions as it thinks fit, including a term or condition requiring any party to –

(*a*) give security,
(*b*) give an undertaking,
(*c*) pay money into court,
(*d*) pay all or any part of the costs of the proceedings, or
(*e*) give a power of re-entry.

(9) Unless the court otherwise directs, the costs of the application shall not be taxed until the general taxation of the costs of the action or matter and, where an earlier taxation is directed, Order 38 shall apply as if the word 'claimed' were substituted for the word 'recovered' wherever it appears.

(10) An appeal shall lie to the judge from any order made by the registrar [district judge] on the application and the appeal shall be disposed of in chambers unless the judge otherwise directs.

(11) An appeal under paragraph (10) shall be made on notice, which shall be filed and served on the opposite party within 5 days after the order appealed from or such further time as the judge may allow.

Extension or abridgment of time
4.—(1) Except as otherwise provided, the period within which a person is required or authorised by these rules or by any judgment, order or direction to do any act in any proceedings may be extended or abridged by consent of all the parties or by the court on the application of any party.

(2) Any such period may be extended by the court although the application for extension is not made until after the expiration of the period.

Application for injunction
6.—(1) An application for the grant of an injunction may be made by any party to an action or matter before or after the trial or hearing, whether or

not a claim for the injunction was included in that party's particulars of claim, originating application, petition, counterclaim or third party notice, as the case may be.

(2) Except where the district judge has power under Order 21, rule 5 or otherwise to hear and determine the proceedings in which the application is made, the application shall be made to the judge and rule 1 (6) shall not apply.

(3) The application shall be made in the appropriate prescribed form and shall –

(*a*) state the terms of the injunctions applied for; and

(*b*) be supported by an affidavit in which the grounds for making the application are set out,

and a copy of the affidavit and a copy of the application shall be served on the party against whom the injunction is sought not less than 2 days before the hearing of the application.

(3A) Where an order is sought ex parte before a copy of the application has been served on the other party, the affidavit shall explain why the application is so made and a copy of any order made ex parte shall be served with the application and affidavit in accordance with paragraph (3).

(4) An application may not be made before the issue of the summons, originating application or petition by which the action or matter is to be commenced except where the case is one of urgency, and in that case –

(*a*) the affidavit in support of the application shall show that the action or matter is one which the court to which the application is made has jurisdiction to hear and determine, and

(*b*) the injunction applied for shall, if granted, be on terms providing for the issue of the summons, originating application or petition in the court granting the application and on such other terms, if any, as the court thinks fit.

(4A) Paragraph (4) (*a*) and (*b*) shall apply, with the necessary modifications, where an application for an injunction is made by a defendant in a case of urgency before issuing a counterclaim or cross-application.

(5) Unless otherwise directed, every application not made ex parte shall be heard in open court.

(6) Except where the case is one of urgency, a draft of the injunction shall be prepared beforehand by the party making an application to the judge under paragraph (1) and, if the application is granted, the draft shall be submitted to the judge by whom the application was heard and shall be settled by him.

(7) The injunction, when settled, shall be forwarded to the proper officer for filing.

Interim payments
12.—(1) Subject to the following paragraphs of this rule, the provisions of RSC Order 29, Part II shall apply in relation to proceedings in a county court except where those proceedings stand referred for arbitration under Order 19, rule 3.

(2) RSC Order 29, rule 10 shall apply with the substitution in rule 10 (4), for the words 'not less than 10 clear days before the return day', of the words 'not less than 7 days before the day fixed for the hearing of the application'.

(3) RSC Order 29, rule 13 (1) shall apply with the substitution, for the

reference to RSC Order 80, rule 12, of a reference to Order 10, rule 11 of these Rules.

(4) RSC Order 29, rule 14 shall not apply but where an application is made for an order requiring the defendant to make an interim payment the court may treat the hearing of the application as a pre-trial review and Order 17 with the necessary modifications shall apply accordingly.

ORDER 15

Amendment

Amendment by order
1.—(1) Without prejudice to Order 5, rules 8 and 11, and rule 2 of this Order, but subject to the following paragraphs of this rule, the court may, in any action or matter, by order allow or direct –

   (*a*) any originating process, pleading or any other document in the proceedings to be amended, or
   (*b*) any person to be added, struck out or substituted as a party to the proceedings,

if the amendment, where falling within sub-paragraph (*a*) or (*b*), is such that the High Court would have power to allow in a like case.

(2) In any case where a relevant limitation period has expired, the reference in paragraph (1) to the power of the High Court to allow the amendment shall be construed, in particular, as a reference to its power to do so subject to the conditions and restrictions imposed by section 35 of the Limitation Act 1980 and the RSC made thereunder.

(3) An order under paragraph (1) may be made on application at the hearing of the action or matter or before the hearing on notice or by the court of its own motion at any stage of the proceedings.

(4) No person shall be added as a plaintiff without his consent signified in writing or in such other manner as may be authorised.

(5) If a summons or other document issued by the court is to be amended pursuant to an order under paragraph (1), the amendment shall be made by the proper officer, and if any other document is to be amended, the amendment shall be made by the party whose document it is and he shall, if authorised or required to do so, file and serve on every other party to the procedings a copy of the document as so amended.

(6) Where by an order under paragraph (1) a person is added or substituted as a defendant, the amended originating process shall, unless the court otherwise directs, be served on him in accordance with the rules applicable to the service of the originating process.

In relation to a person added or substituted as a defendant to a counterclaim this paragraph shall have effect as if for the reference to the amended originating process there were substituted a reference to the amended counterclaim.

Amendment of pleadings without order
2.—(1) Subject to Order 9, rule 2 (3) and the following provisions of this rule, in any action or matter a party may, without an order, amend any pleading of his –

(*a*) at any time before the return day, by filing the amended pleading and serving a copy on every other party, and

(*b*) at any stage of the proceedings, by filing the amended pleading endorsed with the consent of every party to the proceedings.

Where a day has been fixed for the pre-trial review of the action or matter, that day shall be treated as the return day for the purpose of this paragraph.

(2) Where in a default action the plaintiff's claim is amended under paragraph (1) by adding or substituting a claim which could not be made in a default action, the action shall continue as if it has been commenced as a fixed date action.

(3) The court may, of its motion or on the application of the opposite party, disallow an amendment made under paragraph (1) and shall do so where it is satisfied that, if an application for leave to make the amendment had been made under rule 1, leave would have been refused.

(4) Where the plaintiff amends any pleading under paragraph (1) (*a*) he shall not apply for judgment under Order 9, rule 6 until 14 days after the service of the amendment on the defendant.

ORDER 17

Pre-Trial Review

Matters to be considered on pre-trial review
1. On any day fixed for the pre-trial review of an action or matter the registrar shall, subject to the following provisions of this Order, consider the course of the proceedings and give all such directions as appear to be necessary or desirable for securing the just, expeditious and economical disposal of the action or matter.

Securing admissions and agreements
2. On the pre-trial review the registrar shall endeavour to secure that the parties make all such admissions and agreements as ought reasonably to be made by them in relation to the proceedings and may record in the order made on the review any admission or agreement so made or any refusal to make any admission or agreement.

Application for particular direction
3. Every party shall, so far as practicable, apply on the pre-trial review for any particular direction he may desire and shall file and give to every other party notice of his intention to do so, and if an application which might have been made on the review is made subsequently, the applicant shall pay the costs of and occasioned by the application, unless the court otherwise directs.

Rules as to interlocutory applications to apply
4. The provisions of these rules relating to interlocutory applications shall have effect as if the pre-trial review were the hearing of an interlocutory application and accordingly the registrar [district judge] may, on the review, exercise any of the powers exercisable by him on an interlocutory

application and may do so of his own motion if no application is made for the exercise of the power.

Non-appearance by plaintiff
5.—(1) If the plaintiff does not appear on the pre-trial review, the registrar [district judge] may, without prejudice to any other power, proceed with the review in his absence or order the action or matter to be struck out.

(2) Order 21, rules 1 (2) and (3) and 2 (2), shall apply with the necessary modifications, in relation to the striking out of an action or matter under paragraph (1) as they apply in relation to the striking out of proceedings under Order 21, rule 1 (1).

Admission by defendant of plaintiff's claim
6. If, on or before the pre-trial review, the defendant admits the plaintiff's claim or such part thereof as the plaintiff accepts in satisfaction of his claim, the registrar may give such judgment or make such order as he thinks just.

Non-appearance by defendant who has not delivered admission or defence
7.—(1) If the defendant does not appear on the pre-trial review of an action and has not delivered an admission or defence, the registrar may, if he thinks fit, enter judgment for the plaintiff.

(2) If the plaintiff's claim is for unliquidated damages, any judgment entered under paragraph (1) shall be an interlocutory judgment for damages to be assessed, unless at the time of the entry of judgment the plaintiff adduces evidence as to the amount of his damages.

Non-appearance by defendant who has delivered defence
8. If the defendant has delivered a defence but does not appear on the pre-trial review of an action, the registrar [district judge] may, at the request of the plaintiff and upon proof of facts entitling him to relief, give such judgment or make such order as the registrar thinks fit.

Fixing date of hearing
9. On or as soon as practicable after the completion by the registrar [district judge] of his consideration of the matters referred to in rule 1 the proper officer shall, if the action or matter remains to be heard and determined, fix a day for the hearing and give notice thereof to every party.

Pre-trial review in other proceedings
10. If in any proceedings in which no pre-trial review has been fixed the registrar is nevertheless of opinion that the question of giving directions ought to be considered, then, without prejudice to Order 13, rule 2 (4), he may, with a view to obtaining assistance in such consideration, cause notice to be given to the parties requiring them to appear before him on a day named in the notice and thereupon the provision of this Order shall have effect, with the necessary modifications, as if that day were the day fixed for a pre-trial review.

Automatic directions
11.—(1) This rule applies to any default or fixed date action except –

(*a*) an action for the administration of the estate of a deceased person;
(*b*) an Admiralty action;

(c) proceedings which are referred for arbitration under Order 19;
(d) an action arising out of a regulated consumer credit agreement within the meaning of the Consumer Credit Act 1974;
(e) an action for the delivery of goods;
(f) an action for the recovery of income tax;
(g) interpleader proceedings or an action in which an application is made for relief by way of interpleader;
(h) an action of a kind mentioned in section 66(3) of the Act (trial by jury);
(i) an action for the recovery of land;
(j) a partnership action;
(k) an action to which Order 48A applies (patent actions);
(l) a contentious probate action;
(m) a rent action;
(n) an action to which Order 5, rule 5 applies (representative proceedings);
(o) an action to which Order 9, rule 3 (6) applies (admission of part of plaintiff's claim);
(p) an action on a third party notice or similar proceedings under Order 12;
(q) an action to which Order 47, rule 3 applies (actions in tort between husband and wife).

(1A) This rule applies to actions transferred from the High Court as it applies to actions commenced in a county court but (without prejudice to paragraph (2)) where directions have been given by the High Court, directions taking effect automatically under this rule shall have effect subject to any directions given by the High Court.

(2) In an action to which this rule applies –

(a) except where a pre-trial review is ordered pursuant to a direction given under paragraph (4) (a), the foregoing provisions of this Order shall not apply and directions shall take effect automatically in accordance with the following paragraphs of this rule;
(b) where the court gives directions with regard to any matter arising in the course of proceedings, directions taking effect automatically under this rule shall have effect subject to any directions given by the court.

(3) When the pleadings are deemed to be closed, the following directions shall take effect –

(a) there shall be discovery of documents within 28 days, and inspection within 7 days thereafter, in accordance with paragraph (5);
(b) except with the leave of the court or where all parties agree –
   (i) no expert evidence may be adduced at the trial unless the substance of that evidence has been disclosed to the other parties in the form of a written report within 10 weeks; and
   (ii) subject to paragraph (7), the number of expert witnesses of any kind shall be limited to two; and
   (iii) any party who intends to place reliance at the trial on any other oral evidence shall, within 10 weeks, serve on the other parties written statements of all such oral evidence which he intends to adduce;

(c)   photographs and sketch plans and, in an action for personal injuries, the contents of any police accident report book shall be receivable in evidence at the trial, and shall be agreed if possible;

(d)   unless a day has already been fixed, the plaintiff shall within 6 months request the proper officer to fix a day for the hearing and rule 12 shall apply where such request is made.

(3A) Paragraphs (4) to (16) of Order 20, rule 12A shall apply with respect to statements and reports served under sub-paragraph (3) (*b*) as they apply with respect to statements served under that rule.

(4) Nothing in paragraph (3) shall –

(a)   prevent the court from giving, of its own motion or on the application of any party, such further or different directions or orders as may in the circumstances be appropriate (including an order that a pre-trial review be held or fixing a date for the hearing or dismissing the proceedings or striking out any claim made therein); or

(b)   prevent the making of an order for the transfer of the proceedings to the High Court or another county court,

and rule 3 shall apply where an application is made under this paragraph as it applies to applications made on a pre-trial review.

(5) Subject to paragraph (6), the parties must make discovery by serving lists of documents and –

(a)   subject to sub-paragraph (*c*), each party must make and serve on every other party a list of documents which are or have been in his possession, custody or power relating to any matter in question between them in the action;

(b)   the court may, on application, –
   (i)   order that discovery under this paragraph shall be limited to such documents or classes of documents only, or as to such only of the matters in question, as may be specified in the order, or
   (ii)   if satisfied that discovery by all or any of the parties is not necessary, order that there shall be no discovery of documents by any or all of the parties;
   and the court shall make such an order if and so far as it is of opinion that discovery is not necessary either for disposing fairly of the action or for saving costs;

(c)   where liability is admitted or in an action for personal injuries arising out of a road accident, discovery shall be limited to disclosure of any documents relating to the amount of damages;

(d)   the provisions of Order 14 of these rules relating to inspection of documents shall apply where discovery is made under this paragraph as it applies where discovery is made under that Order.

(6) Discovery under paragraph (5) shall not apply in proceedings to which the Crown is a party.

(7) In an action for personal injuries –

(a)   the number of expert witnesses shall be limited in any case to two medical experts and one expert of any other kind;

(b)   nothing in paragraph (3) shall require a party to produce a further medical report if he proposes to rely at the trial only on the report provided pursuant to Order 6, rule 1 (5) or (6) but, where a further report is disclosed, that report shall be accompanied by an amended statement of the special damages claimed, if appropriate.

(8) Where the plaintiff makes a request pursuant to paragraph (3) (*d*) for the proper officer to fix a day for the hearing, he shall file a note which shall if possible be agreed by the parties giving –

(*a*) an estimate of the length of the trial, and
(*b*) the number of witnesses to be called.

(9) If no request is made pursuant to paragraph (3) (*d*) within 15 months of the day on which pleadings are deemed to be closed (or within 9 months after the expiry of any period fixed by the court for making such a request), the action shall be automatically struck out.

(10) Where the proper officer fixes a day for the hearing, he shall give not less than 21 days' notice thereof to every party.

(11) For the purposes of this rule, –

(*a*) pleadings shall be deemed to be closed 14 days after the delivery of a defence in accordance with Order 9, rule 2 or, where a counterclaim is served with the defence, 28 days after the delivery of the defence;
(*b*) 'a road accident' means an accident on land due to a collision or apprehended collision involving a vehicle;
(*c*) 'a statement of the special damages claimed' has the same meaning as in Order 6, rule 1 (7).

(12) Unless the context otherwise requires, references in these rules to the return day in relation to a fixed date action to which this rule applies shall be construed as references to the date on which directions take effect under this rule.

ORDER 19

REFERENCE TO ARBITRATION OR FOR INQUIRY AND REPORT OR TO EUROPEAN COURT

PART I – COUNTY COURT ARBITRATION

Interpretation and application
1. In this Part of this Order, unless the context otherwise requires –
'lay representative' means a person exercising a right of audience by virtue of an order made under section 11 of the Courts and Legal Services Act 1990 (representation in county courts), 'reference' means the reference of proceedings to arbitration under section 64 of the Act, 'order' means an order referring proceedings to arbitration under that section and 'outside arbitrator' means an arbitrator other than the judge or district judge.

2. In this Part of this Order –

(*a*) Rules 3 and 4 apply only to small claims automatically referred to arbitration under rule 3, and
(*b*) Rules 5 to 10 apply to all arbitrations.

Automatic reference to small claims
3.–(1) Any proceedings in which the sum claimed or amount involved does not exceed £1000 (leaving out of account the sum claimed or amount

involved in any counterclaim) shall stand referred for arbitration by the district judge upon the receipt by the court of a defence to the claim.

(2) Where any proceedings are referred for arbitration by the district judge under paragraph (1), he may, after considering the defence and whether on the application of any party or of his own motion, order trial in court if he is satisfied –

(a) that a difficult question of law or a question of fact of exceptional complexity is involved; or
(b) that fraud is alleged against a party; or
(c) that the parties are agreed that the dispute should be tried in court; or
(d) that it would be unreasonable for the claim to proceed to arbitration having regard to its subject matter, the size of any counterclaim, the circumstances of the parties or the interests of any other person likely to be affected by the award.

(3) Where the district judge is minded to order trial in court of his own motion –

(a) the proper officer shall notify the parties in writing specifying on which of the grounds mentioned in paragraph (2) the district judge is minded to order trial in court;
(b) within 14 days after service of the proper officer's notice on him, a party may give written notice stating his reasons for objecting to the making of the order;
(c) if in any notice under sub-paragraph (b) a party so requests, the proper office shall fix a day for a hearing at which the district judge –
  (i) shall decide whether to order trial in court, and
  (ii) may give directions regarding the steps to be taken before or at any subsequent hearing as if he were conducting a preliminary appointment or, as the case may be, a pre-trial review;

and, in the absence of any request under sub-paragraph (c), the district judge may, in the absence of the parties, order trial in court.

(4) For the purposes of paragraph (1), 'a defence to the claim' includes a document admitting liability for the claim but disputing or not admitting the amount claimed.

Restriction on allowance of costs in small claims
4.–(1) In this rule, 'costs' means –

(a) solicitors' charges,
(b) sums allowed to a litigant in person pursuant to Order 38, rule 17,
(c) a fee or reward charged by a lay representative for acting on behalf of a party in the proceedings.

(2) No costs shall be allowed as between party and party in respect of any proceedings referred to arbitration under rule 3, except –

(a) the costs which were stated on the summons or which would have been stated on the summons if the claim had been for a liquidated sum;
(b) the costs of enforcing the award, and
(c) such further costs as the district judge may direct where there has

been unreasonable conduct on the part of the opposite party in relation to the proceedings or the claim therein.

(3) Nothing in paragraph (2) shall be taken as precluding the award of the following allowances –

(*a*) any expenses which have been reasonably incurred by a party or a witness in travelling to and from the hearing or in staying away from home;

(*b*) a sum not exceeding £29.00 in respect of a party's or a witness's loss of earnings when attending a hearing;

(*c*) a sum not exceeding £112.50 in respect of the fees of an expert.

(4) Where trial in court is ordered, paragraph (2) shall not apply to costs incurred after the date of the order.

(5) Where costs are directed under paragraph (2) (*c*), those costs shall not be taxed and the amount to be allowed shall be specified by the arbitrator or the district judge.

The arbitrator
5.–(1) Unless the court otherwise orders, the district judge shall be the arbitrator.

(2) An order shall not be made referring proceedings to the Circuit judge except by or with the leave of the judge.

(3) An order shall not be made referring proceedings to an outside arbitrator except with the consent of the parties.

(4) Where proceedings are referred to an outside arbitrator, the order shall be served on the arbitrator as well as on the parties, but it shall not, unless the court directs, be served on anyone until each party has paid into court such sums as the district judge may determine in respect of the arbitrator's remuneration.

Preparation for the hearing
6.–(1) Paragraph (2) of this rule shall apply unless the district judge –

(*a*) is minded to order trial in court under rule 3 (3) or

(*b*) decides that a preliminary appointment should be held.

(2) Upon the reference to arbitration the district judge shall consider the documents filed and give an estimate of the time to be allowed for the hearing and the proper officer shall –

(*a*) give the parties not less than 21 days' notice of the day fixed for the hearing; and

(*b*) issue directions under paragraph (3) in the appropriate form regarding the steps to be taken before or at any subsequent hearing.

(3) Where proceedings stand referred to arbitration, the following directions shall take effect –

(*a*) each party shall not less than 14 days before the date fixed for the hearing send to every other party copies of all documents which are in his possession and on which that party intends to rely at the hearing;

(*b*) each party shall not less than 7 days before the date fixed for the hearing send to the court and to every other party a copy of any expert report on which that party intends to rely at the hearing and a list of the witnesses whom he intends to call at the hearing.

(4) A preliminary appointment shall only be held –

(*a*) where directions under paragraph (3) are not sufficient and special directions can only be given in the presence of the parties, or

(*b*) to enable the district judge to dispose of the case where the claim is ill-founded or there is no reasonable defence.

In deciding whether to hold a preliminary appointment, the district judge shall have regard to the desirability of minimising the number of court attendances by the parties.

(5) Where the district judge decides to hold a preliminary appointment, the proper officer shall fix a date for the appointment and give to the plaintiff and the defendant not less than 8 days' notice of the day so fixed.

(6) On the preliminary appointment the district judge shall have the same powers as he has under Order 17 on a pre-trial review and he shall –

(*a*) give an estimate of the time to be allowed for the hearing (unless the parties consent to his deciding the dispute on the statements and documents submitted to him); and

(*b*) whether of his own motion or at the request of a party, give such additional directions regarding the steps to be taken before and at the hearing as may appear to him to be necessary or desirable.

Directions given under sub-paragraph (*b*) may include (but shall not be limited to) a requirement that a party should clarify his claim or, as the case may be, his defence.

(7) After the preliminary appointment, the proper officer shall –

(*a*) give the parties not less than 21 days' notice of the day fixed for the hearing; and

(*b*) issue directions under paragraph (3) in the appropriate form regarding the steps to be taken before or at that hearing together with any additional directions given pursuant to paragraph (6) (*b*).

(8) The district judge may from time to time whether on application or of his own motion amend or add to any directions issued if he thinks it necessary to do so in the circumstances of the case.

(9) The following provisions of these rules shall not apply where proceedings stand referred to arbitration:

(*a*) Order 6, rule 7 (further particulars),

(*b*) Order 9, rule 11 (particulars of defence),

(*c*) Order 14, rules 1(2), 3 to 5, 5A and 11 (discovery and interrogatories), and

(*d*) Order 20, rules 2 and 3 (notices to admit facts and documents),

(*e*) Order 20, rule 12A (exchange of witness statements).

Order 11, rules 1, 1A, 3 to 5, 7, 8 and 10 (payments into court) and Order 13, rule 1 (8) (*a*) (security for costs) shall not apply where proceedings stand referred to arbitration under rule 3.

(10) If it appears to the court at any time after a reference has been made (whether by order or otherwise) that there are any other matters within the jurisdiction of the court in dispute between the parties, the court may order them also to be referred to arbitration.

Conduct of hearing

7.–(1) Any proceedings referred to arbitration shall be dealt with in accordance with the following paragraphs of this rule unless the arbitrator otherwise orders.

(2) The hearing may be held at the court house, at the court office or at any other place convenient to the parties.

(3) The hearing shall be informal and the strict rules of evidence shall not apply; unless the arbitrator orders otherwise, the hearing shall be held in private and evidence shall not be taken on oath.

(4) At the hearing the arbitrator may adopt any method of procedure which he may consider to be fair and which gives to each party an equal opportunity to have his case presented; having considered the circumstances of the parties and whether (or to what extent) they are represented, the arbitrator –

(*a*) may assist a party by putting questions to the witnesses and the other party; and

(*b*) should explain any legal terms or expressions which are used.

(5) If any party does not appear at the arbitration, the arbitrator may, after taking into account any pleadings or other documents filed, make an award on hearing any other party to the proceedings who may be present.

(6) With the consent of the parties and at any time before giving his decision, the district judge may consult any expert or call for an expert report on any matter in dispute or invite an expert to attend the hearing as assessor.

(7) The arbitrator may require the production of any document or thing and may inspect any property or thing concerning which any question may arise.

(8) The arbitrator shall inform the parties of his award and give his reasons for it to any party who may be present at the hearing.

Setting awards aside

8.–(1) Where proceedings are referred to arbitration, the award of the arbitrator shall be final and may only be set aside pursuant to paragraph (2) or on the ground that there has been misconduct by the arbitrator or that the arbitrator made an error of law.

(2) Where an award has been given in the absence of a party, the arbitrator shall have power, on that party's application, to set the award aside and to order a fresh hearing as if the award were a judgment and the application were made pursuant to Order 37, rule 2.

(3) An application by a party to set aside an award made by a district judge or an outside arbitrator on the ground mentioned in paragraph (1) shall be made on notice and the notice shall be served within 14 days after the day on which the award was entered as the judgment of the court.

(4) An application under paragraph (3) shall, giving sufficient particulars, set out the misconduct or error of law relied upon.

(5) Order 37, rule 1 (rehearing of proceedings tried without a jury) shall not apply to proceedings referred to arbitration.

Mode of voluntary reference

9.–(1) Except as provided by rule 3, a reference shall be made only on the application of a party to the proceedings sought to be referred.

(2) Unless the court otherwise directs, an application by a party to any proceedings for a reference may be made –

(*a*) in the case of a plaintiff, by request incorporated in his particulars of claim;

(*b*) in the case of a defendant, by request incorporated in any defence or counterclaim of his;

(*c*) in any case, on notice under Order 13, rule 1.

(3) Where an application for a reference is made under paragraph (1) and the proceedings are not referred to arbitration under rule 3, the following provisions shall apply:–

(*a*) Subject to rule 5 (2) and sub-paragraphs (*b*) and (*c*) below, an order may be made by the district judge.

(*b*) If the court is satisfied that an allegation of fraud against a party is in issue in the proceedings, an order shall not be made except with the consent of that party.

(*c*) Where the district judge is minded to grant an application under paragraph (1), the proper officer shall notify the parties in writing accordingly and within 14 days after service of the proper officer's notice on him, a party may give written notice stating his reasons for objecting to the reference; if in any such notice a party so requests, the proper officer shall fix a day for a hearing at which the district judge shall decide whether to grant the application and, in the absence of any such request, the district judge may consider the application in the absence of the parties.

Costs

10. Subject to rule 4, the costs of the action up to and including the entry of judgment shall be in the discretion of the arbitrator to be exercised in the same manner as the discretion of the court under the provisions of the County Court Rules.

ORDER 20

Part IV – Hearsay Evidence

Interpretation and application

14.–(1) In this Part of this Order 'the Act of 1968' means the Civil Evidence Act 1968 and any expressions used in this Part of this Order and in Part I of the Act of 1968 have the same meanings in this Part of this Order as they have in the said Part I.

(2) This Part of this Order shall apply in relation to the trial or hearing of an issue arising in an action or matter and to a reference under section 65 of the Act as it applies to the trial or hearing of an action or matter.

(3) Nothing in this Part of this Order shall apply in relation to a reference under section 64 of the Act.

Notice of intention to give certain statements in evidence

15.–(1) Subject to the provisions of this rule, a party to an action or matter who desires to give in evidence at the trial or hearing any statement which is admissible in evidence by virtue of section 2, 4 or 5 of the Act of 1968 shall, not less than 14 days before the day fixed for the trial or hearing, give notice of his desire to do so to the registrar and to every other party.

(2) Unless in any particular case the court otherwise directs, paragraph

(1) shall not apply to an action or matter in which no defence or answer has been filed; and where a defence or answer is filed less than 14 days before the day fixed for the trial or hearing, any party required to give notice pursuant to paragraph (1) shall apply to the court for an adjournment of the trial or hearing or for such other directions as may be appropriate.

(3) Paragraph (1) shall not apply in relation to any statement which is admissible as evidence of any fact stated therein by virtue not only of the said section 2, 4 or 5 but by virtue also of any other statutory provision within the meaning of section 1 of the Act of 1968.

(4) Paragraph (1) shall not apply in relation to any statement which any party to a probate action desires to give in evidence at the trial of that action and which is alleged to have been made by the deceased person whose estate is the subject of the action.

(5) Where, by virtue of any provision of these rules or of any order or direction of the court, the evidence in any proceedings is to be given by affidavit then, without prejudice to paragraph (3), paragraph (1) shall not apply in relation to any statement which any party to the proceedings desires to have included in any affidavit to be used on his behalf in the proceedings.

Application of RSC
16. RSC Order 38, rules 22 to 25, shall apply to a notice under the last foregoing rule as they apply to a notice under rule 21 of the said Order 38.

Counter-notice requiring person to be called as witness
17.–(1) Subject to paragraphs (2) and (3), any party on whom a notice under rule 15 is served may, within 7 days after service of the notice on him, give to the proper officer and to the party who gave the notice a counter-notice requiring that party to call as a witness at the trial or hearing any person (naming him) particulars of whom are contained in the notice.

(2) Where any notice under rule 15 contains a statement that any person particulars of whom are contained in the notice cannot or should not be called as a witness for the reason specified therein, a party shall not be entitled to serve a counter-notice under this rule requiring that person to be called as a witness at the trial or hearing unless he contends that that person can or, as the case may be, should be called, and in that case he must include in his counter-notice a statement to that effect.

(3) Where a statement to which a notice under rule 15 relates is one to which rule 19 applies, no party on whom the notice is served shall be entitled to serve a counter-notice under this rule in relation to that statement, but the foregoing provision is without prejudice to the right of any party to apply to the court under rule 19 for directions with respect to the admissibility of that statement.

(4) If any party by whom a notice under rule 15 is served fails to comply with a counter-notice duly served on him under this rule, then, unless any of the reasons specified in paragraph (5) applies in relation to the person named in the counter-notice, and without prejudice to the powers of the court under rule 20, the statement to which the notice under rule 15 relates shall not be admissible at the trial or hearing as evidence of any fact stated therein by virtue of section 2, 4 or 5 of the Act of 1968, as the case may be.

(5) The reasons referred to in paragraph (4) are that the person in question is dead, or beyond the seas, or unfit by reason of his bodily or mental condition to attend as a witness or that despite the exercise of reasonable

diligence it has not been possible to identify or find him or that he cannot reasonably be expected to have any recollection of matters relevant to the accuracy or otherwise of the statement to which the notice relates.

Determination of question whether person can or should be called as a witness
18.–(1) Where a question arises whether any of the reasons specified in rule 17 (5) applies in relation to a person particulars of whom are contained in a notice under rule 15, the court may, on the application of any party to the action or matter, determine that question before the trial or hearing or give directions for it to be determined before the trial or hearing and for the manner in which it is to be determined.

(2) Unless the court otherwise directs, notice of any application under paragraph (1) must be served on every other party to the action or matter.

(3) Where any such question as is referred to in paragraph (1) has been determined under or by virtue of that paragraph, no application to have it determined afresh at the trial or hearing may be made unless the evidence which it is sought to adduce in support of the application could not with reasonable diligence have been adduced at the hearing which resulted in the determination.

Power of court to allow statement to be given in evidence
20.–(1) Without prejudice to sections 2 (2) (*a*) and 4 (2) (*a*) of the Act of 1968 and rule 19, the court may, if it thinks it just to do so, allow a statement falling within section 2 (1), 4 (1) or 5 (1) of the Act of 1968 to be given in evidence at the trial or hearing of an action or matter notwithstanding –

(*a*) that the statement is one in relation to which rule 15 (1) applies and that the party desiring to give the statement in evidence has failed to comply with that rule, or

(*b*) that that party has failed to comply with any requirement of a counter-notice relating to that statement which was served on him in accordance with rule 17.

(2) Without prejudice to the generality of paragraph (1), the court may exercise its power under that paragraph to allow a statement to be given in evidence at the trial or hearing if a refusal to exercise that power might oblige the party desiring to give the statement in evidence to call as a witness at the trial or hearing an opposite party or a person who is or was at the material time the servant or agent of an opposite party.

PART V – EXPERT EVIDENCE

Restrictions on adducing expert evidence
27.–(1) Except –

(*a*) with the leave of the court,
(*b*) in accordance with the provisions of Order 17, rule 11, or
(*c*) where all parties agree,

no expert evidence may be adduced at the trial or hearing of an action or matter, unless the party seeking to adduce the evidence has applied to the court to determine whether a direction should be given under rule 37, 38 or 41 (whichever is appropriate) of RSC Order 38, as applied by rule 28 of this Order, and has complied with any direction given on the application.

(2) Nothing in paragraph (1) shall apply to expert evidence which is permitted to be given by affidavit or which is to be adduced in an action or matter in which no defence or answer has been filed or in proceedings referred to arbitration under section 64 of the Act.

(3) Nothing in paragraph (1) shall affect the enforcement under any other provision of these rules (except Order 29, rule 1) of a direction given under this Part of this Order.

Application of RSC
28. RSC Order 38, rules 37 to 44 shall apply in relation to an application under rule 27 of this Order as they apply in relation to an application under rule 36 (1) of the said Order 38.

ORDER 21

HEARING OF ACTION OR MATTER

Non-appearance by plaintiff
1.–(1) If the plaintiff does not appear on the day fixed for the hearing of an action or matter, the court may, without prejudice to any other power, strike out the proceedings or, if the defendant appears, proceed with the hearing in the plaintiff's absence.

(2) Where the court has received from the plaintiff an affidavit which is admissible in evidence by virtue of any Act or rule, he shall be deemed for the purposes of paragraph (1) to have appealed on the day aforesaid and to have tendered the evidence in the affidavit.

(3) Where any proceedings have been struck out under paragraph (1), the court may restore them to the list on application or of its own motion.

Failure by plaintiff to prove claim
2.–(1) If the plaintiff appears at the hearing of an action or matter but fails to prove his claim to the satisfaction of the court, it may, without prejudice to any other power, either nonsuit him or give judgment for the defendant.

(2) Where, after a plaintiff has been nonsuited, or proceedings have been struck out, and costs have been awarded to the defendant, a subsequent action or matter for the same or substantially the same cause of action is brought before payment of those costs, the court may stay the subsequent action or matter until they have been paid.

Non-appearance or admission by defendant
3. If on the day fixed for the hearing of an action or matter the defendant –

(a) does not appear but the plaintiff proves his claim to the satisfaction of the court, or
(b) appears and admits the plaintiff's claim,

the court may give such judgment or make such order as may be just.

Registrar's jurisdiction
5.–(1) The registrar shall have power to hear and determine –

(a) any action or matter in which the defendant fails to appear at the hearing or admits the claim;
(b) any action or matter the value of which does not exceed £5,000;

(*c*) any action in which the mortgagee under a mortgage of land claims possession of the mortgaged land; and

(*d*) by leave of the judge and with the consent of the parties, any other action or matter.

(2) In relation to an action brought to enforce a right to recover possession of goods, or to enforce such a right and to claim payment of a debt or other demand or damages, the reference in paragraph (1) (*b*) to the sum claimed or amount involved shall be construed as a reference to the aggregate amount claimed by the plaintiff, including the value of the goods or, in the case of goods let under a hire-purchase agreement, the unpaid balance of the total price.

(2A) In paragraph (1) (*c*) 'mortgage' and 'mortgagee' have the meaning assigned to them by section 21 (7) of the Act.

(2B) Without prejudice to Order 50, rule 2, a district judge may, at any stage of an action or matter which he has power to hear and determine under paragraph (1) and subject to any right of appeal to the judge, exercise the same powers under section 38 of the Act as the court; but nothing in this paragraph shall authorise the district judge to commit any person to prison.

(3) Nothing in this rule shall prejudice any power conferred by any Act or rule on the registrar [district judge] to hear and determine any other action or matter or authorise the registrar [district judge] to exercise any jurisdiction conferred by any Act or rule on the judge alone.

ORDER 24

Summary Proceedings for the Recovery of Land or Rent

Part I – Land

Proceedings to be by originating application
1. Where a person claims possession of land which he alleges is occupied solely by a person or persons (not being a tenant or tenants holding over after the termination of the tenancy) who entered into or remained in occupation without his licence or consent or that of any predecessor in title of his, the proceedings may be brought by originating application in accordance with the provisions of this Order.

Affidavit in support
2.–(1) The applicant shall file in support of the originating application an affidavit stating –

(*a*) his interest in the land;

(*b*) the circumstances in which the land has been occupied without licence or consent and in which his claim to possession arises; and

(*c*) that he does not know the name of any person occupying the land who is not named in the originating application.

(2) Where the applicant considers that service in accordance with rule 3 (2) (*b*) may be necessary, he shall provide, together with the originating appliction, sufficient stakes and sealable transparent envelopes for such service.

Service of originating application
3.–(1) Where any person in occupation of the land is named in the originating application, the application shall be served on him –

(a) by delivering to him personally a copy of the originating application, together with the notice of the return day required by Order 3, rule 4 (4) (b), and a copy of the affidavit in support, or

(b) by an officer of the court leaving the documents mentioned in sub-paragraph (a), or sending them to him, at the premises, or

(c) in accordance with Order 7, rule 11, as applied to originating applications by Order 3, rule 4 (6), or

(d) in such other manner as the court may direct.

(2) Where any person not named as a respondent is in occupation of the land, the originating application shall be served (whether or not it is also required to be served in accordance with paragraph (1)), unless the court otherwise directs, by –

(a) affixing a copy of each of the documents mentioned in paragraph (1) (a) to the main door or other conspicuous part of the premises and, if practicable, inserting through the letterbox at the premises a copy of those documents enclosed in a sealed transparent envelope addressed to 'the occupiers', or

(b) placing stakes in the ground at conspicuous parts of the occupied land, to each of which shall be affixed a sealed transparent envelope addressed to 'the occupiers' and containing a copy of each of the documents mentioned in paragraph (1) (a).

Application by occupier to be made a party
4. Without prejudice to Order 15, rule 1, any person not named as a respondent who is in occupation of the land and wishes to be heard on the question whether an order for possession should be made may apply at any stage of the proceedings to be joined as respondent, and the notice of the return day required by Order 3, rule 4 (4) (b), shall contain a notice to that effect.

Hearing of originating application
5.–(1) Except in case of urgency and by leave of the court, the day fixed for the hearing of the originating application –

(a) in the case of residential premises, shall not be less than five days after the day of service, and

(b) in the case of other land, shall not be less than two days after the day of service.

(2) Notwithstanding anything in Order 21, rule 5, no order for possession shall be made on the originating application except by the judge or, with the leave of the judge, by the registrar.

(3) An order for possession in proceedings under this Order shall be to the effect that the plaintiff do recover possession of the land mentioned in the originating application.

(4) Nothing in this Order shall prevent the court from ordering possession to be given on a specified date, in the exercise of any power which could have been exercised if the proceedings had been brought by action.

Warrant of possession

6.–(1) Subject to paragraphs (2) and (3), a warrant of possession to enforce an order for possession under this Order may be issued at any time after the making of the order and subject to the provisions of Order 26, rule 17, a warrant of restitution may be issued in aid of the warrant of possession.

(2) No warrant of possession shall be issued after the expiry of 3 months from the date of the order without the leave of the court, and an application for such leave may be made ex parte unless the court otherwise directs.

(3) Nothing in this rule shall authorise the issue of a warrant of possession before the date on which possession is ordered to be given.

Setting aside order

7. The judge may, on such terms as he thinks just, set aside or vary any order made in proceedings under this Order.

ORDER 37

Rehearing, Setting Aside and Appeal from Registrar [district judge]

Rehearing

1.–(1) In any proceedings tried without a jury the judge shall have power on application to order a rehearing where no error of the court at the hearing is alleged.

(2) Unless the court otherwise orders, any application under paragraph (1) shall be made to the judge by whom the proceedings were tried.

(3) A rehearing may be ordered on any question without interfering with the finding or decision on any other question.

(4) Where the proceedings were tried by the registrar [district judge], the powers conferred on the judge by paragraphs (1) and (3) shall be exercisable by the registrar and paragraph (2) shall not apply.

(5) Any application for a rehearing under this rule shall be made on notice stating the grounds of the application and the notice shall be served on the opposite party not more than 14 days after the day of the trial and not less than 7 days before the day fixed for the hearing of the application.

(6) On receipt of the notice, the proper officer shall, unless the court otherwise orders, retain any money in court until the application had been heard.

Setting aside judgment given in party's absence

2.–(1) Any judgment or order obtained against a party in his absence at the hearing may be set aside by the court on application by that party on notice.

(2) The application shall be made to the judge if the judgment or order was given or made by the judge and in any other case shall be made to the registrar.

Setting aside on failure of postal service

3.–(1) Where in an action or matter the originating process has been sent to the defendant or inserted in his letter-box in accordance with Order 7, rule 10 (1) (*b*) or (4) (*a*) or 13 (1) (*b*) or (4) and after judgment has been entered or given or an order has been made it appears to the court that the process did not come to the knowledge of the defendant in due time, the court may of its own motion set aside the judgment or order and may give any such directions as the court thinks fit.

(2) The proper officer shall give notice to the plaintiff of the setting aside of any judgment or order under this rule.

Setting aside default judgment
4.–(1) Without prejudice to rule 3, the court may, on application or of its own motion, set aside, vary or confirm any judgment entered in a default action pursuant to Order 9, rule 6.

(2) An application under paragraph (1) shall be made on notice and, where such an application is made in a default action for a liquidated sum, the proceedings shall be automatically transferred to the defendant's home court if the judgment or order was not given or made in that court.

Non-compliance with rules
5.–(1) Where there has been a failure to comply with any requirement of these rules, the failure shall be treated as an irregularity and shall not nullify the proceedings, but the court may set aside the proceedings wholly or in part or exercise its powers under these rules to allow any such amendments and to give any such directions as it thinks fit.

(2) No application to set aside any proceedings for irregularity shall be granted unless made within a reasonable time, nor if the party applying has taken any step in the proceedings after knowledge of the irregularity.

(3) Where any such application is made, the grounds of objections shall be stated in the notice.

(4) The expression 'proceedings' in paragraph (1), and where it first occurs in paragraph (2), includes any step taken in the proceedings and any document, judgment or order therein.

Appeal from district judge
6.–(1) Any party affected by a judgment or final order of the district judge may, except where he has consented to the terms thereof, appeal from the judgment or order to the judge, who may, upon such terms as he thinks fit, –

(a) set aside or vary the judgment or order of any part thereof, or
(b) give any other judgment or make any other order in substitution for the judgment or order appealed from, or
(c) remit the action or matter or any question therein to the district judge for rehearing or further consideration, or
(d) order a new trial to take place before himself or another judge of the court on a day to be fixed.

(2) The appeal shall be made on notice, which shall state the grounds of the appeal and be served within 14 days after the day on which judgment or order appealed from was given or made.

ORDER 38

Costs

Costs to be regulated by scales
3.–(1) For the regulation of solicitors' charges and disbursements otherwise than for the purposes of rule 18 or 19, there shall be three scales of costs, namely a lower scale, scale 1 as set out in Appendix A and scale 2.

(2) The scales shall have effect subject to and in accordance with the provisions of this Order and any directions contained in the scales.

(3) In relation to a sum of money only, the scales shall apply as follows:–

Sum of money	Scale applicable
Exceeding £25 but not exceeding £100	lower scale
Exceeding £100 but not exceeding £3,000	scale 1
Exceeding £3,000	scale 2.

(3A) The amount of costs to be assessed under the lower scale pursuant to rule 19 shall be determined in accordance with Appendix C and the amount of costs to be allowed on any taxation under scale 1 shall be determined in accordance with Appendix A.

(3B) The amount of costs to be allowed on any taxation of costs under scale 2 shall be in the discretion of the taxing officer and, in exercising his discretion, the taxing officer shall have regard to all the relevant circumstances, and in particular to the circumstances referred to in paragraph 1 (2) of Part I of Appendix 2 to RSC Order 62.

(3C) Where costs are to be allowed on scale 2 –

(a) the bill of costs shall consist of such of the items specified in Part II of Appendix 2 to RSC Order 62 as may be appropriate, set out, except for item 4, in chronological order; and each item (other than an item relating only to time spent in travelling or waiting) may include an allowance for general care and conduct having regard to such of the circumstances referred to in paragraph 1 (2) of Part I of Appendix 2 to RSC Order 62 as may be relevant to that item;

(b) rules 5, 9, 12 to 16, 17 (3) and 19 of this Order shall not apply on any taxation under that scale;

(c) rule 21 (4) of this Order shall apply as if the words after 'party and party' in paragraph (4) (c) were omitted.

(3D) Where costs are awarded on scale 2 to any person, the court may order that, instead of his taxed costs, that person shall be entitled to a gross sum (specified in the order) in lieu of those costs; but where the court so orders and the person entitled to the gross sum is a litigant in person, rule 17 shall apply as if for paragraph (3) there were substituted the following –

'(3) The costs of a litigant in person shall be assessed in accordance with rule 3 (3D) unless the court otherwise orders.'.

(4) Where the sum of money does not exceed £25, no solicitors' charges shall be allowed as between party and party, unless a certificate is granted under rule 4 (6).

(5) In addition to the disbursements shown in the scales the appropriate court fees shall be allowable.

(6) In relation to proceedings referred to arbitration under Order 19, rule 3, this rule is without prejudice to rule 4 of that Order.

Determination of scale
4.–(1) Subject to this Order, the scale of costs in an action for the recovery of a sum of money only shall be determined –

(a) as regards the costs of the plaintiff, by the amount recovered;

(b) as regards the costs of the defendant, by the amount claimed;

but nothing in this paragraph shall apply to an action under the equity jurisdiction or to an admiralty action or an action in which the title to a hereditament comes in question.

(2) In relation to third party proceedings, paragraph (1) shall have effect as if the defendant issuing the third party notice were the plaintiff and the third party were the defendant.

(3) Where in an action to which paragraph (1) applies there is a counterclaim for a sum of money only, that paragraph shall have effect in relation to the costs exclusively referable to the counterclaim as if the references therein to the amount recovered and the amount claimed were references to the amount recovered on the counterclaim and the amount of the counterclaim respectively.

(4) Where an action to which paragraph (1) applies has been transferred from the High Court to a county court and the amount remaining in dispute at the date on which the registrar receives the relevant documents (within the meaning of Order 16, rule 6 (1)) is less than the amount originally claimed, paragraph (1) (*b*) shall have effect as if the reference therein to the amount claimed were a reference to the amount remaining in dispute at that date.

(5) Paragraph (1) shall have effect in relation to garnishee proceedings as if the judgment creditor were the plaintiff and the garnishee or, as the case may be, the judgment debtor were the defendant.

(6) In any proceedings in which the judge certifies that a difficult question of law or a question of fact of exceptional complexity is involved, he may award costs on such scale as he thinks fit.

(7) In proceedings to which none of the foregoing paragraphs applies, costs shall be on such scale as the judge when awarding the costs, or the registrar when taxing or assessing them, may determine.

Discretionary allowances
5. Where in the scales of costs –

(*a*) an upper and a lower sum of money are specified against an item, or
(*b*) the amount to be allowed in respect of an item is directed not to exceed a specified sum, or
(*c*) no amount is specified against an item,

the amount of costs to be allowed in respect of that item shall, subject to rules 9 and 17, be in the discretion of the registrar [district judge] within the limits of the sums, if any, so specified, and in exercising his discretion the registrar shall have regard to all the circumstances to which a taxing officer of the Supreme Court is required to have regard when determining the amount of costs to be allowed in accordance with the provisions contained in paragraph 1 (2) of Appendix 2 to RSC Order 62.

Allowance or disallowance of items by judge
6. Where the costs of any action or matter are to be taxed, the judge may direct that any item in the scale be allowed or disallowed on taxation.

Value added tax
7. In addition to the amount of costs allowed to a party on taxation or assessment in respect of the supply of goods or services on which value added tax is chargeable there may be allowed as a disbursement a sum

equivalent to value added tax at the appropriate rate on that amount in so far as the tax is not deductible as input tax by that party.

Restrictions on allowance of counsel's fees
8.–(1) No costs shall be allowed on taxation in respect of counsel attending before the judge or registrar [district judge] on an interlocutory application, or in respect of more counsel than one attending before the judge or registrar [district judge] on any occasion, unless the judge or registrar [district judge], as the case may be, has certified the attendance as proper in the circumstances of the case.

(2) Unless the judge or registrar at the hearing otherwise orders, no fee to counsel with brief shall be allowed in an action for the recovery of a sum of money only where no defence has been delivered and the defendant does not appear at the hearing to resist the claim.

(3) Where a party appearing by counsel is awarded costs but the costs of employing counsel are not allowed, he may be allowed such costs as he might have been allowed if he had appeared by a solicitor and not by counsel.

Rules of the Supreme Court

ORDER 3

1. 'Month' means calendar month
Without prejudice to section 5 of the Interpretation Act 1978, in its application to these rules, the word 'month', where it occurs in any judgment, order, direction or other document forming part of any proceedings in the Supreme Court, means a calendar month unless the context otherwise requires.

2. Reckoning periods of time
(1) Any period of time fixed by these rules or by any judgment, order or direction for doing any act shall be reckoned in accordance with the following provisions of this rule.

(2) Where the act is required to be done within a specified period after or from a specified date, the period begins immediately after that date.

(3) Where the act is required to be done within or not less than a specified period before a specified date, the period ends immediately before that date.

(4) Where the act is required to be done a specified number of clear days before or after a specified date, at least that number of days must intervene between the day on which the act is done and that date.

(5) Where, apart from this paragraph, the period in question, being a period of 7 days or less, would include a Saturday, Sunday or bank holiday, Christmas Day or Good Friday, that day shall be excluded.

In this paragraph 'bank holiday' means a day which is, or is to be observed as, a bank holiday, or a holiday, under the Banking and Financial Dealings Act 1971, in England and Wales.

4. Time expires on Sunday, etc.
Where the time prescribed by these rules, or by any judgment, order or direction, for doing any act at an office of the Supreme Court expires on a Sunday or other day on which that office is closed, and by reason thereof that act cannot be done on that day, the act shall be in time if done on the next day on which that office is open.

5. Extension, etc, of time

(1) The Court may, on such terms as it thinks just, by order extend or abridge the period within which a person is required or authorised by these rules, or by any judgment, order or direction, to do any act in any proceedings.

(2) The Court may extend any such period as is referred to in paragraph (1) although the application for extension is not made until after the expiration of that period.

(3) The period within which a person is required by these rules, or by any order or direction, to serve, file or amend any pleading or other document may be extended by consent (given in writing) without an order of the Court being made for that purpose.

(4) In this rule references to the Court shall be construed as including references to the Court of Appeal, a single judge of that Court and the registrar of civil appeals.

6. Notice of intention to proceed after year's delay

Where a year or more has elapsed since the last proceeding in a cause or matter, the party who desires to proceed must give to every other party not less than one month's notice of his intention to proceed.

A summons on which no order was made is not a proceeding for the purpose of this rule.

ORDER 10

SERVICE OF ORIGINATING PROCESS: GENERAL PROVISIONS

1. General provisions

(1) A writ must be served personally on each defendant by the plaintiff or his agent.

(2) A writ for service on a defendant within the jurisdiction may, instead of being served personally on him, be served –

    (*a*) by sending a copy of the writ by ordinary first-class post to the defendant at his usual or last known address, or

    (*b*) if there is a letter box for that address, by inserting through the letter box a copy of the writ enclosed in a sealed envelope addressed to the defendant.

       In sub-paragraph (*a*) 'first-class post' means first-class post which has been pre-paid or in respect of which prepayment is not required.

(3) Where a writ is served in accordance with paragraph (2) –

    (*a*) the date of service shall, unless the contrary is shown be deemed to be the seventh day (ignoring Order 3, rule 2 (5)) after the date on which the copy was sent to or, as the case may be, inserted through the letter box for the address in question;

    (*b*) any affidavit proving due service of the writ must contain a statement to the effect that –

       (i) in the opinion of the deponent (or, if the deponent is the plaintiff's solicitor or an employee of that solicitor, in the opinion of the plaintiff) the copy of the writ, if sent to, or, as the case may be inserted through the letter box for, the address in question, will have come to the knowledge of the defendant within 7 days thereafter; and

(ii) in the case of service by post, the copy of the writ has not been returned to the plaintiff through the post undelivered to the addressee.

(4) Where a defendant's solicitor indorses on the writ a statement that he accepts service of the writ on behalf of that defendant, the writ shall be deemed to have been duly served on that defendant and to have been so served on the date on which the indorsement was made.

(5) Subject to Order 12, rule 7, where a writ is not duly served on a defendant but he acknowledges service of it, the writ shall be deemed, unless the contrary is shown, to have been duly served on him and to have been so served on the date on which he acknowledges service.

(6) Every copy of a writ for service on a defendant shall be sealed with the seal of the office of the Supreme Court out of which the writ was issued and shall be accompanied by a form of acknowledgment of service in Form No. 14 in Appendix A in which the title of the Action and its number have been entered.

(7) This rule shall have effect subject to the provision of any Act and these rules and in particular to any enactment which provides for the manner in which documents may be served on bodies corporate.

ORDER 12

ACKNOWLEDGMENT OF SERVICE TO WRIT OR ORIGINATING SUMMONS

1. Mode of acknowledging service

(1) Subject to paragraph (2) and to Order 80, rule 2, a defendant to an action begun by writ may (whether or not he is sued as a trustee or personal representative or in any other representative capacity) acknowledge service of the writ and defend the action by a solicitor or in person.

(2) The defendant to such an action who is a body corporate may acknowledge service of the writ and give notice of intention to defend the action either by a solicitor or by a person duly authorised to act on the defendant's behalf but, except as aforesaid or as expressly provided by any enactment, such a defendant may not take steps in the action otherwise than by a solicitor.

(3) Service of a writ may be acknowledged by properly completing an acknowledgment of service, as defined by rule 3, and handing it in at, or sending it by post to, the appropriate office, that is to say, if the writ was issued out of an office of the Supreme Court at the Royal Courts of Justice, that office, or if the writ was issued out of a district registry that registry.

(4) If two or more defendants to an action acknowledge service by the same solicitor and at the same time, only one acknowledgment of service need by completed and delivered for those defendants.

(5) The date on which service is acknowledged is the date on which the acknowledgment of service is received at the appropriate office.

3. Acknowledgment of service

(1) An acknowledgment of service must be in Form No. 14 or 15 in Appendix A, whichever is appropriate, and, except as provided in rule 1 (2)

must be signed by the solicitor acting for the defendant specified in the acknowledgment or, if the defendant is acting in person, by that defendant.

(2) An acknowledgment of service must specify –

(*a*) in the case of a defendant acknowledging service in person, the address of his place of residence and, if his place of residence is not within the jurisdiction or if he has no place of residence, the address of a place within the jurisdiction at or to which documents for him may be delivered or sent, and

(*b*) in the case of a defendant acknowledging service by a solicitor, a business address (to which may be added a numbered box at a document exchange) of his solicitor's within the jurisdiction;

and where the defendant acknowledges service in person, the address within the jurisdiction specified under sub-paragraph (*a*) shall be his address for service, but otherwise his solicitor's business address shall be his address for service.

In relation to a body corporate the references in sub-paragraph (*a*) to the defendant's place of residence shall be construed as references to the defendant's registered or principal office.

(3) Where the defendant acknowledges service by a solicitor who is acting as agent for another solicitor having a place of business within the jurisdiction, the acknowledgment of service must state that the first-named solicitor so acts and must also state the name and address of that other solicitor.

(4) If an acknowledgment of service does not specify the defendant's address for service or the Court is satisfied that any address specified in the acknowledgment of service is not genuine, the Court may on application by the plaintiff set aside the acknowledgment or order the defendant to give an address or, as the case may be, a genuine address for service and may in any case direct that the acknowledgment shall nevertheless have effect for the purposes of Order 10, rule 1 (5) and Order 65, rule 9.

4. Procedure on receipt of acknowledgment of service

On receiving an acknowledgment of service an officer of the appropriate office must –

(*a*) affix to the acknowledgment an official stamp showing the date on which he received it;

(*b*) enter the acknowledgment in the cause book with a note showing, if it be the case, that the defendant has indicated in the acknowledgment an intention to contest the proceedings or to apply for a stay of execution in respect of any judgment obtained against him in the proceedings;

(*c*) make a copy of the acknowledgment, having affixed to it an official stamp showing the date on which he received the acknowledgment, and send it by post to the plaintiff or, as the case may be, his solicitor at the plaintiff's address for service.

5. Time limited for acknowledging service

References in these Rules to the time limited for acknowledging service are references –

(*a*) in the case of a writ served within the jurisdiction, to fourteen days after service of the writ (including the day of service), or, where that time has been extended by or by virtue of these Rules, to that time as so extended; and

(*b*)   in the case of a writ, served out of the jurisdiction, to the time limited under Order 10, Rule 2 (2), Order 11, Rule 1 (3), or Order 11, Rule 4 (4), or, where that time has been extended as aforesaid, to that time as so extended.

6. Late acknowledgment of service

(1)   Except with the leave of the Court, a defendant may not give notice of intention to defend in an action after judgment has been obtained therein.

(2)   Except as provided by paragraph (1), nothing in these rules or any writ or order thereunder shall be construed as precluding a defendant from acknowledging service in an action after the time limited for so doing, but if a defendant acknowledges service after that time, he shall not, unless the Court otherwise orders, be entitled to serve a defence or do any other act later than if he had acknowledged service within that time.

7. Acknowledgment not to constitute waiver

The acknowledgment by a defendant of service of a writ shall not be treated as a waiver by him or any irregularity in the writ or service thereof or in any order giving leave to serve the writ out of the jurisdiction or extending the validity of the writ for the purpose of service.

8. Dispute as to jurisdiction

(1)   A defendant who wishes to dispute the jurisdiction of the court in the proceedings by reason of any such irregularity as is mentioned in rule 7 or on any other ground shall give notice of intention to defend the proceedings and shall, within the time limited for service of a defence, apply to the Court for –

(*a*)   an order setting aside the writ or service of the writ on him, or

(*b*)   an order declaring that the writ has not been duly served on him, or

(*c*)   the discharge of any order giving leave to serve the writ on him out of the jurisdiction, or

(*d*)   the discharge of any order extending the validity of the writ for the purpose of service, or

(*e*)   the protection or release of any property of the defendant seized or threatened with seizure in the proceedings, or

(*f*)   the discharge of any order made to prevent any dealing with any property of the defendant, or

(*g*)   a declaration that in the circumstances of the case the court has no jurisdiction over the defendant in respect of the subject matter of the claim or the relief or remedy sought in the action, or

(*h*)   such other relief as may be appropriate.

(2)   [*Revoked by RSC (Amendment No. 2) 1983 (S.I. 1983 No. 1181)*.]

(3)   An application under paragraph (1) must be made –

(*a*)   in an Admiralty action *in rem*, by motion;

(*b*)   in any other action in the Queen's Bench Division, by summons;

(*c*)   in any other action, by summons or motion,

and the notice of motion or summons must state the grounds of the application.

(4) An application under paragraph (1) must be supported by an affidavit verifying the facts on which the application is based and a copy of the affidavit must be served with the notice of motion or summons by which the application is made.

(5) Upon hearing an application under paragraph (1) the Court, if it does not dispose of the matter in dispute, may give such directions for its disposal as may be appropriate, including directions for the trial thereof as a preliminary issue.

(6) A defendant who makes an application under paragraph (1) shall not be treated as having submitted to the jurisdiction of the Court by reason of his having given notice of intention to defend the action; and it the Court makes no order on the application or dismisses it, the notice shall cease to have effect, but the defendant may, subject to rule 6 (1), lodge a further acknowledgment of service within 14 days or such other period as the Court may direct and in that case paragraph (7) shall apply as if the defendant had not made any such application.

(7) Except where the defendant makes an application in accordance with paragraph (1) the acknowledgment by a defendant of service of a writ shall, unless the acknowledgment is withdrawn by leave of the Court under Order 21, rule 1, be treated as a submission by the defendant to the jurisdiction of the Court in the proceedings.

ORDER 13

Failure to Give Notice of Intention to Defend

1. Claim for liquidated demand
(1) Where a writ is indorsed with a claim against a defendant for a liquidated demand only, then, if that defendant fails to give notice of intention to defend, the plaintiff may, after the prescribed time enter final judgment against that defendant for a sum not exceeding that claimed by the writ in respect of the demand and for costs, and proceed with the action against the other defendants, if any.

(2) A claim shall not be prevented from being treated for the purposes of this rule as a claim for a liquidated demand by reason only that part of the claim is for interest under section 35A of the Act at a rate which is not higher than that payable on judgment debts at the date of writ.

2. Claim for unliquidated damages
Where a writ is indorsed with a claim against a defendant for unliquidated damages only, then, if that defendant fails to give notice of intention to defend, the plaintiff may, after the prescribed time, enter interlocutory judgment against that defendant for damages to be assessed and costs, and proceed with the action against the other defendants, if any.

3. Claim for detention of goods
(1) Where a writ is indorsed with a claim against a defendant relating to the detention of goods only, then, if that defendant failed to give notice of intention to defend the plaintiff may, after the prescribed time and subject to Order 42, rule 1A, –

(*a*) at his option enter either –
  (i) interlocutory judgment against that defendant for delivery of the goods or their value to be assessed and costs, or
  (ii) interlocutory judgment for the value of the goods to be assessed and costs, or
(*b*) apply by summons for judgment against that defendant for delivery of the goods without giving him the alternative of paying their assessed value,

and in any case proceed with the action against the other defendants, if any.

(2) A summons under paragraph (1) (*b*) must be supported by affidavit and notwithstanding Order 65, rule 9, the summons and a copy of the affidavit must be served on the defendant against whom judgment is sought.

4. Claim for possession of land

(1) Where a writ is indorsed with a claim against a defendant for possession of land only, then, subject to paragraph (2) if that defendant fails to give notice of intention to defend the plaintiff may, after the prescribed time, and on producing a certificate by his solicitor, or (if he sues in person) an affidavit, stating that he is not claiming any relief in the action of the nature specified in Order 88, rule 1, enter judgment for possession of the land as against that defendant and costs, and proceed with the action against the other defendants, if any.

(2) Notwithstanding anything in paragraph (1) the plaintiff shall not be entitled, except with the leave of the Court, to enter judgment under that paragraph unless he produces a certificate by his solicitor, or (if he sues in person) an affidavit, stating either that the claim does not relate to a dwelling-house or that the claim relates to a dwelling-house of which the rateable value on every day specified by section 4 (2) of the Rent Act 1977 in relation to the premises exceeds the sum so specified or of which the rent payable in respect of the premises exceeds the sum specified in section 4 (4) (*b*) of the Rent Act 1977.

(3) An application for leave to enter judgment under paragraph (2) shall be by summons stating the grounds of the application, and the summons must, unless the Court otherwise orders and notwithstanding anything in Order 65, rule 9, be served on the defendant against whom it is sought to enter judgment.

(4) If the Court refuses leave to enter judgment, it may make or give any such order or directions as it might have made or given had the application been an application for judgment under Order 14, rule 1.

(5) Where there is more than one defendant, judgment entered under this rule shall not be enforced against any defendant unless and until judgment for possession of the land has been entered against all the defendants.

5. Mixed claims

Where a writ issued against any defendants is indorsed with two or more of the claims mentioned in the foregoing rules, and no other claim, then, if that defendant fails to give notice of intention to defend, the plaintiff may, after the prescribed time, enter against that defendant such judgment in respect of any such claim as he would be entitled to enter under those rules if that were the only claim indorsed on the writ, and proceed with the action against the other defendants, if any.

6. Other claims

(1) Where a writ is indorsed with a claim of a description not mentioned in rules 1 to 4 then, if any defendant fails to give notice of intention to defend, the plaintiff may, after the prescribed time and, if that defendant has not acknowledged service, upon filing an affidavit proving service of the writ on him and, where the statement of claim was not indorsed on or served with the writ, upon serving a statement of claim on him, proceed with the action as if that defendant had given notice of intention to defend.

(2) Where a writ issued against a defendant is indorsed as aforesaid, but by reason of the defendant's satisfying the claim or complying with the demands thereof or any other like reason it has become unnecessary for the plaintiff to proceed with the action, then, if the defendant fails to give notice of intention to defend, the plaintiff may, after the prescribed time, enter judgment with the leave of the Court against that defendant for costs.

(3) An application for leave to enter judgment under paragraph (2) shall be by summons which must, unless the Court otherwise orders, and notwithstanding anything in Order 65, rule 9, be served on the defendant against whom it is sought to enter judgment.

6A. Prescribed time

In the foregoing rules of this Order 'the prescribed time' in relation to a writ issued against a defendant means the time limited for the defendant to acknowledge service of the writ or, if within that time the defendant has returned to the appropriate office an acknowledgment of service containing a statement to the effect that he does not intend to contest the proceedings, the date on which the acknowledgment was received at the appropriate office.

7. Proof of service of writ

(1) Judgment shall not be entered against a defendant under this Order unless –

- (a) the defendant has acknowledged service on him of the writ; or
- (b) an affidavit is filed by or on behalf of the plaintiff proving due service of the writ on the defendant; or
- (c) the plaintiff produces the writ indorsed by the defendant's solicitor with a statement that he accepts service of the writ on the defendant's behalf.

(2) Where, in an action begun by writ, an application is made to the Court for an order affecting a party who has failed to acknowledge service, the Court hearing the application may require to be satisfied in such manner as it thinks fit that the party is in default of acknowledgment of service.

(3) Where, after judgment has been entered under this Order against a defendant purporting to have been served by post under Order 10, rule 1 (2) (a), the copy of the writ sent to the defendant is returned to the plaintiff through the post, undelivered to the addressee, the plaintiff, shall, before taking any step or further step in the action of the enforcement of the judgment either –

- (a) make a request for the judgment to be set aside on the ground that the writ has not been duly served, or
- (b) apply to the Court for directions.

(4) A request under paragraph (3) (*a*) shall be made by producing to an officer of the office in which the judgment was entered, and leaving with him for filing, an affidavit stating the relevant facts, and thereupon the judgment shall be set aside and the entry of the judgment and of any proceedings for its enforcement made in the book kept in the office for that purpose shall be marked accordingly.

(5) An application under paragraph (3) (*b*) shall be made ex parte by affidavit stating the facts on which the application is founded and any order or direction sought, and on the application the Court may –

(*a*) set aside the judgment; or

(*b*) direct that, notwithstanding the return of the copy of the writ, it shall be treated as having been duly served, or

(*c*) make such other order and give such other direction as the circumstances may require.

8. Stay of execution on default judgment

Where judgment for a debt or liquidated demand is entered under this Order against a defendant who has returned to the appropriate office an acknowledgment of service containing a statement to the effect that, although he does not intend to contest the proceedings, he intends to apply for a stay of execution of the judgment by writ of fieri facias, execution of the judgment by such a writ shall be stayed for a period of 14 days from the acknowledgment of service and, if within that time the defendant issues and serves on the plaintiff a summons for such a stay supported by an affidavit in accordance with Order 47, rule 1, the stay imposed by this rule shall continue until the summons is heard or otherwise disposed of, unless the Court after giving the parties an opportunity of being heard otherwise directs.

9. Setting aside judgment

Without prejudice to r. 7 (3) and (4), the Court may, on such terms as it thinks just, set aside or vary any judgment entered in pursuance of this Order.

ORDER 14

SUMMARY JUDGMENT

1. Application by plaintiff for summary judgment

(1) Where in an action to which this rule applies a statement of claim has been served on a defendant and that defendant has given notice of intention to defend the action, the plaintiff may, on the ground that that defendant has no defence to a claim included in the writ, or to a particular part of such a claim, or has no defence to such a claim or part except as to the amount of any damages claimed, apply to the Court for judgment against that defendant.

(2) Subject to paragraph (3) this rule applies to every action begun by writ in the Queen's Bench Division (including the Admiralty Court) or the Chancery Division other than –

(*a*) an action which includes a claim by the plaintiff for libel, slander, malicious prosecution or false imprisonment, (*b*) [*Revoked.*]

(*c*) an Admiralty action *in rem.*

(3) This Order shall not apply to an action to which Order 86 applies.

2. Manner in which application under rule 1 must be made

(1) An application under rule 1 must be made by summons supported by an affidavit verifying the facts on which the claim, or the part of a claim, to which the application relates is based and stating that in the deponent's belief there is no defence to that claim or part, as the case may be, or no defence except as to the amount of any damages claimed.

(2) Unless the Court otherwise directs, an affidavit for the purposes of this rule may contain statements of information or belief with the sources and grounds thereof.

(3) The summons, a copy of the affidavit in support and of any exhibits referred to therein must be served on the defendant not less than 10 clear days before the return day.

3. Judgment for plaintiff

(1) Unless on the hearing of an application under rule 1 either the Court dismisses the application or the defendant satisfies the Court with respect to the claim, or the part of a claim, to which the application relates that there is an issue or question in dispute which ought to be tried or that there ought for some other reason to be a trial of that claim or part, the Court may give such judgment for the plaintiff against that defendant on that claim or part as may be just having regard to the nature of the remedy or relief claimed.

(2) The Court may by order, and subject to such conditions, if any, as may be just, stay execution of any judgment given against a defendant under this rule until after the trial of any counterclaim made or raised by the defendant in the action.

4. Leave to defend

(1) A defendant may show cause against an application under rule 1 by affidavit or otherwise to the satisfaction of the Court.

(2) Rule 2 (2) applies for the purposes of this Rule as it applies for the purposes of that rule.

(3) The court may give a defendant against whom such an application is made leave to defend the action with respect to the claim, or the part of a claim, to which the application relates either unconditionally or on such terms as to giving security or time or mode of trial or otherwise as it thinks fit.

(4) On the hearing of such an application the Court may order a defendant showing cause or, where that defendant is a body corporate, any director, manager, secretary or other similar officer thereof, or any person purporting to act in any such capacity –

(*a*) to produce any document;

(*b*) if it appears to the Court that there are special circumstances which make it desirable that he should do so, to attend and be examined on oath.

5. Application for summary judgment on counterclaim

(1) Where a defendant to an action in the Queen's Bench Division (including the Admiralty Court) or Chancery Division begun by writ has served a

counterclaim on the plaintiff, then, subject to paragraph (3) the defendant may, on the ground that the plaintiff has no defence to a claim made in the counterclaim, or to a particular part of such a claim, apply to the Court for judgment against the plaintiff on that claim or part.

(2) Rules 2, 3 and 4 shall apply in relation to an application under this rule as they apply in relation to an application under rule 1 but with the following modifications, that is to say –

(*a*) references to the plaintiff and defendant shall be construed as references to the defendant and plaintiff respectively;

(*b*) the words in rule 3 (2) 'any counterclaim made or raised by the defendant in' shall be omitted; and

(*c*) the reference in rule 4 (3) to the action shall be construed as a reference to the counterclaim to which the application under this rule relates.

(3) This rule shall not apply to a counterclaim which includes any such claim as is referred to in rule 1(2).

6. Directions

(1) Where the Court –

(*a*) orders that a defendant or a plaintiff have leave (whether conditional or unconditional) to defend an action or counterclaim, as the case may be, with respect to a claim or a part of a claim, or

(*b*) gives judgment for a plaintiff or a defendant on a claim or part of a claim but also orders that execution of the judgment be stayed pending the trial of a counterclaim or of the action, as the case may be,

the Court shall give directions as to the further conduct of the action, and Order 25, rules 2 to 7, shall, with the omission of so much of rule 7 (1) as requires parties to serve a notice specifying the orders and directions which they require and with any other necessary modifications, apply as if the application under rule 1 of this Order or rule 5 thereof, as the case may be, on which the order was made were a summons for directions.

(2) In particular, and if the parties consent, the Court may direct that the claim in question and any other claim in the action be tried by a Master under the provisions of these rules relating to the trial of causes or matters or questions or issues by Masters.

(3) Without prejudice to paragraph (1), in proceedings to which article 17 (1) of the High Court and County Courts Jurisdiction Order 1991 applies, the Court shall, when giving directions under paragraph (1) of this rule, order that –

(*a*) a statement of the value of the action be lodged and a copy of it served on every other party; and

(*b*) unless a statement is so lodged within such time as the Court may direct, the action be transferred to a county court.

7. Costs

(1) If the plaintiff makes an application under rule 1 where the case is not within this Order or if it appears to the Court that the plaintiff knew that the defendant relied on a contention which would entitle him to unconditional leave to defend, then, without prejudice to Order 62, and, in particular, to

paragraphs (1) to (3) of rule 8 of that Order, the Court may dismiss the application with costs and may, if the plaintiff is not an assisted person, require the costs to be paid by him forthwith.

(2) The Court shall have the same power to dismiss an application under rule 5 as it has under paragraph (1) to dismiss an application under rule 1, and that paragraph shall apply accordingly with the necessary modifications.

8. Right to proceed with residue of action or counterclaim

(1) Where on an application under rule 1 the plaintiff obtains judgment on a claim or a part of a claim against any defendant, he may proceed with the action as respects any other claim or as respects the remainder of the claim or against any other defendant.

(2) Where on an application under rule 5 a defendant obtains judgment on a claim or part of a claim made in a counterclaim against the plaintiff, he may proceed with the counterclaim as respects any other claim or as respects the remainder of the claim or against any other defendant to the counterclaim.

9. Judgment for delivery up of chattel

Where the claim to which an application under rule 1 or rule 5 relates is for the delivery up of a specific chattel and the court gives judgment under this Order for the applicant, it shall have the same power to order the party against whom judgment is given to deliver up the chattel without giving him an option to retain it on paying the assessed value thereof as if the judgment had been given after trial.

10. Relief against forfeiture

A tenant shall have the same right to apply for relief after judgment for possession of land on the ground of forfeiture for non-payment of rent has been given under this Order as if the judgment had been given after trial.

11. Setting aside judgment

Any judgment given against a party who does not appear at the hearing of an application under rule 1 or rule 5 may be set aside or varied by the Court on such terms as it thinks just.

ORDER 14A

Disposal of Case on Point of Law

1. Determination of questions of law or construction

(1) The Court may upon the application of a party or of its own motion determine any question of law or construction of any document arising in any cause or matter at any stage of the proceedings where it appears to the Court that –

(a) such question is suitable for determination without a full trial of the action, and

(b) such determination will finally determine (subject only to any possible appeal) the entire cause or matter or any claim or issue therein.

(2) Upon such determination the Court may dismiss the cause or matter or make such order or judgment as it thinks just.

(3) The Court shall not determine any question under this Order unless the parties have either –

(*a*) had an opportunity of being heard on the question, or

(*b*) consented to an order or judgment on such determination.

(4) The jurisdiction of the Court under this Order may be exercised by a master.

(5) Nothing in this Order shall limit the powers of the Court under Order 18, rule 19 or any other provision of these rules.

2. Manner in which application under rule 1 may be made

An application under rule 1 may be made by summons or motion or (notwithstanding Order 32, rule 1) may be made orally in the course of any interlocutory application to the Court.

ORDER 15

Causes of Action, Counterclaims and Parties

1. Joinder of causes of action

(1) Subject to rule 5 (1) a plaintiff may in one action claim relief against the same defendant in respect of more than one cause of action –

(*a*) if the plaintiff claims, and the defendant is alleged to be liable, in the same capacity in respect of all the causes of action, or

(*b*) if the plaintiff claims or the defendant is alleged to be liable in the capacity of executor or administrator of an estate in respect of one or more of the causes of action and in his personal capacity but with reference to the same estate in respect of all the others, or

(*c*) with the leave of the Court.

(2) An application for leave under this rule must be made ex parte by affidavit before the issue of the writ or originating summons, as the case may be, and the affidavit must state the grounds of the application.

2. Counterclaim against plaintiff

(1) Subject to rule 5 (2), a defendant in any action who alleges that he has any claim or is entitled to any relief or remedy against a plaintiff in the action in respect of any matter (whenever and however arising) may, instead of bringing a separate action, make a counterclaim in respect of that matter; and where he does so he must add the counterclaim to his defence.

(2) Rule 1 shall apply in relation to a counterclaim as if the counterclaim were a separate action and as if the person making the counterclaim were the plaintiff and the person against whom it is made a defendant.

(3) A counterclaim may be proceeded with notwithstanding that judgment is given for the plaintiff in the action or that the action is stayed, discontinued or dismissed.

(4) Where a defendant establishes a counterclaim against the claim of the plaintiff and there is a balance in favour of one of the parties, the Court may give judgment for the balance, so, however, that this provision shall not be taken as affecting the Court's discretion with respect to costs.

3. Counterclaim against additional parties

(1) Where a defendant to an action who makes a counterclaim against the plaintiff alleges that any other person (whether or not a party to the action) is liable to him along with the plaintiff in respect of the subject-matter of the

counterclaim, or claims against such other person any relief relating to or connected with the original subject-matter of the action, then, subject to rule 5 (2) he may join that other person as a party against whom the counterclaim is made.

(2) Where a defendant joins a person as a party against whom he makes a counterclaim, he must add that person's name to the title of the action and serve on him a copy of the counterclaim and, in the case of a person who is not already a party to the action, the defendant must issue the counterclaim out of the appropriate office and serve on the person concerned a sealed copy of the counterclaim, together with a form of acknowledgment of service in Form No. 14 in Appendix A (with such modifications as the circumstances may require) and a copy of the writ or originating summons by which the action was begun and of all other pleadings served in the action; and a person on whom a copy of a counterclaim is served under this paragraph shall, if he is not already a party to the action, become a party to it as from the time of service with the same rights in respect of his defence to the counterclaim and otherwise as if he had been duly sued in the ordinary way by the party making the counterclaim.

(3) A defendant who is required by paragraph (2) to serve a copy of the counterclaim made by him on any person who before service is already a party to the action must do so within the period within which, by virtue of Order 18, rule 2, he must serve on the plaintiff the defence to which the counterclaim is added.

(4) The appropriate office for issuing and acknowledging service of a counterclaim against a person who is not already a party to the action is the central office, except that, where the action is proceeding in the Chancery Division or a District Registry, or is an admiralty or commercial action which is not proceeding in a District Registry, the appropriate office is Chancery Chambers, the District Registry in question or the Admiralty and Commercial Registry, as the case may be.

(5) Where by virtue of paragraph (2) a copy of a counterclaim is required to be served on a person who is not already a party to the action, the following provisions of these rules, namely, Order 6, rule 7 (3) and (5), Order 10, Order 11, Orders 12 and 13 and Order 75, rule 4, shall, subject to the last foregoing paragraph, apply in relation to the counterclaim and the proceedings arising from it as if –

(a) the counterclaim were a writ and the proceedings arising from it an action; and

(b) the party making the counterclaim were a plaintiff and the party against whom it is made a defendant in that action.

(5A) Where by virtue of paragraph (2) a copy of a counterclaim is required to be served on any person other than the plaintiff who before service is already a party to the action, the provisions of Order 14, rule 5 shall apply in relation to the counterclaim and the proceedings arising therefrom, as if the party against whom the counterclaim is made were the plaintiff in the action.

(6) A copy of a counterclaim required to be served on a person who is not already a party to the action must be indorsed with a notice, in Form No. 17 in Appendix A, addressed to that person.

4. Joinder of parties

(1) Subject to rule 5 (1) two or more persons may be joined together in one action as plaintiffs or as defendants with the leave of the Court or where –

(*a*) if separate actions were brought by or against each of them, as the case may be, some common question of law or fact would arise in all the actions, and

(*b*) all rights to relief claimed in the action (whether they are joint, several or alternative) are in respect of or arise out of the same transaction or series of transactions.

(2) Where the plaintiff in any action claims any relief to which any other person is entitled jointly with him, all persons so entitled must, subject to the provisions of any Act and unless the Court gives leave to the contrary, be parties to the action and any of them who does not consent to being joined as a plaintiff must, subject to any order made by the Court on an application for leave under this paragraph, be made a defendant.

This paragraph shall not apply to a probate action.

(3) [*Revoked except in relation to actions which by virtue of section 7 thereof, the Civil Liability (Contribution) Act 1978 does not apply.*]

5. Court may order separate trials, etc.

(1) If claims in respect of two or more causes of action are included by a plaintiff in the same action or by a defendant in a counterclaim, or if two or more plaintiffs or defendants are parties to the same action, and it appears to the Court that the joinder of causes of action or of parties, as the case may be, may embarrass or delay the trial or is otherwise inconvenient, the Court may order separate trials or make such other order as may be expedient.

(2) If it appears on the application of any party against whom a counterclaim is made that the subject-matter of the counterclaim ought for any reason to be disposed of by a separate action, the Court may order the counterclaim to be struck out or may order it to be tried separately or make such other order as may be expedient.

6. Misjoinder and nonjoinder of parties

(1) No cause or matter shall be defeated by reason of the misjoinder or non-joinder of any party; and the Court may in any cause or matter determine the issues or questions in dispute so far as they affect the rights and interests of the persons who are parties to the cause or matter.

(2) Subject to the provisions of this rule, at any stage of the proceedings in any cause or matter the Court may on such terms as it thinks just and either of its own motion or on application –

(*a*) order any person who has been improperly or unnecessarily made a party or who has for any reason ceased to be a proper or necessary party, to cease to be a party;

(*b*) order any of the following persons to be added as a party, namely –

(i) any person who ought to have been joined as a party or whose presence before the Court is necessary to ensure that all matters in dispute in the cause or matter may be effectually and completely determined and adjudicated upon, or

(ii) any person between whom and any party to the cause or matter there may exist a question or issue arising out of or relating to or connected with any relief or remedy claimed in the cause or matter which in the opinion of the Court it would be just and convenient to determine as between him and that party as well as between the parties to the cause or matter.

(3) An application by any person for an order under paragraph (2) adding him as a party must, except with the leave of the Court, be supported by an affidavit showing his interest in the matters in dispute in the cause or matter or, as the case may be, the question or issue to be determined as between him and any party to the cause or matter.

(4) No person shall be added as a plaintiff without his consent signified in writing or in such other manner as may be authorised.

(5) No person shall be added or substituted as a party after the expiry of any relevant period of limitation unless either –

(a) the relevant period was current at the date when proceedings were commenced and it is necessary for the determination of the action that the new party should be added, or substituted, or

(b) the relevant period arises under the provisions of section 11 or 12 of the Limitation Act 1980 and the Court directs that those provisions should not apply to the action by or against the new party.

In this paragraph 'any relevant period of limitation' means a time limit under the Limitation Act 1980 or a time limit which applies to the proceedings in question by virtue of the Foreign Limitation Periods Act 1984.

(6) Except in a case to which the law of another country relating to limitation applies, and the law of England and Wales does not so apply, the addition or substitution of a new party shall be treated as necessary for the purposes of paragraph (5) (a) if, and only if, the Court is satisfied that –

(a) the new party is a necessary party to the action in that property is vested in him at law or in equity and the plaintiff's claim in respect of an equitable interest in that property is liable to be defeated unless the new party is joined, or

(b) the relevant cause of action is vested in the new party and the plaintiff jointly but not severally, or

(c) the new party is the Attorney General and the proceedings should have been brought by relator proceedings in his name, or

(d) the new party is a company in which the plaintiff is a shareholder and on whose behalf the plaintiff is suing to enforce a right vested in the company, or

(e) the new party is sued jointly with the defendant and is not also liable severally with him and failure to join the new party might render the claim unenforceable.

12. Representative proceedings

(1) Where numerous persons have the same interest in any proceedings, not being such proceedings as are mentioned in rule 13, the proceedings may be begun, and, unless the Court otherwise orders, continued, by or against any one or more of them as representing all or as representing all except one or more of them.

(2) At any stage of proceedings under this rule the Court may, on the application of the plaintiff, and on such terms, if any, as it thinks fit, appoint any one or more of the defendants or other persons as representing whom the defendants are sued to represent all, or all except one or more, of those persons in the proceedings; and where, in exercise of the power conferred by this paragraph, the Court appoints a person not named as a defendant, it shall make an order under rule 6 adding that person as a defendant.

(3) A judgment or order given in proceedings under this rule shall be binding on all the persons as representing whom the plaintiffs sue or, as the case may be, the defendants are sued, but shall not be enforced against any person not a party to the proceedings except with the leave of the Court.

(4) An application for the grant of leave under paragraph (3) must be made by summons which must be served personally on the person against whom it is sought to enfore the judgment or order.

(5) Notwithstanding that a judgment or order to which any such application relates is binding on the person against whom the application is made, that person may dispute liability to have the judgment or order enforced against him on the ground that by reason of facts and matters particular to his case he is entitled to be exempted from such liability.

(6) The Court hearing an application for the grant of leave under paragraph (3) may order the question whether the judgment or order is enforceable against the person against whom the application is made to be tried and determined in any manner in which any issue or question in an action may be tried and determined.

13. Representation of interested persons who cannot be ascertained, etc.

(1) In any proceedings concerning –

- (*a*) the estate of a deceased person, or
- (*b*) property subject to a trust, or
- (*c*) the construction of a written instrument, including a statute,

the Court, if satisfied that it is expedient so to do, and that one or more of the conditions specified in paragraph (2) are satisfied, may appoint one or more persons to represent any person (including an unborn person) or class who is or may be interested (whether presently or for any future, contingent or unascertained interest) in or affected by the proceedings.

(2) The conditions for the exercise of the power conferred by paragraph (1) are as follows –

- (*a*) that the person, the class or some member of the class, cannot be ascertained or cannot readily be ascertained;
- (*b*) that the person, class or some member of the class, though ascertained, cannot be found;
- (*c*) that, though the person or the class and the members thereof can be ascertained and found, it appears to the Court expedient (regard being had to all the circumstances, including the amount at stake and the degree of difficulty of the point to be determined) to exercise the power for the purposes of saving expense.

(3) Where, in any proceedings to which paragraph (1) applies, the Court exercises the power conferred by that paragraph, a judgment or order of the Court given or made when the person or persons appointed in exercise of that power are before the Court shall be binding on the person or class represented by the person or persons so appointed.

(4) Where, in any such proceedings, a compromise is proposed and some of the persons who are interested in, or who may be affected by, the compromise are not parties to the proceedings (including unborn or unascertained persons) but –

(*a*) there is some other person in the same interest before the Court who assents to the compromise or on whose behalf the Court sanctions the compromise, or

(*b*) the absent persons are represented by a person appointed under paragraph (1) who so assents,

the Court, if satisfied that the compromise will be for the benefit of the absent persons and that is expedient to exercise this power, may approve the compromise and order that it shall be binding on the absent persons, and they shall be bound accordingly except where the order has been obtained by fraud or non-disclosure of material facts.

ORDER 16

THIRD PARTY AND SIMILAR PROCEEDINGS

1. Third party notice

(1) Where in any action a defendant who has given notice of intention to defend –

(*a*) claims against a person not already a party to the action any contribution or indemnity; or

(*b*) claims against such a person any relief or remedy relating to or connected with the original subject-matter of the action and substantially the same as some relief or remedy claimed by the plaintiff; or

(*c*) requires that any question or issue relating to or connected with the original subject-matter of the action should be determined not only as between the plaintiff and the defendant but also as between either or both of them and a person not already a party to the action;

then, subject to paragraph (2), the defendant may issue a notice in Form No. 20 or 21 in Appendix A, whichever is appropriate (in this Order referred to as a third party notice), containing a statement of the nature of the claim made against him and, as the case may be, either of the nature and grounds of the claim made by him or the question or issue required to be determined.

(2) A defendant to an action may not issue a third party notice without the leave of the Court unless the action was begun by writ and he issues the notice before serving his defence on the plaintiff.

(3) Where a third party notice is served on the person against whom it is issued, he shall as from the time of service be a party to the action (in this Order referred to as a third party) with the same rights in respect of his defence against any claim made against him in the notice and otherwise as if he had been duly sued in the ordinary way by the defendant by whom the notice is issued.

2. Application for leave to issue third party notice

(1) Application for leave to issue a third party notice may be made ex parte but the Court may direct a summons for leave to be issued.

(2) An application for leave to issue a third party notice must be supported by an affidavit stating –

(*a*) the nature of the claim made by the plaintiff in the action;

(*b*) the stage which proceedings in the action have reached;

(*c*) the nature of the claim made by the applicant or particulars of the question or issue required to be determined, as the case may be, and the facts on which the proposed third party notice is based; and

(*d*) the name and address of the person against whom the third party notice is to be issued.

3. Issue, service and acknowledgment of service, of third party notice

(1) The order granting leave to issue a third party notice may contain directions as to the period within which the notice is to be issued.

(2) There must be served with every third party notice a copy of the writ or originating summons by which the action was begun and of the pleadings (if any) served in the action and a form of acknowledgment of service in Form No. 14 in Appendix A with such modification as may be appropriate.

(3) The appropriate office for acknowledging service of a third party notice is the central office, except that, where the notice is issued in an action which is proceeding in the Chancery Division or a District Registry, or is an admiralty or commercial action which is not proceeding in a District Registry, the appropriate office is Chancery Chambers, the District Registry in question or the Admiralty and Commercial Registry, as the case may be.

(4) Subject to the foregoing provisions of this rule, the following provisions of these rules, namely, Order 6, rule 7 (3) and (5), Order 10, Order 11, Order 12 and Order 75, rule 4, shall apply in relation to a third party notice and to the proceedings begun thereby as if –

(*a*) the third party notice were a writ and the proceedings begun thereby an action; and

(*b*) the defendant issuing the third party notice were a plaintiff and the person against whom it is issued a defendant in that action:

provided that in the application of Order 11, r 1 (1) (*c*) leave may be granted to serve a third party notice outside the jurisdiction on any necessary or proper party to the proceedings brought against the defendant.

4. Third party directions

(1) If the third party gives notice of intention to defend, the defendant who issued the third party notice must, by summons to be served on all the other parties to the action, apply to the Court for directions.

(2) If no summons is served on the third party under paragraph (1), the third party may, not earlier than 7 days after giving notice of intention to defend by summons to be served on all the other parties to the action, apply to the Court for directions or for an order to set aside the third party notice.

(3) On an application for directions under this rule the Court may –

(*a*) if the liability of the third party to the defendant who issued the third party notice is established on the hearing, order such judgment as the nature of the case may require to be entered against the third party in favour of the defendant; or

(*b*) order any claim, question or issue stated in the third party notice to be tried in such manner as the Court may direct; or

(*c*) dismiss the application and terminate the proceedings on the third party notice;

and may do so either before or after any judgment in the action has been signed by the plaintiff against the defendant.

(4) On an application for directions under this rule the Court may give the third party leave to defend the action, either alone or jointly with any defendant, upon such terms as may be just, or to appear at the trial and to take such part therein as may be just, and generally may make such orders and give such directions as appear to the Court proper for having the rights and liabilities of the parties most conveniently determined and enforced and as to the extent to which the third party is to be bound by any judgment or decision in the action.

(5) Any order made or direction given under this rule may be varied or rescinded by the Court at any time.

5. Default of third party, etc.

(1) If a third party does not give notice of intention to defend or, having been ordered to serve a defence, fails to do so –

- (*a*) he shall be deemed to admit any claim stated in the third party notice and shall be bound by any judgment (including judgment by consent) or decision in the action in so far as it is relevant to any claim, question or issue stated in that notice; and
- (*b*) the defendant by whom the third party notice was issued may, if judgment in default is given against him in the action, at any time after satisfaction of that judgment and, with the leave of the Court, before satisfaction thereof, enter judgment against the third party in respect of any contribution or indemnity claimed in the notice, and, with the leave of the Court, in respect of any other relief or remedy claimed therein.

(2) If a third party or the defendant by whom a third party notice was issued makes default in serving any pleading which he is ordered to serve, the Court may, on the application by summons of that defendant or the third party, as the case may be, order such judgment to be entered for the applicant as he is entitled to on the pleadings or may make such other order as may appear to the Court necessary to do justice between the parties.

(3) The Court may at any time set aside or vary a judgment entered under paragraph (1) (*b*) or paragraph (2) on such terms (if any) as it thinks just.

7. Judgment between defendant and third party

(1) Where in any action a defendant has served a third party notice, the Court may at or after the trial of the action or, if the action is decided otherwise than by trial, on an application by summons or motion, order such judgment as the nature of the case may require to be entered for the defendant against the third party or for the third party against the defendant.

(2) Where judgment is given for the payment of any contribution of indemnity to a person who is under a liability to make a payment in respect of the same debt or damage, execution shall not issue on the judgment without the leave of the Court until that liability has been discharged.

(3) For the purpose of paragraph (2) 'liability' includes liability under a judgment in the same or other proceedings and liability under an agreement to which section 1 (4) of the Civil Liability (Contribution) Act 1978 applies.

ORDER 18

12. Particulars of pleading

(1) Subject to paragraph (2), every pleading must contain the necessary particulars of any claim, defence or other matter pleaded including, without prejudice to the generality of the foregoing,

(a) particulars of any misrepresentation, fraud, breach of trust, wilful default or undue influence on which the party pleading relies;

(b) where a party pleading alleges any condition of the mind of any person, whether any disorder or disability of mind or any malice, fraudulent intention or other condition of mind except knowledge, particulars of the facts on which the party relies; and

(c) where a claim for damages is made against a party pleading, particulars of any facts on which the party relies in mitigation of, or otherwise in relation to, the amount of damages.

(1A) Subject to paragraph (1B), a plaintiff in an action for personal injuries shall serve with his statement of claim –

(a) a medical report, and

(b) a statement of the special damages claimed.

(1B) Where the documents to which paragraph (1A) applies are not served with the statement of claim, the Court may –

(a) specify the period of time within which they are to be provided, or

(b) make such other order as it thinks fit (including an order dispensing with the requirements of paragraph (1A) or staying the proceedings).

(1C) For the purposes of this rule, –

'medical report' means a report substantiating all the personal injuries alleged in the statement of claim which the plaintiff proposes to adduce in evidence as part of his case at the trial;

'a statement of the special damages claimed' means a statement giving full particulars of the special damages claimed for expenses and losses already incurred and an estimate of any future expenses and losses (including loss of earnings and of pension rights).

(2) Where it is necessary to give particulars of debt, expenses or damages and those particulars exceed three folios, they must be set out in a separate document referred to in the pleading and the pleading must state whether the document has already been served and, if so, when, or is to be served with the pleading.

(3) The Court may order a party to serve on any other party particulars of any claim, defence of other matter stated in his pleading, or in any affidavit of his ordered to stand as a pleading, or a statement of the nature of the case on which he relies, and the order may be made on such terms as the Court thinks just.

(4) Where a party alleges as a fact that a person had knowledge or notice of some fact, matter or thing, then, without prejudice to the generality of paragraph (3), the Court may, on such terms as it thinks just, order that party to serve on any other party –

(*a*) where he alleges knowledge, particulars of the facts on which he relies, and

(*b*) where he alleges notice, particulars of the notice.

(5) An order under this rule shall not be made before service of the defence unless, in the opinion of the Court, the order is necessary or desirable to enable the defendant to plead or for some other special reason.

(6) Where the applicant for an order under this rule did not apply by letter for the particulars he requires, the Court may refuse to make the order unless of opinion that there were sufficient reasons for an application by letter not having been made.

(7) Where particulars are given pursuant to a request, or order of the Court, the request or order shall be incorporated with the particulars, each item of the particulars following immediately after the corresponding item of the request or order.

13. Admissions and denials

(1) Any allegation of fact made by a party in his pleading is deemed to be admitted by the opposite party unless it is traversed by that party in his pleading or a joinder of issue under rule 14 operates as a denial of it.

(2) A traverse may be made either by a denial or by a statement of non-admission and either expressly or by necessary implication.

(3) Every allegation of fact made in a statement of claim or counterclaim which the party on whom it is served does not intend to admit must be specifically traversed by him in his defence or defence to counterclaim, as the case may be; and a general denial of such allegations, or a general statement of non-admission of them, is not a sufficient traverse of them.

(4) [*Revoked.*]

19. Striking out pleadings and indorsements

(1) The Court may at any stage of the proceedings order to be struck out or amended any pleading or the indorsement of any writ in the action, or anything in any pleading or in the indorsement, on the ground that –

(*a*) it discloses no reasonable cause of action or defence, as the case may be; or

(*b*) it is scandalous, frivolous or vexatious; or

(*c*) it may prejudice, embarrass or delay the fair trial of the action; or

(*d*) it is otherwise an abuse of the process of the Court;

and may order the action to be stayed or dismissed or judgment to be entered accordingly, as the case may be.

(2) No evidence shall be admissible on an application under paragraph (1) (*a*).

(3) This rule shall, so far as applicable, apply to an originating summons and a petition as if the summons or petition, as the case may be, were a pleading.

ORDER 20

AMENDMENT

3. Amendment of pleadings without leave

(1) A party may, without the leave of the Court, amend any pleading of his

once at any time before the pleadings are deemed to be closed and, where he does so, he must serve the amended pleadings on the opposite party.

(2)   Where an amended statement of claim is served on a defendant –

(*a*)   the defendant, if he has already served a defence on the plaintiff, may amend his defence, and

(*b*)   the period for service of his defence or amended defence, as the case may be, shall be either the period fixed by or under these rules for service of his defence or a period of 14 days after the amended statement of claim is served on him, whichever expires later.

(3)   Where an amended defence is served on the plaintiff by a defendant –

(*a*)   the plaintiff, if he has already served a reply on that defendant, may amend his reply, and

(*b*)   the period for service of his reply or amended reply, as the case may be, shall be 14 days after the amended defence is served on him.

(4)   In paragraphs (2) and (3) references to a defence and a reply include references to a counterclaim and a defence to counterclaim respectively.

(5)   Where an amended counterclaim is served by a defendant on a party (other than the plaintiff) against whom the counterclaim is made, paragraph (2) shall apply as if the counterclaim were a statement of claim and as if the party by whom the counterclaim is made were the plaintiff and the party against whom it is made a defendant.

(6)   Where a party has pleaded to a pleading which is subsequently amended and served on him under paragraph (1), then, if that party does not amend his pleading under the foregoing provisions of this Rule, he shall be taken to rely on it in answer to the amended pleading, and Order 18, rule 14 (2), shall have effect in such a case as if the amended pleading had been served at the time when that pleading, before its amendment under paragraph (1), was served.

5. Amendment of writ or pleading with leave

(1)   Subject to Order 15, rules 6, 7 and 8 and the following provisions of this rule, the Court may at any stage of the proceedings allow the plaintiff to amend his writ, or any party to amend his pleading, on such terms as to costs or otherwise as may be just and in such manner (if any) as it may direct.

(2)   Where an application to the Court for leave to make the amendment mentioned in paragraph (3), (4) or (5) is made after any relevant period of limitation current at the date of issue of the writ has expired, the Court may nevertheless grant such leave in the circumstances mentioned in that paragraph if it thinks it just to do so.

In this paragraph 'any relevant period of limitation' includes a time limit which applies to the proceedings in question by virtue of the Foreign Limitation Periods Act 1984.

(3)   An amendment to correct the name of a party may be allowed under paragraph (2) notwithstanding that it is alleged that the effect of the amendment will be to substitute a new party if the Court is satisfied that the mistake sought to be corrected was a genuine mistake and was not misleading or such as to cause any reasonable doubt as to the identity of the person intending to sue or, as the case may be, intended to be sued.

(4) An amendment to alter the capacity in which a party sues may be allowed under paragraph (2) if the new capacity is one which that party had at the date of the commencement of the proceedings or has since acquired.

(5) An amendment may be allowed under paragraph (2) notwithstanding that the effect of the amendment will be to add or substitute a new cause of action if the new cause of action arises out of the same facts or substantially the same facts as a cause of action in respect of which relief has already been claimed in the action by the party applying for leave to make the amendment.

ORDER 25

SUMMONS FOR DIRECTIONS

1. Summons for directions

(1) With a view to providing, in every action to which this rule applies, an occasion for the consideration by the Court of the preparations for the trial of the action, so that –

(*a*) all matters which must or can be dealt with on interlocutory applications and have not already been dealt with may so far as possible be dealt with, and

(*b*) such directions may be given as to the future course of the action as appear best adapted to secure the just, expeditious and economical disposal thereof,

the plaintiff must, within one month after the pleadings in the action are deemed to be closed, take out a summons (in these rules referred to as a summons for directions) returnable in not less than 14 days.

8. Automatic directions in personal injury actions

(1) When the pleadings in any action to which this rule applies are deemed to be closed the following directions shall take effect automatically:

(*a*) there shall be discovery of documents within 14 days in accordance with Order 24, rule 2, and inspection within seven days thereafter, save that where liability is admitted, or where the action arises out of a road accident, discovery shall be limited to disclosure by the plaintiff of any documents relating to special damages;

(*b*) subject to paragraph (2), where any party intends to place reliance at the trial on –

(i) expert evidence, he shall, within 14 weeks, disclose the substance of that evidence to the other parties in the form of a written report, which shall be agreed if possible; and

(ii) any other oral evidence, he shall, within 14 weeks, serve on the other parties written statements of all such oral evidence which he intends to adduce;

(*c*) unless such reports are agreed, the parties shall be at liberty to call as expert witnesses those witnesses the substance of whose evidence has been disclosed in accordance with the preceding sub-paragraph, except that the number of expert witnesses shall be limited in any case to two medical experts and one expert of any other kind;

(*d*) photographs, a sketch plan and the contents of any police accident report book shall be receivable in evidence at the trial, and shall be agreed if possible;

(*e*) subject to Order 77, rule 13, the action shall be tried at the trial centre for the place where the action is proceeding or at such other trial centre as the parties may in writing agree;

(*f*) the action shall be tried by Judge alone, as a case of substance or difficulty (Category B) and shall be set down within six months;

(*g*) the Court shall be notified, on setting down, of the estimated length of the trial.

(1A) Nothing in paragraph (1) shall require a party to produce a further medical report if he proposes to rely at the trial only on the report provided pursuant to Order 18, rule 12 (1A) or (1B) but, where a party claiming damages for personal injuries discloses a further report, that report shall be accompanied by a statement of the special damages claimed and, in this paragraph, 'statement of the special damages claimed' has the same meaning as in Order 18, rule 12 (1C).

(2) Paragraphs (4) to (16) of Order 38, rule 2A shall apply with respect to statements and reports served under sub-paragraph (1) (*b*) as they apply with respect to statements served under that rule.

(3) Nothing in paragraph (1) shall prevent any party to an action to which this rule applies from applying to the Court for such further or different directions or orders as may, in the circumstances, be appropriate or prevent the making of an order for the transfer of the proceedings to a county court.

(4) For the purposes of this rule –

'a road accident' means an accident on land due to a collision or apprehended collision involving a vehicle; and 'documents relating to special damages' include

(*a*) documents relating to any industrial injury, industrial disablement or sickness benefit rights, and

(*b*) where the claim is made under the Fatal Accidents Act 1976, documents relating to any claim for dependency on the deceased.

(5) This rule applies to any action for personal injuries except –

(*a*) any Admiralty action; and

(*b*) any action where the pleadings contain an allegation of a negligent act or omission in the course of medical treatment.

ORDER 29

INTERLOCUTORY INJUNCTIONS, INTERIM PRESERVATION OF PROPERTY, INTERIM PAYMENTS, ETC.

I. INTERLOCUTORY INJUNCTIONS, INTERIM PRESERVATION OF PROPERTY, ETC.

1. Application for injunction

(1) An application for the grant of an injunction may be made by any party to a cause or matter before or after the trial of the cause or matter, whether

or not a claim for the injunction was included in that party's writ, originating summons, counterclaim or third party notice, as the case may be.

(2) Where the applicant is the plaintiff and the case is one of urgency such application may be made ex parte on affidavit but, except as aforesaid, such application must be made by motion or summons.

(3) The plaintiff may not make such an application before the issue of the writ or originating summons by which the cause or matter is to be begun except where the case is one of urgency, and in that case the injunction applied for may be granted on terms providing for the issue of the writ or summons and such other terms, if any, as the Court thinks fit.

1A. Cross-examination on assets disclosure affidavit

(1) Where –

(a) the Court has made an order restraining any party from removing from the jurisdiction of the High Court, or otherwise dealing with, any assets,

(b) that party has in compliance with the order, or any order made in connection with it, filed affidavit evidence as to his or any other assets, and

(c) the Court has ordered that that party shall be cross-examined on his affidavit,

the Court may order that the cross-examination shall be conducted otherwise than before a judge, in which case the cross-examination shall take place before a master or, if a master so orders, before an examiner of the Court.

(2) The following provisions of Order 68 shall apply to a cross-examination of a kind referred to in paragraph (1) (c) as if it were a trial with witnesses in the Queen's Bench or Chancery Division and as if the person presiding were the judge –

(a) rule 1 (1) (except the words 'unless the judge otherwise directs'); and

(b) rules 2 (2) and (3) and 8.

(3) A cross-examination of a kind referred to in paragraph (1) (c) shall take place in chambers and no transcript or other record of it may be used by any person other than the party being cross-examined for any purpose other than the purpose of the proceedings in which the order for the cross-examination was made, unless and to the extent that that party consents or the Court gives leave.

2. Detention, preservation, etc., of subject-matter of cause or matter

(1) On the application of any party to a cause or matter the Court may make an order for the detention, custody or preservation of any property which is the subject-matter of the cause or matter, or as to which any question may arise therein, or for the inspection of any such property in the possession of a party to the cause or matter.

(2) For the purpose of enabling any order under paragraph (1) to be carried out the Court may by the order authorise any person to enter upon any land or building in the possession of any party to the cause or matter.

(3) Where the right of any party to a specific fund is in dispute in a cause or matter, the Court may, on the application of a party to the cause or matter, order the fund to be paid into court or otherwise secured.

(4) An order under this rule may be made on such terms, if any, as the Court thinks just.

(5) An application for an order under this rule must be made by summons or by notice under Order 25, rule 7.

(6) Unless the Court otherwise directs, an application by a defendant for such an order may not be made before he acknowledges service of the writ or originating summons by which the cause or matter was begun.

3. Power to order samples to be taken, etc.
(1) Where it considers it necessary or expedient for the purpose of obtaining full information or evidence in any cause or matter, the Court may, on the application of a party to the cause or matter, and on such terms, if any, as it thinks just, by order authorise or require any sample to be taken of any property which is the subject-matter of the cause or matter or as to which any question may arise therein, any observation to be made on such property or any experiment to be tried on or with such property.

(2) For the purpose of enabling any order under paragraph (1) to be carried out the Court may by the order authorise any person to enter upon any land or building in the possession of any party to the cause or matter.

(3) Rule 2 (5) and (6) shall apply in relation to an application for an order under this rule as they apply in relation to an application for an order under that rule.

II. Interim Payments

9. Interpretation of Part II
In this Part of this Order –
> 'interim payments', in relation to a defendant, means a payment on account of any damages, debt or other sum (excluding costs) which he may be held liable to pay to or for the benefit of the plaintiff; and any person who, for the purpose of the proceedings, acts as next friend of the plaintiff or guardian of the defendant.

10. Application for interim payment
(1) The plaintiff may, at any time after the writ has been served on a defendant and the time limited for him to acknowledge service has expired, apply to the Court for an order requiring that defendant to make an interim payment.

(2) An application under this rule shall be made by summons but may be included in a summons for summary judgment under Order 14 or Order 86.

(3) An application under this rule shall be supported by an affidavit which shall –

(*a*) verify the amount of the damages, debt or other sum to which the application relates and the grounds of the application;
(*b*) exhibit any documentary evidence relied on by the plaintiff in support of the application; and
(*c*) if the plaintiff's claim is made under the Fatal Accidents Act 1976, contain the particulars mentioned in section 2 (4) of that Act.

(4) The summons and a copy of the affidavit in support and any documents exhibited thereto shall be served on the defendant against whom the order is sought not less than 10 clear days before the return day.

(5) Notwithstanding the making or refusal of an order for an interim payment, a second or subsequent application may be made upon cause shown.

11. Order for interim payment in respect of damages

(1) If, on the hearing of an application under rule 10 in an action for damages, the Court is satisfied –

- (*a*) that the defendant against whom the order is sought (in this paragraph referred to as 'the respondent') has admitted liability for the plaintiff's damages, or
- (*b*) that the plaintiff has obtained judgment against the respondent for damages to be assessed; or
- (*c*) that, if the action proceeded to trial, the plaintiff would obtain judgment for substantial damages against the respondent or, where there are two or more defendants, against any of them,

the Court may, if it thinks fit and subject to paragraph (2), order the respondent to make an interim payment of such amount as it thinks just, not exceeding a reasonable proportion of the damages which in the opinion of the Court are likely to be recovered by the plaintiff after taking into account any relevant contributory negligence and any set-off, cross-claim or counterclaim on which the respondent may be entitled to rely.

(2) No order shall be made under paragraph (1) in an action for personal injuries if it appears to the Court that the defendant is not a person falling within one of the following categories, namely –

- (*a*) a person who is insured in respect of the plaintiff's claim
- (*b*) a public authority; or
- (*c*) a person whose means and resources are such as to enable him to make the interim payment.

12. Order for interim payment in respect of sums other than damages

If, on the hearing of an application under rule 10, the Court is satisfied –

- (*a*) that the plaintiff has obtained an order for an account to be taken as between himself and the defendant and for any amount certified due on taking the account to be paid; or
- (*b*) that the plaintiff's action includes a claim for possession of land and, if the action proceeded to trial, the defendant would be held liable to pay to the plaintiff a sum of money in respect of the defendant's use and occupation of the land during the pendency of the action, even if a final judgment or order were given or made in favour of the defendant; or
- (*c*) that, if the action proceeded to trial the plaintiff would obtain judgment against the defendant for a substantial sum of money apart from any damages or costs,

the Court may, if it thinks fit, and without prejudice to any contentions of the parties as to the nature or character of the sum to be paid by the defendant, order the defendant to make an interim payment of such amount as it thinks just, after taking into account any set-off, cross-claim or counterclaim on which the defendant may be entitled to rely.

ORDER 32

Applications and Proceedings in Chambers

I. General

1. Mode of making application
Except as provided by Order 25, rule 7, every application in chambers not made ex parte must be made by summons.

2. Issue of summons
(1) Issue of a summons by which an application in Chambers is to be made takes place on its being sealed by an officer of the appropriate office.

(2) A summons may not be amended after issue without the leave of the Court.

(3) In this rule 'the appropriate office' means –

(a) in relation to a summons in a cause or matter proceeding in a District Registry, that Registry;

(b) in relation to a cause or matter in the Chancery Division which is not proceeding in a District Registry, Chancery Chambers;

(c) in relation to a summons in a cause or matter proceeding in the principal Registry of the Family Division, that Registry;

(d) in relation to a summons in an Admiralty cause or matter or a commercial action which is not proceeding in a District Registry, the Admiralty and Commercial Registry;

(dd) in relation to a summons in taxation proceedings in the Supreme Court Taxing Office, that office;

(e) in relation to a summons in any other cause or matter, the Central Office.

For the purposes of this paragraph, a cause or matter in which any jurisdiction is to be exercised by virtue of Order 34, rule 5 (4) by a Master or by the Registrar of a District Registry shall be treated, in relation to that jurisdiction as proceeding in the Central Office, Chancery Chambers or that District Registry as the case may be.

3. Service of summons
A summons asking only for the extension or abridgment of any period of time may be served on the day before the day specified in the summons for the hearing thereof but, except as aforesaid and unless the Court otherwise orders or any of these rules otherwise provides, a summons must be served on every other party not less than two clear days before the day so specified.

4. Adjournment of hearing
(1) The hearing of a summons may be adjourned from time to time, either generally or to a particular date, as may be appropriate.

(2) If the hearing is adjourned generally, the party by whom the summons was taken out may restore it to the list on two clear days' notice to all the other parties on whom the summons was served.

5. Proceeding in absence of party failing to attend
(1) Where any party to a summons fails to attend on the first or any

resumed hearing thereof, the Court may proceed in his absence if, having
regard to the nature of the application, it thinks it expedient so to do.

(2) Before proceeding in the absence of any party the Court may require
to be satisfied that the summons or, as the case may be, notice of the time
appointed for the resumed hearing was duly served on that party.

(3) Where the Court hearing a summons proceeded in the absence of a
party, then, provided that any order made on the hearing has not been perfected, the Court, if satisfied that it is just to do so, may re-hear the summons.

(4) Where an application made by summons has been dismissed without a hearing by reason of the failure of the party who took out the summons
to attend the hearing, the Court, if satisfied that it is just to do so, may allow
the summons to be restored to the list.

6. Order made ex parte may be set aside
The Court may set aside an order made ex parte.

ORDER 38

EVIDENCE

2A. Exchange of witness statements
(1) The powers of the Court under this rule shall be exercised for the purpose of disposing fairly and expeditiously of the cause or matter before it,
and saving costs, having regard to all the circumstances of the case, including (but not limited to) –

(*a*)   the extent to which the facts are in dispute or have been admitted;
(*b*)   the extent to which the issues of fact are defined by the pleadings;
(*c*)   the extent to which information has been or is likely to be provided
by further and better particulars, answers to interrogatories or
otherwise.

(2) At the summons for directions in an action commenced by writ the
Court shall direct every party to serve on the other parties, within 14 weeks
(or such other period as the Court may specify) of the hearing of the
summons and on such terms as the Court may specify, written statements of
the oral evidence which the party intends to adduce on any issues of fact to
be decided at the trial.

The Court may give a direction to any party under this paragraph at any
other stage of such an action and at any stage of any other cause or matter.

Order 3, rule 5 (3) shall not apply to any period specified by the Court
under this paragraph.

(3) Directions under paragraph (2) or (17) may make different provision
with regard to different issues of fact or different witnesses.

(4) Statements served under this rule shall –

(*a*)   be dated and, except for good reason (which should be specified by
letter accompanying the statement), be signed by the intended
witness and shall include a statement by him that the contents are
true to the best of his knowledge and belief;
(*b*)   sufficiently identify any documents referred to therein; and
(*c*)   where they are to be served by more than one party, be exchanged
simultaneously.

(5) Where a party is unable to obtain a written statement from an intended witness in accordance with paragraph (4) (*a*), the Court may direct the party wishing to adduce that witness's evidence to provide the other party with the name of the witness and (unless the Court otherwise orders) a statement of the nature of the evidence intended to be adduced.

(6) Subject to paragraph (9), where the party serving a statement under this rule does not call the witness to whose evidence it relates, no other party may put the statement in evidence at the trial.

(7) Subject to paragraph (9), where the party serving the statement does call such a witness at the trial –

(*a*) except where the trial is with a jury, the Court may, on such terms as it thinks fit, direct that the statement served, or part of it, shall stand as the evidence in chief of the witness or part of such evidence;

(*b*) the party may not without the consent of the other parties or the leave of the Court adduce evidence from that witness the substance of which is not included in the statement served, except –

(i) where the Court's directions under paragraph (2) or (17) specify that statements should be exchanged in relation to only some issues of fact, in relation to any other issues;

(ii) in relation to new matters which have arisen since the statement was served on the other party;

(*c*) whether or not the statement or any part of it is referred to during the evidence in chief of the witness, any party may put the statement or any part of it in cross-examination of that witness.

(8) Nothing in this rule shall make admissible evidence which is otherwise inadmissible.

(9) Where any statement served is one to which the Civil Evidence Acts 1968 and 1972 apply, paragraphs (6) and (7) shall take effect subject to the provisions of those Acts and Parts III and IV of this Order.

The service of a witness statement under this rule shall not, unless expressly so stated by the party serving the same, be treated as a notice under the said Acts of 1968 and 1972; and where a statement or any part thereof would be admissible in evidence by virtue only of the said Act of 1968 or 1972 the appropriate notice under Part III or Part IV of this Order shall be served with the statement notwithstanding any provision of those Parts as to the time for serving such a notice. Where such a notice is served a counter-notice shall be deemed to have been served under Order 38, rule 26 (1).

(10) Where a party fails to comply with a direction for the exchange of witness statements he shall not be entitled to adduce evidence to which the direction related without the leave of the Court.

(11) Where a party serves a witness statement under this rule, no other person may make use of that statement for any purpose other than the purpose of the proceedings in which it was served –

(*a*) unless and to the extent that the party serving it gives his consent in writing or the Court gives leave; or

(*b*) unless and to the extent that it has been put in evidence (whether pursuant to a direction under paragraph (7) (*a*) or otherwise).

(12) Subject to paragraph (13), the judge shall, if any person so requests during the course of the trial, direct the associate to certify as open to

inspection any witness statement which was ordered to stand as evidence in chief under paragraph (7) (*a*).

A request under this paragraph may be made orally or in writing.

(13) The judge may refuse to give a direction under paragraph (12) in relation to a witness statement, or may exclude from such a direction any words or passages in a statement, if he considers that inspection should not be available –

(*a*) in the interests of justice or national security,
(*b*) because of the nature of any expert medical evidence in the statement, or
(*c*) for any other sufficient reason.

(14) Where the associate is directed under paragraph (12) to certify a witness statement as open to inspection he shall –

(*a*) prepare a certificate which shall be attached to a copy ('the certified copy') of that witness statement; and
(*b*) make the certified copy available for inspection.

(15) Subject to any conditions which the Court may by special or general direction impose, any person may inspect and (subject to payment of the prescribed fee) take a copy of the certified copy of a witness statement from the time when the certificate is given until the end of 7 days after the conclusion of the trial.

(16) In this rule –

(*a*) any reference in paragraphs (12) to (15) to a witness statement shall, in relation to a witness statement of which only part has been ordered to stand as evidence in chief under paragraph (7) (*a*), be construed as a reference to that part;
(*b*) any reference to inspecting or copying the certified copy of a witness statement shall be construed as including a reference to inspecting or copying a copy of that certified copy.

(17) The Court shall have power to vary or override any of the provisions of this rule (except paragraphs (1), (8) and (12) to (16)) and to give such alternative directions as it thinks fit.

21. Notice of intention to give certain statements in evidence

(1) Subject to the provisions of this rule, a party to a cause or matter who desires to give in evidence at the trial or hearing of the cause or matter any statement which is admissible in evidence by virtue of section 2, 4 or 5 of the Act must –

(*a*) in the case of a cause or matter which is required to be set down for trial or hearing or adjourned into court, within 21 days after it is set down or so adjourned, or within such other period as the Court may specify, and
(*b*) in the case of any other cause or matter, within 21 days after the date on which an appointment for the first hearing of the cause or matter is obtained, or within such other period as the Court may specify,

serve on every other party to the cause or matter notice of his desire to do so, and the notice must comply with the provisions of rule 22, 23 or 24, as the circumstances of the case require.

(2) Paragraph (1) shall not apply in relation to any statement which is admissible as evidence of any fact stated therein by virtue not only of the said section 2, 4 or 5 but by virtue also of any other statutory provisions within the meaning of section 1 of the Act.

(3) Paragraph (1) shall not apply in relation to any statement which any party to a probate action desires to give in evidence at the trial of that action and which is alleged to have been made by the deceased person whose estate is the subject of the action.

(4) Where by virtue of any provision of these rules or of any order or direction of the Court the evidence in any proceedings is to be given by affidavit then, without prejudice to paragraph (2), paragraph (1) shall not apply in relation to any statement which any party to the proceedings desires to have included in any affidavit to be used on his behalf in the proceedings, but nothing in this paragraph shall affect the operation of Order 41, rule 5, or the powers of the Court under Order 38, rule 3.

(5) Order 65, rule 9, shall not apply to a notice under this rule but the Court may direct that the notice need not be served on any party who at the time when service is to be effected is in default as to acknowledgment of service or who has no address for service.

22. Statement admissible by virtue of section 2 of the Act: contents of notice

(1) If the statement is admissible by virtue of section 2 of the Act and was made otherwise than in a document, the notice must contain particulars of –

(*a*) the time, place and circumstances at or in which the statement was made;

(*b*) the person by whom, and the person to whom, the statement was made; and

(*c*) the substance of the statement or, if material, the words used.

(2) If the statement is admissible by virtue of the said section 2 and was made in a document, a copy or transcript of the document, or of the relevant part thereof, must be annexed to the notice and the notice must contain such (if any) of the particulars mentioned in paragraph (1) (*a*) and (*b*) as are not apparent on the face of the document or part.

(3) If the party giving the notice alleges that any person, particulars of whom are contained in the notice, cannot or should not be called as a witness at the trial or hearing for any of the reasons specified in rule 25, the notice must contain a statement to that effect specifying the reason relied on.

23. Statement admissible by virtue of section 4 of the Act: contents of notice

(1) If the statement is admissible by virtue of section 4 of the Act, the notice must have annexed to it a copy or transcript of the document containing the statement, or of the relevant part thereof, and must contain –

(*a*) particulars of –
(i) the person by whom the record containing the statement was compiled;
(ii) the person who originally supplied the information from which the record was compiled; and

(iii) any other person through whom that information was supplied to the compiler of that record;

and, in the case of any such person as is referred to in (i) or (iii) above, a description of the duty under which that person was acting when compiling that record or supplying information from which that record was compiled, as the case may be;

(b) if not apparent on the face of the document annexed to the notice, a description of the nature of the record which, or part of which, contains the statement; and

(c) particulars of the time, place and circumstances at or in which that record or part was compiled.

(2) If the party giving the notice alleges that any person, particulars of whom are contained in the notice, cannot or should not be called as a witness at the trial or hearing for any of the reasons specified in rule 25, the notice must contain a statement to that effect specifying the reason relied on.

24. Statement admissible by virtue of section 5 of the Act: contents of notice

(1) If the statement is contained in a document produced by a computer and is admissible by virtue of section 5 of the Act, the notice must have annexed to it a copy or transcript of the document containing the statement, or of the relevant part thereof, and must contain particulars of –

(a) a person who occupied a responsible position in relation to the management of the relevant activities for the purpose of which the computer was used regularly during the material period to store or process information;

(b) a person who at the material time occupied such a position in relation to the supply of information to the computer, being information which is reproduced in the statement or information from which the information contained in the statement is derived;

(c) a person who occupied such a position in relation to the operation of the computer during the material period;

and where there are two or more persons who fall within any of the foregoing subparagraphs and some only of those persons are at the date of service of the notice capable of being called as witnesses at the trial or hearing, the person particulars of whom are to be contained in the notice must be such one of those persons as is at that date so capable.

(2) The notice must also state whether the computer was operating properly throughout the material period and, if not, whether any respect in which it was not operating properly or was out of operation during any part of that period was such as to affect the production of the document in which the statement is contained or the accuracy of its contents.

(3) If the party giving the notice alleges that any person, particulars of whom are contained in the notice, cannot or should not be called as a witness at the trial or hearing for any of the reasons specified in rule 25, the notice must contain a statement to that effect specifying the reason relied on.

25. Reasons for not calling a person as a witness

The reasons referred to in rules 22 (3), 23 (2) and 24 (3) are that the person in question is dead, or beyond the seas or unfit by reason of his bodily or mental condition to attend as a witnesss or that despite the exercise of reasonable diligence it has not been possible to identify or find him or that he cannot reasonably be expected to have any recollection of matters relevant to the accuracy or otherwise of the statement to which the notice relates.

26. Counter-notice requiring person to be called as a witness

(1) Subject to paragraphs (2) and (3), any party to a cause or matter on whom a notice under rule 21 is served may within 21 days after service of the notice on him serve on the party who gave the notice or a counter-notice requiring that party to call as a witness at the trial or hearing of the cause or matter any person (naming him) particulars of whom are contained in the notice.

(2) Where any notice under rule 21 contains a statement that any person particulars of whom are contained in the notice cannot or should not be called as a witness for the reason specified therein, a party shall not be entitled to serve a counter-notice under this rule requiring that person to be called as a witness at the trial or hearing of the cause or matter unless he contends that that person can or, as the case may be, should be called, and in that case he must include in his counter-notice a statement to that effect.

(3) Where a statement to which a notice under rule 21 relates is one to which rule 28 applies, no party on whom the notice is served shall be entitled to serve a counter-notice under this rule in relation to that statement, but the foregoing provision is without prejudice to the right of any party to apply to the Court under rule 28 for directions with respect to the admissibility of that statement.

(4) If any party to a cause or matter by whom a notice under rule 21 is served fails to comply with a counter-notice duly served on him under this rule, then, unless any of the reasons specified in rule 25 applies in relation to the person named in the counter-notice, and without prejudice to the powers of the Court under rule 29, the statement to which the notice under rule 21 relates shall not be admissible at the trial or hearing of the cause or matter as evidence of any fact stated therein by virtue of section 2, 4 or 5 of the Act, as the case may be.

27. Determination of question whether person can or should be called as a witness

(1) Where in any cause or matter a question arises whether any of the reasons specified in rule 25 applies in relation to a person particulars of whom are contained in a notice under rule 21, the Court may, on the application of any party to the cause or matter, determine that question before the trial or hearing of the cause or matter or give directions for it to be determined before the trial or hearing and for the manner in which it is to be so determined.

(2) Unless the Court otherwise directs, the summons by which an application under paragraph (1) is made must be served by the party making the application on every other party to the cause or matter.

(3) Where any such question as is referred to in paragraph (1) has been determined under or by virtue of that paragraph, no application to have it determined afresh at the trial or hearing of the cause or matter may be made unless the evidence which it is sought to adduce in support of the application could not with reasonable diligence have been adduced at the hearing which resulted in the determination.

IV. Expert Evidence

35. Interpretation

In this Part of this Order a reference to a summons for directions includes a reference to any summons or application to which, under any of these Rules, Order 25, rules 2 to 7, apply and expressions used in this Part of this Order which are used in the Civil Evidence Act 1972 have the same meanings in this Part of this Order as in that Act.

36. Restrictions on adducing expert evidence

(1) Except with the leave of the Court or where all parties agree, no expert evidence may be adduced at the trial or hearing of any cause or matter unless the party seeking to adduce the evidence –

(*a*) has applied to the Court to determine whether a direction should be given under rule 37 or 41 (whichever is appropriate) and has complied with any direction given on the application or

(*b*) has complied with automatic directions taking effect under Order 25, rule 8 (1) (*b*).

(2) Nothing in paragraph (1) shall apply to evidence which is permitted to be given by affidavit or shall affect the enforcement under any other provision of these Rules (except Order 45, rule 5) of a direction given under this part of this Order.

37. Direction that expert report be disclosed

(1) Subject to paragraph (2), where in any cause or matter an application is made under rule 36 (1) in respect of oral expert evidence, then, unless the Court considers that there are special reasons for not doing so, it shall direct that the substance of the evidence be disclosed in the form of a written report or reports to such other parties and within such period as the Court may specify.

(2) Nothing in paragraph (1) shall require a party to disclose a further medical report if he proposes to rely at the trial only on the report provided pursuant to Order 18, rule 12 (1A) or (1B) but, where a party claiming damages for personal injuries discloses a further report, that report shall be accompanied by a statement of the special damages claimed and in this paragraph, 'statement of the special damages claimed' has the same meaning as in Order 18, rule 12 (1C).

38. Meeting of experts

In any cause or matter the Court may, if it thinks fit, direct that there be a meeting 'without prejudice' of such experts within such periods before or after the disclosure of their reports as the court may specify, for the purpose of identifying those parts of their evidence which are in issue. Where such a meeting takes place the experts may prepare a joint statement indicating those parts of their evidence on which they are, and those on which they are not, in agreement.

39. Disclosure of part of expert evidence

Where the Court considers that any circumstances rendering it undesirable to give a direction under rule 37 relate to part only of the evidence sought to be adduced, the Court may, if it thinks fit, direct disclosure of the remainder.

ORDER 45

5. Enforcement of judgment to do or abstain from doing any act

(1) Where –

(*a*) a person required by a judgment or order to do an act within a time specified in the judgment or order refuses or neglects to do it within that time or, as the case may be, within that time as extended or abridged under Order 3, rule 5, or

(*b*) a person disobeys a judgment or order requiring him to abstain from doing an act,

then, subject to the provisions of these rules, the judgment or order may be enforced by one or more of the following means, that is to say –

(i) with the leave of the Court, a writ of sequestration against the property of that person;

(ii) where that person is a body corporate, with the leave of the Court, a writ of sequestration against the property of any director or other officer of the body;

(iii) subject to the provisions of the Debtors Acts, 1869 and 1878, an order of committal against that person or, where that person is a body corporate, against any such officer.

(2) Where a judgment or order requires a person to do an act within a time therein specified and an order is subsequently made under rule 6 requiring the act to be done within some other time, references in paragraph (1) of this rule to a judgment or order shall be construed as references to the order made under rule 6.

(3) Where under any judgment or order requiring the delivery of any goods the person liable to execution has the alternative of paying the assessed value of the goods, the judgment or order shall not be enforceable by order of committal under paragraph (1), but the Court may, on the application of the person entitled to enforce the judgment or order, make an order requiring the first mentioned person to deliver the goods to the applicant within a time specified in the order, and that order may be so enforced.

6. Judgment, etc. requiring act to be done: order fixing time for doing it

(1) Notwithstanding that a judgment or order requiring a person to do an act specifies a time within which the act is to be done, the Court shall, without prejudice to Order 3, rule 5, have power to make an order requiring the act to be done within another time, being such time after service of that order, or such other time, as may be specified therein.

(2) Where, notwithstanding Order 42, rule 2 (1), or by reason of Order 42, rule 2 (2), a judgment or order requiring a person to do an act does not specify a time within which the act is to be done, the Court shall have power subsequently to make an order requiring the act to be done within such time after service of that order, or such other time, as may be specified therein.

(3) An application for an order under this rule must be made by summons and the summons must, notwithstanding anything in Order 65, rule 9, be served on the person required to do the act in question.

7. Service of copy of judgment, etc., prerequisite to enforcement under r. 5

(1) In this rule references to an order shall be construed as including references to a judgment.

(2) Subject to Order 24, rule 16 (3), Order 26, rule 6 (3), and paragraphs (6) and (7) of this rule, an order shall not be enforced under rule 5 unless –

> (a) a copy of the order has been served personally on the person required to do or abstain from doing the act in question, and
>
> (b) in the case of an order requiring a person to do an act, the copy has been so served before the expiration of the time within which he was required to do the act.

(3) Subject as aforesaid, an order requiring a body corporate to do or abstain from doing an act shall not be enforced as mentioned in rule 5 (1) (ii) or (iii) unless –

> (a) a copy of the order has also been served personally on the officer against whose property leave is sought to issue a writ of sequestration or against whom an order of committal is sought, and
>
> (b) in the case of an order requiring the body corporate to do an act, the copy has been so served before the expiration of the time within which the body was required to do the act.

(4) There must be prominently displayed on the front of the copy of an order served under this rule a warning to the person on whom the copy is served that disobedience to the order would be a contempt of court punishable by imprisonment, or (in the case of an order requiring a body corporate to do or abstain from doing an act) punishable by sequestration of the assets of the body corporate and by imprisonment of any individual responsible.

(5) With the copy of an order required to be served under this rule, being an order requiring a person to do an act, there must also be served a copy of any order made under Order 3, rule 5, extending or abridging the time for doing the act and, where the first-mentioned order was made under rule 5 (3) or 6 of this Order, a copy of the previous order requiring the act to be done.

(6) An order requiring a person to abstain from doing an act may be enforced under rule 5 notwithstanding that service of a copy of the order has not been effected in accordance with this rule if the Court is satisfied that pending such service, the person against whom or against whose property it is sought to enforce the order has had notice thereof either –

> (a) by being present when the order was made, or
>
> (b) by being notified of the terms of the order, whether by telephone, telegram or otherwise.

(7) Without prejudice to its powers under Order 65, rule 4, the Court may dispense with service of a copy of an order under this rule if it thinks it just to do so.

ORDER 58

Appeals from Masters, Registrars, Referees and Judges

1. Appeals from certain decisions of masters, etc. to judge in Chambers

(1) Except as provided by rule 2, an appeal shall lie to a judge in Chambers

from any judgment, order or decision of a Master, the Admiralty Registrar or a Registrar of the Family Division.

(2) The appeal shall be brought by serving on every other party to the proceedings in which the judgment, order or decision was given or made a notice to attend before the judge on a day specified in the notice or on which other day as may be directed.

(3) Unless the Court otherwise orders, the notice must be issued within 5 days after the judgment, order or decision appealed against was given or made and must be served within five days after issue and an appeal to which this rule applies shall not be heard sooner than two clear days after such service.

(4) Except so far as the Court may otherwise direct, an appeal under this rule shall not operate as a stay of the proceedings in which the appeal is brought.

3. Appeals from District Registrars

(1) An appeal shall lie from any judgment, order or decision of a District Registrar in any cause or matter in any Division in the same circumstances and, except as provided by paragraph (2) subject to the same conditions as if the judgment, order or decision were given or made by a master or Registrar in that cause or matter in that Division, and the provisions of these rules with respect to appeals shall apply accordingly.

(2) In relation to an appeal from a judgment, order or decision of a District Registrar, rule 1 shall have effect subject to the modification that for the first reference therein to 5 days and the reference therein to 2 clear days there shall be substituted references to 7 days and 3 clear days respectively.

6. Appeal from judge in Chambers

Subject to section 18 of the Act and section 15 (2) of the Administration of Justice Act 1960 (which restrict appeals) and to Order 53, rule 13, and without prejudice to section 13 of the said Act of 1960 (which provides for an appeal in cases of contempt of court), an appeal shall lie to the Court of Appeal from any judgment, order or decision of a judge in chambers.

ORDER 65

Service of Documents

1. When personal service required

(1) Any document which by virtue of these rules is required to be served on any person need not be served personally unless the document is one which by an express provision of these rules or by order of the Court is required to be so served.

(2) Paragraph (1) shall not affect the power of the Court under any provision of these rules to dispense with the requirements for personal service.

2. Personal service: how effected

Personal service of a document is effected by leaving a copy of the document with the person to be served.

3. Service on body corporate

(1) Personal service of a document on a body corporate may, in cases for which provision is not otherwise made by any enactment, be effected by

serving it in accordance with rule 2 on the mayor, chairman or president of the body, or the town clerk, clerk, secretary, treasurer of other similar officer thereof.

(2) Where a writ is served on a body corporate in accordance with Order 10, rule 1 (2), that rule shall have effect as if for the reference to the usual or last known address of the defendant there were substituted a reference to the registered or principal office of the body corporate and as if for the reference to the knowledge of the defendant there were substituted a reference to the knowledge of a person mentioned in paragraph (1).

4. Substituted service

(1) If, in the case of any document which by virtue of any provision of these rules is required to be served personally or a document to which Order 10, rule 1 applies, it appears to the Court that it is impracticable for any reason to serve that document in the manner prescribed on that person, the Court may make an order for substituted service of that document.

(2) An application for an order for substituted service may be made by an affidavit stating the facts on which the application is founded.

(3) Substituted service of a document, in relation to which an order is made under this rule, is effected by taking such steps as the Court may direct to bring the document to the notice of the person to be served.

5. Ordinary service: how effected

(1) Service of any document, not being a document which by virtue of any provision of these rules is required to be served personally or a document to which Order 10, rule 1, applies, may be effected –

> (*a*) by leaving the document at the proper address of the person to be served, or
> (*b*) by post, or
> (*c*) through a document exchange in accordance with paragraph (2A), or
> (*ca*) by FAX in accordance with paragraph (2B), or
> (*d*) in such other manner as the Court may direct.

(2) For the purposes of this rule, and of section 7 of the Interpretation Act 1978, in its application to this rule, the proper address of any person on whom a document is to be served in accordance with this rule shall be the address for service of that person, but if at the time when service is effected that person has no address for service his proper address for the purposes aforesaid shall be –

> (*a*) in any case, the business address of the solicitor (if any) who is acting for him in the proceedings in connection with which service of the document in question is to be effected, or
> (*b*) in the case of an individual, his usual or last known address, or
> (*c*) in the case of individuals who are suing or being sued in the name of a firm, the principal or last known place of business of the firm within the jurisdiction, or
> (*d*) in the case of a body corporate, the registered or principal office of the body.

(2A) Where –

(a) the proper address for service includes a numbered box at a document exchange, or

(b) there is inscribed on the writing paper of the party on whom the document is served (where such party acts in person) or on the writing paper of his solicitor (where such party acts by a solicitor) a document exchange box number, and such a party or his solicitor (as the case may be) has not indicated in writing to the party serving the document that he is unwilling to accept service through a document exchange,

service of the document may be affected by leaving the document addressed to that numbered box at that document exchange or at a document exchange which transmits documents every business day to that exchange; and any document which is left at a document exchange in accordance with this paragraph shall, unless the contrary is proved, be deemed to have been served on the second business day following the day on which it is left.

(2B) Service by FAX may be effected where –

(a) the party serving the document acts by a solicitor,

(b) the party on whom the document is served acts by a solicitor and service is effected by transmission to the business address of such a solicitor,

(c) the solicitor acting for the party on whom the document is served has indicated in writing to the solicitor serving the document that he is willing to accept service by FAX at a specified FAX number and the document is transmitted to that number; and for this purpose the inscription of a FAX number on the writing paper of a solicitor shall be deemed to indicate that such a solicitor is willing to accept service by FAX at that number in accordance with this paragraph unless he states otherwise in writing, and

(d) as soon as practicable after service by FAX the solicitor acting for the party serving the document dispatches a copy of it to the solicitor acting for the other party by any of the other methods prescribed for service by paragraph (1), and if he fails to do so the document shall be deemed never to have been served by FAX.

Where the FAX is transmitted on a business day before 4 pm, it shall, unless the contrary is shown, be deemed to be served on that day, and, in any other case, on the business day next following.

(3) Nothing in this rule shall be taken as prohibiting the personal service of any document or as affecting any enactment which provides for the manner in which documents may be served on bodies corporate.

(4) In this rule –

(a) 'document exchange' means any document exchange for the time being approved by the Lord Chancellor;

(b) 'business day' means any day other than a Saturday, a Sunday, Christmas Day, Good Friday or a bank holiday as defined in Order 3, rule 2 (5).

ORDER 81

Partners

1. Actions by and against firms within jurisdiction
Subject to the provisions of any enactment, any two or more persons claiming to be entitled, or alleged to be liable, as partners in respect of a

cause of action and carrying on business within the jurisdiction may sue, or be sued, in the name of the firm (if any) of which they were partners at the time when the cause of action accrued.

2. Disclosure of partners' names

(1) Any defendant to an action brought by partners in the name of a firm may serve on the plaintiffs or their solicitor a notice requiring them or him forthwith to furnish the defendant with a written statement of the names and places of residence of all the persons who were partners in the firm at the time when the cause of action accrued; and if the notice is not complied with the Court may order the plaintiffs or their solicitor to furnish the defendant with such a statement and to verify it on oath or otherwise as may be specified in the order, or may order that further proceedings in the action be stayed on such terms as the Court may direct.

(2) When the names of the partners have been declared in compliance with a notice or order given or made under paragraph (1), the proceedings shall continue in the name of the firm but with the same consequences as would have ensued if the persons whose names have been so declared had been named as plaintiffs in the writ.

(3) Paragraph (1) shall have effect in relation to an action brought against partners in the name of a firm as it has effect in relation to an action brought by partners in the name of a firm but with the substitution, for references to the defendant and the plaintiffs, of references to the plaintiff and the defendants respectively, and with the omission of the words 'or may order' to the end.

3. Service of writ

(1) Where by virtue of rule 1 partners are sued in the name of a firm, the writ may, except in the case mentioned in paragraph (3), be served –

- (a) on any one or more of the partners, or
- (b) at the principal place of business of the partnership within the jurisdiction, on any person having at the time of service the control or management of the partnership business there; or
- (c) by sending a copy of the writ by ordinary first-class post (as defined in Order 10, rule 1 (2)) to the firm at the principal place of business of the partnership within the jurisdiction

and subject to paragraph (2) where service of the writ is effected in accordance with this paragraph, the writ shall be deemed to have been duly served on the firm, whether or not any member of the firm is out of the jurisdiction.

(2) Where a writ is served on a firm in accordance with sub-paragraph (1) (c) –

- (a) the date of service shall, unless the contrary is shown, be deemed to be the seventh day (ignoring Order 3, rule 2 (5)) after the date on which the copy was sent to the firm; and
- (b) any affidavit proving due service of the writ must contain a statement to the effect that –
  - (i) in the opinion of the deponent (or, if the deponent is the plaintiff's solicitor or an employee of that solicitor, in the opinion of the plaintiff) the copy of the writ, if sent to the firm at the address in question, will have come to the knowledge of one of the persons mentioned in paragraph (1) (a) or (b) within 7 days thereafter, and

    (ii) the copy of the writ has not been returned to the plaintiff
        through the post undelivered to the addressee.

(3) Where a partnership has, to the knowledge of the plaintiff, been
dissolved before an action against the firm is begun, the writ by which the
action is begun must be served on every person within the jurisdiction
sought to be made liable in the action.

(4) Every person on whom a writ is served under paragraph (1) (*a*) or (*b*)
must at the time of service be given a written notice stating whether he is
served as a partner or as a person having the control or management of the
partnership business or both as a partner and as such a person; and any
person on whom a writ is so served but to whom no such notice is given shall
be deemed to be served as a partner.

4. Acknowledgment of service in action against firm

(1) Where persons are sued as partners in the name of their firm, service may
not be acknowledged in the name of the firm but only by the partners thereof in
their own names, but the action shall nevertheless continue in the name of the firm.

(2) Where in an action against a firm the writ by which the action is begun is
served on a person as a partner, that person, if he denies that he was a partner or
liable as such at any material time, may acknowledge service of the writ and state
in his acknowledgment that he does so as a person served as a partner in the
defendant firm but who denies that he was a partner at any material time.

An acknowledgment of service given in accordance with this paragraph
shall, unless and until it is set aside, be treated as an acknowledgment by
the defendant firm.

(3) Where an acknowledgment of service has been given by a defendant
in accordance with paragraph (2), then –

    (*a*) the plaintiff may either apply to the Court to set it aside on the
        ground that the defendant was a partner or liable as such at a
        material time or may leave that question to be determined at a later
        stage of the proceedings;
    (*b*) the defendant may either apply to the Court to set aside the service of
        the writ on him on the ground that he was not a partner or liable as
        such at a material time or may at the proper time serve a defence on
        the plaintiff denying in respect of the plaintiff's claim either his
        liability as a partner or the liability of the defendant firm or both.

(4) The Court may at any stage of the proceedings in an action in which a
defendant has acknowledged service in accordance with paragraph (2), on
the application of the plaintiff or of that defendant, order that any question as
to the liability of that defendant or as to the liability of the defendant firm be
tried in such manner and at such time as the Court directs.

(5) Where in an action against a firm the writ by which the action is
begun is served on a person as a person having the control or management
of the partnership business, that person may not acknowledge service in the
action unless he is a member of the firm sued.

5. Enforcing judgment or order against firm

(1) Where a judgment is given or order made against a firm, execution to
enforce the judgment or order may, subject to rule 6, issue against any
property of the firm within the jurisdiction.

(2) Where a judgment is given or order made against a firm, execution to enforce the judgment or order may, subject to rule 6 and to the next following paragraph, issue against any person who –

(*a*) acknowledges service of the writ in the action as a partner, or
(*b*) having been served as a partner with the writ of summons, failed to acknowledge service of it in the action, or
(*c*) admitted in his pleading that he is a partner, or
(*d*) was adjudged to be a partner.

(3) Execution to enforce a judgment or order given or made against a firm may not issue against a member of the firm who was out of the jurisdiction when the writ of summons was issued unless he –

(*a*) acknowledges service of the writ in the action as a partner, or
(*b*) was served within the jurisdiction with the writ as a partner, or
(*c*) was, with the leave of the Court given under Order 11, served out of the jurisdiction with the writ, as a partner;

and, except as provided by paragraph (1) and by the foregoing provisions of this paragraph, a judgment or order given or made against a firm shall not render liable, release or otherwise affect a member of the firm who was out of the jurisdiction when the writ was issued.

(4) Where a party who has obtained a judgment or order against a firm claims that a person is liable to satisfy the judgment or order as being a member of the firm, and the foregoing provisions of this rule do not apply in relation to that person, that party may apply to the Court for leave to issue execution against that person, the application to be made by summons which must be served personally on that person.

(5) Where the person against whom an application under paragraph (4) is made does not dispute his liability, the Court hearing the application may, subject to paragraph (3), give leave to issue execution against that person, and, where that person disputes his liability, the Court may order that the liability of that person be tried and determined in any manner in which any issue or question in an action may be tried and determined.

Index

20th Century Photography Museum Ludwig Cologne

Front of dust jacket: Fritz Henle, *Nievis*, 1943, Gruber Collection
Spine of dust jacket: Charlotte March, *Donyale Luna with Earrings for*
"twen", 1966, Gruber Collection
Back of dust jacket: Man Ray, *Lips on Lips*, 1930, Gruber Collection

Concept: Reinhold Mißelbeck
Authors of texts about photographers:
Marianne Bieger-Thielemann (*MBT*), Gérard A. Goodrow
(*GG*), Lilian Haberer (*LH*), Reinhold Mißelbeck (*RM*),
Ute Pröllochs (*UP*), Anke Solbrig (*AS*),
Thomas von Taschitzki (*TvT*), Nina Zschocke (*NZ*)
Reproduction of the images:
Rheinisches Bildarchiv, Cologne
Closing date: January 1996

© 1996 Benedikt Taschen Verlag GmbH
Hohenzollernring 53, D–50672 Köln
www.taschen.com
© on the images rest with VG Bild-Kunst, Bonn,
the photographers, their agencies and estates

Editing and layout: Simone Philippi, Cologne
Design: Mark Thomson, London
English translation: Rolf Fricke, Phyllis Riefler-Bonham
Consultants: Andrew H. Eskind (George Eastman House),
Oscar Fricke (Russian Photohistory)

Printed in Austria
ISBN 3–8228–5867–6

20th Century
Photography
Museum Ludwig
Cologne

TASCHEN

KÖLN LONDON MADRID NEW YORK PARIS TOKYO

The Art of Photography

Marc Scheps

Photography, a 19th-century scientific invention, has – like many other technical innovations of that era – dramatically altered mankind's perception and experience of the world, an effect that continues to this day. The reproduction of a time-constrained reality by the immaterial medium of light, the "freezing" of a visually observable scene, seemed like a miracle, especially in its beginnings. It was, so to speak, the fulfillment of an ancient desire of mankind to create an imaginary world that would be as believable as the real world itself. This mirror image of the real world, chemically recorded on paper, was created in a miracle box, and the resulting pictures, memories of a past time-space situation, formed a visual archive. For the first time, one could record the past not just with written words or painted pictures. Now it could live on in the form of exact images. One could believe in this past as if one had experienced it personally. The photographic image evolved into a collective memory.

At first, the capability of creative interpretation inherent in painted pictures was challenged by the objective realism of the photographic image. Photography appeared to be unaffected by reality. Photographers celebrated the banality of daily life. They had the urge to create an overall record of our world, to assemble an endless collection of pictures into a kind of mega-memory.

The painted picture, the result of a long creative and additive process, could suddenly be replaced by a fast optical, mechanical and chemical process. The photographic image did not initially constitute a direct threat to painting. Its format was restricted by what the lens could cover, the images were black-and-white, and it was dependent on illumination. But even those who recognized the danger that photography posed to painting were fascinated by this new medium and the huge potential that it represented. The invention of photography was, after all, the birth of a new language and as such it should, above all, make possible a new kind of visual communication. This language is not localized, and the flood of photographic images knows no borders. Multiple reproduction and dissemination of these pictures created a virtual reality that has become part of our modern culture.

From this "lingua universalis" evolved an art language. Contingent on and limited by its historical context, this language evolved within the framework of the creative arts of the late 19th century. Photographers conformed to the aesthetics of their time and regarded photography merely as an additional means for visually perceiving and recreating reality. They experimented with this third eye with the intention of thereby enhancing the art of painting.

At the beginning of this century, the awareness grew that the photographic image had achieved autonomy and that it had developed an aesthetic of its own. This autonomy led to a new fertile relationship with painting. Photographers and painters discovered the nearly unlimited possibilities of producing art with this medium, and continued technological advances in this field provided unexpected new ways of doing so. Even so, the history of photography as art evolved independently and parallel to the history of painting. Fear of contact between the two was great, disputes sometimes harsh, a reconciliation seemed hopeless.

Fortunately, a dialog did eventually evolve, and this is undoubtedly one of the most exciting chapters in the visual culture of our century. It was not just a matter of recognizing photography as an art, but definitively eliminating the borders between photography and the creative arts.

In time, photography succeeded in gaining public acceptance. Major artists made a name for themselves with their small black-and-white pictures. Diverse styles expanded the scope. In the end, photography became a significant component of our culture. Modern art meanwhile had questioned its own means, and artists sought new ideas and new means of expression, eager to experiment. Naturally, this also involved photography. Artists like the Russian avant-gardists Alexander Rodchenko and El Lissitzky, the American dadaist and surrealist Man Ray or the Hungarian constructivist László Moholy-Nagy have all created an important body of work, thus becoming pioneers of a development that to this day remains uncompleted. But these artists were to remain exceptions, and the general ranking of photography before the First World War was relatively low. It was not accorded the decisive recognition as "high art". Even the establishment of a Department of Photography at the Museum of Modern Art in New York (which opened in 1929) was to remain an exception, and there were hardly any significant collectors of photographs.

The breakthrough finally occurred in the late fifties and early sixties. The urban world, the media and advertising intrigued artists such as Andy Warhol and Robert Rauschenberg, and photography became an integral part of their creative activities, an expansion of their art. Other artists explored the specificity of the photographic image, like Gerhard Richter, for instance, who regarded photography both as a filter of reality and as an independent pictorial reality.

Photographers now felt more and more attracted by the world of advertising, fashion and the mundane, Horst P. Horst and Richard Avedon being two examples. This resulted in a progressive elimination of media-driven compartmentalization. At last photography achieved museum-worthy status. In addition to the traditional art categories of painting, sculpture, drawing and graphic design, now there was the additional category of photography.

The photography collection at the Museum Ludwig evolved from an art collection. When the photography collection became a separate entity, this dialog was continued judiciously, with an open-minded attitude towards any new trends. Even though it was only created mostly after the museum was founded in 1976, today the collection nevertheless contains about 9300 photographs. The present book of excerpts presents 860 works and profiles 278 photographers. This is the first time that a selection drawn from the entire photography collection of the Museum Ludwig is being published for a broad public. Earlier publications were scientific evaluations of sections of the museum's photography holdings. On the occasion of the 20th anniversary of the museum, it was decided to publish two volumes with the same format, one covering painting and sculpture, and the present one covering 20th century photography. The decisive moment for the establishment of the Department of Photography at the Museum Ludwig was the acquisition in 1977 of the famous L. Fritz Gruber collection. L. Fritz Gruber, a longtime mentor, patron and friend of the museum, has been fostering photography throughout his life. To this day, he is known and respected internationally for his knowledge and love of photography. His worldwide contacts opened many doors, and his collection grew steadily. Parts of his collection were gradually donated to the museum, most recently in 1993 and 1994. The Gruber Collection constitutes the core of the present volume, both in terms of quantity as well as quality. With the help of L. Fritz Gruber, the museum has also been able to acquire many other collectors, and it constantly strives to enhance the collection further with other means. Reinhold Mißelbeck, who has been running the Department of Photography and Video since 1980, performs this task with great dedication, expertise and empathy, in spite of the fact that the means at our disposal are modest. The overall picture is impressive. Nevertheless we are not resting on our laurels but are currently busy planning visions for the collection for the coming years.

With the 1993 exhibition "Photography in Contemporary German Art", we showcased a current development that has mostly taken place in the Rhineland. It pointed to a future emphasis of the collection. With the Richard Avedon Retrospective of 1994 we presented an important photographer who addresses subjects that have fascinated various other artists of his generation: fashion, media, art, politics, poverty, violence and death. At the same time, we experimented with a new kind of photographic exhibition which without doubt will influence exhibitions in the future. This and other exhibitions attest to the symbiosis of artistic media, to mutual stimulation and enhancement of all categories of the creative arts.

With the 1995 exhibition "Celebrities' Celebrities", drawn from the Gruber Collection, we wanted to demonstrate that the great photographers of our time should be equated with all other artists and that the camera is no longer a mere technical aid for creating images that are unforgettable and that have become an integral part of our "musée imaginaire". The present volume is a testimony to the richness of the photographic image, to the creativity of the artists who – with camera in hand – are constantly taking us along on new voyages of discovery. Their artistic experiences are an enrichment of our lives.

The Photography Collection at the Museum Ludwig in Cologne

Reinhold Mißelbeck

The Photography Collection at the Museum Ludwig is the very first collection of photography at a museum of contemporary art in Germany, and it was founded almost simultaneously with the museum itself. Negotiations for founding the Museum Ludwig were completed in 1976, and the acquisition of the Gruber Collection took place barely a year later. Even so, the museum's collection already contained some photographic works before that acquisition occurred, such as *Journeyman* by August Sander, *Studies for Holograms* by Bruce Nauman and two photograms by László Moholy-Nagy. The Wallraf-Richartz-Museum had thus recognized the significance of this medium, and in certain instances it had also acquired individual photographic works. With the Ludwig Collection came a number of major artistic works, such as *Typology of half-timbered Houses* by Bernd and Hilla Becher, *Variable Piece No. 48* by Douglas Huebler, *Birth* by Charles Simonds and *Black Vase Horizontal* by Jan Dibbets. While there was never an emphasis on photography in the Ludwig Collection, these works nevertheless signaled the fact that a photographic collection as part of a museum of modern art has other priorities than a photographic museum per se. The history of photography has never been the guiding theme of the collection's interest. Rather it is the medium of photography as a young field of artistic activity next to painting, sculpture, drawing and printmaking, and as an older one when compared to video, performance or new media. Nevertheless these beginnings can only be considered to be the first hesitant steps of an emerging interest that later matured with the purchase of 887 photographs and the endowment of 200 additional ones from the Gruber Collection.

The Gruber Collection was an auspicious foundation for the museum's photography collection. This single acquisition encompassed an overview of this century's artistic photography, ranging from ebbing Pictorialism, represented by photographs in the work of Heinrich Kühn, Alvin Langdon Coburn and Hugo Erfurth (made in the twentieth century), through American and European Modernism, all the way into the fifties and sixties. This included the most important big names in American straight photography, like Ansel Adams, Edward Weston, Arnold

Newman, Walker Evans, Margaret Bourke-White and Dorothea Lange. But photojournalism was also well represented, with images by Alfred Eisenstaedt, Gordon Parks, Weegee, William Klein and W. Eugene Smith. Experimental trends were represented by the work of László Moholy-Nagy, Man Ray, Herbert List, Philippe Halsman, Chargesheimer, Heinz Hajek-Halke and Otto Steinert. Great names in fashion photography were also included: Cecil Beaton, Richard Avedon, Irving Penn, Horst P. Horst and George Hoyningen-Huene. With a collection of such richness, the Photography Collection of the Museum Ludwig took its place in the vanguard of the most significant photographic collections in Germany, next to those of the Folkwang-Schule in Essen (since 1978 in the Museum Folkwang), the Museum for Arts and Crafts in Hamburg, the first German photographic museum, the Agfa-Foto-Historama in Leverkusen (moved to Cologne in 1986), the photographic collection of the City Museum of Munich (which became the Photographic Museum in 1980). While the last three institutions were photohistory-oriented, and the collections in Essen and in Cologne concentrated on contemporary art, the Museum Ludwig was the only one with a policy of acquiring photographic works by creative artists in addition to fine examples of artistic photography. New acquisitions of images by Ger Dekkers, Peter Hutchinson, Jean Le Gac, Mac Adams and Michael Snow emphatically confirm this policy.

In 1978, another significant selection of photographs arrived in the form of a loan from the Ludwig Collection, consisting of 123 photographs by Alexander Rodchenko and two photograms by El Lissitzky. It was the very first large collection of Russian photographs to be displayed in a German Art Museum. This well-received exhibition and its accompanying publication sent an important signal. Various small exhibitions were also selected from the Gruber Collection, such as "Portraits of Artists" (1977), "Artistic Photography" (1978) and "Reportage Photography" (1979). During these early years, the collection was cared for by Jeane von Oppenheim and Dr. Evelyn Weiss. In 1979, the entire collection of 500 photographs of Cologne architecture by Werner Mantz was acquired, and in the same year the collection was enriched by approximately 2500 prints and their negatives, a part of the Chargesheimer estate.

My task, when I took over the collection in 1980, was to create an inventory of approximately 3000 photographs and to make them gradually accessible to the public. It was during this period that Renate and L. Fritz Gruber made it a custom, highly appreciated by us, to supplement our exhibitions with loans from their collection and subsequently to donate them to the museum. Such was the case with the exhibition "Aspects of Portrait Photography" (1981) and "Glamour & Fashion" (1983). Before then, however, the Mantz Collection had already been curated scientifically in 1982 and presented in an exhibition accompanied by a catalog. This was followed in 1983 by the exhibition "Derek Bennett – Portraits of Germans", which was donated to the collection in its entirety. Then came an exhibition derived from Chargesheimer's estate, which presented an overview of his work and which was also accompanied by a catalog. The Derek Bennett and Chargesheimer exhibitions were the first large traveling exhibitions that were sent on tour by the Photography Collection of the museum.

On the occasion of photokina 1984 we presented a great overview exhibition of the Gruber Collection with the subtitle "Photography of the 20th Century", which was again enhanced by donations. At that time, we also published the first catalog of the entire holdings, with reproductions of the more than 1200 pictures that were currently in the collection. This was the first time that photography in a German photographic collection was curated in the same manner as paintings, sculptures and drawings. Every photograph was accompanied by all the technical data and by specific literature references. The catalog became a reference manual and since then has gone into its third edition. This exhibition, too, went on tour and was displayed in Linz and in Manchester, among other cities. It was the first photographic exhibition which, at the suggestion of Professor Ludwig, was also displayed in East Germany, where it was shown in the gallery of the College for Graphics and Book Art in Leipzig.

The year 1985 was totally dedicated to the planning of the new building and to the move. Even so, it was possible to feature an exhibition of the photographic work of Benjamin Katz, which provided an overview of the set of more than 300 photographs acquired in 1982, which Benjamin Katz had compiled during the course of planning, setting up and displaying the exhibition "Art of the West". There was also an exhibition of architectural photography by Werner Mantz, Hugo Schmölz and Karl Hugo Schmölz, which offered an interesting insight into the work of the three most important architectural photographers in Cologne. Here too, a selection of the best photographs by the Schmölz father and son team were contributed to the collection. Renate and L. Fritz Gruber graciously joined forces with the photography collection of the museum to prepare an exhibition entitled "Photographers Photograph Photographers", which was displayed at the Musée Réattu during the "International Photography Meeting" in Arles. This fascinating exhibition, too, was donated to the museum and, together with the Benjamin Katz collection, formed the basis for the collection's emphasis today on artists' portraits.

On the occasion of the inauguration of the new building, the photography collection presented an expanded, revised and clarified second edition of the catalog of the holdings of the Gruber Collection, along with a similarly designed catalog of all the works that had been acquired by the Museum Ludwig during the past years. For a brief time, the Photography Collection of the Museum Ludwig could claim that it had presented to the public its complete holdings at that time – 5000 pictures, fully illustrated. Only Chargesheimer was presented merely in the form of a selection. This also attests to the extraordinary quality of the photography collection of the museum, because it is certainly not just the great amount of work nor the necessary financial investment that prevents photography collections from publishing truly complete and fully illustrated catalogs of their holdings – it is mostly the fact that too much would be revealed that does not enhance the respective museum's fame.

The second general catalog of the photography collection covered significant expansions in the field of artistic photographs, such as the two albums contributed by Dr. Oppenhoff, with photographs by Johannes Theodor Baargeld, works by Colette, Ger Dekkers, Roger Cutforth, Bernd and Hilla Becher, Jan Dibbets, Braco Dimitrievic, Joe Gantz, Peter Gilles, David Hockney, Douglas Huebler, Peter Hutchinson, Birgit Kahle, Jürgen Klauke, Les Krims, Astrid Klein, El Lissitzki, Marina Makowski, Gordon Matta Clark, Antoni Mikolajczik, Bruce Nauman, Ulrike Rosenbach, Charles Simonds, Michael Snow, Ulrich Tillmann, Andy Warhol and Dorothee von Windheim. Other significant groups of photographs were later added to this, such as the donation by Jeane von Oppenheim of 11 vintage photographs by Lewis Hine, 30 prints by Erwin von Dessauer, and photographs by Gertrude Fehr, Robert Häusser, Fritz Henle, Walde Huth, Arno Jansen, Benjamin Katz, Erika Kiffl, Manfred

Leve, Bernd Lohse, Gabriele and Helmut Nothhelfer, and also Hugo and Karl Hugo Schmölz. But it was not long before the next donation came along. On the occasion of the inauguration, Renate and L. Fritz Gruber filled a room with photographs by Albert Renger-Patsch, Chargesheimer and Man Ray, imparting a photographic accent to the opening festivities, and to which they gave the title of "Pictures of Stillness". Displayed in that room were photographs of machines by Albert Renger-Patsch, a series on *Basalt* by Chargesheimer and *The Milky Way* by Man Ray, a total of 39 photographs. Only a year later, a new exhibition "German Pictorialists" provided an overview of the work of the older generation of German photographers. That exhibition too, was acquired nearly in its entirety over the years that followed, filling gaps in the museum's holdings of photographs taken from the forties to the sixties with works by Ilse Bing, Walter Boje, Rosemarie Clausen, Gertrude Fehr, Hanns Hubmann, Kurt Julius, Peter Keetmann, Fritz Kempe, Edith Lechtape, Willi Moegle, Regina Relang, Toni Schneiders, Anton Stankowski, Pan Walther and Willi Otto Zielke. Others, like Hermann Claasen, Tim Gidal, Robert Häusser, Fritz Henle, Martha Hoepffner, Bernd Lohse, Hilmar Pabel, Karl Hugo Schmölz, Wolf Strache and Carl Strüwe were present in the collection with only a few examples of their work, but since that time have been represented much more adequately. Chargesheimer's 60th birthday provided an occasion for the museum to present the results of additional research work. The show, entitled "Chargesheimer in Person", was dedicated to Chargesheimer's persona, featuring statements from family and friends, school buddies and colleagues from artistic circles. A portfolio of some of his well-known works was issued, and the second half of his estate, containing his meditation musings and gelatin silver paintings, which had been rejected by the trustees in 1979, was acquired. This provided the foundation for an even more intensive study of the work of this artist, which became the subject of more and more scientific research projects at the Art History Institute of the University of Cologne. The results of these projects, which mostly examined the relationship between his photography of ruins and his gelatin silver paintings, were presented in 1994 in the exhibition entitled "Chargesheimer – Chaos Form Archform".

The 80th birthday of L. Fritz Gruber became a celebration that was further enhanced by a publication coupled with an exhibition entitled "L. Fritz Gruber – Highlights and Shadows". In the accompanying catalog, L. Fritz Gruber reviewed his encounters with some of the great photographers of his time. The entire exhibition was later donated to the Museum Ludwig.

In the years that followed, more and more attention was paid to Eastern Europe. Contacts with Leipzig culminated with the transfer of a collection of photographs from the former German Democratic Republic to Cologne. Numerous photographs were contributed after the first overview exhibition of contemporary photography in the former Czechoslovakia in 1990. The exhibition of Czech and Slovak photography travelled to 15 locations in Europe and in America, thus becoming the most successful traveling show of the museum's photography collection.

Soon another estate, the work of Heinz Held, was donated to the museum, almost immediately being presented to the public. Heinz Held had much the same interests as Chargesheimer, of whom Held was a contemporary. He was interested in everyday life, in the banal, in the hard-to-describe, so that he became an interesting counterpoint to the more artistically oriented Chargesheimer. These two photographic legacies provided the Museum Ludwig with the very unusual opportunity of studying two diverse photojournalistic approaches to the same subject.

The retrospective exhibition of fashion photographs by Horst P. Horst in cooperation with *Vogue* was not only a glittering social event, but it had a splendid conclusion with the donation of 40 photographs by this great German-American fashion photographer.

In 1991, years of discussions about an archive of 1500 negatives and 1000 vintage prints by Albert Renger-Patzsch reached an auspicious climax when the Schubert & Saltzer company of Ingolstadt transferred this work to the Museum Ludwig as a permanent loan. The City Museum received the largest selection from the existing duplicates, and the Museum Ludwig received 800 photographs as a donation. By trading additional donated duplicate prints, the museum was able to acquire, among others, landscape and architectural photographs by Albert Renger-Patzsch. After the completion of the research, with which the Photography Section once again lived up to its scientific mission by supporting a dissertation, a new chapter was added to the biography of Albert Renger-Patzsch. After the war ended, Renger-Patzsch photographed not just rocks and trees in Wamel as hitherto assumed, but over a period of 20 years he also completed his most ambitious industrial assignment ever. The exhibition and the catalog "Albert Renger-Patzsch – His Late Industrial Work" was opened at the Museum Ludwig in 1993 and later became a traveling exhibition.

The core category of portraits of artists also received a significant boost during that year, when the City of Bocholt contributed 50 portraits by Fritz Pitz. The latter spent many years as a photographer for the Galerie de France making portraits of artists in the French-Belgian-Dutch language region. A one-man exhibition of his work was created on the occasion of this donation. This acquisition included an experimental work that is of very special interest to the museum, because Fritz Pitz is only the second photographer other than Chargesheimer who was already creating large format 150 x 100 cm photochemical paintings in the early sixties.

In 1992, the couple Irene and Peter Ludwig augmented the museum's collection with the loan of a group of 65 works by Russian photographers. These works complemented the photographs by Alexander Rodchenko that were already on hand and expanded the museum's holdings of Russian constructivist art with outstanding photographic examples of that style.

Gaps in the photography collection were filled not only by donated groups of images, but also by the acquisition of individual works like those of Anna and Bernhard Johannes Blume, Rudolf Bonvie, early photographs by Jürgen Klauke, works by Gina Lee Felber, Gottfried Helnwein, Marina Makowski, Harald Fuchs, Annette Frick, A. T. Schaefer, Krimhild Becker, Piotr Jaros, loaned works from the Ludwig collection and installations by Jenny Holzer and Christian Boltanski. For practical reasons however, installations had to be assigned to the sculpture department.

The 85th birthday of L. Fritz Gruber once again was celebrated by Mr and Mrs Gruber with a generous addition to the museum's photography collection. Still more gaps were filled by gifts of more than 700 photographs during the years 1993 and 1994, which included works by, among others, Alfred Stieglitz, Alvin Langdon Coburn, Edward Steichen, Man Ray, Hugo Erfurth, Hermann Claasen, David "Chim" Seymour, Robert Capa, Franco Fontana. Rolf Winquist, Philippe Halsman, Ernst Haas, Andreas Feininger, Karin Székessy, Gottfried Helnwein, Jürgen Klauke, Ulrich Tillmann and Bettina Gruber.

The Gruber Collection, which continues to be the heart of the museum's photography collection, was once again presented to the public in 1995 in the form of an exhibition entitled "Celebrities' Celebrities", which featured selected portraits of famous personalities made by the best photographers of this century.

A new category, that of nude photography, was added to the subject of artists' portraits in 1995, when Uwe Scheid bestowed a collection upon the museum. In 1991, the Museum Ludwig had displayed an exhibition of photographs from the Uwe Scheid Collection entitled "Picture Lust", which was specially enhanced with images from current work in this field. With the donation of photographs made during the period ranging from the sixties to the nineties and totaling more than 200 images, the museum's photography collection was enriched by additions of major significance: works by Jean Dieuzaide, Lucien Clergue, Joel Peter Witkin, Bettina Rheims, Robert Heinecken, Curt Stenvert, Diana Blok, Toto Frima, Marlo Broekmans, André Gelpke. But the works of earlier photographers such as Wilhelm von Gloeden, Vincenco Galdi, and Franz Roh were also welcome additions. All of this is likely to have made the collection of this topic at the Museum Ludwig the most substantial one in all of Germany. Altogether, not counting the bequest of Heinz Held, the holdings of the photography collection at the Museum Ludwig today cover more than 9300 photographs. The donation by Uwe Scheid gains added significance in light of the fact that the museums of Cologne, which cannot benefit from the financial and political background of state-owned collections, strive to cultivate their 150-year-old tradition of close relations with an art-interested public, with collectors and patrons, whose circles they seek to expand. This is where donations such as that by Uwe Scheid can encourage others to seek a dialog with the Photography Collection at the Museum Ludwig and to enhance its stature.

Adams, Ansel

1902 San Francisco
1984 Carmel,
California

Ansel Adams made his first photographs during a 1916 vacation trip to Yosemite National Park in California. Even then he exhibited the first manifestations of what was to become characteristic of his entire work: a combination of superb photographic skill and a deep admiration for the American landscape.

Adams originally wanted to become a pianist. It was only after an encounter with Paul Strand in 1930 that he discovered that photography was his true medium of expression. Strand's concept of pure photography made a lasting impression on Adams and motivated him to clarify his own intentions. In 1932 he joined photographers Imogen Cunningham, John Paul Edwards, Sonya Noskoviak, Henry Swift, Willard van Dyke and Edward Weston to found the group "f/64". Members of this group dogmatically practiced a style of photography that emphasized the greatest possible depth of field and the sharpest reproduction of details. Fascinated by the precise rendition capabilities of their medium, the photographers particularly favored close-ups of individual subjects. Adams' photograph *Rose on Driftwood* is an example of this tradition.

▲ Ansel Adams
Sierra Nevada, 1944

Gelatin silver print
23.8 x 33.8 cm
ML/F 1977/24

Gruber Collection

▲ Ansel Adams
Zabriskie Point, Death Valley National
Monument, California, 1948

Gelatin silver print, 23.9 x 19 cm
ML/F 1977/30

Gruber Collection

◄ **Ansel Adams**
Rose on Driftwood,
1933

Gelatin silver print
19.5 x 24.1 cm
ML/F 1977/21

Gruber Collection

◄ **Ansel Adams**
Boards and Thistles,
around 1932

Gelatin silver print
23.2 x 16.8 cm
ML/F 1988/57

Gruber Donation

It was in 1941 that Adams created his famous "Zone System", an aid for determining correct exposure and development times for achieving an optimal gradation of gray values. Adams disseminated his photographic ideas and procedures through numerous books and seminars. In 1946 he founded the Department of Photography at the California School of Fine Art in San Francisco. In 1962 he retired to Carmel Highlands.

Adams spent a considerable part of his life as a landscape photographer in America's National Parks, about which he published more than 24 photographic books. During that time, he not only practiced his photography, but he also used his work to generate public interest in the parks, which he supported. He was also instrumental in the creation of new parks. *MBT*

▲ **Ansel Adams**
Canyon de Chelly
National Monument,
Arizona, 1942

Gelatin silver print
37.8 x 47.4 cm
ML/F 1977/26

Gruber Collection

Adams, Mac

1943 Wales
Lives in New York

Photographer Mac Adams, born in Wales in 1943, studied at the Cardiff College of Art from 1961 to 1966 and spent a year at the University of Wales. Later on he moved to New York, where he completed his studies at Rutgers University in 1969. Whereas his early work was very much in the English photographic tradition of the sixties, his *Mystery Environments* are characteristic of his work of the seventies. His preferred subjects are interiors, fictional situations such as *Port Authority (Mystery No. 12)*, which hint at a possible crime. Adams found inspiration for his main subjects in elements of murder mysteries. In *The Toaster*, the shiny metal of this kitchen appliance reflects a woman who, in the second photograph, is already lying on the floor. The toast is burned. This not only suggests a time sequence; the photograph itself also combines objects into a mysterious incident. Adams' conceptual "Narrative Art" also

◄ **Mac Adams**
Port Authority
(Mystery No. 12),
1975

*Gelatin silver print
each 85.5 x 77.5 cm*
ML/F 1979/1352 I-II

includes color photographs and sculptures, whose subjects – an open cupboard, a revolver and a rope – are combined to produce a symbolic charge. In his photographs *Port Authority (Mystery No. 12)* of 1975, Adams used the play of light and shadows to stage people in motion, making the viewer perceive elements of ambiguity. He is less interested in the secret than in the manner the information is conveyed by the objects perceived. He personally characterizes his work as being somewhere between Agatha Christie and Anthony Caro.

Adams has been represented in a number of international exhibitions, such as "documenta VI" in Kassel in 1977, and in Groningen in 1979. The photographer lives and works in New York. *LH*

Arnold, Eve

1913 Philadelphia
Lives in London

Eve Arnold is one of the earliest "Magnum" photographers. From 1947 to 1948 she studied photography under Alexey Brodovitch at the New School for Social Research in New York. In 1951 she joined "Magnum" and became the first woman to take pictures for that agency. She moved to London in 1961 and spent the years that followed as a photojournalist traveling through the former Soviet Union, Afghanistan, Egypt, and China. During the fifties, Eve Arnold created several photographic essays about women from the most diverse levels of society, of whom she wanted to present a realistic, "unretouched" image. It was in this context that she also produced the picture series about Marlene Dietrich and Marilyn Monroe, from which came the illustrations shown here. When Eve Arnold was present at a recording session with Marlene Dietrich in 1954, she was not interested in a conventional, idealized star portrait. During a production pause, she succeeded in capturing a picture of the actress in a pensive, introspective mood, who even then knew instinctively how to stage her body. In a similar, apparently unobserved moment in 1955, Eve Arnold photographed Marilyn Monroe in Illinois. The actress was exhausted and had stretched out on the bed in the hotel, resting her tired feet on the railing of the bed. When Miss Monroe worried whether the pictures that had just been taken would turn out suitably glamorous, the photographer replied: "No... not glamorous – interesting maybe, but not glamorous." *MBT*

▲ Eve Arnold
Marilyn Monroe,
1955

Gelatin silver print
16.2 x 33.4 cm
ML/F 1977/34

Gruber Collection

Atget, Eugène

1857 Libourne near
Bordeaux
1927 Paris

▶ Eugène Atget
Corsets, Boulevard
de Strasbourg, Paris,
around 1905

Gelatin silver print
23.3 x 17.2 cm
ML/F 1977/9

Gruber Collection

▼ Eugène Atget
Versailles, Vase in
Castle Park,
around 1900

Albumen print
21.6 x 18.2 cm
ML/F 1977/14

Gruber Collection

Eugène Atget studied at the Conservatoire d'Art Dramatique in Paris, but he left that school without taking his exams. He went on to act in theaters in the suburbs of Paris, where he met the actress Valentine Delafosse, who was to become his life companion. He had already bought himself a camera in those years and was using it. In 1898, noticing that there was a great demand for photographs of the old Paris, Atget took up photography as a profession. He established a system of working and built up a solid circle of collectors. He initially concentrated on Paris, photographing old buildings, street vendors, architectural details, but especially buildings that were threatened with demolition. In later years, he began to cover the suburbs. As soon as some topics were completed, new ones were started, such as *Parisian Residences, Horse Carriages in Paris* and *Fortifications,* which he initiated between 1910 and 1912. Preoccupied with the safe preservation of his collection, Atget offered it to the Ecole des Beaux Arts in 1920 and received 10,000 francs for his 2621 plates. He then began to produce photographs to serve as subjects for painters, and this took him to the furthest outskirts

of Paris. In 1921 he made portraits of a number of prostitutes in the Rue Asselin for the painter André Dignimont.

Atget refused to take pictures with any camera other than his old wooden 18 x 24 cm camera. He felt that the Rolleiflex Man Ray had offered him worked faster than he could think. He therefore continued to travel with a lot of luggage. When his life companion died, he began a pause in his work. Shortly after he made a portrait of Berenice Abbott in her studio, Atget passed away on the 4th of August of 1927. Berenice Abbott, who had acquired the main portion of his estate in 1928, began to evaluate and to publish his work. She arranged for Atget's

◄ **Eugène Atget**
Prostitute, 1921

Gelatin silver print
23.2 x 17.4 cm
ML/F 1977/1

Gruber Collection

▶ **Eugène Atget**
Organ Player and
Singing Girl, 1898

Gelatin silver print
21.8 x 16.5 cm
ML/F 1977/3

Gruber Collection

work to be exhibited, and in 1930 together with gallery owner Julien Levy initiated the first publication of his photographs, which led to international recognition of Atget's work. *RM*

Richard Avedon studied philosophy at Columbia University in New York City before he became a self-taught photographer. In 1944 he met Alexey Brodovitch, the legendary art director of *Harper's Bazaar*, with whom he worked for many years to come. He attracted a great deal of attention with his book *Observations*, which was published in 1959. Brodovitch did the layout and Truman Capote wrote the text. The book contained mostly portraits of famous personalities and a few fashion pictures. "Have mercy on me", said Henry Kissinger when he was about to have his portrait taken by Avedon. The starkness of his portraits on a white background that brought the very souls of people to the surface was what first caught the attention of the public and the trade.

Avedon achieved extensive publicity with his fashion photographs, in which he expressed his visions of a lively, lifelike world of pictures. He stopped making photographs in his studio and took his models to the streets of Paris, into the cafés and shows. His photograph *Dovima with Elephants, Evening Dress by Dior, Cirque d'hiver, Paris 1955* is Avedon's best known photograph and certainly one of his most unusual ones. It thrives on contrast and yet it is simultaneously an expression of indescribable elegance. This picture marks the beginning of a new era in staged photography. Avedon's fashion photographs, which steadily diminished over the years, and which during the seventies became similar to his portraits, became the standard for an entire generation of photographers.

Not much later he shocked his audience with a series about the slow death of his father Jacob Israel Avedon. In that series he also documented his own relationship with his father, elicited mimicry and expressions from him that he remembered from his youth and which characterized his image of a father figure. But it is also a powerful series about the gradual deterioration of a strong personality and its withdrawal into itself.

With his book *In the American West*, Avedon wanted to expose the myth of the American West, to break up the romanticized world of idyllic cowboys and show another side of that world: day workers and miners, the unemployed and minor public servants, whites, blacks, South Americans. His disenchanting version of the American West caused anger and was perceived as being destructive.

Next he produced a series about the Louisiana State Hospital, a grainy sequence of pictures of mentally disturbed patients, followed by a

► **Richard Avedon**
Dovima with Elephants, Evening Dress by Dior, Cirque d'hiver, Paris, August 1955

Gelatin silver print
24.2 x 19.4 cm
ML/F 1977/39

Gruber Collection

bitter statement against war in the form of a photo essay about victims of napalm in Vietnam. They were his only pictures that showed violence. Avedon was always averse to that subject, because he believed that pictures of violence only bred more violence.

His large format photographic canvasses became a new milestone in the history of photography. Among others, he created portraits of members of the "Warhol Factory", the "Chicago Seven"' the "Ginsberg Family", and the "Mission Council".

His *The Generals of the Daughters of the American Revolution*, 1963, commands a special place among his portraits. With this photograph, Avedon created a group picture with strikingly unconventional composition. Apparently taken during preparations for an official portrait, it is intriguing because of its unusual arrangement and the variety of relationships between the women, who nevertheless remain isolated. The portrait of Charlie Chaplin is equally unconventional, because it suggests a devil. It was created at Chaplin's own request, to express his anger when he had to leave the United States because of his political beliefs. The portrait of the introspective, seemingly painfully concentrating Ezra Pound is the main picture in a series in which that author exposes the full breadth of his emotions and feelings as well as their mimic expression for the camera to record.

On the occasion of the fall of the Berlin Wall, Avedon photographed the jubilant crowd during New Year's Eve 1989. The mood of the pictures of the *Brandenburg Gate* series ranges all the way from boundless

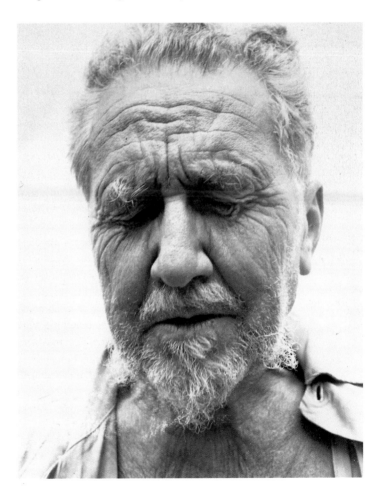

► **Richard Avedon**
Ezra Pound, poet, Rutherford, New Jersey, June 30, 1958

Gelatin silver print
34.1 x 27 cm
ML/F 1977/44

Gruber Collection

joy to expressions of fear of the future. Instead of documenting what he saw, Avedon made a small selection of symbolic constellations, which culminate in the reduced outline of a bald head against the night sky.

Most recently he has made photographs of the Italian nobility, for which he made use, for the first time, of the possibilities of picture collages. The fact that he once practiced photojournalism only came to light again on the occasion of his retrospective show in 1994.

Avedon is considered to be one of the best living photographers. In New York City alone, he can look back on exhibitions in the Museum of Modern Art, the Metropolitan Museum and the Whitney Museum of American Art. The Museum Ludwig in Cologne displayed a large retrospective of his work and his fashion photographs in 1994. In whatever genre he was working, he has always succeeded in applying his own striking approach. *RM*

Alfred Emanuel Ferdinand Grünwald was born in Stettin on the 9th of October 1892. After studying law and political science at Oxford and in Berlin, he was drafted into military service from 1914 to 1918. Upon his return, he wrote articles for the magazine *Aktion* and became involved with the USPD. In addition to his connections with the "Cologne Progressives", he befriended Max Ernst and Hans Arp, with whom he founded the Cologne Dada Group. He called himself Theodor Baargeld, sometimes also Zentrodada or Jesaias. With this Cologne group of artists he published the magazine *Der Ventilator*, and later on the *Bulletin D*. After participating in the exhibition "Early Dada Spring" in Cologne and the "International Dada Fair" in Berlin, Baargeld returned to his studies. Upon graduation he joined a Cologne Reinsurance Company. His albums of mountain photographs contain many of his sequence arrangements. Baargeld succumbed to an accident in the French Alps on the 18th of August 1927. *RM*

Baargeld, Johannes Theodor

(Alfred Emanuel Ferdinand Grünwald)

1892 Stettin, Poland
1927 French Alps

◀▲ Johannes Theodor Baargeld
Mountain Photographs, 1925

Gelatin silver print
6 x 8.5 cm and
5.7 x 8.4 cm
ML/F 1985/29
and 30

Dr. Oppenhoff
Donation

◀ **Pavel Banka**
Untitled, 1984

Gelatin silver print
32.7 x 25.8 cm
ML/F 1995/118

Uwe Scheid
Donation

Banka, Pavel

1941 Prague
Lives in Prague

Pavel Banka studied at the Faculty for Electrical Technology in Prague. In 1976 he began working as a freelance photographer. He favored portraits, but concentrated primarily on staged photography, which already earned him recognition beyond the borders of the Czech Republic in the eighties.

On one hand, his staged sets are based on the concept of the photo performance, which he developed beyond the original work of František Drtikol. On the other hand, he injects surreal aspects into his scene designs, he alters size relationships, arranges bodies in the manner of still lifes. Eroticism is present in his pictures only to a very understated extent. Banka maintains a disciplined formality and simplicity in his compositions, avoiding any distractions or descriptive variations. Instead, he concentrates on a few metaphors, with which he transposes his mystical visions into photographs. *RM*

▶ Micha Bar-Am
Collaborators,
Samaria, West Bank,
1967

Gelatin silver print
24.3 x 31 cm
ML/F 1995/98

As a result of his parents' emigration, Micha Bar-Am spent the years 1936 to 1947 growing up in Haifa. In 1944 he worked on the waterfront, dreaming of becoming a seaman. From 1948 to 1949 he fought for the resistance movement as a member of the Palmach Unit. In 1949 he became a co-founder of the Malkya Kibbutz in North Galilee. He moved to the Gesher-Haziv Kibbutz in 1953, where he initially worked as a blacksmith, but where he also began to take pictures with a borrowed camera. During the Sinai War of 1956 he photographed the desert and the war, and he was able to purchase his first Leica. From 1957 to 1966 he worked for the Israeli army magazine *Bahmahane*. In 1961 the government gave him the assignment of photographing the Eichmann trial. He has been active as a freelance photographer since 1966. In 1967 he met Cornell Capa, with whom he photographed the Six Day War. After that, he became a member of "Magnum" and since then he has been working for the *New York Times*. In 1973 he became the curator of photography at the newly founded Photography Department of the Tel Aviv Museum. Today he is once again working exclusively as a freelance photographer. *RM*

Bar-Am, Micha

1930 Berlin
Lives in Il Ramat
Gan, Israel

▶ **Micha Bar-Am**
Prisoners of War,
Golan Heights, 1970

Gelatin silver print
24.2 x 31.1 cm
ML/F 1995/99

▶ **Micha Bar-Am**
Return from
Entebbe, Ben Gurion
Airport, 1976

Gelatin silver print
24.3 x 24.1 cm
ML/F 1995/100

Mercedes Barros studied photography at the New England School of
Photography and at the School of Visual Arts in New York City. Today
she lives in Cologne, Germany.

Mercedes shows nature in her pictures as part of herself, and she
regards it as endangered. The techniques she applies in creating her
pictures, in part by solarization, in part by the use of chemicals, imparts
the same surface of morbid decay to all her photographic work. Mankind and its civilization is connected to nature through this connecting
element of the dissolution of appearances, which it surrenders to
destruction. The clouds of Chernobyl, which she acknowledged with a
sinister picture in 1988, seem to hover over everything.

Treating the surfaces of her photographic images is a way for Mercedes Barros to execute painterly concepts without having to paint in
the classical sense. This technique enables her to make use of existing
photographic prints and to work on the image of an object instead of
the object itself, so as to present the relationship of different things by
means of a picture. *RM*

**Barros,
Mercedes**

1957 Rio de Janeiro
Lives in Cologne

▲ Mercedes Barros
Chernobyl, 1988

*Gelatin silver print,
mixed media*
82 x 119.5 cm
ML/F 1994/343

◀ Herbert Bayer
Metamorphosis,
1936

Gelatin silver print
25.5 x 34 cm
ML/F 1977/56

Gruber Collection

Bayer, Herbert

1900 Haag, Austria
1985 Montecito,
California

Herbert Bayer was a highly versatile artist. He worked as a typographer, an advertising artist, photographer, painter, sculptor, architect and even as a designer of office landscapes. The ideals of the Bauhaus, where Bayer acquired his artistic education, are fittingly reflected in the creative activities that he pursued during various periods of his life. From 1921 to 1925 he studied at the Bauhaus in Weimar under Johannes Itten, Oskar Schlemmer, and Wassily Kandinsky. In 1925, he took over the printing and advertising shop of the Bauhaus in Dessau, where he was also responsible for the design of Bauhaus printed publications. That is also when he began working with photography, which became his preferred means of expression in the thirties, before he emigrated to the United States. With his photographic work he not only presented himself as a representative of the Bauhaus, but he also showed himself to be especially influenced by the ideas of Surrealism. In this vein, for instance, he created his *Self-portrait* in 1932 that was characteristic of Surrealism, because it blended two levels of reality into a single, traumatic image. Bayer also applied Surrealism in his photographic montage entitled *Lonesome Big City Dweller*, in which the artist's hands float in front of the façade of an inner courtyard in Berlin, with his eyes staring at us from the palms of those hands. A ghostly scene, with which Bayer expressed his criticism of the anonymity of the big city. In his photo-

▲ **Herbert Bayer**
Lonesome Big City Dweller, 1932

Gelatin silver print 34 x 26.9 cm
ML/F 1977/54

Gruber Collection

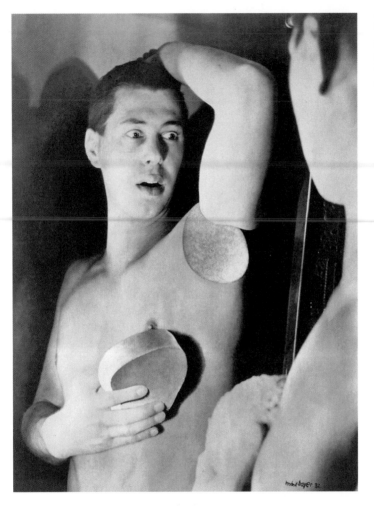

◄ **Herbert Bayer**
Self-portrait, 1932

Gelatin silver print
38.5 x 29.4 cm
ML/F 1977/53

Gruber Collection

graphic sculpture *Metamorphosis*, Bayer reverted to his well-known cover
of the Bauhaus magazine of 1928 by using geometric bodies such as
spheres, cones and cubes as they appeared on that cover. With the
tense arrangement of cubic forms with a landscape as background, he
expressed the theme of the relationship between geometric and natural
forms. *MBT*

► **Cecil Beaton**
Miss Mary Taylor,
1930s

Gelatin silver print
20.6 x 22.9 cm
ML/F 1994/92

Gruber Donation

Cecil Beaton's interest in photography manifested itself quite early, when he started taking pictures of his sisters under the direction of his nanny, who was an amateur photographer herself. He gradually developed a predilection for arty, stylized portrait photographs, inspired by such illustrious predecessors as Baron de Meyer and Edward Steichen. Beaton constructed elaborate backgrounds using showy materials, like mirrors or cellophane, in front of which he posed members of his family dressed in elegant costumes. In his photographs, Beaton did not place the emphasis on persons or clothing, but on the aesthetic effect of the entire atmosphere of the scene. This already suggested his second great talent, that of a stage and costume designer, which only came to fruition much later, between 1940 and 1970.

His first photographic exhibition, in a little-known gallery in London, was an extraordinary success that led to a contract with *Vogue* magazine, for which he was to remain active as a fashion photographer into

Beaton, Cecil

1904 London
1980 Broadchalke
near Salisbury

◄ **Cecil Beaton**
Marilyn Monroe,
1956

Gelatin silver print
25.5 x 20.9 cm
ML/F 1977/58

Gruber Collection

► **Cecil Beaton**
Princess Natalie
Paley, around 1930

Gelatin silver print
23.2 x 19.8 cm
ML/F 1994/91

Gruber Donation

▼ **Cecil Beaton**
The Marx Brothers,
around 1932

Gelatin silver print
9.9 x 18.9 cm
ML/F 1977/79

Gruber Collection

the mid-fifties. He also worked for *Harper's Bazaar*. In the Hollywood of the thirties, he created portraits of film stars in the somewhat surreal ambiances of unused stage sets. In 1937 Beaton was appointed court photographer of the royal family, and during the Second World War he was active as a war correspondent for the British Ministry of Information. The experience gained during the war years influenced the style of his portraits, which became less whimsical and sumptuous, thus becoming clearer and more direct. *TvT*

▲ **Cecil Beaton**
Marlene Dietrich, 1935

Gelatin silver print
24.3 x 19.2 cm
ML/F 1977/60

Gruber Collection

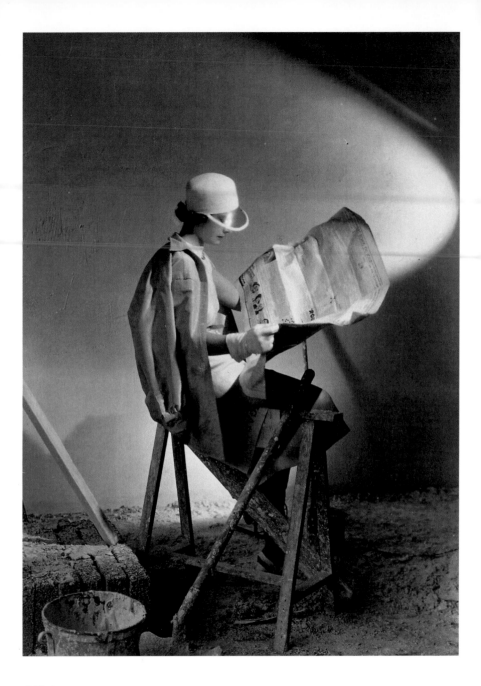

Becher, Bernd

1931 Siegen
Lives in Düsseldorf

Becher, Hilla

1934 Potsdam
Lives in Düsseldorf

Bernd Becher was born in Siegen, Germany on the 20th of August 1931. After completing an apprenticeship in decoration, he studied at the State Academies of Art in Stuttgart and in Düsseldorf, where the co-operation with Hildegard Wobeser began in 1959.

She was born in Potsdam in 1934 and had also completed an apprenticeship in photography and studies at the Academy of Art of Düsseldorf. They married in 1961. Together, they developed the concept of systematic industrial photography with an encyclopedic character.

The work of Bernd and Hilla Becher is entirely specialized in archi-

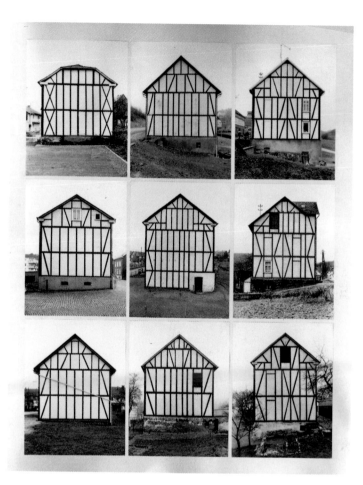

◀ **Bernd and Hilla Becher**
Typology of half-timbered Houses, 1959–1974

Gelatin silver print each 40 x 31 cm in 4 fields of 148.3 x 108 cm
ML/F 1985/34

Ludwig Donation

tecture. It concentrates on average buildings and industrial structures that are based on similar basic layouts and designs. These buildings always have some functional conditions in common, differing only in details, which may stem from tradition, as in half-timbered houses, or from technical requirements, as in industrial architecture. The elements they have in common are usually related to function, whereas the differences often relate to regional peculiarities or local zoning regulations. Bernd and Hilla Becher spent 30 years producing a multitude of water-towers, storehouses, blast furnaces, winding towers, silos and cooling

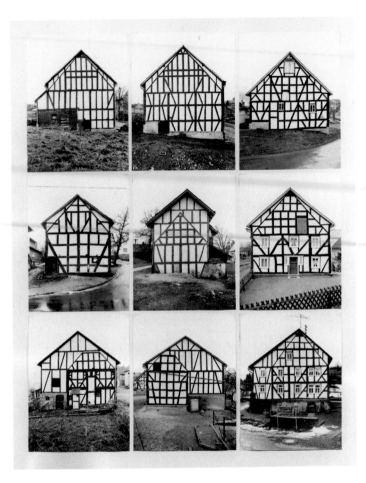

towers, photographed with strictly defined ground rules and systematically arranged in sequences.

It was only the picture sequences that made the methodology of their photographic system apparent. Initially regarded as "Anonymous Sculptures", the conceptional aspect of their photographic work was only discovered by the art trade much later. The recognition of their work sparked attention to the photography of all inanimate objects, generating posthumous public appreciation of the work of artists like Albert Renger-Patzsch or Karl Blossfeldt. The photographic concept of the

◄ Bernd and Hilla Becher
Typology of half-timbered Houses, 1959–1974

Gelatin silver print each 40 x 31 cm in 4 fields of 148.3 x 108 cm
ML/F 1985/34

Ludwig Donation

Becher couple continued to be disseminated through their teaching activities at the most distinguished German school of artistic photography. An important effect of that activity was the recognition by the art scene, for the first time, of technically perfect photographic works. Up to then, the art scene had sought to ignore the technical medium by deliberately neglecting the ground rules of photography. The deciding factor for that change was the connection, by the Bechers, of object and conceptual photography. *RM*

**Becker,
Krimhild**

*1940 Bonn
Lives in Cologne*

▲ **Krimhild Becker**
Untitled, 1989

*Gelatin silver print,
mixed media*
205.2 x 265.4 cm
ML/F 1990/1304

Krimhild Becker studied at the Technical College of Cologne from 1961 to 1965, and she continues working there as a freelance artist.

In the course of her work she developed a specific kind of diptych, in which black-and-white photographs are blended with each other on a silver-colored background. In some of her works, the individual photographs are separated by fluorescent tubes. The illumination of the pictures then corresponds exactly to that of the neon tube, which thus separates and at the same time combines the work. This also imparts a three-dimensional quality to the work. Krimhild Becker speaks through her pictures, if need be she gives the viewer cue words like: *Gravity, Distances, Containers.* Everyday situations and objects are removed from their settings in abstract ways and enhanced into symbols of our being. Removed from their settings of purposeful rationality, Krimhild Becker presents them as cult objects in a world of meanings that confront our functional world. *RM*

At first, Ian Berry was active as an amateur photographer, dreaming of
a career as a journalist. In 1952 he moved to South Africa, where he
worked as a professional photographer for two newspapers, among
them the *Daily Mail*. His work with Tom Hopkinson for the African
magazine *Drum* lasted for more than a year. He produced photographic
series about the Congo, Algeria, the Near and Far East. Berry regards
his photography mainly as social and documentary reporting, which
can accurately depict situations like no other medium. His perspective
is frontal and aimed directly at the event being shown. Whether it is an
uprising in South Africa or a lonesome old woman, his angles seem to
capture emotions on faces as well as the isolation of individual persons
from a distance with the greatest accuracy. The viewer can read Berry's
photographic testimony like a detailed report. The directness of the expression is further reinforced by masterful cropping. The photographer
was a member of the "Magnum" agency, of which he became a vice
president in 1978. His publications *The English* and *Black and Whites.
L'Afrique du Sud* attest to Berry's political-social interests. *LH*

Berry, Ian

1934 Preston,
Lancashire
Lives in London

Biasi, Mario de

1923 Belluno, Italy
Lives in Milan

▼ Mario de Biasi
Sardinia, 1954

Gelatin silver print
30.1 x 24.4 cm
ML/F 1991/44

Gruber Donation

Mario de Biasi was a trained radio technician before he became interested in photography. He began his photographic activity during a visit to Nuremberg in 1945 by teaching himself and by taking a one-year apprenticeship in Germany. His first exhibition came as early as 1948 in Milan. In 1953 he received the award for the best photograph of the year. Starting in 1953, he worked as a photojournalist for the magazine *Epoca*, and his picture series made him a leading figure in Italian photojournalism. In 1956 he began creating documentations, among them the war in Vietnam, the revolt in Prague, papal trips and the earthquake in Sicily. He also created essays for *Epoca* on subjects like "The great parks of Europe" or "Places imagined by authors". To de Biasi, the intensity of every subject he photographed, be it the observation of the eruption of a volcano or snow scenes photographed in Siberia at −65° C, became the pictorial essence of reality. As an author of several photographic books, such as *The Photographer's letter*, he demonstrated his proficiency in portrait, sports and industrial photography. Structural elements, such as judicious symmetry, are important to de Biasi. His photographs stand out because of their unconventional perspectives and their graphic distribution of gray values. In his series with the title *The Third Eye of Nature*, de Biasi provided new insights into nature by working with reduced forms and photographs of light reflections. In 1982, de Biasi received the Saint Vincent Award of journalism. *LH*

▶ **Ilse Bing**
Self-portrait with
Mirrors, 1931

Gelatin silver print
26.6 x 29.8 cm
ML/F 1988/178

Ilse Bing attended the University of Frankfurt in 1920 to study mathematics and physics, but she soon changed to art history. Planning to write her thesis about the architect Friedrich Gilly, she began to take pictures in order to facilitate her research. In 1929 she acquired a Leica, which she used during the 20 years that followed. She started working for the *Illustrierte Blatt* that same year. Her contacts with the avant-garde artists of Frankfurt soon began to influence her photography, which clearly reflected the new way of seeing of the twenties in their choice of subjects and in their perspectives. She became interested in experimental photography, worked with daring perspectives and croppings, with the play of shadows and with reflections. One of her most famous photographs is her self-portrait of 1931, in which she made ingenious use of mirrors to combine a profile and a frontal view of herself. Impressed by an exhibition by Florence Henri, she moved to Paris in 1930. There she worked initially for the Hungarian journalist Heinrich Guttmann before she set out on her own to work on photojournalism, architectural photography, as well as advertising and fashion photography for such magazines as *Vu, Arts et Métiers Graphiques*, and *Le Monde*. Later

Bing, Ilse

1899 Frankfurt/Main
Lives in New York

▲ **Ilse Bing**
Boats and Reflec-
tions on Water, 1931

Gelatin silver print
18.7 x 28.1 cm
ML/F 1988/177

on her photographs also began to appear in *Vogue* and *Harper's Bazaar*.
In 1936 she traveled to New York, where her work was received enthusi-
astically. A year later, in 1937, she married pianist Konrad Wolf, with
whom she emigrated to the United States in 1941. She began working
exclusively in color in 1957, but made all the prints herself. Nevertheless,
it is her black-and-white photography of the thirties and forties that
brought her the greatest recognition. Ilse Bing was a sought-after guest
lecturer, because she had an unforgettably fresh and vivacious way of
motivating young photographers. In Germany, she faded somewhat
from the public eye, until she was rediscovered in the mid-eighties. The
Museum Ludwig in Cologne first displayed her work in 1987 as part of
an exhibition entitled "German Pictorialists". An automobile accident in
1993 almost completely forced her to give up her work and her beloved
travels all over the world during the last two years and to concentrate on
her New York City home. *RM*

Werner Bischof is regarded as one of the leading international photojournalists of the postwar era. He pursued a career that deviated dramatically from his original training. From 1932 to 1936 Bischof studied
at the Arts and Crafts School of Zurich, where his mentor was Hans
Finsler, a photographer devoted to the New Objectivity. Accordingly,
Bischof initially followed a path of precisely arranged and perfectionist
fashion- and object photography. In 1942, Bischof became a full-time
member of the editorial staff of the Swiss magazine *Du*, working primarily as a fashion photographer. In 1945, he traveled all over Europe,
using his camera to document the destruction left behind by war. He
then began to take a greater interest in the international press, which
led him to join the "Magnum" group in 1949. Even though Bischof had
to alter his way of working because of his change to photojournalism, he
nonetheless retained his sensitivity for technical perfection, creativity
with light and a formal composition of his pictures. No more the carefully staged and thought-out photograph in a studio, but live, spontan-

Bischof, Werner

1916 Zurich
1954 Peru

eous moments. In 1951 he received an assignment from the American *Life* magazine to travel to areas plagued by hunger in Bihar province in north and central India. The resulting photographic essay *Famine in India* brought Bischof his first international success. Even though he was deeply moved by the abject poverty of the Indian population, this essay shows him more as an objective observer who maintained his sense of composition even in the most desperate situations. This is exemplified by the accompanying illustration from his India series, in which he rendered the emaciated figures in such a way as to create a powerful composition of vertical and horizontal lines.

In later years Bischof made photojournalistic trips to places such as Japan, Hong Kong, Indochina and Korea, where he became fascinated by children who, despite poverty and war, demonstrated remarkable resilience. In Pusan, Korea, he photographed three youths clad in rags who earned a little money as shoeshine boys at the railroad station. One of Bischof's best known children's photographs is *Boy Playing the Flute near Cuzco, Peru*. Bischof made that photograph only a few days before his fatal accident in the Peruvian Andes. *MBT*

▲ **Werner Bischof**
Hungary, around
1950

Gelatin silver print
33.5 x 28.1 cm
ML/F 1993/124

Gruber Donation

From 1881 to 1884, Karl Blossfeldt completed his apprenticeship as a sculptor and modeler in an art foundry, receiving a scholarship to study at the college of the Royal Prussian Arts and Crafts Museum in Berlin. During numerous study trips to the Mediterranean area, he produced reproductions of plants for educational purposes, there also creating his first photographs of living plants. In 1898 he began to teach at the Arts and Crafts College in Berlin, where he established an archive of plates of plant photographs for use in his teaching activities: "Modeling after living plants", "The plant in the arts and crafts", etc. He continued to expand that archive with the yield from many additional trips. His book *The Original Forms of Art* was published in 1928, two years after his first exhibition, and it made him famous overnight. His second book, *Wonder Gardens of Nature* was published shortly before his death in 1932. *TvT*

Blossfeldt, Karl

1865 Schielo, Germany
1932 Berlin

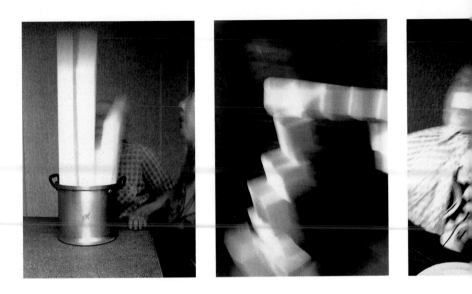

Blume, Anna

1937 Bork
Lives in Cologne and
Hamburg

**Blume,
Bernhard
Johannes**

1937 Dortmund
Lives in Cologne and
Hamburg

Anna and Bernhard Johannes Blume have been working as a team since 1980. Their joint efforts consist primarily of performances which are not intended for the traditional audience for this medium, i.e. a live audience, but exclusively for the camera.

The Blumes present stories, seemingly absurd tales and situations, in which prosaic details from the everyday life of ordinary persons are parodied in a chaotic manner. Their black-and-white photographs are often of larger-than-life proportions and are presented in multi-part sequences. They remind us somewhat of American slapstick comedies, but their subjects are mostly typical of German life and German culture.

In addition to their large format photographic sequences, the Blumes also produce Polaroid prints, which they combine into small, brilliantly colorful collages. These resemble absurd still lifes more than they resemble stories, but here too, the Blumes themselves are the central characters. With their conversation, the artist duo attracts an audience to which it tells its own moralistic story, pointing out that we, too, have to take the roles in our own drama seriously.

Bernhard Blume has studied and taught philosophy, and the photographic work reflects his preoccupation with philosophical questions as well as questions about the nature of truth and its verifiability, about various conditions of being and the existential meaning of life. In the

investigation of these questions, the camera has become a tool as well as a language, so that beneath the surface of the photographs, which at first may seem to portray grotesque melodramas, serious concerns and thoughts are hidden.

An early work entitled *Demonstrative Identification with the Universe = Magic Subjectivism* constitutes a clue for understanding the serious side of the Blumes' photographs, because it points to the fact that their photographs should be interpreted historically as a reaction to the "subjective photography" that dominated artistic photography in Germany during the fifties. They have used the mechanism of the camera, which was presumably designed to produce objective representations of the visible world, in a critical manner – as a means for the critical investigation of our epistemological conditions. That means that they have used it subjectively. *GG*

▲ Anna and
Bernhard Johannes
Blume
Bon appétit!, 1986

Gelatin silver print
5 parts, each
126.8 x 91.1 cm
ML/F 1988/19 I-V

Hypo-Bank
Donation

◀ Radovan Boček
Happening at the
Former Stalin
Monument, 1989

Gelatin silver print
25.3 x 38.5 cm
ML/F 1990/1275

Boček, Radovan

1963 Reykjavík,
Iceland
Lives in Prague

Radovan Boček initially studied foreign trade along with photography at the Public Art College and at the Institute for Applied Photography in Prague. In 1987 he completed his studies of photography at the Motion Picture and Television College (FAMU) in Prague, and in November 1989 he was a co-founder of the "Radost" agency.

Boček at first devoted himself to landscape photography, but he later switched to photojournalism and documentary photography. While his early photographs were very descriptive, later ones conveyed a more vivid impression of the situation, bringing it right to the point. In the autumn of 1989, Boček created a pictorial record of the demonstrations during the peaceful revolution in Prague, describing the situation by means of few pictures and moments. His camera covered the dramatic events from the first intervention by the police to the campaign to elect Václav Havel president of the republic. His photograph *Happening at the Former Stalin Monument* with the undulating star banner and the flag waving above it symbolically expresses the aspirations of people in a powerfully succinct way. *RM*

► Hans-Ludwig
Böhme
Body III, 1991

Gelatin silver print,
mixed media
59.4 x 49.4 cm
ML/F 1995/86

Hans-Ludwig Böhme began studying Germanic and English languages
and literature in Jena, and from 1971 to 1982 he was a teacher at the
children's and youth sports school in Dresden before turning his passion for photography into his profession. Today he can be described as
one of the outstanding German theater photographers. His theater photography does not merely show actors on a stage – it is, in a more realistic sense, choreographed photography. Böhme regards his professional work as being no different from his artistic work. He does not
just seek a pictorial record, but pictures in which he uses photography
and chemistry as creative means for interpreting the given contents,
people, things, spaces and paper collages. The rectangle of a photograph becomes a new stage on which things and people perform. Especially in nude photography, he has been able to use the rectangle of photographic paper to create novel backgrounds for unusual arrangements.
RM

Böhme,
Hans-Ludwig

1945 Coswig, Ger-
many
Lives in Coswig

Boje, Walter

1905 Berlin
1992 Leverkusen

▼ Walter Boje
Man and his Desire,
around 1955

Color print
50.5 x 30.3 cm
ML/F 1989/52

Walter Boje, in addition to his studies of applied economics, which he concluded with a doctorate, also dedicated himself to painting. He used this means to further expand the knowledge he had acquired during an apprenticeship with a restorer of paintings. After serving as an adviser at Berlin University, he became general secretary of the German Academy for Air Research. After the war, he made his hobby into his profession and began working as a photographer. His main interest was theater photography, which he began practicing as early as 1950, using color film and available light. Boje made a creative tool out of mastering the challenge of the low-speed films of that era and the resulting long exposure times. He began to capture motion sequences photographically.

In addition to his practical work, Boje also distinguished himself as an active supporter of professional photography and as an author of numerous articles and books. His 1961 book *The Magic of Color Photography* was probably his most popular one. He performed journalistic work by becoming the editor of the magazine *Der Bildjournalist* and of the *Photoblätter*. Upon completing his activities in the public relations department of Agfa in Leverkusen, he was the director of the Famous Photographers School in Munich from 1969 to 1972. He was the Honorary Chairman of the German Photographic Academy when he passed away in Leverkusen on the 20th of July 1992. *RM*

▶ Gerd Bonfert
D 84-3 (still life),
1991

Gelatin silver print
131.8 x 98.4 cm
ML/F 1992/100

Toyota Donation

For two years now Gerd Bonfert has been applying photography to inter-
pret the phenomenon of the immaterial. The medium he chose for this
purpose is light. At an early stage he scratched light tracks on a blurred
self-portrait, allowing contours to dissipate. In today's pictures light has
become completely independent, separating itself from things. Strictly
speaking, we basically do not see actual objects themselves, only the
diffraction of visible lightwaves around these objects. Thus photography
quite logically does not show the object, but its effects on light. This becomes particularly evident in a series with sculptural elements, where
the illuminated edges of geometrical objects seem to float in a room
that constitutes itself before our eyes with a definable depth. The objects must have been present, otherwise light would not have been
diffracted. As if by magic, their presence is conjured up by the effects of
light, while their material content has disappeared. *RM*

Bonfert, Gerd

1953 Blaj, Romania
Lives in Cologne

Bonvie, Rudolf

1947 Hoffnungstal,
Germany
Lives in
Hoffnungstal

After studying at works schools in Cologne and at the Philosophical Faculty of Cologne University, Rudolf Bonvie first worked on serial projects that dealt with male role clichés. He used a combination of texts and photographs, but he also extended the work into sculptural media and installations, even adding video segments. After various critical artistic commentaries regarding photojournalism, he came upon the problem of human communication in a technical world with its symbols and signals. His photograph *Fighters* stems from that period.

Later on, Bonvie concentrated more and more on the problem of

◄ **Rudolf Bonvie**
Fighters, 1984

Color print
127 x 245 cm
ML/F 1989/198

making portraits, on creating an image for oneself. On one hand, he considers portraits to be a kind of violation of personal integrity, and on the other hand a problem of remembering. In the process, his work becomes more abstract, the photographic part unmasks itself in graininess, while the dubiousness of the authenticity of the photograph documents itself in fragmentation. *RM*

Bourke-White, Margaret

1904 New York
1971 Stanford, Connecticut

▲ Margaret Bourke-White
Mahatma Gandhi, 1946

Gelatin silver print
26.8 x 34.2 cm
ML/F 1977/92

Gruber Collection

The work of Margaret Bourke-White has become symbolic of American political and social-minded photojournalism. Interested mostly in industrial photography since 1928, she received her first major assignment from *Fortune* magazine in 1930, traveling to the Soviet Union, where she became the first foreign reporter to receive permission to photograph Soviet industrial installations. Margaret Bourke-White was one of the founding members of *Life* magazine in 1936, on which her photograph of Fort Peck Dam, then the largest hydroelectric power plant in the world, was used as the first cover picture. During the Second World War, Margaret Bourke-White served as a photographic war correspondent. After the capitulation of Germany, her shocking photographs of liberated concentration camps attracted worldwide attention. In 1946 she traveled to India on assignment from *Life* to document that country's struggle for freedom. In her photograph of Gandhi, she emphasized the spinning wheel, symbol of India's independence, by

► Margaret Bourke-
White
Miners, Johannes-
burg, 1950

Gelatin silver print
24.1 x 17.6 cm
ML/F 1977/90

Gruber Collection

placing it dominantly in the foreground. At the end of 1949, *Life* magazine sent Margaret Bourke-White on assignment to South Africa for a
few months. There, in a gold mine near Johannesburg, at a depth of
nearly 5000 feet (1500 m) and in blistering heat, she made the photograph of the two black miners drenched in sweat – a photograph that
she herself declared to be one of her favorite pictures. *MBT*

Brake, Brian

1927 Wellington,
New Zealand
1988 Auckland

▼ Brian Brake
Untitled (country
healer in China),
around 1950

Gelatin silver print
25.2 x 17 cm
ML/F 1994/107

Gruber Donation

New Zealander Brian Brake became interested in photography in the late thirties. In 1945 he began an apprenticeship with Spencer Digby. Two years later he worked as a cameraman for the New Zealand Film Unit. In the early fifties, a scholarship for the study of color cinematography techniques took him to London. There he became acquainted with members of "Magnum", and in 1955 he joined that association of photographers. He made freelance photographs for such international magazines as *Life, National Geographic* and *Paris Match*, covering Asia, Africa and the Pacific area. In his color essay *Monsoon*, he presented aspects of the monsoon, partly with large portraits of rain-drenched faces, and this earned him the American photographic prize "The Award of Merit". For a time he worked as a journalist in Hong Kong. In 1967 he switched from "Magnum" to the "Rapho" agency. In the seventies he

participated in the creation of a movie film production unit, and during the five years that followed he created eight motion pictures about Indonesia. Brake primarily documented people, their expressions and their living conditions. It did not matter whether the people were in Nigeria, Tibet or Hong Kong; he preferred to emphasize the individual in his or her particular cultural environment. Brake also photographed objects of art. In his book *The Sacred Image*, published in Cologne in 1979, he used a frontal perspective in his photographs of statues of the Buddha to convey the beauty of their stylistically similar, yet individually personalized faces. Brake returned to New Zealand in 1976 and continued to work as a freelance photographer in Auckland until his death in 1988. *LH*

▲ Brian Brake
Chinese ABC,
around 1950

Gelatin silver print
19.9 x 29.8 cm
ML/F 1994/103

Gruber Donation

◄ Brian Brake
Hong Kong, 1959

Gelatin silver print
16.8 x 24.8 cm
ML/F 1977/899

Gruber Donation

Brandt, Bill

1904 Hamburg
1983 London

Bill Brandt became interested in photography during a visit to Vienna in the mid-twenties. In 1929 he moved to Paris, where he worked for three months as an assistant in the studio of Man Ray. There he became acquainted with the art and motion pictures of surrealists. In 1931 he returned to London. From 1931 to 1935 he worked as a freelance photographer, creating a photographic documentation of the social life of the English, which he published in 1936 in the form of a book entitled *The English at Home*. Two years later, in 1938, his picture book *A Night in London* became the English counterpart to Brassaï's successful 1932 book *Paris de Nuit*. During the depression years, Brandt documented life in the industrial cities of England. During the war, he worked for the British Home Office creating picture essays about London and recording the ghostly scenery of empty streets during the London Blitz. His photographs of air-raid shelters and underground stations used as shelters were published in magazines along with Henry Moore's *Shelter Sketchbook Images*, which dealt with the same subjects. While Brandt, during the thirties, concentrated mostly on social themes, cityscapes and architecture, during the forties he more and more made a name for himself in portraiture. His subjects were mostly artists and literati, occasionally businessmen and politicians. Another subject that he favored between 1945 and 1950 was the English countryside. His photograph *Stonehenge*, which was published in the 19 April 1947 issue of the *Picture Post*, stems from that period. The dramatic attraction of this photograph comes from the contrast between the white fields of snow and the stark black silhouette of Stonehenge, which gives that photograph a strong graphic effect.

Stimulated by experiments with a wide-angle camera, Brandt, in the mid-forties, discovered the nude photographed from a distorting perspective. In his nude photographs, he usually concentrated on a detail or, as in the accompanying illustration, on a cropped part of the female body. The sparsely furnished rooms, slightly distorted in the picture, in which Brandt positioned his models, imparted a mysterious, surreal atmosphere to the entire scene. In 1961 Brandt published the results of this phase of his work in a book entitled *Perspectives of Nudes*. *MBT*

▲ **Bill Brandt**
Nude, from the cycle
"Perspectives of
Nudes", 1961

Gelatin silver print
34.9 x 28.9 cm
ML/F 1977/97

Gruber Collection

▲ **Bill Brandt**
Stonehenge, 1947

Gelatin silver print
22.6 x 18.7 cm
ML/F 1977/102

Gruber Collection

▲ **Bill Brandt**
Portrait of a Young
Girl, Eaton Place,
London, 1955

Gelatin silver print
23 x 19.6 cm
ML/F 1977/94

Gruber Collection

Brassaï

(Gyula Halász)

1899 Brasso,
Hungary (now
Brasvo, Romania)
1984 Beaulieu-sur-
Mer, South of France

Gyula Halász, known since 1932 by his pseudonym Brassaï (derived from "de Brasso", his place of birth), came to photography through self-education. He first studied art in Budapest (1918–1919) and Berlin (1920–1922), and soon he was active in circles that included László Moholy-Nagy, Wassily Kandinsky and Oskar Kokoschka. In 1924 he went to Paris as a journalist. There he became acquainted with Eugène Atget in 1925, whose work was to become a constant model for his later work. A year later he met his compatriot André Kertész, whom he often accompanied on assignments and whose photographs he occasionally

◄ **Brassaï**
Sailors' Love, 1932

Gelatin silver print
29.3 x 22.8 cm
ML/F 1977/106

Gruber Collection

used for the documentation of his own work. In 1929 Brassaï borrowed
a camera and made his very first photographs, and soon afterwards he
decided to purchase his own Voigtländer camera. During his extended
wanderings through night-time Paris, Brassaï began, in 1930, to record
the deserted streets and squares of that city. The results of this work
were published in 1932 in his famous book *Paris de Nuit*. Aside from the
aesthetic fascination of the mysterious and stage-set-like architecture,
the photographer also experienced the technical challenge posed by the
extreme lighting conditions for his night-time photographs. During
these nightly sojourns, Brassaï was also fascinated by the activities of
society. In the bars and in the streets he recorded the night owls of the
city, photographing tramps, prostitutes, lovers, dancers and other colorful figures. Among the best known photographs of this period is *The
Prostitute Bijou*. The heavily made-up and opulently bejeweled, heavily-
set Parisian woman attracted Brassaï's camera. However the publica-

▲ Brassaï
Dancers, 1933

Gelatin silver print
22.6 x 29.3 cm
ML/F 1977/112

Gruber Collection

▶ Brassaï
Hospice de Beaune,
around 1950

Gelatin silver print
29.5 x 22.2 cm
ML/F 1977/107

Gruber Collection

tion of that photograph in his book *Paris de Nuit* incensed the old lady, and it took a few banknotes to placate her ire.

In 1932 Brassaï discovered the graffiti on the walls of Paris, and he covered this subject for many years to come. Through his contributions to the surrealist magazine *Minotaure* during the thirties, Brassaï became acquainted with many writers, poets and artists of Surrealism. He began to work for *Harper's Bazaar* in 1937, and he supplied that magazine with many photographic essays about famous literary personalities and artists. In 1962, after the death of Carmel Snow, the publisher of *Harper's Bazaar*, Brassaï gave up photography altogether. From then on, he kept busy making new prints of his photographs and new editions of his earlier books. *MBT*

◀ Bratrstvo
Harvester's Bride,
1989

Gelatin silver print
23.5 x 17 cm
ML/F 1990/1295

Bratrstvo

(Brotherhood)

Founded 1989 in
Prague
Dissolved 1994 in
Prague

Bratrstvo is not the name of an individual artist, but of a group of artists that existed for about four years and which was closely tied to the peaceful revolution of the former Czechoslovakia. The group, formed in 1989, consisted of young artists like Václav Jirásek, Petr Krejzek, Roman Muselik and Zdenek Sokol, who developed a style of staged photography that took a critical and ironical look at the aesthetics of Socialistic Realism. They caricatured the heroic posturings of agricultural workers and soldiers, workers and civil servants. In the beginning, they consistently declined individual photo credits, using the group's name Bratrstvo instead. The group dissolved in 1994. *RM*

▶ Marlo Broekmans
The Wheel or The
Female Christ, 1983

Gelatin silver print
54.7 x 43.1 cm
ML/F 1995/117

Uwe Scheid
Donation

Marlo Broekmans studied at the Pedagogic Academy from 1970 to 1973, and from 1973 to 1977 she studied psychology at the University of Amsterdam. In 1978, she began working as a freelance photographer. From 1979 to 1981 she worked very closely with Diana Blok. This cooperation culminated with the publication of the book *Invisible Forces*. She devised her own themes and followed a specific style, staging her own settings. Marlo Broekmans combined photo-performance with double exposures and used a special way of incorporating the play of light and shadows. These photographs were first published in 1989 as an overview in the book *Marlo Broekmans – The Woman of Light*. Her photographic work concentrates on mythical-psychological aspects, but also on eroticism – an aspect that is especially apparent in her latest work on the subject of "Lovers". Her handling of light diffraction and shadow effects is in the tradition of constructive and cubist worlds of photography. Marlo Broekmans' work found recognition in the eighties not only in the Netherlands, but throughout Europe. *RM*

Broekmans,
Marlo

1953 Hoorn
Lives in Amsterdam

Burri, René

1933 Zurich
Lives in Paris

▲ René Burri
Che Guevara,
Havana, Cuba, 1963

Gelatin silver print
23 × 30
(each 6 × 9.3) cm
ML/F 1984/14

Gruber Donation

From 1950 to 1953, René Burri studied photography under Hans Finsler and Alfred Willimann at the Arts and Crafts College in Zurich. In 1953, thanks to a scholarship, he was also able to take up motion pictures. He made small documentary films and, still in 1953, he was the camera assistant to Ernest A. Heininger for one of the first Cinemascope films about Switzerland. Two years later Burri joined that agency. During the years that followed, he traveled all over the world. The spectrum of his subjects ranged from political reportage to landscapes, architecture, industry and city reports all the way to portraits of prominent artists, architects, and literary personalities. One of his most famous portraits is that of Che Guevara, which became a symbol of the Cuban revolution. During 1960, Burri worked mostly in Germany preparing material for his book *The Germans*, a compilation of Burri's photographs and texts about the Germans by various authors. In 1965 Burri participated in the establishment of "Magnum Films". Together with Bruno Barbey, he opened the Magnum Gallery in Paris in 1982. He has been the art director of the Swiss magazine *Schweizer Illustrierte* since 1988. *MBT*

Harry Callahan initially studied engineering at Michigan State University, and from 1934 to 1944 he worked at Chrysler Motors. In 1938 Callahan became interested in photography. Having attended a lecture by Ansel Adams in 1941, and after seeing one of his exhibitions, Adams became Callahan's great role model. Callahan then began making photographs with a large-format camera. Beginning in 1946, he taught photography at the Chicago Institute of Design, and in 1949 he took over as director of its Department of Photography. During that period, he became friends with Hugo Weber, Mies van der Rohe, Aaron Siskind and Edward Steichen. In 1961, Callahan became the director of the Department of Photography of the Rhode Island School of Design in Providence, RI.

In his photographic work, Callahan showed a predilection for detail shots, to which he often imparted an abstract effect through tight cropping. He liked to experiment with double exposures, and he also used over-exposures to create a graphic effect in his photographs. *MBT*

Callahan, Harry

1912 Detroit,
Michigan
Lives in Atlanta,
Georgia

▲ **Harry Callahan**
Nature, 1948

Gelatin silver print
17.9 x 24.8 cm
ML/F 1984/16

Gruber Donation

▼ **Cornell Capa**
Boris Pasternak,
1958

Gelatin silver print
34 x 22.6 cm
ML/F 1977/114

Gruber Collection

Cornell Capa, born Kornel Friedmann, distinguished himself in the field of photography in three ways: he himself worked as a photojournalist for more than 30 years, he promoted the work of his brother Robert Capa, and he was the founder and director of the International Center for Photography (ICP) in New York City.

Capa became involved with photography when he went to Paris in 1936 and began developing films and making prints for his brother Robert Capa, David Seymour and Henri Cartier-Bresson. Capa emigrated to New York in 1937, where at first he worked for the picture agency "Pix". In 1938 he moved over to *Life* magazine, where he met many photojournalists, who stimulated him to begin his own photographic activities. In 1946 he became a staff photographer at *Life* magazine. In the years that followed, he created approximately 300 photographic essays for that magazine. In 1958, Capa spent six weeks in the Soviet Union creating an essay about the Russian Orthodox Church. During that time he also had the opportunity to meet Russian author and lyric poet Boris Pasternak, who had won the Nobel Prize for literature during that same year, and to take pictures in Pasternak's dacha in Peredelkino. Soon afterwards, the Soviet government prohibited Pasternak from receiving foreign visitors and it also refused permission for him to travel to Stockholm to receive his Nobel Prize.

After founding the International Center of Photography in New York and becoming its director in 1974, Cornell Capa gave up work as a photographer. *MBT*

Robert Capa, born André Friedmann, studied political science at the University of Berlin from 1931 to 1933. He was a self-taught photographer, and in 1931 he started working as a photo lab assistant at Ullstein (a publishing house). In 1932 and 1933 he worked as a photo assistant at Dephot (Deutscher Photodienst, a news agency). In 1933 he emigrated to Paris, where he changed his name to Robert Capa and where he began working as a freelance photographer. His photographs of the Spanish Civil War attracted attention to his name in Paris. His very first series already included the picture entitled *Death of a Spanish Loyalist*, which to this day is still his most famous and much discussed photograph. From then on he concentrated on being a photographic war correspondent. He traveled to China, Italy, France, Germany and Israel. On the 25th of May 1954 he was fatally injured in Thai-Binh, Vietnam. His death was the tragic consequence of his own motto "If your pictures aren't good enough, you aren't close enough". His talent for pointedly conveying the feelings and suffering of people in civil wars or rebellions in a single picture earned him great admiration.

A quality that transpires throughout Capa's pictures is his fascination for the fine edge along which humans proceed between the will to

Capa, Robert

(André Friedmann)

1913 Budapest
1954 Thai-Binh,
Vietnam

▲ **Robert Capa**
D-Day, 1944

Gelatin silver print
22.7 x 34.1 cm
ML/F 1977/115

Gruber Collection

▲ **Robert Capa**
Untitled (Wounded
Soldier), 1944

Gelatin silver print
22.9 x 34.1 cm
ML/F 1993/134

Gruber Donation

▶ **Robert Capa**
Transporting a
Wounded Soldier in
a Wheelbarrow, 1944

Gelatin silver print
26.5 x 34.1 cm
ML/F 1993/143

Gruber Donation

▶ **Robert Capa**
Sicilian Campaign,
1944

Gelatin silver print
35.6 x 27.9 cm
ML/F 1993/142

Gruber Donation

live and the urge for self-destruction. His obsession with his work made
him the most famous war correspondent of this century. But Capa did
not just set standards for photography and perform exemplary work.
His work is also a manifesto against war, against injustice and oppression. The Robert Capa Gold Medal Award has been presented in his
honor since 1955. The International Fund for Concerned Photography
was initiated by him. His brother Cornell Capa founded the International
Center for Photography in New York partly for the purpose of preserving
the work of Robert Capa and for making it accessible to the public. *RM*

▲ Robert Capa
Untitled (Blind
People), 1950

Gelatin silver print
25.3 x 34.6 cm
ML/F 1993/141

Gruber Donation

▶ Robert Capa
Infantry Soldiers in
Trojana, Italy, 1943

Gelatin silver print
25.4 x 34.3 cm
ML/F 1993/137

Gruber Donation

► **Robert Capa**
A "Time Out" of
War, Sicily, 1943

Gelatin silver print
22.7 x 34.3 cm
ML/F 1993/146

Gruber Donation

► **Robert Capa**
March to the Prison
Camp, France, 1944

Gelatin silver print
24.6 x 34.2 cm
ML/F 1993/136

Gruber Donation

Cartier-Bresson, Henri

1908 Canteloup
Lives in Paris

▲ Henri Cartier-Bresson
Sunday on the Banks of the Marne, 1938

Gelatin silver print
27.5 x 39.9 cm
ML/F 1977/141

Gruber Collection

▶ Henri Cartier-Bresson
Rue Mouffetard, Paris, 1958

Gelatin silver print
37.2 x 25.1 cm
ML/F 1977/126

Gruber Collection

Henri Cartier-Bresson attended the Ecole Fénélon and the Lycée Condorcet in Paris before studying painting under Cotenet from 1922 to 1923 and under André Lhote from 1927 to 1928, both in Paris. After that, he completed his studies of painting and philosophy at Cambridge University. His career as a photographer began in 1931. After participating in an ethnographic expedition to Mexico, he began working as a freelance photographer. In 1932, gallery owner Julien Levy hosted his first solo exhibition. In 1935, he learned about motion picture photography from Paul Strand. After that he worked as a camera assistant for Jacques Becker and André Zvoboda and also for Jean Renoir. In 1937 he made documentary films in Spain, and in 1940 he became a prisoner of war of the Germans in the state of Baden-Württemberg.

After escaping in 1943, he joined the MNPGD, a French underground resistance movement. After 1945 he once again turned to freelance photography. He authored many books illustrated with his photographs, among them *The Decisive Moment, Changing China* and *The World of Henri Cartier-Bresson*. In 1970 he married the photographer Martine Franck.

Cartier-Bresson is a living legend. Hardly any other photographer

▲ Henri Cartier-
Bresson
Seville, Spain, 1933

Gelatin silver print
27.2 x 41.1 cm
ML/F 1977/130

Gruber Collection

has been cited so often as exemplary of one of the great capabilities of photography: capturing a moment. In Cartier-Bresson's view, it is not just any moment, as it is in 99% of the millions of pictures made every day, for him it is "le moment décisif", the decisive moment that expresses the essence of a situation.

This photographer worked for nearly all the great international newspapers and magazines of the world. Together with Robert Capa, David "Chim" Seymour and George Rodger, he founded the "Magnum" group, and his travels took him to India, Burma, Pakistan, China, Indonesia, Cuba, Mexico, Canada, Japan and the former USSR.

Today Cartier-Bresson no longer takes pictures, having returned to his original passion of painting and drawing. Those who lament this may not have taken his earlier pronouncements seriously enough: "Actually, I am not at all interested in the photograph itself. The only thing I want is to capture a fraction of a second of reality."

Thanks to the Gruber Collection, the Museum Ludwig owns some of the most famous photographs by Cartier-Bresson, such as *Prisoner of War Camp in Dessau, Germany*, where he captured the moment when a

▲ **Henri Cartier-Bresson**
Srinagar, Cashmere, 1948

Gelatin silver print
27.3 x 39.9 cm
ML/F 1977/140

Gruber Collection

◄ **Henri Cartier-Bresson**
Shanghai, 1949

Gelatin silver print
27.7 x 39.9 cm
ML/F 1977/139

Gruber Collection

◄ Henri Cartier-Bresson
Alberto Giacometti, 1961

Gelatin silver print
24 x 16.5 cm
ML/F 1977/151

Gruber Collection

▲ Henri Cartier-Bresson
Henri Matisse, 1944

Gelatin silver print
26.3 x 39.9 cm
ML/F 1977/143

Gruber Collection

former prisoner recognized the person who had denounced her and who had brought her into that camp. Or *Rue Mouffetard, Paris*, a street scene showing a small boy with a proudly raised face bringing home two bottles of red wine. There is also the frequently published *Seine Boatman*, showing a glimpse at the cabin of a freight barge, with the barge master in the foreground looking at his family standing in the doorway. Even the dog assumed an expectant pose. The most often published picture, however, has to be *Sunday on the Banks of the Marne*, a picture that epitomizes the idylls of the Sunday picnic. The river is as calm as a lake, fishing lines hang from the tied-up boats, and two couples sit on the grass with their backs to the viewer. The plates have been eaten clean, the last glass of red wine is just being poured. The picture expresses tranquility, yet it contains everything that one would associate with a typical French picnic. Every one of Cartier-Bresson's photographs contains its own specific tension. In his photograph *Shanghai*, one can feel the anxious shoving of the people eagerly trying to get to the bank counter. It is as if the crowdedness has spilled over into the picture and the photographer tried to squeeze as many people as possible into it. The portrait of Giacometti is also particularly charming. A sculpture in each hand, he is walking across his studio, his blurred, forward-leaning figure resembling the dark sculpture of a thin walking man in the foreground. Those who did not understand Giacometti up to then, will certainly do so after one look at Cartier-Bresson's photograph.

Cartier-Bresson repeatedly emphasized that one could not learn to make photographs. He himself was blessed with an enormous talent for perception and ability to react, and he had the uncanny sense always to be at the right place at the right time in situations that interested him, and then to press the button precisely when he perceived the situation to culminate. He would then have snatched a fragment of reality from passing into oblivion, playing a trick on time, as it were. To Cartier-Bresson, the concept that photography is capable of faithfully reproducing reality, that it contains the possibility of truth, is of major importance. His kind of photography is possible only when the above is the premise. Because the moment in question, the one that is deemed as "decisive", is so only in the situation that was experienced, it requires this direct relationship to reality in order to be understood as "decisive".

▼ Henri Cartier-Bresson
Galant vert,
Paris, 1953

Gelatin silver print
24.6 x 36.3 cm
ML/F 1988/85

Gruber Donation

In this sense, Cartier-Bresson was an astute observer, a man of the eye, who knew what he wanted and what interested him. He once compared himself to a fisherman who had a fish at the end of his line. The most important thing was to approach his quarry cautiously, and to strike at just the right moment. *RM*

▲ **Henri Cartier-Bresson**
Prisoner of War Camp in Dessau, Germany, 1945

Gelatin silver print
17.2 x 24.5 cm
ML/F 1977/150

Gruber Collection

Chargesheimer

(Karl Heinz
Hargesheimer)

1924 Cologne
1971 Cologne

Karl Heinz Hargesheimer attended the College of Commerce in Cologne, where his teachers noticed his anti-National-Socialist attitudes. In 1942 he had a lobe of one of his lungs inactivated in order to evade military conscription. Based on his abilities, he was then accepted into the photographic curriculum of a Cologne factory school without the respective prerequisites. There are conflicting reports about his life between 1944 and 1947. It is said that he disappeared into the Alsace and that he was in a concentration camp. He himself kept silent about this period. In 1948, on the occasion of a story for the magazine *Stern*, he gave himself the name Chargesheimer. During the late forties, he and his friend Günther Weiß-Margis planned his first publication about the war-ravaged city of Cologne, but the aestheticized nature of his pictures found no willing publisher. His first gelatine-silver experiments and abstract sculptures were also created during that period. From 1950 to 1955 he was a lecturer at the BiKla School in Düsseldorf. In 1956, L. Fritz Gruber exhibited his work at Photokina. In 1957 he started a series of photo books, all of which caused a furore: *Cologne intime, Unter Krah-*

◄ **Chargesheimer**
Konrad Adenauer,
1954

Gelatin silver print
29.2 x 33.8 cm
ML/F 1977/172

Gruber Collection

nenbäumen, *In the Ruhr Region, Romanesque Style on the Rhine, People at the Rhine, Berlin – Pictures of a Big City* and *Interim Balance Sheet.* These books demonstrated to the trade that he not only had a specific outlook, but also new concepts about utilizing his pictures in books and bringing them to people's attention.

This series concluded in 1962, and Chargesheimer dedicated himself to the stage. He was a stage designer and director in Bonn, Cologne, Brunswick, Hamburg, Vienna and Kassel, busied himself with kinetic sculptures, his meditation mills. In addition, he took up his abstract photography and light graphics again, with which he attempted to break into the art trade. But it was not until the eighties that the signific-

ance of this experimental photography was recognized. Chargesheimer received the Cultural Award of the German Society for Photography in 1968 and the Karl Ernst Osthaus Prize from the city of Hagen in 1970. In 1978, his estate was donated to the Museum Ludwig in Cologne, and his meditation mills and light graphics followed in 1989. The scholarship for the furtherance of photography sponsored by the city of Cologne has been named after him since 1986. Chargesheimer, an early exponent of inter-media art, is now recognized internationally for his significance as an avant-gardist. These successes had no bearing on the fact that he became embroiled in a personal crisis that was also heavily fanned by social developments. His book *Cologne 5:30 AM* in which he focused intensely on the spread of concrete in his home town of Cologne from the point of view of a conceptional city portrait, even rejecting a foreword already written by Heinrich Böll, became his legacy. He died under mysterious circumstances on New Year's eve in 1971.
RM

▲ **Chargesheimer**
Ballet Break,
around 1963

Gelatin silver print
59.4 x 49.5 cm
ML/F 1980/172

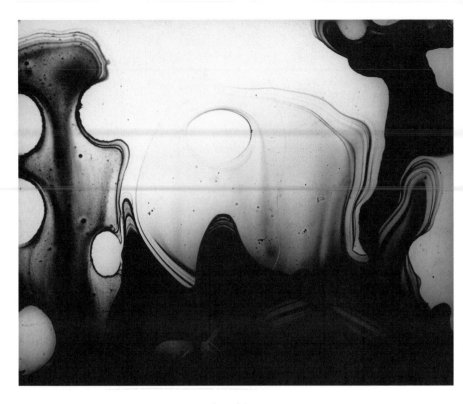

▲ **Chargesheimer**
Musical Reflection
(gelatin silver print
painting)
(Wagner), 1949

*Gelatin silver print,
mixed media*
39.7 x 48.6 cm
ML/F 1994/66

▲ Chargesheimer
Untitled (gelatin
silver print painting),
around 1962

Gelatin silver print,
mixed media
49.5 x 59.5 cm
ML/F 1994/68

Claasen,
Hermann

1899 Cologne
1987 Cologne

▲ **Hermann Claasen**
Christ among the
Ruins, 1945

Gelatin silver print
28 x 38.6 cm
ML/F 1987/170

Hermann Claasen was only 14 years old when he began making photographic experiments with a camera made from a cigar box. After the col-
lapse of his parents' textile business, where he too had worked, the self-
taught Claasen made the daring move to professional photography.

His photographic archive was destroyed during a bombing raid in
1942. During the war he photographed the ruins and the people in
Cologne and its surroundings. These photographs are among the most
gripping documents of the destroyed city. His unforgettable picture
Christ among the Ruins is a symbolic memorial against war. Life with
crude improvisation, the daily battle for bare necessities, they were all
chronicled by Claasen. A selection of these pictures was published in
1947 in the book *Songs in the Furnace,* supplemented by an exhibition in
the Eigelsteintor city gate in Cologne under the title "Cologne – the
Tragedy of a City". Since his death, the District Savings Bank of Cologne
has been sponsoring the Hermann Claasen Prize, a scholarship to
foster young photographers. *RM*

► **Hermann Claasen**
Cologne Cathedral,
seen from the south,
1944

Gelatin silver print
33.3 x 43.2 cm
ML/F 1987/168

◄ **Hermann Claasen**
Neumarkt Square in
Cologne, first day-
light bombing raid,
1944

Gelatin silver print
30.4 x 40.4 cm
ML/F 1993/156

Gruber Donation

Clausen, Rosemarie

1907 Berlin
1990 Hamburg

▶ Rosemarie Clausen
"Endgame" by
Samuel Beckett, 1968

Gelatin silver print
59.8 x 45.1 cm
ML/F 1989/42

▼ Rosemarie Clausen
Marcel Marceau,
1964

Gelatin silver print
58 x 45 cm
ML/F 1989/40

After first studying art, Rosemarie Clausen began an apprenticeship in photography in Berlin in 1925. She took a special interest in the theater and until 1933 worked with theater photographer Elli Marcus. She soon became a familiar person in theater circles, having the opportunity to photograph the great actors and actresses of her time. She established her own studio and worked primarily at the state playhouse at the Gendarmenmarkt, where Gustaf Gründgens became the director in 1934. In 1938 she published her first picture book, *People Without Masks*, in which she presented her theater photography. After the end of the war, Rosemarie Clausen moved to Hamburg, where she practiced photography at the Hamburg Studio Theatres, at the Theater in the Room, and in the German Playhouse. In 1947 she met the playwright Wolfgang Borchert and photographed the premiere of his play *The Man Outside* in the Hamburg Studio Theatres. In 1968, Samuel Beckett staged his *Endgame* on the workshop stage of the Schiller Theater in Berlin. Rosemarie Clausen photographed that play in dim light, in many gradations of grainy gray values, occasionally applying unsharpness.

Rosemarie Clausen's work stretched over more than half a century, largely elevating theater photography into a concept of its own. She worked in two of the most important theater centers of Germany, over the decades photographing and interpreting many great actors in the most diverse roles. Her pictures are optically frozen moments of thespian poetry, with a profound sensitivity for the expressiveness of human mimicry. *UP*

Clergue, Lucien

1934 Arles
Lives in Arles

▲ Lucien Clergue
Bullfight, around
1960

Gelatin silver print
24.7 x 37.3 cm
ML/F 1984/23

Gruber Donation

After finishing high school, Lucien Clergue began to take pictures in his spare time. In 1954, he had his first public exhibition with 50 portraits of actors, all of them impersonating Julius Caesar. Next he produced a series of photographs of traveling acrobats, taken in the wartime ruins of Arles, and a series of pictures of dead animals. In 1956 he started his series *Nudes of the Sea* which made him known around the world. They represented a novel interpretation of bodily shapes and of the treatment of surfaces in combination with water and light. By candidly staging eroticism in his pictures, Clergue furthermore openly broke with the tradition of prude rendition of nudes that dominated photography in the fifties. He did not place chaste young women in the landscape, neither did he aim for the usual untouched landscape and untouched femininity. Instead he used water, light and waves to impart a sensuous radiance to the female body. In 1957 he illustrated the book *Memorable Bodies* by Paul Eluard. In 1959 he began his intensive photographic study of the Camargue, its swamps, plants, and its waters. In this subject, too, he bridged the distances to the objects, creating an extraordinary immediacy of things in his pictures. He also worked on a photographic series about the topography of Arles, and he kept a daily photographic log for

► Lucien Clergue
From the series:
Nudes of the Sea,
around 1975

Gelatin silver print
49.9 x 60.6 cm
ML/F 1995/119

Uwe Scheid
Donation

Jean Cocteau's film "The Testament of Orpheus". Over a period of many
years, he used his camera to observe Picasso at work, and he also photographed bullfights in the arena. In 1961 he took many trips abroad and
decorated a hall in the Rockefeller Center in New York. In 1962 he visited
Brasilia and Rio de Janeiro, beginning a new series of his *Nudes of the
Sea*. In 1971 he made a film for his friend Pablo Picasso for Universal
Pictures. In 1970 he founded the Rencontres Internationales de la Photographie in Arles, which he served as artistic director for 25 years. The
Rencontres Internationales de la Photographie were captivating because
of their liveliness and freshness, which were greatly enhanced by the
quaint southern charm of the city of Arles. He has been teaching at the
University of Marseilles since 1976. In 1979 he became the first person
to receive a doctor's degree in photography, and since then he has been
teaching at the New York School for Social Research. In 1980 he was
named "Knight of the National Order of Merit" of France. *RM*

◄ Alvin Langdon
Coburn
Semi-nude,
around 1905

Photogravure
8.3 x 10.3 cm
ML/F 1984/24

Gruber Donation

**Coburn,
Alvin Langdon**

1882 Boston
1966 Colwyn Bay,
North Wales

Alvin Langdon Coburn belongs to the generation of photographers who brought about the change from the pictorialism of the 19th century to an avant-garde-oriented style of photography.

It was during a visit in 1899 to a distant cousin in London, art photographer Fred Holland Day, that Coburn became definitely fascinated with photography. As early as 1902 he opened his own studio in New York. There Coburn became acquainted with Alfred Stieglitz, in whose magazine *Camera Work* he published some of his photographs as photogravures. Through the circle of artists around Stieglitz, Coburn soon became familiar with the avant-gardistic trends of the art. Inspired by that trend, he began to explore new forms of expression with photography. He experimented with extreme perspectives and developed a strong interest in structures and abstract formations. In 1912 he left New York and went to Great Britain, where he remained to the end of his days. There he had friendly contacts among members of the English group of cubists founded by Ezra Pound and called "Vorticists". This connection inspired Coburn's "Vortographs", in which he achieved a cubist fragmentation of forms by using reflecting prisms.

► Alvin Langdon
Coburn
St. Paul's Cathedral
from Ludgate Circus,
around 1905

Photogravure
38.2 x 28.6 cm
ML/F 1977/183

Gruber Collection

In addition to his avant-garde creativity, Coburn also made a name for himself with portraits of famous contemporary personalities, which he published in 1913 and 1922 in his two volumes entitled *Men of Mark*.
MBT

▲ **Alvin Langdon Coburn**
London Bridge, 1905

Photogravure, 12.2 x 10 cm
ML/F 1993/165
Gruber Donation

▲ **Alvin Langdon Coburn**
The Bridge at Ipswich,
around 1904
Photogravure, 19.4 x 15 cm
ML/F 1995/7
Gruber Donation

◀ **Serge Moreno**
Cohen
Marie-Jo Lafontaine,
1991

Color print
40.3 x 32.6 cm
ML/F 1993/168

Gruber Donation

Cohen, Serge
Moreno

1951 Portes-Les-
Valence, France
Lives in Paris

Aside from a six-month period as an assistant to Daniel Frasnay in
Paris, Serge Cohen is a self-taught photographer. After various auxiliary
jobs and a few black-and-white assignments for the supplement of the
Frankfurter Allgemeine Zeitung, he had the opportunity of proving his talent to art director Willy Fleckhaus. In 1982, his first picture essay was
published in the *Frankfurter Allgemeine Magazin,* for which he has since
become a staff photographer.

Cohen is active in architectural and landscape photography and in
photojournalism, but it is his staged portrait photography that made
him famous. He succeeds in creating a portrait that stays on one's
mind and that remains associated with the sitter. He provokes by depicting the sitter in roles that spring from his imagination after an intense study of his subject. *UP*

► **Serge Moreno Cohen**
Richard Avedon, 1994

Gelatin silver print
25.8 x 30.7 cm
ML/F 1994/124

Gruber Donation

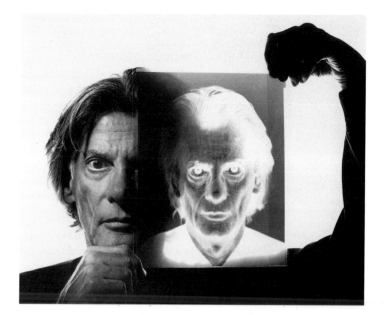

◄ **Serge Moreno Cohen**
Jasper Johns, 1986

Color print
27.7 x 40.4 cm
ML/F 1993/169

Gruber Donation

Colette

1947 Tunisia
Lives in New York
and Munich

Colette began painting while she was still in her youth. In the year 1970, she completed her first performance with *Hommage à Delacroix*, which was the beginning of an artistic career devoted to the oneness of art and life. Then came street works, actions and performances on streets and public squares, followed by her "living environments" and the "windows", in which she remained motionless in a selected pose with an elaborate arrangement of fabrics and lace. Her titles were *Cinderella's Dream*, *Rag Doll* or *Justine as Joan of Arc*. Meanwhile, her home became a "living environment". There her activities produced sculptures, objects and photographic works that should not be regarded as relics of those activities, but as parallel developments. Colette is unquestionably a multi-media artist who assumes various roles of historical women for certain phases of her work, which she then combines directly with her everyday life. Colette has convincingly implemented Marcel Duchamp's idea of aesthetic behavior throughout her entire artistic career. In recent years, she has withdrawn somewhat from performance art, working more intensively in the fields of object art, painting, and photographic work. Some of her more recent themes have been *Call C for Scandal*, *Mata Hari and the Stolen Potatoes* or *The Bavarian Adventure*. Her "Magic Code", which threads through her artistic work like a credo, simultaneously signals her personal creed: "T. M. for Deadly Feminine". *RM*

▲ Colette
Real Dream, 1975

Mixed media
82 x 197 cm
ML/F 1994/1

Uwe Scheid
Donation

► Stephen
D. Colhoun
Laughing Woman
with Cup, around
1955

Gelatin silver print
27.7 x 26.2 cm
ML/F 1977/907

Gruber Donation

Stephen D. Colhoun's career as a professional photographer began in 1950. He soon became a well-known glamour photographer for leading magazines and advertising agencies. His advertising assignments ranged from watches to automobiles, but he became best known for his fashion photography.

Colhoun's photograph *Laughing Woman with Cup* was taken for an advertisement for brassieres. While the fore- and background are pleasantly blurred, a band of sharpness diagonally traverses the center of the picture. Here we see the neckline of a woman, with her head leaning back so far that only her wide open, laughing mouth is visible in the picture. This ingenious contrast between sharp and blurred areas, visible and hidden elements place the observer in the role of a voyeur. *MBT*

**Colhoun,
Stephen D.**

Born in 1921

Cosindas, Marie

Born in Boston, Massachusetts
Lives in Boston

Marie Cosindas studied design at the Modern School of Fashion Design in Boston and painting at the Boston Museum School. From 1945 to 1960 she worked as an illustrator and designer. In 1960 she established herself as a photographer in Boston. She attended photography workshops conducted by Ansel Adams (1961) and Minor White (1963/1964). In subsequent years she herself taught courses in photography, including the Colorado College Summer Photo Workshops in Colorado Springs from 1972 to 1978, and she also taught at various American Institutions.

As a trained painter, it was in keeping with Marie Cosindas' temperament to be intrigued by color, so that it is not surprising that she took up color photography at a time when black-and-white photography was still the favorite with most photographers. She began experimenting with this medium in the early sixties and sought to achieve the greatest possible brilliance and perfection with colors. She dispensed with artificial light, used various filters and experimented with different developer times and temperatures. In 1962, Marie Cosindas became one of the first photographers to explore the possibilities of Polaroid instant print material successfully. She was always very meticulous with technical aspects of her work. Cosindas paid the same painstaking attention to her compositions, which she organized to the last detail. Her portrait sessions became well known for her thorough familiarization with her subjects and for the quality of the resulting portraits themselves. In addition to human faces, Marie Cosindas was fascinated by old dolls, masks and fabrics, which she arranged in romantically enchanting still-life tableaus. *MBT*

▼ Marie Cosindas
Still Life with Flowers, 1976

Polaroid
24 x 19 cm
ML/F 1984/26

Gruber Donation

Carel Cudlin studied social law before entering the College for Film and Television (FAMU) in Prague. From 1988 to 1989 he was a staff photojournalist for the weekly newspaper *Mlady Svet,* and since then he has been working for picture agencies in Prague and in Paris. In 1989, Cudlin used his camera to record the mass exodus of citizens of the German Democratic Republic, and he documented the crowds at Lobkovicz Palace, the West German Embassy in Prague. His photographs show people helping one another to climb over walls, they show the draining of a state. In his photographs of the "velvet revolution" in Czechoslovakia in November 1989, Cudlin concentrated on gestures of solidarity and moments of poignant symbolism, such as the removal of a Soviet star from a building, or the cutting of barbed wire at the Hungarian border. Cudlin has a keen sensitivity for the power of expression of certain gestures and actions, and he has a refined talent for conveying this in his photographs. *RM*

Cudlin, Carel

1960 Prague
Lives in Prague

▲ **Carel Cudlin**
At the German Embassy, Prague, 1989

Gelatin silver print
22.6 x 34.2 cm
ML/F 1990/1326

Cutforth, Roger

1944 England
Lives in Terlingua,
Texas

Roger Cutforth studied at the Nottingham College of Art from 1962 to 1966 and at the Ravensbourne College of Art from 1963 to 1966. After emigrating to New York he taught drawing and photography at various colleges.

Cutforth created his first photographic sequences in the early seventies, calling them *Personal Space*. With the size of the figure remaining unchanged, he enlarged the surrounding field in order to demonstrate the proportional relationships among things. In films that he made between 1973 and 1975, Cutforth conducted similar investigations of the relationship of human beings with the image space surrounding them.

In 1977 and 1978, Cutforth continued to utilize the medium of photographic sequences for his landscape photography. He sought out hard-to-reach locations in the American west, far removed from civilization. There he photographed a particular part of the scenery at different times of the day, usually early in the morning, at noon and in the early evening. His sequences always consisted of three landscape photographs with identical cropping. The appearance of the landscape is different in each picture as a result of different lighting conditions, but because of the identical cropping, the information about the formation of the landscape remains unchanged. By means of such a juxtaposition of the changed and the unchanged, the observer is stimulated to compare nuances and variations that are to be discovered especially in the changes in color, shadows and light. Unlike a motion picture, such a photographic sequence does not convey a seamless description of the evolving scene. The charm of the photographic sequence lies more in the intervals of time between exposures, which serve to enhance the illustration of the passing of time by means of changes in the rendition of the subject. *MBT*

▲ **Roger Cutforth**
Bighorn Canyon,
Montana, 1978

Color print
3 photographs,
each 61.2 x 61.2 cm
ML/F 1979/1354 I-III

After an apprenticeship in photography, Bruce Landon Davidson studied photography at the Rochester Institute of Technology in Rochester, NY in the early fifties. Following that, he studied painting, philosophy and photography under Herbert Matter, Alexey Brodovitch and Josef Albers at Yale University in 1955. After that he worked as a freelance photographer in New York, Paris and Los Angeles, serving such international magazines as *Live, Esquire* or *Vogue*. He has been a member of the "Magnum" group since 1958, and he also teaches at a variety of institutions.

Davidson concerns himself with subjects of everyday reality. He photographs drug addicts and criminals, and he documents street scenes and demonstrations. He followed the changes in America during the late fifties and early sixties with great empathy. He had a special interest in social groups like the beatniks, precursors of the hippies with unconventional attitudes, in suburban environments and other contemporary subjects. Davidson's photographs convey impressions that are typical of our times. *UP*

**Davidson,
Bruce Landon**

1933 Oak Park,
Illinois
Lives in New York

▲ Bruce Davidson
Young Couple, 1958

Gelatin silver print
16.9 x 24.2 cm
ML/F 1977/909

Gruber Donation

Dekkers, Ger

(Gerrit Hendrik
Dekkers)

1929 Borne,
Netherlands
Lives in Giethoorn

Gerrit Hendrik Dekkers studied at the Art Academy in Enschede in the
Netherlands from 1950 to 1954. Before that, he served in the Dutch
Army in Indonesia from 1948 to 1950. In 1954 he married Hilda Hart-
suiker, with whom he had two children, Henriette and José. Between
1954 and 1976, he worked as a freelance artist in Enschede, and since
then in Giethoorn.

Dekkers first attracted public attention in 1969 with an exhibition of
his precise, sober landscapes at the Stedelijk Museum in Amsterdam.
In 1971 he started his serial photography, which enabled him to depict
evolving events. These photographic series can illustrate changes in a
cultural landscape that are due to the intervention of mankind, but they
can also illustrate spatial shifts such as a change of the artist's position
within a given space, or the clarification of scenic relationships. To accomplish this, he uses the square format and color photography, completely dispenses with the presence of any human beings, and positions
the horizon precisely in the center. In a horizontal arrangement of the
pictures, the horizons line up, forming a continuous line that traverses
all the pictures. When the photographs are arranged in a square field,
he achieves a regular image pattern that pervades the entire picture
arrangement. Dekkers utilizes this method of pictorial recording, which
dispenses with subjective decisions and which always abides by these
established rules, and he focuses on the cultivated landscape of the
Netherlands, on tree plantations, hedges, fields, gardens and dikes. The
alignments and the perspective of regularly stepped rows cause the observer to be consciously aware of the landscape and to study it. In particular the new polders, which were created entirely by human hands,
provide Dekkers with manifold possibilities for analysis. The polder is,
for all intents and purposes, paradigmatic for cultivated landscapes.

Orchard near Emmeloord, photographed in the first of the new polders, with which the original plan called for the Ijsselmeer to be completely drained in a series of steps, is one of the best known examples of these alignings. It is symmetrical around an axis, both in the horizontal as well as in the vertical direction, the only difference being that a row of trees, parallel to the horizon, moves into the picture in seven steps from left to right.

Dekkers' art can be classified as lying somewhere between conceptual art and land art, with photography being utilized with a documentary purpose. But since Dekkers arrived at such a concept from a background of photography, he places significantly more emphasis on the technical perfection of his photographs than many of his artistic colleagues. Dekkers' work proves that the differentiation between artists who make photographs and conceptually working photographers can no longer be defined, and that it can only be established biographically.

In his own work, he distinguishes between series that show a close relationship to land art, because they depict situations in which the soil has obviously been cultivated and altered by human hands, and other photographic series, which he regards as "objets trouvés" in the context of landscapes. But it is only through his photography that we become aware of them and acknowledge them with their sometimes surreal appearance. In spite of the occasional determinisms that are a priori in Dekkers' endeavors, his work is not guided purely intellectually by reflective thought processes. He is enough of a photographer to accept the eye and perception as the second important axiom of his work and to let the visual experience precipitate the decision for a particular picture subject. *RM*

▲ **Ger Dekkers**
Orchard near
Emmeloord, 1974

Color print
50 x 50 cm,
altogether 50 x 350 cm
ML/F 1985/35

◄ Erwin von
Dessauer
Children on the
Beach, around 1933

Gelatin silver print
28 x 25.3 cm
ML/F 1983/182

**Dessauer,
Erwin von**

1907 Valparaiso,
Chile
1976 Rio de Janeiro,
Brazil

Erwin von Dessauer studied photography under Willy Zielke at the
Bavarian State College for Photographic Imaging. In 1933 he accepted
an offer from a magazine to settle in Rio de Janeiro. His photographs
depicting the life of simple people were created during numerous trips
across the South American continent. It is evident from his photographs, especially from his pictures of religious ceremonies like
macumba, that he had a talent for being accepted by people. He was
particularly interested in genre portraits, which he produced on an extensive scale for the "Ballet Folklórico Brasileiro". It can be detected in
many of his photographs that his eye was trained by a master of object
photography. In spite of their seemingly incidental nature, photographs
like *At the Water* and *Children on the Beach* are composed with great precision. *RM*

▲ Erwin von Dessauer
At the Water, around 1939

Gelatin silver print, 35 x 27 cm
ML/F 1983/181

Dibbets, Jan

1941 Weert
Lives in Amsterdam

After studying to become an arts teacher at the Academy for Creative and Constructive Arts in Tilburg, Jan Dibbets began his career as a minimalist painter in Amsterdam. In 1967 he received a scholarship to study in England. There he discovered photography and made it the mainstay of his now conceptually oriented art. Still young at the time, the Dutch artist achieved international recognition with a series of photographs entitled *Perspective Correction* (1967-1969). With this series, he questioned the illusion of perspective in paintings, at the same time challenging the notion that the camera cannot lie. One of the photographs from this series, for example, shows a trapezoid that Dibbets had painted directly on a white wall of his studio. But perspective distortion in the picture makes the trapezoid appear as a square. With photographs such as this one, Dibbets assured himself a place among the spiritual fathers of photographic concept art – next to artists like John Baldessari, Douglas Huebler and Ugo Mulas.

One of the significant objectives of concept art is to illustrate a scientific abstract notion in a descriptive, clarifying manner. This is to bring phenomena of reality determined with a scientific method closer to the direct range of human experience and perceptual capabilities. For Dibbets, the phenomenon of movement in and through time is the subject of numerous works. Dibbets is concerned with the visualization of this phenomenon, which, although it can be verified scientifically, is not readily visible. Jean-Christoph Ammann wrote the following about this artist: "Dibbets does not question reality in photography, he questions the reality of photography itself. In doing so, he does not address the object, but the 'way of seeing' of the camera [...]. For Dibbets, to uncover the seeing mechanism of the camera means to introduce a recognition process that causes reality to be perceived as a photographic reality, not as a surrogate."

In his photographic work *Film-Painting: Black Vase Horizontal* (1972), Dibbets moves a motion picture camera past a vase at a uniform distance. This movement, which takes places in a room in a timed sequence, is visualized objectively by the simultaneous display of the film strip. With each new location of the vase within the picture area, it simultaneously indicates the respective position of Dibbets as he moves past the vase.

The course of time and an action taking place during that course of time are graphically illustrated by simultaneously showing – and this is

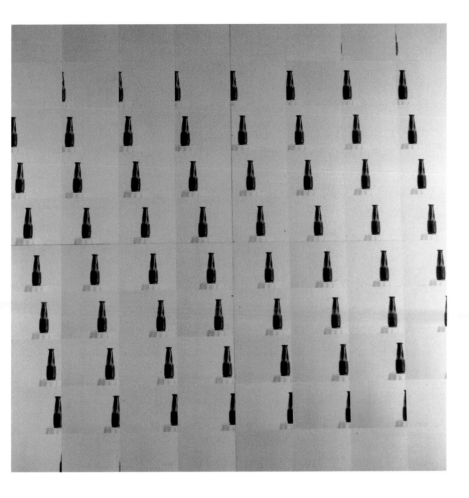

not possible in real time – the successive progression of a time sequence. For Dibbets' artistic endeavors, the motion picture camera is
assigned the role of a measuring instrument that records the slightest
changes that occur in space and time. *GG*

▲ **Jan Dibbets**
Film-Painting: Black
Vase Horizontal,
1972

*80 photographs
mounted on alu-
minum plates,
each 24 x 19 cm,
altogether
190 x 192 cm*
ML/F 1985/36

Ludwig Donation

Dieuzaide, Jean

1921 Grenada-sur-
Garonne
Lives in Toulouse

▲ Jean Dieuzaide
Nude in the Woods,
1975

Gelatin silver print
30.3 x 40.3 cm
ML/F 1995/120

Uwe Scheid
Donation

Jean Dieuzaide's career as a photographer began on the 19th of August 1944, when he took pictures of the liberation of his home town of Toulouse. In 1945, he began working as a photojournalist for various newspapers and weekly magazines. In 1951 he settled down as a photographer in Toulouse. His famous picture of the great surrealist *Dalí in the Water, Cadaqués,* was made during a 1951 trip to Spain.

During the fifties, Dieuzaide discovered his predilection for the structures of things. His close-up pictures of sea mud, in which the photographer found fascinating formations, became his most famous photographs of this genre. In 1974 he published this series under the title *My Adventure with Tar.* In 1963 Dieuzaide was among the founders of the "Libre Expression" group, which believed in "subjective photography" and in the ideas of Otto Steinert. Until 1981, Dieuzaide operated a gallery in Toulouse, in which he provided a display forum for members of the "Libre Expression" group. Dieuzaide closed his studio in 1986. *MBT*

▲ Jean Dieuzaide
Dalí in the Water, Cadaquès, 1951

Gelatin silver print, 31 x 24.5 cm
ML/F 1984/31

Gruber Donation

◄ Herbert Döring-
Spengler
Untitled, 1990

Cibachrome
50.5 x 50.5 cm
ML/F 1995/181

Uwe Scheid
Donation

**Döring-
Spengler,
Herbert**

1944 Cologne
Lives in Cologne

Since the mid-eighties Herbert Döring, a self-taught photographer, has
been exploring the possibilities of the Polaroid. He began to make
notches in the fresh film and to separate the layers. He also combined
Polaroid with video, making references to art-historical models and
utilizing unusual materials. His method of working might best be described as an attempt to break down the media at his disposal into their
component parts, to search out previously undiscovered elements, and
finally to recombine the whole. The blending takes place emotionally, in
the light of his feelings, not in accordance with any rational considerations. He is one of the most creative personalities in his field, ever capable of springing a surprise, and always intent on moving on to new
ground. His pictures start out as simple photos or video sequences, are
subjected to color changes, are captured on Polaroid, heated, ripped
apart, dried, in turn employed together with their new carrier as a slide,
or re-photographed, finally to yield up a Cibachrome print. *RM*

► Robert Doisneau
Café des Halles,
Paris, Tramp, 1952

Gelatin silver print
29.9 x 23.9 cm
ML/F 1977/209

Gruber Collection

Originally trained as a lithographer, Robert Doisneau embraced in 1929
a new interest as a self-taught photographer. He regarded photography
as the ideal medium for recording life during his wanderings through
Paris. His career as a professional photographer began in 1934 at the
Renault works in Billancourt, where he was employed until 1939 as an
industrial and advertising photographer. Also in 1939 he decided to become an independent photojournalist, but still in that same year the war
forced him to give up his dream of becoming a freelance photographer.
He served in the French army until 1940, and from then until the end of
the war, he worked for the résistance. Even so, he did not entirely interrupt his work as a photographer. Instead, he tried to earn a little money
by producing postcards. In 1949, Doisneau signed a contract with the
fashion magazine *Vogue,* for which he worked as a full-time staff photographer until 1952 and from then on as a freelance photographer.
Through his activities for *Vogue,* the photographer became acquainted
with high-society circles, for which, however, he did not have as much
sympathy as he did for the common people in the streets. He also did

**Doisneau,
Robert**

1912 Gentilly
near Paris
1994 Paris

▲ **Robert Doisneau**
The Bride near
Gégène, 1948

Gelatin silver print
30.5 x 23.9 cm
ML/F 1977/204

Gruber Collection

► **Robert Doisneau**
Gate of Hell,
Boulevard de Clichy,
Paris, 1952

Gelatin silver print
30.4 x 24 cm
ML/F 1977/211

Gruber Collection

not enter the annals of photography as a fashion photographer. What
made Doisneau famous was his "street photography". In countless
snapshots, he humorously, but not without empathy, documented life
in the suburbs of Paris.

   This resulted in a number of photographs that have become icons
of the French way of life. The most famous example is the *Kiss in front of*
the Palace of City Hall, which has been reproduced by the million, and
which more than any other picture became the symbol of young, bois-
terous love in a big city. As a "street photographer", Doisneau was on

▲ **Robert Doisneau**
Pablo Picasso in Vallauris with Françoise Gilot, around 1950

Gelatin silver print
21.9 x 18.9 cm
ML/F 1977/213

Gruber Collection

▶ Robert Doisneau
The Little General,
1950

Gelatin silver print
27.9 x 23.9 cm
ML/F 1977/215

Gruber Collection

the same level as Brassaï, Willy Ronis and Izis, with whom he shared a
joint exhibition at the Museum of Modern Art in New York in 1951. Like
Brassaï, Doisneau loved to wander through the streets of night-time
Paris in order to record the life of marginal society. It was during such
nightly excursions that he made the well-known photograph of the hobo
Coco, a failed soldier of the Foreign Legion, and the photograph of a
dock worker lying on his bed dreaming of the pin-up girls of his wall
decorations. Doisneau himself called this picture a parody of a masculine man. *MBT*

▲ Robert Doisneau
Dreams of a Tattooed Man, 1952

Gelatin silver print, 27.3 x 23.9 cm
ML/F 1977/205

Gruber Collection

At the beginning of this century, when Dora Kallmus, who later worked under the name Madame D'Ora, decided to become a photographer, this was an unconventional choice of profession for a woman from her social level. That is why she was only permitted to take courses in theory at the Graphic Education and Experiments Institute in Vienna, and she was not allowed to take practical courses. In spite of this obstacle, Madame D'Ora decided to open a studio in Vienna. She learned the fundamentals of portrait photography from Nicola Perscheid in Berlin. In 1907, together with Arthur Benda, whom she met at Nicola Perscheid's place in Berlin, she opened her studio in Vienna. Benda took care of the technical part of photography. Madame D'Ora dedicated herself to the arrangement and the staging of the photographs, for which she was influenced by the Viennese Art Nouveau. In 1917 Benda designed a lens that softened the contours in a picture. This soft-focus effect became a trademark of Madame D'Ora's early photographs, which sometimes gave the impression of having been taken through a frosted glass plate. She continued to use this technique when she opened a studio in Paris in 1924. It was only after the Second World War

Madame D'Ora

(Dora Kallmus)

1881 Vienna
1963 Frohnleiten,
Styria, Austria

▲ **Madame D'Ora**
Rosella Hightower,
1955

Gelatin silver print
21.3 x 30.9 cm
ML/F 1984/32

Gruber Donation

▲ **Madame D'Ora**
Marquis George de
Cuevas, 1955

Gelatin silver print
25.5 x 26.3 cm
ML/F 1977/222

Gruber Collection

that Madame D'Ora changed from soft focus to precise sharpness. She used this new technique between 1953 and 1955, when she produced an extensive series of photographs of the Marquis de Cuevas and his dance theater.

There was also a change in her choice of subjects after the war. She was no longer interested just in glamour and the good life. For instance, she took her camera to Paris slaughterhouses. Fascinated by this subject, she sought to create abstract views of it, arranging it in virtually poetic still-life compositions. *MBT*

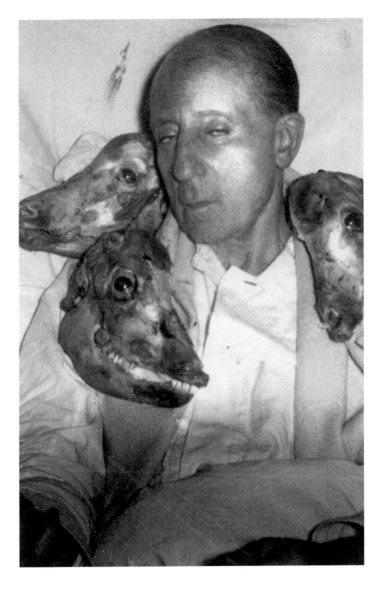

◀ František Drtikol
Salome, 1923

Bromoil print
22.8 x 28.7 cm
ML/F 1984/34

Gruber Donation

▶ František Drtikol
Nude, around 1920

Gelatin silver print
11.8 x 8 cm
ML/F 1993/172

Gruber Donation

Drtikol,
František

1883 Príbram,
Bohemia
1961 Prague

František Drtikol was one of the most famous photographers of the twenties and thirties in the former Czechoslovakia, and he also enjoyed an international reputation. His work was largely forgotten after he gave up photography in 1935, only to gain renewed recognition in the early seventies.

From 1901 to 1903, Drtikol enjoyed a well-founded education at the Bavarian State Institution for Photography in Munich. In 1910, after completing his military service and after spending three years in Príbram, Drtikol went to Prague, where he experienced public recognition of his work for the first time. Drtikol specialized in portraiture and nude photography, showing himself stylistically influenced by Romanticism and Symbolism. It was during this period that the feminine figure of Salome first appeared in his photographs, which continued to fascinate him during his entire work. During the twenties, Drtikol's style underwent significant changes: he began to emphasize and arrange space with man-sized geometrical forms, he developed the creative possibilities of light into virtually expressionistic dramaturgy, and he reduced his nudes to torsos or individual limbs. *MBT*

◀ Harold
E. Edgerton
Milk Drop, 1936

Gelatin silver print
39.5 x 49.9 cm
ML/F 1977/229

Gruber Collection

**Edgerton,
Harold E.**

1903 Fremont,
Nebraska
1990 Boston

Harold E. Edgerton studied at the University of Nebraska from 1921 to 1925 and at the Massachusetts Institute of Technology in Cambridge, MA from 1926 to 1927, where he began to teach in 1928. As an independent photographer he developed stroboscopic photography of high-speed kinetic action. A large number of his photographs became milestones of "high speed photography" and he received numerous international awards.

Stroboscopic photography is a technique for capturing and depicting kinetic action and timed events in distinct steps. Edgerton used strobe flash for recording fast action on film. The photographs were made in a darkened room, using numerous exposures per second. This also became a scientific tool, because it made the fine details of such fast-occurring events become visible for the first time.

One of Edgerton's most famous photographs is his *Milk Drop,* which shows the delicate, crown-shaped form created by a milk drop when it strikes a thin layer of milk on a plate. A physical event that is familiar to scientists is transformed into a liquid sculpture that can only be made visible by means of Edgerton's photographic technique. *UP*

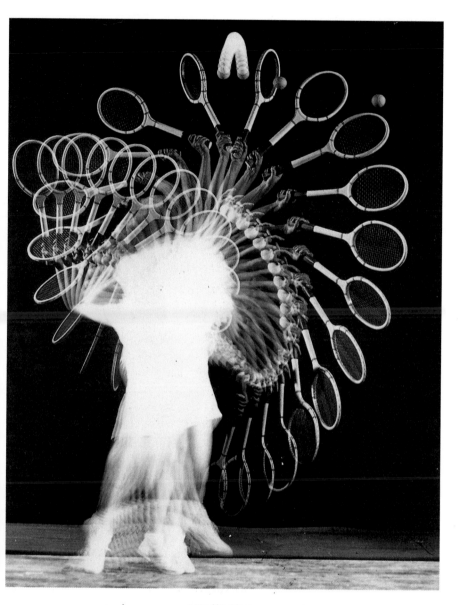

▲ Harold E. Edgerton
Tennis Player, 1938

Gelatin silver print
24 x 19 cm
ML/F 1977/224

Gruber Collection

Alfred Eisenstaedt was only 13 years old when he began taking pictures with a Kodak camera that he had received as a gift. During the inflation period after the First World War, he made a living as a belt and button salesman for a company in Berlin. In his spare time he practiced photography as a hobby and began to experiment with cropped photographic enlargements. His activities as a freelance photographer began when his photograph of a female tennis player was published in the *Weltspiegel*, followed by other publications in the *Berliner Tageblatt*. In 1929, he decided to make photography his profession, and he began to work for the "Pacific and Atlantic Picture Agency".

His first assignment, a photographic report of the awarding of the Nobel Prize to Thomas Mann in 1929, already earned him great recognition. During those years he made many portraits that became famous, of such personalities as, among others, Marlene Dietrich; George Bernard Shaw, but also Joseph Goebbels, Hitler and Mussolini. In addition, he also produced a report about the war between Italy and Ethiopia. He worked for the *Berliner Illustrirte Zeitung* and other tabloids in Berlin and Paris.

Eisenstaedt, Alfred

1898 Dierschau, Germany
1995 Oak Bluffs, Massachusetts

▲ **Alfred Eisenstaedt**
American Ballet, 1938

Gelatin silver print
16.2 x 24.1 cm
ML/F 1977/237

Gruber Collection

◀ **Alfred Eisenstaedt**
V-Day, 1945

Gelatin silver print
24 x 15 cm
ML/F 1977/242

Gruber Collection

◄ **Alfred Eisenstaedt**
Marlene Dietrich,
1928

Gelatin silver print
24.7 x 26.8 cm
ML/F 1977/247

Gruber Collection

Concerned about the political situation in Germany and hoping for
better work opportunities, Eisenstaedt emigrated to America in 1935 and
began working for *Harper's Bazaar, Vogue* and *Town and Country*. Eisenstaedt arrived in New York just as *Life* magazine was being launched,
and he became a member of its full-time staff right from its beginning
in early 1936. Up until 1972, when *Life* magazine temporarily ceased publication, he had worked on more than 2500 assignments, and he produced photographs for more than 90 cover pages. As a photojournalist,
Eisenstaedt was not specialized in a specific field. Nevertheless, his

▲ **Alfred Eisenstaedt**
Mussolini in Venice,
13.6.1934

Gelatin silver print
19.1 x 24.4 cm
ML/F 1988/64

Gruber Donation

photographs of people were the ones that earned him a place in photographic history. He not only photographed countless famous personalities in politics and culture, but also unknown people in everyday situations. One of his most famous photographs is *V-Day*, a snapshot of a passionate kiss during a victory parade of sailors on Times Square at the end of the Second World War. Eisenstaedt is regarded as a pioneer of available light photography, because early on he dispensed with flash photography in order to preserve the ambiance of natural lighting. Peter Pollack wrote the following comment about Eisenstaedt: "The strength of his photographs lies in the simplicity of their composition. Eisenstaedt's portraits clearly reveal the spirit and the character of a person, regardless of whether that person is famous or unknown. The intimacy of his pictures make the viewer feel like a participant, as if he was present, standing next to the photographer."

Eisenstaedt was honored with numerous international awards and he counts among the most published photojournalists in the world. *TvT*

Elsken,
Ed van der

1925 Amsterdam
1990 Edam

▲ **Ed van der Elsken**
Hongkong, 1960

Gelatin silver print
31 x 40.5 cm
ML/F 1988/79
Gruber Donation

▶▲ **Ed van der Elsken**
Girl Refugee,
Hongkong, 1960

Gelatin silver print
15.8 x 23.4 cm
ML/F 1977/252
Gruber Collection

▶ **Ed van der Elsken**
Durban, South Africa,
1960

Gelatin silver print
23.9 x 30.2 cm
ML/F 1977/255
Gruber Collection

Dutchman Ed van der Elsken completed his studies of art in his home town, later moving to Paris to work as a freelance photographer. He also became a correspondent for a Dutch newspaper. Many of this politically active photographer's socio-critical pictures and films were made during a trip around the world. At first he worked only in black-and-white, taking up color later on. In a photographic series about jazz, created between 1955 and 1961, he did not use flash illumination, because he considered it important to preserve the atmosphere and the emotions of the moment in natural light conditions. Elsken published *Sweet Life* in 1963, along with numerous photographic books about Amsterdam, Japan and China. Elsken expressed the drama of social injustice in a pictorially concentrated manner with photographs like the one of the careworn, strained face of a Chinese girl, or the one of the South African apartheid situation. Both with genre studies of the subculture of Amsterdam as well as the photographic short story *Love on the left Bank*, Elsken expressed his interest in people on the margins of society, who are never shown in representative reports about a country. *LH*

**Engelskirchen,
Hein**

1908 Krefeld
1985 Krefeld

After an apprenticeship in a home-weaving shop, Hein Engelskirchen made a trip to Paris, during which he discovered the camera and thus his later profession. After serving in the war, he was exceptionally admitted to an examination at the handicrafts chamber, and he spent the rest of his life as a successful photographer, creating illustrations for advertising and for industry. Their richness in color, but also the combined precision of detail and panorama-like overview, in particular of his photographs of the Bayer-Uerdingen works, are reminiscent of a way of seeing industrial installations that later became known worldwide, especially through the Becher school.

Engelskirchen worked with enormous energy, and he never sought publicity. That is why some of his photographs, like *Wallpaper Designer,* are world-famous classics whose author is not generally known. His estate was divided among the Kaiser Wilhelm Museum in Krefeld, the Museum Ludwig in Cologne, and the archive of the Photographic Academy in Leinfelden. *RM*

▲ Hein
Engelskirchen
Bayer-Uerdingen,
around 1965

Color print
29.4 x 40 cm
ML/F 1993/91

▲ **Hein Engelskirchen**
Wallpaper Designer,
around 1955

Gelatin silver print
24.9 x 40.5 cm
ML/F 1993/97

Engelskirchen | 155

Erben, Li

1939 Blauda,
Czechoslovakia
Lives in Munich

▼ Li Erben
Daoist Temple,
Mount Taishan, 1986

Color print
30.3 x 23.8 cm
ML/F 1987/104

After a photographic apprenticeship with Stuttgart fashion photographer Walde Huth, followed by studies at the Institute for Photojournalism, Li Erben began to photograph Munich life in its beergardens and streets, in parks and in the hustle and bustle of its carnival. After that she found her strength in the field of portrait photography of personalities from the arts, music and literature. She made portraits of Ingmar Bergman and Liv Ullmann, Isabel Adjani and Roman Polanski, Federico Fellini and Jane Birkin, Arthur Rubinstein and Marc Chagall. During that time she met stage director Victor Vicas, whom she later married in Paris. During her time in Paris, she worked primarily as a still photographer in movie productions, but she also continued making portraits of actors, and she began working as an assistant stage director. When her husband passed away, she became a stage director herself, and in the eighties she specialized in international co-productions. She took advantage of her countless trips to create pictorial reports. Among these was the colorful series about China and Chinese life: people who camp in railway stations, hikers on Taishu mountain, old men who take their caged birds to parks to let them sing, the dense throng of cyclists, rituals and processions. Li Erben presents a lively image of China in the mid-eighties, in its transition from communist uniformity to the liberalization of customs. Today she lives with the architect Dieter Walz in Munich. *RM*

▲ **Li Erben**
Kufu, 1986

Color print
30.3 x 23.8 cm
ML/F 1987/108

◀ **Li Erben**
The First of May in
Tiananmen Square,
Beijing, 1986

Color print
30.5 x 23.8 cm
ML/F 1987/99

Erben | 157

Eremin, Yuri

1881 Kasanskaja on
the Don
Died 1948

▼ Yuri Eremin
Street in Buchara
with Camels, 1928

Gelatin silver print
37.8 x 26.3 cm
ML/F 1992/121

Ludwig Collection

Parallel to the constructivist and realistic tendencies of the Russian avant-garde, pictorial photography in the Soviet Union also enjoyed a revival in the twenties. This was the time during which Yuri Eremin was successful with his impressionistically poetic photographs. Trained as a painter at the Moscow School of Painting, Art and Architecture, he later dedicated himself entirely to photography. As a staff member of the magazine *Fotograf*, which was published between 1926 and 1929, Eremin was of the opinion that photography should be regarded as one of the creative arts. He preferred to work with a soft-focus lens and bromoil techniques, thus assuming a stylistic position that was contrary to the photographic avant-garde of his country. Beginning in the mid-thirties, Eremin was active as a reporter and correspondent for the magazines *Izvestiya, SSSR na stroike,* ("USSR under Construction"), *Ogonek* and *Smena*. Eremin specialized in the subjects of landscapes and architecture, but he was also inspired by genre scenes of cities during his extensive trips through Russia and Western Europe.

In the photograph *Street in Buchara with Camels,* Eremin documented the oriental atmosphere of this city in the south of the USSR. With the view of a street through a shaded archway, Eremin imparted a special charm to his picture: the darkened figures and the portion of the archway in the foreground create a foil-like contrast with the bright, sun-drenched background, enhancing the impression of depth in the picture. *MBT*

Stefan Erfurt studied French literature at the Sorbonne in Paris from 1978 to 1980. From 1980 to 1981, he worked as an assistant in a photography and video studio. From 1981 to 1987, he studied photography under Professor Inge Osswald at the University of Essen. Since 1985 he has been contributing regularly to the *Frankfurter Allgemeine Magazin*, and also to *Vanity Fair* and to the *Sunday Times*. Erfurt stood out particularly because of his unconventional photographic reports. He dared to distance himself from the customary style of photojournalism and to let motion blur become part of his pictures. In his view, the essence of a picture lay not in the precision of reproduction, but in its expression of atmosphere and vitality. His search for the fusion of the moment with the subjective perception of the photographer found an incentive with his discovery of Polaroid instant imaging material as the medium best suited to his interests. These large format images are even more dedicated to forever preserving the fleeting moment than his black-and-white reportages. *RM*

Erfurt, Stefan

1958 Wuppertal
Lives in New York
and Berlin

▲ **Stefan Erfurt**
The Odeon, 1985

Gelatin silver print
25.6 x 37.7 cm
ML/F 1985/32

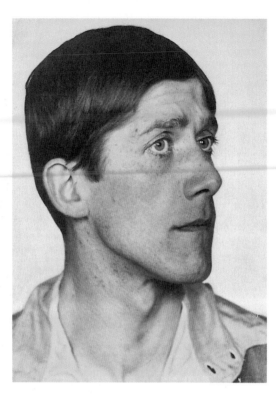

◀ Hugo Erfurth
Oskar Kokoschka,
1927

Bromoil print
38.4 x 28.4 cm
ML/F 1977/267

Gruber Collection

▶ Hugo Erfurth
Mrs Schuller,
around 1930

Oil pigment print
49.3 x 33.3 cm
ML/F 1977/262

Gruber Collection

Erfurth, Hugo

1874 Halle on the
Saale
1948 Gaienhofen on
Lake Constance

Hugo Erfurth was one of the most significant portrait photographers of his time. In 1895 he began an apprenticeship under court photographer Wilhelm Höffert, and in 1896 he took over the Schröder Studio in Dresden. In 1906 the photographer purchased the Lüttichau Palace in Dresden, in which he installed a studio for "modern and artistic photographic pictures", the so-called Erfurth imagery. Here he welcomed personalities from politics, business and the arts as his clients.

Erfurth cultivated a rather sober style of portraiture. He usually dispensed with characterizing or decorative settings, choosing instead to concentrate entirely on the face of the sitter.

In 1934 he moved to Cologne and opened a studio that was destroyed during the 1943 bombing raids on that city. After the war, the photographer retired to Gaienhofen on Lake Constance. *MBT*

▲ **Hugo Erfurth**
Mrs Fähndrich, around 1930

Oil pigment print, 48.8 x 38.3 cm
ML/F 1977/258
Gruber Collection

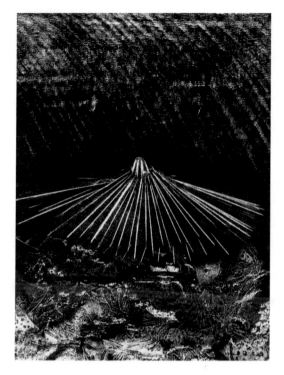

► **Max Ernst**
Photograph of a
rubbing, around
1936

Gelatin silver print
25.8 x 20 cm
ML/F 1984/37

Gruber Donation

The artist Max Ernst studied philosophy, psychology and art history in
Bonn. In 1919 he was a co-founder of the Dada movement in Cologne,
and in 1921 he joined the surrealists of the Paris avant-garde under
André Breton. Ernst utilized a great variety of techniques to express his
visions, among them collages, scraping, decalcomanias and oscillation.
Ernst invented the frottage (rubbings), which makes chance the liber-
ator of fantasy. He discovered this technique by accident when he transferred the texture of a wooden floor to paper by rubbing it with a pencil.
He incorporated this picture fragment in his work and subjected it to
his creativity.

A process that constitutes a combination of drawing and photography is the cliché verre, which is a handmade glass cliché that is
printed and reproduced with light. Ernst also utilized this technical
variation of the etching. *UP*

Ernst, Max

1891 Brühl
1976 Paris

◄ Walker Evans
Children in Alabama,
1936

Gelatin silver print
18 x 22 cm
ML/F 1984/39

Gruber Donation

Evans, Walker

1903 St. Louis,
Missouri
1975 New Haven,
Connecticut

Walker Evans, who originally wanted to become a writer, discovered his passion for photography at the end of the twenties. He began his career as a photographer with picture series about Victorian architecture in America and a reportage about the political unrest in Cuba in 1933. His early work already exhibited his objective, highly detail-conscious outlook, which was to earn him his fame as one of the most talented documentary photographers of his time. He himself described his photographs as "documentary in style", and he gave himself the challenge of maintaining the purity of the art of photography. In October 1935, Evans joined the Farm Security Administration (FSA), which was a federal authority during the Roosevelt era that developed aid programs for small farmers and tenant farmers during the years of the Great Depression. In this project, photography was used as evidence, documenting the abject poverty of the rural population for dissemination to a broader public – a project that combined political and socio-critical, documentary and aesthetic interests in an unprecedented manner. His efforts for the FSA became the most important segment of Evans' work. Using the same objective precision with which he had earlier photographed the architecture of his country, Evans was now recording the life of the poor. It was

▶ **Walker Evans**
Louisiana, 1936

Gelatin silver print
24.2 x 18.9 cm
ML/F 1984/38

Gruber Donation

during this period that he made the photograph of the skeptical but proud farm worker who appears in the picture entitled *Louisiana,* as well as the photograph of the two children dressed in meager rags who appear in the photograph entitled *Children in Alabama.*

In 1938, one year after Evans had finished his work for the FSA, the Museum of Modern Art in New York honored the achievement of this photographer with a solo exhibition, the very first that this museum dedicated to a photographer. *MBT*

Fehr, Gertrude

1895 Mainz
1996 Territet,
Switzerland

▶ **Gertrude Fehr**
Solarised Torso,
around 1935

Gelatin silver print
41 x 29 cm
ML/F 1987/158

▼ **Gertrude Fehr**
Odile, around 1940

Gelatin silver print
20.3 x 25.5 cm
ML/F 1987/159

Gertrude Fehr studied photography in the studio of Eduard Wasow and at the Bavarian State Educational Institute for Photography in Munich. She then operated a studio for theater and portrait photography in the Schwabing area of Munich until 1933. During the Third Reich era she moved to Paris, where she and her husband, the painter Jules Fehr, opened their own school of photography, which they called PUBLI-phot. Influenced by the Paris art scene, with which she maintained close contact, she began to experiment. She was particularly fascinated by the work of Man Ray, which motivated her to work with techniques like solarization, collages and abstractions. In doing so, she ventured into a type of work that is extremely unconventional for professional photographers. When the circumstances of war forced her to close the school, she clung to the idea of a photographic school and, immediately following her move to Switzerland, she founded a new school for photography, which she called "Ecole Fehr".

In 1945, she turned the school over to the public domain represented by the Ecole des Arts et Métiers in Vevey, where she continued to teach for another 15 years. Gertrude Fehr radiated a great influence as a teacher. Among her pupils were such successful photographers as Monique Jacot, Yvan Dalain and Jeanloup Sieff. Since 1960, Gertrude Fehr has limited her work to freelance photography, devoting herself mostly to portraiture. In Germany, her work remained forgotten for a long time. Exhibitions in the City Museum of Munich and at the Museum Ludwig in Cologne brought it back to the attention of the German public. Gertrude Fehr remained active into her advanced age and even changed residence and studio once again at more than 90 years of age. *RM*

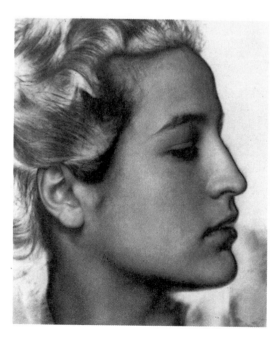

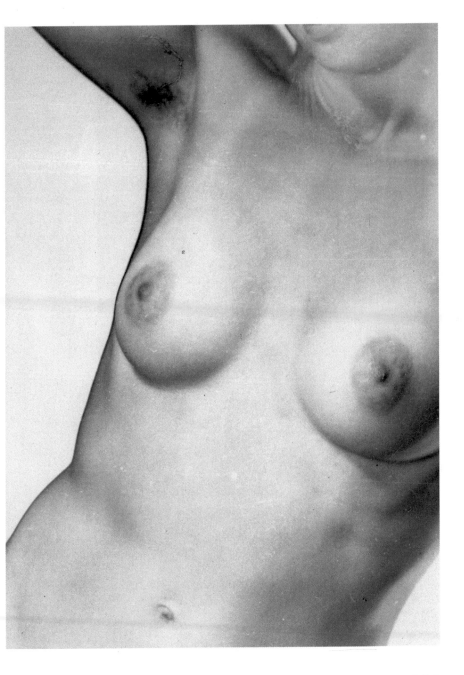

◄ **Gertrude Fehr**
Threepenny Opera,
Munich, 1933

Gelatin silver print
28.8 x 22 cm
ML/F 1983/192

► **Gertrude Fehr**
Hans Arp, around
1950

Gelatin silver print
28.7 x 22.4 cm
ML/F 1983/195

▼ Andreas Feininger
Detail of a Bivalve
Clam, around 1972

Gelatin silver print
34.5 x 27 cm
ML/F 1993/185

Gruber Donation

Andreas Feininger spent his youth in Germany, where he studied at the Bauhaus in Weimar and at the State School of Architecture in Zerbst. At first he worked as an architect in Dessau and in Hamburg, but towards the end of the twenties he began to be interested in photography. His first publications about photography appeared in 1930. In 1932 Feininger emigrated to Paris, where he initially worked for Le Corbusier. Later on he founded his own company for architectural and industrial photography in Stockholm. In 1939 he moved to New York and devoted himself entirely to photography. He worked for *Life* magazine and was considered to be one of the founders of contemporary photojournalism. After that period, he concentrated exclusively on the publication of his own books.

Feininger has a unique way of combining picture contents with formal criteria such as structures, picture composition and perspective. His photographs of New York are always structured architectonically, conforming to the rectangle of the picture, and never seeming like views

through a frame. The basic principle of his photographic work is especially evident in the example of picture composition, which he himself describes as "clarity, simplicity and structure". But he simultaneously demands that pictures must say something to the observer. To him, technical perfection is never an end in itself. Photographs like *New York, Cruiser United States* (1952) or *New York, Midtown Manhattan at 42nd Street* (1947) convey his architectonic outlook, the rigorous structure and the intensity of his pictures in a powerful way.

In his photojournalistic work for *Life* magazine, Feininger placed particular emphasis on a judicious combination of picture content and picture expression.

According to Feininger, the story has to be told by the pictures themselves, so that the accompanying text can be reduced to a minimum. If the content is the prerequisite for a picture, then its organization and its composition determine its quality. Feininger himself observed this fundamental principle of journalistic work during his many years at *Life* magazine, thus helping to shape the image of this publication.

Feininger's photography covers the entire spectrum of photographic activity: from lively street scenes to carefully composed city views, from nearly abstract landscapes to minute details of plants, stones, shells or sculptures. He masters the narrative as well as the strictly composed picture, and he accomplishes the blending of both criteria in his photojournalistic reports. *RM*

▲ **Andreas Feininger**
New York, Entrance
to a Discotheque,
around 1964

Gelatin silver print
26.5 x 34.1 cm
ML/F 1993/193

Gruber Donation

▲ **Andreas Feininger**
New York, Cruiser
United States, 1952

Gelatin silver print
26.7 x 34.2 cm
ML/F 1993/192

Gruber Donation

▶ **Andreas Feininger**
New York, Midday,
around 1964

Gelatin silver print
26.6 x 34 cm
ML/F 1993/191

Gruber Donation

▲ **Andreas Feininger**
New York, Midtown
Manhattan at 42nd
Street, 1947

Gelatin silver print
25.3 x 34.2 cm
ML/F 1993/190

Gruber Donation

▶ **Andreas Feininger**
New York, Brooklyn
Bridge, 1948

Gelatin silver print
26.6 x 34.1 cm
ML/F 1993/195

Gruber Donation

Felber, Gina Lee

1957 Zweibrücken,
Germany
Lives in Cologne

Gina Lee Felber, a graduate of the Technical College of Cologne, developed a quiet, restrained style of staged photography. Her work is representative of the fictitious, of the arranged in two ways. Her self-built picture objects originally served the exclusive purpose of being photographed. In the meantime, however, they have become exhibition subjects in their own right. They are unreal interiors, rooms populated with strange wire figures and objects made of paper and glue, artificial miniature worlds, which she fits out, illuminates, and then photographs.

This introduces a second abstraction, a second staging through the kind of illumination, because Gina Lee Felber does not employ her photography to obtain an exact reproduction of the miniature worlds created, but uses them only as a model for the creation of a sort of shadow play. Hardly anything recognizable is recorded in her photographs. One senses a solid wall, yet in another spot it turns out to be transparent. A tapestry of threads, grids, figures and heads unfolds in front of us, about whose correlations the titles, such as *Evocation, Night Moth* or *Shadow Conversation* also provide no clues. We are faced with events in three-dimensional space, even if the latter regularly converts into a plane. Because of this interpretive and altering photography, her wire sculptures have absolutely no disillusioning effect on her photographic work. But this also proves that neither one is a by-product of the other, or that the sculptures and photographic works speak an entirely different language independently of each other. *RM*

◀ **Gina Lee Felber**
Evocation, 1991

Gelatin silver print
128 x 188 cm
ML/F 1991/685

Fieger, Erwin

1928 Toplei,
Czechoslovakia
Lives in Castelfranco
di Sopra, Italy

After moving to Germany, Erwin Fieger was drafted into the army in 1944. He then studied graphic design and typography at the State Academy for the Creative Arts in Stuttgart. In 1960 he resolved to make photography his profession and settled in Italy and in Germany. He concentrated on color photography and undertook extensive journeys through England, Japan, Mexico and India, always following his own conceptions. Fieger was not willing to accept assignments that restricted his conceptions. He worked only for a few selected magazines, such as *Life*, *Réalités, Queen, Town* and *twen*. He always worked with a view to publications, which he meticulously serviced and published. Fieger also made a name for himself as a sports photographer at numerous Olympic Games, and he published books about the Olympiads in Sapporo, Munich, Innsbruck and St. Moritz. His book about India, which he planned over a period of many years as a journey from the source of the Ganges river all the way to its mouth, and which was lavishly printed, is magnificent. *RM*

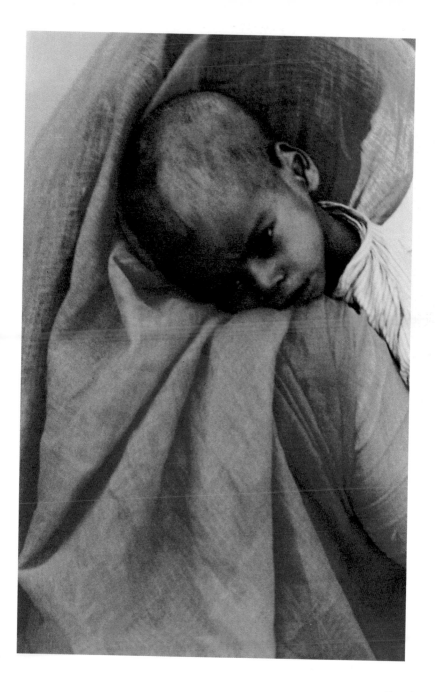

Finkelstein, Nat

1933 New York
Lives in Amsterdam
and New York

Nat Finkelstein learned photography from Alexey Brodovitch, the legendary art director of *Harper's Bazaar*. During the sixties he worked as a photojournalist for the picture agency "Black Star", reporting primarily on the political developments of the subculture of New York City. In the course of this work he met Andy Warhol, whom he photographed with his co-workers at the Warhol Factory. Because of his constant presence, he was able to make photographs of great intensity and intimacy, furnishing an insider's view of that famous studio.

After his break with Warhol, Finkelstein turned to political activities, and it was only in the early eighties that he returned to photography. He again devoted himself to the underground, but he developed a style that could be interpreted as a revival of pop art principles. He delved into the new media, mixed video and color photography and manipulated the pictures with a computer. Today many of his originals are laser prints. In many of his important works, pictures of the subculture are arranged into a solemn altar composed of still and moving pictures. *RM*

▲ Nat Finkelstein
Warhol Factory,
1964/1967

Gelatin silver print
30 x 40 cm
ML/F 1994/5 b

▲ **Nat Finkelstein**
Warhol Factory,
1964/1967

Gelatin silver print
30 x 40 cm
ML/F 1994/5 e

◀ **Nat Finkelstein**
Warhol Factory,
1964/1967

Gelatin silver print
30 x 40 cm
ML/F 1994/5 f

Fischer, Arno

1927 Berlin
Lives in Leipzig

▲ Arno Fischer
Berlin, 1958

Gelatin silver print
33.4 x 50.1 cm
ML/F 1991/171

Arno Fischer is considered to be one of the most outstanding exponents of classical photojournalism in eastern Germany. He had studied in the drawing and sculpture class of the Käthe Kollwitz School in Berlin, later continuing his studies of sculpture under Professor Drake at the Art College of Berlin and under Professor Gonda at the College for the Creative Arts in Berlin Charlottenburg. Encouraged by his teacher, he came upon photography, to which he later devoted all his attention. He photographed people in their social environment, dramatically describing everyday situations and scenes in the German Democratic Republic, but also in the USA. The scene in Berlin showing people, isolated and depressed, sitting among the ruins, is an impressive document of the postwar situation in Germany. Fischer worked for numerous publications, such as *Sybille, Freie Welt* and *Das Magazin*, and in 1967 he was a member of the "Direkt" group. In 1985, following various teaching assignments in Berlin and Leipzig, he became a professor of photography at the College for Graphic design and Book Art in Leipzig. *RM*

► Hannes
Maria Flach
Nude, around 1922

Bromoil print
39.6 x 27 cm
ML/F 1984/40

Gruber Donation

Hannes Maria Flach completed an apprenticeship as a businessman, after which he found a job as a representative at the AEG firm in Düsseldorf. In his spare time he was an active amateur photographer and he became a member of the German Association of Amateur Photographers. In 1925 he participated for the first time in a photographic exhibition. In 1928 he opened his own studio in Cologne-Zollstock. He worked as a freelance photojournalist, which enabled him to give up his job as a representative. Flach's work is strongly characterized by the Cologne progressives. He died in 1936 as a result of maltreatment by a member of the SS. *RM*

Flach, Hannes Maria

1901 Cologne
1936 Cologne

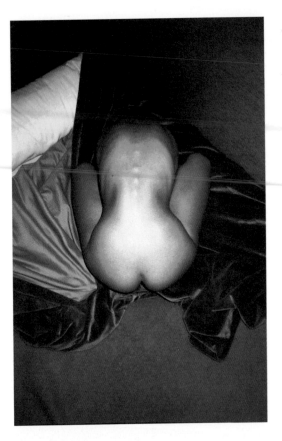

Fontana, Franco

1933 Modena
Lives in Modena

In 1961, Franco Fontana devoted himself completely to photography. In 1964, the magazine *Popular Photography* published his first portfolio, and in 1970 he published his first book, *Modena una Città*. In the seventies his most important subjects were landscapes, which he reduced to abstract basic structures. The horizontal is usually the structural element which, in the form of a horizon, the border of a field, a street or a beach, subdivides the picture area. Restrained and rigorous as the composition was, it was invigorated by intensive, even luminous colors, a creative principle that he also applied to other subjects. In addition to his photographic activity, Fontana also made a name for himself as the organizer of the San Marino International Photomeeting. *RM*

◄ **Franco Fontana**
Beach and Ocean,
1973

Color print
20.2 x 29.4 cm
ML/F 1977/917

Gruber Donation

▶ **Franco Fontana**
Puglia, 1971

Color print
20.2 x 29.7 cm
ML/F 1977/916

Gruber Donation

► Annette Frick
The Toiletries of
Venus, 1990

Color print
212.5 x 142.3 cm
ML/F 1994/2

Uwe Scheid
Donation

Annette Frick studied art in the motion picture class of Robert van
Ackeren. Aside from her artistic work, she campaigned vehemently for
work opportunities for young and alternative artists, founded the Harbor Salon, and was one of the initiators of artistic life on the Cologne
Rheinau Harbor.

    Annette Frick's photographic works deal with feminine history and
feminine sexuality in an aggressive way. This challenging attitude stems
from the consideration that suppression is actually a result of fear, so
that it is not a matter of demanding rights, but of grabbing them and
publicly demonstrating this fact. In this context, Annette Frick's art is
highly political, though she does not misunderstand her art as propaganda. She understands and utilizes the suggestive power of symbolic
images. *RM*

Frick, Annette

1957 Bonn
Lives in Cologne

◀ **Toto Frima**
Untitled, 1985

SX 70 Polaroid print
8 x 8 cm
ML/F 1993/217

Gruber Donation

▶ **Toto Frima**
Untitled, 1988

Polaroid print
87.5 x 56 cm
ML/F 1995/125

Uwe Scheid
Donation

Frima, Toto

1953 The Hague
Lives in Amsterdam

After quitting her studies at an agricultural school, Toto Frima moved to Amsterdam. From 1970 to 1979 she lived there with a painter, for whom she also posed as a model. It was during this period that she created her first Polaroid images, which were to become her most important medium throughout her entire career. During the first years, she used a Polaroid SX 70 camera, with which she recorded her staged sets on the small square format. While doing that, she did not slip into other roles, but always remained herself. She demonstrates how this self changes and is finally converted into the woman herself by means of the multitude of views. This is magnified by her adopting the 50 x 50 cm Polaroid format, which requires more careful staging and more intense working, because the camera is not constantly and arbitrarily available. On the other hand, Toto Frima developed a type of multi-part work steps, in which framed photographic components are assembled into diptychs or triptychs, with the cut edges remaining visible. This reduction into individual elements reduces the tendency of de-individualizing the pictures within their assemblage. Toto uses herself to introduce us to woman as the universe. *RM*

Fuchs, Harald

1954 Rehau
Lives in Cologne

From 1974 to 1978 Harald Fuchs studied graphic design under Professor Erwin Grießel at the Technical College in Würzburg. He continued his studies of graphics from 1978 to 1982 with Professor Rudolf Schoofs at the State Academy for the Creative Arts in Stuttgart and then settled down as an independent artist in Cologne.

In his work, Fuchs concerns himself with natural science research, with astronomy, geometry, anthropology, and with the myths that are also traditionally associated with these subjects. The purposeful association of these elements results in pictures that challenge the views from the former as well as from the latter premise. Fuchs is keenly interested in models of seeing, understanding and interpreting given situations. For the content of his large format photographic works, his installations and lightboxes, he selects not nature itself, but culturally conditioned views of nature. With their penetration of multi-layered levels of imagery, they elucidate the relativity of understanding natural contexts, demonstrating at the same time the extent to which they are related. *RM*

▲ Harald Fuchs
Ashes, from the
series: Structural
Superiority, 1986

Gelatin silver print
78 x 114 cm
ML/F 1988/190

► **Peter H. Fürst**
Hat with Flower,
1971

Color print
50.1 x 39.8 cm
ML/F 1987/27

Peter H. Fürst received his training in his parents' photographic studio. He later visited the Graphic Educational and Experimental Institute in Vienna, working also in the Agfa testing laboratory and in the studios of several photographers. In 1960 he opened his own studio in Cologne. In the years that followed, he dedicated himself to architectural, industrial, and advertising photography. He enjoyed his first big success with a photographic series about the Père Lachaise cemetery in Paris, which he produced on his own initiative.

But his breakthrough as an internationally recognized photographer came in the field of fashion and beauty photography. As the leading photographer of underwear in Germany, he soon earned the nickname "Prince of Lingerie". He was a trendsetter in this field. He lifted it out of the boudoir atmosphere and arranged settings of an entirely different sort, as he did in his series *Hommage à Anton Räderscheidt*. His photograph from that series *Danielle in a Black Basque* was printed as a sensational picture in all the major newspapers. *RM*

Fürst, Peter H.

1939 Leoben,
Austria
Lives in Cologne

▲ **Peter H.Fürst**
Danielle in a Black Basque –
Hommage à Anton
Räderscheidt, 1983

Gelatin silver print
50 x 40 cm
ML/F 1989/181

► **Hideki Fujii**
Untitled (Tableau of
four photographs),
1970s

Color print
14.3 x 9.4 cm
ML/F 1993/219
IV, II, V, I

Gruber Donation

Hideki Fujii was already interested in photography while he was still in school. He began his studies at Nihon University in Tokyo in 1954 and even then assisted Japanese portrait photographer Shotaro Akiyama in his studio. In 1957 Fujii joined the magazine *Fukuzo (Costume)* as a fashion photographer. Three years later, in 1960, he changed over to the Nihon Design Center, which is an advertising agency, and began working there as a commercial photographer. After another three years, in 1963, he became an independent photographer. In 1980 Fujii started a series about Japan and its geishas. In 1984 he became acquainted with Max Factor, who introduced him to the model Hiromi Oka, with whom the photographer went on to work for several years. Hideki Fujii was honored as a fashion and advertising photographer through many exhibitions and awards well beyond the borders of Japan. *MBT*

Fujii, Hideki

1934 Tokyo
Lives in Tokyo

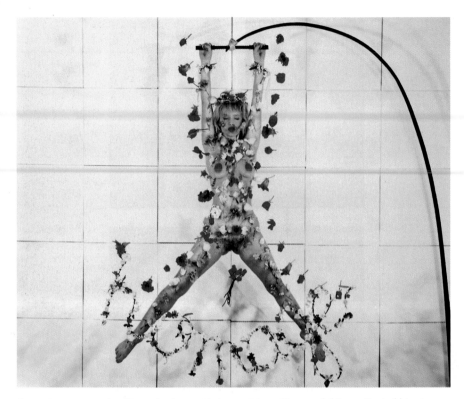

Gantz, Joe

1954 Cincinnati,
Ohio
Lives in Los Angeles

▲ Joe Gantz
Homage II, from:
The Possibility for
Love, 1985

Color Print
77 x 92.8 cm
ML/F 1995/130

Uwe Scheid
Donation

Joe Gantz had an early interest in writing, and this motivated him to study literature at the University of Wisconsin. He then delved into socio-critical research, which he supplemented with photographic documentation. In 1983 he founded the "View Film and Video" company, in which he produced a number of video series with his brother Harry Gantz. The series all addressed the subject of socio-critical research in a novel conceptual way. "People Arguing" and "Taxicab Confessions" were produced along similar guidelines, as was his photographic sequence *Couples*. He would come over with video and photographic equipment whenever one of his volunteer models contacted him by telephone. Earlier, with his photographic series *Inching towards a Leap of Faith, If it's done right, it is* and *The Possibility for Love,* he had investigated various aspects of human relationships. In his latest sequence, Gantz uses a computer to explore Christian and mythological subjects in a hyperrealistic way. *RM*

▶ **Joe Gantz**
From the series:
Self-portraits, 1985

Color print
50.7 x 60.8 cm
ML/F 1986/82

◀ **Joe Gantz**
From the series:
Self-portraits, 1985

Color Print
50.8 x 60.8 cm
ML/F 1986/210

Garanger, Marc

1935 Ezy-sur-Eure,
Normandy
Lives in Paris

Marc Garanger's photographic career began during the time of his military service, which he absolved in Algeria in 1960. At the time, the French army was using all the means at its disposal in its efforts to suppress the Algerian independence movement. In order to gain better control of the population, citizens were to be given French personal identification papers. Garanger was given the assignment of photographing local citizens. He made his pictures outdoors, using a white wall as a neutral background. This resulted in nearly 2000 portraits, at times 200 per day. The majority of the people he photographed were women, who were first compelled to unveil their faces in public. In a sense, this transformed the camera into a weapon with which the population was being culturally demeaned. Later on Garanger made the following comment about these unusual photographs: "I could feel the silent but intense resistance from close proximity. And I want my pictures to be a testimony to that. All the photographs that I made during two years in Algeria should protest against the terror that I have seen." The photographer published a selection of these pictures in his 1982 book *Algerian Women*.

▼ Marc Garanger
Algerian Woman,
1960

Gelatin silver print
40.4 x 30.4 cm
ML/F 1984/51

Gruber Donation

In April 1989, Garanger traveled to Louisiana at the invitation of Kodak to test its new Ektar color film. As a result of this trip, Garanger, in cooperation with the author Yves Berger, published the photographic book *Louisiana, Between Heaven and Earth*, in which he documents the fascinating nature and the lively doings of the population of this southern American state. *MBT*

▶ Jack Garofalo
Wedding, 1972

Gelatin silver print
39.9 x 28.8 cm
ML/F 1977/282

Gruber Collection

Jack Garofalo became known primarily for his social documentary
reports about Pakistan and about the USA. In his 1971 photographic
series *Conflicts in Pakistan* he presented gripping pictures of the war and
of the violent anarchy.

His approach was different when he recorded life in the slums in
big American cities. Then it became critical, yet affectionate. He shows
cheerful children's faces amongst garbage and ruins, youths dancing
in front of a movie house, others forming a defensive group. All these
pictures are filled with tension and movement, including those of the
wedding of a black couple, which he photographed in 1972. The smiling
couple and the bridesmaids and flower children are standing in a
shower of rice and flowers. The brilliant white dresses of the women are
in sharp contrast with the dark suits of the men, and all of them are
smiling under a drizzle of rice. *NZ*

Garofalo, Jack

Born 1924
Lives in Paris

◄ **André Gelpke**
Pin-up Wall Self-
portrait, 1984

Gelatin silver print
25.3 x 25 cm
ML/F 1995/113

Uwe Scheid
Donation

Gelpke, André

1947 Beienrode,
Germany
Lives in Zurich

From 1969 to 1974, André Gelpke studied photography under Otto
Steinert at the Folkwang School of Composition in Essen. In 1975,
Gelpke, together with Rudi Meisel and Gerd Ludwig, founded the
"VISUM" picture agency, which Gelpke left only one year later in order
to work as a freelance photographer. He made many trips, which took
him across Europe, to North and Central America, and to India and
Nepal. Gelpke relies less on "found" pictures, preferring to photograph
situations he has deliberately sought out. His type of photography set
the style for the development of "visualism" in Germany, especially during the seventies. His many years as a photojournalist become evident
in his choice of subjects. In his work, Gelpke distinguishes between two
complementary categories: monologues (in the sense of self-observa-
tion), and dialogs (the relationship with the surroundings). *TvT*

When Arnold Genthe traveled to the United States after completing his studies in philology, he had no intention of settling there, nor was he thinking of becoming a photographer. He had accepted an invitation to teach for two years as a private tutor in San Francisco. Fascinated by this city, particularly by the lively hustle and bustle of Chinatown, he soon decided to buy a camera in order to record his impressions. His first photographs were already so successful that he was able to display them in several exhibitions on the west coast. In 1897 he became independent and established his own studio in San Francisco. He rapidly gained a reputation as an outstanding portrait photographer, and his premises were visited by many prominent personalities.

In April 1906 Genthe lost his entire property during the great earthquake in San Francisco. Only his negatives of Chinatown survived, because they were stored in the safe of a bank. Soon after the catastrophe, Genthe bought himself a new camera, with which he proceeded to create an impressive documentation of the aftermath of the disaster. These photographs, and those of Chinatown, are today valued for their great historical relevance.

In 1908 Genthe moved his studio to New York, where he continued to be recognized as a talented portrait photographer. This is were he made, among many others, his well-known portraits of Greta Garbo.

Genthe, Arnold

1869 Berlin
1942 New Milford, Connecticut

▲ Arnold Genthe
San Francisco, Earthquake, 1906

Gelatin silver print
24.7 x 33.5 cm
ML/F 1993/283

Gruber Donation

◄ **Arnold Genthe**
Anna Pavlova,
around 1925

Bromide print
33.5 x 24.3 cm
ML/F 1977/287

Gruber Collection

► **Arnold Genthe**
Greta Garbo, 1925

Bromide print
33.6 x 23 cm
ML/F 1977/288

Gruber Collection

Genthe photographed her before she had her great successes, and it is said that his portraits were a decisive factor in bringing about the discovery of this star. Another field of special interest for Genthe was dance photography. He photographed numerous famous dancers, among them Anna Pavlova and Isadora Duncan. *MTB*

Gibson, Ralph

1939 Los Angeles
Lives in New York

▼ Ralph Gibson
From: The Somnam-
bulist, 1968

Gelatin silver print
31.4 x 20.8 cm
ML/F 1988/84

Gruber Donation

Ralph Gibson studied photography from 1956 to 1960, while he was still doing his military service in the US Navy. After his discharge, he attended the San Francisco Art Institute from 1960 to 1961. In 1962 he became an assistant to the famous social documentary photographer Dorothea Lange. In 1969 Gibson went to New York, where he became an assistant to Robert Frank, who was making the film "Me and My Brother". Still in that same year, he founded "Lustrum Press", a publishing house through which he published his own books as well as those of other photographers.

In his photographic work, Gibson first concentrated on black-and-white photography. He especially preferred grainy films in order to lend a more graphic effect to his photographs. For subjects, he had a preference for fantastic and surrealistic scenes, which he staged with fragments and excerpts from reality. He liked to use a wide-angle lens for deliberate spatial distortion in order to accentuate the dynamics and tension in his pictures. One of his most successful "Ghost" series was *The Somnambulist* of 1968, which included the picture of the silhouette of a hand in bright light coming through a partly opened door. According to L. Fritz Gruber, this photograph has become the photographer's "signature icon". *MBT*

▶ Ralph Gibson
From: The Somnam-
bulist, 1968

Gelatin silver print
24 x 15.6 cm
ML/F 1993/226

Gruber Donation

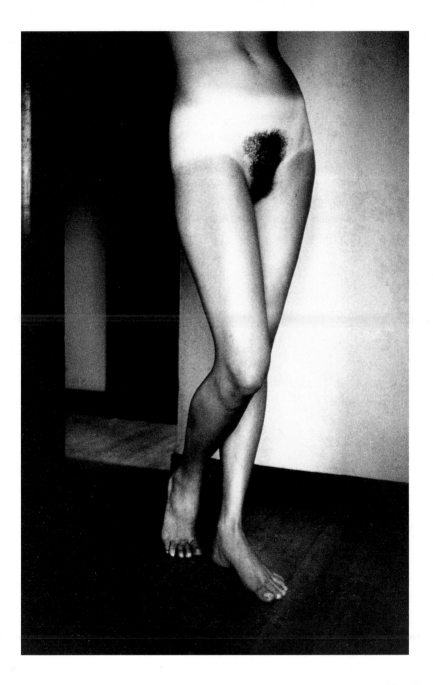

Gidal, Tim N.

(Ignaz Nachum
Gidalewitch)

1909 Munich
1996 Jerusalem

▼ **Tim N. Gidal**
Cheerful Self-
portrait, 1940

Gelatin silver print
17.5 x 12 cm
ML/F 1989/68

Ignaz Nachum Gidalewitch, son of an eastern orthodox Jewish family, became an early member of the Zionist movement, where he also experienced his first photographic impulses. From 1928 to 1931 he studied law, art history and history at the Universities of Munich and Berlin. After succeeding in having one of his pictures published in the *Münchner Illustrierte Presse* in 1929, he adopted the name Tim N. Gidal and dedicated himself entirely to photojournalism. He left Germany in 1933 and continued his studies in Basle, concluding them in 1935 with a thesis on photojournalism and the press. During the same year, he spent two months in Palestine, emigrating there shortly afterwards. Working as a freelance photographer, he soon belonged, together with Kurt Hübschmann and Felix H. Man, to the team of photographers of the *Picture Post*. The photographic reports of that time became the core of the magazine. His photograph *Face* shows a world premiere: the very first television transmission in the Deutsches Museum in the year 1930. In 1940, Gidal returned from a trip to Asia with a reportage about Mahatma Gandhi, which earned him worldwide success. In 1942 he joined the British Army as a volunteer and worked until 1944 as the chief reporter for the army magazine *Parade*. In 1947 Gidal returned to work as a freelance photographer in Jerusalem, from where he traveled throughout Europe. In 1948 he settled in the USA, where he worked for *Life* magazine and where, beginning in 1955, he lectured at the New School for Social Research. Later Gidal became a professor at the Hebrew University in Jerusalem. *RM*

▲ **Tim N. Gidal**
Face, 1930

Gelatin silver print
24.5 x 19.2 cm
ML/F 1989/72

◀ Krzysztof
Gieraltowski
Andrzy Gwiasda
Inzyniew, 1981

Gelatin silver print
59.9 x 40 cm
ML/F 1991/127

**Gieraltowski,
Krzysztof**

1938 Warsaw
Lives in Warsaw

Krzysztof Gieraltowski is regarded as one of Poland's leading photographers. He studied in Gdansk and Lodz. Beginning in 1961, he became more involved with the subjects of industry and fashion in connection with numerous advertising campaigns in Europe. Since 1976 he
has concentrated on portraiture, photographing portraits of politicians,
writers, musicians, actors, scientists, including many members of the
opposition party Solidarnosc. Over time, this has resulted in a fascinating portrait of the Polish intelligentsia, of a society in turmoil. He concentrates on the depiction of facial features and what they express about
the individual. To that end, he asks his subjects to reveal something
about themselves through facial expressions and gestures, and he usually stages his pictures in motion, dramatically and full of tension. *RM*

▶ **Peter Gilles**
Regression, Action
Relic, Museum Lud-
wig, Cologne, 1985

*Gelatin silver print,
mixed media*
216.5 x 126.5 cm
ML/F 1986/221

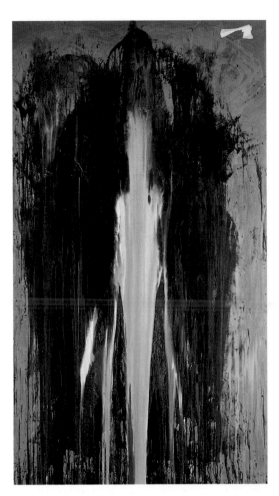

Peter Gilles attracted attention in the seventies through actions that involved the spilling of his own blood. The myth that has been conjured
by blood, especially by human blood, since the dawn of mankind motivated him to an intensive intellectual investigation of ancient African
cultures. In this quest, he came upon the fields of physical and psychic
borderline situations and the opportunities they presented for making
photographs of extreme sensitivity and intense tension. These pictures
are the direct outpouring of feelings, of fear and of emotion. *RM*

Gilles, Peter

1953 Cologne
Lives in Cologne

Gloeden, Wilhelm von

1856 Volkshagen, Germany
1931 Taormina, Sicily

▼ Wilhelm von Gloeden
Taormina, 1901

Gelatin silver print
16.9 x 22.3 cm
ML/F 1995/114

Uwe Scheid
Donation

Wilhelm von Gloeden studied art history in Rostock and painting in Weimar until a lung ailment compelled him to move to Taormina in Sicily in 1877/1878. The experience in that small village was to become a turning point in his life. Von Gloeden was fascinated by the natural pride of its inhabitants and by the liberal atmosphere that he encountered there. He learned photography from a cousin in Naples, Wilhelm von Plüschow, who was already established as a portrait and nude photographer, and from Giovanni Crupi. In 1880 he began to photograph landscapes and typical scenes for postcards. His first outdoor nude pictures were made in 1890, when he began photographing young men from Taormina in classical antique poses. He used landscapes, the seashore, terraces and inner courtyards to stage his visions of these youngsters in an ideal, Homeric-idyllic life. In 1899 the Photographic Society of Berlin invited him to present a lecture on outdoor photography. He became known internationally towards the end of the 19th century. In 1908 he photographed the big earthquake in Sicily and Calabria.

Von Gloeden's prominence lasted until the outbreak of World War I, at which time he was forced to leave Taormina for four years. The fascists condemned his photographs as obscene, and they destroyed the greatest part of his glass negatives and prints after he died in the thirties. It was only in the late sixties and the early seventies that von Gloeden was rediscovered. The cult of the androgynous propelled him into fame as one of the outstanding nude photographers of this century. *TvT*

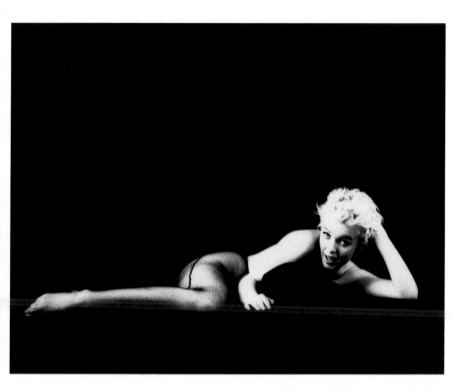

Milton H. Greene began taking pictures when he was 14 years old. He was an assistant to Eliot Elisofon, Maurice Baumann and Louise Dahl-Wolfe. He was only 19 when he established his own studio, in which he later photographed stars like Judy Garland, Cary Grant, Grace Kelly, Elizabeth Taylor, Sammy Davis Jr. and Marlene Dietrich. Greene worked for a particularly long time with Marilyn Monroe, whom he met in 1953 during a photographic assignment for *Look* magazine. With her co-operation he founded "Marilyn Monroe Productions" and over a period of four years he created a large quantity of photographic icons of this star. The two movies "Bus Stop" and "The Prince and the Showgirl" were also made during that period. Greene was active on an international level as a fashion and portrait photographer for such magazines as *Life, Vogue* and *Harper's Bazaar. TvT*

**Greene,
Milton H.**

1922 New York
Died in 1985

▲ **Milton H. Greene**
Marilyn Monroe,
1956

*Gelatin silver print
34.2 x 26.3 cm*
ML/F 1995/121

Uwe Scheid
Donation

Gruber, Bettina

1947 Cologne
Lives in Cologne

Bettina Gruber studied at the College for the Creative Arts in Berlin and then concentrated on photography and video. She was also active as a professional writer. Her artistic work is infused with poetic humor. She skillfully uses historical events, myths or everyday occurrences to create picture stories, either as film and music presentations or compressed into a single photographic image.

For a time she cooperated with Ulrich Tillmann and Maria Vedder in order to work on campaigns. She developed joint video concepts with Maria Vedder, with whom she created the videos *Mama's Little Pleasure (1984)*, *Big Brother Blues (1986)*, *Catfish Tango (1986)* and *Anubis' Heart Attack (1988)*, for which they were jointly awarded the 3rd Marler Video Prize.

Up to then it had not been noticed how slyly caustic these films were, in their contents and also with regard to the perfectionist television industry. Her settings with children's toys, hand-cobbled props and lighting manipulations presented fantasy worlds that were also lateral swipes against the hidden directive that video art would be much more attractive if it could avail itself of the same technical possibilities as videoclips.

With her video work, Bettina Gruber proved that it is not necessary to work perfectly with the medium, or to have perfect technical equipment in order to develop an independent artistic visual language with video. Bettina Gruber often created her photographic work in conjunction with her video work by selecting some of the best situations and then isolating them in the form of photographs. Her photograph *Creatures of the Night* evolved from one of these video projects, and it shows her with an indispensable component of her art: her dog Flicki. *RM*

▼ **Bettina Gruber**
Creatures of the
Night, 1990

Color print
14.8 x 14.5 cm
ML/F 1990/235

Gruber Donation

▶ Ara Güler
Allah (God), 1956

Gelatin silver print
36.5 x 28.8 cm
ML/F 1988/70

Gruber Donation

Ara Güler is considered to be one of the most widely-known international creative artists. He met Marc Riboud and Henri Cartier-Bresson
in 1956 and became a member of the "Magnum" agency. In 1961 a number of photographic editors selected Ara Güler as one of the seven best
photographers in the world. "Time Life" chose him at that time to become their Middle East correspondent. Not much later, he was also appointed by *Paris Match* and the German magazine *Stern* to become their
photographic reporter in the Middle East.

In the eighties, Güler was already able to look back on trips all over
the world.

Güler supplied the press in Europe and in America with a different
kind of picture of people, but also of art and archaeology – pictures like
the one of two dark-robed figures contrasted against a white wall with
the sweeping Arabic writing spelling the word "Allah". *NZ*

Güler, Ara

1928 Istanbul
Lives in Istanbul

**Gursky,
Andreas**

1955 Leipzig
Lives in Düsseldorf

Andreas Gursky studied at the Folkwang School of Creativity in Essen
and at the State Art Academy in Düsseldorf, where he became a master
pupil of Bernd Becher in 1985. His large-format color photographs are
heavily influenced by the work of his mentor. They radiate audacity and
dynamism, and contain an intense if frozen energy. Gursky's pictures
stand out because of his unusual attention to small details, events,
figures and patterns, as compared to the drawing-like objects and isolated forms that are so typical of Becker's work. Gursky's subjects are
topical situations and landscapes. His pictures capture the intensity and
density of human activities as well as the pace of their movements.

Gursky's large-format color photograph *Paris-Montparnasse* (1993)
shows an anonymous multi-story housing block for the working class, a

characteristic symbol of life in a post-industrial megalopolis. As in Richard Estes' photo-realistic paintings of depopulated big cities, in Gursky's portrait of an apartment house complex, too, human beings play a subordinate role. The composition of the picture is systematic and conceptual, cold and distant. There is no staging by the artist, the young Becher scholar merely presents, without comment, that which already exists. But the bleakness and isolation of his objective photography convey, even without any critical commentary by the artist, a clear and unequivocal point of view. *GG*

▲ **Andreas Gursky**
Paris-Montparnasse,
1993

*Color print,
mixed media*
180 x 350 cm
ML/F 1995/97

Ludwig Collection

Haas, Ernst

1921 Vienna
1986 New York

▲ Ernst Haas
Rose, 1970

Color print
28 x 35.3 cm
ML/F 1993/241

Gruber Donation

Ernst Haas discovered his passion for photography early on – in his own words, when he was still a child. His emotional photographs of the arrival of the first train with returning prisoners of war in 1950, when he was a freelance journalist for the magazines *Der Film* and *Heute*, earned him a lot of attention. Soon afterwards, he joined the "Magnum" agency. Beginning in 1951, Haas used primarily color film as a freelance photographer for *Life, Look, Vogue* and *Holiday*. This resulted in the reportage about New York entitled *Images of a Magic City* and the sports reportage *The Magic of Color in Motion*. Haas began to distance himself more and more from sensationalistic photojournalism. In 1964 he produced "Days of Creation" for John Houston's film "The Bible". The corresponding book *Creation* was published in 1971. Now the photographer began to experiment with audiovisual techniques. *Flower Show* and the portfolio *Flowers*, produced in 1983, demonstrate that details of flowers were important subjects in his late work. Shortly before he died unexpectedly in 1986, Haas presented his audiovisual show *Abstracts. NZ*

◄ **Ernst Haas**
Time Life Building,
around 1955

Color print
56.5 x 37.8 cm
ML/F 1983/125

Gruber Donation

Ill. p. 214/215:
Ernst Haas
Homecoming,
1947–1950

Gelatin silver print
ca. 18 x 12 cm
ML/F 1983/122, 123,
124 and
1993/245, 246, 249,
252, 253

Gruber Donation

Häusser, Robert

1924 Stuttgart
Lives in Mannheim

Robert Häusser grew up in Stuttgart, and it was there that in 1934 he bought his first camera obscura for 1 German mark. After graduating from high school, he studied at the College for Graphic Design in Stuttgart from 1941 to 1942. He was a soldier in 1944 and 1945. In 1946 he married Elfriede Meyer, with whom he had a daughter named Renate. From 1946 to 1952 he lived as a farmer on his parents' farm in the Brandenburg Marches. It was there that he made his first portraits of farmers from the surrounding area. In 1950 he began to study under Professor Heinrich Freytag and Professor Walter Hege at the School of Applied Arts in Weimar. He became a member of the German Society of Photographers (GDL), where he was active as a member of the jury and of the presiding committee. In 1952 he moved to Mannheim, where he established a studio for photography.

▼ **Robert Häusser**
The 21 Doors of
Benito Mussolini,
1983

*Gelatin silver print
each 39 x 28 (alto-
gether 140 x 200) cm*
ML/F 1986/93

In 1969 he was a founding member of the Association of Freelance Photodesigners (BFF). Häusser was also very active in cultural politics, and he was a member of the German Association of Artists, the Mannheim Academy for the Creative Arts, the "Darmstadt Secession". In the German Society of Photographers (GDL), he held the offices of business manager, president, and vice-president.

Within the framework of these functions, he initiated a programmatic reorientation of this society, a self-critical examination of its role in the Third Reich, and its reorganization as the German Photographic Academy (DFA).

Häusser made his living with the publication of numerous pictorial books about cities and landscapes, as well as with his work on behalf of artists. This led to close friendships and to the accumulation of an outstanding collection of art. But his main interest lay in his own artistic endeavors, which can be classified into various phases of work. During the first phase of his work, his photographs were mostly narrative, but with a dramatic, heavy and somber expression. During the years 1952 to 1954 he changed to a bright period, creating light and delicate pictures that often seemed more like drawings than photographs. As a result of his work on the parental farm in Brandenburg, farm life always inter-

▲ **Robert Häusser**
In the Housemaid's
Room, 1960

Gelatin silver print
48.8 x 59.3 cm
ML/F 1993/285

Gruber Donation

ested him as well, as evidenced in his series *Home Slaughtering,* a photographic essay in six pictures. Häusser became more and more interested in political subjects and in human fringe situations, like loneliness, bleakness, desperation and death.

His series *The 21 Doors of Benito Mussolini* is one of his principal works. The 21 doors represent the 21 years of the Mussolini government, and they were all in the Duce's villa, just as Häusser photographed them. The pictures are accompanied by the Mussolini statement: "When a man fails together with his system, then the case is ir-

◀▲ **Robert Häusser**
Wing 1-7, 1976

Gelatin silver print
45.5 x 44 cm
ML/F 1993/284

Gruber Donation

revocable." His sequence *Wing* shows his interest in formal compositions and sequential work. In recent years, numerous publications and
retrospective exhibitions have brought his work to greater public attention. For his accomplishments in photography and its recognition as an
art form, and for his cultural-political commitment, as well as for his
overall artistic achievements, Häusser was awarded the title of Professor. *RM*

Heinz Hajek-Halke spent his early childhood in Argentina. Returning to Berlin, he studied at the Royal School of the Arts from 1915 to 1917. After serving in the army, he continued his studies under Professor Ortik and the engraver Baluscheck. He started designing posters for movie companies and worked for the publishing house Dr. Dammert. From 1923 to 1925 he was a fisherman in Hamburg. His first attempts at photography stem from the year 1924. He worked as a press photographer, receiving much inspiration from the photojournalist Willi Ruge. In 1925 he began making his first experimental photographs.

Beginning in 1927, he worked together with the publisher of the *Deutsches Lichtbild*. In 1933 he began his scientific research in the field of microorganisms and macrophotography. In 1937 he traveled to Brazil, where he produced a pictorial essay about a snake farm. In addition, he created abstract pictures and photograms. Starting in 1939, he worked for the German army as an industrial and aerial photographer at the Dornier works. In 1945 he became a prisoner of war of the French, but he escaped and started a snake farm for the production of poison for the pharmaceutical industry. In 1947 he went back to working as a photojournalist and experimental photographer. In 1949 he was a co-founder of the "fotoform" group in Saarbrücken, with whom he participated in their exhibitions. In 1955 he began teaching at the College for the Creative Arts in Berlin as a professor of graphic design and photography. Hajek-Halke is considered to be one of the leading German photographers of the postwar era, who successfully represented photography as an art form, especially with his photomontages and photograms.
RM

▼ Heinz
Hajek-Halke
A Dealer's Shirt, 1955

Gelatin silver print
23.6 x 17.7 cm
ML/F 1977/1006

Gruber Donation

Before entering the photographic profession, Chadwick Hall worked as an editor and theater critic for the magazine *The Nation*. At first he worked for *GQ* and *Esquire* magazines as a fashion photographer and portrait photographer of famous personalities. In 1965 he and his wife, photographer Christa Peters, moved to Europe, where he worked for the magazines *Harper's Bazaar, Elle, Vogue, Queen* and *Stern*. Hall attended events at the College of Design in Ulm, and he also gave lectures in New York. As founder and former president of "The Photographers' Association", he directed the production of advertising films before becoming more specialized in documentary films. He is under contract to the William Morris agency as a scriptwriter. In 1969 he produced a documentary film about Leni Riefenstahl. *MTB*

Hall, Chadwick

1926 New York
Lives in London

▲ Chadwick Hall
Untitled, 1976

Color print
35.8 x 23.6 cm
ML/F 1994/155

Gruber Donation

Halsman, Philippe

1906 Riga, Latvia
1979 New York

▲ **Philippe Halsman**
Dalí Atomicus, 1948

Gelatin silver print
26.6 x 33.3 cm
ML/F 1977/300

Gruber Collection

Philippe Halsman is one of the most original and inventive portrait photographers of our century. Before he turned to photography, Halsman studied electrical engineering in Dresden. It was only in 1928, when he went to Paris, that he established himself as an independent fashion and portrait photographer. In 1940 he emigrated to the USA, where he took on numerous assignments for *Life* magazine. In 1959 he published his successful series entitled *Jump Pictures*, which were photographs of prominent personalities performing jumps in front of his camera. This series is characteristic of the witty humor that permeated all his work. Equally characteristic is the surrealistic touch of his work, which can be ascribed to his friendship with Salvador Dalí. Halsman worked jointly with Dalí on various projects for more than 30 years, expressing the painter's ideas with the medium of photography. *MBT*

▲ **Philippe Halsman**
Dalí's Skull of Nudes,
around 1950

Gelatin silver print
10.8 x 8.8 cm
ML/F 1993/268

Gruber Donation

▲ **Philippe Halsman**
One-Eyed Dalí, 1954

Gelatin silver print
10 x 7.9 cm
ML/F 1993/269

Gruber Donation

▶ **Philippe Halsman**
Mona Lisa Dalí, 1953

Gelatin silver print
33.9 x 23 cm
ML/F 1977/304

Gruber Collection

▲ **Philippe Halsman**
Dancer, around 1946

Gelatin silver print
34.1 x 28 cm
ML/F 1977/302

Gruber Collection

▲ **Philippe Halsman**
Untitled (Pregnant
Woman and Cat),
around 1950

Gelatin silver print, 11.5 x 9 cm
ML/F 1993/273
Gruber Donation

Hamaya, Hiroshi

1915 Tokyo
Lives in Oiso, Kana-gawa-Ken, Japan

▼ Hiroshi Hamaya
A Rice-planting Woman, 1955

Gelatin silver print
29.7 x 19.9 cm
ML/F 1977/312

Gruber Collection

Hiroshi Hamaya started taking pictures at the age of 15. He founded a photographic club in 1933 and in the same year began working for the "Oriental Photographic Manufacturing Company". In 1937 he established himself as an independent freelance photographer. Hamaya quickly became known and in 1940, like many of his colleagues, he went to Manchuria as a photographic war correspondent. Between 1945 and 1952 Hamaya lived in Takada, later moving to the town of Oiso near Tokyo. In 1960 he joined the "Magnum" agency. During the years that followed, Hamaya made many trips to America and Europe.

Hamaya documented the life of his countrymen in many photographic essays. One of the best known of these essays was his series about the Niigata region. Over a period of about 20 years, Hamaya repeatedly photographed the simple life in this countryside, which is covered with snow for three quarters of the year.

In addition to such photographic essays, Hamaya also made a name for himself with his aerial color photographs of landscapes, which he made from an aircraft. Quite unlike Hamaya's photographic reportages, human beings no longer play any roles in his aerial views. The imposing formations of nature speak for themselves in these impressive documents of natural history.
MBT

▶ Hiroshi Hamaya
Women Washing, around 1955

Gelatin silver print
29.9 x 20 cm
ML/F 1977/323

Gruber Collection

Heinecken, Robert

1931 Denver,
Colorado
Lives in Los Angeles

After completing his studies at the University of California at Los Angeles, Robert Heinecken began teaching drawing, design and laboratory techniques there in 1960. In addition to his teaching activities at several American universities and art colleges, Heinecken has also been working as a freelance photographer since 1960. In his work he delves into the subject of elementary human drives and behavior patterns, such as sexuality, violence or social competitiveness. Occasionally he combines sexual images with pictures from social and political realms, thus establishing connections between individual and collective behavior.

Heinecken enjoys using pictures from a variety of media, including magazines, television, even mail-order catalogs. He uses the visual methods of advertising in order to impart a comparable subliminal effect to his work. With the changes of color and black-and-white, photograph and contour line, Heinecken concentrates precisely on those signals of the advertising industry with whose props he composes many of his pictures. The broad spectrum of his techniques includes gelatin silver print, printing on existing picture material, collage, lithography, photogram, photographic emulsions on canvas and environment. Heinecken often combines pictures with texts. The versatility and the provocative effect of his works are echoed in the verdicts of art critics, who have labeled him as typically American, a satirist, chauvinist, guerrilla, dadaist, surrealist and anti-purist.

▼ Robert Heinecken
Porno Photo Litho,
1969

Mixed media
24.3 x 24.9 cm
ML/F 1995/115

Uwe Scheid
Donation

In his work *Porno Photo Litho* Heinecken utilized existing pornographic pictures and layered them until they became unrecognizable. In the tangle of seemingly abstract and dark forms, it is only upon a closer look that one can discern faces and female body shapes. *TvT*

► **Heinz Held**
Willy Fleckhaus behind a Henry Moore Sculpture, 1953

Gelatin silver print
23.4 x 30 cm
ML/F 1988/60

Gruber Donation

At the end of the forties, Heinz Held was the manager of an art gallery in Cologne and a freelance journalist before an exhibition arranged by Otto Steinert entitled "Subjective Photography" inspired him to begin taking pictures himself. It was not long before photography became his most important activity after writing. He worked as a freelance photographer and journalist for a variety of German and European newspapers and magazines and he published several art travel guides. Numerous journeys took him through nearly all the European countries and to Africa, America and the Middle East. Between 1960 and 1963, Held operated the first private photographic gallery in Germany, in which he exhibited mostly journalistic photography.

Held's philosophy about photography is evident in several of his essays and in his book *The Magic of the Banal*, published in 1960. Held was sensitive to the ethical problems of photography, and he generally photographed people from a judicious distance. In addition, he did not pursue the culminating "decisive moment", but the less dramatic, sometimes melancholy human expression that is found in unspectacular everyday situations and actions. *TvT*

Held, Heinz

1918 Zeitz, Germany
1990 Cologne

▲ Heinz Held
Untitled (Girl with
Balloon), around 1960

Gelatin silver print
29.8 x 23.8 cm
ML/F 1995/95

► Heinz Held
London, Picadilly
Circus, 1946

Gelatin silver print
29.5 x 22.8 cm
ML/F 1995/96

▲ **Heinz Held**
Untitled (Lovers and
Policeman),
around 1960

Gelatin silver print
22.2 x 29.1 cm
ML/F 1995/94

▶ **Heinz Held**
Dortmund, 1948

Gelatin silver print
16.4 x 22.5 cm
ML/F 1995/91

▲ **Heinz Held**
Hungarian Refugees,
Andau, 1956

Gelatin silver print
29.4 x 22.9 cm
ML/F 1995/93

Helnwein, Gottfried

Gottfried Helnwein studied at the College for Graphic Design and Research in Vienna from 1965 to 1969. The first modest perfomances took place during this time. From 1969 to 1973 he studied painting at the Academy for the Creative Arts in Vienna and, concerned about everyday violence tolerated apathetically by the public, began a series of hyperrealistic paintings of injured children. In 1970 he and two fellow students staged a performance under the slogan *The Academy is on Fire.* In 1973 he created his first magazine cover for the publication *Profil.* In 1981 he began a series about trivial heroes of the present, and he also initiated a photographic working group whose work was later published under the name *Faces.* Helnwein worked with the media of painting and photography, created stage sets and performances, and campaigned for doing away with the separation of art into categories such as entertaining art and serious art. With this in mind, he published his work on posters and on the covers of large magazines. He also took his art to the streets, as he did in 1988 with *The Night of the Ninth of November* on the occasion of the "International Photo Scene Cologne" between the Museum Ludwig building and the main railway station in Cologne. Helnwein is regarded as one of the most important, politically committed artists in Germany, considering public reaction to be part of his artistic work in the sense of conceptual art. He is always seeking new ways to disseminate that work. *RM*

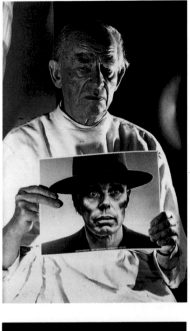

Henle, Fritz

1909 Dortmund
1993 Virgin Islands

▶ Fritz Henle
Pablo Casals, 1972

Gelatin silver print
23.4 x 23.9 cm
ML/F 1990/230

▼ Fritz Henle
Grandma Moses,
around 1947

Gelatin silver print
31 x 27.4 cm
ML/F 1977/332

Gruber Collection

Fritz Henle was only 15 years old when he began taking pictures. After a brief period as a physics student in Munich, he turned to photography. The first publication of one of his photographs, a view of a blast furnace in his home town, took place when he was only 20. Hannah Seewald noticed his work and arranged for his admission to the Bavarian State College for Photography in Munich, where he completed his studies with an honors diploma. Soon afterwards he spent a year in Florence working on an assignment to photograph art treasures of the Renaissance.

The pictures he made of the Toscana during that same period attracted the attention of the steamship line "Lloyd Tourismus", for whom he traveled all over Italy during 1934. In the years 1935 and 1936 he was able to make photographs in China and in Japan. In 1936 he photographed on assignment for "Time-Life", and his pictures were published in *Fortune* magazine. His subsequent trip to America enabled him to establish connections with *Life* magazine, which facilitated his emigration to the USA. He became a US citizen in 1942. Henle photographed the USA as a freelance photojournalist working for a variety of magazines, such as *Fortune, Life* and *Harper's Bazaar*. From the beginning, the Rolleiflex camera was his trademark and America his subject. He mastered the square format with great skill, combining in it both balance and tension. During his active years, he became known as "Mr. Rollei", the personification of the professional photographer.

In 1958 he gave up his studio in New York and settled in St. Croix on the Virgin Islands, where he married his favorite model. Henle, who always strove to accentuate the positive aspects of life and to emphasize them in his pictures, found pristine beauty on the islands, and he considered it his special duty to pass it on. Fritz Henle achieved outstanding fame as a nude photographer, especially in the fifties, and this was

To the artist photographer
Fritz Henle

Pablo Casals

1972

▲ **Fritz Henle**
Frida Kahlo with
her Monkey, 1943

Gelatin silver print
21.5 x 21.7 cm
ML/F 1989/100

the subject of his book *Fritz Henle – Figure Studies*. But he also made
portraits of great personalities of our century, cultivating a special
relationship with the two Mexican artists Diego Rivera and Frida Kahlo.
His uncomplicated philosophy of life enabled him to retain his vitality
and his energy into the last years of his life.

From St. Croix, Henle frequently visited Europe for extended
periods, because he did not want to lose contact with his homeland,
his colleagues, and museums. In 1989 he succeeded in having his
photographs of Paris published, which were made within a short

period of time in 1939. Soon afterwards, his home town of Dortmund organized a large retrospective of his work at the Museum of Art and Art History. He had already donated his archive many years earlier to the University of Texas at Austin, TX, where he had been cataloging it over the years and where he rediscovered many pictures that he had long since forgotten. *RM*

▲ **Fritz Henle**
Nievis, one of Diego
Rivera's models,
1943

Gelatin silver print
23.2 x 22.5 cm
ML/F 1989/137

Henri, Florence

1893 New York
1982 Compiègne,
France

Florence Henri became known in the twenties and thirties as a trendsetting photographer of the New Vision. Her first artistic endeavors were in the medium of painting. Florence Henri studied painting in Berlin and Munich, and in 1924 she went to Paris to attend the Académie André Lhotes and the Académie Moderne, which were directed by Fernand Léger and Amédée Ozenfant. In 1927 she successfully applied for the preparatory course at the Bauhaus in Dessau. There she was inspired in particular by László Moholy-Nagy, under whose influence she began to take an interest in photography. While her course was still in progress, she already began familiarizing herself with the creative possibilities of this medium, and under the guidance of her teacher experimented with unconventional perspectives, multiple exposures, montages, reversal of tonal values and the like.

Florence Henri returned to Paris in 1929. At this point, she had already earned broad recognition for her photographic work and was invited to participate in such important exhibitions as "Contemporary Photography" in Essen and "Film and Photo" in Stuttgart. Photography caused her painting to recede more and more into the background. In Paris Florence Henri began to specialize in portraiture. Her models were mostly celebrities from the artistic and intellectual circles of Paris. In addition, she also created a series of anonymous portraits, so-called

▼ Florence Henri
Günther and Carola
Peill, 1957

Gelatin silver print
17.3 x 16.7 cm
ML/F 1983/13

Carola Peill
Donation

Portrait Compositions. Utilizing unusual perspectives and rigorous and intimate croppings in these pictures, the photographer overcame any distance she might have had towards portraiture.

Another important category in the work of Florence Henri consists of her *Compositions with Mirror.* In these dense arrangements of fruit, plates, reels of thread, perfume bottles or purely geometric objects that were thought out to the last detail, and by the use of one or more mirrors, she succeeded in upsetting the familiar central perspective spatial

arrangement of photography. With this fragmentation of picture planes, Florence Henri reverted to the cubist form elements of her early abstract paintings on one hand, and on the other she showed the definite influence of Constructivism in her clear, constructed still-life compositions with the resulting structuring line arrangements. In her 1957 portrait of Günther and Carola Peill, Florence Henri still made use of this style of visual expression of the twenties and thirties by positioning the couple behind the banister of a staircase. The rods of the banister thus became a constructivist structuring element of the picture's composition.

Florence Henri left Paris in 1963 to retire in the small village of Bellival in Picardy, where she gave up photography altogether and devoted herself entirely to her original vocation of abstract painting. *MTB*

▲ **Florence Henri**
Composition II, 1928

Gelatin silver print
17.2 x 23.9 cm
ML/F 1976/6 IV

Hill, David Octavius

1802 Perth, Scotland
1870 Edinburgh

▼ **David Octavius Hill**
Self-portrait,
around 1843

Calotype
19.8 x 14.6 cm
ML/F 1977/336

Gruber Collection

David Octavius Hill, who entered history as one of the most important portrait photographers, was actually a landscape painter and lithographer. He resorted to photography only as an aid for executing an unusual assignment that he was given in 1843. He was commissioned to paint a group portrait of the 457 men and women who participated in the founding convention of the Free Church of Scotland in Edinburgh. At the suggestion of his friend Sir David Brewster, Hill decided first to photograph all the delegates individually, and then to use the resulting pictures as guides for rendering their facial features correctly in the painting of the group. He was fortunate in securing the cooperation of a competent photographer, Robert Adamson, who had opened a photographic studio in Edinburgh a short time earlier. Even though the photographs were initially intended as a sort of memory aid, the two men did not concentrate exclusively on the facial features of their clients. Instead they created elaborate and well-composed portraits in the style of

painted portraits of their time. Some of their portraits, those that show ladies robed in luxuriant silk garments, are even reminiscent of Dutch painting of the 17th century. Nearly all the portraits were made outdoors, with exposure times of several minutes. As backdrops they used an open-air studio on Carlton Hill and the baroque monuments of Greyfriars Cemetery.

▶ **David Octavius Hill**
Mr Rintoul, Editor
of the *Spectator*,
1844–1848

Photogravure
21.6 x 15.9 cm
ML/F 1995/26

Gruber Donation

Hill and Adamson worked as a team. Hill was regarded as the project leader and as the one who set the artistic tone. Yet Adamson's role, too, appears to have been greater than that of a mere craftsman. Be that as it may, Hill gave up his photographic activities for a time when Adamson died prematurely in 1848. Photographs that Hill made later with a new partner did not reach the quality of earlier photographs made with Adamson's creative input. *MBT*

Hilsdorf, Jacob

1872 Bingen,
Germany
1916 Frankfurt on
Main

▼ Jacob Hilsdorf
Cosima Wagner, 1911

Gelatin silver print
22.5 x 16 cm
ML/F 1993/290

Gruber Donation

Along with Rudolf Dührkoop, Nicola Perscheid and Hugo Erfurth, Jacob Hilsdorf was one of the great portrait photographers of the turn of the century. Unfortunately his work, unlike that of his colleagues, lay forgotten for decades, until it was rediscovered and newly appreciated at the end of the seventies.

Jacob Hilsdorf, like his brother Theodor, learned the craft of photography in the studio of his father Johann Baptist Hilsdorf in Bingen. After completing his apprenticeship, he served as an assistant for a time with Nicola Perscheid in Leipzig. In 1897 Hilsdorf took over his father's studio, and he soon made a name for himself as a talented portrait photographer. His clientele was made up of personalities from the nobility, politics, high finance and the creative arts. His contemporaries particularly appreciated Hilsdorf's talent for conveying something of his sitter's character and psyche in his photographs. During lengthy portrait sittings, which often took place in the model's home rather than in the studio, he would strive to elicit the most natural expression by engaging the sitter in intensive conversation.

During the controversy about the artistic recognition of photography that raged around the turn of the century, Hilsdorf assumed "a forceful front against the 'artist delusions' affected by some of his colleagues" (*German Art and Decoration*). On one hand, Hilsdorf had no ambition to impart a painterly look to his photographs by doing subsequent work on them. On the other hand, he suffered from the "limitations" of photography as compared to painting, lamenting: "It will remain a hybrid art." *MBT*

► **Siegfried Himmer**
The Release on
the Apple, Bettina
Gruber, 1974

Gelatin silver print
40 x 30 cm
ML/F 1995/227

Gruber Donation

Siegfried Himmer completed his apprenticeship in photography in
Wunsiedel and proceeded to study under Professor Hannes Neuner at
the State Academy for the Creative Arts in Stuttgart. From 1965 to 1972
he worked with four partners who called themselves the "Graphicteam
Köln". He has been operating his own studio since 1972, working on assignments from Lufthansa, Bayer AG, Hapag Lloyd, Köln-Düsseldorfer,
Adam Opel AG, and has also published his work in the magazine *Capital*. Himmer stands out because of the great precision of his photographs, and also because of his unconventional pictorial interpretations. In his still-life photographs, he combines classic arrangements
with dramatic use of color in order to generate strong expressiveness in
his pictures. His picture *The Release on the Apple* is a satire of the surreal picture ideas of the seventies, particularly those associated with the
name Sam Haskins. *RM*

Himmer,
Siegfried

1935 Dresden
Lives in Cologne

Hine, Lewis Wickes

1874 Oshkosh, Wisconsin
1940 New York

▲ Lewis W. Hine
Untitled, around 1910

Gelatin silver print
11.8 x 16.9 cm
ML/F 1986/139

Jeane von Oppenheim Donation

▶ Lewis W. Hine
Glass Factory, 1908

Gelatin silver print
16.7 x 11.8 cm
ML/F 1986/138

Jeane von Oppenheim Donation

Lewis W. Hine was the outstanding exponent of social documentary photography in America. He dabbled in various fields before enrolling in the University of Chicago, and in 1900 he moved to New York City to study at New York University. He returned for one summer to the University of Chicago and then went back to New York City to study social work at Columbia University. Encouraged by his friend Frank A. Manny, Hine began to take photographs in 1904. He realized that the camera was an important instrument, both for his investigations as well as for the evaluation of the findings of those investigations. He concluded his pedagogical studies in 1905. He taught at a photographic club, which he also managed and which two years later was joined by Paul Strand. He started working for the National Child Labor Committee (NCLC) in 1906 and he continued working with that organization until approximately 1917. In 1908, under the auspices of the NCLC, he photographed children working in coal mines and factories. In 1909, the Child Welfare League used his photographs in its campaign against child labor. During further travels throughout the USA, Hine documented the social conditions of children, and he also gave lectures on behalf of the Na-

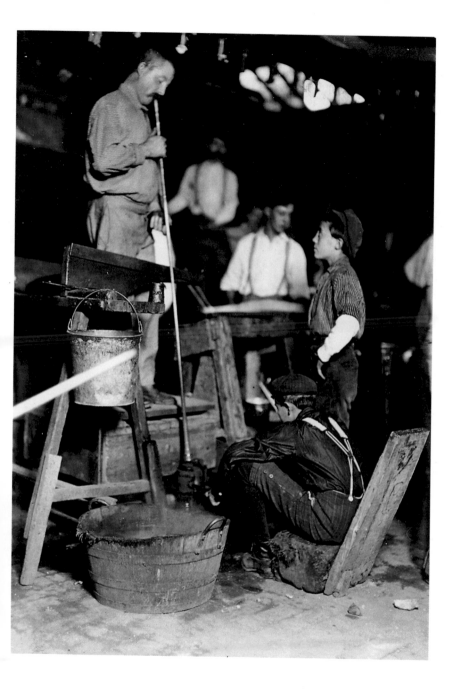

▲ **Lewis W. Hine**
New England
Country Store,
around 1910

Gelatin silver print
12 x 17 cm
ML/F 1986/135

Jeane von Oppen-
heim Donation

▶ **Lewis W. Hine**
Untitled (Hickory,
North Carolina),
1908

Gelatin silver print
11.8 x 16.9 cm
ML/F 1986/140

Jeane von Oppen-
heim Donation

▲ **Lewis W. Hine**
At Work in a Glass-
blowing Works, 1909

Gelatin silver print
11.7 x 16.8 cm
ML/F 1986/136

Jeane von Oppen-
heim Donation

◄ **Lewis W. Hine**
Newsboys, 1909

Gelatin silver print
11.4 x 16.6 cm
ML/F 1986/143

Jeane von Oppen-
heim Donation

tional Child Labor Committee. In 1918 Hine joined the Red Cross, which dispatched him to France. From there he also traveled to Italy and to Greece, returning to New York in June 1919. There he changed his emphasis from an objective, clear documentation without emotion to a more interpretive style of photography. His advertising was now headlined "Lewis Wickes Hine, Interpretive Photography". With his photographs of workers he sought to demonstrate that it was not the machine, but man who created affluence. In 1930, Hine was given the assignment of documenting the gigantic construction project of the Empire State Building. The resulting images, which Hine regarded as "Industrial Interpretation", are probably the most famous of Hine's photographs. *MBT*

▲ **Lewis W. Hine**
Oyster Openers, 1913

Gelatin silver print
9.2 x 11.4 cm
ML/F 1986/141

Jeane von Oppenheim Donation

◄ **Lewis W. Hine**
Untitled, around 1910

Gelatin silver print
16.9 x 11.9 cm
ML/F 1986/145

Jeane von Oppenheim Donation

Hockney, David

1937 Bradford,
England
Lives in London
and Los Angeles

▲ **David Hockney**
Two Lemons and
Four Limes, 1971

Color print
18 x 24 cm
ML/F 1983/109

▶ **David Hockney**
Yves Marie Sleeping,
1974

Color print
24 x 18 cm
ML/F 1983/108

David Hockney studied at the Bradford College of Art and then, from 1959 to 1962, continued his studies at the Royal College of Art in London. Starting in 1963, he taught at several universities in the USA. Together with his academic colleagues Allan Jones, Ronald B. Kitaj and Peter Phillips, Hockney developed an English variant of American Pop Art. It is distinguished by its inclusion of ironic and playful elements in its art. In his swimming-pool pictures, Hockney combines accuracy of rendition with the dissolution of the picture surface in the water.

Hockney's photographic work remained unknown to the public for a long time. In his large format collages of Polaroid SX 70 images, which were exhibited worldwide during the eighties, Hockney made use of cubist elements, such as penetration of picture surfaces, repetition, and the shifting and reversal of values within the composition. *RM*

Hoepffner, Marta

1912 Pirmasens,
Germany
Lives in Kressbronn

▶ Marta Hoepffner
Absurd Canyon, 1950

Gelatin silver print
39.5 x 29.8 cm
ML/F 1989/76

▼ Marta Hoepffner
Firebird, 1940

Gelatin silver print
29.7 x 22.2 cm
ML/F 1989/82

In her youth, Marta Hoepffner was interested in the natural sciences. Her first artistic inspiration came from a relative named Hugo Ball. After her parents moved to Frankfurt on Main in 1928, Marta Hoepffner earned her tuition money by doing office work. After one semester at the Arts and Crafts School in Offenbach, she began studying painting, graphic design and photography at the School for the Arts in Frankfurt on Main, where she derived a great deal of motivation from her teacher, Professor Willi Baumeister. This is also where she became aware of photography as an artform. When the Nazis discharged Baumeister, Marta Hoepffner left the art school and opened her own studio in 1934, where she conducted photographic experiments and created photographic montages and abstract photograms in addition to running her photographic business. After her studio was destroyed in wartime 1944, she moved to Hofheim in the Taunus Region. Here she created her first interference pictures with polarized light. Many of her photographs were inspired by the composition principles of contemporary artists such as Giorgio Morandi and Wassily Kandinsky. In 1949 she was joined by her sister in founding the private Marta Hoepffner Photographic School. The curriculum, which also included theory, was based on the principles of the Bauhaus. The first color photograms were created in 1956. In 1966 she developed her first "variochromatic light objects". In 1971 she moved to Kressbronn on Lake Constance and gradually turned her teaching activities over to her assistant Irm Schoffers. Since 1975 she has only been freelancing. *RM*

Marlin Hoepffner 1950

▲ **Marta Hoepffner**
Composition with
Bottles, 1945

Gelatin silver print
34.8 x 28 cm
ML/F 1989/79

► **Marta Hoepffner**
Nude, Movement,
Solarization, 1940

Gelatin silver print
39.6 x 26.7 cm
ML/F 1989/78

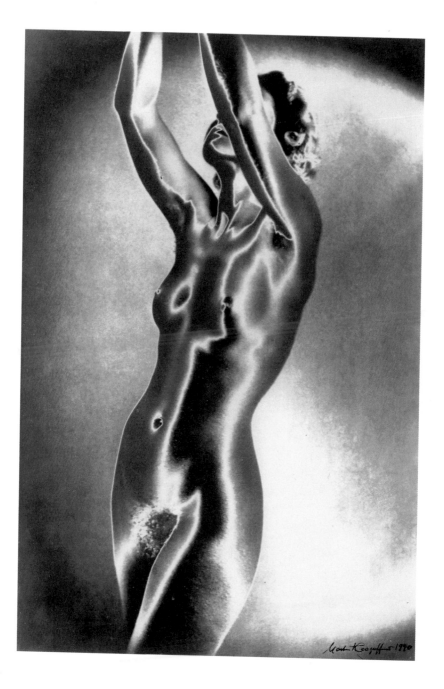

Horst, Horst P.

(Paul Bohrmann)

1906 Weißenfels,
Germany
Lives in New York

▶ **Horst P. Horst**
Mainbocher Corset,
Paris, 1939

Gelatin silver print
24.2 x 19.2 cm
ML/F 1984/66

Gruber Donation

▼ **Horst P. Horst**
Coco Chanel, Paris,
1937

Gelatin silver print
20.6 x 19.7 cm
ML/F 1977/340

Gruber Collection

After a short-lived interest in architecture and an apprenticeship with Le Corbusier in Paris that bored him, Horst P. Horst was attracted to photography through his friend George Hoyningen-Huene. Janet Flanner of the *New Yorker* discovered his pictures in a small exhibition in a bookstore in Paris-Passy. This led to his first job at *Vogue*, the magazine to which Horst was to remain loyal as a fashion photographer for the rest of his life.

Horst may not have revolutionized fashion photography, but he certainly perfected it. The second generation in fashion photography still had to define fundamental concepts for the photographic approach to fashion. How representative or realistic should a fashion photograph be, how much should the respective fashion design be the center of photographic interest, and how much could the photographer's creative concept prevail over these precepts?

What characterizes Horst's photography is his conception of beauty. Horst had undertaken intensive studies of classical poses, he studied Greek sculpture and classical painting, and he devoted particularly meticulous attention to details such as the positioning of hands, because he was aware of the fact that most people did not know what to do with their arms and hands during photography. The combination of

judicious poses and bearings, sparse accessories and simple but skillful lighting is typical of what is often described as Horst's illusionist talent. He magically transformed simple boards of wood into exquisite furniture. cardboard rolls into antique columns and plaster figures into marble sculptures. Whatever he photographs, he transforms everything into elements of his classical, idealized world. But in no way does he suggest that this idealized world now is reality. He leaves it as fiction, as the projection of an ideal conception of beauty. His beauty is distant, cool

◄ **Horst P. Horst**
Elsa Schiaparelli, Paris, 1937

Gelatin silver print, 35.2 x 27.5 cm
ML/F 1992/181

R. Wick Donation

▲ **Horst P. Horst**
Helen Bennett, Paris, 1936

Gelatin silver print, 35.2 x 27.5 cm
ML/F 1992/198

R. Wick Donation

◄ **Horst P. Horst**
Hands, Hands, 1941

Gelatin silver print
35.2 x 27.5 cm
ML/F 1992/185

R. Wick Donation

▲ **Horst P. Horst**
Still Life, 1937

Gelatin silver print
35.2 x 27.5 cm
ML/F 1992/175

R. Wick Donation

▲ **Horst P. Horst**
Vogue Cover, 1938

Color print
41 x 41 cm
ML/F 1992/199

R. Wick Donation

and unapproachable, erotic and seductive, but only as a figment of the mind, like a dreamworld far beyond all animal instincts. This distance between his photographs and reality makes him an artist of his time, who, even though he loves the material world, the illusions of advertising, of beauty and of fashion, and photographs it with devotion, is aware of its illusory character and for that very reason reveres it. *RM*

▲ **Horst P. Horst**
Around the Clock,
New York, 1987

Gelatin silver print
35.2 x 27.5 cm
ML/F 1992/196

R. Wick Donation

Horvat, Frank

1928 Abbazia, Italy
Lives in Paris

▶ **Frank Horvat**
In the Dressing
Room, 1963

Gelatin silver print
39 x 26 cm
ML/F 1977/346

Gruber Collection

▼ **Frank Horvat**
Fellini and a Model,
1963

Gelatin silver print
39.9 x 27.1 cm
ML/F 1977/345

Gruber Collection

Frank Horvat, whose father was a physician, fled to Lugano in 1939 and attended high school there. In 1944 he sold his stamp collection in order to buy a used camera. After returning to Italy, he studied drawing at the Accademia di Brera in Milan. In 1951 he submitted his first photographic essay about southern Italy, which was published by the magazine *Epoca*. His very first color photograph was on the cover. That year he traveled to Paris for the first time, where he met Robert Capa and Henri Cartier-Bresson. In 1952 he traveled to India at his own expense. The photographs that he made there were published by *Paris Match*, *Picture Post* and *Life* magazine. In 1955, Edward Steichen selected some of his pictures for the legendary exhibition "The Family of Man". In 1958 Frank Horvat began working for *Jardin des Modes, Elle* and *Vogue*. He became a member of the "Magnum" agency in 1959, but remained there for only three years. In 1964 he started working for *Harper's Bazaar, twen* and *Elle*. During those years, he began to concentrate more and more on fashion photography.

Horvat is a highly versatile photographer who masters the most varied subjects, ranging from landscape and fashion photography to portraits. He is also very interested in experimentation. He began to stage his settings in the style of old masters, and more recently he has been using computers for picture montages in the surrealistic tradition. *RM*

Hoyningen-Huene, George

1900 St. Petersburg
1968 Los Angeles

▶ **George Hoyningen-Huene**
Bathing Suits by
Izod, 1930

Gelatin silver print
28.8 x 22.6 cm
ML/F 1992/207

R. Wick Donation

▼ **George Hoyningen-Huene**
Greta Garbo, 1951

Gelatin silver print
34.2 x 26.6 cm
ML/F 1977/349

Gruber Collection

George Hoyningen-Huene is considered to be one of the great exponents of fashion photography of the twenties and thirties. His career began after he moved to Paris in 1920, where he took up a great variety of jobs. He worked as a movie extra and studied painting. It was during this period that he also developed close contacts with the Paris art scene, befriending such legendary figures as Kiki de Montparnasse and Jean Renoir. He soon made a name for himself as a talented fashion draftsman, and his work was published in *Harper's Bazaar* and *Fairchild's Magazine*. In 1925 he was hired by *Vogue*. It was approximately at that time that he began to turn more and more to photography, starting to work as an assistant to the American photographer Arthur O'Neill. A year later Hoyningen-Huene made his first fashion photographs for *Vogue* and thus gained entry into this field, in which he was particularly active in the years from 1926 to 1945. Many of his photographs from this period reflect his fascination with Surrealism and his interest in Greek antiquity. Flawless compositions with well-balanced lighting are as much a trademark of this photographer as are the inclusion of classical Greek props and surrealistic effects.

In 1935 Hoyningen-Huene moved to New York, and in 1936 he began working almost exclusively for *Harper's Bazaar*. In 1943 he published his picture books *Hellas* and *Egypt*. In 1946 he went to Hollywood, where he became a sought-after portrait photographer of American movie stars, and where he also became active in motion pictures, especially short features. *MBT*

◀ Hanns Hubmann
Willy Brandt kneel-
ing at the Monu-
ment to the Warsaw
Ghetto, 7 Dec.1970

Gelatin silver print
49.9 x 49.8 cm
ML/F 1987/174

▶ Hanns Hubmann
Reception in Beverly
Hills, Zsa Zsa Ga-
bor, Curd Jürgens
and Louella Parsons,
the Hollywood gos-
sip columnist, 1957

Gelatin silver print
31 x 22.5 cm
ML/F 1987/179

**Hubmann,
Hanns**

1910 Freden
Lives in Kröning

Hanns Hubmann studied at the Technical College in Darmstadt, but he
soon became interested in photography, and in 1931 moved to Munich
in order to study photography at the Bavarian State Institute for Photography. His first Leica photographs already brought him success. Upon
his return to Germany from working for the administration of the St.
Moritz health resort, he was arrested for alleged propaganda lies
against the Nazis. Barely avoiding a concentration camp, he went underground for a while, reappearing in 1935 to work for the *Berliner Illustrierte Zeitung*. In 1936 he moved to Berlin, from where he traveled to
America. In 1937 he published a reportage about the Spanish Civil War.
In 1939 he began working for *Life* magazine and in 1941 he was drafted
to become a war correspondent for *Signal*. In 1945 he began working for
the latter's American equivalent, the *Stars and Stripes*. He traveled to
every continent, interesting himself primarily in political and sports
events. His photograph of *Willi Brandt kneeling at the Monument to the
Warsaw Ghetto* is a picture that became synonymous with an event and
which was published around the world. *RM*

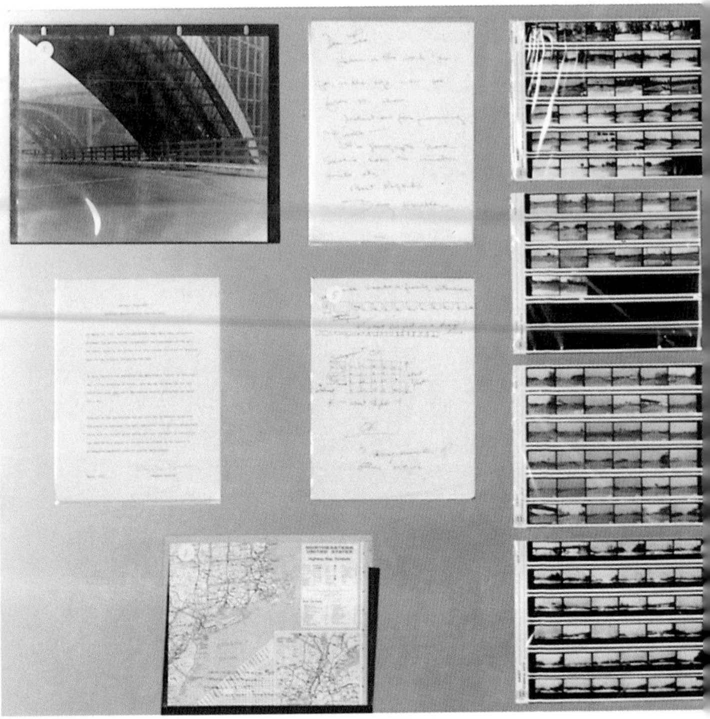

**Huebler,
Douglas**

1924 Ann Arbor,
Michigan
Lives in Bradford,
Massachusetts

Like Allan Kaprow and Joseph Kosuth, Douglas Huebler is both an artist
as well as an art critic and theoretician. In Huebler's conceptual work of
the seventies the documentation of his projects played a significant role
– not least because that is the only way they are perceivable to a viewer.

As an example, for his *Variable Piece No. 48* (1971), Huebler assembled documentation of an art project. In a statement that is as much a
part of the work as a series of photographs, a road map, a letter to New
York gallery owner Leo Castelli and a sketch of the arrangement of the
photographs, Huebler describes the idea behind the project. On the 13th
of May 1971 he made more than 650 photographs along the way from
his adoptive home town of Bradford, Massachusetts, to the Leo Castelli
Gallery in New York City.

These pictures document the totality of the optical impressions that
he encountered on his way. Every photograph was made from a specific
spot on the highway, in the direction of travel and looking as far as the

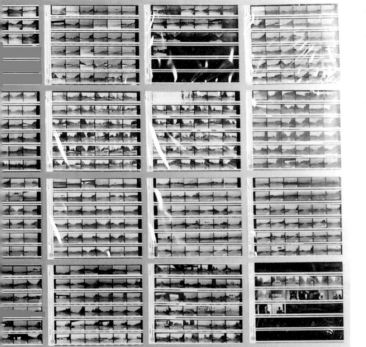

◄ **Douglas Huebler**
Variable Piece
No. 48: Document
for the entire visual
"Appearance" as far
as the eye can see,
1971

Collage, Gelatin silver
print, printed piece,
sketches
210 x 97 cm
ML/F 1985/37

Ludwig Donation

eye could see. Huebler then had someone else select the "most aesthetic" view from the entire crop of photographs and he displayed an appropriately enlarged print of that view along with the rest of the documents.

Huebler is not especially interested in aesthetic problems, even if the enlargement of the New York bridges still has a particular photographic appeal. In general, less emphasis is placed on the quality of the photographs than on the best possible capture of the various optical phenomena. According to Huebler, "These documents are not necessarily interesting on an aesthetic level, meaning that they are not intrinsically 'works of art'. I use these documents to record a condition of absolute coexistence between 'picture' and 'language'." *GG*

◀ Peter Hutchinson
J-Blue Jay, 1974

Color print
50.5 x 75.7 cm
ML/F 1979/1351 I

Hutchinson, Peter

1930 Thornton Heath, Surrey, UK
Lives in New York

Like Joseph Kosuth, conceptual artist Peter Hutchinson is interested in the abstract definition of words and things. Together with Jean Le Gac, Bill Beckeley, Mac Adams and Roger Welch, Hutchinson belonged to a subgroup of Concept Art that became known in New York during the seventies as narrative or descriptive art. These artists combined the systematic analysis of art with poetic stories in which the artist/author often also acted as the main protagonist.

With his three-part work *J-Blue Jay* (1974) from his *Alphabet Series*, Hutchinson explores the connotation of the letter "J". He combined photographic images, anecdotal text and three-dimensional letter shapes in order to explore their elementary properties. In his text about the letter "J", the artist wrote: "I had been reading 'Memories, Dreams and Reflections' by Carl Jung and was sitting outside my cottage in Provincetown trying to 'let go' as Jung described it, 'sink into my unconscious and have a mystical, mythical experience'. Nothing happened except that my head began to throb strangely. At that moment a bird alighted on the seat of my bicycle a few feet away. It was a Blue Jay. It looked at me for a few moments as though it carried some important message." *GG*

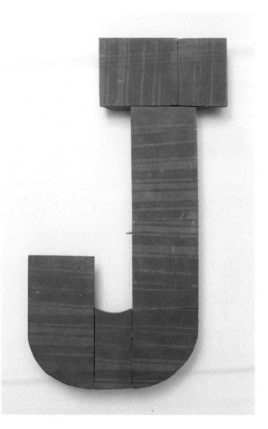

► **Peter Hutchinson**
J-Blue Jay, 1974

Handwritten text
panel
50 x 75.7 cm
ML/F 1979/1351 II

Blue Jay

The letter "J" from the Alphabet Series

I had been reading "Memories, Dreams and Reflections" by Carl Jung and was sitting outside my cottage in Provincetown trying "to let go" as Jung described it, "sink into my unconscious and have a mystical, mythical experience. Nothing happened except that my head began to throb strangely. At that moment a bird alighted on the seat of my bicycle a few feet away. It was a Blue Jay. It looked at me for a few moments as though it carried some important message.

► **Peter Hutchinson**
J-Blue Jay, 1974

Wood, ceramics
ca. 35.5 x 23 x 2.5 cm
ML/F 1979/1351 III

Huth, Walde

1923 Stuttgart
Lives in Cologne

Walde Huth originally wanted to become an actress or a mime, but she acceded to her father's wishes for her to take up studies, on a trial basis, at the State School for Applied Art in Weimar. There she experienced light as a formative, creative medium and began to be interested in photography. After completing her studies she started working in the color film processing division of Agfa in Wolfen. In 1945 she earned a living for herself and her parents with portrait photography and with photographic assignments. In 1953 she opened a studio for fashion and advertising photography in Stuttgart. Her work for the *Frankfurter Illustrierte Zeitung* provided her with an entry into fashion photography in Paris and in Florence. This resulted in an exclusive contract with the *Frankfurter Illustrierte Zeitung*. Walde Huth's open-air fashion work and her talent for bringing fashion and architecture into an expressive relationship found great acceptance. In 1955 Walde Huth turned down a contract with *Vogue* and, after marrying Cologne architectural photographer Karl Hugo Schmölz, opened a joint studio for fashion, advertising, architectural and furniture photography.

▼ **Walde Huth**
Ambre, from:
Fashion of the
Times, 1962

Gelatin silver print
51.7 x 50.5 cm
ML/F 1989/107

After her husband passed away in 1986, she dissolved his additional large studio and concentrated entirely on making photographs according to her own conceptions. Her photographic cycles *One Hundred Unwritten Letters, One Hundred frozen Steps, Eyed Existence, Foamborn, Became a Figure* or *Busts, Bosoms and other Delicacies* exemplify her very individual approach to staged photography, to photographic found objects, and to serial photography. *RM*

▲ Walde Huth
Patricia, Evening
Robe by Jacques
Fath, Paris 1953

Gelatin silver print
57.4 x 49.7 cm
ML/F 1989/110

▲ **Walde Huth**
Lucky Décolleté,
Dress by Dior,
Paris, 1955

Gelatin silver print
35.2 x 21.9 cm
ML/F 1983/110

Gruber Donation

▶ **Walde Huth**
33rd letter from the
cycle: One Hundred
Unwritten Letters,
1979

Color print
40.5 x 28.5 cm
ML/F 1982/16

▶▶ **Walde Huth**
7th letter from the
cycle: One Hundred
Unwritten Letters,
1979

Color print
40.5 x 28.5 cm
ML/F 1982/5

▶ **Walde Huth**
51st letter from the
cycle: One Hundred
Unwritten Letters,
1979

Color print
40.5 x 28.5 cm
ML/F 1982/20

▶▶ **Walde Huth**
9th letter from the
cycle: One Hundred
Unwritten Letters,
1979

Color print
40.5 x 28.5 cm
ML/F 1982/7

Ignatovich, Boris

1899 Lutzk, Ukraine
1976 Moscow

▲ Boris Ignatovich
Hermitage, 1929

Gelatin silver print
36.7 x 45 cm
ML/F 1992/131

Ludwig Collection

Boris Ignatovich began his professional career as a newspaper editor and journalist in Moscow in 1918. From 1922 to 1925 he worked mostly for humor magazines like *Lore* or *The Laughing Man*. In 1923 he also took up photography and during the years that followed worked as a photographer and correspondent for various magazines. He achieved his first success with a photographic essay about village subjects. In the late twenties, Ignatovich had close contacts with Alexander Rodchenko, with whom he founded the photography section of the "October Group" in 1930. The friendly relationship with Alexander Rodchenko had a marked influence on Ignatovich's photographic style. He enjoyed taking pictures from extremely low or high camera positions, and through these unconventional viewing angles he discovered a new way of looking at everyday life. A sightseeing flight over Leningrad presented him with new opportunities in his search for unconventional perspectives.

▲ **Boris Ignatovich**
Isaac Cathedral,
1930

Gelatin silver print
19 x 24 cm
ML/F 1992/124

Ludwig Collection

◄ **Boris Ignatovich**
Smokestacks and
Factories of a
Leningrad Industrial
Complex, 1931

Gelatin silver print
13 x 18 cm
ML/F 1992/125

Ludwig Collection

▲ **Boris Ignatovich**
Leningrad Docks
with Aircraft Wing,
1929

Gelatin silver print
16.5 x 23.5 cm
ML/F 1992/126

Ludwig Collection

▶ **Boris Ignatovich**
Factory Window,
1929

Gelatin silver print
24 x 17.8 cm
ML/F 1992/127

Ludwig Collection

He created bird's-eye views such as *Smokestacks and Factories of a Leningrad Industrial Complex,* in which architecture is rendered as an abstract-constructivist composition.

After 1929 Ignatovich was the leading photographer, together with Rodchenko, of the magazine *Daijosch*. During that period, Ignatovich particularly enjoyed the use of symbols, slogans and picture captions, which he applied not just as intellectual supplements to his photographs, but in which he also saw forms with their own graphic appeal.

After the war Ignatovich devoted himself especially to landscape and portrait photography, concerning himself also with the opportunities of color photography. *MBT*

Ionesco, Irina

1935 Paris
Lives in Paris

▼ Irina Ionesco
Nude with Two
Doll's Heads,
around 1973

Gelatin silver print
39.2 x 39.4 cm
ML/F 1984/69

Gruber Donation

Irina Ionesco spent her childhood in Romania and moved to Paris in 1951. She traveled for several years and busied herself with painting before becoming interested in photography. In March 1974 she exhibited her photographs in the Nikon Gallery in Paris and attracted a great deal of attention. In the years that followed, her pictures were published in numerous publications, such as *Femmes sans tain*, *Nocturnes* and *Temples aux miroirs*. In many of her picture series she alludes to situations reminiscent of those described in the novels of Alain Robbe-Grillet, in particular *Memories of the Golden Triangle*: lavishly dressed women, bedecked in jewels and in motionless poses, provocatively offering themselves partly disrobed, often wearing leather chokers, bracelets, gloves or corsages to conjure hints of possibly impending or perhaps already existing violence. In her photographs, Irina Ionesco conjures up a world of beautiful women in connection with eroticism and death. Irina Ionesco's photographs became controversial because she used her own pubescent daughter as a model, depicting her in poses that were no less erotically suggestive than they would be with more mature models. Her photography always seemed to move along the fine line between purely erotic pictures and artistic compositions, and she had to struggle for the recognition of her earnestness. Today the content of her photographs is closer to the spirit of the times than ever before, and at present her pictorial expression can even be considered as restrained. In this respect she can be regarded as a trendsetter in her field. *RM*

Gottfried Jäger completed an apprenticeship as a photographer and studied at the State College for Photography in Cologne. In 1960 he became a lecturer in photographic technology at the School of Arts and Crafts in Bielefeld. In 1973 he became a professor of artistic fundamentals of photography and photographic design at the Professional College of Bielefeld. Jäger devoted himself to experimental photography and the effects of light, concentrating on a so-called "generative photography". He concerned himself with photographic series and with investigations of vision and perception, and he created the concept of "image-conveying photography" on a systematically constructive basis. In 1970 he developed so-called "apparatus art" and since 1980 he has been delving into color developments, color cycles and color spectra as well as the plain colorfulness of photographic paper.

Jäger was also a very successful teacher, and he founded a school in Bielefeld that has significant influence on the development of contemporary artistic photography in Germany. Aside from that he was an effective president of the German Photographic Academy (formerly "GDL", the Society of German Photographers), whose new orientation he was instrumental in bringing about. His writings, particularly "Image-conveying Photography" are regarded as standards in the field of experimental and fundamental photography. *RM*

Jäger, Gottfried

1937, Burg near
Magdeburg
Lives in Bielefeld

▲ **Gottfried Jäger**
Two Squares, a
three-part photo-
graphic work, 1983

*Gelatin silver print
each 24.5 x 24.5 cm*
ML/F 1985/161 I-III

Jansen, Arno

1938 Aachen
Lives in Cologne

Arno Jansen grew up in Düsseldorf, and in 1959 he began studying photography under Professor Otto Steinert at the Folkwang School in Essen. In 1974 he became a professor at the Technical College in Cologne. During the years of his teaching tenure, the Technical College of Cologne graduated numerous artists who today are known internationally and who devote themselves to photography.

Jansen grew up in a generation that, even though it was based largely on "subjective photography", more and more followed impulses emanating from America, for instance from Ralph Gibson or Lee Friedlander, who brought "visualism" to Europe in the seventies. While "visualism" possesses certain parallels to "subjective photography", it is however less constructive and rational, oriented less towards the Bauhaus. Instead, it is more emotion based and it observes less from the outside than it does from the inside. Jansen dedicated himself to this sensitive outlook on evolution and decay, he assisted a little with arrangements, and beyond that he observed with calm but also with anticipation the changes taking place around him in time, eventually making his photographs when time had left sufficient traces. Jansen thus evolved into a master of the clear transposition of the natural chaos that he observed. As much as he did not like to intervene in the events of his decaying still-life arrangements, his pictures are equally strongly characterized by his insistence on perfection. From the judiciously undertaken, well-balanced illumination to the carefully selected camera position, everything was designed to achieve a maximum of clarity in the composition. Jansen pursued his main subject of still-life photography both in black-and-white as well as in color, which he kept very subdued, although he also did not shirk from a saturated blue color as a background.

In the eighties, Jansen discovered another subject: portraits of mature women. They intrigued

▼ Arno Jansen
Heating Period, 1975

Gelatin silver print
40.3 x 30.5 cm
ML/F 1988/92

Gruber Donation

him for the same kind of reasons as his still-life pictures did: the tension-filled relationship of still evident beauty and feminine radiance and approaching decline.

With the closing of the Technical College of Cologne, Jansen lost his professorship, whereupon he devoted himself entirely to his own pursuits. *RM*

▲ **Arno Jansen**
My Ex, 1975

Gelatin silver print
40 x 30.1 cm
MLF 1994/183

Gruber Donation

◀ **Piotr Jaros**
Embrace, 1994

Gelatin silver print
191 x 200 cm
ML/F 1994/9

Jaros, Piotr

1965 Myslenice

Piotr Jaros studied at the College of Art in Cracow until 1989, and since then he has been working in the fields of photography and installations. An important theme in his staged photographs are the relationships and interactions between people. The large-format black-and-white enlargements from his series *Embraces* depict couples sitting in stiff poses in front of a neutral background. Familiar from Christian iconography, the subject of Madonna and Child is applied to same-sex and opposite-sex relationships. A paradoxical effect is generated by the fact that the individuals appear indifferent and unemotional, in spite of the proximity and intimacy signaled by their bodily contact. Because they are life-size, the portraits in the exhibit situation combine with the space of the observer and confront him with their static presence. *TvT*

▶ **Dimitri Jermakov**
Tiflis on the Banks
of the Kura River,
around 1895

Gelatin silver print
22 x 28.8 cm
ML/F 1994/339

Gruber Donation

Dimitri Jermakov completed his training at the Military School of Topography. In 1870 he made a number of photographs of Georgian architectural monuments, which he signed on the back as "Artistic Photograph by His Highness the Shah of Persia". In the same year, Jermakov
opened a photographic studio in Tiflis. Between 1870 and 1915 he traveled through Persia, the southern coast of the Crimea, Central Asia and
the Northern Caucasus. Jermakov worked on new methods for the manufacture of collodion plates and he also made sketches for a mobile laboratory. In 1874 he was decorated by the French Photographic Society.
During the war between Russia and Turkey, between the years of 1877
and 1878, Jermakov was a photographer for the military mail department of the general staff of the Caucasus Army. In 1883 he was named
Art Photographer of the Archaeological Society of Moscow. Commissioned by the French expert on oriental matters Jean Mourier, he made
photographs of wall paintings in various churches in 1884. In 1889 he
published his *Historical Photo Album of Georgia*. During his active time,
Jermakov assembled a total of 127 albums. Today a large collection of
his work and his equipment is in the Historical Museum of Georgia.
MBT

**Jermakov,
Dimitri**

around 1845/48
Tiflis, Georgia
around 1915/17 Tiflis

Johnston, Alfred Cheney

1885 New York
1971 Oxford,
Connecticut

Alfred Cheney Johnston was already an amateur photographer while he was studying art at the School of Fine Arts in New York City. His career as a glamour photographer began when Flo Ziegfeld hired him as the official photographer of his show dancers, the Ziegfeld Girls. Johnston perfected a wonderfully titillating skill of making his dressed models look nude. He photographed all the silent movie stars of the twenties, among them the Dolly Sisters, Gloria Swanson, Mae Marsh, the Fairbank Twins, as well as Lillian and Dorothy Gish.

His photographs shaped the image of Hollywood of that decade. Johnston was a master of the art of draping, of only partially covering models with fabrics and lace, so that the stars did not have to undress and still appeared disrobed to their fans. That skill soon earned him the nickname "Mr Drape".

With the end of the silent movie era, his fame also began to fade. Other photographers followed in his steps and portrayed the heroines of the new era. Johnston's work lay forgotten for many years and it was only recently rediscovered in the USA. There is practically no demand for his photographs in the art market. The L. Fritz Gruber Collection is

▲ Alfred Cheney
Johnston
Dolly Sisters, 1923

Gelatin silver print
Diameter: 26 cm
ML/F 1977/354

Gruber Collection

▲ Alfred Cheney
Johnston
Blanche Satchell,
1925

Gelatin silver print
32.5 x 26.3 cm
ML/F 1977/363

Gruber Collection

▲ **Alfred Cheney Johnston**
Gloria Swanson, 1920

Gelatin silver print
34 x 26.5 cm
ML/F 1977/359

Gruber Collection

one of the very few European collections that can boast a large body of his work and that has regularly exhibited and published it since 1983.

Johnston continued his work for another seven years after Ziegfeld passed away, and in 1940 he retired to his country home in Oxford, CT, where he devoted himself to nude photography until he died. *RM*

▲ **Alfred Cheney Johnston**
Reclining Nude,
around 1950

Gelatin silver print
24 x 32.9 cm
ML/F 1977/366

Gruber Collection

**Jüttner,
Burkhard**

1952 Delmenhorst
Lives in Bonn

Burkhard Jüttner studied photography with Arno Jansen at the Cologne Factory Schools. In 1972 he embarked on study tours to Spain and Northern America. In 1974 he became an assistant to Professor L. Fritz Gruber, in charge of artistic aspects of Photokina. In 1975 he undertook study tours of Northern Africa, Spain, and France. Following his exams he became a master student under Professor Arno Jansen. From 1978 to 1981 he taught at the Technical College of Cologne. Since then he has been working as photojournalist based in Bonn. In 1980 he founded a portrait studio with a workshop gallery for artistic photography. In 1983 he founded a photographic production company. In 1995 he expanded its scope by adding an on-line imaging agency called "Vintage" for artistic photography with emphasis on travel photography and artistic portraiture.

Since taking his first photographs, Jüttner – in the tradition of visualism – pursued a type of photography following an underlying conceptualism. Thus his thematic picture sequences of the seventies were later increasingly structured on the laws of immanent contradiction. Jüttner took pictures of bathing beaches and hot-dog stands in opposite seasons and formulated starkly composed views of absolute emptiness. He

▼ Burkhard Jüttner
The Queen of Fried
Foods, 1987

Gelatin silver print
13.9 x 25 cm
ML/F 1989/3

contrasted truncated advertising billboards with their adjacent environment – the pavement, a landscape or a fence in the background. Jüttner's photographs appear to obey the strict laws of the documentary and still be pure products of imagination. In particular his beach scenes satisfy a high degree of what could be called "photographic minimalism". Frequently, his comparisons are so astounding that they appear to be stage productions. Still, Jüttner has never allowed himself to be affected by current trends such as the large format or image manipulation, but, once he had discovered it, has remained faithful to the small format, to "straight photography", and to the principle of technical perfection. *RM*

▲ **Burkhard Jüttner**
Roncalli Circus, 1976

Gelatin silver print
21.5 x 14.5 cm
ML/F 1994/187

Gruber Donation

▲◄ **Burkhard Jüttner**
War Veterans, 1975

Gelatin silver print
22.3 x 15.2 cm
ML/F 1977/950

Gruber Donation

Julius, Kurt

1909 Hanover
1986 Kirchheim

▶ **Kurt Julius**
Margot Hielscher,
1949

Gelatin silver print
38.9 x 29.2 cm
ML/F 1991/100

▼ **Kurt Julius**
Hildegard Knef, 1947

Gelatin silver print
40.5 x 30.3 cm
ML/F 1991/96

Kurt Julius studied photography at the Bavarian State Educational Institute for Photography in Munich. Upon completing his education with distinction, he worked nationally, as well as internationally, in various photographic studios from 1931 to 1938. After receiving his diploma as master photographer he took over his father's studio in Hanover. In 1943 his apartment and studio were destroyed during an air raid and Julius lost his entire archive. He spent 1944 in a labor camp from which he managed to escape in 1945. After the end of the war he returned to Hanover, set up a new studio and devoted subsequent years to portrait, advertising, architectural and theatrical photography. In addition, he acted as photojournalist at movie studios in Göttingen, Hamburg, and Munich.

The first edition of *Stern* magazine in 1948 showed a portrait by Julius, the famous face of the young actress Hildegard Knef. Between 1949 and 1979 Julius documented all the opera and ballet performances and stage plays of the National Theater of Lower Saxony in Hanover.

In 1980 he finished his contract work, and he and his wife moved back to Kirchheim in the vicinity of Munich. There, he continued to work exclusively on a freelance basis, mostly portrait studies, for example, a series on his neighbors or his photographer colleagues. His portraits are composed unconventionally and frequently imply an individual's ambiance in an understated manner. *RM*

Kahle, Birgit

1957 Cologne
Lives in Cologne

▲ Birgit Kahle
Untitled, 1983

Gelatin silver print
50.7 x 50.7 cm
ML/F 1985/138

Birgit Kahle began her collaboration with performance artist and painter Peter Gilles toward the end of the seventies. In part she documented his performances in photographs, in part she included herself, while sometimes she made herself the object of photographic productions. This latter idea, finally developed into her own artistic methodology. Her first cycle, *Fear is Man's Best Friend*, which was directed at external threats, as well as at internal ones brought about by disease, resulted in immediate success in the arts world. In the years following she developed her projections with increasing simplicity, arrived at cuts and tears in large for-

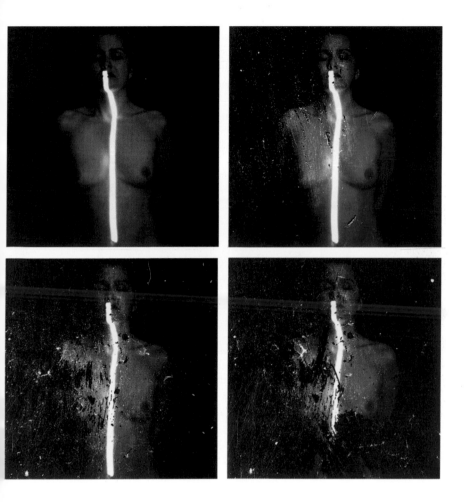

mats, and in later series re-composed her image fragments to create new collage-like works. Finally, in her Polaroid series she arrived at the question of the perceptibility of the beyond and its existence, conveyed through the perceptibility of the pictures themselves. Being an artist couple, Birgit Kahle and Peter Gilles thrive on the constant, reciprocal stimulation of their work. *RM*

▲ **Birgit Kahle**
Untitled, 1984

*Gelatin silver print
each 50.7 x 50.7 cm*
ML/F 1984/134 I-V

◀ Yousuf Karsh
Jawaharlal Nehru,
around 1949

Gelatin silver print
31.3 x 25.3 cm
ML/F 1977/376

Gruber Collection

Karsh, Yousuf

1908 Mardin,
Armenia
Lives in Ottawa,
Canada

"The never-ending fascination for the people I photograph rests in what I call their internal strength. It is part of the hard-to-define secret hidden within everyone, and the attempt to capture this on film has been my life's work." This is how portrait photographer Yousuf Karsh has described the attraction of his work.

In 1924, aged 16, Karsh emigrated to Canada, where he came under the care of his uncle, George Nakash, an established photographer. That is when Karsh discovered his enthusiasm for photography and, with the aid of his uncle, learned the fundamentals of the art. In 1928 George Nakash succeeded in securing an apprenticeship for his nephew with Boston portrait photographer John H. Garo, to whom Karsh owes a well-trained observant eye for the great masters of painting and art in general. In 1932 Karsh opened his own portrait studio in Ottawa. There, he quickly acquired the reputation of an exceptionally talented portrait photographer, whose clientele included high-ranking individuals in politics, science and the arts. In 1941 Karsh achieved his international breakthrough with his famous portrait of Winston Churchill. This pic-

▲ **Yousuf Karsh**
Winston Churchill,
1941

Gelatin silver print
31 x 25.3 cm
ML/F 1977/369

Gruber Collection

◄ **Yousuf Karsh**
George Bernard
Shaw, 1943

Silver bromide print
33.8 x 26.9 cm
ML/F 1977/372

Gruber Collection

ture of a grouchy, critical Churchill appeared on the title page of *Life*
magazine and to this day it is still one of the most reproduced portraits.

In his work Karsh did not restrict himself to his own studio. He actually preferred to take portraits of his sitters in their own familiar environment. Karsh published his portraits in numerous photographic volumes
and frequently revealed the pictures' histories in brief anecdotes. *MBT*

▲ **Yousuf Karsh**
Martha Graham, around 1959

Gelatin silver print
32.6 x 26.4 cm
ML/F 1977/375

Gruber Collection

▶ **Benjamin Katz**
André Kertész, 1980

Gelatin silver print
28.3 x 21.6 cm
ML/F 1985/93

Gruber Donation

▶▶ **Benjamin Katz**
Georg Baselitz, 1977

Gelatin silver print
29.2 x 22 cm
ML/F 1983/150

Katz, Benjamin

1939 Antwerp
Lives in Cologne

▲ **Benjamin Katz**
Marcel Broodthaers
and Marie-Puck
Broodthaers, 1972

Gelatin silver print
21.5 x 28.5 cm
ML/F 1983/155

▶ **Benjamin Katz**
The König Brothers,
Paul Maenz Gallery,
Cologne, 1981

Gelatin silver print
30.9 x 23.9 cm
ML/F 1982/308

▶▶ **Benjamin Katz**
Markus Lüpertz,
1979

Gelatin silver print
28.5 x 21.5 cm
ML/F 1983/151

Benjamin Katz moved to Berlin in 1956. There he studied at the Academy of Fine Arts under professors Jaenisch, Böhm and Lortz. Between 1958 and 1959 Katz was a member of the youth ensemble under the direction of Thomas Harlan. In 1963 he and Michael Werner founded the Galerie Katz/Werner. After barely one year he and his partner separated and he operated the gallery by himself until 1969. His staged over 60 exhibitions, showing artists such as Markus Lüpertz, Georg Baselitz, Marcel Broodthaers, and Antonius Höckelmann. In 1972 Katz settled in Cologne and made photography his medium of choice. He evolved into the chronicler of the Rhine art scene, with Cologne and Düsseldorf as the main centers.

Benjamin Katz did mostly freelance work, but especially during the eighties he also frequently collaborated with museums, in particular the Museum Ludwig in Cologne, where he was commissioned to document the large exhibition "Art of the West" in 1981. However, he also documented other large events in great detail, such as the exhibitions "From Here On", "Picture Fight" and "documenta IX".

Even after turning to photography, his artist friends from his gallery days remained an important subject for him. He took pictures in studios and pubs, at exhibitions, gallery openings and artists' parties and documented exhibition set-ups and performances. Katz is not only an

outstanding portrait photographer, he has also developed essay-like picture sequences to perfection. Situations come alive when three or four
closely related image sequences capture the gist of a situation in an almost movie-like manner. He often recognizes something in otherwise
inconsequential moments that is characteristic of the people who are
involved. It is in those situations at the periphery of action that his extraordinary sense for the essence blossoms out.

By now his archive has developed into an inexhaustible source for
all those who organize exhibitions or who publish books. There is hardly
anyone in the art scene, be it artist, collector, gallery owner, museum
director, critic or journalist, who has not been captured by his camera at
least once. *RM*

▲ **Benjamin Katz**
Nam June Paik and
Reinhold Mißelbeck
with Shigeko Kubo-
ta's Buddhas, 1986

Gelatin silver print
30.5 x 24 cm
ML/F 1987/132

▶ **Benjamin Katz**
James Lee Byars,
1981

Gelatin silver print
30.9 x 23.9 cm
ML/F 1982/189

▶▶ **Benjamin Katz**
Joseph Beuys, 1981

Gelatin silver print
23.9 x 30.9 cm
ML/F 1982/196

◀ Peter Keetman
Reflecting Drops,
1950

Gelatin silver print
23.2 x 30.3 cm
ML/F 1989/46

▶ Peter Keetman
Thousand and One
Faces, 1957

Gelatin silver print
30.3 x 23.3 cm
ML/F 1989/48

Keetman, Peter

1916 Wuppertal-
Elberfeld, Germany
Lives in
Marquartstein

Peter Keetman received his first photographic inspirations from his father, who was a serious amateur photographer. At the age of 19 he attended the Bavarian State Educational Institute for Photography in Munich, where he obtained his apprentice's diploma in 1937. After two years at the studio of Gertrud Hesse in Duisburg he worked as an industrial photographer for the C. H. Schmeck Company in Aachen. In 1944 he returned from military service seriously wounded and unable to work. Nevertheless he continued his studies at the aforementioned Institute in the master's program and then studied under Adolf Lazi in Stuttgart. Following his legendary exhibition in Neustadt/Hard in 1949, Keetman was one of the founding members of the "fotoform" group. Together with the other members of this group (Toni Schneiders, Wolfgang Reisewitz, Ludwig Windstoßer, Siegfried Lauterwasser and Heinz Hajek-Halke) he showed his first pictures at Photokina in 1950. Keetman became known internationally through his experimental work, in particular *Reflecting Drops*. RM

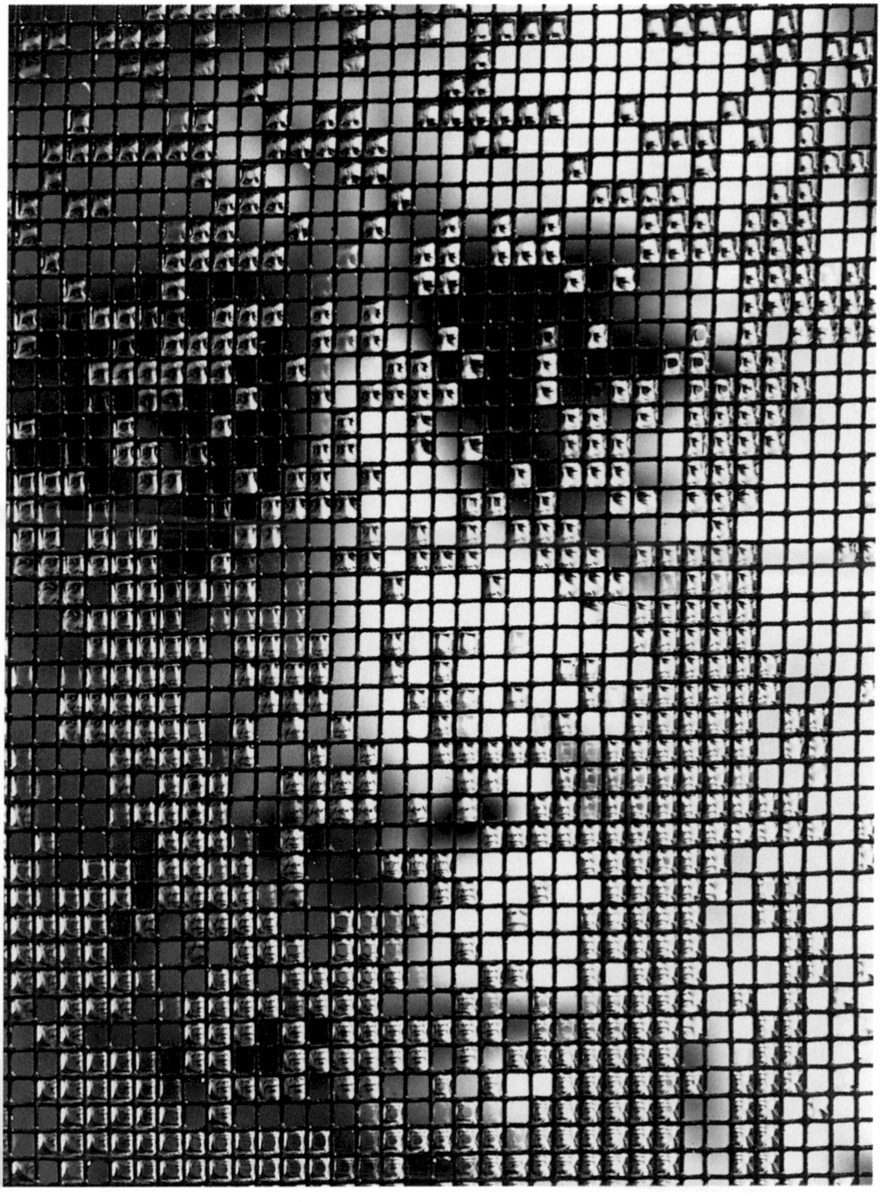

◄ **Peter Keetman**
Volkswagen Plant,
1953

Gelatin silver print
30.2 x 23.1 cm
ML/F 1989/49

▲ **Peter Keetman**
Screw Pump, 1960

Gelatin silver print
30.2 x 23.6 cm
ML/F 1989/44

Keetman | 323

Keiley, Joseph Turner

1869 New York
1914 New York

▼ Joseph T. Keiley
A Small Piece of
Paris, 1907

Glycerin Platinotype
19.1 x 14 cm
ML/F 1995/35

Gruber Donation

Joseph Turner Keiley began as a lawyer on Wall Street in New York City before turning to photography and participating in amateur exhibitions. In 1899 he became a member of the "Camera Club" and, as one of four American members elected to the "Linked Ring" in London, he participated in this club's photographic salon exhibitions. He and Alfred Stieglitz were friends. Together they worked on improving tone values in the development of platinum prints. In addition, they experimented with mercury and uranium salts in order to impart platinum prints with more realistic flesh tones. Keiley wrote phototechnical and historical articles for *Camera Notes*, a journal which Stieglitz had been publishing since 1896. In 1902 Stieglitz founded "Photo Secession", and Keiley was among the founding members, who included such famous photographers as Frank Eugene, Gertrude Käsebier and Edward J. Steichen. The object of "Photo Secession" was, among other things, to "promote photography as a means of artistic expression". In 1903 Keiley participated in the Salon Photographique des Photo-Clubs Paris. At the same time he was a member of the editorial committee of Stieglitz's publication *Camera Works*. This unique journal published not only the works of "Photo Secession" members but also of European photographers, including Heinrich Kühn, Hans Watzek, Frederick H. Evans and Julia Margaret Cameron, who was already dead at that time. *AS*

▲ Joseph Turner
Keiley
The Last Hour, 1901

Photogravure
12.1 x 19.2 cm
ML/F 1995/31

Gruber Donation

▶ Joseph Turner
Keiley
Portrait of Miss de
C., (Mercedes de
Cordoba), 1902

Photogravure
12 x 16 cm
ML/F 1995/32

Gruber Donation

Kempe, Fritz

1909 Greifswald,
Germany
1988 Hamburg

Following an apprenticeship in photography with his father, Fritz Kempe
set up his own studio for industrial and advertising photography in
Berlin. In 1945 he settled in Hamburg, where he worked as an editor and
publisher. Between 1949 and 1974 he was director of the State Regional
Picture Center Hamburg. In 1952 he founded the Hamburg Collection
for the History of Photography which has its present home in the Museum of Fine and Industrial Arts. This made him the founder of one of
the first photographic collections in a museum. His photographic works
have concentrated on portraits, although he is mainly credited for his
organizational and publishing activities. His publications have contributed significantly to the recognition of photography as an artistic
medium. *RM*

Keresztes, Lajos

1933 Budapest
Lives in Nuremberg

After graduating from high school, Lajos Keresztes worked in a graphic arts office in Budapest. However, when the Soviets crushed the 1956 uprising, he fled to Austria and then to Germany. In 1957 he began to study architecture in Munich and, in the context of graphic design, discovered photography. Following his studies of photography at the Technical College of Cologne, Keresztes settled in Nuremberg in 1963, where he set up a studio and devoted himself to subjects such as fashion, cosmetics, calendars, magazine illustrations and advertising.

In his photography he continued in the realm of graphic design. In particular in his series *Light-Symbols-Language* he combined linguistic, photographic and graphic media. Symbols and photography were largely interwoven. At times the photograph was reduced to geometric forms, at times these forms were painted or drawn on the image. Texts were used as counterpoints.

In subsequent years, Keresztes concentrated mainly on purely photographic work, although he remained faithful to his interest in minimal images, cropped sections, geometric forms, simple symbols, and color relationships. In the tradition of visualism, the incidental, for example a colored area, is pushed to the center, drawing the eye to the incidental. The picture *Atlantis, Signals of Imagination* from the year 1982 shows just such a structured and colored relationship. It is also an example of his talent for using close croppings for making a picture come to the point. Since handing his professional studio over to his son in 1992, he has devoted himself exclusively to subjects of his own preference. *RM*

▼ Lajos Keresztes
Titicaca, Bolivia,
1988

Color Print
50 x 40 cm
ML/F 1995/90

▲ **Lajos Keresztes**
Atlantis, Signals of
Imagination, 1982

Color Print
30.5 x 41.1 cm
ML/F 1993/303

Gruber Donation

Kertész, André

1894 Budapest
1985 New York

As a young man André Kertész found a photographic manual in an attic and decided to become a photographer. After the death of his father, however, he first attended the Academy of Commerce and, like his foster father, worked in the Budapest stock market. In 1913 he acquired his first camera, an Ica. In 1914 he served in the Austro-Hungarian army. One year later he began to work seriously as a photographer. He was wounded and for a year was paralyzed. All of his negatives were destroyed in 1918 and he returned to the stock market. In 1922 he received an honorary diploma from the Hungarian Association of Photography. Between 1922 and 1925 he lived in Paris, where he sold prints for 25 francs in order to make a living. During this time he began his collaboration with the *Frankfurter Illustrierte*, the *Berliner Illustrirte*, the *Nationale de Fiorenza*, *Sourire*, *Uhu*, and *Times*. In Paris he began his series *Distortions*. In 1927 he had his first solo exhibition and in 1928 met Brassaï, whom he introduced to photography. Kertész acquired his first Leica and did documentaries for *Vu*. In 1933 he married Elisabeth Sali and published his first book on children. Three years later he emigrated to New York and signed a contract with Keystone. In 1937 his began his as-

▼ André Kertész
Esztergom, Hungary,
Swimmer, 1917

Gelatin silver print
19 x 24.7 cm
ML/F 1977/394

Gruber Collection

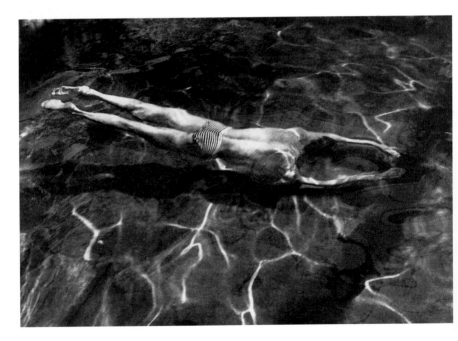

sociation with *Vogue, Harper's Bazaar, Collier's, Coronet,* and many other magazines. In 1944 he became an American citizen. He attempted to bring over his negatives from Paris, but more than half were lost in transit. From 1949 to 1962 he worked continuously for Condé Nast.

After a serious disease, Kertész decided to cancel all his contracts and work exclusively as a freelance photographer. In addition to many honors, he received an honorary doctorate from the Royal College of Art and he was also made a member of the French Legion of Honor. Many of Kertész's photographs, for example *The Fork, Esztergom, Swimmer,* the *Park Bench,* or *Mondrian's Atelier,* are now among the most famous photographs of this century. *RM*

▲ **André Kertész**
The Fork, 1928

Gelatin silver print
19.4 x 24 cm
ML/F 1977/381

Gruber Collection

◄ **André Kertész**
Paris, 1930

Gelatin silver print
19.4 x 23.5 cm
ML/F 1977/391

Gruber Collection

► **André Kertész**
My Friend Brassaï,
1963

Gelatin silver print
24.5 x 17.7 cm
ML/F 1977/388

Gruber Collection

► **André Kertész**
Park Bench, 1962

Gelatin silver print
16.6 x 24.7 cm
ML/F 1977/383

Gruber Collection

▲ **André Kertész**
Avenue Junot, 1927

Gelatin silver print
24.2 x 19.6 cm
ML/F 1977/389

Gruber Collection

▶ **André Kertész**
Champs Elysées, 1930

Gelatin silver print
24.5 x 18 cm
ML/F 1977/384

Gruber Collection

Kiffl, Erika

1939 Karlsbad,
Western Bohemia
Lives in Düsseldorf

▲ **Erika Kiffl**
Untitled, from:
Stone Age, 1979

Gelatin silver print
22.5 x 22.5 cm
ML/F 1986/207

▲▶ **Erika Kiffl**
Untitled, from: The
Kingdom of Signs –
Homage to Roland
Barthes, 1984

Gelatin silver print
80 x 80 cm
ML/F 1986/179

Between 1957 and 1959 Erika Kiffl studied under Joseph Fassbender at the Technical College of Krefeld. Thereafter, until 1961, she studied graphic arts, layout and photography under Walter Breker at the Arts Academy of Düsseldorf. Until 1965 she was art director of the magazine *Elegante Welt* in Düsseldorf. Since 1978 she has been a freelance photographer. The Museum Ludwig owns several of her works of the late seventies showing artists in their studios and still-life pictures. Erika Kiffl has been dealing with this topic for 20 years. "Artists' studios and what takes place there have always held an exceptional fascination which both paralyzed and inspired me." In 1990 the "Rounds 1979 – 1989" was published, presenting a selection of over 600 photographic works resulting from photos of this art academy. Scenes in studios appear sensitive and discreet. In particular when the artist is not pictured, the atmosphere is shaped by work, transition, and openness. Erika Kiffl's works reflect creativity, be it in the form of an unfinished piece of art, an artist in motion, or material in a space. The works from the group *Stone Age* show excerpts of sculptures photographed by her in museums in Europe and the USA. By emphasizing a part of a sculpture – a dynamic view from below or light cast over parts of it – stones appear to trade their static nature for a moment of dynamism in a temporary release from rigidity brought about by the photographer. *AS*

▲▲ **Erika Kiffl**
Gerhard Richter,
1977

Gelatin silver print
22.5 x 22.5 cm
ML/F 1986/200

▲ **Erika Kiffl**
Joseph Beuys'
Studio, 1978

Gelatin silver print
22.5 x 22.5 cm
ML/F 1986/185

▲▲ **Erika Kiffl**
Ulrike Rosenbach
during her Perfor-
mance: My Power is
my Lack of Power,
1978

Gelatin silver print
22.5 x 22.5 cm
ML/F 1986/182

▲ **Erika Kiffl**
Konrad Klapheck

Gelatin silver print
22.5 x 22.5 cm
ML/F 1986/194

Kimura, Ihei

1901 Shitaya, Tokyo
1974 Tokyo

▶ **Ihei Kimura**
Basket Carriers, 1957
Gelatin silver print
26.2 x 17.2 cm
ML/F 1977/389
Gruber Collection

▼ **Ihei Kimura**
Child in Playpen, 1957
Gelatin silver print
26 x 17 cm
ML/F 1977/401
Gruber Collection

Ihei Kimura learned photography in the autodidactic manner. In 1924 he opened his own photostudio in Nippori, Tokyo. Together with Iwata Nakayama and Yasuo Nojima, both experimental photographers, he founded *Koga* (photo image), a photographic journal. Right from the publication of the first issue *Koga* was intended to be regarded as an instrument of pure photography – away from abstraction and experiments without camera, but aimed at the world of objects and the art of realism called "Shashin". In 1933, together with Yonosuke Natori, graphic artist Hiroshi Hara and others, Kimura founded the "Nihon Kobo" (Japan Studio) Association, which fostered the integration of photography with other crafts. In the first exhibition of the "Nihon Kobo", group action photographs by Kimura were shown. In so doing, the group promoted photography as art for a specific purpose. Within one year of the group's founding, basic discussions among group members led to defections and new foundations. Together with other defectors, Kimura formed "Chuo Kobo". Like "Nihon Kobo", this group stood for realism and the close connection between photography and society, but it took a more radical stance. Following the foundation of the International Society for Culture, an institution for the dissemination of Japanese culture internationally, Kimura became a member of the photographic section in 1934. In 1938 and between 1940 and 1944 Kimura was in Manchuria as a war photographer. In the fifties he worked as a reportage photographer on several trips to Europe. *MBT*

Klauke, Jürgen

1943 Kliding
Lives in Cologne

Jürgen Klauke studied at the College of Art and Design in Cologne and at first worked mainly in the field of drawing. In 1970 he began working with photography, using himself as a model. In 1971, in his book *I and I, Day Drawings and Photographic Sequences*, he provided an insight into his work hitherto. He considered provocation to be an important tool for compelling the consumer of art to contemplate. In his earlier self-portraits he presented himself decorated with the accessories of a society hungry for sex yet incapable of love. Remarkably early on he used himself as an object of the androgynous, a topic which is currently ubiquitously dominant in society, the arts and media. He realized many of his topics in the form of videos, but the photographic sequence remained his central medium. From the very beginning, his sequences dealt with questions of sexuality, the psyche, identity relative to the body and its marketing, seeing his own body only as a stand-in and as an example. Even political behavior, belief in authority and obedience play a part in some of his sequences. Of essence, however, is also the humor which has been added to serious subjects and which ultimately suggests despair, as if laughter were the only way to deal with one's inability to effect change.

His cycle *Formalizing Boredom*, created between 1979 and 1980, was Klauke's breakthrough to international fame. He developed a pictorial language of stricter, yet less transparent rules of behavior that were characterized by isolation and by an inability to communicate, but which were followed by the protagonists who appeared in the pictures. This was the first time he laid out his cycles in the form of multi-part, tabular displays, which added a meditative and simultaneously prosaic tone. In Klauke's art there is an exceptional congruence between work and person or art and life, which other artists often labor strenuously to achieve. With him this is a matter of course and effortless. Klauke frequently gives the impression of being one of the last bastions of rebelious resistance to the excessive laxness and comfort of present-day society. His presence at his performance art has a persuasive effect, because his art and its message are obviously important to him. One of his more recent cycles, *Pro Securitas*, for the first time distanced itself somewhat more from his own person and, at the same time, pursued the goal of penetration and formal strength. By linking a skeletal reduction of forms to monumental size, it is not only the self-portrait that allows an association with relics. *RM*

▲ **Jürgen Klauke**
Formalizing Bore-
dom, 1979–80

Gelatin silver print
each 180 x 110 cm
ML/F 1985/40 I-V

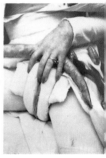

▲ **Jürgen Klauke**
Self-performance,
1972/73

Gelatin silver print
each 56.8 x 41.9 cm
ML/F 1987/128

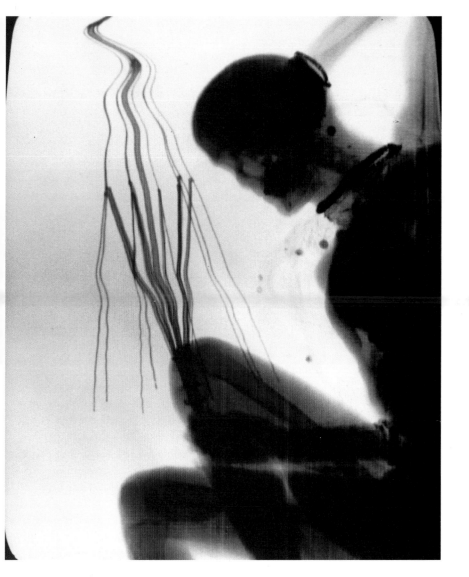

▲ **Jürgen Klauke**
Self-portrait, from:
Pro Securitas, 1987

Gelatin silver print
60.8 x 51.6 cm
ML/F 1993/304

Gruber Donation

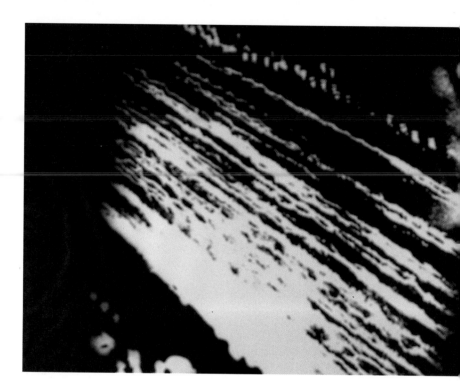

Klein, Astrid

1951 Cologne
Lives in Cologne

Between 1973 and 1977 Astrid Klein attended college in Cologne. At the beginning of the eighties, when she went public with her large-format black-and-white works, she struck the nerve of the times. Just as it became fashionable no longer to let photographs stand on their own, but to edit and manipulate them, she presented photographic work that made precise statements, that took a stand and that showed clear reasons for having been manipulated.

Astrid Klein was not striving for painterly effects, for a blurring of photographic contours, but edited her photographs in order to achieve a greater clarity of content. She used mostly already printed, screened images, related them to topics picked up by the tabloid press, cut them out, enlarged, singled them out and reassembled them so that abstract or systematic relationships in the pictures would suddenly become transparent and obvious. Still, there is always a disquieting residue, because editing is obvious, screening is too distinct and the authenticity of

a straight photograph is lost. With her treatment, the message by the press denounces itself as piecework, as pretense and as fiction, containing only fragments of truth. Astrid Klein has maintained and improved this approach to her art for nearly two decades, at times scaled down and then again enhanced and embellished. *RM*

▲ **Astrid Klein**
30.1.33, 1983

Gelatin silver print
126 x 345 cm
ML/F 1983/157

◀ **Astrid Klein**
Installation,
Kunsthaus Kassel,
1983

*Gelatin silver print,
mixed media, wall
painting*
220 x 294.5 cm and
220 x 290 cm
ML/F 1995/22

Donation
Prof. Jacobs

Eine peinigende Vorstellung: daß von
einem bestimmten Zeitpunkt ab die
Geschichte nicht mehr *wirklich*
war. Ohne es zu merken, hätte die
Menschheit insgesamt die Wirk-
lichkeit plötzlich verlassen; alles,
was seitdem geschehen sei, wäre gar
nicht wahr; wir könnten es aber nicht
merken. Unsere Aufgabe sei es nun,
diesen Punkt zu finden, und so lange
wir ihn nicht hätten, müßten wir in
der jetzigen Zerstörung verharren.

Klein, William

1928 New York
Lives in Paris

▲ William Klein
Rome, Guard at
Cinecittà, 1959

Gelatin silver print
27.4 x 30.4 cm
ML/F 1977/418

Gruber Collection

With his shots of the fifties and sixties, William Klein created an uncompromising rejection of the then prevailing rules of photography. His artistic career began in 1948 in Paris, where he trained as a painter. He discovered his passion for photography in the early fifties. Initially Klein utilized it as an abstract tool of expression, but he soon became fascinated with its possibilities for dealing with the real world. In 1954 Alexander Liberman, then art director at *Vogue,* hired the young photographer for his fashion magazine. This launched Klein's career as a fashion photographer, a journey marked by his ambivalent and ironic approach to the world of fashion. He did not want to continue with mundane fashion poses, but wanted to take "at last real pictures, eliminating taboos and clichés". Klein worked with unconventional wide-

► **William Klein**
Playing Children
with Gun, 1954/55

Gelatin silver print
23 x 30.4 cm
ML/F 1977/419

Gruber Collection

◄ **William Klein**
Tokyo, 1961

Gelatin silver print
24 x 29.8 cm
ML/F 1977/411

Gruber Collection

Backstage Alaïe, Paris 1986 ... To Faur Happy Birthday & so more." Bill Klein 1988

To Renata with love & kisses .... Backstage Goalisti, Paris 1985 Bill Klein 1988

to Fritz Happy Happy Birthday & many happy returns ♡ Bill

angle and telephoto pictures, with unconventional lighting and flash effects and with intentional motion blurs. Although he worked for *Vogue* until 1966, he did not consider fashion photography to be his real calling but rather what he calls "serious photographs". By that he meant uncompromising, unadorned documentaries about large cities like New York, Rome, Moscow, and Tokyo. Books about these cities enabled him to enjoy great successes. Around 1961 Klein gave up still photography – with the exception of a few jobs for newspapers and advertising – in favor of motion pictures. His politically committed and unconventionally produced motion-picture contributions put him in the position of a maverick. Only at the beginning of the eighties did Klein start to take still pictures again. At this time his earlier shots were rediscovered and given recognition. *MBT*

▲ **William Klein**
Entrance to a Sumo
Arena, Tokyo, 1987

*Gelatin silver print,
mixed media*
30.4 x 40.4 cm
ML/F 1994/194
Gruber Donation

◀▲ **William Klein**
Backstage, 1988

Gelatin silver print
30.5 x 40.3 cm
ML/F 1993/306
Gruber Donation

◀ **William Klein**
Backstage, 1985

Gelatin silver print
30.3 x 40.5 cm
ML/F 1993/307
Gruber Donation

◄ **Barbara Klemm**
Peter Handke, 1973

Gelatin silver print
28.5 x 39.5 cm
ML/F 1984/146

Gruber Donation

Klemm, Barbara

1939 Münster
Lives in
Frankfurt on Main

Photojournalist Barbara Klemm received her training in a photographic studio in Karlsruhe. At the beginning of 1959 she found employment with the *Frankfurter Allgemeine Zeitung (FAZ)*, starting as an engraver. Since 1970 she has been a photographer on the editorial staff, concerned mainly with the features section and politics. In this capacity Barbara Klemm documents daily events in the fields of economics, politics, and culture. Her works are usually titled only with location and year, a sign of her attitude of being an observer who participates, but who does not take a superior stand by means of an unusual perspective. Barbara Klemm's individual shots depict events of historical value and political arenas which, despite their modesty, illustrate characteristic moods of the moment. Her work, including the travel supplement of the *FAZ* keeps this journalist frequently on the move. The collection includes the photograph *Leonid Breschnev with Willy Brandt* from 1973. The people she photographs act unobserved, the camera appears not to exist. Still, the situations captured by Barbara Klemm are distinguished by their surprising perspectives and moments. Her method of cropping gives a feeling of balance based on aspects of form and composition, irrespective of the spontaneity of the moment when the picture was taken. In the eighties, Barbara Klemm's portraits of artists revealed another dimension of her work. Her photographs of her father, the painter

▶ **Barbara Klemm**
Fritz Klemm, 1968

Gelatin silver print
39.3 x 29.1 cm
ML/F 1984/147

Gruber Donation

Fritz Klemm, in 1968, of George Segal in 1971, and of Peter Handke in 1973 place her subjects in their environment from a distance, conveying an impression of their work and attitudes. *LH*

Koelbl, Herlinde

1939 Lindau
Lives in Munich

Herlinde Koelbl is a self-taught photographer who began taking pictures in 1975. She has worked for magazines such as *Stern, Zeit Magazin, New York Times,* and other illustrated magazines. As a photojournalist she traveled to many countries and on one such occasion produced a documentary on the Intifada that included pictures reminiscent of Biblical scenes.

Her artistic work has always focused on publications. The subjects she chose were always treated with a view to publication. Her very first book *The German Living Room* created a sensation in 1980. Without disclosing their full names, she took pictures of well known as well as unknown people in their homes providing a surprising look into their "expanded self". In her publication *Fine People* she removed the mask of High Society after attending receptions, parties, gallery openings, and fashion shows with her camera and by observing not the activities themselves, but the people, their clothes and their behavior. In this way the title proved to be ironic. The book revealed a broad spectrum of not so fine appearances. Ranging from vain self-presentation and greed at

▲ Herlinde Koelbl
Robert Mapple-
thorpe, 1983

Gelatin silver print
22.7 x 22.6 cm
ML/F 1985/101,
102, 103

Gruber Donation

the buffet to older gentlemen who surround themselves with decorative young women, *Fine People* is a book about human weaknesses and vices.

One of her first picture cycles called *Men* caused a furor because it depicted male nudes photographed by a woman. They showed clearly that a woman photographs men in a different manner than a man. This does not involve concentrating only on the gender. There are photographs of intellectuals with bodies untouched by body building, or gentle photographs of old men. Herlinde Koelbl takes pictures not only of bodies, body parts or skin surfaces; she takes pictures first and foremost of human beings, thereby making her male nudes significantly different from the ubiquitous female nudes.

One of her most comprehensive and labor-intensive projects was *Jewish Portraits*. Herlinde Koelbl did not restrict herself to finding Jewish personalities of German intellectual history all over the world in order to make portraits of them. She created her portraits based on an intense dialog, which required that she prepare herself thoroughly with the sub-

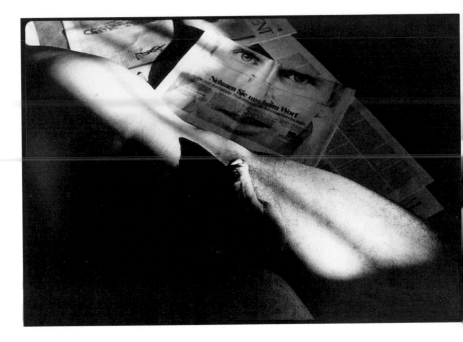

stantial works of her subjects. As a result, *Jewish Portraits* became an overview of still living German-speaking Jewish intellectual greats and also an intelligent introduction to their work as provided by the records of the conversations.

In her most recent, very brief and completely differently conceived – large format – picture sequence of Turkey, she uses the subject of slaughter as a reminder of old myths associated with that topic. Different from the high-tech abattoirs in industrial countries, in the rural areas of Turkey sheep and lambs are still slaughtered ritually as they have been for hundreds of years. With a few large color pictures Herlinde Koelbl seeks to awaken memories of such events in us. *RM*

◀ **Les Krims**
A Marxist View;
Madam Curious;
Bark Art; Art Bark
(for Art Park); a
Chinese Entertain-
ment; Irving's Pens;
Something to Look
at Spotting Upside
Down; Hollis's
Hersheys; and
4 Women Posing,
1984

45.2 x 34.1 cm
ML/F 1995/126

Uwe Scheid
Donation

Krims, Les

(Leslie Robert
Krims)

1942 New York
Lives in New York

Beginning in 1960, Les Krims studied fine arts at the Cooper Union
School of Art and Architecture and at the Pratt Institute in New York. He
began taking pictures at this time, and by 1966 he had had his first solo
exhibition. He held several teaching positions in photography at a
number of fine arts colleges. Since 1967 Krims has been working as a
freelance photographer. Between 1971 and 1972 he produced three conceptual series, all published at the same time: *Little People of America*
describing people of short growth, *The Deerslayers* featuring hunters and
The Incredible Case of the Stack O'Wheat Murders on imaginary murders.
His works are provocative, sometimes exhibiting a rough, dark humor
and a disturbing mercilessness. His Polaroid shots of the project
Fictcryptokrimsographs of 1975 show his sexual fantasies. They are at
once grotesque and fascinating. Krims is provocative in order to bare
the complexities of the "American Way of Life" and thus to rub salt in
the wounds of the observer. *AS*

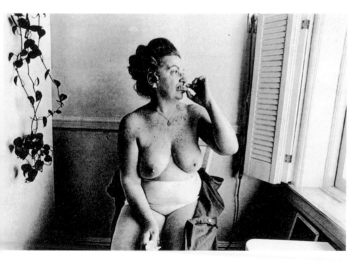

▲ Les Krims
The Static Electric
Effect of Minnie
Mouse On Mickey
Mouse Balloons,
1969

Gelatin silver print
11.4 x 17.2 cm
ML/F 1982/1086

◄ Les Krims
Untitled (Mummy's
Teeth), 1971

Gelatin silver print
11.4 x 16.8 cm
ML/F 1982/1088

Krull, Germaine

1897 Wilda-Posen,
Poland
1985 Wetzlar,
Germany

▼ Germaine Krull
Pont Transbordeur,
Marseille, 1926

Gelatin silver print
19.8 x 14.4 cm
ML/F 1980/2 XI

Germaine Krull left her home in 1916 and moved to Munich in order to study photography. She opened her first portrait studio in Munich in 1919, and one year later she started one in Berlin. During subsequent years Germaine Krull worked in Amsterdam for magazines such as *Der Querschnitt, Die Dame,* and *Varieté.* During her tours of the harbor, the photographer was impressed by the gigantic cranes, which she photographed. When Germaine Krull moved to Paris in 1924, she first worked as a fashion photographer, even though from the very beginning she was interested in the observation of technical constructions and buildings. Germaine Krull's pictures of the Eiffel tower in Paris appeared in the very first issue of the magazine *Vu.* She was one of the first women photographers to create a new type of technical product without spectacular imaging rhetoric. Her first book entitled *Metall* was published in

1927. Germaine Krull's friendship with Sonia and Robert Delaunay, Man Ray, André Kertész, and Eli Lotar created a foundation for close cooperation at various newspapers and on various projects. She received advertising projects from Citroën and Columbia Records. Similarly, she insisted on unconventional realism and shots capturing the moment. During the War Germaine Krull spent time in Brazil and Africa for the organization "France Libre". In 1946 she worked as a war correspondent in Indochina. After 1965 she lived in seclusion in a Tibetan enclave in Northern India, taking hardly any pictures at all. Germaine Krull's last works were small experimental color photographs called "Silpagrams".
LH

Michel Szulc Krzyzanowski was born in the Netherlands in 1949 as the son of Polish parents. Until 1969 he studied at the St. Joost Academy in Breda and the Royal Academy at Den Bosch. After purchasing a Leica M3 in 1970 he began to concentrate on two subjects. On one hand he produced photographic sequences in black-and-white with details of people in front of lonely landscapes, and on the other hand he devoted himself to sociological reportage. In 1971 Krzyzanowski participated in an exhibition for the first time. In the years that followed, he produced sequences entitled *Women in Camden, London,* in 1972, *People in the Street, s'Hertogenbosch,* and *Living and Working, Arles,* in 1974. The last title refers to a sociological project by Krzyzanowski, for which he took pictures of the same man, at work and at home with his family, in similar poses but with a changed social background. In 1976 he created the sequence *Being Naked, Amsterdam,* and the series *Neem nou Henny.* Krzyzanowski's interest lies in social phenomena, which he examines in a conceptual manner and then brings into an aesthetic form. This aspect is expressed in particular in his last work on authors in Surinam *Deep Rooted Words,* where he expands the sequence into an essay. *LH*

Krzyzanowski, Michel Szulc

1949 Oosterhout, Netherlands
Lives in Amsterdam

▲ **Michel Szulc Krzyzanowski**
Untitled (Nude in the Water), around 1985

Gelatin silver print
19.8 x 29 cm
ML/F 1993/322

Gruber Donation

**Kudojarow,
Boris**

1898 Tashkent,
Usbekistan
1974 Moscow

▲ **Boris Kudojarow**
October Revolution
Celebration, around
1935–1940

Gelatin silver print
26 x 37 cm
ML/F 1992/153

Ludwig Collection

From 1917 to 1920 Boris Kudojarow was a member of the Red Army, afterwords working for several years as an amateur photographer. Starting in 1926 he became a professional photographer for *Russfoto* (later *Union-foto*). In 1931 he became a foreign correspondent for the magazine *Sojusfoto*. Between 1930 and 1932 Kudojarow was a member of the "October" group, an association of artists of various genres and different avant-garde media. Bold perspectives and cropping place his photographic works of the thirties firmly in the tradition of photographic Constructivism, stylistically oriented to the photographs of Alexander Rodchenko and Boris Ignatowich. During the Second World War Kudojarow became famous for his shots of life in beleaguered Leningrad (now St. Petersburg). After the War he worked as a photojournalist for *TASS. MBT*

▲ **Boris Kudojarow**
Dynamo Soccer
Game, around
1935–1940

Gelatin silver print
23.6 x 38 cm
ML/F 1992/154

Ludwig Collection

◀ **Boris Kudojarow**
Five Young Sports-
women, 1930s

Gelatin silver print
26.2 x 40.1 cm
ML/F 1992/150

Ludwig Collection

Already during his school years, at the age of 13, Heinrich Kühn conducted his first photographic experiments by casting collodion plates
himself and printing his pictures on salt paper. In 1894 at the "Vienna
Camera Club" he met photographers Hugo Henneberg and Hans
Watzek. From this meeting evolved a lively and close cooperation. Together they perfected printing with precious materials and introduced
color gum bichromate printing into artistic photography. Beginning in
1897 they signed their photographs with a clover leaf. Alfred Stieglitz,
among others, was an important partner for Kühn in the exchange of
ideas, because both fought for the ideas of artistic photography. Later
on their views evolved in different directions. Stieglitz was open to photographic trends influenced by modern art, whereas Kühn appeared to
adhere to his ideas that meanwhile had become conventional. In 1914
Kühn attempted to pass on his endeavors by founding a school for
artistic photography. *MBT*

Kühn, Heinrich

1866 Dresden
1944 Birgitz, near
Innsbruck

▲ **Heinrich Kühn**
Miss Mary, 1908

Gum bichromate print
29.3 x 23.6 cm
ML/F 1977/425

Gruber Collection

▶ **Hans-Wulf Kunze**
From: Living Spaces,
1982

Gelatin silver print
23.9 x 35.5 cm
ML/F 1991/136

Hans-Wulf Kunze grew up in Magdeburg. Between 1977 and 1982 he studied photography under Helfried Strauß at the College for Graphic Design and Book Art in Leipzig. Then he worked as a freelance photographer in Magdeburg. During this time he created his photographic series *Living Spaces*, in which he offered a spotlight-like insight into the living conditions of people in the former German Democratic Republic (GDR). Kunze developed a photographic concept built on the official doctrine of documentary photography, but with a different outlook. There is no longer a trace of the glorification of the feats of Socialism and a depiction of happy people. His perspective is subjectively critical, the tone of his photographs always gloomy. Kunze created a somber picture of society in the GDR. Beyond the general image of the GDR, he dealt with specific projects in those years, in particular the photographic challenge of various factories and the Mansfeld Combine. In 1991, together with the author Ludwig Schumann he launched the project *Border Spaces*. In 1992 he continued his studies under Helfried Strauß at the College for Graphic Design and Book Art in Leizpig. *RM*

**Kunze,
Hans-Wulf**

1955 Dresden
Lives in Magdeburg

**Lange,
Dorothea**

1895 Hoboken,
New Jersey
1965 San Francisco

▲ **Dorothea Lange**
Field Worker,
Texas, 1936

Gelatin silver print
24.5 x 32.5 cm
ML/F 1977/440

Gruber Collection

"Hands off! I do not molest what I photograph, I do not meddle and I do not arrange." That was one of the principles of American photographer Dorothea Lange, whose work has provided one of the most committed social documentaries of photography in our century.

Following her studies at Columbia University in New York under Clarence H. White between 1917 and 1919, Dorothea Lange started out as an independent portrait photographer in San Francisco. Shocked by the number of homeless people in search of work during the Great Depression, she decided to take pictures of people in the street to draw attention to their plight. In 1935 she joined the Farm Security Administration (FSA) and reported on living conditions in the rural areas of the USA. In an unflinchingly direct manner she documented the bitter poverty of migrant workers and their families. Dorothea Lange's pictures not only showed the hopelessness and despair, but also the pride and dignity with which people endured their circumstances. One of the most famous and most frequently published photographs of the FSA

▲ **Dorothea Lange**
Migrant Mother,
California, 1936

Gelatin silver print
32.8 x 26.1 cm
ML/F 1977/442

Gruber Collection

◄ **Dorothea Lange**
Toqueville, Utah,
1953

Gelatin silver print
25.8 x 23.4 cm
ML/F 1977/437

Gruber Collection

project is *Migrant Mother*, the portrait of a Californian migrant worker
with her three children. The face of the young woman is marked by
wrinkles, the gaze full of worry directed in the distance. To the right
and left the two older children, seeking protection, lean against her
shoulders, hiding their faces from the camera, while the small baby has
fallen asleep on its mother's lap. This highly concentrated, tightly composed image has made Dorothea Lange an icon of socially committed
photography. *MBT*

▲ **Dorothea Lange**
White Angel Bread-
line, 1933

Gelatin silver print
31.1 x 25.6 cm
ML/F 1977/435

Gruber Collection

**Lartigue,
Jacques-Henri**

1894 Courbevoie,
France
1986 Nice

▲ Jacques-Henri
Lartigue
Delaye Grand Prix,
1912

Gelatin silver print
20.8 x 28.7 cm
ML/F 1977/431

Gruber Collection

"People say: 'I do not trust my eyes'. Myself, I always trust them, my eyes. But there are days when they bring me slightly too much astonishment." This was expressed by French photographer Jacques-Henri Lartigue at the age of only 15. His father, a passionate amateur photographer, introduced him to photography when he was only six years of age and had him take his first pictures. Two years later he received his first camera as a gift. From then on he recorded everything he liked. This included the remarkable activities and hobbies of the well-to-do Lartigue family, such as kite-flying, racing with automobiles, home-made motorcycles and steerable bobsleds. Equipped with increasingly better and more sophisticated cameras, Lartigue was able to take his first action shots in 1904. He was particularly fascinated by the possibility of freezing motion in a picture. Accordingly, he photographed friends, members of his family or the household staff at play with a ball, hunting butterflies, playing tennis or simply jumping in the air. Another subject he pursued with passion was airplanes. Between 1908 and 1910 he created a collection of shots of all types of airplanes and numerous pion-

▲ Jacques-Henri
Lartigue
Bois de Boulogne,
1911

Gelatin silver print
21.1 x 29.2 cm
ML/F 1977/430

Gruber Collection

◄ Jacques-Henri
Lartigue
Auteuil, 1912

Gelatin silver print
22.2 x 29.1 cm
ML/F 1977/433

Gruber Collection

eers of aviation. When the family moved to Pairs in 1911, Lartigue discovered the eccentric world of fashion in the Bois de Boulogne. Courtesans, worldly ladies and actresses became his favorite subjects. In 1915 Lartigue decided to become a painter, which was not, however, a detriment to his enthusiasm for photography. More and more he developed into a photographic chronicler of society and cultural life, which he captured beginning with the Belle Epoque, through Art Déco and into the eighties. In 1963 Lartigue's work was honored with a large solo exhibition in the Museum of Modern Art in New York. As a result, his photographic activities were also recognized internationally because, significantly, this retrospective was dedicated not to Lartigue the painter but to Lartigue the photographer. *MBT*

Lawler, Louise

1947 Bronxville,
New York
Lives in New York

Louise Lawler belongs to a generation of post-modern artists who reveal the position of art and its mechanisms in modern society. The main topic of her works is the presentation of art in the context of the world of art. In her photographic "picture collages" she shows, for example, works of art in public and private environments and, in so doing, refers to the place of art and artist's place in the market economy. The artist introduces a gallery, a museum or a private collection, whereas usually the opposite applies. She brings the social traditions of art to the foreground – features which determine the function, location, and importance of a piece of art. Photographs such as these, which document the "Arrangement of Pictures" in private or museum collections, illustrate the societal purpose to which art is subjected once it has left the artist's studio. When these so-called installation photographs are shown in museums or private collections, i.e., when the documentation itself becomes art, the problems involved assume an additional dimension. Who should be credited with the work? The artist herself or the artists whose works are depicted in the photograph? Or possibly the museum which acquired the works and has arranged them in a different context?

▼ **Louise Lawler**
Two Pictures, 1992

Gelatin silver print
42 x 55 cm
ML/F 1994/4a

Ludwig Collection

Did You Get What You Deserved?
More Than You Deserved? Less?

► **Louise Lawler**
Two Pictures, 1994

Gelatin silver print
42 x 55 cm
ML/F 1994/4b

Ludwig Collection

In this way the mechanisms of presentation are questioned, and the claim of originality has become irrelevant. The reversal of roles illustrated by Louise Lawler's installations and photographic works, however, is of a symbolic nature because it still takes place within a tradional context of art. The relationship between artist and institution is reflected and questioned, but it remains intact. Like a spy, the photographer sabotages the mechanisms of museum presentation of art. At the same time, however, her own works take these mechanisms into account. "An exhibition, that is the selection of pieces of art by a curator, is based on work which has already been accomplished. I believe that the work of an artist is part of a cumulative endeavor. It is 'made possible', presented/recognized by the dominant culture. It is victim (product) as well as perpetrator (producer)", writes Louise Lawler. *GG*

Lazi, Franz

1922 Stuttgart
Lives in Stuttgart

Franz Lazi completed his apprenticeship in photography under his father, Adolf Lazi, who is considered to be the "old master" of large-format object photography and who founded the Lazi School in 1950. After completing his training, Franz Lazi was in military service from 1941 to 1945 and an American prisoner of war until 1947. The richness of his understanding and experience is owed to extended studies in the USA. In 1947 he earned his master's diploma in Stuttgart and began working out of his own studio as an independent industrial and advertising photographer. He is a member of the German Society of Photographers, the German Society for Photography and many international photographic associations. The portrait he made of Willi Baumeister substantiates Franz Lazi's interest in dealing with art and the artist. His partially cropped face becomes part of an abstract composition that establishes a relationship with the work of Willi Baumeister. For his many photographic works produced outside Germany, Lazi has received the German Federal Cross of Merit. In addition to participating in many exhibitions he has given lectures in Great Britain, Northern Ireland, Switzerland, and the USA. Since 1965 Lazi has also devoted himself to motion pictures, producing experimental and advertising films, films for television, and films of virgin landscapes. His shots of volcanic eruptions were carried out under sometimes life-threatening conditions, resulting in fascinating images. During this time he has traveled throughout the world, including Greenland and the Antarctic. In 1979 he published his book *Antarctic*. He began taking pictures early on, in particular in color: "I was one of the first photographers after the war who developed their color films themselves." *AS*

▼ Franz Lazi
Willi Baumeister,
1955

Gelatin silver print
29 x 23.2 cm
ML/F 1977/960

Gruber Donation

Robert Lebeck studied political science in Zurich and in New York. His 23rd birthday was a turning point in his life. On that day his wife presented him with a Retina 1A camera. On July 15 1952, Lebeck had his first photograph published in the *Heidelberger Tagesblatt*. His first great success came in 1955 – the publication of a report in *Revue* magazine. The same year he was appointed director of the Frankfurt office of *Revue*. His breakthrough came in 1960, in Africa, with his work for *Kristall* magazine. In 1966 Lebeck joined *Stern*.

His earlier photographic documentaries in black and white and his later ones in color were produced by this self-taught photographer with a minimum of technology. Pictures like *The Stolen Sabre* or *Robert Kennedy's Funeral* went around the world. Lebeck's photography characterized the style of *Stern* photojournalism in a lasting manner. *NZ*

Lebeck, Robert

1929 Berlin
Lives in Hamburg

▲ **Robert Lebeck**
The Stolen Sabre,
Leopoldville, 1960

Gelatin silver print
50.7 x 60.7 cm
ML/F 1991/256

▶ **Robert Lebeck**
Robert Kennedy's
Funeral, 1968

Gelatin silver print
23.9 x 30.4 cm
ML/F 1988/61

Gruber Donation

▲ **Robert Lebeck**
Jayne Mansfield, Berlin, 1961

Gelatin silver print, 61.4 x 50.7 cm
ML/F 1991/257

Lechtape, Edith

1924 Herne
Lives in Strasbourg

▼ **Edith Lechtape**
LXVIII/10, 1983

Gelatin silver print
57 x 49.3 cm
ML/F 1990/236

Between 1941 and 1942 Edith Lechtape trained as an actress under Heinz Moog in Bochum. Afterwards she worked for one year at the German Theater Lille, then at the National Theater in Weimar, the People's Stage in Dresden and the State Theater in Dresden. In the mid-fifties she acted at the Hamburg Studio Theaters and on the city stages of Bochum, Dortmund, Essen, and Wuppertal. She played mostly character roles. For example, she played the parts of Clytemnestra and Mother Courage.

In 1967 she met Antoine Weber, who had been taking an interest in photographic techniques for 20 years. He encouraged Edith Lechtape to turn to photography as well. Since 1972 they have created painted-over and drawn-over photographs. Edith Lechtape went public for the first time at an exhibition in 1974. In 1977 she developed her first sculpture-pictures, which are collages of portrait sculptures which she had photographed. These works incorporate predominantly the parts of her face – eyes and mouth. The works were first shown at an exhibition in 1978. After Weber's death in 1979 she continued her photographic work by herself. Her assembled works appear to resemble a conglomeration of bunched-up paper more than a planned collage. Eyes, mouth, and nose are the only constants. She sees her self-portraits as an extension of her acting, an act of change and disguise, slipping into the most varied faces. *RM*

▲ **Edith Lechtape**
LXV/4/Z 6 U, 1983

Gelatin silver print
50.6 x 41.9 cm
ML/F 1990/232

L' ANTENNE
EN HAUT
DE L'ARBRE
ET LE
FUTUR GARAGE
étaient ce que
l'on voyait tout
d'abord en arri-
vant chez le
peintre au début
de son installa-
tion à Etampes
dans les années
1972-1973.

L'INFERNALE ZONE INDUSTRIELLE EN AVAL DE ROUEN
Entre les voies l'endroit où le peintre fut mêlé
à des évènements d'un ordre particulier n'ayant
rien à voir avec l'art et qui, bien que personne
en définitive ne portât plainte contre lui, contri-
buèrent à assombrir cette période de sa vie.
Il ne reviendra à l'art que dans les années 70.

FRONTISPICE DE : "LE PEINTRE AUX SCABIEUSES",
le meilleur ouvrage consacré à l'artiste.
"... J'étais très jeune et prêt à être impressionné
durablement par n'importe quelle forme d'art quand
le hasard me fit passer devant la vitrine d'un mar-
chand de tableaux."

UN PEINTRE PHOTOGRAPHE !
Cette unique photo prise par le peintre au cours
d'un long voyage devait beaucoup amuser les siens
quand la précieuse pellicule une fois développée
fut découverte presque vierge !

Le Gac, Jean

1936 Alès, France
Lives in Paris

Jean Le Gac belongs to a subgroup of Concept Art which became known in the seventies in New York as narrative or story-telling art. On numerous trips the French artist composed diaries and records, documents of the remarkable and everyday. Between 1968 and 1971 his art consisted of performance, travel, and activities documented with photographs, picture postcards, and texts in so-called "notebooks". In the seventies he shifted his interest to the problems of reality and fiction, on which Le Gac produced ironic comments, for example, by intertwining his own biography with the fictitious character of Florent Max. In his series *The Scabious Painter* (1977) he combined photographs and writing. "In the

CE QUI RESTE
DU CHATEAU
DE
ROBERT LE DIABLE
où,parmi les cou-
leuvres lourdes,
lentes,et les lé-
zards à qui il
sifflait pour les
charmer "Gloria,
alleluia..",le
peintre faisait
ses premières po-
chades sur des
cartons de cheni-
serie.

LA MARE PAR TEMPS DE NEIGE(Photo conservée par la famille)
C'est là,qu'une nuit,ils virent au moment de la pon-
te une telle procession de crapauds que le peintre
plein de répugnance,voulant quand même franchir l'
obstacle à grandes embardées,vit le jeune Storge
descendre de la voiture et comme un petit démon,é-
carter du chemin à pleines mains les étrons vivants.

LE CHEMIN DES DOUANIERS QUI DOMINE
L'ANSE DE TREGUEZ (Finistère)
où à l'âge de quatre ans on retrouva tout en
sang le peintre,grimpé sur un banc,terrorisé
par d'hypothétiques lions !

VU DES REMPARTS L'ETAT ACTUEL DU JARDINET
Le 6 avril 1951 c'est de cet endroit,qu'assis les
pieds dans le vide et dessinant sur un carnet ce
qu'ils appelaient "Les Etranges Figures du Jardin
Roques",qu'un camarade de lycée du peintre tomba
accidentellement et se tua.

linguistic forms of everyday media and tools of illustration he makes the observer a detective in search of the artist's fictitious 'vocation'. He offers the photograph as a means for reporting and, with the installation and film as a tool for simulation, can disclose events, encounters, memories discussed by the corresponding text without disclosing the fictitious 'painter'." (Quoted from: Jean Le Gac, "The Phantom Painter", 1992). *GG*

▲ Jean Le Gac
The Scabious Painter, 1977

Color Print
85.5 x 85.5 cm
ML/F 1979/1353 I-VIII

Leibovitz, Annie

1949 Warterbury,
Connecticut

Lives in New York

Annie Leibovitz spent her childhood and youth in different states of the USA. During this time she experienced her first significant encounter with photography by way of her family's photo albums. Her earliest role models among prominent photographers were Henri Cartier-Bresson and Jacques-Henri Lartigue. In 1970 Annie Leibovitz began her studies of fine arts and photography at the San Francisco Art Institute. In the same year she submitted a portfolio to the art director of *Rolling Stone* magazine, Robert Ingsbury, and scored her first success. Jann Wenner, publisher of the magazine, took the young photographer with him to New York, where she was to take pictures during an interview with John Lennon. Within one month her Lennon portraits were published on the cover of *Rolling Stone*. In 1973 Annie Leibovitz became chief photographer of this magazine until she switched to *Vanity Fair* in 1983.

"It is really fun to take pictures with me. Sometimes I put people in mud. Sometimes I hang them from the ceiling." This is how Annie Leibovitz sees herself working. Indeed, her portraits of stars from the world of music, motion pictures, the theater, the arts, literature or politics catch the eye because of their original, lively arrangements. She does not portray a sober, serious hailing of the stars, rather she adds a dose of wit, humor, and irony to the picture. Annie Leibovitz, who is currently considered the American photographer of the stars, prepares her portrait sessions very meticulously and usually consults with her subjects many days prior to the portrait appointment date. Only because of her intense and personal interaction with her models is this photographer successful in cajoling her subjects into the desired, frequently fun and humorous poses. "When I say I want to take a picture of someone, it really means I want to get to know that person."

Annie Leibovitz' photographic sequence of the collector couple Renate and L. Fritz Gruber is undoubtedly an unusual example of her work: she dispenses with all elaborate staging and captures the lovingly embracing couple with an apparently spontaneous "snapshot". *MBT*

► **Annie Leibovitz**
Renate and L. Fritz
Gruber, 1989

Gelatin silver prints
3 photographs,
each 21.2 x 25.2 cm
ML/F 1993/324-326

Gruber Donation

Le Va, Barry

1941 Long Beach,
California
Lives in New York

▲▶ **Barry Le Va**
Extensions, 1971

*Gelatin silver prints
18 photographs,
each 16 x 23.5 cm*
ML/F 1985/38

The art of Barry Le Va does not readily follow any particular direction or movement. Rather it is related to ideas and questions posed in other areas such as psychology, physics, or architecture. Between 1969 and 1971 Le Va worked with photography in exterior space. In this context he explored problems of dimensions, the location of the observer, the determination of locality, and position. Le Va's concern was "to use an external situation which is normally not viewed as a cohesive form or mass and create a consciousness for its essential elements – volume, edges, height, length, width – by means of one specific act which I would shoot from different distances" (Le Va). Such "landscape" work represents the attempt to move as far away as possible from the production of objects. The problem of the continuum of space and time plays an important part in this case because this continuum cannot be captured in a physical object. In this manner the process of seeing becomes a subject of its art. It deals with the expansion of the sculptural, which allows a comparison of his work with that of his sculptor-colleagues Richard Serra, Carl Andre, or Robert Morris. *GG*

Extension

Barry Le Va 1971

◀◀ **Manfred Leve**
Prepared WC, from:
Exposition of Music,
Parnass Gallery,
Wuppertal, 1963

Gelatin silver print
23.8 x 16.2 cm
ML/F 1986/97

◀ **Manfred Leve**
Random Access with
Magnetic Head,
from: Exposition of
Music, Parnass
Gallery, Wuppertal,
1963

Gelatin silver print
23.8 x 16.2 cm
ML/F 1986/101

Leve, Manfred

1936 Trier
Lives in Nuremberg

Manfred Leve grew up in Düsseldorf and studied law, Middle Eastern cultures, art history, and philosophy at universities in Cologne, Freiburg, Munich, and Berlin. Since then he has been working as a lawyer. He is currently employed at the Federal Institute of Labor in Nuremberg.

He has been interested in the arts since his youth and he began observing the art scene in Düsseldorf in his early school days. He already enjoyed photography during those years and began to record art events with his camera. He gained contact with artists and became friends with Sigmar Polke, whose life and work he has documented extensively. He attended the performance and Fluxus concerts at the gallery Parnass in Wuppertal and recorded these unrepeatable events. In the course of the years he developed a comprehensive archive of the art scene around Düsseldorf, including artists' portraits, openings, and performance. Leve's coarse-grained images focus on the fleeting, transient aspects of the moment, and they show that photography is the only medium that can prolong the lifespan of an art event. *RM*

▲▲ **Manfred Leve**
Wolf Vostell at Paik's
Record-Shashlik,
from: Exposition of
Music, Parnass
Gallery, Wuppertal,
1963

Gelatin silver print
23.8 x 16.2 cm
ML/F 1986/125

▲ **Manfred Leve**
Untitled, from: Expo-
sition of Music, Par-
nass Gallery, Wup-
pertal, 1963

Gelatin silver print
16.2 x 23.8 cm
ML/F 1986/127

▲▲ **Manfred Leve**
Untitled, from: Expo-
sition of Music, Par-
nass Gallery, Wup-
pertal, 1963

Gelatin silver print
16.2 x 23.8 cm
ML/F 1986/119

▲ **Manfred Leve**
Nam June Paik,
Karl Otto Götz,
from: Exposition of
Music, Parnass
Gallery, Wuppertal,
1963

Gelatin silver print
16.2 x 23.8 cm
ML/F 1986/106

▲ **Manfred Leve**
Untitled, 1986

Color print
50.8 x 60.9 cm
ML/F 1986/215

▲ **Manfred Leve**
Sound Object, 1986

Gelatin silver print
16.2 x 23.8 cm
ML/F 1986/117

Leve | 393

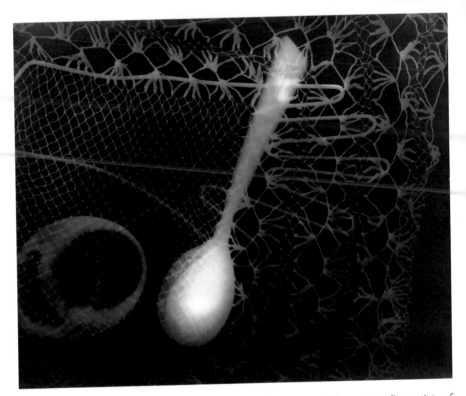

Lissitzky, El

1890 Portchinok,
near Smolensk
1941 Moscow

▲ El Lissitzky
Composition with
Spoon, around 1924

Gelatin silver print
23.4 x 29 cm
ML/F 1979/1404

Ludwig Collection

As early as the twenties El Lissitzky was one of the outstanding artists of
the Russian avant-garde. Trained as an architect, he made a name for
himself in painting, typography and photography as an innovative intellectual, contributing significantly to the implementation and dissemination of constructivist and suprematist ideas. He became famous for his
Proun work. *Proun* was a "project to affirm the new", with which Lissitzky envisioned the utopia of constructing a new space which was also
intended to be the symbolic image of a new societal order to be established.

Lissitzky experimented in the field of photography from the early
twenties and he was mainly interested in photomontages and photograms. He arranged preferably everyday objects such as spoons, pliers,
glasses, and lace doilies on photographic paper, but unlike László
Moholy-Nagy, he did not attempt to create an immaterial light space. In
an article published in 1929 he summarized his ideas on photogram

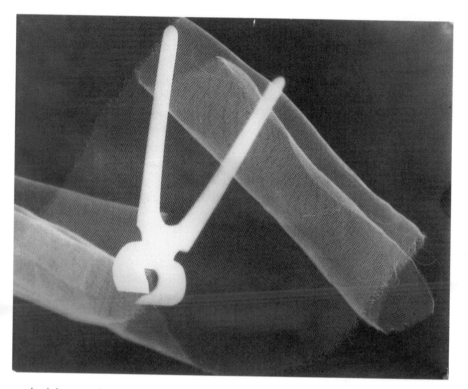

methodology, in which he acknowledged the greater expressive force of photographic images: "The language of photography is not the language of the painter, and the photograph has properties which are not accessible to painters. These properties are intrinsic in the photographic material itself and must be developed if photography is to be turned into art, into a photogram."

Lissitzky utilized photograms and montages to design advertisements and posters. One of his most monumental projects in the area of photomontage was the photographic frieze he assembled of newspaper clippings and photographs for the Soviet pavilion at the international press exhibition "Pressa" in Cologne (1928). *MBT*

▲ El Lissitzky
Composition with
Pliers, around 1924

Gelatin silver print
23.4 x 29.1 cm
ML/F 1979/1405

Ludwig Collection

List, Herbert

1903 Hamburg
1975 Munich

▼ Herbert List
Athens, 1937

Gelatin silver print
30.7 x 23.8 cm
ML/F 1977/972

Gruber Donation

Herbert List entered photographic history as a master of the "fotografia metafisica". He started out with an apprenticeship in business and, between 1926 and 1928, traveled to South American coffee plantations, before returning to work as an attorney and partner in his father's business in Hamburg. Besides his profession he was always interested in the artistic life of his environment. At the end of the twenties he discovered his passion for photography. His friend Andreas Feininger, who had just completed his architectural studies at the Bauhaus, introduced him to the technical fundamentals of his field. Fascinated by the paintings of the Surrealists, List took advantage of their ideas and magical image changes in his photographs. He placed objects in alien, unfamiliar contexts or staged encounters between uprooted fragments of reality and attempted "to capture the magic of appearance in the picture". In 1936 political circumstances forced List to leave Germany, his home. Without means he went to London and made his hobby his profession. Already by the end of the thirties he could record a breakthrough as a successful photographer. In 1937 List and photographer George Hoyningen-Huene traveled to Greece. List's interest in Greek mythology and his preference for Surrealism were especially nurtured among antique ruins. On Lycabettos' hill in Athens he shot a series on the topic of covering and uncovering. An individual covered in a white robe posed in the habit of theatrical stage appearances in the landscape and played with the ambiguity of front and back, male and female. In the case of the picture shown here, List allowed confusion to reign supreme by using a mirror to play reality and its mirror image against each other.

After the War List returned to Germany and settled in Munich,

▲ **Herbert List**
Santorin, 1937

Gelatin silver print
28.5 x 23.1 cm
ML/F 1977/969

Gruber Donation

▲ **Herbert List**
Lycabettos, 1937

Gelatin silver print
28.1 x 23.2 cm
ML/F 1977/971

Gruber Donation

► **Herbert List**
George Hoyningen-
Huene, Glyphada,
1937

Gelatin silver print
28.9 x 22.5 cm
ML/F 1977/968

Gruber Donation

using it as a base for many trips in the years that followed. In 1962
he gave up photography and devoted himself to the collection and
identification of Italian drawings. *MBT*

Lohse, Bernd

1911 Dresden
1995 Burghausen

▲ **Bernd Lohse**
That's Life in the
USA, 1937

Gelatin silver print
16.1 x 23.4 cm
ML/F 1989/94

▶ **Bernd Lohse**
Bookkeeper at the
Minolta Company,
Osaka, 1951

Gelatin silver print
39 x 28.5 cm
ML/F 1985/147

By the age of 14 Bernd Lohse had already established himself as a picture and text author on the subject of photography. Following his studies he began training at Scherl, a large publishing house, where he soon advanced to editor in picture services. His photographic essays appeared mostly in the *Neue IZ* and in the *Berliner Illustrirte*. Soon Lohse was part of a small group of top-notch German reporters.

His topics never included sensational events or the world of politicians and the famous. Instead he strove to present the reader with the characteristics of everyday life in other countries. During World War II Lohse was drafted as a photojournalist. He was wounded and discharged before the war ended, and he moved to Bavaria.

There, in 1946, he was hired as editor of *Heute* magazine. In addition, he produced the *Foto-Spiegel* and later *Foto-Magazin* for Heering, a publishing house. As a reporter he toured Japan, Korea, the USA, and numerous other countries.

In 1955 Lohse became chief editor at a book-publishing company. In addition, in 1964, he and Walter Boje became editors of *Photoblätter* and later of the *Bildjournalist*. After retiring, Lohse devoted himself mostly to

◄ **Bernd Lohse**
Old Scotland Lives,
1936

Gelatin silver print
23.5 x 16.5 cm
ML/F 1989/97

► **Bernd Lohse**
French Married
Couple, 1938

Gelatin silver print
23.3 x 17.5 cm
ML/F 1989/93

book reviews. Today his library, the "Visual Collection", is part of the
photographic library of the Museum Ludwig in Cologne. *RM*

Lynes,
George Platt

1907 East Orange,
New Jersey
1955 New York

▲ George Platt
Lynes
Henri Cartier-
Bresson, around
1930

Gelatin silver print
19.1 x 23 cm
ML/F 1977/473

Gruber Collection

Before becoming interested in photography, George Platt Lynes was fascinated by the idea of becoming a writer. He sought contact with the literary avant-garde and, in the twenties, set out to write a novel. In 1925,
at the age of 18, he took his first trip to France and, while staying in
Paris, became friends with Gertrude Stein, Jean Cocteau, and the
painter Pavel Tchelitchew. A desire emerged in him to become the publisher of the most important authors of his time. After his return to New
York he actually did publish books by Gertrude Stein, René Crevel, and
Ernest Hemingway. In 1927 Lynes, under the guidance of a local professional photographer, began to take pictures of his numerous famous
friends. A year later he exhibited these portraits in his Park Place Book
Shop. Photography gradually became his profession, and in 1932 he was
able to open his first professional studio in New York. One year later he
began to publish his portraits and fashion shots in magazines such as

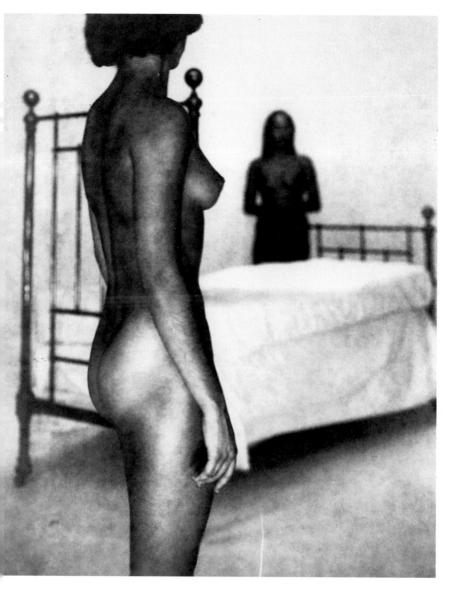

▲ **George Platt Lynes**
Two Nudes, around 1940

Gelatin silver print
24.2 x 19.5 cm
ML/F 1977/482

Gruber Collection

▲ **George Platt Lynes**
Female Nude by a
Stone Block, 1944

Gelatin silver print
25.1 x 20.3 cm
ML/F 1977/472

Gruber Collection

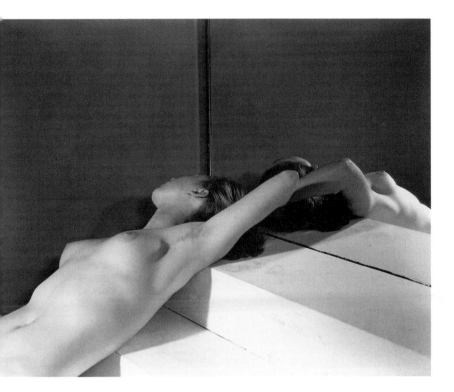

Town and Country, Harper's Bazaar, and Vogue. Lynes' style took its lead from the European avant-garde and, in particular, Surrealism. In 1942 Lynes left New York, moved to Hollywood and became director of the Vogue studio. In 1947, deeply in debt, he returned to New York. Lynes was unable to regain his earlier commercial success and wealth. During his later years Lynes focused increasingly on erotic male nudes. This brought him neither compensation nor fame, but it increasingly continued to dominate his work. Just before his death Lynes destroyed a large number of his negatives and archived documents because he feared that many of his photographs might be misunderstood. *MBT*

▲ **George Platt Lynes**
Nude in the Mirror, around 1945

Gelatin silver print
19.4 x 24.1 cm
ML/F 1977/470

Gruber Collection

Macků, Michal

1963 Bruntál,
Czech Republic
Lives in Olomouc

▲ **Michal Macků**
Untitled (No. 6),
1989

Gelatin silver print
51.5 x 64.5 cm
ML/F 1991/101

Michal Macků studied at the Technical Faculty of the Technical College at Brno and then worked at the Sigma Research Institute in Olomouc. Between 1986 and 1989 he studied photography in Prague and at the Public College of Fine Arts in Olomouc. Macků is one of the young Czech photographers who, following their first public exposure in Europe as part of the exhibition "Contemporary Czechoslovak Photography" at the Museum Ludwig in Cologne, were met with immediate enthusiasm and then passed on from one festival to the next, receiving numerous invitations to exhibitions. His pictures of naked people in stretched poses are indeed impressive: the photosensitive layer of the photographic paper has been peeled off, creased, and replaced to give the appearance that the subject's skin has been removed. Macků's expressive experimental photography struck many people's core of current existential fears in a time of political and economic change. *RM*

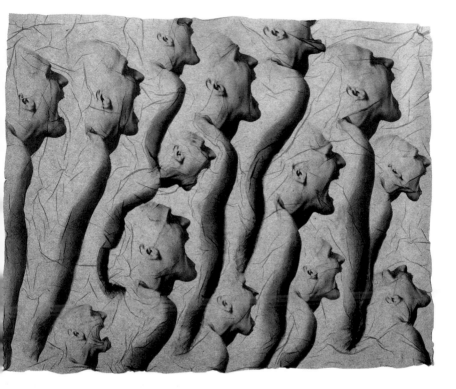

▲ **Michal Macků**
Untitled (No. 8),
1989

Gelatin silver print
36.8 x 47.8 cm
ML/F 1995/124

Uwe Scheid
Donation

◄ **Michal Macků**
Untitled, 1989

Gelatin silver print
49 x 63 cm
ML/F 1995/248

Uwe Scheid
Donation

◀ Eva Mahn
From: Shadow
Images, 1983

Gelatin silver print
48.1 x 48.1 cm
ML/F 1995/123

Uwe Scheid
Donation

Mahn, Eva

1947 Aschersleben,
Germany
Lives in Halle/Saale

Between 1965 and 1970 Eva Mahn studied art history, history, and art
pedagogy at Ernst-Moritz-Arndt University in Greifswald and at the University of Leipzig. Then she became an academic assistant in the departments of teaching, research, and publications at the College of Fine
Arts and Design, Burg Giebichenstein in Halle. After earning her doctorate she became director of the art collection at the college. Between 1969
and 1974 she collaborated with Günter Rössler in the area of photography and since then she has been active as an independent photographer. For a while she concentrated on erotic photography and on the
subject of shadow images. Between 1977 and 1984 she worked for the
cultural monthly *Das Magazin*, designed posters, theater programs, and
worked in the pharmaceutical industry. Between 1992 and 1993 she participated in the project *Departure to Freedom* which she used to address
the situation of young people in East Germany. In 1994 she received a
scholarship at the Ahrenshoop Artists' Residence, where she created the
series *Cross-border Commuters – Ahrenshoop Portraits*, which dealt with
the employment situation after the opening of the border between East
and West Germany. Her most recent series again deals with the young
generation, which is adapting to the situation quite differently from her
own generation. This is a photographic approach to young people following the theme *Departure to Freedom – A Document of Change. RM*

1 1978 Marina Makowski gave up being a book dealer and devoted her-
elf to the arts. From the very beginning she concentrated on photo-
raphy and, one year later, she began to participate in exhibitions. To
his day she adheres firmly to the formal creative principles on which
er art is based. Her literary roots manifest themselves in her large-for-
nat, black-and-white triptychs in the form of text passages of different
engths, which mostly read like excerpts from fantasy or science fiction
ovels. Yet these are not descriptions that she found somewhere; they
re her own, individually tailored to the specific situation shown in a pic-
ure. Her severely rastered photographs are mostly taken from video
nd television movies, and they show the characteristic structures of
hese media. Her texts and images describe intimidating situations,
cenes of threats, and of being exposed. They are about anonymous
ower, technology devoid of a soul, or a government that monitors
verything, where people are pigeonholed, either as blind executive
ower or as victims. *RM*

**Makowski,
Marina**

Born 1956
Lives in Berlin

ZUM ERSTEN MAL GESTATTETE MAN IHR
DIE TEILNAHME AN DEN VERSUCHEN. IHR
PLATZ LAG ETWAS ERHÖHT, UND SIE
KONNTE AUF DAS GESCHEHEN HINUN-
TERBLICKEN, OHNE DIE ANDEREN DURCH
IHR DABEISEIN ZU STÖREN. IN DER VOR-
HERGEGANGENEN LANGEN ZEIT DES WAR-
TENS AUF DIESEN MOMENT HATTEN DIE
DINGE (DIE SIE NUN ERLEBTE) IN IHRER
VORSTELLUNG EINE MYSTISCHE, IRREALE
DIMENSION ANGENOMMEN; STUNDEN-
LANG HATTE SIE SICH DIESEN ANGENEH-
MEN UND SIE SCHAUDERND MACHENDEN
VISIONEN HINGEGEBEN UND FÜHLTE SICH
WÄHRENDDESSEN WEIT FORT VON IHREM
TATSÄCHLICHEN AUFENTHALTSORT UND
DEN DAMIT VERBUNDENEN WIRKLICHKEI-
TEN. GLEICHZEITIG EMPFAND SIE IHREN
KÖRPER ALS DEN DEUTLICHEN BEWEIS EI-
NER ANWESENHEIT, DIE FÜR SIE JEGLICHE
BEDEUTUNG VERLOREN HATTE. TATSÄCH-
LICH LIESS MAN SIE BEI DIESEM ERSTEN
MAL NOCH NICHT WIRKLICH EINBLICK
NEHMEN; VÖLLIG AM RANDE STEHEND
WAR SIE WEDER DEN TABUS NOCH DEN RI-
TUELLEN VORSCHRIFTEN UNTERWORFEN,
DIE DEN HINTERGRUND BILDETEN ZWI-
SCHEN DER HANDLUNG UND DEM WISSEN
DARUM.

◀ **Marina Makowski**
75/86 I-III, 1986

*Gelatin silver print
each 79 x 109 cm*
ML/F 1990/62 I-III

Toyota Donation

Mantz, Werner

1901 Cologne
1983 Eijsden,
Netherlands

When he was only 14 years old Werner Mantz began to take pictures with an Ernemann camera, and he achieved his first financial success with the sale of his own picture-postcards of the flood disaster of 1920 in Cologne. Following his studies at the Bavarian Education and Research Institute for Photography in Munich, he opened his first studio i Cologne in 1921, where he made portraits and advertising photographs. In 1926 he met Wilhelm Riphahn in conjunction with a project for the Pickenhahn barber salon and within a short period of time became his "house photographer". This led him to the Gemeinnützige Aktiengesellschaft für Wohnungsbau (a residential construction corporation). He subsequently took pictures for all its member architects. In 1968 Mantz withdrew to Eijsden in the Netherlands, where he embarked on his second career as a photographer of children. *RM*

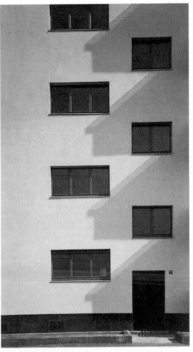

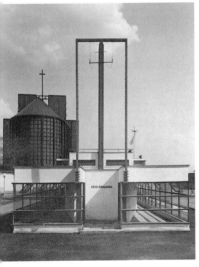

Mapplethorpe, Robert

1946 New York
1989 New York

▲ R. Mapplethorpe
Self-portrait as a
Woman, 1980

Gelatin silver print
35.2 x 35 cm
ML/F 1984/76

Gruber Donation

At first Robert Mapplethorpe wanted to become a musician, but he eventually decided to study painting at the Pratt Institute in Brooklyn. In 1968 he met the singer Patti Smith with whom he moved to the now legendary Chelsea Hotel in Manhattan in 1970. Under the influence of his friend John McEndry, curator for printed art and photography at the Metropolitan Museum of Art, New York, Mapplethorpe began to take an interest in photography, collecting old photographs. Initially he only made montages from photographs that he found, but in 1972 he began to take pictures with a Polaroid camera.

Mapplethorpe's preferred subjects were classical themes such as still-life scenes, flowers, portraits, and nudes, all of which he recorded in rigorous compositions with an extremely precise photographic style. He caused a sensation in particular with his nudes, which defined eroticism and homosexuality with a virtually relentless arrogance. The openness with which Mapplethorpe approached in particular the male gender, and which disclosed his own homoerotic tendencies even resulted in the confiscation of his photographs at one of his exhibitions. *MBT*

▲ **Robert Mapplethorpe**
Untitled (male nude), 1981

Gelatin silver print
38.1 x 38.5 cm
ML/F Dep. 1989/209

Jeane von Oppenheim Donation

▲ **Robert**
Mapplethorpe
Untitled (male
nude), 1980

Gelatin silver print
35.4 x 35.4 cm
ML/F Dep. 1989/208

Jeane von
Oppenheim
Donation

▶ Charlotte March
Satyric Dancer, in
memory of André
Kertész, 1985

Cibachrome print
30.9 x 20.7 cm
ML/F 1991/273

From 1950 to 1954 Charlotte March attended the Alsterdamm School of
Art in Hamburg. Since 1956 she has been an assistant professor at the
Master School of Fashion in Hamburg. In 1955 she spontaneously decided to take up photography, and since 1961 has had her own studio in
Hamburg. She works mostly in fashion and advertising photography in
Germany, France, and England. A series entitled *Girls and Fashion* from
the sixties shows Charlotte March's style. The models frequently look
directly at the viewer. They embody personality, self-confidence, and a
certain aloofness. In 1973 Charlotte March said: "I am uninhibited
when I take pictures of nude girls. I find that as normal as photographing a coffee pot. I would be rather more inhibited photographing an un-
dressed man, because of the eroticism between man and woman." Four
years later her book *Man oh Man! A Proposal for the Emancipation of the*

**March,
Charlotte**

1930 Essen
Lives in Hamburg

▲ **Charlotte March**
Trevor in Bathing
Trunks for "twen"
magazine, 1967

Cibachrome print
61 x 50.8 cm
ML/F 1991/280

Attractive Man was published. In this book we read: "A beautiful man is still suspect. In particular, of course, among men." She took photographs of men in all kinds of poses: in the style of classic pin-ups, child-like playing with rabbits, like fauns cavorting through nature, stripping, swimming, in bed. The descriptions deal with the subject in the liberated speech of the seventies as cultivated by magazines like *Pardon* and *twen*. Nude men – photographed by a woman – caused this book to become quite a sensation. *AS*

▲ **Charlotte March**
Donyale Luna with Earrings for "twen" magazine, 1966

Gelatin silver print
40 x 39.9 cm
ML/F 1991/276

Gruber Collection

◄ **Mary Ellen Mark**
Untitled, 1972

Gelatin silver print
25.6 x 17.4 cm
ML/F 1994/213

Gruber Donation

Mark,
Mary Ellen

1940 Philadelphia
Lives in New York

After studying art and completing her university studies in photojournalism, Mary Ellen Mark has been working as a freelance photographer since 1966. Her genre is social documentary photojournalism, and her intention is to photograph fringe groups of society in an explanatory and direct style. Her reports are never sensation-mongering, and they always seek to be compassionate and not to denigrate the dignity of those portrayed. This is true of the prostitute in India in her project *Falkland Road* (1981) and of a photographic series of the eighties with children living in the Bronx, the homeless, junkies, and the handicapped. Her technically perfect and creative photos are rooted in the tradition of W. Eugene Smith and Dorothea Lange. In 1994 she was awarded the Erich Salomon Prize by the German Society for Photography (DGPh). AS

Matta Clark, Gordon

1948 New York
1978 New York

Gordon Matta Clark studied architecture at Cornell University in New York and literature in Paris in 1963. Being an architect, he was interested not only in new buildings but also in the problems of social tensions in cities, the destruction and demolition of buildings. In his work he combines drawing, sculpture, architecture, photography, motion pictures, and performance art. In the early seventies he made movies of demolition events and from 1973 photographed sections of houses. Empty buildings, just before being torn down, were his subjects. His intervention snatched them from oblivion and made them a reference to history and to the destruction of their continuity. The *Office Baroque* project was created in 1977 in an abandoned office building in Antwerp in memory of the 400th birthday of Peter Paul Rubens. Because officials would not give him permission to carry out his original changes to the façade of the building, he prepared new plans for its internal rooms. In September he explained: "My first five-story building offered unique opportunities and I wanted to elicit an almost musical phrase, i.e. a fixed set of elements should permeate all the stories. On account of an unexpected event – rings left by a teacup on a drawing – I ended up grouping the piece around two semi-circular areas with slightly different diameters. They began on the first floor and created the guiding motif, limited by floors and the roof. Wherever these circles intersected, a peculiar row-boat-like hole was formed, which changed from one story to the next, defined by beams and existing space. In this project, now called 'Office Baroque', the arrangement of large spaces (large, open offices at the bottom; small interconnected rooms at the top) defines how the formal elements of uninterrupted round disks change into shrapnel-like splinters and pieces, in particular in the areas where they abut to borders and walls. In addition to the element of surprise and the loss of orientation caused by this work, it provides a particularly satisfying intellectual model." At the same time, the photographic work is reflected formally by the "splittings" of the house – the film material was cut into pieces and reassembled: "The camera is not meant to capture the moment but act as a stage for a plot which has not yet been completed." *AS*

▶ Gordon Matta Clark
Office Baroque, Antwerp, 1977

Cibachrome print
102 x 77 cm
ML/F 1983/1

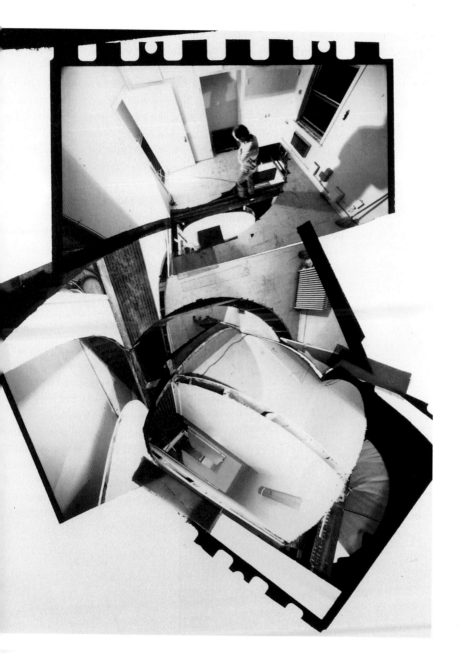

Maywald, Willi

1907 Kleve
1985 Paris

From 1925 to 1928 Willi Maywald attended fine arts schools in Cologne and Krefeld. From 1928 to 1931 he studied at the College of Creative Arts in Berlin, earning his living during this time as an assistant in motion picture studios. In 1931 he moved to Paris, where he worked with Harry Meerson, a photographer, until 1934. He then opened his own studio for portraits, journalism, architecture, and fashion. He began collaborating with a number of magazines, including *Femina, Harper's Bazaar, Vogue, Réalités, Picture Post, Life, Elegante Welt,* and *Photo Prisma*. Between the years 1935 and 1942 he spent his summers in Cagnes-sur-Mer where he shot the sequences *Renoir's Garden* and *Monet's Garden* which were first published in *Verve* magazine. Between 1939 and 1940 he was interned in several camps in France. In 1942 he began his portrait series of famous people from the worlds of theater, the fine arts, and literature. Among others, he shot portraits of Marc Chagall, Le Corbusier, Pablo Picasso, Joan Miró, and Jean Cocteau. Between 1942 and 1946 he lived in Switzerland, where he contributed to a number of magazines. Finally, in 1946 he opened a new studio in Paris and became a photographer with

▼ Willi Maywald
Jacques Heim,
Fashion Photo-
graphy, 1950s

Gelatin silver print
27.2 x 23.9 cm
ML/F 1993/336

Gruber Donation

Christian Dior. He is equally as famous for his fashion photography as for his portraits – with his artists' portraits being exceptional. In 1949 he compiled them into a book entitled *Artists at Home*, published at the time when an exhibition with the same title was opened, which met with immense public response. Shortly before his death in 1985 Maywald published his memoirs. *RM*

▲ Willi Maywald
Dress by Jacques
Fath, 1950s

Gelatin silver print
30.3 x 24 cm
ML/F 1993/343

Gruber Donation

McBean, Angus

1904 Newbridge,
South Wales
1990 Suffolk

Angus McBean discovered his passion for photography when he was quite young. However, before embarking on becoming a professional photographer, he worked in an antiques business in London's West End, where he learned how to restore old furniture. At the beginning of the thirties McBean went to the theater and became successful as a make-up artist and set designer. In 1934 he worked as an assistant in the studio of Hugh Cecil, opening his own studio in London the following year. Soon he earned a reputation as being an excellent theater photographer and portrait photographer of famous actors. At this time McBean's work was marked by wit and great inventive imagination, and his elaborate productions reflected the photographer's interaction with the art of Surrealism.

▼ Angus McBean
Audrey Hepburn,
1951

Gelatin silver print
27.9 x 22.3 cm
ML/F 1977/487

Gruber Collection

When the theaters in London were forced to close during World War II, McBean moved to Bath. In 1945 he opened a new studio in London and became number one among British theater photographers. Even after the war he maintained his humorous, surreal style as evidenced by *Self-portrait* from the year 1947: The grinning head of the photographer appears like a ghost on the stairs.

One of his most famous photographs of the post-war era was the portrait of the as yet unknown Audrey Hepburn. She emerges like an antique bust from a desert divided by classical columns. As an advertising poster for a cosmetic product, this portrait was seen in display windows throughout the country and it ultimately provided the young model with access to the motion picture studios of Hollywood, thereby marking the beginning of a meteoric career.

In the fifties and sixties, in addition to his theater photographs McBean also took numerous photographs for album covers of pop records. His most popular shot

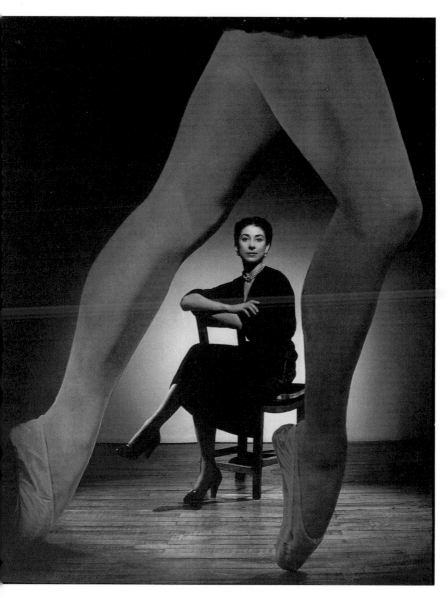

▲ **Angus McBean**
Margot Fonteyn,
1951

Gelatin silver print
37.6 x 29.8 cm
ML/F 1977/485

Gruber Collection

◀ **Angus McBean**
Penelope Dudley-
Ward, 1938

Gelatin silver print
28.8 x 23.9 cm
ML/F 1977/486

Gruber Collection

in this area was undoubtedly his picture of the laughing Beatles as
they leaned over the railing of a balcony. This picture traveled around
the world on the cover of the LP "Please, Please Me".

In the early seventies McBean sold his house in London and his
studio in Islington. A large number of his photographs went to Harvard
University. At the age of 70 he finally retired from the business of photography altogether. *MBT*

▲ **Angus McBean**
Self-portrait, 1947

Gelatin silver print
28.8 x 23.4 cm
ML/F 1977/484

Gruber Collection

McBride, Will

1931 Saint Louis,
Missouri
Lives in Frankfurt
on Main

Will McBride started out by studying art and art history in New York. At the same time he trained as an army officer, ending up stationed in Würzburg. Even though he had dealt with photography during his studies, McBride learned to value photography as an independent medium of expression in Germany. His first topic was the life of soldiers in the Würzburg barracks.

In 1956 he took up residence in Berlin as an independent photographer. From there he produced photographic reports for the magazines *Life, Stern, Quick*, and especially *twen*. In the sixties he developed more and more into one of the most significant photographic chroniclers of the political and social scene – especially of student protests – in the Federal Republic of Germany of that era. In this context he not only dealt with public events. Many of his works provide insight into the intimate spheres of human existence.

For him, photography always meant the challenge of people and things, and the capture of continuous change. Not least for this reason, it was characteristic of his working style that he conveyed history with a photo essay in the form of a sequence or series of images.

In 1972 McBride moved to Tuscany where he continued working as a photojournalist. In 1980 he returned to Germany where he resumed painting and sculpting. *MBT*

◄ **Will McBride**
Konrad Adenauer,
1965

Gelatin silver print
26 x 39.4 cm
ML/F 1977/905

Gruber Donation

▲ **Will McBride**
Overpopulation,
around 1969

Gelatin silver print
26.7 x 40.5 cm
ML/F 1995/122

Uwe Scheid
Donation

◄ **Will McBride**
Barbara in our Bed,
1959

Gelatin silver print
24 x 37.2 cm
ML/F 1977/489

Gruber Collection

◄ **Duane Michals**
Nude, 1972

Gelatin silver print
12.1 x 17.8 cm
ML/F 1977/513

Gruber Collection

▶ **Duane Michals**
Paradise Regained,
1968

Gelatin silver prints
6 photographs,
each 16.6 x 24 cm
ML/F 1977/510

Gruber Collection

Michals, Duane

1932 McKeesport,
Pennsylvania
Lives in New York

Duane Michals is not one of those photographers who use photography
to create an image of reality. Instead, he has tried repeatedly to cross
the borders of reality, to blend reality and dream. He himself once said:
"I believe in the invisible. I do not believe in the visible .... For me, reality
resides in intuition and imagination, and in the small voice in my head
which says: 'Isn't that extraordinary?!'"

Between 1951 and 1953 Michals studied at the University of Denver
and in 1956 attended the Parson School of Design in New York. He took
his first photographs in 1958 on a trip through the Soviet Union. Toward
the end of the fifties he settled in New York as a freelance photographer,
worked for fashion and entertainment magazines such as *Vogue, Esquire, Mademoiselle, Show*, or *New York Times*, and specialized in portrait
photography. Even at that time his sense for cryptic, at times dream-like,
productions showing his interest in Surrealism manifested itself. In
1963 Michals visited René Magritte, whose paintings he had long found
exciting. The series of portraits of this artist is considered a peak of
Michals' art because he succeeded in portraying not only Magritte the
person but also his world of artistic ideas.

Especially Michals' self-staged photo sequences became famous,
which sought to overcome the restrictions of the single picture. "I was
not satisfied with the individual picture because I could not bend it to
provide additional disclosure. In a sequence the sum of pictures indic-

...ates what cannot be said by a single picture." Michals used three to fifteen shots to compose picture stories which, however, were not usually complete narrations but mysterious events meant to raise questions and to entice the viewer into further contemplation. By using photo sequences Michals translated picture stories, frequently accompanied by descriptions, of everyday events so ubiquitous in the photojournalism of the fifties and sixties into an artistic statement.

◀ **Duane Michals**
Andy Warhol, 1973

*Gelatin silver prints
3 photographs,
each 8.7 x 12.3 cm*
ML/F 1988/47

Gruber Donation

In 1966 Michals began to provide his photographs with hand-written titles which he then expanded into more and more detailed explanations. In some cases they even became independent literary texts. With these verbal elaborations Michals wanted to increase the recognition value of his otherwise strictly visual story-telling skill. At the same time he provided the "mechanical" imaging tool of photography with a personal, graphic touch. Later on he enhanced this effect in his photo-paintings, in which he combined photography with graphics and painting by overpainting his pictures. *MBT*

▲ **Duane Michals**
Ludmilla Tshernina,
1964

Gelatin silver print
12.3 x 18 cm
ML/F 1993/359

Gruber Donation

◄ Antoni
Mikolajczyk
Light-Drawing, 1980

Gelatin silver print
60 x 67 cm
ML/F 1982/1380

**Mikolajczyk,
Antoni**

1939 Siemianowice,
Poland
Lives in Lodz

Between 1962 and 1967 Antoni Mikolajczyk attended the Visual Arts Department of the University of Torun. From 1964 to 1969 he was a member of the group "Zero 61". Between 1967 and 1969 he was assistant for
visual projects at the Visual Arts Department of the University of Torun.
Thereafter, from 1971 to 1977, he was a professor at the Academy of Arts
at Lodz and since then he has been teaching at the Academy of Arts at
Posen. Mikolajczyk deals with space and light in his sculptural as well
as his photographic work. His camera captures the motion of light in
space, yet in other series, like *Light-Drawings*, it itself moves in order to
allow static light to draw lines. In a third variant, the motion of the camera strikes that of space. This results in images of great expressiveness,
which includes the use of color. Already in the seventies Mikolajczyk
was in contact with Western institutions that staged exhibitions, which
is why his work is linked more closely with those artistic traditions than
the work of many of his colleagues. *RM*

▶ Willi Moegle
Ulm, View of the
Cathedral Square,
1933

Gelatin silver print
49.8 x 55.6 cm
ML/F 1985/1

Willi Moegle completed an apprenticeship in chemigraphy. In 1922 he worked for the State Office for Historical Preservation in Stuttgart and began to take photographs there. In 1927 Moegle set up his own studio and took pictures for architects, interior architects, and graphic designers. In 1944 his studio was destroyed during an air raid and he worked with his step-brother, Arthur Ohler, for five years. In 1950 he was able to open a new studio of his own, where he mainly took pictures for porcelain and glass manufacturers and also for furniture companies. In the fifties his reserved factual style impacted the appearance of the advertising of numerous companies in Germany. In 1959 Moegle set up his studio in Obereichen. He entrusted his long-time associate Hansi Müller-Schorp with its management. His activities on behalf of the German Society of Photographers (GDL) have had a lasting influence on this organization of photographers working in the artistic field. *RM*

Moegle, Willi

1897 Stuttgart
1989 Leinfelden

Ill. p. 438:
Willi Moegle
Silk-Spinning Plant
in Biberach/Riss,
1948–1949

Gelatin silver print
42.5 x 32.8 cm
ML/F 1991/119

Ill. p. 439:
Willi Moegle
Prototypes –
Apothecary Bottles,
1954

Gelatin silver print
59.8 x 35.8 cm
ML/F 1991/125

Moholy, Lucia

1894 Karolinenthal,
near Prague
1989 Zollikon, near
Zurich

▲ Lucia Moholy
Wassily and Nina
Kandinsky in their
Dining Room, 1926

Gelatin silver print
19.4 x 25.1 cm
ML/F 1988/59

Gruber Donation

Lucia Schulz studied art history and philosophy and in 1915 began work as an editor for various newspapers and publishing houses. In 1920 she met László Moholy-Nagy, whom she married in 1921. Beginning in 1922 the couple worked together on photographic experiments. After her husband was called to the Bauhaus in Weimar, Lucia Moholy began an apprenticeship as a photographer and produced numerous portraits of Bauhaus teachers and friends. In 1926 she documented the construction of the new Bauhaus in Dessau and took numerous product pictures for Bauhaus workshops. In 1928 she and Moholy-Nagy went to Berlin, where they continued to work together until their separation in 1929. In 1933 Lucia Moholy emigrated to London. There, in 1933, she published a much-cited cultural history of photography entitled *One Hundred Years of Photography*. *MBT*

▲ Lucia Moholy
Bauhaus Dessau,
Workshop Wing, 1926

Gelatin silver print
34.7 x 28.4 cm
ML/F 1977/523
Gruber Collection

◄ László
Moholy-Nagy
Bauhaus Balconies,
1925

Gelatin silver print
8.2 x 6.1 cm
ML/F 1977/1144

Gruber Donation

Moholy-Nagy, László

1895 Bácsborsod,
Southern Hungary
1946 Chicago

Although the Hungarian László Moholy-Nagy considered himself a painter and not a photographer, he is now considered as one of the pioneering innovators in photography in the twenties.

Initially Moholy-Nagy had decided on a career as a lawyer, but this plan was interrupted by World War I. In 1914 he was drafted for war duty into the Austro-Hungarian army. During his stay in a military hospital in 1915 he made his first chalk and ink drawings.

After the war he decided to devote himself to the arts entirely and abandoned his legal studies. In 1920 Moholy-Nagy went to Berlin, where he established contacts with the "Sturm" group, dadaists, and constructivists. There he met Lucia Schulz, who was to become his wife and with whom he worked on photographic experiments during the years that followed. He became famous, however, because of his photograms, the earliest of which can be dated back to the fall of 1922.

▲ László
Moholy-Nagy
Ascona, 1926

Gelatin silver print
37.8 x 30.3 cm
ML/F 1977/531
Gruber Collection

Das Tänzerpaar Olly & Dolly Sisters

In 1923 Walter Gropius invited Moholy-Nagy to go to the Bauhaus
in Weimar. There he directed first the metal workshop and then the
preliminary courses after Johannes Itten had left the Bauhaus. Although
there was no independent photographic course at the Bauhaus at the
time of Moholy-Nagy (it was instituted only in 1929 after the arrival of
Walter Peterhans), he is considered to be one of the pioneers of this
medium, becoming the representative of Bauhaus photography per se.
Among other things, he owes this reputation to his publication *Painting,*

Photography, Motion Pictures, which he published in 1925 as the eighth volume of the *Bauhaus Books*.

This constituted the publication of the first definitive text on the topic of photography at the Bauhaus. Moholy-Nagy tried to clarify the relationship between painting and photography, promoting a clear separation between the two media. While he considered painting as creating with color, he used photography for the examination and depiction of the phenomenon of light. For him photography was not mainly an auxiliary tool for intensifying human vision – as was frequently the case in the twenties – but a new artistic medium. In his aforementioned book *Painting, Photography, Motion Pictures* Moholy-Nagy also coined the term "photo sculpture or relief" for his photomontages. He understood them to be the following: "They are composed of different photographs, a [...] method for testing simultaneous illustration, compromising penetration of the visual and the humor of the word, mysterious connection of the most realistic imitative means growing into the imaginary. Yet, they can tell stories at the same time, be concrete, truer to life 'than life itself'."

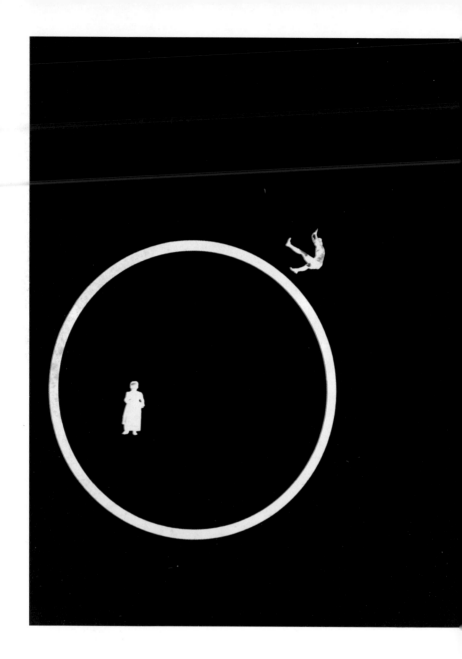

After the Bauhaus had moved to Dessau in 1926, Moholy-Nagy remained there for two more years as a teacher, before moving to Berlin in 1928. In 1929 he participated in assembling the famous Stuttgart Werkbund exhibition "Film and Photo" (FIFO), where he himself was represented with 97 photographs, photoreliefs, and photograms. In 1934 Moholy-Nagy emigrated to Amsterdam and from there to London. In 1937 he moved to Chicago, where he became director of the newly founded Association of Arts and Industries design school, which he renamed the New Bauhaus. Only one year later, the New Bauhaus closed down. In 1939 he and other artists founded their own School of Design.

In addition to his artistic work, Moholy-Nagy left behind comprehensive theoretical works dealing with questions of painting and photography. He always endeavored to make photography a medium with the same artistic value as painting. *MBT*

▲ **László Moholy-Nagy**
The Spiral Turn of the Room, 1925

Gelatin silver print
13.4 x 18.3 cm
ML/F 1988/101

Gruber Donation

Ill. p. 452:
László Moholy-Nagy
Photogram, 1924

Gelatin silver print
39.8 x 29.8 cm
ML/F 1971/53

Ill. p. 453:
László Moholy-Nagy
Photogram, 1924

Gelatin silver print
39.7 x 29.8 cm
ML/F 1971/54

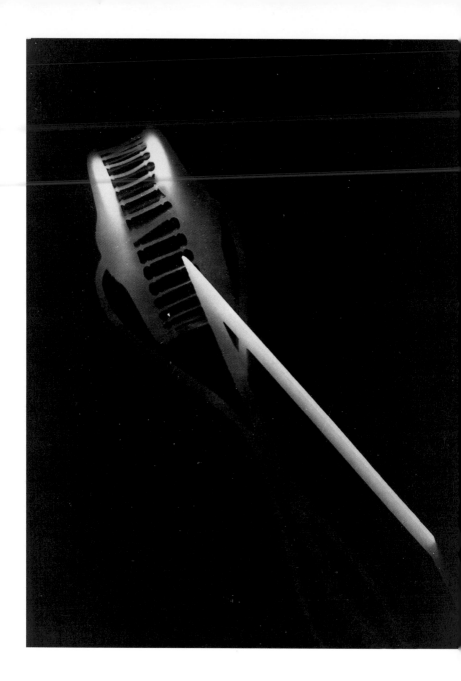

Morath, Inge

1923 Graz
Lives in Roxbury,
Connecticut

▼ Inge Morath
Dominguin, 1955

Gelatin silver print
25.4 x 16.8 cm
ML/F 1977/517

Gruber Collection

After studying Romance languages and literature in Berlin and Bucharest, Inge Morath worked as a journalist for the press and radio before turning to photography and studying under Simon Guttman in London, who is considered to be one of the fathers of modern photo-journalism. She has been a member of the "Magnum" group in Paris and New York since 1953. Inge Morath has worked with Ernst Haas and with Henri Cartier-Bresson, whose assistant she was from 1953 to 1954. In 1956 she had her first solo exhibition and her first book *War on Sadness*. Photographic journeys took her to Europe, Africa, the Orient, the USA, the USSR, China, Japan, Thailand, and Cambodia. Her photographic reports appeared in well-known magazines such as *Life*, *Paris Match*, *Holiday*, and the *Saturday Evening Post*. She has been married to the American author Arthur Miller since 1962. He wrote the text for her book *In Russia* (1969). Inge Morath's photographs are characterized by great sensitivity. In 1975 she herself characterized her work: "Before I tackle a project, I want to know its background, immerse myself in its civilization and at least learn the fundamentals of its language. Then I have more freedom to reach what Cartier-Bresson calls the decisive attitude of the photographer. He took his pictures with one eye open, observing the world through a viewfinder, and the other eye closed, looking into his own soul." *AS*

▶ **Martin Munkacsi**
Torso, 1944

Gelatin silver print
33.8 x 27.4 cm
ML/F 1977/541

Gruber Collection

The Hungarian Martin Munkacsi taught himself photography. His work
as painter and sports reporter for a Budapest newspaper was helpful in
that endeavor. In 1927 he worked for the Ullstein publishing house in
Berlin as a photojournalist for the magazines *Dame, Studio,* and *Berliner
Illustrirte*. Later Munkacsi freelanced for international newspapers. In
1933 he emigrated to the USA, where he worked as a fashion photographer for *Harper's Bazaar* and in 1936 he became a full-time staff
member of *Life* magazine. In the forties Munkacsi became one of the
most highly paid and sought-after photojournalists in the USA.
Munkacsi's action shots captured spontaneity and used unconventional
viewing angles. He applied his experience in sports photography to
fashion photography. He took pictures from extreme angles, frequently
bird's eye views, of professional models as well as ordinary people
outdoors and in motion. His photographs of masses of people and of
individuals appear natural, presenting fashion without artifice in daily
life and within real contexts. Until his death Munkacsi was also active as
a cameraman and light designer in motion pictures. *LH*

Munkacsi,
Martin

(Martin Marmorstein)

1896 Koloszvar,
Hungary
1963 New York

Muybridge, Eadweard

(Edward James Muggeridge)

1830 Kingston-upon-Thames, England
1904 Kingston-upon-Thames

▲ **Eadweard Muybridge**
Motion Studies/
Animal Locomotion,
Plate 48, 1887

Photo print
32.7 x 25.3 cm
ML/F 1977/543

Gruber Collection

Eadweard Muybridge left England in 1850 in order to seek his fortune in America. There he met the daguerreotypist Silas Selleck, who won him over to this medium. Between 1856 and 1867 he again lived in England, but he returned to San Francisco where he formed a partnership with Selleck in a gallery. He became famous for his landscape views of the Yosemite Valley taken with a large plate camera. These were followed by views of the Pacific Coast, an Alaskan expedition, and his specialization in industrial photography. Muybridge became famous for his motion studies, which he began in 1872 by attempting to capture a galloping horse in photographic pictures. In 1877 he expanded his experiment by placing twelve cameras next to each other in order to be able to record the running horse in all its phases of movement. His books *Animal Locomotion* and *The Human Figure in Motion* appeared during his lifetime. Fastened next to each other and viewed in a zoetrope, photographs became moving pictures for the first time. Muybridge himself used similar equipment to project his images on a screen and is therefore considered to be a pioneer of cinematography. *AS*

In 1884 Moisei Nappelbaum began an apprenticeship at the Boretti Studio. In 1887 he left Minsk and undertook an extensive journey through Russia, Poland, and the USA, where he worked in New York, Philadelphia, and Pittsburgh. In 1895 he returned to Minsk and opened a studio for portrait photography. In 1910 he worked in St. Petersburg for the newspaper *The Sun of Russia*. In 1919, when the government moved to Moscow, Nappelbaum set up the first state photographic studio. In the twenties he participated in many international exhibitions and in the thirties became one of the most successful portrait photographers of famous party leaders and personalities from the cultural and artistic realm. In 1935 he became the only Soviet photographer to receive the title "Artist of Merit of the Republic" for his 50 years of work. In 1958 he published his autobiography *From Trade to Art*. *MBT*

**Nappelbaum,
Moisei**

1869 Minsk
1958 Moscow

Nauman, Bruce

1941 Fort Wayne,
Indiana
Lives in Pasadena,
California

Bruce Nauman is one of the most significant practitioners of Concept Art in the USA. Although he frequently used photography and film, in particular in the years from 1967 to 1970, he viewed these media merely as forms of documentation for capturing his "Body Art". For Nauman, photography constituted an interesting alternative to traditional media because it offered the advantage of being fast, technologically simple, and (still) unencumbered by the prejudices of the art world.

His *Studies for Holograms* (1970) are based on a 1967 motion picture entitled "Thighing". In 1968 he created his first series of holograms projected on glass and gave it the title *Making Faces*. In 1967 Nauman created a drawing of five unnatural lip positions. On this drawing he wrote the note: "Both lips folded toward the outside; mouth open, upper lip pulled down by the right forefinger; both lips stretched tightly over teeth – mouth open. As above, but with mouth open. Both lips are compressed from the side with the thumb and the forefinger of the right hand." In the series of hologram studies Nauman pulled his face in a similar manner, expanded and stretched in exaggerated forms ending in the absurd. These studies are reminiscent of child's play or abnormal behavior. "I think I was interested in doing something extreme", Nauman said about this work. "Had I only smiled, it would not have been worth a picture. It would have been sufficient to make a note that I did it. I also could have made a list of things which one can do. But then there was the problem with holograms which require an expression strong enough that one would not think so much of the technical aspect."

In a series of motion pictures he explored the problem of hiding behind a mask. About the motion-picture "Art Make-Up" (1967–1968) Nauman said: "'Make-Up' is not necessarily anonymous, but still somehow distorted; something behind which one can hide. It does not advertise or reveal anything. The tension in the work frequently tells of that. One does not get what one does not get."

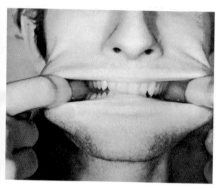
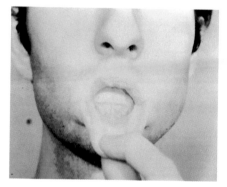

◄▲ **Bruce Nauman**
Studies for
Holograms, 1970

*Screen prints
5 sheets,
each 66.2 x 66.2 cm*
ML/F 1970/32 I-V

◄ **Angela Neuke**
Secretary General
Gorbachov is
expected, Andrews
Air Force Base,
Washington, DC,
1987

Color print
50.6 x 61 cm
ML/F 1993/363

Gruber Donation

Neuke, Angela

1943 Berlin
Lives in Cologne

Between 1963 and 1966 Angela Neuke studied photography under Otto Steinert at the Folkwang School of Creativity in Essen. In 1967 she became independent and worked for various magazines and newspapers. Since 1980 she has been a professor at the General College of Essen. Her series *National Theater – Media Circus* was much acclaimed. Angela Neuke observed the preparations for the obligatory photographic pictures at official government receptions and similar events. However, because she did not wait for the backdrops to be finished or take the prescribed position of the photographers, she documented not only the expected perspective with staged groupings but also the preparations for the production. In this way she unmasks the arrangement as such, denouncing as theater what appears so relaxed and normal in newspaper photographs. In particular Angela Neuke's color photographs show a distinctly new language of imaging and a specific topic which exposes and questions what is apparently known. *RM*

► **Floris Michael Neusüss**
Artificial Landscape, 1985

Color print
17.8 x 25.8 cm
ML/F 1988/45

Gruber Donation

Floris Michael Neusüss studied photography at the Arts and Crafts School of Wuppertal and at the Bavarian State Educational Institute for Photography in Munich. In 1960 he completed his photographic training with Heinz Hajek-Halke at the College of Creative Arts in Berlin. Already in 1957 he was interested in free, artistic photography. He began with surreal photomontages and photograms, and, in the seventies, developed the nudogram – life-size shadow outlines of nudes, and later of clothed people.

Since the early seventies Neusüss has been conducting a class for experimental photography at the Art Academy of Kassel. There he founded the college gallery as well as the collection and edition of "Fotoforum" Kassel. Both in theory and practice, he dealt with the relationship of photography and art.

His exhibitions featuring environmental pollution with pictures like *Photo Recycling Photo* and *Photography, Patience, and Boredom* between the years 1982 and 1985 caused quite a furor.

At the beginning of the eighties he created *Artificial Landscapes*, abstract chemical works which looked like reduced excerpts of landscapes or large horizons. Beginning in 1986 he created a new series, his *Night Images*, photographs which are arranged outdoors at night. With his

Neusüss, Floris Michael

1937 Lennep, Germany
Lives in Kassel

◀ Floris Michael
Neusüss
Night Images I, 1988

Gelatin silver print
50.5 x 37 cm
ML/F 1993/364

Gruber Donation

artistic work, teaching and publications, Neusüss has significantly
stimulated discussion about the imaging tradition of experimental, in
particular camera-less, photography. *RM*

◀ **Floris Michael Neusüss**
Nudogram, 1966

Gelatin silver print on canvas
231 x 104 cm
ML/F 1979/1155

Gruber Donation

**Newhall,
Beaumont**

1908 Lynn,
Massachusetts
1993 Santa Fe,
New Mexico

Beaumont Newhall studied art history at Harvard University, in Philadelphia, and in Paris. Between 1933 and 1934 he was an associate in the De
partment of Arts and Crafts of the Metropolitan Museum of Art in New
York. In 1935 he became librarian of this museum. During this time he
was able to prepare his legendary exhibition "Photography 1839 to 1937"
which opened to the public in 1937. In conjunction with this exhibition
he wrote and published the catalog *History of Photography*. In it he described in an exemplary manner not so much the technical development
of the medium, but rather the artistic accomplishments of the photographers, their aesthetics and their approaches, from the perspective of
an art historian. *History of Photography* was kept up to date with numerous revisions and new editions until the seventies, and to this day it is
considered to be the standard reference in photographic history.

In 1940 Newhall was placed in charge of the photographic division
of the Museum of Modern Art, working as its curator until 1945. In 1948
he went to the George Eastman House in Rochester, New York, acting
as its director from 1958 to 1971. In 1967 he was one of the founding
members of "The Friends of Photography at Carmel" and he also lectured at various universities. In 1971 Newhall moved to the University
of New Mexico to become a professor of art. *MTB*

Since his childhood and youth, Arnold Newman exhibited a talent for drawing and painting. After completing school he began the study of art at the University of Miami, which he had to interrupt because of financial difficulties. At the age of 20 he took a job in a portrait studio in Philadelphia. This was to be the beginning of his successful career as a photographer. Between 1938 and 1942 Newman concentrated on social documentary work, which he shot in the black districts of West Palm Beach, Philadelphia, and Baltimore. In the early forties he specialized more and more in portraits, becoming the star photographer of artists, literary personalities, musicians, and other famous people. Newman developed his own particular style in this field called the "environmental portrait". This refers to Newman's peculiarity of including in the portrait objects characteristic of the portrayed person and of taking the photograph in an environment typical of that person, thereby associating the subject with his work and with the world of ideas. Newman, who did not want to feel himself restricted to the concept of the "environmental portrait", considered the symbolic content of his pictures to be of particular importance. Of his work he said: "I am not so much interested in documentation, but would like to use the means of the steadily expanding language of my medium to express my impressions of the individual."
4BT

Newman, Arnold

1918 New York
Lives in New York

▲ **Arnold Newman**
Igor Strawinsky, 1946

Gelatin silver print
18.3 x 34.4 cm
ML/F 1977/557

Gruber Collection

◄ **Helmut Newton**
Self-portrait with
Wife and Model,
1981

Gelatin silver print
22 x 22 cm
ML/F 1987/3

Gruber Donation

► **Helmut Newton**
Jenny Kapitän in the
Pension Florian,
Berlin, 1977

Gelatin silver print
20 x 13.4 cm
ML/F 1988/50

Gruber Donation

Newton,
Helmut

1920 Berlin
Lives in Monte Carlo

Helmut Newton, born in Germany, carrying an Australian passport and living in Monaco undoubtedly is a cosmopolitan who cultivates this image with relish. The fact that many of his photographs are created in hotel suites is certainly part of this image. Newton trained with Yva, a Berlin photographer who was famous for her fashion, portrait, and nude photographs. Following his training, he spent several years in Australia and Singapore, and then lived in Paris for 25 years. He worked for the French, British, American, and Italian issues of *Vogue*, but also for *Elle, Marie Claire, Jardin des Modes, American Playboy, Nova,* and *Queen*. In addition, he took regular assignments for *Stern* and *Life* magazines.

Today, there are not many photographers who manage to polarize the art world quite like Newton. It is divided into his community of fans, who admire his pictures, and his bitter enemies, who want to qualify him as fashion gadfly or woman-hater. In fact, in fashion, beauty, and nude photography Newton has created a new style which is successful

Dear Fritz, Here is the print you wanted, Herr Professor. There is a story attached to this photo: I've slept in this bed for 10 nights, it's in the Pension Florian in the Giesebrechtstrasse corner of Kurfürstendamm. it's the original "Salon Kitty", famous Nazi brothel, the cellar

▲ **Helmut Newton**
They Are Coming,
1981

Gelatin silver print
22.6 x 22.8 cm
ML/F 1984/132

Gruber Donation

because it betrays a deep sense for the signs of the time. His linking of
offensive self-portrayal and voluntary subjugation with a preference for
tall, large-boned, and self-assured women strikes the nerve of the dilemma in which women and the women's movement are still mired –
to have their share of participation in society and still not want to relin-
quish the traditional identity of a woman, or to experience the fact that
the process of redefinition is difficult and painful. Masculine women,
the trend to the androgynous, is his response to the not yet found identity of the new role. Newton's photography demonstrates the most di-

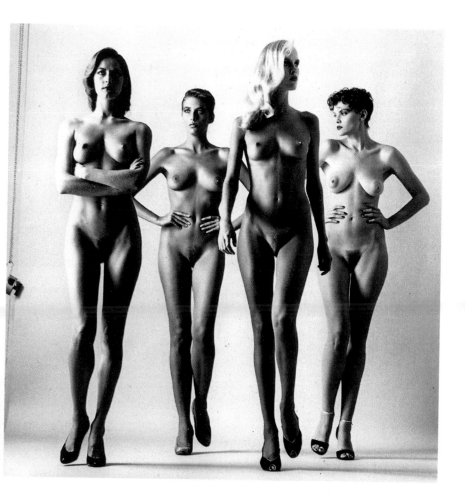

verse facets of types of women who have developed in this situation. He does not do this in a critical but in a sensuous manner, thus drawing the wrath of the women's movement, which has resulted in many a law-suit. *RM*

▲ **Helmut Newton**
They Are Coming,
1981

Gelatin silver print
22.4 x 22.8 cm
ML/F 1984/133

Gruber Donation

► Helmut Newton
Untitled, Paris, 1973

Gelatin silver print
30.3 x 40.5 cm
ML/F 1993/370

Gruber Donation

▼ Helmut Newton
Roselyne,
August 1975

Gelatin silver print
90 x 134 cm
ML/F 1990/68

Gruber Donation

► Helmut Newton
Violetta des Bains,
1979

Gelatin silver print
40.3 x 30.3 cm
ML/F 1993/368

Gruber Donation

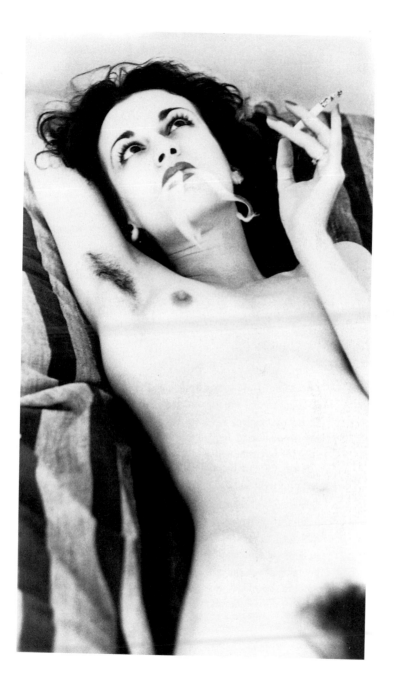

**Nothhelfer,
Gabriele**

1945 Berlin
Lives in Berlin

**Nothhelfer,
Helmut**

1945 Bonn
Lives in Berlin

▲ **Gabriele and
Helmut Nothhelfer**
Father and Son at
the Industrial Fair,
1974

Gelatin silver print
21 x 29.5 cm
ML/F1985/25

Between 1967 and 1969 Gabriele and Helmut Nothhelfer studied at the Lette School in Berlin and between 1969 and 1970 at the Folkwang School of Creativity in Essen. They have been living in Berlin since then, and in addition to doing freelance assignments they work at the Technical University of Berlin and at the Free University of Berlin. Gabriele and Helmut Nothhelfer have been working on a portrait of the Germans since the early seventies. They photograph them in public, at events, festivities, and demonstrations. Conspicuous in their pictures is the loneliness of those portrayed, even in crowds of people and at happy occasions, at a rock festival, or even while dancing. The stereotypical answer of the satiated post-war German to the question of how things are going becomes evident: "they must". Loneliness as the result of inner emptiness and lack of perspective in times of outward wealth create the tenor of the contemplative mood of the Nothhelfers' photography. *RM*

▲ Gabriele and
Helmut Nothhelfer
Dancing Couple
at Whitsuntide
Concert, Berlin, 1974

Gelatin silver print
21 x 29.5 cm
ML/F 1985/24

▶ Gabriele and
Helmut Nothhelfer
Roman Catholic
Man, Feast of
Corpus Christi,
Berlin, 1974

Gelatin silver print
21 x 29.5 cm
ML/F 1985/23

◄ **Hilmar Pabel**
Heinrich Böll in
Prague, 22 August
1968

Gelatin silver print
41.1 x 59.7 cm
ML/F 1977/564

Gruber Collection

▶ **Hilmar Pabel**
Returning Home,
1947

Gelatin silver print
top left: 23.9 x 17 cm
top right: 29.1 x 20.6 cm
bottom left: 29 x 20.5 cm
bottom right:
29.4 x 20.4 cm
ML/F 1994/14-17

Pabel, Hilmar

1910 Rawitsch,
Silesia
Lives in Rimsting,
Germany

Hilmar Pabel grew up in Berlin and studied Germanic languages, literature and Journalism under Prof. Dovifat between 1930 and 1932. Until 1933 he worked as photojournalist for, among other publications, *Neue Illustrierte* magazine. He was drafted as a photographer during World War II and worked primarily for *Signal* magazine. Pabel became famous worldwide on account of his missing child tracing efforts in cooperation with the Bavarian Red Cross and Rowohlt publishing company: "Missing Children Look for their Parents." After the war he began working as a photojournalist for *Quick* magazine, traveling around the globe and visiting countries such as Japan, Syria, Indochina, India, Pakistan, Mexico, the USSR, the People's Republic of China, Saudi Arabia, and Egypt. In the sixties he worked exclusively for *Stern* magazine, then as a freelance photographer. His reports on Mother Theresa, the Vietnam War, and the Prague Spring traveled around the world. Individual fates on the fringes of world politics were always most important to him because they reflect the consequences of politics most dramatically. In 1985, 50 years after Sven Hedin, he led a small team along the Silk Road. Immediately afterwards this indefatigable photographer set himself a new goal: "Around the world at the age of 80". *RM*

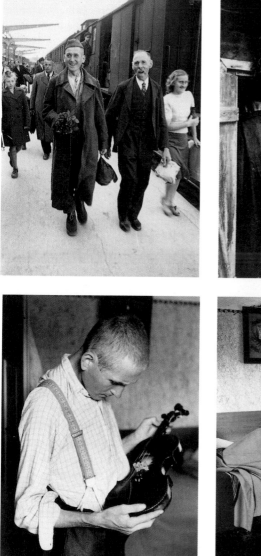

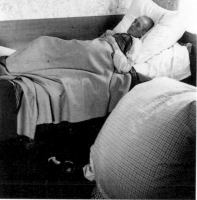

Parkinson, Norman

(Ronald William
Parkinson Smith)

1913 London
1990 London

▼ **Norman
Parkinson**
Fashion photograph,
around 1965

Gelatin silver print
36.6 x 26.9 cm
ML/F 1977/562

Gruber Collection

Between 1931 and 1933 Norman Parkinson trained with court photographer Splaight Sons. One year later he opened a studio together with Norman Kibblewhite. Parkinson worked for *Harper's Bazaar* magazine and *The Bystander*, a society newspaper. At the end of the thirties this fashion and portrait photographer distinguished himself with new standards of capturing a "natural aura" in his models, and he strove to suggest action and activity in his photographs. Still, Parkinson did not view himself as an artist but as an implementer who knew how to use his camera. Starting in 1945, he spent five years making photographs for *Vogue*. His wife, actress Wenda Rogerson, presented haute couture in Parkinson's new, unpretentious style. Following the European lead, he strove to get away from static photographs. Thus he placed his models in front of unusual props and presented them in special imaging perspectives. For example: hat fashions in front of skyscrapers. Parkinson took a similar approach in his portrait series of famous people in 1951.

One example is the shot of Algernon Blackwood, an author, whose close-up picture was taken on his balcony. The shot of Wenda Rogerson in an exquisite cashmere suit next to a cowboy has a similar surreal effect; attention is drawn by high-contrast confrontation. Parkinson also took portraits of well-known actors and singers such as Audrey Hepburn, the Beatles, and every member of the British royal family. After 1963 he worked as an independent photographer for international newspapers. He lives on Tobago island. *LH*

► **Gordon Parks**
Gloria Vanderbilt,
1960

Gelatin silver print
34.3 x 25.9 cm
ML/F 1977/576

Gruber Collection

Gordon Parks is the son of a day laborer and he is the youngest of 15 children. He grew up in his sister's house in Minneapolis until his brother-in-law threw him out at the age of 16. He made a living as a bus-boy and musician until, seeing pictures of the Farm Security Administration and a weekly newsreel with photographer Norman Alley, he bought a used Voigtländer Brillant camera and began to take pictures. He started out with fashion photography and, beginning in 1942, also worked for the Farm Security Administration. Between 1949 and 1970 he worked as a photojournalist for *Life* magazine. He portrayed the lives of people in the Southern United States and in Brazilian slums, as well as those of fashionably dressed rich people in New York and Washington. He portrayed artists and produced a touching report about black leader Malcolm X. His pictorial reports from the slums of Harlem, to which he had access being black himself, opened the eyes of white Americans to their own divided country. He became most popular because of his motion

Parks, Gordon

1912 Fort Scott,
Kansas
Lives in New York

◄ **Gordon Parks**
Red Jackson in "The
Harlem Gang Story",
1948

Gelatin silver print
24.2 x 19.1 cm
ML/F 1977/575

Gruber Collection

pictures, in particular "The Learning Tree" of 1969, and because of his
mystery stories, which for the first time had a black as hero. Through his
exemplary career, Parks, who could not be hired by Alexey Brodovitch
because of the color of his skin, has contributed greatly to the recognition of blacks in American life. *RM*

▲ **Gordon Parks**
Portrait of the
Harlem Story, 1948

Gelatin silver print
32.2 x 26.5 cm
ML/F 1977/566

Gruber Collection

Penn, Irving

1917 Plainfield,
New Jersey
Lives in New York

After studying design under Alexey Brodovitch, Irving Penn worked as a graphic artist at the Philadelphia Museum School of Industrial Art. In 1938 he moved to New York and began freelancing. In 1943 he produced his first cover picture for *Vogue*, a still life. Since then his photographs have appeared regularly in *Vogue* and other magazines. Since 1951 he has been taking pictures for individual clients all over the world. Like Richard Avedon, Penn is mainly known for his work as a fashion photographer. Unlike his counterparts, Penn is not interested in photography outside the studio, let alone shots in streets and cafés. All his life he has remained faithful to photography in the studio, under very specific lighting conditions, allowing cognoscenti of his work to distinguish between his pictures taken in Paris and those taken in New York. Despite these fundamental differences in approach, Penn also sees the interest in the human being as central to his work. In his fashion photographs, the personality of the model is always given considerable play, so that his pictures at times appear close to being portraits. His series, such as his 1949 assignment for *Vogue* to photograph fashion that is characteristic of the first half of the 20th century in five shots, appear to have been customized for the model – the scene depicting the fifties with the relaxed pose and dress almost allowing us to forget that this is a fashion shot, were it not for the repeated subtle background color.

The significance of this background only becomes clear when one remembers that even his portraits, his series on British and French small business people and skilled workers, his shots of people in Morocco, Benin, or New Guinea feature that background. The background is Penn's stage, on which he allows his models to act. Be it fashion or portraits, he detaches people from their own social context, isolating them to draw greater attention to their idiosyncrasies. Indeed, by con-

▼ Irving Penn
Jean Cocteau,
Paris, 1948

Gelatin silver print
27.7 x 25.5 cm
ML/F 1977/599

Gruber Collection

sistently using the same background, he both highlights the individual,
pulling him or her out of anonymity, and draws to the clothing. For
Penn, every piece of clothing, as soon as it is presented on a specific
stage, becomes fashion. From the viewpoint of cultural history, this idea
can certainly be justified, even if the style of clothing of earlier centuries
changed at a somewhat slower pace. In his series of pictures taken of
carpenters, lesser employees, and workers in England and France, Penn
removed their different uniforms and work-clothes from their practical
purpose and presented them as a fashion phenomenon. Likewise, these

▲ **Irving Penn**
Pablo Picasso, 1957

Gelatin silver print
34.1 x 34.1 cm
ML/F 1977/591

Gruber Collection

◄ **Irving Penn**
Marlene Dietrich,
1950

Gelatin silver print
48.7 x 38 cm
ML/F 1977/581

Gruber Collection

▲ **Irving Penn**
Max Ernst and
Dorothea Tanning,
New York, 1947

Gelatin silver print
24.2 x 19.1 cm
ML/F 1988/27

Gruber Donation

intentions were expressed in his portraits of native inhabitants of New Guinea, whose tribal dress was defined in terms of fashion. Even the scars on the skin of the girls from Benin are suggested to the viewer in this sense. At the same time, these pictures enhanced the idea of the portrait, with people being perceived as individuals.

Penn published a number of highly acclaimed books. In particular his *Moments Preserved* and *Worlds in a Small Room* caused a sensation in the European world of photography. This was made particularly obvi-

▲ **Irving Penn**
Cecil Beaton, 1950
Gelatin silver print
33.9 x 32.9 cm
ML/F 1977/587
Gruber Collection

◄ **Irving Penn**
The Bonapartist
Armand Fevre, 1950
Gelatin silver print
32.5 x 23 cm
ML/F 1993/374
Gruber Donation

▲ **Irving Penn**
Lisa with Roses, 1950

Gelatin silver print
41.5 x 34.5 cm
ML/F 1993/378

Gruber Donation

▶ **Irving Penn**
Fashion, 1950

Gelatin silver print
47.9 x 35.8 cm
ML/F 1983/130

Gruber Donation

▲ **Irving Penn**
Lisa Fonssagrives,
1950

Gelatin silver print
39.4 x 31.6 cm
ML/F 1977/579
Gruber Collection

▲ Irving Penn
The 1910s, 1949

Gelatin silver print
39 x 39 cm
ML/F 1977/590

Gruber Collection

ous by the publication of the retrospective, containing topics in a random sequence, which he put together with John Szarkowski in 1984. For Penn, as for other great photographers of our time, his own photographic interest and photography performed under contract become one in the course of the years. He uses these as an expression of a view of the world, an interest in the medium of photography which offers the opportunity to approach his fellowman and his environment for distinctive interpretation. *RM*

▲ Irving Penn
The 1920s, 1949

Gelatin silver print
43.1 x 39.5 cm
ML/F 1977/608

Gruber Collection

► Irving Penn
The 1930s, 1949

Gelatin silver print
40.9 x 31.8 cm
ML/F 1977/578

Gruber Collection

◀ **Irving Penn**
The 1940s, Dorian
Leigh, 1949

Gelatin silver print
41.9 x 32.8 cm
ML/F 1977/582

Gruber Collection

▲ **Irving Penn**
The 1950s, Dorian
Leigh and Evelyn
Tripp, 1949

Gelatin silver print
38.7 x 38.8 cm
ML/F 1977/584

Gruber Collection

Petrussow, Georgii

1903 Rostow,
Ukraine
1971 Moscow

▼ **Georgii Petrussow**
Caricature of Rodchenko, 1933-1934

Gelatin silver print
29 x 40 cm
ML/F 1992/161

Ludwig Collection

Between 1920 and 1924 Georgii Petrussow worked as a bookkeeper in a bank, devoting his spare time to his hobby of photography. In 1924 he moved to Moscow, where he made his hobby his profession by working as a photojournalist for the trade union papers *Metallist* and *Rabochichmik*. Between 1926 and 1928 he worked for *Pravda*. Petrussow specialized in industrial topics. Between 1928 and 1930 he took the post of departmental head of information at the Magnitogorsk mine in the Ural mountains, where he produced a documentary about the building of this plant. During subsequent years Petrussow worked as an associate for the newspaper *USSR under Construction*, creating many photographic essays on the subject of heavy industry. In 1931 he joined the group "October" and worked closely with photographers of the avant-garde, to whom he owed significant encouragement. Photographers like Alexander Rodchenko or Boris Ignatovitch affected his style and encouraged him to use bold perspectives and to experiment with photography – as he did, for example, by using a double exposure for *Caricature of Rodchenko* (1933–1934).

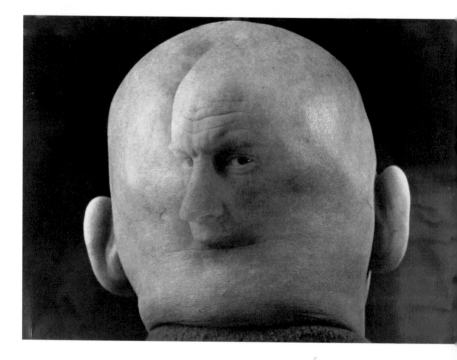

▶ Georgii Petrussow
Soldiers with
Helmets, 1935

Gelatin silver print
30 x 25 cm
ML/F 1992/159

Ludwig Collection

During World War II he worked with Petrussow as a war reporter
for the Soviet Office of Information and the newspaper *Izvestiya*. In
April 1945 he reached Berlin with the first troops and used his camera
to document the Soviet occupation of the city. Between 1957 and 1971
he worked in the USA for the newspaper *Soviet Life*, published by the
"Nowosti" press agency. In 1967 he was honored with a solo exhibition in Berlin. *MBT*

◄ **Georgii Petrussow**
Dam, 1934

Gelatin silver print
54.4 x 41 cm
ML/F 1992/162

Ludwig Collection

▶ **Georgii Petrussow**
Monument to
Workers and Peasant
Women, around
1936-1937

Gelatin silver print
49 x 36.6 cm
ML/F 1992/163

Ludwig Collection

◄ **Wolfgang Pietrzok**
Squashing 127/10 I,
1992

Color print
50 x 50 cm
ML/F 1993/398

Gruber Donation

**Pietrzok,
Wolfgang**

1949 Eilum,
Germany
Lives in Etzling, near
Saarbrücken

Between 1970 and 1971 Wolfgang Pietrzok studied art pedagogy at the Arts and Crafts School of Hanover, and between 1971 and 1975 he studied fine arts and art history at the Arts Academy of Kassel. Since then he has been working as an art teacher, organizer of exhibitions, and photographer in Saarbrücken and Etzling. In his work Pietrzok has combined artistic activism and his experience at the Arts Academy of Kassel with the concept of photo-performance art. Here, the square of the glass plate proves to be his special universe, in which the body is reduced to a black imprint or where it appears to have been frozen in battle, where body parts are reassembled puzzle-like to form a new physical entity. On a large pane of glass covered with blue ink he has male and female models take poses that are partly derived from movement, but which nonetheless are the result of the exact planning of his multi-piece work. To be sure, Pietrzok's work has been affected by the anthropomorphic images of Yves Klein, but in his case the imprint of the body is but one element of his photography. Decisive is the photographic momentum of tension resulting from focus, the absence of focus, of imprint and transparency. By blurring the color, the image becomes a dialog of expressive color tracks, imprints of body parts, which are often deformed and alienated themselves, and of vague looks at rounded parts of the body through spots where the glass is blank and

transparent. At times, in particular in his most recent work, the freezing of phases of motion could be called a memory of color that has accurately captured positions and attitudes that have changed in the meantime. Pietrzok's "Ecrasements" are marked by a dance-like ease, whereas deformities and outlines of ribs in his earlier black-and-white work were reminiscent of injuries. In those instances the happy ballet on the square shape inadvertently becomes a dance of death. *TM*

▲ **Wolfgang Pietrzok**
Squashing 20/16,
1989

Gelatin silver print
30.8 x 50.2 cm
ML/F 1993/400

Gruber Donation

Pitz, Fritz

1923 Bocholt,
Germany
Lives in Bocholt

After completing his apprenticeship in his parents' business, Fritz Pitz studied photography at the School of Creative Crafts in Weimar. Following a master program he participated in numerous international exhibitions in the fifties. In 1963 he began his long-term association with the Galerie de France with portraits of artists represented there. These included Henry Moore, Hans Hartung, Emil Schumacher, Salvador Dalí, Paul Delvaux, Lynn Chadwick, Ossip Zadkine, George Mathieu, André Masson and Joseph Beuys. In 1970 he was one of the first photographers to have an opportunity for a show at the Louvre.

Pitz is one of those portrait artists who follow a traditional pattern. His portrait studies dispense entirely with backgrounds that would allow conclusions regarding those depicted.

▼ Fritz Pitz
Karel Appel, 1964

Gelatin silver print
97.8 x 78 cm
ML/F 1992/11

Donation of the
City of Bocholt

Portraits of artists especially often include such hints in the form of a painting or a sculpture. Pitz, however, focuses on the face and frequently even crops the head in order to intensify his approach to physiognomy. He approaches faces like a sculptor, modeling heads and facial lines out of the dark with the help of light. The most significant aspect of Pitz' skill is his ability to stand back and to size up the person before him, to challenge and at the same time to put that person at ease in order to elicit the essence of a person. He has also employed unconventional darkroom techniques that have yielded prints of extraordinary precision and depth. In addition to his portraiture, it has always been important to Pitz to create abstract works, to be active as a painter in the realm of surreal expressionism in the circle of the "Cobra" group. *RM*

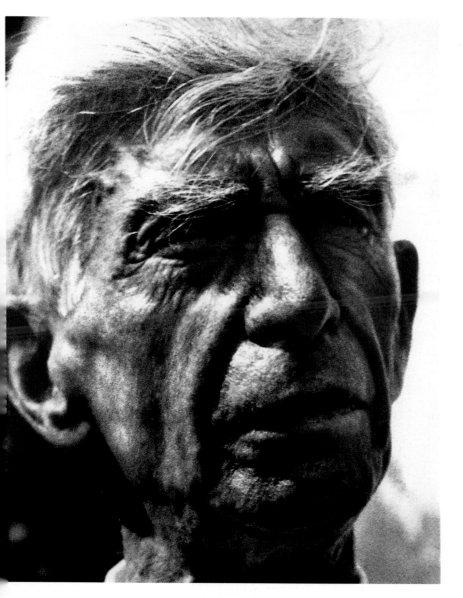

▲ **Fritz Pitz**
Ossip Zadkine, 1960

Gelatin silver print
97.8 x 87 cm
ML/F 1992/14

Donation of the
City of Bocholt

▲ **Fritz Pitz**
Paul Delvaux, 1965

Gelatin silver print
64.7 x 87.5 cm
ML/F 1992/37
Donation of the
City of Bocholt

▲ **Fritz Pitz**
Henry Moore, 1969

Gelatin silver print
64.7 x 87.5 cm
ML/F 1992/26
Donation of the
City of Bocholt

Pocock, Philip

1954 Ottawa, Canada
Lives in Cologne

▲ **Philip Pocock**
East Berlin, 1984

Cibachrome print
49.5 x 33.9 cm
ML/F 1994/230
Gruber Donation

▲▶ **Philip Pocock**
Kreuzberg, 1984

Cibachrome print
49.2 x 33.2 cm
ML/F 1994/213
Gruber Donation

▶ **Philip Pocock**
Mawlianmee, 1989

Cibachrome print
101.6 x 76 cm
ML/F 1994/8
Uwe Scheid Donation

Philip Pocock, a Canadian of Irish descent, completed his formal education at the New York University Film School under Haig Manoogian in 1979. Since then he has been active as an artist in the field of new media. After living in Toronto, Marseilles and New York, he moved to Cologne in 1991, where he has been working ever since. In his early years of artistic development he produced color photographs on Cibachrome, and his first book entitled *The Obvious Illusion: Cibachromes from the Lower East Side* was published in 1982. In 1982 he departed from this type of photographic image reproduction and began to experiment. He developed a completely new type of photochemical painting on Cibachrome, at times painting illusionary versions of baroque paintings with themes such as *Venus* or *Daphne*, but he also experimented with a type of dot painting that was strongly reminiscent of Australian Aboriginal painting. He constantly sought to fuse opposites in his work, as he did in *Mawlianmee*, where he combined pornography and abstraction. *RM*

◄ **William Boyd Post**
Winter Weather,
from: Camera
Work 6, 1904

Photogravure
15.1 x 16.5 cm
ML/F 1995/36

Gruber Donation

Post, William Boyd

1857 New York
1925 Fryeburg, Maine

William B. Post, a New York financier by profession, was a prominent amateur photographer in the 1890s. His picturesque shots of young ladies in idyllic scenes appeared regularly in the photographic magazines of his time. Shortly after the founding of the "Photo Secession" by Alfred Stieglitz in 1902, he joined this group, whose goal was "to promote photography as a means of artistic expression". One year earlier, in 1901, Post had moved to Fryeburg, Maine, where he focused mostly on two topics: lily-covered lakes and snowy landscapes. Snow was a particular challenge to him, to bring out the subtle nuances of the interplay of light and shadows on the white surfaces. *Winter Weather*, one of this photographer's most famous shots, proves Post's talent for composition. Post boldly positioned the large white area of the snowy field, divided only by a diagonal path, below the lone farm house at the upper edge of the picture. *MBT*

▶ **Barry Pringle**
Nude, 1977

Gelatin silver print
17.7 x 12.7 cm
ML/F 1984/88

Gruber Donation

Barry Pringle studied at the Guilford School of Arts and later at the
Royal College of Arts in London. After completing his studies he began
his photographic career and worked with numerous publishing houses.
Pringle has devoted himself mainly to two themes: the erotic child picture and the still-life. They are particularly distinguished by the simplicity of their composition. Pringle is interested in the beauty of one
single object or a smaller number of similar objects, be they corn cobs
or stalks of leeks, and directs his eye at the differences in similar things.
The use of lighting is particularly significant in all his photographs, still-
life pictures as well as nudes, and it is his specific way of emphasizing
his way of seeing things. *RM*

Pringle, Barry

1943 South Africa
Lives in Copenhagen

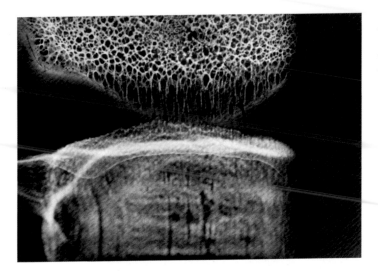

Rajzík, Jaroslav

1940 Hradec
Lives in Prague

Jaroslav Rajzík attended a technical school and then studied photography at the Motion Picture and Television Faculty in Prague. In 1966
he began to teach there. In 1981 he became assistant professor and
was head of the Motion Picture and Television Faculty in Prague between 1987 and 1990. In his work Rajzík has pursued the tradition of
experimental photography of the twenties. His work concentrates on
geometric abstraction, but not so much in the area of camera-less
photography, but rather in the arrangement of pure light phenomena
and light refraction, a photographic trend originated by Alvin Langdon
Coburn, the father of the vortograph. At the same time, his work has
roots in the visualism of the seventies and in the geometric light experiments of the Czech pioneer of experimental photography, František
Drtikol. Rajzík's adherence to the experimental tradition has been of
great importance to Czech photography and it has been particularly
fruitful in teaching the younger generation of Czech photographers. *RM*

► **John W. Rawlings**
Lynn Fontanne, 1958

Gelatin silver print
33.5 x 26.3 cm
ML/F 1977/614

Gruber Collection

John Wilsey Rawlings, the fashion, theater and portrait photographer, had a number of different jobs before being hired as an amateur photographer by Condé-Nast. He was sent to England to establish and head the *Vogue* studio there. In 1945 Rawlings moved to New York to open his own studio. In addition to his work for the American edition of *Vogue*, he also wrote photographic books, such as *100 Studies of the Figure*. In 1966 Rawlings published *The Model*, based on more than three years of work with the same model. Rawlings considers it most important for the model to arrive at a pose naturally, so that he would mostly record situations. Rawlings also propagates the art of omission, for example by masking the background. His body studies clearly show that movements can be as characteristic as a look. *LH*

**Rawlings,
John Wilsey**

1912 Ohio
Lives in New York

Ray, Man

(Emmanuel
Rudnitzky)

1890 Philadelphia,
Pennsylvania
1976 Paris

Man Ray first studied art by taking night courses at various schools, including the National School of Design in New York. Between 1908 and 1912 he studied drawing at the Francisco Ferrer Social Center in New York. In 1911 he began to work as a painter and sculptor. He was one of the first abstract painters of the USA and had close contact with the avant-garde of European art. In 1915 he began to turn to photography, working as a freelance photographer, movie-maker, and painter. In 1917 he was co-founder of the New York Dada group. In 1921 he went to Paris, where he worked closely with the surrealists for a number of years. In addition to his artistic activities he accepted commercial projects, especially in the areas of portrait and fashion photography. When the Germans invaded Paris in 1940, he returned to the USA, where he lived in Hollywood until 1950 and where he taught painting and photography. In 1951 he returned to Paris, remaining there until his death.

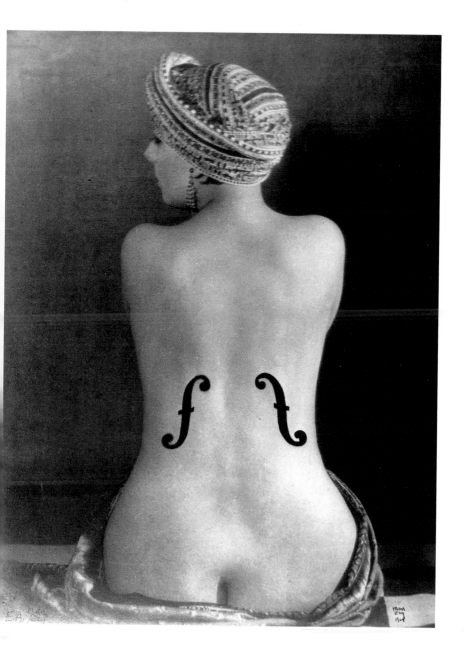

▲ **Man Ray**
Jean Cocteau, 1922

Gelatin silver print
36.5 x 30 cm
ML/F 1977/617

Gruber Collection

▲ **Man Ray**
Pablo Picasso,
1932–1933

Gelatin silver print
29.9 x 23.9 cm
ML/F 1977/632

Gruber Collection

◄ **Man Ray**
Lee Miller, 1929

Gelatin silver print
28.9 x 22.2 cm
ML/F 1977/643

Gruber Collection

▶ **Man Ray**
Lips on Lips, 1930

Gelatin silver print
22.9 x 17.5 cm
ML/F 1977/620

Gruber Collection

Man Ray is considered to be one of the most important pioneers of contemporary photography. His photographs broke new ground, especially in the experimental sector. Together with Lee Miller he developed the solarization process, which he used mostly in portraits but also in nude photography. With his "rayographs" he provided an important impetus to camera-less photography. His friendship with avant-garde artists of his time paved the way for the recognition of photography in the artistic context. Man Ray is one of the first artists whose photographic works have been valued more in the world of the arts than his paintings or sculptures. *RM*

▲ **Man Ray**
Solarization, 1929

Gelatin silver print
24.6 x 32.4 cm
ML/F 1977/646

Gruber Collection

◄ **Man Ray**
Dora Maar,
around 1936

Gelatin silver print
27.1 x 21 cm
ML/F 1988/39

Gruber Donation

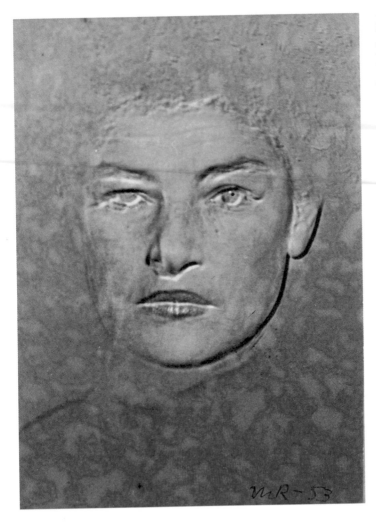

◀ **Man Ray**
Juliet, 1953

Gelatin silver print
17.5 x 12 cm
ML/F 1988/38

Gruber Donation

▶ **Man Ray**
The Veil, around
1930

Gelatin silver print
27.9 x 21.5 cm
ML/F 1988/37

Gruber Donation

Ill. p. 524:
Man Ray
Max Ernst, 1935

Gelatin silver print
24.9 x 19.8 cm
ML/F 1977/634

Gruber Collection

Ill. p. 525:
Man Ray
Coco Chanel,
1935/1936

Gelatin silver print
22.1 x 15.7 cm
ML/F 1977/621

Gruber Collection

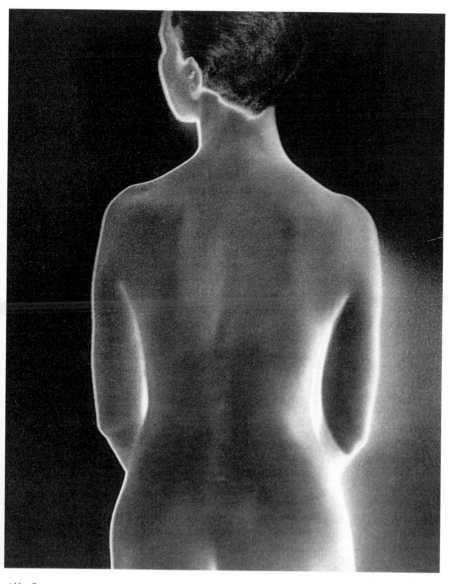

◄ **Man Ray**
Untitled (rear view
of nude), 1920/1934

Gelatin silver print
23 x 17.6 cm
ML/F 1993/408

Gruber Donation

▲ **Man Ray**
Untitled (solarized rear
view of nude), 1920/1934

Gelatin silver print
25 x 20 cm
ML/F 1993/409

Gruber Donation

Relang, Regina

1906 Stuttgart
1989 Munich

Regina Relang's exposure to the arts began at her parents' home. After graduating from high school, she studied painting, first in Stuttgart, later in Berlin and Paris, where she was greatly impressed by Amédée Ozenfant. Following her exams, however, she changed her mind about the teaching career she had planned originally and started to teach herself photography.

In 1933 she began to travel as a photojournalist through Southern Europe. After stays in France, Spain, Turkey, and Corsica, she achieved her first success with a report on "Fishermen in Need" in Portugal. In 1936 she met the stateless Russian Arkadii Kuzmin, who later was to become her husband. After trips to Southern France and Yugoslavia she began to turn to fashion photography in 1938.

She landed a contract with *Vogue* in Paris, London, and New York, and during these years had her first successes with *Shoes Walk Around a Tree* and *The Glove Ballet*. World War II broke out while she was on a photographic assignment in Spain and she returned to Germany, where she worked for Deutscher Verlag, a publishing house in Berlin and Vienna. Between 1940 and 1942 she took pictures for *Die Dame* in Berlin. In 1944 the house where she was born in Stuttgart was completely destroyed. After the war she moved to Munich and opened her new studio. During this time she worked with every leading fashion journal and enjoyed particularly good contacts with the magazine *Madame*. In 1951 she began to report twice a year on fashion shows in Paris, Florence, Rome, and Berlin.

After the death of her husband in 1971 she also turned to independent artistic work and, in this regard, was mainly interested in the merging of art and photography. These early examples of staged photography with fashionably dressed models placed in familiar contemporary settings are distinct, in particular because of the rich use of colors. Regina

▼ **Regina Relang**
Shoes Walk Around
a Tree, 1936

Gelatin silver print
25.6 x 23.8 cm
ML/F 1989/129

Relang continued working as a photographer until she passed away. During her later years she donated her collection to the photographic museum at the City Museum of Munich. *RM*

▲ **Regina Relang**
The Glove Ballet,
1936

Gelatin silver print
25.3 x 23.4 cm
ML/F 1989/127

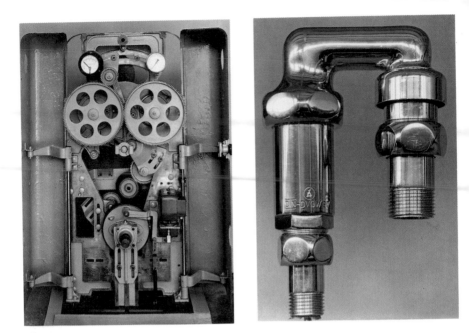

Renger-Patzsch, Albert

1897 Würzburg
1966 Wamel, near
Soest

▲ Albert Renger-Patzsch
Ring-spinning Machine, Head-stock, 1961

Gelatin silver print
22.4 x 16.6 cm
ML/F 1986/240

▲▶ Albert Renger-Patzsch
Pipe Air-Release Valve, 1961

Gelatin silver print
22.3 x 15.6 cm
ML/F 1990/898

Albert Renger-Patzsch, like August Sander, Karl Blossfeldt, or László Moholy-Nagy, was one of the photographers whose name became synonymous with the photography of the twenties. Being a firm opponent of so-called artistic photography, Renger-Patzsch developed a precise photographic style that strove for an exact reproduction of form, which made him a leading German exponent of the factual rendition of industrial and technical subjects. He became symbolic of the contemporary enthusiasm for technical progress and its abundance of new shapes. In publications such as *The World is Beautiful* (1928), *Pioneering Technology* (1928), and *Lübeck* (1928), he couched his industrial photographs in a programmatic context. These pictures are documents and aesthetic guides of a technological age.

As a proponent of factual, realistic photography that should always be subject to its imaging technique, Renger-Patzsch clearly distanced himself from the artistic trends affected by Moholy-Nagy. In the eyes of Renger-Patzsch, who understood photography to be more of a skill, the experiments and new viewpoints of the photographic avant-garde appeared more and more like an artistic fad, and he literally mocked them

▲ **Albert Renger-Patzsch**
Advertising Picture for the
Jena Works, around 1935
Gelatin silver print, 38 x 28.2 cm
ML/F 1977/655, Gruber Collection

► Albert Renger-Patzsch
Katharina Mine, 1954

Gelatin silver print
22.4 x 14.3 cm
ML/F 1993/112

◄ Albert Renger-Patzsch
Blast Air Heater in the Herrenwyk Furnace, 1927

Gelatin silver print
37.8 x 27.9 cm
ML/F 1977/660

Gruber Collection

Ill. p. 534, top left:
Albert Renger-Patzsch
Weeping Willow Tree, Aasee, Münster, around 1962

Gelatin silver print
22.5 x 16.4 cm
ML/F 1991/213

Ill. p. 534, top right:
Albert Renger-Patzsch
Reinhard Forest, Oak Tree, around 1962

Gelatin silver print
22.5 x 16.4 cm
ML/F 1991/216

Ill. p. 534, bottom left:
Albert Renger-Patzsch
Spruce Trees, around 1962

Gelatin silver print
22.5 x 16.6 cm
ML/F 1991/222

Ill. p. 534, bottom right:
Albert Renger-Patzsch
Fern Beech Tree, around 1962

Gelatin silver print
22.2 x 16.7 cm
ML/F 1991/219

▲ **Albert Renger-Patzsch**
Bulk Turneny, Card
Cylinder, 1950s

Gelatin silver print
16.6 x 22.4 cm
ML/F 1986/250

n his critique of the exhibition "Film and Photo" of 1929: "Their recipe
or success: type from the top or from the bottom, maximize or minim-
ze enormously, the trash-can is the most grateful subject."

In 1944 Renger-Patzsch, who lived in Essen at that time, lost his
tudio during an air raid. After the war he and his family moved to the
mall village of Wamel near Soest. In the fifties and sixties Renger-
atzsch became well known mostly as a photographer of landscapes
nd architecture. The fact that he continued to take industrial photo-
raphs was not recognized for a long time. Only in 1993 was he honored
or this aspect of his later works by the Museum Ludwig in Cologne on
he occasion of the exhibition "Albert Renger-Patzsch: Late Industrial
hotography". *MBT*

1952 Neuilly-sur-
Seine
Lives in Paris

Before becoming a photographer, Bettina Rheims worked as a fashion model, actress, art dealer, and journalist. In 1978 she began making portrait photographs and while doing so, she devoted special attention to black-and-white prints. A series of nudes of fairground strippers and acrobats was published in *Egoïste* in 1980. During the following year she had her first two solo exhibitions, in the Centre Georges Pompidou and nude portraits in the Texbraun Gallery, Paris.

In 1982 she began a series of animal portraits which were exhibited in 1983 in Paris in the Texbraun Gallery and in 1984 in the Daniel Wolf Gallery in New York. She worked for magazines, took her first fashion shots and photographs for record covers and movie posters. From 1984 on, in cooperation with the "Sygma" agency, she created photographic essays and portraits of celebrities. In 1986 she produced a number of advertising films, several video clips, and the leader for a feature film. She worked equally on portraits, fashion, and advertising photographs. At the same time she prepared a retrospective covering ten years of her photographic work for the "Photographic Space in Paris". Accompanying this presentation, which took place in 1987/1988, "Paris Audiovisuel" published a book. Her work was well received by the press and reviews appeared in *Le Monde, Le Figaro,* and *Le Matin.* Various photographic magazines *(Photo, Photographic Magazine, Annual Photography, Collector Photography)* and journals *(Paris Match, Stern)* published portfolios of her work.

In 1989 the Musée de l'Elysée in Lausanne exhibited Bettina Rheims' pictures. In the same year her book *Female Trouble* was published in Germany, France, and Japan. Simultaneously, the City Museum of Munich and the Parco Gallery, Tokyo, and Sapporo sponsored exhibitions. In 1990 she completed a series of portraits entitled *Modern Lovers*, which was first exhibited at the Palais des Beaux-Arts in Charleroi, Belgium. The Maison Européenne de la Photographie in Paris opened with this exhibition, and a book with the same title appeared in France, Germany, and Japan. In 1992 *Spies* and *Behind Closed Doors* were published, the latter with a text by Serge Bramly. From 1992 to 1993 *Behind Closed Doors* was shown at exhibitions in the Galerie Maeght in Paris, the Hamiltons Gallery in London, and the Galerie Bodo Niemann in Berlin. In 1994 *Animal* was published and Bettina Rheims received Le Grand Prix de la Photographie de la Ville de Paris. Her work is represented in numerous public and private collections in Europe, the USA, and Japan. *RM*

Riboud, Marc

1923 Lyon
Lives in Paris

▲ Marc Riboud
Applause for
Churchill, 1954

Gelatin silver print
33.1 x 49.4 cm
ML/F 1977/666

Gruber Collection

▶ Marc Riboud
Hunger in the
Congo, 1961

Gelatin silver print
29.5 x 19.7 cm
ML/F 1993/416

Gruber Donation

Marc Riboud's interest in photography began at the age of 14, when his father gave him a Kodak Pocket camera. After having fought in the French Resistance during World War II, he studied mechanical engineering at the Ecole Centrale in Lyon from 1945 to 1948. In 1951 he became a freelance photographer and, in 1952, joined the "Magnum" agency in Paris. In 1959 he became European vice president of this world-famous photographic cooperative and served as its president between 1975 and 1976. Riboud's work stands for sensitive photojournalism reporting on misery from travels all over the world, for example, Africa, China, and Vietnam, not with exposures of great dramatic gestures but with moving insight reaching into small details. Riboud performs his journalistic work not only in classic black-and-white but also in color, where exquisite composition and finesse of color are expertly applied. A selection of his publications includes *Women of Japan* (1951), *Ghana* (1964), *Face of North Vietnam* (1970), *Visions of China* (1981), *Gares et Trains* (1983). AS

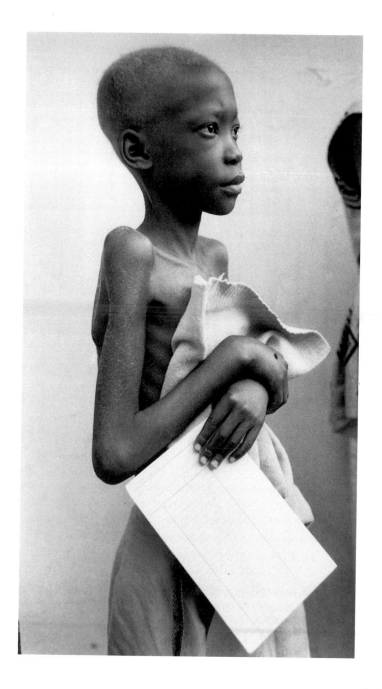

Richter, Evelyn

1930 Bautzen
Lives in Leipzig

From 1948 to 1952 Evelyn Richter studied photography under Pan Walther and Franz Fiedler in Dresden. Between 1953 and 1956 she studied at the College of Graphic Design and Book Art in Leipzig. She was a member of the Association of Creative Artists and worked on a freelance basis between 1956 and 1980. Between 1958 and 1962 she was a member of the group "Operation Photography" in Leipzig. Since 1980 she has been teaching at the College of Graphic Design and Book Art in Leipzig, first as head of the school of photography, then as lecturer, and since 1992 as full professor. Evelyn Richter never could accept conditions in the GDR (the former East Germany) and was constantly subjected to more or less open criticism. In spite of the fact that she was re-

▲ **Evelyn Richter**
Receptionist at
Leipzig Town Hall,
around 1975

Gelatin silver print
19.3 x 29.7 cm
ML/F 1988/67

Gruber Donation

garded as one of the country's leading contemporary photographers, she was refused a professorship at her college before the dissolution of the GDR. Even though she was permitted to travel to the West, where she had been celebrated since the eighties, she was denied recognition at home. Her photographic journalism, along with her ingrained critical stance, exerts a great influence on the younger generation. *RM*

► **Alexander Rodchenko**
Photomontage for LEF, Nr. 3, 1923

Gelatin silver print, mixed media
16.5 x 14.5 cm
ML/F 1978/1020

Ludwig Collection

Alexander Rodchenko was one of the most versatile artists in the Russia of the twenties and thirties. Between 1910 and 1914 he studied under Nikolai Feshin and Georgii Medvedev at the Arts College of Kasan, where he met his future wife Varvara Stepanova. In 1914 he moved to Moscow and attended the Stroganov School of the Arts. There Rodchenko met Kasimir Malevich and Vladimir Tatlin, and during the years that followed he evolved into one of the leading artists of the Russian avant-garde. He worked as a sculptor, painter, and graphic artist, designed posters for movie theaters, businesses and factories, and designed book covers and furniture. In 1921 his triptych *Pure Colors: Red, Yellow, Blue* was a masterpiece of absolute painting.

Between 1922 and 1924 Rodchenko turned increasingly to photomontages as related to poster art and book design. Especially famous were his illustrations of Vladimir Mayakovski's poetry *Pro éto* (About This), in which that poet proclaims his love for Lilia Brik. In his montages Rodchenko tried to create a visual image of Mayakovski's verses, thereby creating a unique connection between photomontage and constructivistic form. As he did in his other, earlier montages, Rodchenko

Rodchenko, Alexander

1891 St. Petersburg
1956 Moscow

► **Alexander Rodchenko**
Stairs, 1930

Gelatin silver print
27 x 40 cm
ML/F 1978/1048

Ludwig Collection

► **Alexander Rodchenko**
Girl with Leica, 1934

Gelatin silver print
40 x 29 cm
ML/F 1978/1072

Ludwig Collection

◄ **Alexander Rodchenko**
Photomontage for Mayakovski's Pro éto, 1923

Gelatin silver print, mixed media
22.5 x 14 cm
ML/F 1978/1018

Ludwig Collection

used existing photographic originals in *Pro éto*, i.e. not photographs he
produced himself. Only in 1924, when he was less and less able to find
suitable picture material for his montages, did Rodchenko reach for the
camera, at last recognizing photography as the artistic medium of his
era. Because pictures can be taken with a camera from every position,
photography, in Rodchenko's opinion, corresponded to the active eye
of man. Therefore, photography was predestined to render, in a representative manner, the confusing impressions to which modern big city
dwellers are exposed. By using bold and unusual perspectives, he
wanted to liberate photography from conventions and from the standard belly-button perspective and thus he evolved into a distinct pioneer
of photographic Constructivism. In 1928 he wrote in his manifesto-like
text *Ways of Contemporary Photography*: "In order to educate man to a
new longing, everyday familiar objects must be shown to him with totally unexpected perspectives and in unexpected situations. New objects
should be depicted from different sides in order to provide a complete
impression of the object." In 1928 Rodchenko, who had given up painting in favor of photography in 1927, bought himself a Leica which, because of its handy format and quick operation, became his preferred

ool for his work. This camera enabled him to realize to excess his ideas of unusual camera positions, severe foreshortenings of perspective, and views of surprising details. Increasingly Rodchenko's photography was dominated by the artistic element of the line. He liked to integrate elements such as grids, stairs, or overhead wires in his photographic compositions, converting them into abstract constructivistic line structures. *Stairs* of 1930 and *Girl with Leica* of 1934 are undoubtedly among the most famous photographs of this kind.

In 1930 Rodchenko became a founding member of the "October" group, the most important organization for photographic and cinematographic art of that time. Between 1933 and 1941 he also worked for the journal *SSSR na stroike (USSR under Construction)* which he had founded together with Varvara Stepanova. *MBT*

▲ Alexander Rodchenko
Gears, 1930

Gelatin silver print
6.5 x 10 cm
ML/F 1978/1106

Ludwig Collection

◄ Alexander Rodchenko
Pine Tree, 1925

Gelatin silver print
39.9 x 25.8 cm
ML/F 1978/1103

Ludwig Collection

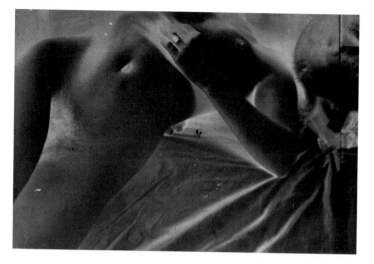

◀ Alexander
Rodchenko
Hot Air Balloon,
1927

Gelatin silver print
40 x 29 cm
ML/F 1978/1053

Ludwig Collection

▶ Franz Roh
Untitled, 1930

Gelatin silver print
22.2 x 15.2 cm
ML/F 1995/127

Uwe Scheid
Donation

Beginning in 1908, Franz Roh studied philosophy, literature, history, and art history in various cities of Germany. From 1916 to 1919 he was assistant to Heinrich Wölfflin in Munich, were he obtained his doctorate.

In 1919 Roh began to work as an independent writer and art critic for various newspapers. Between 1922 and 1923, encouraged by his work in contemporary art, he began to produce collages and experimental photographs. In his photographic work, which was created mostly between 1923 and 1933, he favored abstractions, such as negative prints, photograms, or the superimposed printing of several negatives. Employing these techniques, he created a fantasy world of images where, among other things, female nudes are superimposed on architectural and nature photographs.

In 1929 Roh and Jan Tschichold published the epoch-making book *Photographic Eye*, which was the first documentation of experimental photography besides László Moholy-Nagy's Bauhaus book. The time of National Socialism became a time of internal emigration for Roh, during which he worked on his collages and wrote his book *The Unrecognized Artist*, which appeared in 1948. It was only toward the end of his life that Roh went public with his own artistic work and exhibited his collages in galleries. *TvT*

Roh, Franz

1890 Apolda,
Germany
1965 Munich

Rohde, Werner

1906 Bremen
1990 Worpswede

Originally Werner Rohde wanted to become a painter like his father. In 1925 he attended the Arts and Crafts School at Burg Giebichenstein in Halle, studying painting under Erwin Hahs. It was at this time that Rohde took up photography. Initially, he considered this medium a by-product of his artistic development, but increasingly came to recognize it as a separate means of expression. It was because of Hahs that Rohde also discovered his love for motion pictures, in particular Charlie Chaplin. In many of his self-portraits he makes reference to his idol by taking pictures of himself wearing a white mask or white make-up and a black bowler hat.

After Rohde had left Burg Giebichenstein in 1927, and before finishing his studies, in order to learn the trade of glass-painting from his father, he concentrated more on his photographic work. He aligned himself with the avant-garde trends of the New Vision and experimented with bold perspectives, double exposures, photomontages, or exciting light effects. In 1929 he achieved his first success. He showed a few photographs at the photographic avant-garde's famous exhibition "Film and Photo" in Stuttgart. In 1935 his companion and future wife Renata Bracksieck introduced Rohde to Berlin gallery owner Karl Nierendorf, who asked him to take pictures of his friends and artists at the gallery.

After the war Rohde settled with his wife in Worpswede. There he devoted himself again to glass-painting and verre églomisé, utilizing the medium of photography only for reproducing his glass paintings. *MBT*

▶ Ulrike Rosenbach
and Hildegard
Weber
It Became a Matter
of Life and Death,
Museum Ludwig,
Cologne, 1985

Gelatin silver print
59.7 x 50.4 cm
ML/F 1985/155

Between 1964 and 1969 Ulrike Rosenbach studied sculpture under Prof. Joseph Beuys at the Art Academy of Düsseldorf, where she became a master student. Since 1972 her work has concentrated on video productions, in particular video installations and performance art. Her artistic work is based on her own experiences of life, questioning the historical position of women in society and exposing structures of oppression. Traditional notions and images of women become the mirror in which she reflects the fundamental problems of women in society. Her video work deals with subjects such as Venus, the Amazon, or Hercules as a counterpoint and also introduces occasional connections with Far Eastern philosophies and trains of thought. *It Became a Matter of Life and Death* was created in 1985 on the occasion of a performance at the Museum Ludwig in Cologne. Hildegard Weber studied at the Technical College, Cologne. She has documented the work of a number of artists in addition to her own. *RM*

**Rosenbach,
Ulrike**

1943 Bad Salzdetfurth,
Germany
Lives in Homburg

**Weber,
Hildegard**

1939 Kleve, Germany
Lives in Cologne

◀ **Sanford H. Roth**
Joan Crawford, 1958

Gelatin silver print
27 x 34.5 cm
ML/F 1977/670

Gruber Collection

Roth,
Sanford H.

1906 Dresden
1962 New York

Sanford H. Roth was a self-taught photographer. From the very beginning he worked as a freelance photographer. In 1946 he moved to Paris and began working for numerous international magazines, including *Life, Harper's Bazaar, Paris Match, Collier's, Oggi,* and *Elle.* The main focus of his work was portraits. He included just enough ambiance in his images to characterize the personality's essential traits. For example, he positioned Alfred Hitchcock exactly as the great director himself liked to portray himself for a few moments in his films – half hidden, peeking from around the corner of a house. He portrayed Joan Crawford as a mirror image sitting at a make-up table. Roth dealt with artists in a special manner and took portraits of almost all the famous ones. From 1954 on, he lived and worked mostly in Rome. *RM*

▶ Harry C. Rubicam
At the Circus,
around 1907

Heliogravure
15.6 x 19.3 cm
ML/F 1995/37

Gruber Donation

Harry C. Rubicam moved to Denver in 1897, where he was an agent for "Fidelity and Casualty Co." insurance company. In 1903 he became a member of the New York based group "Photo Secession". His picture *At the Circus*, using the complex technique of heliogravure, appeared next to those of Gertrude Käsebier, Edward J. Steichen, Alfred Stieglitz, and others in issue No. 17 of 1907 of *Camera Work*. This book showed that art photography was splitting into two directions, which could be defined as "pictorial against straight photography". While photographs based on symbolist art were still prevalent, new picture ideas were beginning to emerge that were to blossom a short time later in Paul Strand's work and especially in the photographs of the twenties. In Rubicam's photograph taken under the canvas of the circus tent, daylight filters down on spectators' heads, an artist standing on a white horse with her arms gracefully extended rides around in a ring that is cropped on the right side. The composition is well thought out, without being artistically stilted, and it relies on the photographic elements of image composition and the effectiveness of an everyday subject. *AS*

**Rubicam,
Harry C.**

1871 Philadelphia
1940 Denver

Rubinstein, Eva

1933 Buenos Aires,
Argentina
Lives in New York

▲ **Eva Rubinstein**
Bed in Mirror, 1972

Gelatin silver print
14.7 x 21.4 cm
ML/F 1984/93

Gruber Donation

▶ **Eva Rubinstein**
Standing Nude, 1972

Gelatin silver print
20.7 x 14.1 cm
ML/F 1984/92

Gruber Donation

Eva Rubinstein, daughter of Arthur Rubinstein, grew up in Paris and studied ballet under Mathilde Kszesinska in Paris. In 1939 her family emigrated to the USA, where Eva Rubinstein attended the French High School in New York. Beginning in 1941, she attended ballet school in California, where she studied under Bolm, Bekefi, and finally under Oboukhoff and Nemtchinova in New York. Between 1951 and 1952 she studied acting in Los Angeles, where she took part in productions and studied modern dance under Bella Lewitzky. In 1953 she settled in New York and danced at the Balanchine School and at the Martha Graham School. Until the sixties, Eva Rubinstein devoted herself exclusively to dance, but after her divorce she turned to photography, taking courses at the New York Institute.

She participated in workshops given by Lisette Model and Diane Arbus and began to travel. In addition, she devoted herself to portrait and nude photography. In 1973 she photographed the Yom Kippur War on the Golan Heights and at the Suez Canal. In 1974 she began to teach photography at various colleges throughout Europe and the USA. *RM*

▲ **Erich Salomon**
Aristide Briand at the League
of Nations, 1928

Gelatin silver print, 37.2 x 29.5 cm
ML/F 1984/98

Gruber Donation

Between 1906 and 1909 Erich Salomon studied zoology and engineering in Berlin, followed by law in Munich and Berlin. Between 1914 and 1918 he was on war duty in the German Reichswehr. He was taken prisoner of war and became an interpreter and spokesman for the prisoners at a French camp. After World War I he worked at the stock exchange, then in a piano factory, eventually founding a rental business for automobiles and motorcycles with sidecars. In 1926 he joined the Ullstein publishing house, where he was responsible for public relations work. There he was exposed to photography, which motivated him to acquire his first camera, an Ermanox. In 1928 he attracted attention with a series of pictures he had taken with a hidden camera in a courtroom. These pictures were published in the *Berliner Illustrirte*, which compensated him with two months' wages. He then left the Ullstein publishing house and began working as a freelance photographer for such publications as the *Berliner Illustrirte Zeitung, Müncher Illustrierte Presse, Fortune, Life, Daily Telegraph*, and also for the Ullstein publishing house.

Salomon, Erich

1886 Berlin
1944 Auschwitz

▲ **Erich Salomon**
Summit Conference, Chamberlain, Stresemann and Briand, 1928

Gelatin silver print
26.1 x 35.1 cm
ML/F 1977/690

Gruber Collection

▲ **Erich Salomon**
Immertreu Trial,
1928

Gelatin silver print
27.7 x 36 cm
ML/F 1977/675

Gruber Collection

▶ **Erich Salomon**
Observers at the
League of Nations,
1928

Gelatin silver print
27.7 x 35.9 cm
ML/F 1977/672

Gruber Collection

◄ **Erich Salomon**
Interview with
Fridtjof Nansen in
Geneva, 1928

Gelatin silver print
29.8 x 39.6 cm
ML/F 1977/691

Gruber Collection

► **Erich Salomon**
Hugo Eckener in
conversation with
Oskar von Miller at
the Hotel Esplanade,
Berlin, around 1930

Gelatin silver print
29.9 x 39.9 cm
ML/F 1977/695

Gruber Collection

Salomon's way of photographing political and social events made him the founder of modern political photojournalism. He had an inimitable gift for being everywhere without being noticed and thus his photographs reflect accurate observation. He took advantage of his Ermanox camera and its large aperture lens, as well as high-speed glass plates, which made intrusive flash unnecessary. His pictures gave the viewer the feeling of actually being present at the events he portrayed. It was Aristide Briand who, during a political debate from which journalists had been excluded, finally discovered Salomon and exclaimed: "There he is, the king of the indiscreet!"

Following his emigration to the Netherlands, Salomon was discovered by the National Socialists in Scheveningen and, being a Jew, he was sent to Theresienstadt and later to Auschwitz, where he, his wife and son Dirk were murdered. *RM*

▲ **Erich Salomon**
American newspaper magnate William Randolph Hearst in his castle La Cuesta Encantada, California, 1930

Gelatin silver print
28.3 x 36 cm
ML/F 1977/694

Gruber Collection

▲ **Erich Salomon**
King Fuad of Egypt
with Hindenburg,
1930

Gelatin silver print
17.7 x 23.7 cm
ML/F 1988/80

Gruber Donation

▶ **Erich Salomon**
Max Liebermann,
around 1905

Gelatin silver print
28.4 x 36 cm
ML/F 1977/692

Gruber Collection

▲ Erich Salomon
Marlene Dietrich, 1930

Gelatin silver print
each 28.3 x 36 cm
ML/F 1977/697-702

Gruber Collection

Sander, August

1876 Herdorf,
Germany
1964 Cologne

After working in the mines for seven years and serving in the military,
August Sander studied painting in Dresden between 1901 and 1902. His
intention was to enhance his artistic skills, in order to apply them to his
interest in photography, which he had developed on numerous trips and
while working at many photographic businesses in Berlin, Magdeburg,
Leipzig, Halle, and Dresden in 1898 and 1899. Finally, in 1902, he moved
to Linz, where he first worked at Studio Greif and then, in 1904, founded
the August Sander Studio for artistic photography and painting. In 1909
he returned to Cologne, where he founded his studio in Lindenthal in
1910. There he began his life's work, *People of the 20th Century*, which
occupied him into the fifties. In the thirties he got into trouble with the
National Socialists on account of his son's political activities, causing
him in those years to devote himself almost exclusively to taking pictures of landscapes in the Rhine River area and in old Cologne. Prior to
that, by publishing the *Mirror of Germany* and *Face of the Times*, he was

◄ **August Sander**
Publisher, 1923/1924

Gelatin silver print
22.5 x 16.7 cm
ML/F 1977/708
Gruber Collection

► **August Sander**
Heinrich Hoerle,
around 1928

Gelatin silver print
22.8 x 16.7 cm
ML/F 1977/711
Gruber Collection

►► **August Sander**
Prof. Dr. Wilhelm
Schaefer, around 192

Gelatin silver print
22 x 15.9 cm
ML/F 1977/736
Gruber Collection

► **August Sander**
The Architect Prof.
Dr. Hans Poelzig,
Berlin, 1928

Gelatin silver print
28.4 x 19.4 cm
ML/F 1977/748
Gruber Collection

►► **August Sander**
The Scholar Max
Scheler, 1925

Gelatin silver print
26.9 x 19.4 cm
ML/F 1977/745
Gruber Collection

Ill. p. 572:
August Sander
Albert Fischbach as a
Hunter with Dog,
arround 1910

Gelatin silver print
14.6 x 10.1 cm
ML/F 1989/27
Lotte Lohe Donation

Ill. p. 573:
August Sander
Pharmacist Linz,
around 1907

Gelatin silver print
47 x 32.4 cm
ML/F 1977/747
Gruber Collection

▲ **August Sander**
Porter, 1929

Gelatin silver print
28.3 x 22.5 cm
ML/F 1993/433

Gruber Donation

▶ **August Sander**
Unemployed, 1928

Gelatin silver print
22.5 x 14.2 cm
ML/F 1977/735

Gruber Collection

able to accomplish at least the initial stage of his idea of an encyclopedic and systematic picture of the German people. Finally, in 1980, his
son Gunther, collaborating with Ulrich Keller, published the combined
work under the original title *People of the 20th Century*. After the destruction of his studio and archive in 1944, Sander moved to Kuchhausen in
the Westerwald region, where he continued working under the most
primitive conditions. His name was almost forgotten in Cologne until

◀ **August Sander**
Photograph for a
Sanka Advertise-
ment, 1925

Gelatin silver print
20.8 x 15.1 cm
ML/F 1977/723

Gruber Collection

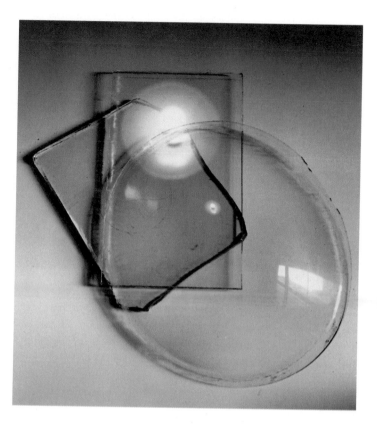

► **August Sander**
Glass Panes, 1924

Gelatin silver print
18.6 x 17.5 cm
ML/F 1988/118

Gruber Donation

.. Fritz Gruber showed his work at photokina in 1951 and arranged for his pictures of old Cologne to be taken over by the Museum of the City of Cologne.

Sander's portrait work constitutes an important contribution to the recognition of photography as an art. Today, his systematic approach is viewed as an early example of conceptual art, which was also not without influence on the development of the creative arts. He is now considered to be Germany's internationally best-known photographer of this century. *RM*

Saudek, Jan

1935 Prague
Lives in Prague

▲ Jan Saudek
Lips with Drop, 1974

Gelatin silver print
15.8 x 22.8 cm
ML/F 1993/443

Gruber Donation

▶ Jan Saudek
Super Striptease,
1982

Gelatin silver print,
colorized
each 16.2 x 12.2 cm
ML/F 1984/107

Gruber Donation

To a great extent Jan Saudek's work is marked by two circumstances his childhood, when he and his twin brother Karl were interned in a centration camp, where only by sheer luck they escaped the experim of Josef Mengele, and by visiting the exhibition "The Family of Man", which he considered an expression of the deep need for familial harmony and which made him aware of photography as a means of expression.

Between 1950 and 1952 Saudek studied at the School of Industrial Photography in Prague, before taking various jobs in farming and in numerous factories. He has been interested in photography since the earl fifties and he stages his own pictorial reality. Saudek was one of the first Czech photographers whose work became known in the West and this earned him the suspicion of the Czech government until the eighties.

His photographs, initially black and white, later in color, revolve around sexuality and the relationship between men and women, old ag and youth, clothing and nudity. Generally, he takes an antagonistic approach to attain powerful pictorial effects. To accomplish this, Saudek sometimes uses strong imaging language, reminiscent of the coarse ribaldry of medieval sexual life, an impression which is enhanced by the always unchanged, drab ambiance of his pictures. Frequently, he stages scenes in which couples appear alternately dressed and naked, young

◀ Jan Saudek
Untitled (Sugar),
1975

Gelatin silver print
14.6 x 11.9 cm
ML/F 1994/258

Gruber Donation

▶ Jan Saudek
Untitled (Rear View
of Nude), around
1985

Color print
22 x 16.8 cm
ML/F 1993/442

Gruber Donation

Ill. p. 582:
Jan Saudek
Untitled, around
1986

Gelatin silver print
17.1 x 11.5 cm
ML/F 1994/254

Gruber Donation

Ill. p. 583:
Jan Saudek
What an Unlucky
Girl, 1983

Gelatin silver print
13.9 x 9 cm
ML/F 1994/256

Gruber Donation

girls reappear pregnant, and children grow older. Without artifice
Saudek's photography reaches into life at its fullest. His direct language
very quickly met with lively acclaim in the art world. *RM*

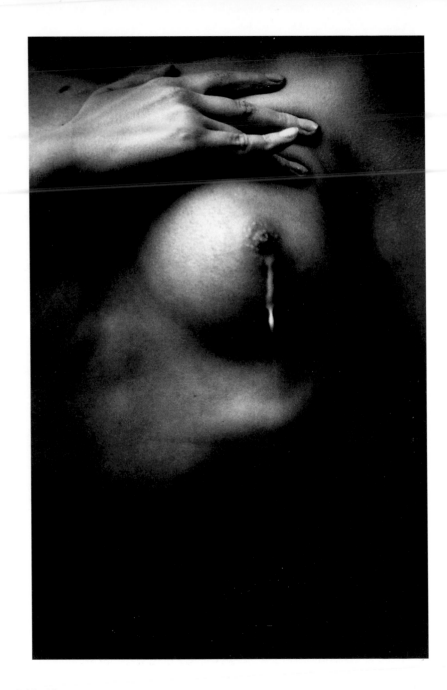

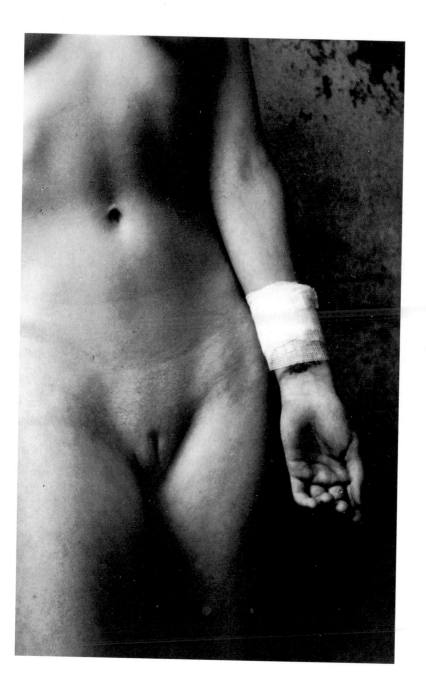

Sawada, Kyoichi

1936 Aomori, Japan
1970 Cambodia

Kyoichi Sawada became known as a press photographer who worked for "United Press International" during the Vietnam War. Sawada's interest in photography began early in life. At the age of 20 he became a newspaper editor in Tokyo. In 1965 he had himself transferred to Vietnam in order to experience the reality of war with his own eyes. He received several international awards, such as the first prize of "World Press Photo" in 1965 and the Pulitzer Prize for his picture *Flight to Freedom* in 1966. The human drama of grief and terror, expressed by the distorted faces of four children and their mother who were able to flee an attack on their village by swimming for their lives, tells of the reality of the Vietnam War.

Sawada's pictures document the suffering of civilians under the rule of soldiers, as well as wounding and pain on both sides. *Time* magazine called this photojournalist "the best, certainly the most daring photographer working for UPI in Indochina". Sawada risked his life numerous times on his many assignments to isolated territories of war. On October 28, 1970, Sawada was killed while on a photographic assignment in Cambodia. *LH*

▲ Kyoichi Sawada
Flight to Freedom,
1960

Gelatin silver print
25.2 x 39.3 cm
ML/F 1977/751

Gruber Collection

Hajime Sawatari studied photography with Kishin Shinoyama at the Faculty of Fine Arts of Nihon University in Tokyo. Between 1963 and 1966 he belonged to a circle of permanent employees at the Nihon Design Center in Tokyo. Since then, however, he has been active as a freelance photographer, working both in motion picture and fashion photography, and also as a photojournalist for *Asahi Camera*. In 1966 he worked as a cameraman for the movie "The Tomato Ketchup Emperor". Here he already showed his inclination for fantasy themes. In 1968 he married Hiroko Arahari, with whom he had a daughter. Between 1969 and 1980 Sawatari kept a studio in Roppongi. In 1973 he was awarded the annual prize of the Japanese Photographic Association. In that year he published his series *Alice*, which earned him the nicknames "Brother Alice" and "Gilles de Rais of the Camera" for years to come, influencing his image as a photographer of young girls and women. In 1979 he was named Photographer of the Year in Tokyo. Since 1980 he has had a studio in Minami Aoyama in Tokyo. *RM*

Sawatari, Hajime

1940 Tokyo
Lives in Tokyo

▲ Hajime Sawatari
Untitled (Girl on Stairs) from the series: Alice, 1973

Color print
10 x 13.2 cm
ML/F 1984/110

Gruber Donation

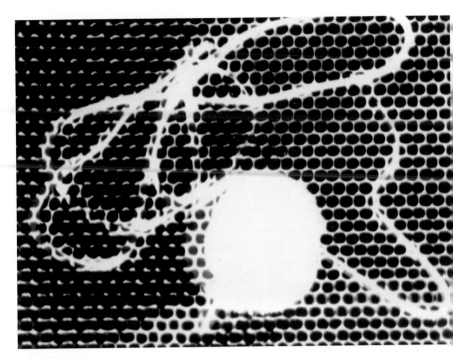

Schad, Christian

1894 Miesbach,
Germany
1982 Keilberg,
Spessart

▲ **Christian Schad**
Shadograph 15, 1960

Gelatin silver print
10.5 x 14.1 cm
ML/F 1977/752

Gruber Collection

▶ **Christian Schad**
Shadograph 20,
1960

Gelatin silver print
23.5 x 17.7 cm
ML/F 1977/753

Gruber Collection

From 1913 to 1914 Christian Schad studied painting for two semesters at the Academy of Creative Arts in Munich. In 1915 he avoided war duty and until 1920 lived as a painter and graphic artist in Zurich and Geneva.

Through Walter Serner, with whom he worked at his newspaper *Sirius* in Zurich, he remained in touch with Zurich dadaists Hans Arp, Hugo Ball and Tristan Tzara while he was in Geneva. During his time in Geneva he discovered camera-less photography while experimenting with "found objects" and photographic papers. These photographs, of which he produced approximately 30 in 1919, are the first artistic photograms – actually preceding the work of Man Ray and László Moholy-Nagy. Since 1936 they have been called "Shadographs", a name first coined by Tristan Tzara. Not until 1960 did Schad use this technique again, creating a comprehensive late work.

His was a restless spirit. Between 1920 and 1925 he lived in Naples and in Rome, then in Vienna and, from 1928 on, in Berlin. Beginning in 1935, when he was unable to support himself with painting alone, he

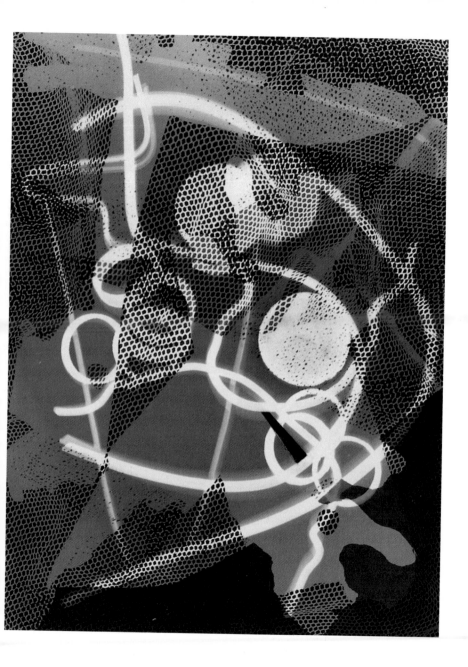

◄ **Christian Schad**
Shadograph 24b,
1960

Gelatin silver print
15.6 x 11.5 cm
ML/F 1993/512

Gruber Donation

worked temporarily in various other professions. Following the destruction of his studio during an air raid in 1943 he moved to Aschaffenburg, and finally, in 1962, settled in Keilberg in the Spessart region. *RM*

A. T. Schaefer started out studying painting and design at the Arts and Crafts School of Hanover, taking an interest in sculptures and painting. In the late seventies he began to work more and more with the medium of photography and since 1981 has been devoting himself exclusively to this technology. In photography he discovered possibilities of exploring the phenomenon of color and its perception in a more authentic manner than it was possible to do with painting. Photography creates color as a function of light, and vision is subject to the same conditions. Schaefer investigates the vividness of photographic color against the backdrop of Goethe's Theory of Colors, seeing it as an opportunity for transforming its teachings in a novel, visual manner. Whereas his early work investigated mainly the possibilities offered by pure color spectra, in particular the color red, his cosmic images of the series *Skieron* offered subtle colors, in particular in tones of deep black and blue, as well as variations of white. What appears to be the result of experimental photography, reminiscent of the macrocosm and microcosm, is in fact the result of pure "straight photography". *RM*

Schaefer, A. T.

1944 Enningerloh, Germany
Lives in Stuttgart

▲ A. T. Schaefer
MB 29, 1990

Cibachrome print, acrylic paint
234 x 120 cm
ML/F 1991/149

◀ **Ivan Schagin**
Spasky Tower,
around 1935–1939

Gelatin silver print
56.6 x 41.4 cm
ML/F 1992/137

Ludwig Collection

Schagin, Ivan

1904 Jaroslaw
1982 Moscow

Ivan Schagin left home when he was quite young in order to earn his living as a sailor. In 1924 he moved to Moscow, where he pursued different activities. During this time he began to take an interest in photography. In 1930 he made his hobby his profession and began working as a press photographer for the newspapers *Nascha shizn, Kooperativnaya* and *Selchosgis*, the national publisher for agricultural matters. In the thirties Schagin specialized in the contemporary subject of technical progress and took a number of pictures of the Red Army. Between 1933 and 1950 Schagin worked as a photojournalist for the central youth newspaper, *Komsomolskaya Pravda*, as well as for *SSSR na stroike (USSR under Construction)*. During World War II Schagin worked as a reporter at various fronts. Beginning in 1950, he produced photographic volumes and reports for "Isogis", a government-operated publishing house, and for *Sowjetskij khudozhnik, Progress, Pravda*, and "Nowosti", the press agency. *MBT*

After arriving in Moscow, Arkadii Samoilovich Shaikhet began working
as a retoucher for a portrait photographer. In 1924 he turned to photojournalism and worked for *Rabochaya gazeta* and *Ogonek*. He became
a member of the Union of Russian Proletarian Photoreporters (ROPF),
on whose avant-garde style he had an influence. At that time his work
dealt mainly with the new life under Socialism, in particular the heroic
struggle of the individual. Together with Max Alpert and Solomon Tules,
he prepared a pictorial report covering 24 hours in the life of steel-
worker Fillipov, which presented an image of the high standard of living
of Soviet industrial workers and which was strongly tinged by propaganda. Also, Shaikhet worked for newspapers such as *SSSR na stroike
(USSR under Construction)* and the *Workers Illustrated Newspaper*. During
World War II he was at the front, working as a war reporter. *RM*

**Shaikhet,
Arkadii
Samoilovich**

1898 Nikolajew
1959 Moscow

◄ **Arkadii S. Shaikhet**
Steel Furnace, 1935

Gelatin silver print
37.7 x 24.7 cm
ML/F 1992/146

Ludwig Collection

◄ **Arkadii S. Shaikhet**
Moving Locomotive,
1935–1939

Gelatin silver print
38.9 x 58.5 cm
ML/F 1992/143

Ludwig Collection

► **Arkadii S. Shaikhet**
Tower at Red Square,
1936–1940

Gelatin silver print
43 x 28.5 cm
ML/F 1992/140

Ludwig Collection

**Scheffer,
Michael**

1953 Schmalkalden,
Germany
Lives in Leipzig

▲ Michael Scheffer
From: City, 1987

*Gelatin silver print
42.2 x 63.8 cm*
ML/F 1991/194

After graduating from high school, Michael Scheffer began an apprenticeship as a surveyor. Between 1974 and 1977 he was a forest worker in the area of the Eastern Harz. Until 1982 he worked as skilled surveyor. Between 1982 and 1987 he studied photography under Prof. Arno Fischer at the College of Graphic Design and Book Art in Leipzig. Since then he has been working as a freelance photographer and has been a member of the "EIDOS" group in Berlin. Scheffer's photography depicts the mundane, banal, and yet it has a disquieting effect on the viewer because of its lack of sharpness, its tight cropping and the direct access permitted by photography. In his pictures Scheffer duplicates the view of the citizen of the former East Germany. Concentrating on the immediate environment to simulate an apparently accidental look into private life, it is in fact the absence of social contexts that conveys the feeling of impending threat. *RM*

Regina Schmeken started out studying art history and German art and literature at the University of Essen, and it was only in 1976 that she became a self-taught photographer. As early as 1978 she received the Prix de la Critique in Arles and, in 1984, was awarded a grant for photography by the City of Munich. Since 1986 she has been working in Munich for the *Süddeutsche Zeitung*. In addition to her professional activities, Regina Schmeken has been continuing her artistic work. Following picture series resulting from trips to New York, Paris, and Montreal, her series of photographs of slaughterhouses caused a sensation. She did not produce a photographic report, but concentrated on a few shots illustrating the burden and sorrow of the slaughterers and the slaughtered. The focal point was the relationship between humans and the bodies of animals, being intertwined in a symbiotic, fateful relationship. Her most recent publication *Closed Society* demonstrates that she has maintained her artistic force in her professional work. *RM*

Schmeken, Regina

1955 Gladbeck, Germany
Lives in Munich

▲ **Regina Schmeken**
New York, 1981

Gelatin silver print
25 x 37.2 cm
ML/F 1988/86

Gruber Donation

Schmölz, Hugo

1879 Sonthofen,
Germany
1938 Cologne

▲ **Hugo Schmölz**
Glass Roof over the
Staircase of the Po-
lice Headquarters in
Düsseldorf, 1934

Gelatin silver print
16.5 x 22.4 cm
ML/F 1986/24

▶ **Hugo Schmölz**
Handrail, 1932

Gelatin silver print
47.8 x 35.1 cm
ML/F 1986/25

Hugo Schmölz studied photography under Richard Eder and attended a trade school in Kempten. In 1896 he began to work as an assistant in a studio. In November 1911 he and portrait photographer Eugen Bayer founded a studio in Cologne-Nippes. Schmölz concentrated on architectural photography. The architect Wilhelm Riphahn was one of his most important clients. During this time Schmölz also took pictures for Dominikus Böhm, Theodor Merrill, Adolf Abel, Bruno Paul and others, and he worked as a press photographer. His sober, factual style made its mark on the architectural photography of his time. He had an exceptionally congenial relationship with Dominikus Böhm. In 1924 he and Eugen Bayer parted ways and Schmölz opened his own photographic business. After Schmölz's death, his son Karl Hugo operated the business under the name "Fotowerkstätte Hugo Schmölz" well into the fifties. *RM*

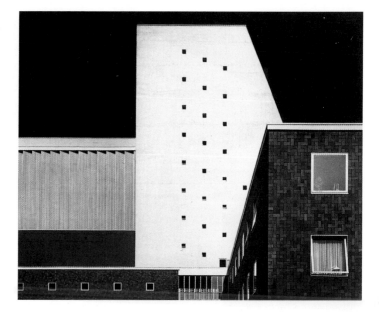

◄ Hugo Schmölz
Staircase with Clock,
Teacher Training
College, Bonn, 1933

Gelatin silver print
21 x 15 cm
ML/F 1986/18

► Karl Hugo
Schmölz
The Cologne Opera,
Architect Riphahn,
1959

Gelatin silver print
48 x 58.6 cm
ML/F 1989/196

Because his father Hugo Schmölz was an architectural photographer, Karl Hugo Schmölz was exposed to photography early on. In the thirties he began accompanying his father on photographic assignments. He took pictures for architects, including Adolf Abel, Bruno Paul, Dominikus Böhm, Gottfried Böhm, Wilhelm Riphahn, and Rudolf Schwarz. When his father died in 1938, the close cooperation he had had with his father enabled Karl Hugo to continue contract work for their business "Fotowerkstätte Hugo Schmölz" without interruption. Karl Hugo Schmölz returned to his home town after serving in World War II and documented the wartime destruction with a large-format camera. This was one of the few photographic topics that he covered without an assignment, as did his father, who had photographed the city of Cologne during the twenties and thirties. His factual approach creates a completely different tone from the emotional view taken by Hermann Claasen. The continuation of his work for the great architects of the Rhineland resulted in an impressive documentation of the reconstruction of the city of Cologne. In conjunction with this, he also took a comprehensive series of pictures of Augustusburg Castle in Brühl.

At the same time Schmölz accepted more and more advertising

**Schmölz,
Karl Hugo**

1917 Weissenhorn,
Germany
1986 Lahnstein

◄ **Karl Hugo Schmölz**
Hohenzollern Bridge,
1946

Gelatin silver print
60 x 44 cm
ML/F 1989/192

▲ **Karl Hugo Schmölz**
View from Cologne Cathedral
onto Wallraf Square, 1946

Gelatin silver print
61 x 48 cm
ML/F 1989/195

Schmölz, K. H. | 601

◀ **Karl Hugo Schmölz**
St. Alban, 1959

Gelatin silver print
60.9 x 43.7 cm
ML/F 1989/193

▲ **Karl Hugo Schmölz**
The East Choir of Cologne
Cathedral, 1938

Gelatin silver print
53.9 x 45 cm
ML/F 1989/191

Ill. p. 604:
Karl Hugo Schmölz
Staircase, WRM/ML,
Detail, 1986

Gelatin silver print
23.2 x 16.5 cm
ML/F 1986/153

Ill. p. 605:
Karl Hugo Schmölz
Main Floor, WRM,
1986

Gelatin silver print
22.8 x 16.2 cm
ML/F 1986/164

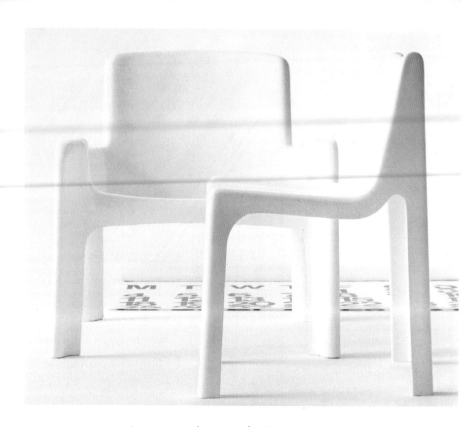

assignments, took pictures for Westag and concentrated especially on furniture photography. Today, his archive holds Germany's most comprehensive documentation of 30 years of living in Germany, from Interlübke to Eugen Schmidt, from Thomé to Draenert. He was masterful in portraying suggested home décor through the effective arrangement of even the simplest furniture. Following his marriage to Walde Huth, a photographer in Stuttgart, they set up a joint studio under the name "schmölz + huth", thus adding fashion and portrait photography to their range of services. The last assignment he accepted was to take pictures of the new Museum Ludwig in Cologne, but he was unable to complete it. Nevertheless, his "test pictures" had already established the most important focal points of this building, setting the standards for the task. *RM*

◄ Dietmar
Schneider
Meret Oppenheim,
1982

Gelatin silver print
17.1 x 23 cm
ML/F 1990/69

**Schneider,
Dietmar**

1939 Breslau
Lives in Cologne

Dietmar Schneider has been living in Cologne since 1945. In the sixties he gave up his profession to devote himself to art management. He became the driving force of the Cologne art scene and was famous for bringing art to a broader spectrum of the public. His project "Current Art on High Street" involved the display of art in shop windows. Because of his connections with businesses, he was successful in arousing their interest in art at a time when they were only accustomed to sponsorships of sports. He promoted artists and committed himself to an art award given by the "4711" perfume company.

As a sideline, he has always documented art events and taken portraits of artists. In this way he has compiled an almost encyclopedic collection of portraits of artists and art events in Cologne over the past 30 years. Also, many artists have used his photographs as a starting point for manipulation. *RM*

Between 1936 and 1939 Toni Schneiders took an apprenticeship as a photographer. He used his first Leica, which he bought in 1938, until the fifties. During World War II he spent some of his time as a war reporter in Italy and France. After being released from captivity, he again set up his own studio in Meersburg on Lake Constance in 1948. In 1949 he co-founded "fotoform". In 1950 he took over the direction of Werner Mannsfeld's studio, a position which was to influence his later work. In 1951 he settled in Lindau. In 1953 he traveled to Ethiopia, Sardinia, Crete, Yugoslavia, Scandinavia, and Japan. During the years that followed he built a comprehensive archive of photographs of buildings and land-scapes that were published in numerous calendars and picture books.
RM

Schneiders, Toni

1920 Urbar
Lives in Lindau

Schrammen, Eberhard

1886 Cologne
1947 Lübeck

▼ Eberhard
Schrammen
Untitled (Self-
portrait), 1930

*Gelatin silver print,
stencil photogram*
23.8 x 17.9 cm
ML/F 1993/523

Gruber Donation

Eberhard Schrammen studied at the Art Academy of Düsseldorf and at the Archducal Saxonian College of Creative Arts in Weimar. Under Henry van de Velde he cultivated additional contacts with the Arts and Crafts Academy and expanded his studies with numerous trips. In 1914 he participated in the "Burga" exhibition of the German Association of Artists in Leipzig and, as a result, shared the Villa Romana Award in Florence. He was drafted during World War I, after which he participated in the merging of the former Arts and Crafts College and the Academy of Art into the State Bauhaus of Weimar. He was a student of Oskar Schlemmer, publisher of the first Bauhaus journal, *Der Austausch*, master teacher of the carpentry workshop, and he built furniture. In 1925 he joined the Gildenhall Cooperative of Commercial Artists and also became a member of the German Crafts Association.

Schrammen remained active as an artist, painter, graphic artist, and writer. There is little evidence of his written work. Even his art was forgotten for many years until it was rediscovered by L. Fritz Gruber, who donated a number of Schrammen's works to the photographic collection of the Museum Ludwig. Schrammen worked especially in the field of pattern photograms, a technique he developed that is particularly suitable for illustrations in books and newspapers. Schrammen considered himself a craftsman and universal artist who integrated applied work in his understanding of art. *RM*

► Gundula Schulze
el Dowy
Tamerlan, Berlin,
1984

Gelatin silver print
39.7 x 55.6 cm
ML/F 1995/128

Uwe Scheid
Donation

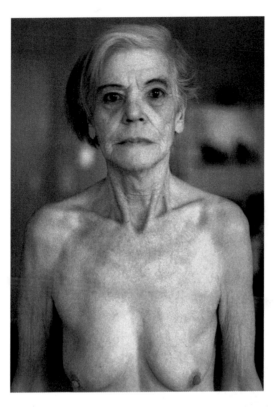

Gundula Schulze el Dowy trained as an industrial trader and attended a college of advertising and design in Berlin before studying photography under Horst Thorau at the College of Graphic Design and Book Art in Leipzig between 1979 and 1984. Initially, her photographic work dealt with black-and-white cycles of social criticism. Near her apartment at the Prenzlauer Berg she took pictures of people in the backyards of East Berlin. The unbeautified, yet also sensitive photographs in this series show people in the Scheunenviertel area, the Pfarrstraße, at work or in the slaughterhouse. In 1983 she changed to color photography. Her international breakthrough came when she participated in the exhibition "Private Photography" in the USA in 1987 and in the Rencontres Internationales de la Photographie in Arles in 1988. *TvT*

**Schulze
el Dowy,
Gundula**

1954 Erfurt
Lives in Berlin

Seidenstücker, Friedrich

1882 Unna
1966 Berlin

Friedrich Seidenstücker became interested in photography at an early age. When he was only 17, he built his own camera from a cigar box, using the lens from a laterna magica. From 1902 to 1903 he studied mechanical engineering, first in Hagen, later in Berlin. There he developed close connections with artists of his time and began to take pictures of them. His first major series was created in the Berlin Zoo, and it showed the specific sense of humor which was evident in much of his work. His powers of observation and his feeling for the comical in everyday situations made him an extraordinary chronicler of Berlin's daily life. Between 1914 and 1918 he worked in the Zeppelin building in Potsdam. From 1919 to 1922 he studied sculpture at the Arts College in Berlin, after which he decided to make a profession out of his artistic inclinations. Between 1922 and 1930 he made frequent trips to Munich, Paris, Berlin, and Rome and he participated in numerous exhibitions, but he was unable to make a living with his art. Therefore, he decided to be-

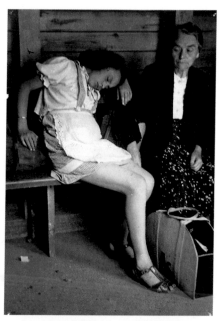

...come a photographer and entered into a contract with the Ullstein publishing house. He became a chronicler of Berlin life, took pictures in
Pomerania and Prussia and produced photo-reports for *Berliner Illustrirte*. He became famous, in particular, for his pictures of daily life in
Berlin and for his *Puddle Jumpers*, young women and girls in summer
dresses who with legs spread, at times umbrella in hand, jumped over
puddles onto the sidewalk. *RM*

◀ **Michel Seuphor**
Mondrian Studio,
1929

Gelatin silver print
20.4 x 27.8 cm
ML/F 1980/355 VI

**Seuphor,
Michel**

(Michel Berckelaers)

1901 Antwerp
1989 Paris

It was in school that Michel Berckelaers used his pseudonym "Seuphor" for the first time, having derived that name as an anagram of the word "Orpheus". At the end of World War I he joined the Flemish movement and published a number of battle pamphlets. In 1921 he founded the newspaper *Het Overzicht*, which dealt with abstract art and which was joined by such artists as Robert Delaunay, László Moholy-Nagy, Fernand Léger, Kurt Schwitters, and others. Following several trips between 1922 and 1924, he ceased publishing his newspaper in 1925.

In 1925 Seuphor began to turn to photography. He developed into a chronicler of the Paris art scene and took portraits of many of his artist colleagues. Together with Joaquín Torres García, he founded the group "Cercle et Carré" in Paris. Between 1937 and 1948 he withdrew to Anduze in Southern France and worked for the magazine *L'Aube*, publishing autobiographical novels, essays, and poetry. From 1943 to 1944 Seuphor was active in the Resistance. In 1951 he returned to Paris and worked as the French correspondent for the American *Art Digest*. He published books on contemporary art, devoted himself intensely to drawing, and worked as an art critic. *RM*

Peter Sevriens was a sailor for many years before he began trading in antiques in Germany. This business eventually led him to be interested in making art objects. The unusual aspect of all his objects is the inclusion of photography. In this context he does not restrict himself to making collages of photographs, but includes in his works like a leitmotif a camera, parts of a camera, or reconstructed camera-like objects. On one hand, he understands the camera as an object that may be used and defamiliarized in many ways, and on the other he recognizes its facilitating function between reality and perception. In some of his early works this is still evident in a quiet and reserved manner. Lined up and tied up are a fragment and a photograph of the fragment, a shell and a photograph of the shell, a stone and a photograph of the stone, etc. on a clean background reminiscent of an archeological collection or a museum display. In the center is the camera, the evidence. In his more recent works Sevriens increasingly cultivates his ironic, provocative discourse with the camera. It is worked into the art, from the old folding camera to the expensive Leica. It has to be incorporated in things which it was originally meant to record from a distance – the camera itself becomes the subject. *RM*

Sevriens, Peter

1942 Venlo, Netherlands
Lives in Meinerzhagen, Germany

◄ **Peter Sevriens**
Untitled, 1991

Metal, photography, mixed media
149 x 50 cm
ML/F 1991/286

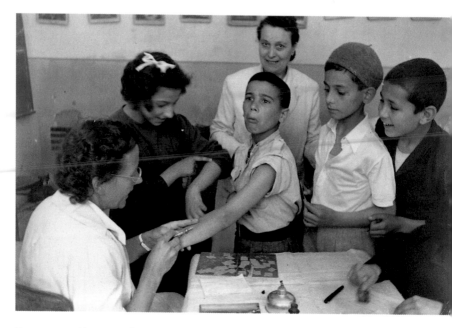

Seymour, David

1911 Warsaw, Poland
1956 Suez, Egypt

▲ **David Seymour**
School Vaccination,
around 1948

Gelatin silver print
15.9 x 24 cm
ML/F 1994/273

Gruber Donation

David Seymour grew up in Warsaw and in Russia. After finishing high school, he began to study art and photography at the Leipzig Academy of Graphic Arts. After completing his studies in 1931 he moved to Paris, where he continued his training at the Sorbonne until 1933. There, he also assumed the pseudonym "Chim", by which he was known to most of his friends and colleagues. He became an independent photographer and, beginning in 1934, was able to publish his work regularly in the magazine *Regards*. In Paris, Seymour became friends with Henri Cartier-Bresson and Robert Capa.

In 1936 Seymour, a passionate liberal and anti-fascist, went to Spain. With his camera he captured the terror of civil war, documenting soldiers fighting at the front and the daily life of the civilian population in the back country. His pictures of air raids on Barcelona earned him worldwide recognition as a photojournalist.

In 1939 Seymour returned to Paris, went from there to Mexico, and in the same year settled in New York. Between 1942 and 1945 he was in the US Army in photo-reconnaissance and as an interpreter. After World War II he traveled for UNESCO to Czechoslovakia, Poland, Hungary, Germany, Greece, and Italy to record the effects of war on children. In

▲ David Seymour
Greece, Evacuation of
Children, around 1940

Gelatin silver print
23.7 x 19.3 cm
ML/F 1993/502

Gruber Donation

◀ **David Seymour**
Untitled,
around 1947

Gelatin silver print
13.6 x 11.3 cm
ML/F 1994/275

Gruber Donation

▶ **David Seymour**
Untitled,
around 1948

Gelatin silver print
21.2 x 19.8 cm
ML/F 1994/276

Gruber Donation

1949 UNESCO published the result of this work in the book *Children of Europe*. Beyond this assignment, children remained his favorite and most impressive photographic theme.

In 1947 Seymour, together with his friends Henri Cartier-Bresson, Robert Capa and George Rodger founded the international picture agency "Magnum". When Robert Capa died, Seymour took over the presidency of the agency. Nine years later, in 1956, Seymour traveled to Greece to study antique monuments when the Suez Crisis escalated into war. The photographer went to Suez via Cyprus. He was killed in Suez on November 10 of that year by Egyptian machine-gun fire while he was reporting on an exchange of prisoners. *MBT*

Shinoyama, Kishin

1930 Tokyo
Lives in Tokyo

▲ Kishin Shinoyama
Two Rear Views of
Nudes, 1968

Gelatin silver print
19.8 x 30.6 cm
ML/F 1977/764

Gruber Collection

Kishin Shinoyama, the son of a Buddhist monk, was supposed to follow in his father's footsteps and become a monk at his temple. Instead, he let his brother take his place and opted in favor of photography. Between 1961 and 1963 he studied photography at Nihon University in Tokyo. Between 1961 and 1968 he worked for the Light-House advertising agency in Tokyo. In 1966 he was awarded the Prize for Young Photographers by the Japanese Association of Critics, and his first pictures were published in *Camera Mainichi*. Since 1968 Shinoyama has been working as a freelance photographer in the areas of fashion, sports, advertising, and the press. In 1970 he was honored by the Japanese Association of Photographers as Photographer of the Year. He became known as a photographer of nudes, and his pictures were exhibited at photokina. His nudes attracted attention because he did not adhere to conventions, but rendered highly formalized views of the body. Shinoyama saw nude photography as a modeling problem encountered by a sculptor, leading him at times to create abstract forms. In 1974 he caused an international sensation with his series on the Tattooing House in Yokohama. He was the first photographer to provide images of the world of traditional tattooing art by Japanese artist Kuniyoshi.

▲ **Kishin Shinoyama**
Brown Lily, 1968

Gelatin silver print
18.8 x 18.7 cm
ML/F 1977/766

Gruber Collection

Shinoyama followed this up with a quiet, almost meditative study of traditional Japanese houses and gardens, offering the European world an intimate glance at the Japanese way of life. Nevertheless, he continued to pursue nude photography with great intensity. In 1985 he published *Shinorama*, a series for which he photographed nude dancers with nine cameras triggered at the same time, so that the final picture was composed of as many parts. In 1990 he also employed the large format with his photographic series *Tokyo Nude*, for which he arranged panorama-like

▲ **Kishin Shinoyama**
The Birth, 1968

Gelatin silver print
18.4 x 18.2 cm
ML/F 1977/765

Gruber Collection

overviews of nudes to create a surreal world which is illuminated artificially and populated by doll-like beings. Today, Shinoyama is considered to be one of the leading Japanese photographers, representing the generation that brought recognition to Japanese photography all over the world. *RM*

▲ **Kishin Shinoyama**
Nude Over Fence, 1969

Color print, 23.1 x 18.2 cm
ML/F 1977/767

Gruber Collection

Sieff, Jeanloup

1933 Paris
Lives in Paris

▼ Jeanloup Sieff
Homage to Seurat,
1964

Gelatin silver print
30 x 20 cm
ML/F 1984/114

Gruber Donation

In 1953 Jeanloup Sieff studied literature, journalism and photography at the Vaugirard School of Photography in Paris. A year later he studied photography in Vevey in Switzerland. He began his career as a freelance journalist in Paris, working for *Elle* as a photojournalist and fashion photographer between 1955 and 1958. Following a brief membership in "Magnum" in 1959, during which he reported from Greece, Turkey and Poland, he worked as a freelance photographer until 1961, winning the "Prix Niepce" in the same year. Since then, he has photographed fashion for all the important magazines, including *Harper's Bazaar, Glamour, Esquire, Look, Vogue,* and *twen,* in both the USA and Europe.

Sieff is also a celebrated photographer of nudes. One of his stylistic tools is the wide angle, which gives his nudes a feeling of dreaminess, suggesting a kind of distance of the naked models, even though they are often looking directly at the camera. Sieff is less known for his excellent landscape photographs. *Black House* of 1964 is an early example of this genre – a picture that indicates the dramatizing effect of a 28 mm lens and the virtuosity with which Sieff captures in his black-and-white photographs on the one hand the textures of wood and red grass and on the other silhouettes, shadows and sky formations. *AS*

► Jeanloup Sieff
Black House, 1964

Gelatin silver print
30 x 20 cm
ML/F 1984/113

Gruber Donation

**Simonds,
Charles**

1945 New York
Lives in New York

In his miniaturized cities, such as *Park Model/Fantasy* (1974–1976)
in the collection of the Museum Ludwig in Cologne, Simonds demonstrates the evolutionary process of an imaginary people, the "Little
People", in various stages: from a "linear" via a "circular" to a "spiral"
culture. Simonds' "Little People" are nomadic. Their settlements,
landscapes and ritual spaces can usually be found in easily overlooked corners and niches of modern, largely devastated big cities.
For Simonds the life of these invisible people is based on faith, on
a special attitude to nature, and on close ties to the earth. The
theme of his *Park Model* and related works is always excavation, in the
historical as well as psychological sense.

Simonds' interest in cultural and psychological relationships between man and his environment, the earth, is expressed in different
ways – from a plane of personal imagination up to a social metaphor.
"I have an interest in the earth and in myself, or in my body and the
earth, in what happens when they are intertwined with each other or
with all the related things, symbolically and metaphorically, such as
my body as the body of all humans, or the earth as the place where we
all live."

In his private rituals, which he documents in films or photographs,
Simonds goes in search of the tracks of human evolution. In his photographic series *Birth* of the year 1970, a human figure appears – the artist
himself – from a reddish rock. This, too, concerns an evolutionary process of man, as well as his being in harmony with nature, in harmony
with his environment. Like many of his photographic works, *Birth* is
a series of still images derived from filming a performance. In other
works, for example *Body/Landscape* (1974), the artist's body forms a

mountain landscape, in which he writhes in the nude in a field of mud. His body is born to the earth and at the same time of the earth.

Simonds' work is closely linked with the land and body art of the seventies. Dennis Oppenheim, for example, made an 8 mm film in 1970 entitled "Petrified Hand", in which he gradually covered his right hand with stones, thus making it invisible. In his large-scale project "Earthworks", the land-art artist Michael Heizer "made drawings" with and on the earth. "My personal association with earth is quite real. I like lying in earth. [...] my work with earth satisfies an extremely fundamental desire", says Michael Heizer. In all cases man finds his way back to nature, and the injured relationship between man and his environment is healed. *GG*

▲ **Charles Simonds**
Birth, 1970

Color prints
20 photographs,
each 18.6 x 23.6 (alto-
gether 49 x 145) cm
ML/F 1979/1166 I–XX

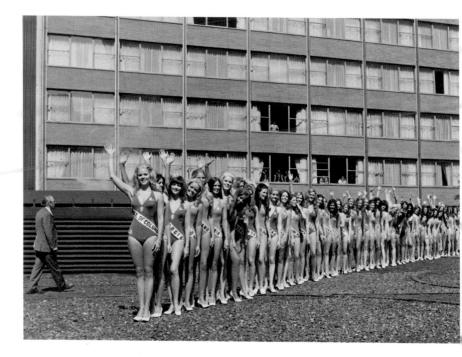

Slavin, Neil

1941 New York
Lives in New York

▲ Neal Slavin
Miss USA Pageant
and Miss Universe,
1973

Gelatin silver print
24.2 x 33.5 cm
ML/F 1984/115

Gruber Donation

Between 1959 and 1963 Neil Slavin studied painting, graphic design and photography at Cooper Union School. In 1961 he received a scholarship to study at Oxford. In the same year he worked as a photographic assistant at the Guggenheim Museum in New York. Since then he has been working as a freelance graphic designer and photographer for *Fortune*, *Newsweek* and *Stern*, among others. Since 1975 Slavin has been working in his own studio as well as workshops at colleges including the famous School of Visual Arts in New York. Slavin has become especially known for two publications which could be called sociological photographic project studies: *When Two or More are Gathered Together* (1976) and *Britons* (1986). Since 1973 he has addressed the phenomenon of groups, clubs, and organizations, which he carefully composes in group pictures with the concerned interest of an anthropological researcher. The technically brilliant color photographs used for *Britons* were created with a 20 x 24 inch Polaroid Instant Camera. *AS*

▶ W. Eugene Smith
Pride Street,
Pittsburgh, 1955

Gelatin silver print
34.7 x 23.2 cm
ML/F 1977/776

Gruber Collection

"Humanity is worth more than a picture of humanity, which ultimately can serve only for exploitation." This is the credo of W. Eugene Smith, who has rendered outstanding services to photojournalism with his extraordinary political and social commitment.

In 1933 Smith took his first photographs and, a short time later, managed to sell them to various newspapers. In 1936 he received a scholarship for photography at Notre Dame University in Indiana. Thereafter he moved to New York, where he studied under Helene Sanders at the New York Institute of Photography. In 1937 and 1938 Smith worked as a photojournalist for *Newsweek* before moving to the "Black Star" agency as a freelance photographer. Between 1939 and 1942 he had a contract with *Life* magazine. During World War II

Smith,
W. Eugene

1918 Wichita, Kansas
1978 Tucson,
Arizona

Smith worked as a war photographer in the South Pacific, where he took some of his most impressive pictures, for which he paid with serious injuries caused by grenades. After the war and after his recovery – his wounds required 32 operations altogether – Smith returned to *Life* magazine.

During subsequent years he had an impact on the photography of this magazine, because he wanted to do away with the conventional approach of using pictures as mere illustrations to accompany the text, wanting instead to give greater emphasis to the pictures themselves. As a result of this, Smith was instrumental in the development of the independent form of the photo-essay. One of his most famous pieces of journalism in this regard was the photographic series on a Spanish village, published in *Life* in 1951. Because the editor had room for only 17 pictures, a supplement with an additional eight pictures was added. Here, the photographs – completely according to Smith's concept – were presented entirely on their own strength, without any text.

In 1955 Smith left *Life* magazine to work with the "Magnum" agency, a relationship that he kept up until 1959. During subsequent years the

◀ **W. Eugene Smith**
Self-portrait in the
Rear View Mirror,
around 1963

Gelatin silver print
26.6 x 34.5 cm
ML/F 1977/768

Gruber Collection

▶ **W. Eugene Smith**
Albert Schweitzer,
1949

Gelatin silver print
26.7 x 34.2 cm
ML/F 1977/773

Gruber Collection

► **W. Eugene Smith**
Tennessee Williams,
1948

Gelatin silver print
34 x 26.1 cm
ML/F 1977/771

Gruber Collection

photographer discovered the book as a suitable medium for publishing
his photographs. By using this medium, he could exercise complete
control over the presentation of his photographs.

   In memory of Smith's immense human commitment, the International Center of Photography in New York has been awarding the W.
Eugene Smith Memorial Fund Scholarship since 1980. *MBT*

Snow, Michael

1929 Toronto,
Canada
Lives in Toronto

▼ Michael Snow
Imposition, 1976

Color print
160 x 96 cm
ML/F 1985/39

In the early fifties, Canadian Michael Snow attended the Ontario College of Art, marrying artist and film-maker Joyce Wieland in 1959. The multi-faceted talents of Snow manifested themselves in his activities as a photographer, musician, artist, and film-maker. He sees his photography influenced by painting and sculpting rather than by photographic technology. In 1961 Snow began with his *Walking Women* series and created new forms and environments with various arrangements of many small pictures of details of persons. In 1962 he introduced *Four to Five*, a montage of twelve rectangular photographs with sections of a walking woman in various contexts, thereby establishing new spatial and optical relationships. The vertical arrangement of the two central pictures alone assures the curiosity of the viewer, triggering the necessary search for a new pictorial reality. In this context Snow considers important the process and the new arrangement of the individual parts, which indirectly illustrate the progress of the woman. Snow's work with motion pictures and his photography exhibit many similar elements. The environment *Field/Champ* (1973–1974) includes 99 rectangular photographs with details of plants. Since 1955 Snow has been a professor at the University of Toronto, receiving several awards and a Guggenheim grant. In 1977 he was represented in the Canadian pavilion at the Biennale in Venice and at "documenta VI" in Kassel. *LH*

Frederick Sommer showed an interest in photography early on, but first he studied landscape architecture at Cornell University in Ithaca, New York. Between 1931 and 1935 Sommer lived as a painter and occasional photographer in Arizona. His acquaintance with Alfred Stieglitz convinced him to devote himself entirely to photography. In 1936 he met Edward Weston, whose tone value scale impressed him especially. Shortly thereafter, the young photographer began to work with an 18 x 24 cm camera.

    Sommer's preferred subjects were rock fissures and the expansive landscape of Arizona. In 1939 he created a series of grotesque still-life photographs depicting the heads and entrails of chickens with impressive precision. This series also reflects his interest in the art of Surrealism, which stemmed from his friendship with the painter Max Ernst, whom he froze "in stone" in a famous portrait taken in 1946. *MBT*

Sommer, Frederick

1905 Angri, Italy
Lives in Prescott, Arizona

▲ **Frederick Sommer**
Max Ernst, 1946

Gelatin silver print
19.2 x 24.1 cm
ML/F 1977/785

Gruber Collection

◄ **Erich Spahn**
Mixco Viejo,
Guatemala, 1992

Gelatin silver print
160 x 160 cm
ML/F 1995/131

Locher Donation

Spahn, Erich

1957 Weiden,
Germany
Lives in Amberg

Following an apprenticeship in photography in Regensburg, Erich
Spahn studied painting and photography at the Academy of Arts in
Kassel and he became the fifth-generation photographer to follow in
the footsteps of his ancestors. From 1980 to 1981 he attended a master
class at the Bavarian State Institute of Photography in Munich. His
photographic work relates to the tradition of the abstract-concrete, to
structures, stone patterns or light and shadow effects, and he uses cropping techniques in order to carry out minimal changes with horizontal,
vertical, or diagonal shifts, axial rotations, counter-movements, or color
changes from one picture to the next. The image is conceived in his
mind and composed in the camera. *RM*

► Erwin Olaf
Springveld
From the series:
Chessmen, 1988

Gelatin silver print
37.4 x 37.4 cm
ML/F 1990/54

Deutsche Leasing
Donation

Between 1977 and 1980 Erwin Olaf (Erwin Olaf Springveld) attended a school for journalism in Utrecht. Since 1981 he has been working as a freelance photographer for the homosexual scene in the Netherlands and for various international papers such as *Gai-Pied, The Advocate, Rosa Flieder,* and *Gay-krant.*

In 1968 he secured a contract to produce all the covers for *Vinyl,* a magazine for young people. During subsequent years his magazine covers, posters and record covers were highly successful. In 1988 he achieved his breakthrough with the first publication of his series *Chessmen,* earning him international recognition. It was published in *Focus* and awarded first prize for Young European Photographers by Deutsche Leasing. Since then he has been working predominantly for newspapers. In 1990 he published his next picture series entitled *Blacks.* Since then he has also been working as a movie director. In 1991 he made the 30-minute-long film "Tadzio". *RM*

**Springveld,
Erwin Olaf**

1959 Hilversum,
Netherlands
Lives in Amsterdam

Springs, Alice

(June Brown)

1923 Melbourne
Lives in Monaco

▼ **Alice Springs**
Helmut Newton as a
Nun, 1975

Gelatin silver print
7.3 x 11.7 cm
ML/F 1985/80

Gruber Donation

Alice Springs was an actress when she met Helmut Newton, to whom she had been recommended as a model. She is a self-taught photographer. She ended up as a photographer because she substituted at short notice for Newton, who was ill with a cold. Her pictures published under his name were successful and encouraged her to try her hand in this field. She concentrated on portraits and currently works for a number of magazines such as *Vanity Fair*. Alice Springs does not interfere with her pictures. She allows subjects to be free and she waits for moments that seem important to her. Because she usually takes portraits of people in an environment familiar to them, relaxed situations may develop, which are of decisive importance to her method. Since 1990 Alice Springs has been photographing her models with a video camera, which enables her to review the recorded material at leisure and to print out those moments that appear important to her. In so doing, she is not attempting to cloud her method, but to utilize the structure of the video image as a tool characteristic of her work. *RM*

▶ **Alice Springs**
Untitled (Rear View)
around 1970

Gelatin silver print
29.5 x 20 cm
ML/F 1993/505

Gruber Donation

Stankowski, Anton

1906 Gelsenkirchen
Lives in Stuttgart

▼ Anton Stankowski
Self-portrait, 1938

Gelatin silver print
23.9 x 26.2 cm
ML/F 1991/109

Between 1921 and 1926 Anton Stankowski apprenticed as a painter of religious motifs, after which he studied under Prof. Max Burchart at the Folkwang School of Design in Essen. Between 1929 and 1937 he worked as a painter and graphic designer at a then famous Zurich advertising agency. During that time Stankowski began to experiment in the field of photography. He produced collages and photomontages and was interested in photograms. At the same time he used photography as an essential tool for his graphic designs. In 1937 Stankowski moved to Stuttgart. There his design work, which was derived from the fundamental idea that art and applied art are inseparable, had an influence on the vision of many companies. In addition, he maintained close connections with solid artists such as Richard Paul Lohse, Carlo Vivarelli, or Herbert Mattar. After the war and captivity Stankowski returned to his studio and, in addition to his design work, acted as chief editor of the *Stuttgarter Illustrierte*. Stankowski led the way in many branches of photography. In the twenties he already produced photographic series on industrial landscapes. As far as their stylistic orientation was concerned,

these early photographs were based on photographic Constructivism, yet they already contain the concept of photography of inanimate objects. In the forties he experimented with heated gelatin silver layers as did his contemporary, Chargesheimer, who developed gelatin silver painting at that time. In the fifties he created the first examples of Op Art, producing them in black and white and integrating optical effects which only became effective when the viewer moved. In 1953 he created his first nudograms. Because they were created in the context of his professional work, they especially satisfied his claim that artistic work and applied work should not be

▲ **Anton Stankowski**
Nudogram, 1954

Gelatin silver print
59.7 x 48.3 cm
ML/F 1991/102

▲ **Anton Stankowski**
Children's Pavement
Drawing, 1929

Gelatin silver print
23.8 x 30.4 cm
ML/F 1991/107

▶ **Anton Stankowski**
Notre Dame, 1930

Gelatin silver print
11.2 x 8.1 cm
ML/F 1991/103

perceived as contradictory but as equivalent. He always combined innovative artistic work with the requirements of advertising and design. On the one hand he utilized photography in a supportive function for his design work, but on the other used it as an independent medium of equal importance. Taking this approach, Stankowski proved to be an artist who has consistently carried the spirit and tradition of the Bauhaus and the constructivists forward into the present. *RM*

Stano, Tono

1960 Zlaté Moravce
Lives in Prague

▲ Tono Stano
Current Relation-
ship, 1988

Gelatin silver print
43.3 x 52.3 cm
ML/F 1990/1324

Locher Donation

Tono Stano studied at the College of Arts and Crafts in Bratislava and then pursued photography at the Prague Film Faculty. At this school, a group of young photographers formed who developed a new type of staged photography. It included Miro Svolik, Peter Zupnik, Rudo Prekop, Vasil Stanko, and Martin Strba. Fantastic scenes using models in a studio are characteristic of their creative work. They exhibit humor, irony, and hidden metaphors, and frequently refer to mythological traditions. Many times these works deal with the problem of human re- lationships and sexuality.

In this group, Stano is the one who minimizes his imagery the most. He dispenses with narrative moments and concentrates on a restrained pictorial language and simple symbols. *RM*

► **Christian Staub**
Warming Up, 1953

Gelatin silver print
26.5 x 26.5 cm
ML/F 1993/103

Christian Staub conducted his first photographic experiments with a
pinhole camera. However, while in Paris between 1938 and 1940, he devoted himself to surrealistic painting. After meeting André Lhote he embraced Cubism for a while. Upon his return to Switzerland in 1940, he
realized that he could not make a living with his paintings and decided
to study photography under Hans Finsler at the Arts and Crafts School
of Zurich. Between 1943 and 1946 he worked as a freelance photographer for magazines such as *Du* and *Annabelle*. After meeting Willi
Maywald, he was encouraged to try fashion photography and society
portraits. In 1956 he went to New York for the first time. Between
1958 and 1963 he taught at the College of Design in Ulm. Then, between
1963 and 1966, he lectured in photography at the National Design Institute Ahmadabad in India. In 1966 he taught at the University of California in Berkeley and since 1967 has been teaching at the University of
Washington in Seattle. Staub, who has always been interested in photo-

Staub, Christian

1918 Menzingen,
near Zug,
Switzerland
Lives in Seattle,
Washington

▲ Christian Staub
Regensburg, 1962

Gelatin silver print
24.4 x 26.6 cm
ML/F 1993/106

graphic experimentation, has created distortions of architecture and nudes, worked on sequences and, in his photograph of St. Severin, alluded to Robert Delaunay and his cubist fragmentation of a space. Recently he has been using a panoramic camera with a movable lens to take pictures of spaces, making the viewer feel transported into the scene. *RM*

▶ **Christian Staub**
St. Severin, Paris,
Homage to Delau-
nay, 1975

Gelatin silver print
34.2 x 14.4 cm
ML/F 1993/107

◀ Edward Steichen
George Frederick
Watts, from: Camera
Work 2, 1903

Photogravure
21.2 x 16.5 cm
ML/F 1995/47

Gruber Donation

▶ Edward Steichen
Rodin, from: Camera
Work 2, 1903

Photogravure
21.2 x 16.2 cm
ML/F 1995/38

Gruber Donation

Steichen, Edward

1879 Luxembourg
1973 West Redding,
Connecticut

Edward Steichen, who was born in Luxembourg, grew up in the USA after his family emigrated in 1881. Between 1894 and 1898 he studied under Richard Lorenz and Robert Schade at the Milwaukee Art Students' League and was an apprentice in a lithographic business in Milwaukee.

Steichen painted, was interested in photography and, in 1895 began working in the style of artistic photography. During subsequent years he successfully participated in photographic exhibitions in America and in Europe. Despite his early commitment to photography, Steichen continued to pursue his career as a painter.

In an early self-portrait taken in 1901, Steichen drew attention to his double role. Although acting as a photographer, he deliberately took the pose of a painter. In his eyes, apparently the rich tradition of the medium of painting was a more suitable medium for depicting artistic genius than was the medium of photography. Nevertheless, he ultimately decided in favor of photography. In 1923 he broke entirely with

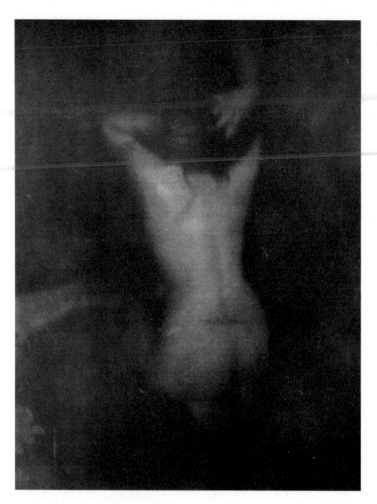

◄ **Edward Steichen**
Dolor, from: Camera
Work 2, 1903

Photogravure
19.3 x 14.9 cm
ML/F 1995/42

Gruber Donation

► **Edward Steichen**
Small Round Mir-
rors, from: Camera
Work 14, 1906

Photogravure
14.2 x 21.4 cm
ML/F 1995/51

Gruber Donation

his vocation as a painter by single-handedly burning those of his paintings that were in his possession.

In 1902 Steichen became one of the founding members of "Photo
Secession", which was initiated by Alfred Stieglitz in New York. By
spending several years in Paris and by taking extended trips throughout Europe, Steichen became familiar with local avant-garde art and
arranged exhibitions for artists in the USA, particularly in Stieglitz' famous Gallery 291 in New York.

▲ Edward Steichen
The Brass Bowl, from:
Camera Work 14, 1906

Halftone print
19.3 x 16.3 cm
ML/F 1995/54

Gruber Donation

▶ Edward Steichen
Eleonora Duse, 1903

Photogravure
17.7 x 13.5 cm
ML/F 1994/290

Gruber Donation

During World War I, Steichen served as a photographer in the Air Force and in the Marines, an assignment that was to change his photographic style fundamentally. The precision required by aerial photographs honed his eye and taught him to appreciate the beauty of non-manipulated photography.

In 1923 Steichen became the chief photographer at Condé-Nast, where he was responsible especially for the fashion magazines *Vanity Fair* and *Vogue* until 1938. During these years he advanced to become one of the best-paid fashion and portrait photographers of his time.

After World War II, the now 67-year-old photographer embarked

▲ **Edward Steichen**
William M. Chase, from: Camera Work 14, 1906

Photogravure, 20.7 x 16.1 cm
ML/F 1995/48

Gruber Donation

▲ Edward Steichen
The Flatiron Evening, from: Camera Work 14, 1906

Three-color halftone print, 21 x 15.9 cm
ML/F 1995/55

Gruber Donation

◄ Edward Steichen
Laughing Boxes,
New York, 1921

Silver bromide print
24.4 x 19.4 cm
ML/F 1977/80

Gruber Collection

► Edward Steichen
George Washington
Bridge, 1931

Gelatin silver print
24.1 x 19.4 cm
ML/F 1988/72

Gruber Donation

on a second career. He became director of the photographic department
of the Museum of Modern Art in New York, organizing numerous exhibitions. His "Family of Man", representing not only a photographic
concept but also a moral ideal, became world famous. This exhibition
was meant to be a "mirror of the essential unity of man worldwide".
MBT

▲ **Edward Steichen**
Self-portrait, 1929

Gelatin silver print
25.1 x 20 cm
ML/F 1977/786

Gruber Collection

▲ **Edward Steichen**
Charlie Chaplin, 1931

Silver bromide print
25 x 19.8 cm
ML/F 1977/790

Gruber Collection

▲ **Edward Steichen**
Marlene Dietrich, 1935

Silver bromide print
24.2 x 19.3 cm
ML/F 1977/791

Gruber Collection

▲ Edward Steichen
Gloria Swanson, 1926

Silver bromide print
24.2 x 19.3 cm
ML/F 1977/810

Gruber Collection

Steinert, Otto

1915 Saarbrücken
1978 Essen

Otto Steinert, who made history as an outstanding personality of German post-war photography, started out wanting to become a physician. In 1934 he began to study medicine, graduating in 1939. After World War II he worked as a doctor in residence in Kiel from 1945 to 1947. Simultaneously, however, he taught himself photography, eventually giving up his profession as a physician to pursue his passion for photography. In 1948 he became the director of the photographic class at the State College of Arts and Trades in Saarbrücken. There he, Peter Keetman, Ludwig Windstoßer, and others, founded the group "fotoform" in 1949, which was dedicated to rekindling people's awareness of the photographic design possibilities and modes of expression of the pre-war avant-garde, which had been suppressed by the dictatorial cultural policy of the National Socialists. In 1951 Steinert organized the first of three exhibitions whose title "subjective photography" was to become synonymous with a whole new direction in style. In the second catalog of this small series of exhibitions Steinert explained: "We feel all the more

▶ **Otto Steinert**
Dancer's Mask, 1952

Gelatin silver print
34.5 x 26.5 cm
ML/F 1977/817

Gruber Collection

obligated [...] to encourage all efforts to work actively and creatively on the synthesis of the creative, contemporary photographic image and to generate a genuine relationship with photographic image quality." High-contrast prints, radical cropping, abstract structures, surreal-looking situations, negative prints, and solarizations became the favorite forms of expression espoused by Steinert and his students. Their idols were photographers such as Man Ray and especially László Moholy-Nagy.

In 1959 Steinert accepted an invitation to teach at the Folkwang School of Design in Essen, where he directed the photography work group until he passed away. During these years Steinert not only acted as a photographer and teacher, but also assembled an excellent photographic collection. *MBT*

► **Curt Stenvert**
New Dimensions of
Cosmology or: Out-
side Like Inside, 1985

Collage, mixed media
70 x 51 cm
ML/F 1995/116

Uwe Scheid
Donation

Curt Stenvert studied painting, sculpting, theater and motion picture
sciences in Vienna. Following an initial involvement with German Expressionism and Futurism, he became co-founder of the Vienna School
of Fantastic Realism. His motion studies, however, concentrated on the
development of a synthesis of Futurism, Constructivism, and Cubism.
After a few years of making films ("The Raven", "Venice"), he turned to
object art in 1962, writing his manifesto on "Functional Art of the 21st
Century". Stenvert was active as an object artist, producing his series
Human Situations as well as photocollages, verse-collages, screened
prints, and watercolor paintings. In the seventies he began to paint
again and developed pictures that implemented his idea of a process
perspective with motion studies and a gold background. *RM*

Stenvert, Curt

(Curt Steinwendner)

1920 Vienna
1992 Cologne

Stern, Bert

1929 New York
Lives in New York

Bert Stern is a self-taught photographer. In 1951 he was a cameraman for the US Army in Japan. Since 1953 he has been working as a fashion and advertising photographer. He was one of the first to design newspaper advertisements in color that were difficult to distinguish from editorial picture pages. His style can be circumscribed with words such as glamour, romanticism, and delicacy: "If you want to be seduced by the camera, by a man who can fall in love with any object, go see Bert Stern", is how a publisher characterized him. His outstanding abilities in portrait photography were especially noticeable in *Louis Armstrong*, a picture taken around 1959 on the occasion of an advertising campaign for an early Polaroid film. The sharpness of detail and gradation of the black-and-white tones was perfect to a point that the client considered it "too good", but still had it printed. But without doubt the most famous of Stern's photographs are those he took of Marilyn Monroe. They were shot during her last photographic session for *Vogue* magazine at a Los Angeles hotel in June of 1962, six weeks before she died. In the course of three days Stern shot almost 2700 pictures, including portraits, fashion photographs and nudes, which were published in the 1992 picture book *The Complete Last Sittings* and which attest to the unique intimacy and understanding between model and photographer during that session. At that time *Vogue* published a total of eight of the black-and-white shots. Bert Stern became increasingly successful during the sixties, but his photographs of Marilyn Monroe remained very special: "In the course of the years I noticed that the pictures we had taken together now belonged to everyone. What we created had grown beyond me. Somehow they slipped away from me and into the dreams of everyone." *AS*

▼ **Bert Stern**
Eartha Kitt, around 1956

Gelatin silver print
28.1 x 27.4 cm
ML/F 1977/824

Gruber Collection

▲ **Bert Stern**
Louis Armstrong,
around 1959

Gelatin silver print
41.9 x 34.5 cm
ML/F 1977/821

Gruber Collection

Alfred Stieglitz was the son of a well-to-do German-Jewish family. He studied engineering and photographic chemistry in Berlin, where he trained under Hermann Wilhelm Vogel, the inventor of orthochromatic film.

Initially, he was particularly interested in the functional, scientific aspect of his studies of photography. His first works, oriented to conventional photography, were created in 1883 in Berlin. In 1890, at the age of 26, he returned to New York. Because he had quickly reached the technical limits of photography, Stieglitz began to look for new methods of exposure and processing. Together with Joseph T. Keiley, he invented "pure photography", using the gelatin process.

In the 1890s Stieglitz worked in gravure printing and also wrote articles for photographic journals. Photographs of this time, including *A Street in Sterzing, South Tyrol*, and *Sun Rays, Paula* show his intense interest in lighting conditions and their effects, such as light stripes created by Venetian blinds as shown in the latter of the aforementioned photographs. There is also a certain influence of German genre painters evident in Stieglitz' understanding of imagery.

In 1893 he created his first successful photograph of snow, and three years later he made his first night-time photograph. Also in 1893 Stieglitz became the publisher of *American Amateur Photographer* and in 1897 of *Camera Notes*.

In 1902 Stieglitz, Edward Steichen, and Alvin Langdon Coburn founded "Photo Secession" and the journal *Camera Work*. The title "Photo Secession" was selected in honor of Symbolism and of the Vienna Secession. The photographers of "Photo Secession", including Gertrude Käsebier, Clarence H. White, and Frank Eugene, did not so much see mimetic qualities in photography, but the spiritual expression of the artist himself. In the aesthetics of his pictures Stieglitz emphasized his own perception, totally independent of any viewing tradition. Despite the group's goal of artistic aesthetics, Stieglitz' photography remained quite untouched by these ideas. Symbolic titles like *The Hand of Man* can still be found here and there, but his main subjects in those years were the city of New York and the formal, architectural aspects of its buildings.

In 1905 he opened Gallery 291, which derived its name from its location on 291 Fifth Avenue in New York City, where Stieglitz introduced the European avant-garde to Americans. His newspapers and the presenta-

▲ **Alfred Stieglitz**
The Steerage, 1907

Heliogravure
19.7 x 15.8 cm
ML/F 1982/1

▲ **Alfred Stieglitz**
The Mauretania, from:
Camera Work 36, 1911

Photogravure
20.9 x 16.3 cm
ML/F 1995/59

Gruber Donation

▲ Alfred Stieglitz
In the New York Central
Yards, from: Camera
Work 36, 1911

Photogravure
19.4 x 15.9 cm
ML/F 1995/69

Gruber Donation

▲ **Alfred Stieglitz**
A Dirigible, from:
Camera Work 36,
1911

Photogravure
17.8 x 18 cm
ML/F 1995/63

Gruber Donation

tion of modern European artists in the USA place Stieglitz in the center of photography and art of the early twenties.

In 1917, the last year *Camera Work* was published, he met Georgia O'Keeffe, a photographer and later his life companion, whose pictures he exhibited in 1926 in his second gallery, the Intimate Gallery. As a result of numerous photographs he took of Georgia O'Keeffe Stieglitz' portrait photography set new standards, exhibiting unadulterated directness and the search for objective truth through "pure photography". As is obvious from a voluminous exchange of letters, Stieglitz' friendship with newspaper illustrator Arthur G. Dove was of great importance. In

1929 Stieglitz' second gallery was closed. Soon he opened another one, "An American Place", which he operated until his died. Regardless of the fact that he managed his gallery more on idealistic than commercial lines, Stieglitz saw himself mainly as a photographer who wanted to convey what he saw – his "idea photography". In 1922 he photographed a series of clouds at Lake George, which were of an abstract nature. *LH*

▲ **Alfred Stieglitz**
Aeroplane, from:
Camera Work 36,
1911

Photogravure
14.4 x 17.6 cm
ML/F 1995/62

Gruber Donation

◄ **Alfred Stieglitz**
Excavating in New York, from: Camera Work 36, 1911

Photogravure
12.7 x 15.8 cm
ML/F 1995/65

Gruber Donation

▶ **Alfred Stieglitz**
End of the Line, from: Camera Work 36, 1911

Photogravure
12.2 x 15.9 cm
ML/F 1995/70

Gruber Donation

◄ **Alfred Stieglitz**
At the Pool, from:
Camera Work 36,
1911

Photogravure
12.6 x 15.9 cm
ML/F 1995/67

Gruber Donation

► **Alfred Stieglitz**
The Swimming
Lesson, from:
Camera Work 36,
1911

Photogravure
14.9 x 23.1 cm
ML/F 1995/66

Gruber Donation

Stock, Dennis

1928 New York
Lives in the
Provence, France

▼ Dennis Stock
New Orleans, 1961

Gelatin silver print
19.4 x 24 cm
ML/F 1994/298

Gruber Donation

Following a photographic apprenticeship with Gjon Mili (1947–1951), Dennis Stock worked as a freelance photographer for *Life, Paris Match, Look, Geo,* and *Queen,* among others. He has been a full member of the "Magnum" photo-agency since 1954. In 1951 *Life* magazine already awarded him the first prize for young photographers for his picture series on refugees from East Germany. From the late fifties into the seventies he worked as a chronicler and portrait photographer of the jazz scene (picture book, *Jazz World,* 1959), where he accompanied musicians on all sorts of locations, on the stage, during rehearsal, on the way home in the early morning after a gig in a club. In addition to his publications and reports on Italy, Japan, California, and Alaska, he became known for his plant impressions. His encounter with James Dean in 1955 made Stock famous. In 1956 his *Portrait of a Young Man, James Dean,* was published. He photographed him in Hollywood, New York, and in his home in Indiana. By taking the picture *James Dean in Times Square, New York City* in 1955, showing the actor with shoulders raised, hands deep in his coat pockets, cigarette dangling from the corner of his mouth on a street wet from rain, Stock created an icon that symbolized the cult around the movie star who died young and who was the idol of an entire generation. That picture has been reprinted on thousands of posters and postcards, and it remains in everyone's mind to this day. *AS*

► **Wolf Strache**
Relay Race, 1936

Gelatin silver print
40 x 30 cm
ML/F 1988/16

Wolf Strache obtained his doctorate in political science in Cologne and
Munich. After working for just one year for the Ullstein publishing
house in Berlin, he began his career as a freelance photojournalist. His
first picture books were published in 1936. His work as a photographer
and writer was interrupted by World War II, when he had to serve in the
Foreign Office. Later on he was drafted to become a photographic reporter for the German air force. His photographic style is strongly based
on the New Vision and its extreme perspectives. Some of his photographs of the destruction in Germany, such as *Berlin, Kurfürstendamm
After a Major Air Raid*, became world famous because of their powerful
symbolism. In 1945 Strache moved to Stuttgart. He published a broad
spectrum of photographic picture books with topics relating to culture,
art history, natural science, and geography. He used different publishers, but he also published his own series of books *The Beautiful Books*.
In 1955 he began publishing the annual *The German Photograph*, which

Strache, Wolf

1910 Greifswald,
Germany
Lives in Stuttgart

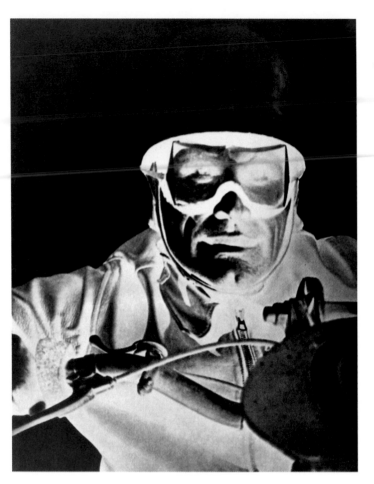

◄ **Wolf Strache**
Dirt Track Rider, 1956

Gelatin silver print
38 x 30 cm
ML/F 1988/18

► **Wolf Strache**
Berlin, Kurfürsten-
damm After a Major
Air Raid, 1942

Gelatin silver print
40 x 30 cm
ML/F 1988/17

has been presenting outstanding work by German photographers for 25 years. Today, it is considered one of the most important documents of recent German photographic history. Between 1971 and 1985 he was the secretary-treasurer of the Association of Freelance Photo-Designers.
RM

Strand, Paul

1890 New York
1976 Orgeval, France

In 1909 Paul Strand completed his studies under Lewis Hine at the Ethical Cultural School in New York. Hine introduced him to Alfred Stieglitz, the founder of "Photo Secession" and the publisher of *Camera Work*. Strand began producing abstract photographs in 1915. In 1917, the last double-edition of *Camera Work* was dedicated exclusively to Strand's photographs. He imparted this medium with a new direction in style, called "straight photography" ever since. The traditional orientation to painting was replaced by a self-assured exploration of the genuinely photographic, where the charm is frequently found in the mundane, in a structure, or in the shadow of the world of things, in excerpts and rhythms. *Abstraction, Shadows of a Veranda, Connecticut* (1916) is representative of this style. Strand's works cover almost all subjects, including portraits and documentary pictures, landscapes and plant photography, architectural themes and photographs of machines and industrial sites. *AS*

Strauß, Helfried

1943 Plauen
Lives in Leipzig

▶ **Helfried Strauß**
From: Sanssouci, 1982

Gelatin silver print
45 x 30 cm
ML/F 1991/182

▼ **Helfried Strauß**
From: Sanssouci, 1982

Gelatin silver print
448 x 30 cm
ML/F 1991/181

Between 1963 and 1965 Helfried Strauß studied singing and voice at the Conservatory in Halle, after which he sang for two years at the theater of the City of Cottbus. Between 1967 and 1972 he studied photography at the College of Graphic Design and Book Art in Leipzig. From 1973 to 1976 he was a photojournalist for *Freie Welt* in Berlin. Between 1976 and 1979 he completed additional studies at the aforementioned college, becoming an assistant and, in 1980, its director of the photography program. He has been a professor there since 1993. Strauß is a photographer who has always been meticulous in preparing and carrying out his projects. He is not only interested in successful individual pictures, but also in completed self-contained projects. He adopted this method of working when in the former East Germany it was anything but politically expedient to do so. He documented religious folk customs of the

Sorbs dating back hundreds of years, daily life in Moscow, and the life and work of ferrywoman Brigitte Höfgen in Grimma, which he was only able to publish in book form after German reunification. One of his most extensive projects is the documentation of parks designed by landscape architect Peter Joseph Lenné, where he devotes equal interest to preserved, as well as modified or destroyed parks. In his view, the history of the park is as important as its original design. Another series deals with the sculptures in Sanssouci. Here he examined the relationship of sculptures and space, and in another series he approached parts of the sculptures so closely that their surfaces began to look deceptively like living skin. *RM*

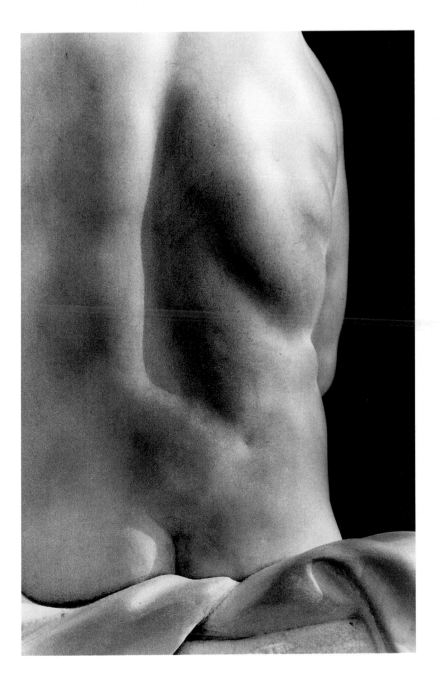

Strelow, Liselotte

1908 Redel, Pomerania
1981 Hamburg

After attending a private school in Neustettin, Liselotte Strelow began to study agronomy and then, from 1930 to 1932, photography at the Lette-Verein in Berlin. In 1933 she was an assistant to Sys Byk in Berlin, where between 1933 and 1938 she was subsequently employed by Kodak AG. In 1936 she completed her training with a diploma. In 1938 she set up a studio at Kurfürstendamm in Berlin, later working as a freelancer for various papers such as the *Frankfurter Allgemeine, Die Welt, Der Spiegel,* and *Theater der Zeit.* Her camera of choice was a Rolleiflex, which influenced her style. In 1943 she moved to Neustettin where she devoted herself mainly to landscape photography. Between 1945 and 1950 she set up a studio in Detmold and began to work on theater photography with Gustaf Gründgens at the Düsseldorf Theater. In 1949 she had her first solo exhibition. One year later Liselotte Strelow moved to Düsseldorf, from where she traveled extensively. Her work was very successful and the name "Strelow" became synonymous with fine portrait photography. She also cultivated the portrait in her theater photography. She made portraits of socially and culturally prominent people of her time, she was official photographer at the Wagner Festivals from 1952 to 1962,

◀ **Liselotte Strelow**
Alice Bettina
Constance Gruber,
1960

Gelatin silver print
28.2 x 23 cm
ML/F 1993/532

Gruber Donation

and she received numerous awards, including the Cultural Award of the
German Society for Photography (DGPh) and the David Octavius Hill
Medal of the Society of German Photographers (GDL). Between 1959
and 1962 she was the chief photographer at the theaters of the City of
Cologne, and in 1966 received the Adolf Grimme Prize. She lived in
Munich between 1969 and 1976, and in Hamburg from 1977 until she
died after seven cancer operations. *RM*

► Carl Strüwe
Plant Thorns, 1933

Gelatin silver print
23.8 x 18.4 cm
ML/F 1991/87

Carl Strüwe apprenticed in lithography and studied at the Arts and
Crafts School of Bielefeld. His interest in photography emerged during
that time. At the beginning of the twenties he was employed as a commercial artist at a large graphic arts company in Bielefeld. In the course
of his activities, which included the design of logos, packages, and
posters, he discovered photography as a new medium. Between 1924
and 1952 Strüwe traveled to Italy, the Alps, and Africa. His publication
Hohenstaufen in Italy – Pictures and Words of 1986 goes back to that
time. In 1926 he produced his first micro-photographs, a subject that
continued to fascinate him. After his book *Shapes of the Microcosm –
Form and Design of a World of Images* first appeared in 1955, his name
was inseparably linked with micro-photography. *RM*

Strüwe, Carl

1898 Bielefeld
1988 Bielefeld

▲ Carl Strüwe
Notched Butterfly Pro-
boscis. Roll-up Mecha-
nism, from the series:
Forms of Structure and
Motion, 1928
Gelatin silver print
22.7 x 18.5 cm
ML/F 1991/83

► Carl Strüwe
Archetype of Adaptation.
Ocean Rhythms in the Struc-
ture of A Sea Algae, from
the series: Original Images,
Symbolic Images, 1930
Gelatin silver print
24.5 x 19 cm
ML/F 1991/84

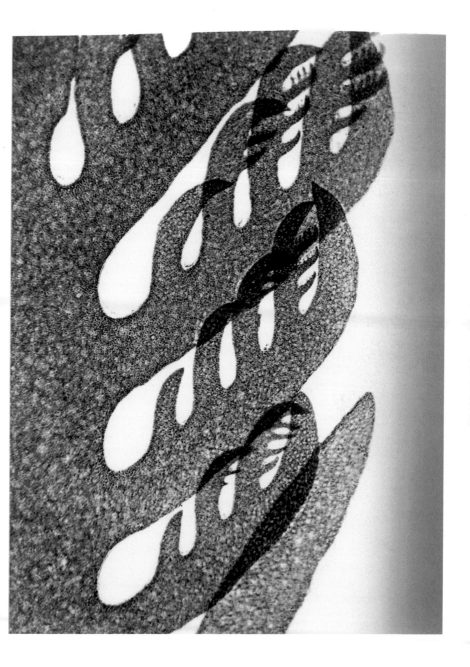

Sudek, Josef

1896 Kolín, Bohemia
1976 Prague

▲ Josef Sudek
Untitled
(panorama), around
1950

Gelatin silver print
14 x 37.8 cm
ML/F 1993/506

Gruber Donation

Following an apprenticeship as a bookbinder, Josef Sudek served as a soldier in World War I. In 1916 he was seriously injured in Italy, losing his right arm. After spending three years in hospitals he decided to become a photographer. In 1920 he became a member of the Prague Club for Amateur Photographers, going on to study photography for two years under Karel Novak at the National School of Graphic Art in Prague. Together with Jaromir Funke and other photographers he founded the Czech Photographic Association in 1924. In the twenties he shot a series of photographs of the reconstruction of St. Vitus Cathedral (Portfolio *Svazy Vit*, 1928) which earned him the title of official photographer of the City of Prague. Until 1936 Sudek was co-publisher and illustrator of the magazines *Panorama* and *Zijeme*, at the same time carrying out advertising and portrait work in his own studio. Sudek used an 1894 Kodak panoramic camera (negative format 10 x 30 cm) to produce an extensive series of views of Prague, which was only published in 1959. Beginning in 1940, he used mostly large-format cameras because he was fascinated by the possibilities of contact prints. Sudek is considered a master of the still life and of nature shots. The objects in his still-life pictures are illuminated with lyrical sensitivity. Diffused daylight, direct sunlight, or a cloudy sky provide an extremely melancholy, romantic, and at times sinister atmosphere despite the realistic rendition. Following a large exhibition in 1974 at the George Eastman House in Rochester, New York, he was honored two years later on the occasion of his 80th birthday with retrospectives in Prague and Brno in his home country. *AS*

► **Josef Sudek**
Untitled (cherry
blossom), around
1940

Gelatin silver print
29.3 x 22.3 cm
ML/F 1993/507

Gruber Donation

► **Josef Sudek**
Park and Bridge,
1964

Gelatin silver print
11 x 17.2 cm
ML/F 1984/117

Gruber Donation

Székessy, Karin

1939 Essen
Lives in Hamburg

▼ **Karin Székessy**
Nude with Mask and
Fish, 1973

Gelatin silver print
27.9 x 22.2 cm
ML/F 1993/508

Gruber Donation

Karin Székessy grew up in Hertfordshire, England, where she decided to become a photographer. In 1954 she began to take pictures with her first Leica. Following high school in Düsseldorf, she studied photography under Prof. Hans Schreiner in Munich from 1958 to 1960. In 1959 she gave birth to her son Oliver. Since 1960 she has been living in Hamburg, where she works as a freelance photographer and takes portraits of famous people. Between 1960 and 1963 she collected dolls, which she photographed, publishing the pictures in different newspapers such as *Die Zeit, Die Welt*, und *Süddeutsche Zeitung*. Between 1962 and 1967 she produced a series of photographs of *Contemporaries*. From 1963 until 1967 she worked for *Kristall* magazine, which published her pictures of politicians and children in the big city. Between 1967 and 1970 she worked for *Brigitte, Zeitmagazin, Konkret*, and *Photo* and began to photograph nudes. She developed her very own style with long-legged models posing in unconventional ways, frequently alluding to historical prototypes in paintings. In conjunction with this type of work, a congenial collaboration developed with painter and sculptor Paul Wunderlich, with whom she published the book *Correspondences* in 1976, which expressed the harmony of their perceptions. Karin Székessy took photographs of Paul Wunderlich's paintings and it is difficult to say who had the greater influence on whom. In 1971 she married Paul Wunderlich. From 1970 to 1971 she worked with *Orion Press* in Japan and with *twen, Brigitte, Knoll International*, and *Zeitmagazin*. In 1972 her daughter Laura was born. During subsequent years she also photographed advertising campaigns, among others for Draenert-Möbel, a furniture company, and for Ergee-Strümpfe, a stocking com-

► **Karin Székessy**
Mask in Easy Chair,
1980

Gelatin silver print
23.9 x 29 cm
ML/F 1994/280

Gruber Donation

◄ **Karin Székessy**
Girls and Plants,
1989

Gelatin silver print
24.7 x 37.2 cm
ML/F 1994/281

Gruber Donation

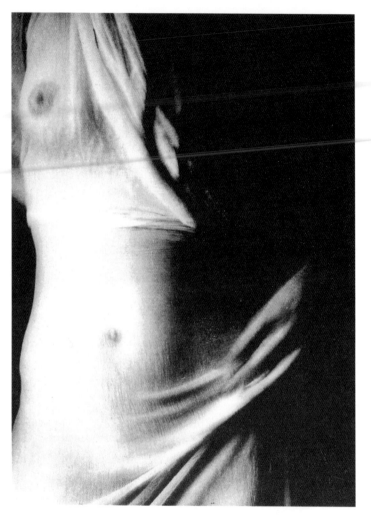

◀ **Karin Székessy**
Torso (at Studio VII),
1974

Print-out, colorized
27.1 x 19.9 cm
ML/F 1993/511

Gruber Donation

▶ **Karin Székessy**
Dance with Cactus,
1990

Gelatin silver print
30.8 x 22.3 cm
ML/F 1994/284

Gruber Donation

pany. Her photographs and publications have won many prizes. In the eighties she took an interest in another topic, over and above her photography of young women; she took advantage of her travels to Italy, France, Japan, and the USA to photograph a series of melancholy southern landscapes. *RM*

◄ Ulrich Tillmann
The Artist and his
Work, 1989

Gelatin silver print
23.3 x 22.3 cm
ML/F 1994/309

Gruber Donation

**Tillmann,
Ulrich**

1951 Linnich
Lives in Cologne

Ulrich Tillmann was born in Linnich in 1951. He studied photography at
the Technical College of Cologne and art history, theater, motion-picture,
and television sciences at the University of Cologne. From 1978 to 1985
he operated the "Gallery without a Gallerist", an exhibition space for experimental photography, video art, and film. From 1977 to 1987 he lectured at universities in Cologne, Wuppertal, and Düsseldorf. Since 1986
he has been employed at the Agfa Foto-Historama in Cologne.

**Vollmer,
Wolfgang**

1952 Marburg
Lives in Cologne

Between 1978 and 1984 Wolfgang Vollmer studied liberal arts and artistic photography under Arno Jansen at the Technical College of Cologne. Between 1982 and 1985 he operated the "Gallery without a Gallerist" together with Ulrich Tillmann. In 1985 Vollmer began lecturing
at various German universities. Since 1994 he has been teaching in
the department of design of the Technical College of Würzburg.

Tillman and Vollmer worked very closely together in the mid-eighties. In 1984 they created the cycle *Masterpieces of Photographic Art*, which proved that some of the most famous pictures in the history of photography, such as Irving Penn's portraits of Pablo Picasso, can be attributed to unknown, only recently discovered predecessors. *RM*

▲ N.N. Pablo Gruber, from: Masterpieces of Photographic Art, Tillmann and Vollmer Collection, 1984

Gelatin silver print
30 x 30 cm
ML/F 1993/539

Gruber Donation

▲ Mariana Swanson, 1987, from:
Masterpieces of Photographic Art,
Tillmann and Vollmer Collection

Gelatin silver print, 32.6 x 27.3 cm
ML/F 1994/308

Gruber Donation

▶ Paul Outerbridge (attributed to), Woman
with Kitchen Gloves and Trap-the-Cap Caps,
from: Masterpieces of Photographic Art,
Tillmann and Vollmer Collection, 1987

Color print, 40.1 x 29.9 cm
ML/F 1994/302

Gruber Donation

Tourdjman, Georges

1935 Casablanca, Morocco
Lives in Boulogne

▼ Georges Tourdjman
Alexey Brodovitch, 1964

Gelatin silver print
37.5 x 24.7 cm
ML/F 1988/68

Gruber Donation

Beginning in 1956, Georges Tourdjman was an assistant producer. In 1963 he moved to New York to study photography. His teachers Ike Weegler and especially Alexey Brodovitch had a decisive influence of Tourdjman's subsequent career. In 1964 this Moroccan photographer went to Paris to freelance, and during the following years obtained advertising contracts with Chanel, Dior, L'Oréal, Air France Maroc and several French automobile companies. Tourdjman designed many cover pages for international magazines such as *Marie-France, Queen, Kodak International Photography*, and *Stern*, and he was responsible for over 50 advertising movie spots. His portrait photographs of the eighties depicting major artists and photographers such as Man Ray, Robert Doisneau and his teacher Brodovitch share a remarkable intensity of expression, obtained on the one hand by a frontal, direct look at the viewer

and on the other hand by a certain intimate ambiance. For example, by contrasting the painted portrait and the persons, he has imparted the double portrait of the Prévert brothers with a certain clownish aura. This creates a teasing picture-within-a-picture confusion, because the painting almost emphasizes the characters more than the realistic photograph does. In other black-and-white work the photographer emphasizes cropping, diagonals, and effects like reflections on a table or in the lenses of spectacles. Tourdjman has conducted several workshops in Arles, on portraits in 1976 and on nudes and portraits in 1984. These were followed by several solo exhibitions in Paris, Arles, and Bordeaux. Tourdjman lives and works in France. *LH*

► Judith Turner
Untitled, 1984

Color print
30.4 x 20.2 cm
ML/F 1986/168

Judith Turner graduated with a Bachelor of Fine Arts from Boston University. She has been interested in photography since 1972, concentrating largely on architectural photography. She has worked for numerous newspapers and magazines in Europe and in America. Her first publication was entitled *Five Architects*, and it brought her instant international fame. Other exhibitions followed at the Tel Aviv Museum, the International Center of Photography in New York, and at Princeton University in New Jersey. Judith Turner works in black and white as well as in color, valuing pure, clear colors. She is considered to be one of the best architectural photographers in the USA. *RM*

Turner, Judith

Born in Atlantic City
Lives in New York

Ueda, Shoji

1913 Sakaiminato,
Japan
Lives in
Sakaiminato-shi

▲ **Shoji Ueda**
Silhouette Pro-
cession, 1978

Color print, satiny
23.8 x 36.2 cm
ML/F 1984/121

Gruber Donation

Shoji Ueda completed his formal training under Toyo Kikuchi at the Oriental School of Photography. Ueda opened his first studio in his home
town in 1933. Ueda points out that, because in Japan photography is not
held in the same high esteem as painting, he fostered the new age with
a cosmopolitan way of thinking. He is frequently called a "poet of images". Ueda's main subjects are people set in landscapes, such as the
sand dunes of the Samin region. The staged character of his pictures is
conspicuous in his publication *Dunes* of 1978, and also in *Children the
Year Round*. A person, be it in the form of a rear view of a nude, a man
with a bowler hat, or a child, is the extraneous object in the dunes with
an infinite expanse of sky. Frequently the horizon provides the only
boundary, and spatial concepts are often suspended. Ueda plays with
artificial perspective tricks in nature. Clothes hangers, carpets, and
bowler hat, are often used to confuse perspective viewing.

Since 1975, Ueda has been a professor at the Kyushyn Sangyo University in Sakaiminato-shi. *LH*

► Umbo
Sinister Street, 1928

Gelatin silver print
29.8 x 22.8 cm
ML/F 1981/574

From 1921 to 1923 Umbo studied at the Bauhaus in Weimar. In 1926 he produced photomontages for Walter Ruttmann's film "Berlin". He made the acquaintance of Paul Citroen, the painter, who introduced him to photography. The actress Ruth Landshoff became his preferred model for his innovative portraits, a combination of the broad view of the motion picture and the classical portrait. He adopted the pseudonym Umbo, and his pictures of large cities, portraits and photograms earned him international acclaim as one of the leading German avant-garde artists of the twenties. His style influenced the photojournalism of "Dephot" (German Picture Agency). During the time of the National Socialist regime he joined the resistance movement, and his agency was closed. During World War II Umbo lost his entire archive, and his significance went unrecognized until he was finally rediscovered in 1978 as a pioneer of modern art. *RM*

Umbo

(Otto Maximilian Umbehr)

1902 Düsseldorf
1980 Hanover

Vogt, Christian

1946 Basel
Lives in Basel

After completing his training as a photographer at the Crafts School in Basel, Christian Vogt traveled and worked as an assistant in Will McBride's studio in Munich. Since 1970 Vogt has been working successfully out of his own studio in Basel, serving advertising clients and magazines such as *Du, Camera, Photo, Playboy, Time-Life,* etc. He has received numerous prizes and awards, including the photokina Prize in Cologne in 1972, the Grand Prix of the Phototriennale Fribourg in Switzerland 1975, and the Prize of the Art Directors' Club of Germany in 1978.

Parallel to his work in commercial photography, Vogt also pursues his personal artistic interests in photography. In 1972 he had his first solo exhibition in Basel, and in 1980 he published the photographic volume *Christian Vogt, Photographs,* which was followed in 1982 by *In Camera, Eighty-Two Photographs with Fifty-Two Women.* He prefers the implementation of a pictorial concept in large cycles. In the seventies, for example, he created the series *Images of Clouds,* with distinctly surrealist overtones reminiscent of René Magritte, and a *Red Series, Blue Series,* and *Yellow Series.* Of particular importance among his works has been the *Frame* series, in which he used a photographed frame to define and change the cropping of the picture. With these pictures he connected with the conceptual art of those years, but also related to Land Art and its methodology of surveying and archiving certain

▲▶ **Christian Vogt**
Portraits, Duane
Michals I–III, 1976

*Gelatin silver print
each 14 x 21 cm*
ML/F 1985/111–113

Gruber Donation

positions in a landscape. The *Frame* series was meant to illustrate the fact that an event is the result of certain conditions, which themselves make these circumstances transparent in the picture. In addition, this series demonstrated the extent to which a change in these parameters caused a change in the image.

In his nude photography, which was temporarily pre-eminent during the eighties, he preferred a subtle approach to the subject, which was sometimes created in dialog with the women. For the project *In Camera* he asked over 50 women to come to his studio, inviting them to select their own poses in front of a curved, colored background. The only condition was that an open wooden crate had to appear in the picture. This resulted in very aesthetic, intimate, humorous, and narrative photographs. *AS*

Vormwald, Gerhard

1948 Heidelberg
Lives in Paris

Between 1966 and 1971 Gerhard Vormwald studied commercial art and liberal arts at the Applied Arts School in Mannheim. In 1970 he began working as a stage photographer for the National Theater of Mannheim. In addition, he accepted advertising assignments and created photographic illustrations for magazines. In 1975 he created his first photographic productions. In 1983 he moved to Paris, where he established himself as photographer for advertising, magazines and cover pages. Vormwald earned the reputation of a pioneer of staged advertising photography inspired by surreal ideas. The particular attraction of his photographic interpretation was that the physically impossible appeared real in the picture. Vormwald's photographic worlds of photographic images could be considered precursors of computer-generated virtual worlds of images. His flying African, who made every viewer wonder how something like this was possible, became the symbol of this development and was published as such all over the world. But Gerhard Vormwald also increasingly showed his humorous side, as demon-

strated by his photograph of several gentlemen lined up to be measured with a surveyor's staff. In the nineties he distanced himself from producing virtual worlds and turned to a rather obvious form of artifice. Countering the trend that he himself had launched and that was now booming by way of the computer, he began to be interested in pictorial arrangements more reminiscent of a world of Arcimboldo. He used everyday objects, kitchen utensils, rubbish, flowers and food to cobble assemblages, fantasy arrangements that quite obviously are not what they pretend to be, but which assert themselves as ironic statements about that comical world. These photographs too, attest to humor and to obvious fun with surprising and amusing picture ideas, and they are evidence of a fantasy world in which utilitarian thinking is eccentric. He produced these new Cibachrome prints at his own initiative. In 1989 Vormwald opened a studio in the country, devoting himself more and more to his own ideas. *RM*

◄▲ **Gerhard Vormwald**
St. Oskar the Gourmet, 1992

Color print
53.7 x 41.8 cm
ML/F 1995/82

Gruber Donation

▲ **Gerhard Vormwald**
Mykons, Paris, 1992

Color print
53.6 x 43 cm
ML/F 1995/83

Gruber Donation

Walther, Pan

1921 Dresden
1987 Bangkok

Pan Walther became aware of photography through his father. After attending the Waldorf School he studied photography in The Hague and in Dresden, where he founded a studio in 1945. After obtaining his diploma as a master photographer in 1946, he worked as a freelance photographer concentrating on portraits, first in Dresden and then, beginning in 1950, in Münster. In addition, he taught for more than 30 years at various colleges, both in Cologne and, since 1963, in Dortmund. There, with single-minded determination, he succeeded in consolidating his own photography classes into an autonomous department with the name "Subject Group Photo-Film-Design", and he soon gave it its own individual profile. His portraits, heads precisely modeled in light, have been regarded as classics for many years. Walther loved dramatic light that brings his faces out of the dark. In addition to people prominent in politics, literature, the arts, and theater, he devoted equal enthusiasm to unknown people he encountered and whose faces he found fascinating. During his many journeys he often had an opportunity encounter peasants, workmen and gypsies whose faces had been etched by the rigors of life and labor.

▼ Pan Walther
The German Michel,
from the series:
Think About It, 1983

Color print
29.8 x 30 cm
ML/F 1991/110

In addition to this classic theme, Walther developed several sequences of staged photography in the latter works of his life which dealt with the problems of present-day life. These picture series were produced in color and in the manner of photographic performance art. For example, an ode to human stupidity he presented like a fight against a windmill in the form of a Japanese swordfighter holding a club and wrapped in toilet paper and entitled *Think About It*, or the ecological wave which he satirizes in the form of a green catalyst in the thicket of his overgrown garden. Finally, he also addressed the nuclear threat, posing in a rubber suit and gas mask. These later works again demonstrate Walther's fundamentally rebellious attitude and his conviction

of the unity of art and life. Being a pugnacious contemporary, he was always able to earn his colleagues' respect at all times, and he succeeded in producing convincing work and in creating surprises. *RM*

▲ **Pan Walther**
Fighter in the Japan-Look, from the series: Think About It, 1983

Color print
28 x 30.2 cm
ML/F 1991/111

Warhol, Andy

1928 Pittsburgh
1987 New York

Andy Warhol, the son of Czech immigrants, studied at the Carnegie Institute of Technology in Pittsburgh from 1945 to 1949 and started out as a graphic artist in advertising. In 1960 he decided to become an artist and began by painting comic strip figures. His love of money and fame motivated him to search for themes that were as banal as they were provocative: money bills, soup cans, catastrophes, criminals, and stars such as Marilyn Monroe, Elvis Presley, and Robert Rauschenberg. His connections, such as his friendship with Henry Geldzahler, who at that time was a curator at the Metropolitan Museum of Art, helped Warhol to achieve his dream of world fame. In his studio, called "The Factory", he produced screen prints almost in assembly-line fashion. He promoted the ideal of being a machine and of producing art that is equivalent to money – ideally one would convert money into art. In his art, Warhol concentrated completely on the world of consumers and thus became the star and protagonist of American Pop Art. While he was active in the field of painting, screen-printing, and sculpture, Warhol also constantly took photographs. His book *Andy Warhol's Exposures*, published in 1980, containing his casual portraits of the New York art scene, caused a scandal. Warhol provided an insight into the private life of high society in a provokingly artless manner, popping flash pictures of the goings-on with a cheap camera. Shortly thereafter, his patched-together architectural shots appeared, and they were no less of a surprise. The triple portrait of Peter Ludwig is one of the photographic variants of Warhol's large-format work in the possession of that collector. *RM*

▲ Andy Warhol
Three Portraits of
Peter Ludwig, 1980

Color print
each 12.9 x 12.9 cm
ML/F1980/1375

Ludwig Collection

After completing high school, Jürgen Wassmuth began an apprentice-ship in industrial administration, after which he studied economics in Mannheim. In 1981 he decided to change to photography and began to study under professor Ulrich Mack at the Technical College of Dort-mund. In 1982 he married Annette Hitzegrath, and his daughter Anna was born in 1984. Since 1985 Wassmuth has been a graduate photo-graphic designer and freelance photographer for architectural and in-dustrial photography. He has had a studio in Dortmund since 1987. He is a lecturer at the Parsons School of Design in New York and in Paris. In the eighties he undertook numerous study tours of France, Denmark, Poland and Greece, and he also organized the international FOCUS workshop in New York and in Dortmund. In 1988, while on a two-month study tour in New York, Wassmuth produced a comprehensive series of pictures on the architecture of this city. He repeatedly succeeded in pre-senting entirely new perspectives of buildings that were otherwise famil-iar from countless conventional pictures. He has been lecturing at the Technical College of Dortmund since 1989. *RM*

Wassmuth, Jürgen

1955 Balve, Germany
Lives in Dortmund

▲ **Jürgen Wassmuth**
Flatiron Building,
New York, 1988

Gelatin silver print
30.7 x 40.3 cm
ML/F 1993/553

Gruber Donation

Webster, Christine

1958 Pukekohe,
New Zealand
Lives in Dunedin
and Paris

▼ Christine Webster
Post Crucifixion,
1988

Cibachrome print
156.3 x 95 cm and
25.1 x 25 cm
ML/F 1989/180 I–II

Between 1976 and 1979 Christine Webster studied at Massey and Victoria Universities, as well as at Wellington Polytechnic. In 1982, 1984, and 1988 she was the recipient of the Queen Elizabeth II Arts Council Grant and in 1989 received a scholarship through Agfa Hong Kong. Christine Webster's large-format works deal with myths and traditions that have defined the image of women and the relationship of the sexes through history. By setting picture and word ambiguously opposite each other, she alludes to handed-down meanings while at the same time questioning them in order to suggest new meanings. In so doing, she consciously establishes references to the traditional Tableau Vivant in Victorian salons. She herself arrived at these scenes at Victoria University while studying theater and began to take pictures of her fellow students on the stage. In her current work she deliberately plays with the idea of a voyeuristic look and erotic imagery in order to arouse interest and simultaneously to pose a critical challenge.

Christine Webster considers herself an artist who formulates the feminine viewpoint of sexuality and relationship between the sexes. Despite the complexity of its content, Christine Webster's work concentrates on formal execution and perception, limiting itself to what is essential. Text and picture are separate, and people, glowing reddish yellow, emerge from the darkness of the black background. Initially she served as her own model, but today she works more and more with partners. While it may appear unusual for an artist from New Zealand to address European myths and traditions, the discussion of the role of women in society is a topic discussed in all cultures. Christine Webster's art, which has also been successful in Western Europe, has quickly brought her into contract with the international art world. *RM*

POST CRUCIFIXION

▲ **Christine Webster**
Game Bird, 1987

Cibachrome print
each 154 x 85.7 cm
and 25 x 85.7 cm
ML/F 1987/155 I–IV

Weegee

(Arthur H. Fellig)

1899 Zloczwe
1968 New York

▼ **Weegee**
Nikita Khrushchev,
1959

Gelatin silver print
22.7 x 19 cm
ML/F 1977/845

Gruber Collection

"WEEGEE... I have never met a better name or a better photographer." This is how famous American sensationalist photographer Arthur H. Fellig, called Weegee, saw himself. In 1910 he and his family emigrated from Austria to New York, where he grew up in poor conditions on the Lower East Side. In 1914 he quit school prematurely in order to help support his family. He held jobs as a candy salesman and street photographer, finally becoming an assistant to a photographic dealer. After he left his family at the age of 18, he took occasional jobs at train stations and shelters for the homeless until he found a job taking passport pictures. At 24 he went to "Acme Newspictures", a photo-agency for newspapers. There, he worked predominantly as a laboratory technician in the darkroom and occasionally helped to take pictures of fires at night and of other catastrophes.

In 1935 Weegee started working as a freelance photojournalist. With absolute obsession he chased sensational events such as traffic accidents, violent crimes, and catastrophic fires. He sent these pictures to the tabloid press. "Photos by Weegee, the famous", read the self-assured stamp on the reverse side of his press photographs. Because of

friendly contacts he had with policemen of the Manhattan Police Headquarters, Weegee was informed of all crimes and accidents as quickly as the policemen themselves. In 1938 he even received official permission to install a police radio in his car. This unusual privilege frequently enabled him to be first at the scene and, no less important for the tabloid press, he could be the first to submit photographs to his editor. This collaboration with the Manhattan Police Headquarters lasted for about ten years. During that time he produced over 5000 photographic reports – according to Weegee's own estimates – making him the most famous picture

▲ **Weegee**
Money Stocking in
the Bowery, 1944

Gelatin silver print
24.1 x 19.8 cm
ML/F 1977/849

Gruber Collection

chronicler of New York at that time. In his photographs he captured traces of the Great Depression with anguishing directness. To this day, his work constitutes an impressive documentation of life in modern large cities marked by violence, brutality, and mercilessness. As a balance to this miserable side of life, Weegee began taking pictures of High Society in 1938. These photographs reflect a sarcastic opinion of the rich, decadent stratum of society.

The intensity radiated by Weegee's photographs is also based on a crassly realistic style, paired with a tendency toward expressionistic staging. He liked to use strong flashlight, producing dramatic effects of light and shadow and harsh black-and-white contrasts. Whether these effects are the result of the requirements of the tabloid press or whether he exercised his artistic creativity is not important. The fact is that today his work is justifiably valued for its stylistic uniqueness, making this photographer's work a milestone of photojournalism.

▲ Weegee
Policeman with Dog,
1950

Gelatin silver print
23 x 18.9 cm
ML/F 1977/846

Gruber Collection

▲ **Weegee**
Onlookers, 1936

Gelatin silver print
30 x 27.3 cm
ML/F 1977/836

Gruber Collection

In 1947 Weegee moved to Hollywood, where his first book, *Naked City* (1945), was made into a motion picture. He remained in this center of the motion-picture industry, working as technician and actor in small parts. During that time he collected material for his new book *Naked Hollywood*. In 1952 he returned to New York and produced mainly caricatures of personalities in politics and society. To accomplish this, Weegee developed a kaleidoscope for his camera, calling it a "Weegeescope". In

1961 he published his autobiography, *Weegee by Weegee*, in which he summarized: "I had taken famous pictures of an infamous decade [...] I had photographed the soul of the city that I knew inside out and that I loved." *MBT*

▲ **Weegee**
Coney Island Crowd,
1940

Gelatin silver print
19.1 x 23.5 cm
ML/F 1977/839

Gruber Collection

▲ Weegee
Simply Add Boiling
Water, around 1950

Gelatin silver print
21.4 x 17.5 cm
ML/F 1977/834

Gruber Collection

▲ Weegee
The Human Cannon-
ball, 1952

Gelatin silver print
23.9 x 19.7 cm
ML/F 1977/844

Gruber Collection

Weston,
Edward

1886 Highland Park,
Illinois
1958 Wildcat Hill

▲ Edward Weston
Nude, 1936

Gelatin silver print
19.1 x 24.1 cm
ML/F 1977/855

Gruber Collection

The photographer Edward Weston is considered to be a pioneer and one of the most consistent representatives of American "straight photography".

His career in photography began in 1902, when he received a camera as a gift from his father and began to take a passionate and committed interest in the possibilities of this medium. At first he taught himself and started traveling as a portrait photographer. In 1908 he attended the Illinois College of Photography and then went to Los Angeles, where he worked as a retoucher and a laboratory assistant in a photographic studio.

In 1911 he opened his own studio in Tropoico (now Glendale), California. Here, as earlier, Weston worked mainly with the soft-focus lens in the style of painterly Pictoralism. During subsequent years he earned the reputation of a successful, respected photographer who was honored with numerous prizes and exhibitions. Between 1921 and 1922 a

▲ Edward Weston
Nude, 1936

Gelatin silver print
24.5 x 19.3 cm
ML/F 1977/850

Gruber Collection

◄ **Edward Weston**
Nude, 1934

Gelatin silver print
9.2 x 11.8 cm
ML/F 1988/51

Gruber Donation

► **Edward Weston**
Willie, 1941

Gelatin silver print
24.3 x 19.2 cm
ML/F 1988/51

Gruber Donation

change began to take place in Weston's photographic work. He began to enjoy experimenting, seeking abstract motives, unusual viewing angles and lighting conditions. He photographed fragments of faces and nudes, and began to use soft-focus techniques instead of sharply focusing lenses. In 1922, during a visit to his sister May in Middletown, Ohio, he took his first industrial photographs of the Armco Steelworks. These photographs mark the actual turning point of his career.

From now on Weston produced only precise, detailed, and extremely sharp photographs. His change of style was enhanced by his acquaintance with photographers Alfred Stieglitz, Charles Sheeler, and Paul Strand, whom he met during that same year in New York.

In 1923 Weston left his family and moved to New Mexico with his son Chandler and Tina Modotti, a young Italian woman who was his model, his pupil, and later his lover. Together, the three kept a studio until 1926. Weston established contacts with Mexican intellectuals and artists, including Diego Rivera, Frida Kahlo, and others. Weston specialized not only in portraits but also in nudes and still-life pictures, and from 1924 to 1925 he also devoted himself intensely to close-ups. These particular photographs demonstrate this photographer's extraordinary sense for the texture of surfaces, which he depicted with an exquisite

richness of nuances in black-and-white tones on his photographic paper, giving them an almost tactile quality.

"Presentation instead of interpretation" was one of Weston's much-quoted mottoes. To him, presentation meant the attempt to illustrate "things per se", to show their essence. About his photograph of a head of cabbage he wrote in 1933: "In the cabbage I sense the entire secret of life's force; I am baffled, emotionally excited, and, because of my way of presenting, I can communicate to others why the shape of the cabbage is this way and no other, and what its relationship is to all other forms." Even though Weston explained realism, presentation, and not interpretation, as being of artistic concern to him, it is his rigorously designed compositions of nature and of natural objects that frequently impress viewers, because they evoke absolutely ambivalent interpretations and associations of forms.

In 1932 Weston, Ansel Adams, Imogen Cunningham, and others

founded the group "f-64", which was to evolve into an important forum of "straight photography". In 1937 Weston received a grant from the John Simon Guggenheim Memorial Foundation, becoming the very first photographer to receive this honor. This grant allowed him to travel through California and its neighboring states for two years.

In the mid-forties he became ill with Parkinson's disease, which forced him to give up photography in 1948. *MBT*

◀ **Edward Weston**
Pelican, 1942

Gelatin silver print
19.2 x 24.1 cm
ML/F 1977/854

Gruber Collection

▶ **Edward Weston**
Cabbage Leaf, 1931

Gelatin silver print
19.3 x 24.8 cm
ML/F 1977/856

Gruber Collection

► Edward Weston
Armco Steel, Ohio,
1922

Gelatin silver print
23.5 x 17.1 cm
ML/F 1977/857

Gruber Collection

▲ **Edward Weston**
Rock, Point Lobos, 1930

Gelatin silver print, glossy
24 x 19.2 cm
ML/F 1977/862
Gruber Collection

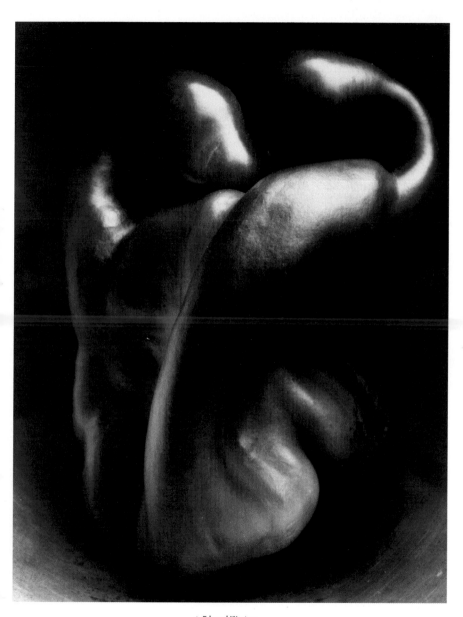

▲ **Edward Weston**
Pepper, 1930

Gelatin silver print
24 x 19.2 cm
ML/F 1977/864
Gruber Collection

Wilp, Charles

1934 Berlin
Lives in Düsseldorf

▼ Charles Wilp
Untitled (Rear View
of Nude), 1972

Gelatin silver print
29.5 x 39 cm
ML/F 1993/557

Gruber Donation

In 1950 Charles Wilp began to study psychology, journalism, and music, training also as a photographer and movie maker. In 1953 he worked on the Brasilia project with the architect Oscar Niemeyer in Rio de Janeiro. One year later his first "Photos of Emptiness" were created during his collaboration with Yves Klein and Jean Tinguely. In 1958 Wilp joined the group of artists "New Realism" as a movie maker. In 1959 his "Photos of Emptiness" were exhibited together with works by Klein, Tinguely, Arman, Jesus Raphael Soto, and Franco Fontana. While collaborating with this group of artists, Arman created the *Portrait of Charles Wilp* in 1961. Between 1962 and 1964 Wilp made several movies about projects by Christo, Tinguely, Arman, and Fontana. In 1965 he began making advertising photographs, in which he incorporated the aesthetics of Pop Art. Wilp received several international awards for his Volkswagen advertisements. His advertising campaign for Afri-Cola was particularly successful. The novel aesthetics of advertising that he developed consisted mainly of the merging of erotic and psychedelic image effects. In 1970 he received the assignment to create a pop portrait of Chancellor Willy Brandt's cabinet. In 1972 he had a one-man exhibition at "documenta V" entitled "Consumer Realism". He designed the stage props and wrote the music for the "Consumer's Opera" during the XX Olympic Games in Munich in 1972. During subsequent years he also concentrated on political portraits. Since the mid-eighties Wilp has been working as "Artronaut" on projects in which he expresses space travel and high technology in the artistic mode.
TvT

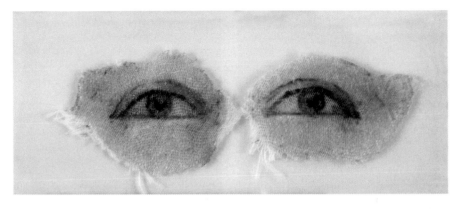

In Dorothee von Windheim's work, photography often plays the part of notes made with pictures instead of writing, similar to protocols or entries in a journal, telling of the processes in which her works of art are formed, developed, and changed. Dorothee von Windheim studied under Dietrich Helms and Gotthard Graubner (1965–1971) at the College of Creative Arts in Hamburg. With a grant she received from the German Academic Foreign Service, she went to Florence and apprenticed with a restorer. She has been professor at Kassel Polytechnic since 1989. Towards the end of the sixties she began working with life-size images of figures on pieces of cloth. These ghostly silhouettes of bodies were created with techniques such as etching, burning, rubbing, or burying, and they are suggestive of mythological, psychological, and religious themes (like the famous "Turin Shroud"). Other projects are *Strappo*, pieces of cloth with stucco removed from a wall; *Tree Cloths*, in which the trunk of a tree is wrapped in cloth and the pattern of the bark is then transferred to the cloth by the rubbing technique; and *Wine Cloths*, sheets that are stretched in vineyards to protect the vines from birds. Dorothee von Windheim has participated in numerous important exhibitions, including "documenta VI" in Kassel in 1977, Women Artists of the 20th Century in Wiesbaden in 1990, and the Biennale in Venice in 1995. A major solo exhibition was organized by the Wiesbaden Museum in 1989. *AS*

Windheim, Dorothee von

1945 Volmersdingen, near Minden, Germany
Lives in Cologne

▲ **Dorothee von Windheim**
One of the Eleven Thousand Pairs of Eyes from among the Followers of St. Ursula, 1984

Photographic emulsion on gauze between two plates of glass
9 x 21 cm
ML/F 1986/217

Winquist, Rolf

1910 Gothenburg,
Sweden
1968 Stockholm

▲ **Rolf Winquist**
Dancer in Medea,
around 1957

Gelatin silver print
29.4 x 23.3 cm
ML/F 1977/874

Gruber Donation

▲▶ **Rolf Winquist**
Dancer Gertrud Frith
in Medea, around
1957

Gelatin silver print
28.7 x 22.6 cm
ML/F 1977/873

Gruber Donation

Rolf Winquist studied photography under David Sorbon in his home-town of Gothenburg. In 1939 he was hired as an assistant by the Ake-Lange Studio in Stockholm. In the same year he became the chief photographer of the Ateljé Uggla in Stockholm. Under his direction that studio became one of the best known addresses in Sweden. Winquist was a portrait, advertising, and fashion photographer. His early portraits showed the influence of English and German photographers, whereas his later work featured sensual studies of women reminiscent of American fashion journals and Hollywood glamour shots. Distanced on the one hand, and sensitive on the other, his photography appears to place more emphasis on a physical impression than on an intellectual background. This is apparent in his portraits of women and children. Winquist photographed famous Swedish people and, during his spare time acted as an amateur, photographing people in the street. He published articles in various newspapers under the titles "Bildmässig fotografi" in 1947 and "Engelska Bilder" in 1959. He managed the Ateljé Uggla until he passed away in 1968. *LH*

▶ Joel Peter Witkin
Courbet in Rejlander's Pool, 1985

Gelatin silver print
38.2 x 37.9 cm
ML/F 1995/129

Uwe Scheid
Donation

At first, Joel Peter Witkin worked as a technician in a studio producing dye transfer prints and then as an assistant in two photographic studios. After that he worked as a military photographer. In 1967 he began to freelance, becoming the official photographer for City Walls Inc. in New York. Later on he studied at the Cooper Union School of Fine Arts in New York, where he obtained his Bachelor of Arts degree in 1974. After receiving a scholarship for poetry at Columbia University in New York, he completed his studies at the University of New Mexico at Albuquerque with a Master of Fine Arts degree, and he currently teaches photography at that school. In the eighties, Witkin shocked the public with photographs of misshapen people, of parts of corpses, and by staging events of church history, frequently citing known masterpieces in a morbid way. Many of his works are reminiscent of Hieronymus Bosch. Even though he is a maverick, he has gained acceptance in the established art scene. *RM*

**Witkin,
Joel Peter**

1939 New York
Lives in Albuquerque,
New Mexico

Wolf, Reinhart

1930 Berlin
1988 Hamburg

Until 1954 Reinhart Wolf studied psychology, literature and art history in the USA, Paris, and in Hamburg. He was already interested in photography in his youth, and this interest matured into his decision to make his hobby his profession. He began his study of photography at the Bavarian State Institute of Photography in Munich, completing it in 1956. Wolf settled in Hamburg and set up a studio. In 1969 he started moving into the "studio-house" which he designed, adding a studio for advertising films to this studio for advertising photography. In addition to his professional work, he pursued topics of personal interest, with which he caused a sensation even among the broader public. His first success was a publication of his picture series of American buildings. Conceived quite differently from conventional New York-style photography, he used an 18 x 24 cm camera to take pictures of façades of buildings, mostly by taking elevators to the top floors of skyscrapers. In 1977 he traveled to Georgia and in 1979 to New York in order to create his series *Faces of Buildings*. This large-format book, for which he received many awards, set the standard for a different type of architectural photography. Shortly afterwards *Stern* magazine asked him to take pictures of castles in Spain. During his two trips in 1981 and 1982 he created his picture

◄ **Reinhart Wolf**
Vienna, Hofburg,
1983

Color print
19.5 x 24.5 cm
ML/F 84/126

Gruber Donation

series *Castles of Spain*. Wolf's independent projects became more and more central to his work and philosophy. Most important in this context is the fact that his professional photography became increasingly affected by his freelance work, so much so that the boundaries became blurred. This was evident especially in his food photography, which culminated in 1987 in the publication *Japan – Culture of Eating* and which exhibited a quality of high artistic standards. By taking pictures of Japanese cuisine, mostly on his small hotel night table, he broke all the rules of commercial food photography and created images that embodied Japanese sensibilities to a very high degree while expressing them in the medium of photography. *RM*

▲ **Reinhart Wolf**
Washing and
Changing Hall for
Miners, Stadthagen,
1978

Color print
17.2 x 23.2 cm
ML/F 1984/129

Gruber Donation

Wolff, Paul

1887 Mulhouse,
upper Alsace
1951 Frankfurt on
Main

Paul Wolff started out by studying medicine, planning to become a doctor. In 1920, while exercising his profession, he came into contact with photography, and in 1926 was fortunate enough to win a Leica at a photographic exhibition in Frankfurt. Wolff became a pacesetter for 35 mm photography in the realms of professional photography and photojournalism. He illustrated numerous books and wrote theoretical discourses on the use of the 35 mm format. In doing so, he helped to make this format popular for serious applications. In 1930 photography became his second profession. He taught many students how best to use a Leica, gave instructions on new perspectives and viewing angles, and in 1934 published his experiences in a book entitled *My Experiences with the Leica*, which he dedicated to Oskar Barnack, the inventor of the Leica. In 1948 he published another book on taking pictures with a Leica, and this time his topic was color photography. Wolff, who never specialized in a topic or concept, but who took pictures of everything he found interesting and suitable, was mainly a theoretician, technician, and image designer of photohistorical importance. In this regard he greatly affected amateur photography in the fifties and thus certainly contributed to the exceptionally high level of photographic technology in Germany. *RM*

▼ **Paul Wolff**
New York, Fifth
Avenue West, 1932

Gelatin silver print
23.2 x 17 cm
ML/F 1984/131

Gruber Donation

▶ **Paul Wolff**
Steel Cable
Manufacture,
around 1936

Gelatin silver print
23.7 x 17.8 cm
ML/F 1984/130

Gruber Donation

◄ Wols
Cassis, 1940–1941

Gelatin silver print
15.4 x 15.4 cm
ML/F 1979/148

Gruber Donation

Wols

(Alfred Otto
Wolfgang Schulze)

1913 Berlin
1951 Paris

Alfred Otto Wolfgang Schulze, alias Wols, worked as a photographer for 16 years. During the last ten years of his life he devoted himself mainly to drawing and painting. After his death his work as a painter became known, famous and celebrated, but no one was interested in his photographs. Only with the generally growing interest in the medium of photography did Wols' photography begin to attract attention.

This unexpected success came in 1937 with a request for the fashion pavilion at the World Fair. This is when the young photographer received his pseudonym Wols. This name, as his wife Gréty recalls, was "the product of an accident". The then director of the House of Lanvin sent a telegram to Wolfgang Schulze asking him to come to his office. During the transmission the name was mutilated into "Wols", but Schulze considered it a good solution. The photographs shown at the "Pavilion of Elegance" were promptly published under the name "Wols".

By far the greatest part of Wols' photographs consists of portraits.

He always took a series of pictures, photographing people in many different poses. Occasionally he would make up to two dozen exposures of the same person; of Nicole Bauban he even took more than 40 pictures.

As a photographer, Wols did not develop any new techniques or theories. Neither was he interested in daring perspectives, special camera settings, or details. He was no virtuoso with the camera, and did not want to create a new vision. It was always his way of seeing and his world that he portrayed, a world that was lonely and cold. When he photographed Paris, his pictures showed empty streets, sleeping tramps, steep stairs, and always grids. Many of the people whose portraits he took had their eyes closed. Sometimes Wols took pictures of only part of a person – an arm, a hand, a foot. His strange affection for fragmentation and for the inorganic becomes ever more obvious upon

▶ **Wols**
Gutter, Paris,
around 1937

Gelatin silver print
15.9 x 15.4 cm
ML/F 1979/1147

Gruber Donation

closer study of his photographs. Most amazing are his still-life pictures, his pictures of objects: strange, bizarre compositions peaked to psychic obsession with images of a broken doll in the gutter or of dead, skinned birds. The elements of an apparent reality become psychograms of a soul. He never misused, adulterated, or manipulated the medium of photography.

Ewald Rathke wrote as follows about Wols' photographs: "Wols increasingly arranged objects that did not match and that did not belong together, placing them in a contradictory environment. The realities of his compilations lost their individuality and they simultaneously combined into a new entity. The sense of the familiar was eliminated and recognition impeded. The substance of the external form was removed, the spatial relationship rearranged, the field of view narrowed. But, paradoxically, that is precisely what enhances the physical presence of the object in the picture." In one of his many aphorisms, Wols himself confirmed the fact that chance always played an important role for him:

◄ Wols
Section of Road,
around 1937

Gelatin silver print
19.9 x 15.4 cm
ML/F 1977/1153

Gruber Donation

"Chance is a great master because it is actually not an accident. Chance
exists only in our eyes. It is an assistant to the Master's 'Universe'." *GG*

Zelma, Georgii

1906 Tashkent,
Uzbekistan
1984 Moscow

▲ Georgii Zelma
Military Exercise.
Tanks and Airplanes,
around 1920–1924

Gelatin silver print
28 x 42 cm
ML/F 1992/106

Ludwig Collection

▶ Georgii Zelma
Covered Street in
Asia with Man and
Small Child, 1926

Gelatin silver print
10.7 x 8.1 cm
ML/F 1992/109

Ludwig Collection

In 1921 Georgii Zelma joined the camera club of his school. At that time he took pictures with a Kodak 9 x 12 cm box camera. During subsequent years he worked at the "Proletkino" motion-picture studio and with the "Russfoto" agency, which forwarded his documentary photographs to the foreign press. In 1924 Zelma returned to Tashkent as the "Russfoto" correspondent for Uzbekistan and Central Asia.

He published many of his pictures in *Prawda Wostoka (Truth of the East)*. In the thirties he was on the staff of *SSSR na stroike (USSR under Construction)* magazine, producing major reports such as *The USSR Viewed From the Sky* and *Ten Years of Soviet Republic in Jakutia*. During World War II Zelma was a combat reporter for *Izvestiya* in Odessa and Stalingrad among other places. After the war he worked for the magazine *Ogonjok* and for the "Nowosti" press agency.

Many of Zelma's works show the influence of the Russian photographic avant-garde. Thematically, his work covers a spectrum ranging from military exercises, demonstrations, factory and farm workers, all the way to ethnological subjects. *MBT*

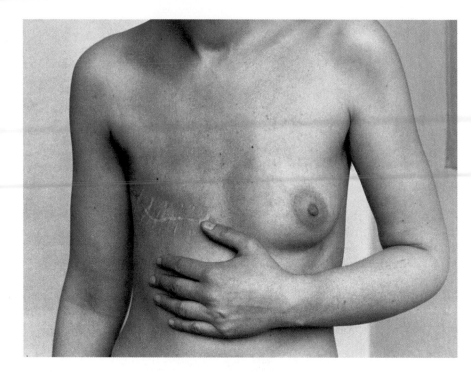

Zeun, Renate

1946 Radebeul
Lives in Berlin

After finishing high school, Renate Zeun trained to become a beautician, going on to study photography from 1978 to 1979 by taking a correspondence course at the renowned College of Graphic Design and Book Art in Leipzig. In 1988 she became a member of the Association of Creative Artists. In 1986 she published the book *Afflicted, Images of My Cancer*, in which she addresses the subject of breast cancer. These photographs are as effective in the form of a sequence as they are as individual pictures. They offer the viewer an opportunity for reflection and empathy in the often taboo area of disease, suffering, fear, and death. In 1987 she created the sequence *Mrs. Anneliese St. – Clinic for Oncology, Berlin,* about which she said: "I hope that these photographs encourage reflection and discussion, and that it might be a step on the way for those who are healthy to be able to meet those who are sick in an understanding and uninhibited manner." *AS*

▲ Renate Zeun
Hand on Body, from:
Afflicted, Images of
My Cancer, 1983

Gelatin silver print
17.8 x 23.8 cm
ML/F 1991/147

In 1921, following his studies of railroad technology in Tashkent, Willy
Otto Zielke and his family moved to Munich. There he attended the
Bavarian State Educational Institute of Photography. Beginning in 1928
he was a teacher who influenced the evolution of numerous photographers, including Hubs Flöter, Kurt Julius, and Erwin von Dessauer. In
those years he also began to create motion pictures, achieving such a
great success with his first film "Unemployed" that he was motivated to
make another motion picture called "The Steel Animal" on the occasion
of the 100th anniversary of the Nuremberg-Fürth railway. In addition to
his motion-picture work, Zielke also became known for his photography
of objects, his brilliant technique, and his unconventional perspectives.
He was experimenting with color photography as early as 1933. In the
fifties he was Chargesheimer's predecessor at the BIKLA School in Düsseldorf. *RM*

Zielke,
Willy Otto

1902 Lodz, Poland
1989 Bad Pyrmont

◄ Georgii Zimin
Still Life with Comb
and Scissors,
1928–1930

Gelatin silver print
23.7 x 29.5 cm
ML/F 1992/104

Ludwig Collection

Zimin, Georgii

1900 Moscow
1985 Moscow

► Georgii Zimin
Still Life with Light
Bulb, 1928–1930

Gelatin silver print
24 x 18 cm
ML/F 1992/102

Ludwig Collection

Between 1914 and 1917 Georgii Zimin attended the Stroganov School of Arts for Industry in Moscow. Between 1918 and 1920 he studied at SWOMAS and from 1921 at WCHUTEMAS, the center of suprematist and constructivist art in revolutionary Russia. El Lissitzky, who was also teaching there at that time, was creating his first photograms. During this time Zimin designed decorations for agitprop events celebrating May Day in Moscow, and he cultivated contacts with the group "Art of Motion" at the Academy of Sciences in Moscow. In the late twenties he tried his hand at experimental photography by creating his own photograms. His work is characterized by great simplicity and clarity while using few pictorial elements. His still-life pictures abstain from any narrative content and, with their simple arrangement, they not only resemble the photograms of El Lissitzky but also the first experiments of Henry Fox Talbot. *RM*

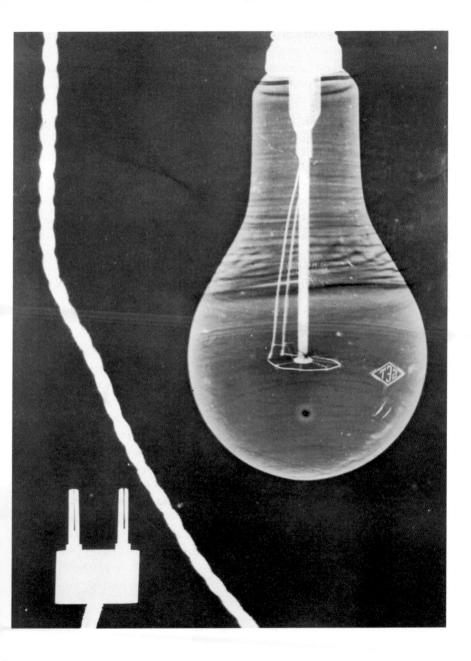

**Židlický,
Vladimír**

1945 Hodonin
Lives in Brno

Vladimír Židlický studied photography under Prof. Jan Smok and Prof. Jaroslav Rajzík at the Prague Faculty of Film. Between 1977 and 1988 he worked at Hodonin's art gallery, where he organized numerous photographic exhibitions and initiated a collection of photography. Between 1977 and 1982 he was the head of the Photography Department at the School of Applied Arts in Brno and in 1982 became the director of that school. Židlický's work represents a new beginning for Czech photography. It is closer to painting and drawing than to photography. He began manipulating the technical process of producing a print, devising a technique of light-drawing that he blended with the photographic image. Thus his photographic work stands between photographic imaging and experimental, abstract photography. With his light-drawings, Židlický creates cosmic spaces into which he places human bodies. Some of his compositions move so weightlessly in the image plane that they are reminiscent of baroque figures in church cupolas. His nudes appear to float in an abstract space, integrated in a network of lines and areas with which he composes the structures of his pictures. Frequently, these lines and structures are the result of light effects, while many others suggest rather destruction, leading one to suppose some violent treatment of the negative, which also affects the integrity of the nude figures. In many of his photographs the latter only play a subordinate role, incorporating themselves in the abstract drawings and becoming dark silhouettes. Židlický has developed an expressive blend of light-drawing and nude photography. He is considered to be one of the leading Czech artists of the middle generation. *RM*

▼ Vladimír Židlický
Dramatic Figure,
1985

Gelatin silver print
45.5 x 40.5 cm
ML/F 1990/1283

Piet Zwart initially became known as a typographer and designer of interior spaces and craft objects. In 1924, encouraged by the constructivist El Lissitzky, Zwart for the first time integrated a photogram into
advertising that he was designing for the "Dutch Cable Factory" in Delft.
A few years later, when he received a request from the same company to
handle the typographic design for a catalog of cable products, he recognized that photography, because of its capability for exact reproduction
of materials and structures, was predestined for this task. The catalog,
which was published in 1928, was an enormous success, meeting with
acclaim beyond the borders of the Netherlands. His precise pictures, as
well as his utopian ideas of the possibilities of technology, set the standards for the Dutch photographic avant-garde during the years that followed. *MBT*

Zwart, Piet

1885 Zaandijk, near
Amsterdam
1977 Leidschendam,
near The Hague